RAINER ON FILM
Thirty Years of Film Writing in a
Turbulent and Transformative Era

BY PETER RAINER

Published by:

Santa Monica Press LLC
P.O. Box 850
Solana Beach, CA 92075
1-800-784-9553
www.santamonicapress.com
books@santamonicapress.com

Printed in the United States

Santa Monica Press books are available at special quantity discounts when purchased in bulk by corporations, organizations, or groups. Please call our Special Sales department at 1-800-784-9553.

ISBN-13 978-1-59580-077-0

Library of Congress Cataloging-in-Publication Data

Rainer, Peter, 1951-
[Works. Selections.]
Rainer on film : thirty years of film writing in a turbulent and transformative era / by Peter Rainer.
    pages cm
 ISBN 978-1-59580-077-0 (pbk.)
1. Motion pictures. 2. Motion pictures—Reviews. I. Title.
PN1995.R27 2013
791.43'75—dc23
                    2013002641

Cover design by Future Studio
Back cover photo: Mary Knox Merrill/ *The Christian Science Monitor*

For my parents, John and Barbara Rainer

CONTENTS

CHAPTER 2
YOUNGISH TURKS

CHAPTER 3
AUTEURS

CHAPTER 4
STEVEN SPIELBERG

CHAPTER 5
ABOUT ACTING, STAR ACTORS, AND ACTING STARS

CHAPTER 6
SOME MASTERPIECES

CHAPTER 7
DOCUMENTARIES

CHAPTER 8
ISSUES (MOSTLY HOT-BUTTON)

CHAPTER 9
COMEDIES (INTENTIONAL AND UNINTENTIONAL)

Intentional

Unintentional

CHAPTER 10
LITERARY AND THEATRICAL ADAPTATIONS

CHAPTER 11
MISCELLANY: BOOK REVIEWS AND CRUISE SHIPS

INTRODUCTION

Some of my very first memories are of movies. My hazy recollection of Kirk Douglas and the giant squid in *20,000 Leagues Under the Sea* may not qualify as Jungian or Freudian or primal or prelapsarian, but it tells me that movie love is bred in the bone. I suspect this is true for most people who care about movies.

I started watching them regularly when I around six or seven, on the New York TV show *Million Dollar Movie*, which replayed the same film over and over throughout the week. The show always opened with Max Steiner's soaring theme from *Gone with the Wind*, which initially proved confusing when I finally saw *Gone with the Wind*. I am convinced that *Million Dollar Movie* set an entire crop of kids on the road to a critic's connoisseurship. By week's end, you could just about memorize how a movie was put together, whether it was *The Hunchback of Notre Dame* with Charles Laughton or *The Body Snatchers* with Boris Karloff. I fashioned a pantheon and peopled it with my own roster of stars.

Bogart was, for many years, chief luminary. He wasn't just a tough guy—a prerequisite for me in those days—he was a tough guy with a cruel and curdling humor. He came wreathed in cigarette smoke that was like Hollywood hellfire. His wily, insinuating baritone, which could rise suddenly to a maniac's crescendo, was the obbligato of my pulp fantasies.

Around this time, in the mid-sixties, my father bought me a copy of *Agee on Film*, which had recently come out in paperback. This book remains for me the most rapturous of discoveries. The impassioned way Agee wrote about movies, including many of the forties Bogart films, legitimized my time in the dark (as, later, he helped legitimize my desire to become a critic). I would set my alarm clock so I could watch as many Agee-anointed films as possible on *The Late Late Show*: *The Story of G. I. Joe*, *Hail the Conquering Hero*, *The Best Years of Our Lives*, and *The Treasure of Sierra Madre* (again and again). The experience of watching films like these in the dead of night had an illicit tingle. It made me feel as if I were part of a secret society, and sure enough, in the years ahead, I met many other supplicants of the sect—an entire film generation of them. I became a fixture at the New York revival houses and film societies. Hallowed ground for me was the Bleecker Street Cinema, where a typical double bill might be *La Grande Illusion* and *Un Chien Andalou*; the New Yorker on Broadway and Eighty-Eighth Street, where I first saw *Citizen Kane* and freaked out at *Freaks*; and, close by, the Thalia, which sloped upward and gave many a vagrant trying to sleep it off his first taste of Fellini.

The New Yorker had a massive wall of directors' head shots in the lobby, a murderers' row of mugs (Dovzhenko, Dreyer, Huston, Hitchcock *ad gloriam*). Inside the theater's low-lit entryway was a big, ledger-like book where you could write down screening recommendations. I would puzzle through other people's wish lists, poring over the pages as if they were leaves in an illuminated manuscript. Not enough is made, I think, of the replenishing role that movie theaters play in the whole tone of a movie lover's experience. At least this was true before Twitterized patrons crammed the cubicles of the fifteen-plexes.

Back then, paradise was seeing *Dr. No* and *Potemkin* on the same day. I loved the way movies could reach high and low. This was, after all, a time when students were still required to memorize Joyce Kilmer's "Trees." Movies were a splendid rebuke. Pauline Kael's first collection, *I Lost It at the Movies*, came out around this time, and the elegant rowdiness of her writing, her high-lowness, was unlike anything else; plus, unlike Agee's, her reviews were for the most part about the fairly recent movie scene, which made their immediacy even greater for me.

I read Dwight Macdonald religiously in *Esquire*. I loved biblical epics—this was, as a critic friend of mine describes it, my Pre-Taste Period—and Macdonald left them flapping in the wind (his takedown of *The Greatest Story Ever Told* is officially the Funniest Review Ever Written.) Manny Farber's essays, which were later collected in *Negative Space*, laid bare a strange and beautiful mindscape, brambly as hell. The pile-on of pronouncements continued with such critics as Stanley Kauffmann (still very much at it, illustriously, in his nineties), John Simon, and Andrew Sarris, whom I recognized as a kindred obsessive list-maker. None of these critics seemed to agree with each other on much of anything. The free-for-all was exhilarating, and also somewhat perplexing. I was accustomed to canons. By the time I entered college, I was pretty sure I wanted to be a film critic. I wanted to be in the cult. I wanted to try out my ideas in print and see if I could progress from idiot savant to savant.

For three years in the early seventies—between anti-war rallies and other extracurricular frolics—I was the chief critic for my college newspaper, the Brandeis *Justice*. I also helped program the college film society. I would bound onstage, offer bumbling preambles about mise en scène, and then signal the projectionist to start up *Ugetsu*. My audience, both in print and in the screening rooms, was captive. Films were much more central to the zeitgeist then, and the best of them were much better. I could write about *Five Easy Pieces*, or *McCabe and Mrs. Miller*, or *Straw Dogs*, or *The Godfather*, and the *Justice* would be dumped in bundles in front of the student union building and the reviews would be hashed out that day in the dining halls and dorms. My professors would argue with me about what I wrote. There was a marvelous urgency to all this, and my experience was not atypical. The big reason so many movie critics came out of my generation is that we all passed through the same ether.

I was wide-eyed enough in those days to regard film criticism as a calling rather than a profession. My rude awakening came several years later, while I was film critic for *Mademoiselle* magazine (my first review was of *Chinatown*). A higher-up declared that, forthwith, every story in the magazine had to answer at least one of two questions: "How do I dress?" and "How can I get laid?" My column held in for a while longer, perhaps because of its date-night utility concerning that second question.

When I began writing film reviews for the *Los Angeles Herald Examiner*, a big city daily where I happily spent most of the eighties, I hooked into a vast dynamo of late-breaking deadlines and bottom lines. The critic business, it seems, was an adjunct of the news business. Critics and crime reporters, having perhaps more in common than not, worked side by side. I would sweat over *Places in the Heart* and hear next to me, "Was the head completely severed?"

Being a film critic in Hollywood was (and is) especially risky. It's a company town. The knives come out. Reacting to negative reviews, movie companies would pull ads, hoping to guillotine the offender. Remarkably, my editors at the massively money-losing "*Her-Ex*" didn't cave. This honorableness is the exception, and not only in L.A. Wherever lucrative advertising money is to be had—and there's less of it to go around in these digital days—there will be problems. One reason movie critics, that endangered species, often can't be heard anymore above the din of the marketplace is that many of their outlets have become co-opted, subtly and not-so-subtly, by the studios, or by conglomerates or publishers or editors cozying up to the studios. For a lot of critics now, no longer just the blurb whores, being quoted in the ads is part of one's job description. Critics comply by running their deathless prose through the blurb-o-matic. In the quote ads, the studios reproduce the publication's logo. Quid pro quo.

There is a gilded nostalgia now for the critic wars of yore, but it's remarkable how little traction those wars have had. Auteurism/anti-auteurism, midcult/masscult, white elephant art versus termite art, movies versus cinema—these came out of a time when the way you talked about movies was as important as the movies themselves. (With my fingers fervently crossed, I trust that the current death-of-the-movies hoo-ha will prove no more predictive than that old controversy over the death of the novel, not to mention God, although our Incredible Shrinking Screens, alas, bode best for pygmy cineastes.) But the dirty little secret of film criticism is that system-building is, thankfully, damn near impossible. You start out a theoretician and end up an impressionist. Film is such a *confusing* art form. Norman Mailer once said, "Literature haunts our intellect, movies haunt our dreams." If you're lucky, they do.

Years ago, when Hollywood churned out nonstop slews of teen pix—or was this only yesterday?—I questioned whether I was in the right profession. I questioned the movie medium itself. Where were the movies with the richness of, say, great novels? It was important for me to know that movies could be great in that way. If the essence of what I was writing about was, even from a purely entertainment level, negligible, then why bother? Then a friend said to me, "What about the films of Satyajit Ray?" He could have named a dozen others, but I was already off and running, jolted back to sanity.

A great movie is, almost by definition, perplexing, because it scrambles our radar. Movies are like magic acts. You are constantly trying to peek behind the curtain; you want to be fooled, and you don't want to be fooled. You want to be mesmerized, but charlatanism is rife, and sometimes charlatans mutate into geniuses, and then back again. New Waves wash ashore, leaving a bubbly wake of broken shells and, occasionally, a pearl.

If you stay a critic long enough, you grow old right alongside the movie stars you came up with. When I was a kid, I could watch Bogart in revivals and he was both fully alive to me and a memento mori. His iconography was freestanding and for all time. When I watch an actor like Dustin Hoffman now, or Robert De Niro, my responses are much more complicated. So many of the actors who meant so much to my college generation have nestled into comfy, spoofy character roles. It's tempting to see this as an erasure of our pasts, a betrayal. Why should this be? It is because of the extraordinary, spooky intimacy of film itself. If you care enough about movies, the trajectory of, say, an actor's career, or a director's, inevitably becomes a part of one's own autobiography. But I hasten to add that autobiographies get rewritten all the time, some old timers have held up quite well indeed, and, like any other self-respecting Lothario, this critic is always on the prowl for fresh ecstasies.

This book should not be mistaken for a comprehensive survey. The vagaries of the profession do not allow for that. It covers three decades of reviews and essays written during an especially turbulent and transformative film era, drawn from my years at big-city papers, city magazines and monthlies, alternative weeklies, and national newspapers. With the exception of a few trims and minor restorations, the reviews remain the same as when they were written. In a number of instances, especially in my writings over the years on Richard Pryor, Stanley Kubrick, Sylvester Stallone, Eddie Murphy, and film noir, I have retained a few repetitions, which seemed preferable to messing with the original constructs. Here and there I have added postscripts, but I have resisted the fetish, not to mention the impossibility, of bringing things "up to date." These pieces are best approached as snapshots in time, captured in the heat of the moment.

The book begins with a divided chapter on movies either exasperatingly overrated upon their release (sometimes no longer) or deserving of much greater attention (often still true). Next is a section on young, or youngish, turks who are represented here, in most cases, by the films that first made their reputations, and one on major directors that focuses on key films or entire careers. Because of his centrality to the movie scene, Spielberg, about whose films I have not always held a fixed position, gets his own chapter. The section on actors covers both individual performers and larger issues, including the dearth of good movie roles for women (that old perennial, alas). I love writing about acting and, as someone who sees about 250 films a year, I am immensely grateful that a good performance is often reason enough to sit through even a middling movie.

Next is a chapter on masterpieces. They are toughest to write about, which is one reason I love writing about them. The chapter on documentaries brings together some of my thoughts on such directors as Ross McElwee, Agnès Varda, and Frederick Wiseman. (If I had become a filmmaker instead of a critic, I would have wanted to be Fred Wiseman.) Following this is a lengthy value-pack of essays on violence in the movies, sexual harassment, racism, politics right and left, male weepies, children's films, all things noir, video art, and the Passions of both Christ and Thelma and Louise. Comedies, both intentional and unintentional, come next (really, what is one to do with *The Messenger: The Story of Joan of Arc* except lance it?). The ensuing section on literary adaptations is meant to justify that oft-asked question: "Why did you major in English?"

None of these chapter compartments are intended to be watertight. Masterpieces, comedies, duds, documentaries—all these and more can be found willy-nilly throughout the book. The chapter headings are suggestive rather than definitive.

I close things out with a miscellany. Because I have also written about books, and because I love the essay form, I have included pieces on both Montaigne (who would have made a great film critic) and on Alexander Theroux's *Primary Colors*, which is the most cinematic book ever not written about the movies. A travel essay I wrote about a movie-ish cruise in the south of France is included as proof that critics do occasionally get out in the sun.

PETER RAINER
Los Angeles, California

CHAPTER 1

OVERRATED, UNDERSEEN

OVERRATED

American Beauty

Lester Burnham (Kevin Spacey) in *American Beauty* is a big zero with a boring desk job whose highlight of the day is masturbating in the shower. Then he goes through a life change and is supposedly reborn. I say "supposedly" because the new Lester, apart from being more buff and gruff and wide-eyed, isn't a big improvement on the old Lester—he's zero and a half. This is not, however, how we are meant to respond to him: *American Beauty* is a movie in which not only Lester but practically all the other characters are designed to confound our preconceptions and unfold their secret selves. In most cases, though, this two-step agenda comes across as simply one kind of shallowness giving way to another.

The tag line to the film's title is "Look closer," and we're pressed by Sam Mendes, the celebrated theater director (*Cabaret*, *The Blue Room*) making his movie-directing debut, and his screenwriter, Alan Ball, a TV-comedy writer who was co-executive producer of *Cybill*, to look closer at the archetypes of Anytown Americana. Lester's real-estate-agent wife, Carolyn (Annette Bening), for example, with her pasted-on smiles and cast-iron coif, has the veneer of a perfect suburban wifey-wife, but she holds Lester in deep contempt. So does their teenage daughter, Jane (Thora Birch), who undergoes a transformation of her own when she falls for Ricky (Wes Bentley), the mental-case video-voyeur classmate next door who, of course, turns out to be not so much nuts as "mad"— the way romantic poets are mad. He sees beauty where you would least expect to find it, and that's what *American Beauty* wants to do, too.

But why should we trust this simplistic film's notions of the ineffable? Mendes has been quoted in the *New York Times* as saying that *American Beauty* "sounds like some dreadful sitcom on speed," adding that "it's not [that] at all. It's so filled with loneliness, and beneath the surface, it's very funny." The sitcom connection is apt, though—and, by now, overfamiliar. *The Truman Show* and *Pleasantville* have already raked over much of this turf, and some of us didn't buy it then, either. These movies express outrage that the Ozzie-and-Harriet lives we never really believed in anyway are false. Maybe some sort of Hollywood-boomer midlife crisis explains why we're now getting all these films in a row. Moviemakers who feel betrayed by the cheery sitcoms of their adolescence can now take it out on all the rest of us and, as a bonus, get points for profundity, too.

There's something else afoot in *American Beauty*. Lester is not only the anti-Ozzie Nelson, he's also a counterculture washout who smoked dope and partied in the sixties and now has nothing to show for it. Why should we care about him? What ideals did he leave behind? We're never really told. The filmmakers apparently don't feel the need to fill out Lester's character; it's as if he were fated to become a drone by the country's straitjacket culture. Carolyn is also a casualty of the culture. She says that "my job is selling an image, and part of my job is living that image," but real life keeps getting in the way. When she can't sell a house, she goes into a screaming fit, bawling and slapping herself and smearing her makeup. She's in awe of the local real-estate king (Peter Gallagher), who has florid, soap-opera good looks and seduces her with his success talk. Their roll in the hay emboldens her, giving credence to the enlightened notion that all she needed was to get laid.

Unlike Lester or Jane, Carolyn is never really brought into the realm of our sympathy; she's a facade selling facades. When Lester, swigging a beer, tries to get amorous with her and calls upon their fun-loving past, she warms a bit and then pushes him away, fearing the beer will spill onto her expensive couch. We're supposed to understand, of course, that what Carolyn really fears is closeness, but she's too villainized in our eyes for that to sink in. Although both actors pull out the stops—Spacey alternates fey snideness with moist wistfulness, while Bening does a contortionist's number on her smile muscles—there is hardly anything in either of their performances to indicate even a faded blush of marital longing.

The filmmakers want us to know that we can't choose what will liberate us; we have to be prepared for transcendence to come from the unlikeliest sources—like, for example, from the weirdo Ricky, whose video of a white plastic bag swirling around in the wind he describes to a rapt Jane as "the most beautiful thing I've ever filmed." Because of the prominence Mendes gives this clip, we're supposed to agree. Ricky, who deals dope to fund his video habit, is the son of a brutally repressive marine ex-colonel (Chris Cooper)—is there any other kind?—and a catatonic mother (the wonderful Allison Janney, underused), and so, in the best sentimental juvenile-delinquent tradition, his troubles are bought off, justified. Ricky, the new-style hippie, is balanced out by the rejuvenated, superannuated hippie Lester, who buys the kid's weed, drops out of the rat race, and finds his own measure of transcendence in the person of a stuck-up cheerleader pal of Jane's, Angela (Mena Suvari), whom he repeatedly fantasizes festooned in rose petals. In these moments, he gets a lulling look of complete repose; he looks post-coital without ever having had the coitus.

It's difficult for us to know how to take Lester's rebirth. His yearning for his daughter's friend has incestuous overtones that are never developed, and in a movie about the tyranny of facades, it doesn't help Lester's credibility that, long before he gets to really know her, he's enamored by Angela's all-American, blonde-haired, blue-eyed cheerleader looks. Because this middle-aged guy is so dimensionless, his supposed entrancement comes across more like plain old chickie lust. Angela looks like every Hollywood movie producer's second wife.

American Beauty plugs into a widespread boomer paranoia that, like Rip Van Winkle Lester here, we've wasted away our past twenty years in a kind of coma, and now it's too late to change. What gives the movie its air of seriousness is the attempt to spiritualize this emptiness; Mendes really loves his floating plastic bags and rose petals. The film is like a sportier, homegrown version of all those Antonioni-ish movies about the depleted upper-middle classes zombified by regret. It flatters its audience by turning burnout and midlife itch into tragic states, but a zero in torment is still a zero.

(New York, 1999)

In the Mood for Love

In the Mood for Love, the new film from Hong Kong writer-director
Wong Kar-wai, is like a fashion show of images; the camera placements
and color coordinations come to us right off the runway. Wong is best
known in this country for *Chungking Express*, which turned contemporary Hong Kong into an oscillation of glittery shards, and his new film is
stylistically at just about the opposite extreme—it's as languorous as the
earlier film was frenetic. But beneath it all, Wong is still essentially the
same artist who places a higher premium on show-offy technique than
on content. His movies have a high decadence quotient; we always feel as
if we're marinating in a gorgeous insubstantiality.

In the Mood for Love is set in 1962 Hong Kong, but almost all of it
is shot indoors, in apartments and noodle shops and office buildings. It's
possible to discern a faint outline of social observation in the way the
film's characters separate out into indigenous Cantonese Chinese and
immigrants from the mainland, but such subtleties will be lost on most
Westerners. Wong really isn't interested in sociology, anyway. His Hong
Kong is basically a mood-memory realm drawing on old-fashioned Hollywood romance. Wong is a bit like Fassbinder in the way he burnishes
and fetishizes kitsch. He's unlike Fassbinder in that his films don't pull
you into a great big Teutonic funk; there's nothing punishing in his approach. But trying to gorge on the visuals of *In the Mood for Love* is a bit
like trying to make a banquet of cotton candy. That Wong frames his
confection in an art-gallery window doesn't make it any less candied.

Tony Leung's Mr. Chow is a journalist who has moved with his
wife into a rented room in an apartment occupied by Shanghai immigrants; his new next-door neighbors are Mrs. Chan (Maggie Cheung)
and her businessman husband. Both Chow and Chan are often left by
themselves; their respective spouses, working late or away on business,
are virtually absent from the film. The revelation that they are having an
affair draws Chow and Chan together in a casual, platonic way at first—
they rehearse with each other what they will say when they confront their
mates—but it is only with the passage of time, and many changes of costume from Maggie Cheung, that the relationship deepens. If that's the
right word. Nothing really deepens in this film; instead, what we get is a

more resonant shallowness. Hands touch and are pulled back; eyes lock and lower; partial smiles are exchanged. It's all so coy that you half expect Wong to go all the way into parody. But what he really wants is to fashion a love poem from parody; he wants us to see the lyricism in all this straight-faced mooniness. What's touching isn't so much the plight of these repressed lovebirds but rather Wong's desire to summon something rapturous from it (the soundtrack contains generous selections of Nat King Cole singing in Spanish). Wong is a romantic in a very timeworn tradition, but the change of venue from Hollywood to Hong Kong gives his film, at least for some, the illusion of strangeness.

Wong uses his actors in the same decorative way that he uses everything else. Despite the fact that he won the Best Actor award in Cannes last year, Tony Leung seems to be not so much performing as posing. He broods blankly and cocoons himself in curlicue rings of cigarette smoke while Maggie Cheung, pretty as a mannequin, is bathed in amber light and deep shadow. Dietrich and Von Sternberg, to name the highest exponents of Hollywood art kitsch, could get away with this sort of thing because they understood how deep-down sexy all that fancy preening could be. Dietrich was both a hoot and a turn-on—the mockery of our wooziest romantic fantasies, and also their perfect embodiment. To really succeed with his new film, Wong would need stars who radiated that kind of impossible allure. Perhaps he realizes he doesn't have them, which explains why he's always playing peekaboo with them, camouflaging their dullness. They need his help. On the other hand, Wong is the sort of director whose camera gives equal weight to objects and to people: an office clock has the same emotional temperature, the same poignancy, as a close-up of Mr. Chow or Mrs. Chan. For Wong, people are living decor.

He generally works without a detailed script and keeps his actors in the dark about what he's up to, and yet the dialogue for his new film is replete with romantic sentiments and clichés that we are probably meant to regard not as howlers but as classics: Mrs. Chan tells her adorer, "I didn't think you'd fall in love with me"; he tells her that he's leaving her because she won't leave her husband, and so on. American art-house audiences who dismiss this cornball stuff when it's homegrown don't seem to have a problem buying it as exotica. Maybe these audiences aren't so quick to reject the corn after all. They still want it, but they also want the respectability of believing it's all intended to be hip, postmodern. Seeing our pop-pulp dreams recast in another culture can be fun; sometimes, as in the case of films like *Breathless* or *Shoot the Piano Player*, it can be much more than that—it can give us an entirely new reading of our own movie-mad mythology. *In the Mood for Love* has novelty value, I suppose, and plenty of pretty camera moves, but it's not really a movie you can warm to. Those Hollywood weepies may have been sopping with sentimentality, but at least the sobs were delivered on schedule; the men who made those movies knew what their audiences expected. Wong Kar-wai tricks up the schmaltz with a lot of avant-garde filigree. He's that most suspect of hybrids: a pop-schlock aesthete.

(New York, 2002)

Good Will Hunting

The Gus Van Sant film *Good Will Hunting* is like an adolescent's fantasy of being tougher and smarter and more misunderstood than anybody else. It's also touchy-feely with a vengeance.

Is this the same director who made *Mala Noche* and *Drugstore Cowboy*? Those films had a fresh way of seeing. We may have been watching blasted, detached outcasts, but he brought us up close to them, almost erotically close. In those films, and portions of *My Own Private Idaho*, he managed to turn the blank cool of his hustlers and wayfarers into something lyric and impassioned.

Good Will Hunting, starring Matt Damon and Robin Williams, is a commercial for the restorative power of love. It's shaggy and "tender"—a hard-sell masquerading as a soft-sell (those are the worst kind). And what's being sold are recycled goods. Instead of showing us new ways to feel, Van Sant plays up all the old, dull ways. He embraces mawkishness as if it were manna.

At least Van Sant didn't write the script. That dubious distinction belongs to Damon and Ben Affleck, who has a supporting role. Damon plays Will Hunting, a twenty-one-year-old South Boston tough who works as a janitor at MIT. Will likes to joyride and booze it up with his Southie buddies. He's perpetually pumped, with a hefty rap sheet—assault, grand theft auto, the works.

He's also—and here's the rub—a supergenius. Orphaned, Will spent his youth in and out of foster homes and never attended college. And yet his mind is so wizardly that he can reduce a smarty-pants Harvard student to jelly. Will's genius exists as a way to one-up people who look down on him. When a famous MIT math professor, Dr. Lambeau (Stellan Skarsgård), challenges his students to solve a real braincracker, Will takes one look at the classroom chalkboard after hours and writes in the solution—anonymously.

Lambeau tracks down Will in police custody. (He's in jail because he pulverized a snooty guy he recognized from kindergarten.) In awe of this Einstein-in-the-rough, Lambeau agrees to act as Will's mentor in exchange for the police dropping the assault rap. As part of the deal, he must also secure psychological counseling for Will. After a series of comically bad matches, the boy is placed with Sean McGuire (Robin Williams), a community college therapist and old classmate of Lambeau's who, like Will, has an Irish, South Boston pedigree.

This is where the film makes a beeline for Hokumsville. To begin with, Sean and Lambeau are not just friends but uneasy rivals; while Lambeau went after academic hosannas, Sean disdained glory and ambition and lived a blissful wedded life—until his wife's death two years ago. With his rumply jackets and hair sprouting everywhere, Sean is a fuzzball in mourning. He may be brilliant, but he's burned out by loneliness. And just in case we don't register what a holy man he is, we also discover for good measure that he was a) a combat soldier in Vietnam, b) an abused child, and c) a Red Sox fanatic.

Sean is the perfect therapist for Will because both are hurting inside. At least that's what we're supposed to think. While Lambeau is exhorting Will to realize his stratospheric potential, Sean, once he breaks through the boy's barriers, counsels him to "do what's in your heart." Guess who wins?

Good Will Hunting—even the title is irritatingly touchy-feely—offers itself up as a film about a genius who needs to allow himself to be vulnerable. He's isolated by his outcast upbringing and, presumably, by his terrific intelligence. But the filmmakers aren't really interested in what Will is really like. They set him up as a prodigy only to bring him down to normalcy. Their point is: matters of the heart trump matters of the mind. Will may be a brain, but it turns out he's as angry and confused as us dullards. The film seems designed to cajole audiences into embracing their averageness. It's saying, "Will is a genius, but he needs love just like the rest of us."

Most Hollywood movies about prodigies exist on this same dumb-ed-down plane—the most recent offenders being *Searching for Bobby Fischer* and Jodie Foster's *Little Man Tate*. What you rarely get in these movies is any sense of the *specialness* that comes with genius. In popular culture, it's impolite to elevate genius; it smacks of—gasp—elitism. But why should we be asked to identify with geniuses only insofar as they resemble ourselves? Isn't this just narcissism passing itself off as humility?

In *Good Will Hunting*, there are at least four people trying to connect with Will. Besides Lambeau and Sean, there's Will's best buddy Chuckie (Affleck), who wants Will to break free of South Boston and use his smarts to make a better life for himself, and Skylar (Minnie Driver), a wealthy Harvard premed student he falls in love with and who, of course, loves him for "himself."

But the voice we are most meant to heed is Sean's. It's he who challenges Lambeau's dreams of glory for the boy by retaliating with: "Maybe he doesn't want to do what you want." Lambeau is like Salieri in *Amadeus* in reverse—he is embittered and belittled by Will's genius, but wants it to flourish. And Sean is like the psychiatrist in *Equus* in reverse—he doesn't envy the boy's gifts, but envies Will's capacity to blast through his defenses and feel like ordinary folk. Sean, of course, also reaps wisdom from Will; like his patient, he learns to feel again.

Will's ongoing normalization is thick with psychobabble. At his big bawling breakthrough, Sean embraces him and says over and over, "It's not your fault." The guy whose face he pounded for that kindergarten slur might have a different opinion. The filmmakers go in for this kind of sentimental victimology because it relieves Will of any responsibility for his actions. He's just this abused, hurt kid.

But suppose Will's behavior and complications came about not only because he grew up working-class and abused, but because of the nature of his genius? The filmmakers don't really explore that possibility, because to do so would turn Will into an elite. And yet, surely the way a genius sees the world has great bearing on how he lives in it. The crux of *Good Will Hunting* ought not to be how *normal* genius can be but, rather, how provocatively *different* it can be.

Because Will's gifts are not explored except as a sidelight, we never even get the sense of elation he might feel at solving a monumental math problem—or, more to the point, his frustration in *not* solving a problem. Everything comes so easy to him that we are never permitted to see his passion for the way his mind works. The filmmakers' notions of genius are rudimentary; Will is like some brainiac who grasps solutions painlessly and reels off reams of facts stored in his photographic memory. This is a dolt's idea of genius—Will comes across as a human parlor trick.

Still, despite his showing off, Will clearly is clamping down on his "potential." He doesn't want to release his gifts to the world because, we are made to feel, the world doesn't deserve them. *Good Will Hunting* offers up a society in which the uses of intelligence are all corrupt. Lambeau sends Will on an interview that turns out to be for a job in military decoding. This, of course, gives Will the opportunity to get all self-righteous about using his brains to kill innocent people in unjust wars. Saint Will. The film, of course, doesn't posit any ways in which Will's genius might be used for peace-making—we never see *those* job interviews.

Will's sanctification also has its working-class-hero side. When, for example, he demolishes with his brain a preppie snoot in a Cambridge bar, we're meant to recognize that, for Will, intellectual confrontation doubles as class war. But surely Damon, who was a Harvard undergraduate, must know that gifted South Boston students have attended the university on scholarship. If Will has closed himself out of the academy, it's not the academy's fault—despite what the film implies.

Damon—as actor, not as co-screenwriter—is the best thing about *Good Will Hunting*. His performance isn't particularly modulated, but he carries an impending sense of violence that keeps his scenes on edge. Will's first meeting with Sean, in which the patient humiliates his therapist by intuitively homing in on his weakness, is unsettling and multilayered in a way the rest of the film isn't. It suggests a cruelty underneath Will's showing off. And Driver brings some freshness to her rather unfresh role.

Williams doesn't. He's so swaddled in good intentions that he might as well be playing a teddy bear. Williams must feel a personal connection to this movie—he has, after all, been "normalizing" his own genius in the movies for a long time now, to his detriment and ours.

Good Will Hunting pretends to face up to the big questions. Here's one it avoids: What if the cost of Will's anguish was a great scientific discovery? Suppose his life was a godawful psychotherapeutic mess, but out of it came the Unified Field Theory or a cancer cure? This is not something the filmmakers confront. They're content to send Will on his merry way as a self-realized good guy. What matters to them is that he loves himself.

(New Times, 1997)

Far From Heaven

In Todd Haynes's *Far From Heaven*, set in middle-class suburban Hartford in 1957, the characters are armored in autumnal tones—green swing coats and plaids and orange gloves. Autumn itself appears to have utilized the services of a costume designer; the dazzling foliage is all of a piece with the plumage and the big, bright hairdos of the Hartford ladies, chief among them Cathy Whitaker (Julianne Moore), whose voice seems honeyed with matronly bliss and who is the dutiful wife to Frank (Dennis Quaid), a sales executive, and mother to a pair of picture-perfect children. Cathy's home-and-hearth tableau is almost unreal in its supernal comfiness—a sure sign that reality will soon set in.

The central upheaval in *Far From Heaven* occurs when Cathy accidentally discovers Frank kissing a man. Devastated, but still the perfect wife, she encourages him to see a doctor who will "cure" him. As Frank moves ever farther away from Cathy, she grows closer to her gardener, Raymond Deagen (Dennis Haysbert), a widowed black man with a young daughter who is a bedrock of nobility. Haynes retains the costuming and color schemes of the fifties "women's picture" while bringing to the foreground sexual and racial issues that were safely nestled into the background of such movies as *Magnificent Obsession* and *All That Heaven Allows*, directed by that master of high-toned kitsch, Douglas Sirk. He's trying to turn the subtext of those movies into the text of his own. In so doing, he is also drawing a parallel between the repressions of the fifties, at least as they appeared in Sirk's movies, and our current era, which, by implication, is still far from halcyon.

In other words, *Far From Heaven* is a thesis movie, artfully worked out and played with the utmost seriousness. Haynes and his actors sustain a tone of principled detachment, never winking at us or betraying the slightest hint of facetiousness or camp. In effect, Haynes is deconstructing those Rock Hudson-Jane Wyman-Lana Turner weepies while also paying homage to their seriousness. He's making the movie that Sirk might have made if Sirk hadn't had to work everything out in code.

For some of us, there were never any great hidden depths to decipher in those weepies, and so *Far From Heaven* can at times seem rather precious. It's a form of intellectual vanity, I think, to ascribe great artistic value to whatever mists our eyes; it's a ploy that allows us to keep our dignity in the process of losing it. The Sirk movies certainly had more texture and craft than the slick ladies'-magazine fiction that was their literary equivalent, but their upholstered sentimentality and leaden acting is something else again. Rock Hudson as iconic hero? Puh-leeze.

At the same time, it could be argued that whatever was subterranean in the Sirk movies is better off for being so; it could also be argued that *Far From Heaven* loses rather than gains strength from being explicit. And yet, the film's most emotionally effective moments are precisely the ones that wouldn't have turned up in a fifties Hollywood film. "I know it's a sickness," Frank says of his homosexuality, "because it makes me feel despicable." In moments like this, Quaid gets right to the quick of a man who is incinerated with self-loathing. Frank's story is ultimately a sideline to what Cathy endures, but it's the most lacerating aspect of the movie, and the single instance where Haynes's lush and finicky homage breaks through to something raw.

Julianne Moore manages to bring some emotional levels to Cathy, but she's stuck in the iconic mode; Cathy's homemaker's pride and politesse mask her suffering. (Just because a Lana Turner role is being played by a real actress doesn't mean the role is redeemed.) Her increased emotional intimacy with the righteous Raymond sets the whole town talking, and Cathy must once again endure an unfulfilled love. In the movie's terms, she is left behind because she is a woman.

It's odd that Haynes, having upended the sexual dynamic of the traditional women's picture, should otherwise settle for such stereotyping, even though, in the case of Raymond, the stereotype is ostensibly positive. Raymond, like Cathy, is too good to be true. In the end, Haynes may not be terribly interested in reworking the old weepie clichés; if he were, then Raymond wouldn't endure with such dignity the prejudices of his time and Cathy wouldn't be so sorrowfully cast off. *Far From Heaven* ultimately achieves the same sentimentality as the Sirk films, and in much the same way—it elevates female sacrifice into an aesthetic. The movie isn't about suffering, really. It's about how you look when you suffer, how you dress up for it. Style is all.

(New York, 2002)

Shine

When we first see the character of middle-aged Australian David Helfgott (Geoffrey Rush) in *Shine*, he's standing in the driving rain and tapping at the window of a wine bar after closing time. Let inside by a sympathetic waitress, he keeps up a nonstop nonsensical patter that makes him sound like a Lewis Carroll character on speed. Returned to his rundown rooming house, David flops out on the floor—a wind-up toy temporarily at rest. We then flash back about thirty years to his childhood in the fifties, and realize with a jolt that this stringy-haired, wild-eyed jabberer was once a piano prodigy. *Shine*, which continues to whirl in and out of flashback in a manner intended to be "musical," is about how David came to be what he is. It's also about his redemption.

Helfgott is a real pianist and dubs most of the piano playing in *Shine*. Director Scott Hicks and his screenwriter, Jan Sardi, have incorporated those elements of his actual life that suit their purposes—his giftedness, followed by a breakdown that placed him in mental hospitals for years, and his triumphant return to the concert stage. They've also gone in for some rather heavy embroidery work.

The central piece of embroidery is the character of David's father, Peter (Armin Mueller-Stahl), who is made out to be an abusive, toughlove martinet who single-handedly sets up David's breakdown. The real Peter, by some of his children's accounts, was a sweet-tempered soul who wished only the best for his children, but it's crucial for *Shine* to have such a villain in order to victimize—and beatify—David.

The old-worldly Peter fits the job description—he's a Freudian nightmare. What saves him from total ogre status is that his mania for keeping his family in harness draws on the loss of his parents, and his wife's sisters, in the Holocaust. Emigrating from Poland to Australia shortly before the war, he is determined his own family will survive—which, in his eyes, means staying all together in Australia. When David wins a scholarship to study music in America—presented to him by no less than Isaac Stern—Peter swats it down.

As a young boy (Alex Rafalowicz) and, later, as a spindly teenager (Noah Taylor), David has the wary insularity of a kid who lives mostly inside his own head. David's paradox is the standard romantic-artist movie paradox: He's the crazy-saintly genius. The disharmony of his mind is cleared away by the harmoniousness of his art. This gawky nerd who looks like Waldo and seems balanced on the verge of derangement can still get it together to tune the planets with his playing.

This art-house romantic-genius conceit is old-hat Hollywood, but tricked up in outback duds and given a true-confessions cachet, it can seem brand new. *Shine* has impressed a lot of people who wouldn't give Cornel Wilde's Chopin in *A Song to Remember* a second thought. They're not all that far apart.

In most cornball Hollywood movies about great classical musicians—such as *A Song to Remember*, or *Song of Love*, with Paul Heinreid's Schumann cracking up on the podium—the music-making is sweet torture for its practitioners. Their agonies are supposed to be what art is all about. And so it is with *Shine*. When David finally works up Rachmaninoff's Third Piano Concerto—the piece his father always wanted him to conquer—he seems more than masterful; he seems possessed. It is at this concert that David snaps, after defying Peter in order to take up a scholarship at the London College of Music. Following a long convalescence, he becomes the gibbering holy fool we glimpsed at the beginning—the man standing in the rain.

The most generous take on this material, I suppose, is that it's an allegory on the disasters of the Holocaust—the destruction of families begets the destruction of families. Peter survives but in a sense is destroyed, and so, for a time, is David. But Hicks is after something even more elemental—he wants to show us how love can vanquish the darkness. The love here is David's passion for music; later it is the love of a woman (Lynn Redgrave) who charts his stars and becomes his soulmate—and his wife. Standing in for the dark forces are his father and the anonymous hospital workers who give him electroshock and discourage him from playing the piano. It's when he takes up the piano again—tapping out "Flight of the Bumblebee" to an amazed audience at that wine bar—that David is resurrected. He may be a holy fool, but propped up by his loved ones' tender ministrations, he fights his way back to a form of sanity through his playing.

The people who care for David treat him like an adorable pet—part infant, part wizard. Hicks plays up the adult David's infantilism, giving us long cascading sequences with him bouncing high in the air backed by Vivaldi, or jumping naked into the waves and bounding like an overgrown tyke. We're supposed to regard this childlike stuff as a protective device—a way for David to seal himself off from the horrors of the adult world and play out the childhood he never enjoyed. But the childishness is also meant to have metaphorical weight; it represents the wonderment in him that allows for his genius.

Either way, there's something a bit condescending in this view of David. It turns his misery and redemption into a species of child's play. His art, and his suffering, are reduced to a kind of quirky fabled quaintness—much as Glenn Gould's was in that overrated art-house rave of a few years back, *Thirty-Two Short Films About Glenn Gould.*

It's significant that the reasons for David's breakdown are laid at his father's feet—even though the split between the valiant introvert that David was and the screw-loose jabberer he becomes is so decisive that some sort of neurological explanation is probably a lot closer to the truth. But physiology doesn't play as well as Freud in these romances, so David's condition and treatment are made fuzzy throughout. So is his recovery into music. He doesn't even really need to practice. None of those boring scales and arpeggios for us—that might put a damper on the "mystery" of it all. His genius, which as a boy appeared to arrive complete, returns again fully formed.

Hicks has a rather middle-brow take on David's genius. The pieces we hear him pound out are mostly grand-scale showstoppers, such as the Rachmaninoff, or tricky finger exercises, such as "Flight of the Bumblebee." The real Helfgott, on the soundtrack, is impressively dexterous in his renditions, but he isn't given much chance to play softly and lyrical-ly—just a few swabs of Chopin here and there. But people who think great piano playing means fancy-fingered, mile-a-minute marathons will get the message: This guy's a genius. (By this standard, so was Liberace.)

There are some impressive performances in *Shine.* All three Davids are superb, and they match up. Geoffrey Rush, celebrated in Australia for his stage work, gives a tricky, propulsive rendition of David's manic joy-ousness. (He also bears an uncanny resemblance to James Woods.) Nich-olas Bell is remarkably good as David's first piano tutor; John Gielgud, as David's tutor in London, is imperious and large-souled—he's the Good Father to Peter's Bad Father. Googie Withers, as the elderly woman who befriends David in Australia, is a plush matron whose passing represents the film's most delicately sad moment. Lynn Redgrave makes her charac-ter's dawning, bewildered love for David seem like a revelation.

Performers such as these help tone up the proceedings. They root the movie in human feeling, even when the filmmakers are trying to snow us. But snow may be what audiences want from *Shine.* The audience that once cooed over the romantic malaise in *Five Easy Pieces* may have found a sunny nineties substitute. The ga-ga uplift in *Shine* knocks the malaise right out of your head—along with just about everything else.

(*New Times*, 1996)

Your Friends and Neighbors

As the lights came up after a screening of the Neil LaBute movie, *Your Friends and Neighbors*, a colleague next to me growled disapprovingly, "That was a *nasty* movie." For LaBute—whose divisive debut film, *In the Company of Men*, is probably the worst date-movie ever made—this com-ment would no doubt come as the highest praise. He's the kind of writ-er-director who doesn't think he's giving us a good time unless he's making us squirm. He has a horror filmmaker's mindset—except LaBute doesn't resort to bloodletting. He does it all with words. He wants to make our skin crawl by demonstrating how morally depraved people can be.

But the funny thing about this prince of darkness is that he's really a softy. Beneath all his men-and-women behaving badly scenarios beats the bleeding heart of an innocent who can't bear the bad news. He's aghast at the ugliness of the species, which, given how much ugliness is out there in plain view, makes him a bit of a johnny-come-lately. Despite all this hoo-ha, there's something ho-hum about LaBute's amazement at what people are capable of doing to each other. I mean, what else is new? In *Your Friends and Neighbors*, he's having a high old time giving himself the creeps. For the rest of us, it's all kind of . . . well . . . nasty.

LaBute is fond of saying that the people in his movies are representative only of themselves—that no larger sociological implication should be extracted. But clearly, this is a coy ploy. *In the Company of Men* was about two corporate players who set out to woo a deaf-mute employee in order to unceremoniously dump her as vengeance against all women. In *Your Friends and Neighbors*, LaBute is once again scourging upscale urbanites. There's something unseemly about the way he goes after this crowd. He may be throwing rabbit punches, but behind them is an Old Testament wrath. The wrath is way out of proportion to the target.

Jerry (Ben Stiller), for example, is a nerdy college drama professor who is miserably cohabitating with Terri (Catherine Keener), a shrew who makes her living writing ad copy for such products as tampons. We are first introduced to this couple in the throes of passion—his passion, at any rate. Terri can't stand his play-by-play vocalizing and, in mid-hump, tells him so (she's right; he does talk too much). Terri just wants to get down. Maybe she doesn't even want that. "It's not a time for sharing," she says. Thanks for sharing.

Then there's our other fun couple. Mary (Amy Brenneman), a journalist, and Barry (Aaron Eckhart), who works in some unspecified white collar managerial job. As with Jerry and Terri, we first see them in bed. (LaBute is big on these plot parallelisms, as if to demonstrate that human behavior is as quantifiable as a theorem.) Barry is depicted as a big lug in the bedroom; Mary, wordless and unsatisfied, is a big mope. He ends up making love with his favorite partner—his hand.

Cary (Jason Patric), a bachelor and also—God help us—an obstetrician, is first introduced to us as he tape-records his own sex talk while doing sit-ups in his sleek apartment. He's rehearsing his Lothario spiel for his bedmates, but the real object of his lust is clearly himself. He's as autoerotic as Barry—a stud whinnying in his own stable.

LaBute intersects the lives of these people in a flat, diagrammatic style that is part *Carnal Knowledge*, part David Mamet, part Geometry 1A. Barry and Cary are buddies—at least in the LaBute manner, which means they're comfortable enough around each other to share dirty confidences. Jerry is friends with them, too, but he doesn't trust Cary, and he initiates a tryst with Mary. Needless to say, the tryst fizzles. Jerry pouts and apologizes and Mary goes into her mope. But Terri gets wind of the goings-on and, furiously jealous, initiates with considerably more success her own affair, with Cheri (Nastassja Kinski), an art gallery assistant.

Mary, Barry, Terri, Cheri, Cary, Jerry—all these rhyming names. LaBute wants to lump them all together in order to mow them down. Actually, these names appear only on the credits. In the movie, no one is addressed by name, for that "anonymous," archetypal effect. Unidentified, these people could be anybody, even *you*. The city in which the movie takes place is also unidentified, no doubt for the same reasons. In general, LaBute does his best to strip his characters and their environment of any specifying traits. No one has any kids, parents, or family that we can see; no other friends or neighbors intrude. Their jobs are, at best, sketched in. In any given scene, LaBute never allows more than three or four players to be seen or heard, and he films the monologues and dialogues very close-in, for that clinical, depersonalized effect. But it's no great feat to depersonalize people if you eliminate most of what makes them human. LaBute stacks the deck; he wants to demonstrate how maggoty everybody is, and he does so by showing us only characters with sex on the brain.

There are bound to be people who will argue that the film makes us uncomfortable because it exposes the beastliness beneath. Our lives really *are* all about sex. We're more scuzzily one-dimensional than we'd like to admit.

What I think this defense misses is the fact that people are only one-dimensional until you get inside their heads. For a supposedly serious filmmaker, LaBute has an awfully narrow concept of human nature. That's why the people in *Your Friends and Neighbors* remain "types." They don't learn from experience, and they don't change. We don't even see what might once have attracted them to each other. They're just specimens in LaBute's insectarium.

Basically what he's saying is this: We're all crumb-bums and dupes. Men are unworthy of women, who are not worth it anyway. This is the way it's always been; human nature doesn't change. The rituals LaBute exposes are, in his view, the same male-female screw sessions that dramatists have been delineating since the Greeks. Only the names—or, in this case, the no-names—have changed.

By setting his movie in an upscale milieu, LaBute is implicitly condemning the middle class for having the effrontery to seek its pleasures. This is a very old game. The counterculture used to play it in the sixties; now the reactionaries have stepped up to the plate. It's not just that these friends and neighbors are scum—they're *bourgeois* scum. What could be worse? LaBute doesn't want to let any joy into the picture; if he did, it might expose how rigged and shallow his cynicism is. A fun couple in bed would explode his depresso thesis. No one in *Your Friends and Neighbors* gets any pleasure from anything. The closest approximation is when the heterosexual Cary delivers a rapt three-minute monologue to his "friends" about the intense personal fulfillment he received sodomizing a student who snitched on him in high school.

It's significant that Cary, despite all his tape-recorded warm-up sex talk, is never shown actually sleeping with anyone. What we see instead are pre- or post-coital sessions with Cary rasping at his bedmates, who are usually off-camera. For him, the rasp is the real sex. Humiliating others—his male friends as well as his women—turns him on. Cary is the most compelling character in the movie because at least he doesn't make any bones about who he is. He may get dangerously high inhaling the fumes of his own hellfire, but his radar is in fine working order; without prompting, he catches the vibrations of discontent in his friends' bedrooms. Jason Patric, who also co-produced the film, has been a bland brooder in his other movies. Here, his malevolence is all-of-a-piece with his lethal handsomeness and square-cut jaw. When Cary moves in on Terri in a bookstore and is rebuffed, he glides back into her with such cool ferocity that it's like watching a shark attack. He's a predator.

LaBute, ironically, comes along at a time when romantic love is once again being sentimentalized on-screen. Hollywood in the feminist era never really figured out what to do with guys and gals; the solution, more often than not, was to jettison women to the fringes altogether. They became ornamental adjuncts in the male action-fantasy universe.

In the shimmer of post-feminist Hollywood, men and women are once again starting to act coy and googly-eyed around each other. You can see this in a lot of the big-studio romances, ranging from *Titanic* and *The Mask of Zorro* to even a gross-out romp like *There's Something About Mary*. But you also see it in the acclaimed smaller stuff, such as *Sliding Doors* or the just-released *Next Stop Wonderland*. The low-budget, "independent" sector is playing the same ga-ga game as the big leagues. We've skipped over the tensions of male-female relations in the feminist era and gone directly back to the halcyon days of "Some Day My Prince (or Princess) Will Come."

With this in mind, it's easy to overvalue LaBute's funk. He comes on like a spoiler, and with his clinician's camera and killer dialogue, he certainly holds you. But he's not really going against the romantic sentimentality of the day—he's just demonstrating how awful life is without it. In a way, he's perhaps even more of a traditionalist than the Hollywood treacle-meisters. It's possible they are just dispensing their fluff as a commercial expediency, but LaBute seems genuinely horrified by the prospect of sex without love. That's why he flays his characters so mercilessly. He wants these bourgeois elites to *pay* for their sins. What I want to know is, who appointed this guy judge, jury, and executioner?

(New Times, 1998)

Fight Club

A cynical exercise in designer existentialism, *Fight Club* has that raw-sleek look that often shows up in fragrance or jeans commercials, and yet the film supposedly is all about how consumerism and the corporate culture destroy us—or, to be more specific, men. Intended as a great big howl of a movie, it comes closer to being a mammoth snit fit—a snit fit with pretensions (the worst kind).

Edward Norton plays the film's nameless narrator in a nameless city. (Beware of films set in nameless cities; they're out to sell you something.) Early in the movie, sodden with insomnia, he renews himself for a time by attending self-help groups for the terminally ill, embracing and weeping right along with his fellow twelve-steppers, who think he is one of them. This conceit has its black-comic possibilities, but the narrator is crying for himself before we've had much of a chance to find out who he is, and when we learn more, there's still not much there. His condo is outfitted to the gills by Ikea, but the poor sap remains unfulfilled; his job as recall coordinator for a major auto company involves flying around the country checking on accidents to determine how cost-effective it would be for the company to lie low. He's the Organization Man as Everyman, and his little life is just waiting to be exploded.

The blandness of his days, played out in look-alike plane seats and hotel rooms, is interrupted when he meets Tyler (Brad Pitt), who wears loud-print shirts and leather jackets and sunglasses indoors. Tyler talks like a cross between a Bowery Boy and a Buddhist sage, and he's everything the poor sap apparently isn't. After the narrator's condo mysteriously blows up, he goes to live with Tyler in his condemned house near a toxic-waste site. This trickster makes ends meet working a projector at a movie house, where, for sport, he splices a few frames from a porno film—just enough to cause subliminal discomfort—into the evening's family-entertainment fare. He also makes soap, which, as we see from an escapade where he and his housemate raid the dumpsters of a liposuction clinic, derives from human fat. He gets a kick from selling the soap back to lipo-sucked ladies.

The pair's greatest achievement, though, is the creation of Fight Club, where, in a hidden-away city basement, men congregate and pummel one another in order to experience the liberating effects of pain. We're treated to a succession of these head-splitting, blood-frothing spectacles, whose participants, led by Tyler, eventually form a cult-like terrorist militia aimed at taking out corporate America. The narrator, increasingly repulsed by Tyler's commando cruelties, tries to sabotage the sabotage.

In its muzzy mix of paleo-men's-movement musings and bone-crunch, *Fight Club* could be the god-awful offspring of the WWF's Vince McMahon and Lionel Tiger, or of the Susan Faludi of *Stiffed*. Clearly something deep and bellowing is going on here. These men, disenfranchised by franchise-mad America, are the rabid battalions Starbucks hath wrought; zonked by malaise, they can feel alive only when they hurt. Director David Fincher and screenwriter Jim Uhls, adapting the cult novel by Chuck Palahniuk, want us to know that, like Tyler, we men are all living in a toxic dump, and it's called America. Even though Tyler turns into a scourge by the end, his rantings are meant to resonate. We've all been deluded by advertising, he says; we've had no great wars or Depressions to preoccupy our testosterone. What's a poor primal guy to do?

Fight Club rolls out its indictments and its Zen koans, but what it really resembles, perhaps unknowingly, is the squall of a whiny and essentially white-male generation that feels ruined by the privileges of women and a booming economy. (The underclass, which would feel excluded from this argument, isn't much of a factor in *Fight Club*—this is a well-to-do guys' whine.) Fear of castration is a running theme throughout. So is stigmata imagery, for that holy, martyred effect. The male squadron in *Fight Club*, vaguely homoerotic, is striking a blow for atavism, but it's the kind of tribal tom-tom atavism that doesn't allow for women who might also be enraged by the hollowness of corporate culture; the film doesn't even have the wit to recognize that that culture might itself just be a more lustrous and galvanized form of blood lust. (Haven't these filmmakers spent any time in Hollywood's corridors of power?) Except for an appearance by Helena Bonham Carter, playing a grungy vixen who moves in with the guys, the film is pretty much female-free in its front ranks—although serious sport is made of a twelve-stepper turned Fight Clubber (Meat Loaf Aday) whose steroids have given him D-cup dimensions. This is how pathetically low the men in *Fight Club* have sunk—they've sprouted breasts! Even Marx could not have foreseen this baleful result of a capitalist free-market economy.

As part of the new growth industry in masculinist socio-pop fantasias, *Fight Club* at least has the distinction of being lively, like an acid-rock show (Camille Paglia will want to take a look). It's all hepped up about the vileness of materialism, and so, of course, David Fincher unleashes on us his vast array of TV-commercial-derived whammies. The film is a hard sell about no-sell. (Nothingness here looks awfully burnished.) Brad Pitt jangles like a lethal jitterbug, and Edward Norton, with his gift for making anonymity frightening, is perfectly cast. But I hope this film isn't going to be given the brink-of-the-millennium treatment by deep-think commentators. Idea-wise, *Fight Club* has about as much going on in its head as an afternoon with Oprah. Actually, Oprah may have the edge.

(New York, 1999)

Zero Dark Thirty

Kathryn Bigelow's troubling, infuriating *Zero Dark Thirty* is about Maya (Jessica Chastain), a CIA agent whose obsessive single-mindedness eventually lands Osama bin Laden in a body bag. Like Ahab, she is fixated on her prey to the exclusion of all else. Bigelow and her screenwriter, Mark Boal, who also collaborated on *The Hurt Locker*, deny Maya virtually any backstory. We know almost nothing about her life away from the film's decade-long hunt. She's a cipher—a vengeance machine with flame-red hair.

Bigelow began this project when bin Laden was still on the run, but changed course when he was tracked down and killed by Navy SEALS on May 2, 2011, in the assault on his compound in Abbottabad, Pakistan. As in *The Hurt Locker*, which was about an American bomb disposal unit in Iraq, Bigelow doesn't expend a lot of energy putting the action into a political context. *Zero Dark Thirty* is essentially, or at least ostensibly, an action thriller. But since we already know the outcome of the SEAL operation, which occupies the final half hour of this more than two-and-a-half hour movie, the film's narrative has a methodical sameness. This is a nuts-and-bolts cinematic dossier on how the job was done.

What I find troubling and infuriating is that, by turning the hunt for bin Laden into a glorified police procedural, Bigelow neutralizes the most controversial and charged aspects of this story. (To no avail, I might add; the film is controversial anyway.) George W. Bush is never shown, ditto Dick Cheney, Iraq is AWOL, and Barack Obama is only glimpsed in a 2008 campaign interview. This is a bit like making a movie about the D-Day invasion without referencing FDR or Eisenhower.

Actually, it's much worse, since the film traffics in scenes of torture. Its first full sequence, in fact, has a CIA officer, Dan (Jason Clarke), brutally interrogating a man (Reda Kateb) suspected of having information about bin Laden's courier while Maya, new to all this, observes in hushed compliance. The waterboarding and pummeling and all the rest are presented as instrumental in bin Laden's eventual capture. Mission accomplished, sort of.

In a recent *New Yorker* piece on Bigelow, the political reporter Dexter Filkins wrote:

According to several official sources, including Dianne Feinstein, the head of the Senate Intelligence Committee, the identity of bid Laden's courier, whose trail led the CIA to the hideout in Pakistan, was not discovered through waterboarding. 'It's a movie, not a documentary,' Boal said. 'We're trying to make the point that waterboarding and other harsh tactics were part of the CIA program.'

In the article, Bigelow adds: "The film doesn't have an agenda, and it doesn't judge. I wanted a boots-on-the-ground experience."

But by not enlarging or contextualizing the meaning of the waterboarding scenes, by avoiding any sense of political partisanship, Bigelow is, in effect, judging. It's difficult to look at these sequences in a vacuum, which is how she wants us to respond to them. I am not arguing that she should have denounced waterboarding per se. Let's say, for the sake of argument, that these brutalities helped bring down bin Laden. This is a possibility that anti-torture advocates on both sides of the aisle, if they are honest with themselves, must acknowledge. The problem I have with *Zero Dark Thirty* is that, for the sake of a "boots-on-the-ground" experience, it mucks around in matters of great gravity without ever really getting its hands dirty. Imagine what Costa-Gavras, who made *Z*, or Gillo Pontecorvo, who made *The Battle of Algiers*, would have done with this material.

Dan, the almost sadistically enthusiastic interrogator, is portrayed as basically one of the guys. Maya, who is admiringly called a "killer" by her colleagues, has so little emotional resonance that she might as well be a cyborg. (She is based on a real person.) Bigelow fatuously turns her into an existential hero at the end, a lost soul whose life has no meaning once bin Laden is taken out. This is a fancy way of covering up the fact that Maya is a blank. (Is Bigelow saying that, in the "war on terror," only the blanks can get the job done?)

By showing scenes of torture without taking any kind of moral (as opposed to tactical) stand on what we are seeing, Bigelow has made an amoral movie—which is, I would argue, an unconscionable approach to this material. I don't understand those critics and commentators who denounce this film's amorality and then go on to laud the movie anyway—as if a film's moral stance, or lack of, was incidental to its achievement.

Are we so cowed and wowed by cinematic technique that we can afford to lobotomize ourselves in this way?

(*The Christian Science Monitor*, 2012)

UNDERSEEN

Wild Bill

Wild Bill, starring Jeff Bridges, is Walter Hill's best film in years. It's a movie about the self-destructive power of myth. By the end, Hill makes that self-destruction seem like the archetypal American story. Wild Bill Hickok's extended demise is like a dirge for our national innocence. That innocence, if it ever really flourished, was lost long ago.

James Butler "Wild Bill" Hickok was "created" by a country bent on inventing a unique past for itself. Even while he was alive—and long after he was shot in the head in a bar at thirty-nine by a drifter named Jack McCall—he was the stuff of dimestore-novel puffery. With his fringed buckskin and ivory-handled Colt Navy pistols and flowing hair—as if daring the Indians to scalp him—Hickok was the Gentleman of the West who fought in the Civil War as a Union scout and tamed the boomtowns of the last frontier. He was also, as the movie rams home, a hounded, spooked, closed-off man, and a natural-born killer. Hill and Bridges make you understand how he might have been torn apart by the schism. They are torn apart by it, too. *Wild Bill* careens back and forth between tall-tale hallucination and stark, harrowing realism.

Bridges's Wild Bill has the hollowed-out look of someone who can no longer connect with other people except as moving targets; with his eyesight failing, the world has become a shadowed shooting gallery. He never knows what horror will fall into the light. There's a near-perfect matchup between the way Bridges looks in this movie and the way Wild Bill, in photos, appeared in his heyday as a marshal of Hays City and Abilene in the early 1870s. When he looks up from the poker table or steps out into the mud-sloshed cow-town streets, there's an almost obscene complacency to his gaze; he's measuring you for a coffin.

But the gaze has begun to turn inward by the time *Wild Bill* hits its stride. Hickok—making his last stand in the gold-rush town of Deadwood in the Dakota Territory, drinking and playing cards and living uneasily off his legend—retreats again and again to an opium den and wafts into a dreamy, troubled doze. His rockabye nightmares, photographed in bleached-out black-and-white, shake up the movie. Reveries about shootouts and the Cheyenne and a woman he may once have loved, Susannah Moore (Diane Lane), have a combustible, powder-burned look. After a spell, they usually explode into a pure, blinding white, as if the visions could no longer be contained by the mind that imagined them.

It is the conceit of this movie that Hickok's killer, Jack McCall (David Arquette), was Susannah's son. Jack's fixation with destroying Wild Bill has a gruesome inevitability. He has the scrubbed, clean-cut look of an all-American nut case; believing his mother was wronged by Hickok, his face is lit up with vengeance like a jack-o'-lantern. Hickok's encounters with Jack grow progressively more troubling to him. At first, he slams him into the mud—he's just another kid trying to make a name for himself. But, as the boy moves against him in the darkness of the opium den, or closes in for the kill with hired killers in tow, Hickok senses the fatedness of the pursuit. Jack is like an avenging angel—crazed but righteous—and Hickok feels a kinship with him. He needs the boy to complete his legend. In the Thomas Babe play *Fathers and Sons*, upon which Hill very loosely drew for his screenplay (along with wisps from Pete Dexter's novel *Deadwood*), Jack is Hickok's son. But *Wild Bill* doesn't need that Oedipal twirl. Jack isn't Hickok's son in the movie, but they have a blood closeness anyway. Without fully realizing it, they each require the other for completion.

Hickok can savor his own demise because, in a sense, it's the only remaining action in his life. There's a scene in which Hickok, busting up a brawl in the streets, mistakenly shoots his own deputy. He seems aghast at his own fury—and is left cruelly alone with his act.

The history books on Hickok usually mark this moment as a turning point; he is said to have never recovered from it. Hill doesn't make the sequence quite so epochal, but, even so, it keeps sounding throughout the rest of the film like a soft, unfading chord. What's horrific about the moment—for Hickok and for us—is how casually life can be taken away.

Hickok may have been a natural-born killer, but he had his scruples. He reportedly once said, "The killing of a bad man shouldn't trouble one any more than killing a rat or an ugly cat or a vicious dog." But what about the killing of a good man, a friend?

Until this moment in Abilene, Hickok's masculine code, his almost dandyish sense of personal style, probably precluded him from believing himself to be a bad man. Violence may have been the armature of his life, but he strode into battle not as the aggressor but as the avenger—the righter of wrongs. In *Wild Bill*, each time he moves in for the kill, there's a ritualistic fervor in the act. He has a confident killer's sense of fair play. When he is called out of a saloon to square off with a half-crazed man in a wheelchair (Bruce Dern), Hickok straps himself into a wheelchair, too. Fair's fair. When he tracks down Jack's hired killer, his vengeance is magically swift.

It's a crowning, defining moment for Hickok because, at long last, after Abilene, he needs to act out once again his own sense of heroism. We need to see the heroism, too. Hill understands that an anti-western like *Wild Bill* still requires the kinds of legends and rituals that drew us to westerns in the first place—if only to subvert them. The film's tone is enraged nostalgia, and Hill is the artist as magisterial spoilsport; he never allows us to sink into the timeworn comforts of the genre.

And Jeff Bridges never allows us to regard Wild Bill as a fable-in-motion. He's not corny or clever; there's no actor's vanity in anything he does. Bridges is a supremely naturalistic actor playing a supernaturalistic role; that's the source of the tension in his performance, unlike Ellen Barkin's stock turn as Calamity Jane. We can see how Hickok has wearied of playing himself in public. Still, he goes through the motions when he's out in the saloons, as much for self-protection as for vanity. He's a trooper.

The demythologizing of our American heroes isn't a new tactic in the arts. It's old hat. If a movie came out now that plumped for a mythic Hickok, it would probably seem far more radical and perverse than anything in *Wild Bill*. Yet audiences are still hooked by homilies. They like their revisionism pint-size; jumbo-size would be un-American. This may explain why MGM, nervous about the film's reception, held up the release of *Wild Bill* for six months.

This may also explain why Robert Altman's movies, which often royally upend our American mythologies, usually flop with audiences. And last year Ron Shelton's subversive *Cobb* was excoriated. Ty Cobb was *already* known to be a crumb-bum. Why the shock? *Cobb* got inside the exasperating craziness of why we are drawn to the terrible people who sometimes become our myths.

  Wild Bill isn't as muscular or rollicking as *Cobb*, but it's hunting the same big game. It's about hanging onto myth, even when you know it's a cheat. The terrible comedy of *Wild Bill* is it makes you ache for something you know in your bones didn't really exist anyway.

(*Los Angeles*, 1995)

Joe Gould's Secret

At its best, *Joe Gould's Secret*, starring Ian Holm and its director, Stanley Tucci, and based on a pair of legendary *New Yorker* profiles by Joseph Mitchell, has some of the same qualities as Mitchell's prose: plangent intelligence and an empathy that's practically a state of grace. Mitchell's profiles of Gould, the Harvard-educated Greenwich Village cadger and layabout and crackbrained philosopher, were written twenty-two years apart, with "Professor Seagull" appearing in 1942 and "Joe Gould's Secret" in 1964, seven years after Gould's death. Gould claimed to be compiling the longest book ever written, *An Oral History of the World*, which would give voice to everyone he encountered, especially the lowlifes and the dispossessed and the banished. He fancied himself a gutter Gibbon, and his antics, such as imitating seagulls, whose speech he believed he had deciphered, or performing a Chippewa dance in the middle of a Village soirée, were also his shtick. In the forties in New York, it was possible for someone like Gould to play the performing monkey for radical bohemia and make just enough to get by. He was even welcomed as a regular into some of the local clubs and hangouts, because his "authenticity" drew in the tourists looking to do a little slumming with the art set. He got close to the likes of e. e. cummings, who wrote a poem about him, and a snatch of his musings was once published in the magazine *The Dial*, which first published *The Waste Land*.

In the movie, which was scripted by Howard A. Rodman, Ian Holm's Joe Gould isn't quite as yammery as he appeared on the page. It would have been off-putting if he were. Gould lives in Mitchell's prose as a "character" of genius—the Flying Dutchman of the Village—but on the screen, his yowlings have been brought down to a manageable level. Holm's Gould is a character, all right, but he's also a believable person. The art of Holm's performance, of the entire movie, in fact, is in the way it humanizes the guy's weirdnesses and caterwaulings so we can spot the man beneath the grimy, exfoliating beard and rheumy eyes. There is no more satisfying moment in current movies than the one here, where Mitchell first walks over to Gould for an interview and the old sot's face expands into delight like one of those speeded-up shots of a flower unfolding.

There is a tendency in movies of this sort to place a nimbus around such a man, and *Joe Gould's Secret* doesn't entirely escape that trap. Gould is portrayed not just as a figure of resonant derangement but also as something more: a too sensitive soul who suffers for our bourgeois sins. Gould may be a dissembler in the particulars, but mainly he is shown to be a truth-teller, which is what we, too, would be if we weren't hemmed in by fuddy-duddy convention. In fact, so goes the movie, if we look within ourselves, we may perhaps discover our own inner Joe Gould. "He's a freak," says a cop about him to the proprietor of a diner Gould frequents. "We're all freaks," comes the reply. This is a disservice to Joe Gould, who could out-freak just about anybody.

The film also sets up a simpatico relationship between Gould and Mitchell—the two Joes—that's a bit too freaky-deaky. We're supposed to see both men as loners who feel at home only among other loners. Gould is an expatriate of illustrious Massachusetts lineage; Mitchell is a refugee from the South, from North Carolina, and he retains a Southerner's slow-cooked courtliness. Mitchell is shown with his wife (Hope Davis) and two daughters in scenes of snuggly harmony but, perhaps unintentionally, these moments feel weightless, as if we were observing a charade of what domestic bliss should be. Still, the hokiness of this lonely-hearts-club stuff is greatly alleviated by the extraordinary subtlety of the performers, particularly Tucci, who manages the extraordinary feat of turning a sounding board into a feeling, full-fledged character. There is a moment halfway through the film when Mitchell, weary of being hounded by Gould, hides from him in the *New Yorker* building while a receptionist lies about the writer's whereabouts, and the riven look on Tucci's face shows you how hollow Mitchell feels at that moment. Very few movies have ever dramatized as well as this one how a subject can take over a writer. Gould gets to Mitchell, not just as the subject of a profile but on a deeper, more elusive level; he's spooked by him, by the unreachableness of him. Gould is like some avenging imp who challenges Mitchell's complacencies about his profession. In approaching Gould and writing about him, Mitchell has entered into another person's life, and now, both literally and figuratively, he can't shake the guy. Noting at the end that Mitchell, who died in 1996, never published anything after his final Gould piece, the filmmakers make perhaps too large and sentimental a presumption about the men's relationship, but the presumption also has the ring of truth. If Joe Gould in this film is a bit like one of the mad, delusional barflies in *The Iceman Cometh*, then Joseph Mitchell is like that play's Larry Slade, who, alone in the end, is stripped of all illusion. He knows Joe Gould's secret, and he's stricken by it.

(New York, 2000)

Babe: Pig in the City

The advance word on *Babe: Pig in the City* was that it was "problematic"—studiospeak for uncommercial. Its benefit premiere in Los Angeles had been canceled amid dire rumors that the picture was too scary, too loud, too violent, too everything. This piqued my interest. *Babe II: Dark Meat*—what a concept! The first *Babe* was such a transcendently charming experience that redoing it wouldn't have worked anyway; it would be like trying to be a virgin again. Better to shake things up.

As it turns out, the new *Babe* isn't the horror show that was rumored. But it's certainly more raucous and rough-edged than the original. Arguably, it's even better. George Miller, the co-producer and co-writer of *Babe*, has directed and co-scripted the sequel, and his *Mad Max* dark roots are showing. The set pieces have a hearty grotesqueness, and the action is full-throttle. The film's showcase sequence is an extended chase in which the wee pig is pursued by a pit bull, and it has as much vroom as anything in *The Road Warrior*. I can understand why the executives at Universal were concerned; this sort of thing doesn't bode well for the franchise. So what? *Babe: Pig in the City* is every bit as funny as its predecessor, but it's funny in a screwier, twistier way.

By bringing the pig into the urban hell of strays and pet impounders, Miller—with his co-writers, Judy Morris and Mark Lamprell, and his animal trainers and animatronic experts—opens up a brave new world. Babe is the country rube in the big city, but he's also the rube as holy fool. By the film's end, his goodness triumphs over the Gotham grunge. ("I'm just a pig on a mission," he says.) In *Babe*, he was a leader of sheep. Now he's a leader of men—and ducks, chimps, poodles, even pit bulls. His innocence proves cast-iron.

Babe is first brought to the city by Farmer Hoggett's ovoid wife, Esme (Magda Szubanski), in a botched plan to feature him in a fair and use the fee to stave off the farm's foreclosure. They end up residents in a four-story rooming house—the Flealands Hotel—catering to pets. From its attic lookout, Babe surveys the skyline—it's the shot used in ads for the film—and sees a scrunched mélange of Manhattan, Hong Kong, Hollywood, Paris. It's an intimidating vista. By contrast, the rooming house is a romper-room oasis. The rickety, dark-toned majesty of the place suits its denizens, including the courtly orangutan Thelonius; Bob the hepcat chimp and his wife, Zootie, and brother, Easy; and, among other squallers and squawkers, a Neapolitan mastiff, an English bulldog, and a fleet-fingered capuchin monkey. If Charles Dickens had created a bestiary, it might have resembled this one. It's positively jovial with oddity.

Miller doesn't ask us to recognize the humanness of these critters. He doesn't go in for a lot of goopy anthropomorphism. Instead, he exults in his menagerie's animalness. In *Babe: Pig in the City*, being an animal is the highest station in life. The people we see—not just the porcine Esme but also her flamingo-thin husband, Farmer Hoggett (James Cromwell), and the rooming-house landlady (Mary Stein), with her whippet profile, and the chipmunk-cheeked clown Fugly Floom (Mickey Rooney)—haven't quite achieved the full-fledged look of their bestial counterparts. They're honorary members of the club, animals-in-transition.

The film is full of exemplary gestures, like the way Thelonius attempts to save his goldfish friend from marauding animal impounders without thinking to save himself; or the pelican who transports the wisequacking Ferdinand the duck in his bill before releasing him high above the city with the words "Farewell, noble duck." Flealick the arthritic terrier spins out in a chase and has an enchanted, end-of-life reverie in which he leaps loose-limbed at butterflies. And then there's Babe's finest moment, when he suddenly wheels around in that pit bull chase and calmly asks his pursuer, "One simple question. Why?"

Babe doesn't comprehend why animals—or people—self-destructively play out their natures. The pit bull clues him in: "I have a professional obligation to be malicious." And yet, when Babe's generosity redeems his attacker, it's as if all of evolution had suddenly been overruled. Babe brings together dogs and cats, pink poodles and pit bulls. Kids barred from this movie by wary parents are missing out on a helluva role model.

Still, I don't want to overstate the film's goody-goodyness. *Babe: Pig in the City* is no *Gandhi*. It's also not an archetypal quest. In interviews, Miller has attempted to frame Babe as a mythic hero, à la Joseph Campbell and all that jazz. But this is not at all how we experience the porker. (Miller blabbed the same line when he made the *Mad Max* movies, and *Lorenzo's Oil*, too. He's got myth-on-the-mind.) If the new *Babe* should be compared to anything, it's to those epic questers the Marx Brothers. Whether he admits it or not, Miller is a gonzo first and an educator second—a distant second. His new film is too *spirited* to be instructional. It's all over the place. At times it seems to summon up the whole history of show business, from fleabag vaudeville animal-novelty acts to the latest in animatronic whoop-de-doo. The animals are like the apotheosis of all the performing pets we've ever seen in the movies; each one is a stunner, and because they can talk, they're more vivid—and, for that reason, a bit more nightmarish, too. They assume personalities that remind us of everybody from Mafiosi to the Beats, and the shock is in how easily we buy the transformation. After a while, there's no dissonance at all; the alternate universe has become the real universe.

Miller loves the clangor of butting high culture with low. It's no accident that the Hollywood sign sits across from the Eiffel Tower in his skyline. Once again, as in the original *Babe*, he mixes in music from Saint-Saëns's Third Symphony—and it has never sounded better than when it's being trilled by singing mice. Elvis and Edith Piaf are similarly mouseketeered. He has the film's narrator say: "You can't always put things back together, but sometimes you can look at things afresh," and that's what he's done here. He's bid a frenzied farewell to the old *Babe* and given us a delirious new joyride.

(New York, 1998)

A Cry in the Dark

Fred Schepisi's *A Cry in the Dark* is an unremitting, almost magisterial vision of a horrific, true-to-life incident.

In the spring of 1980, Michael Chamberlain (Sam Neill), a Seventh-Day Adventist pastor, and his wife, Lindy (Meryl Streep), along with their two sons and nine-week-old daughter, Azaria, vacationed in the Australian Northern Territory at Ayers Rock, Australia's most popular tourist attraction (and a sacred Aboriginal site).

One evening, at a crowded campsite in the vicinity, a dingo (a wild Australian dog similar to the coyote) was seen scampering away from the tent where Azaria slept. Inside the bloodstained tent, Azaria was gone. A massive search ensued, but neither the baby nor the dingo was ever found.

Slowly, inexorably, what appeared at first to be a personal tragedy for the Chamberlains turned into a national witch hunt, as Lindy was charged with the killing of her baby. Cleared by the first inquest, Lindy, in a trial remarkable for its dubious evidence, ultimately was convicted of murder and, though pregnant, sentenced to life imprisonment. She served three and a half years before new evidence and judicial leniency resulted in her release in September of this year.

Given the opportunities for sensationalism, Schepisi and his co-screenwriter, Robert Caswell, adapting John Bryson's 1986 book *Evil Angels*—his furious defense of the Chamberlains—have done a remarkably lucid job of depicting Australia's hysteria over this case. *A Cry in the Dark* is so devoid of pulp that it's liable to be condemned by some in much the same terms as Lindy was—as too freakishly *calm* to be believable.

But the calm is only on the surface. The film, with its true-story/ human-interest/courtroom drama trappings, may have the superficial elements of a made-for-TV movie, but it has a resonance that comes from the filmmakers' deep, abiding sympathy for the Chamberlains' flinty resolve. Schepisi's great cinematographer, Ian Baker, shot the movie in wide-screen Panavision, and the vistas suggest larger meanings: waiting-to-be-tapped sources of power.

Schepisi recreates the story not only as a family tragedy but as a national tragedy. There's a tamped-down fury to his work here, a measured rage at the spectacle of prejudices unleashed. Schepisi's anger goes beyond the reformer's; it's an expression of cosmic disgust.

And yet Schepisi and Meryl Streep make you understand how it is that Lindy Chamberlain, with her hard manners and jet-black bangs, could give the country the cold creeps. Given the film's high intelligence, a more sentimental approach would have been another form of sensationalism. Schepisi acknowledges the differentness of the Chamberlains without acceding to the popular view of their "otherness." The film implies that their Seventh-Day Adventism inspired fear—and therefore hatred—in a populace all too willing to believe in secret sacrificial rites. Lindy herself becomes a human sacrifice in the public's own blood sport; she and Michael are made to embody her detractors' darkest impulses. (Michael, convicted as an accessory to the crime, was allowed to remain home with the two boys and, after her birth inside prison, his baby girl.)

Lindy's prosecution hinged in large part on the disbelief among white Australians that a dingo—the national mascot—could carry off a baby. But the point is made in the film (as in Bryson's book) that the Aborigines, several of whom tracked Azaria's disappearance, knew the truth to be otherwise. Yet the Aborigines were never brought in for testimony. In *A Cry in the Dark*, religious intolerance and racism are linked. Victimization makes for strange bedfellows: Seventh-Day Adventists and Aborigines.

The link is also made between religious intolerance and sexuality—Lindy's. Schepisi understands, as Carl Dreyer also did in *Day of Wrath*, just how intimately imputations of witchery are bound up with sexuality. Schepisi eroticizes Lindy for us; in one of her first scenes, in bed with her husband, she has a glow, a lushness, as if the armor of public rectitude had been cast aside, gently. She has a totally unselfconscious beauty in sequences like these.

On the witness stand, or giving interviews before the incessant TV camera crews, Lindy doesn't yield up her sorrows easily; but we know they are there because we've seen her in private, unveiled. It's a matter of almost religious principle that she not reveal her vulnerability to the hordes. Still, there's a sensual edge to her defiance, and her accusers pick up on it. It's what gives her sharpness its sting.

A Cry in the Dark may be the most quietly uncondescending film ever made about religious fundamentalists. Schepisi can humanize Lindy and Michael and their fellow congregationalists because he isn't repelled by their rectitude; he can locate the human being inside the dogma. (Schepisi may have a special sensitivity for religious subjects. His first film, the elating, semi-autobiographical *The Devil's Playground*, set in a Marist boys' seminary, was the work of a filmmaker who could look back on his incarceration with a fond sanity.)

It's clear in *A Cry in the Dark* that Michael and Lindy's staunchness has a lot to do with their belief in the Second Coming, when they will be reunited with Azaria. When they state for the cameras that "nothing happens in the world unless God allows it," it's a way of comforting themselves, even if the public mistakes their covenant and brands them unfeeling. Michael is surprisingly media-savvy, but he's no profiteer. He has a preacher's yen to spread the word, but he's not out to convert anybody, really. He's just using the worldly materials so promiscuously at his disposal to justify his own fearsome condition.

Like Schepisi, Meryl Streep and Sam Neill have a gift for humanizing characters traditionally ill-treated in the movies. Streep sounds preternaturally Aussie—she has truly become Our Lady of the Accents. But her latest makeover is no stunt. Her performance is an attempt to make us understand how Lindy's principled, almost drab straightforwardness was her only purchase on heroism. Streep takes her cue from Lindy; there's no special pleading in her acting, no grandstanding. She makes you accept Lindy on her own ornery, embattled terms.

Sam Neill works so subtly with Streep that, for long stretches of the film, they seem to be communicating in code. Lindy and Michael share a sense of privilege based on faith, but the film is at its most ambiguously moving when it shows us how that faith is tested. In the wake of Azaria's disappearance, the Chamberlains never renounce their beliefs, but they move through the film in a state of controlled shock. They're waiting for some sign, some clue as to why this is happening to them. We can sense in their bewildered, fortified smiles the hysteria underneath. Although they may not realize it, the truest sign of grace in their ordeal is that they stayed together. After you've seen *A Cry in the Dark*, you'll know why.

(Los Angeles Herald Examiner, 1988)

Madadayo

Akira Kurosawa's thirtieth and last film, *Madadayo*, was completed in 1992 and, criminally, is only now being shown in the U.S. (he died in 1998). It's customary to call a master director's final film a summation, or a leave-taking, but most often this sentiment is bunk; artists don't get to pick their moments with such precision. And yet, certain lucky filmmakers do manage to pull off what amounts to an orchestrated valedictory. John Huston did it when he made *The Dead*, which is voluminously rich in its intimations of mortality. *Madadayo* is similarly concerned with the approaches of death, and of what it means to have lived a good life.

It's an extremely formalized work, a series of mostly stationary set pieces, and it will disappoint viewers who still think of Kurosawa as the thunderous, supple master of films like *Seven Samurai* and *Yojimbo*, or a later work like *Ran*, which, by a fine piece of timing, is currently in national rerelease. Kurosawa has always somewhat mistakenly been called the most Western of Japanese directors. Partly this is because a number of his movies were remade by Hollywood, or were derived from writers ranging from Shakespeare and Dostoevsky to Ed McBain, but it's also because his vigorous multi-camera technique in his most famous movies broke with the traditional orthodoxies of masters like Yasujiro Ozu. You can go through an entire festival of Ozu films without spotting a single tracking shot; his imagery has a stilled, sacramental quality. And yet Kurosawa's imagery can have this quality, too, and no more so than in *Madadayo*, in which a lifetime of moviemaking—Kurosawa was eighty-three when he made it—seems to have pared down his technique to its essentials. We are looking at the work of a director who no longer needs to charge the screen with dynamism in order to achieve his effects. He's reaching for something more quietly ineffable, a rigorous splendor. He asks his audience to contemplate, in a kind of communal silence, the beauty of the imagery, and the beauty of the emotion behind the imagery.

Madadayo is a celebration of a professor beloved by his university students. It begins in 1943 as Hyakken Uchida (Tatsuo Matsumura) announces to his class his plan to retire, after thirty years of teaching, in order to write books. Professor Uchida was a real person who taught German literature and wrote novels and essays and haiku on subjects ranging from locomotives to the wartime Tokyo air raids, but Kurosawa doesn't provide us with the contours of an academic life; his professor is not so much an actual person as a vivid essence. Uchida is an idealization of grace, and Kurosawa's identification with him is total. This man, we are made to feel, is the fulfillment of the director's own best self.

The film is marked by a series of birthday tributes to Uchida put on by his students, starting with the professor's sixtieth and culminating in his seventy-seventh and, perhaps, last. In the years between, in a variety of mostly dry, sweetly comical situations, we see Uchida and his wife (Kyôko Kagawa) play host to the students, who at first cannot stand to see their *sensei* living in such cramped circumstances and organize to find him more spacious quarters. They are honored to watch over him. When Uchida's much-doted-upon cat is lost, sending him into a deep depression, the students form a search party. They never think to make light of his grief. He suffers because, as one of the pupils says with pride, "his sensitivity and imagination are beyond us." And yet the students also recognize what Uchida's wife realizes, too—that he has never really grown up. Uchida is revered by his students both for his calm wisdom and for his childlike bemusement, which is perceived as a kind of holy innocence. Uchida makes his final birthday speech to the children and grandchildren of his students, and in this moment he seems a perfect fusion of man and cherub; his rapport with these young ones is without a trace of condescension. "Find something in life you are able to treasure," he tells them. Uchida is a man whose kindness has saved him from despair.

It is poetically perfect that Kurosawa closes the film with a dream of Uchida's in which the old man imagines himself as a boy. Kurosawa's dream sequences have always been transcendent, and this brief final scene is so quietly devastating that it summons up, in a rush, the profoundest melancholy. Throughout the film we have seen the students and Uchida play a children's game; they ask him if he is ready to pass into the afterlife, and he responds heartily, "*Madadayo*," which means "No, not yet." In his dream, Uchida conjures this hide-and-seek game between children and that boy, and the screen at the end is filled with a lustrous wash of colors. They are the colors of a sky in which the sun could be rising—or setting.

(*New York*, 2000)

Trouble in Mind

Alan Rudolph has always had a prodigious ease as a filmmaker and a prodigious pretentiousness as an idea man. In movies like *Welcome to L.A.* and *Remember My Name*, you could take pleasure in the way he moved the camera and framed his compositions, but his characters talked as if they had spent too much time in deprivation tanks. If you melted down their dialogue, it would make a great paste wax—you could shine your furniture with it. Last year's *Choose Me* was dubbed the Rudolph movie for people who don't like Rudolph, but I still didn't care much for it. A lot of what people took to be satirical and funny just seemed like the usual Rudolphisms to me, with a twirl or two.

Trouble in Mind is unmistakably an Alan Rudolph film; it retains some of his arch swooniness. But it's also a captivating, bizarre film noir fantasia. The best part of *Choose Me* was the lyrical opening sequence in the street, scored to Teddy Pendergrass; Rudolph extends the pleasure of that scene—its sensual tingle—throughout most of *Trouble in Mind*. He does in this film what I think he was mistakenly credited with doing in *Choose Me*. Along with his extraordinary cinematographer, Toyomichi Kurita, he turns his pretensions into cracked, lyric flights of fancy. It's funny in the dank, brittle way that some of the best films noirs were, when they were at their most tough-guy poetic, and it's as dreamy and trancelike as those films sometimes were, too. Rudolph can do anything he wants to in this movie—his style is so perfected that the film has the effect of a single, uninterrupted camera move through noir corridors and drizzly cityscapes.

Kris Kristofferson is the blasted, bitter hero who, in the best film noir tradition, sees his salvation in a young, unsullied woman. A cop who spent a long stretch in the clink for the vengeance shooting of a mob-ster, Kristofferson's Hawk has returned to his haunt—the grayish Rain City, in an unspecified future where language and currency have subtly changed and the militia is a presence in the streets. He takes a room above the breakfast diner run by an old flame, Wanda (Genevieve Bujold), and spends a lot of time gazing out of his window (he constructs a cardboard miniature model of the street scene) and picking at his ham and eggs in the diner downstairs. The diner is Edward Hopperish, with a neon glow. Even in daylight, its denizens seemed slugged and depleted. They're like vampires sapped of their strength when the cold light hits their faces. It's a familiar grungy tableau, and yet Rudolph makes it like nothing you've ever seen: a busboy swats roaches with addled aplomb, a black poet (Joe Morton) sits in a booth wreathed in plumes of cigarette smoke and spews screwy, philosophy-major blank verse.

This poet is also a low-level gangster looking for a partner, and he finds him in Keith Carradine's Coop, a country boy who brings his girl-friend, Georgia (Lori Singer), and their baby girl to the big city to make a score. That's a great noir theme—the corrupting influence of the big bad city. (It was also a central theme in silent films; Rudolph makes us under-stand the visual and thematic links between noir and movies like Mur-nau's *Sunrise* and *City Girl*, passages in Griffith, even Keaton.) Rudolph plays around with this theme. Once Coop falls in with crooks, he whoops it up in sordid little fleabag-hotel-room orgies and leaves his girlfriend in-creasingly open to the tough-tender ministrations of Hawk, who's in love with her innocence. Every time we see Coop, his clothes become flashier, his features more jagged. His hair, swooped into a warlock's pompadour, becomes more outré. By the end of the film, Carradine resembles Willem Dafoe's comic-book villain in Walter Hill's *Streets of Fire*, with his lurid nostrils and vampire's widow's peak. And yet he's not scary, just pathetic. This rube is like a futurist noir version of the small-timers who come to Hollywood and immediately go for the open-shirt-and-medallion look. Rudolph turns Coop's corruptibleness into an absurdist joke.

He also turns Coop into something of an artwork. Noir characters, at their best, were always poetic conceits. Rudolph takes the conceit a step further. The people in *Trouble in Mind* are like centerpieces in their own private museum. They take the light like showcase sculptures, and they're coordinated with the decor: the huge deco palace of Rain City's kingpin gangster, played by Divine (without the female-impersonator accoutrements); Hawk's cinderblock apartment; a Chinese restaurant, with its loud red and golds; Georgia's opium-den yellow room. Joe Morton (the mute "Brother from Another Planet") is an artwork, too. He's burnt ocher to Coop's gilded white lily. Rudolph has a jangly modern artist's love of visual collision. In *Choose Me*, Susan Scott's image-text paintings were on the walls of Genevieve Bujold's apartment, and movie posters were used pop-art style in Rae Dawn Chong's digs. In *Trouble in Mind*, Rudolph uses sculptor Dale Chilhuly's elegant glassworks. Joe Morton's apartment is like a Zen computer nut's pad, and Divine's mansion has a towering cylindrical Lucite fish tank. Rudolph filmed in Seattle, and he uses the Space Needle in one scene as though it were specially designed for the film. Like most of the movie, it has a piquant abstract quality.

Noir movies have always distinguished themselves with their look. The inky expressionist visual designs, framed in highly contrasting shades of black and white, were like the leopard skins of the characters, the stories. There have been a few color noirs (*Chinatown*, *Farewell My Lovely*), but no one has ever reworked the genre the way Rudolph has in *Trouble in Mind*. He's taken the genre's inherent visual elegance and brought it into the realm of abstract art. He's given film noir a modernist, out-of-the-mainstream flavoring. He can stage a shoot-out in a deco mansion and make it look like *Hellzapoppin'* at the Guggenheim.

You would expect the actors to fade into the ozone with a movie this designed-to-the-teeth, but they bring their own stylishness to the piece. Kristofferson is strong and brooding; Bujold is tart, like a nouveau Ida Lupino. Keith Carradine is loonily intense—he doesn't point up for the audience his overweening pompadour. Lori Singer could have been more resonant, and Divine—in the Sydney Greenstreet role—isn't wonderful (this is his first time playing a man). But even the bad acting in this film is all of a piece with Rudolph's off-kilter design. And he uses Mark Isham's pop-rock-jazz fusion score to lull the audience into the design, into the mood. It's true that you can grate your teeth on some of the lines in this movie—at one point, Kristofferson says, "You gotta be nice to your friends because without them, you're a total stranger." But highfalutin dialogue is no stranger to noir. Charles Brackett and Raymond Chandler and Ben Hecht came up with some lulus in their day. It's part of the texture of the movies. There was always something slightly absurd about film noir, with its doom-tinged aura and moody-blues people.

Trouble in Mind finally locates a filmic universe for Rudolph's artificial-world gifts. He's never seemed so at home.

(Los Angeles Herald Examiner, 1985)

A Modest Proposal

Reviewers sometimes overrate the underseen. In the run-up to their year-end awards, most critics' societies indulge in last-minute in-house lobbying for their favorite films, often the more pretentious and overblown, the better. Fed up, I posted a gag e-mail to the members of the Los Angeles Film Critics Association on the eve of our vote. At least one of the members wasn't sure I was kidding and thought I was attacking the New Romanian cinema.

> Friends:
>
> I know there is little time before we vote, but I just recently saw something that certainly would qualify for honors if only enough critics could see it. I refer to *Wha?*, the debut film from a young Tuvan director named Mr. Mxypltk who currently resides in the Cotswolds in Lower Slaughter after attending film school in Tanganyika.
>
> *Wha?* is about a dyslexic ventriloquist who is kidnapped by rabid followers of Walter Benjamin, and it is unlike any movie I have ever seen—or not seen, for that matter. Since it did not play locally, I have taken the liberty of having screeners sent to all members by midnight tonight.
>
> I realize that its eight-hour running time may prove an obstacle to some, but since almost two of those hours are blank leader—an extended homage, apparently, to the closing frames of Bresson's *Le Journal d'un Curé de Campagne*—there is ample time for bathroom breaks.
>
> This film could change the face of cinema. I know it changed mine.

CHAPTER 2

YOUNGISH TURKS

SPIKE JONZE

Being John Malkovich

Being John Malkovich is the most comically strange and original movie of the year. Like most one-of-a-kind films, it exists almost entirely within its own wiggy frame of reference, and yet, by touching on so many aesthetic conundrums, it's the art film of the moment—or the moment just ahead. Dazzlingly singular movies aren't often this much fun. The director, Spike Jonze, and his screenwriter, Charlie Kaufman, both making their feature-film debuts, transform their notions about the nature of celebrity and time and inspiration into a kind of metaphysical vaudeville. Imagine Pynchon or Nabokov or Borges with a neo-slacker's absurdist spin, and add to it something far more mysterious, a feeling for the crawl spaces in our pop-cult consciousness. There's more going on inside this movie's brainpan than in many a pretentious European import, or stateside equivalent, and yet, in the best American tradition, it wears its intelligence lightly. Only after the film is over do you realize the passion and melancholy that also went into it. *Being John Malkovich* may turn out to be the latest word in cutting-edge hip, but it's just about the least *cynical* hip movie ever made.

The filmmakers at once parody and dignify the earnestness of the self-conscious artist, personified here by Craig Schwartz (John Cusack), a dejected puppeteer who believes himself unemployable because he "raises issues." He does, but that's probably not the only reason he's unemployable; he's also one ornery prima donna. He creates a mini-ballet called *Dance of Despair and Disillusionment*, featuring a puppet with a painted-on face identical to Craig's, which, incidentally, resembles Jesus's; he stages on the streets of New York a lyrical marionette play featuring Abélard and Héloïse, concluding with the two medieval lovebirds, separated by a cell wall, simulating sex. (A father, watching his young daughter gape at the sight, punches out the puppetmaster.) Craig has the ratty, blasted look of a street person who could be bonkers or some kind of visionary (or both). His idea of existence is simple and self-pitying: *I think, I feel, I suffer.* He's a poseur but also highly gifted. Enthralled by his own expressiveness, he's the master of his play-act domain.

Craig's wife, Lotte (Cameron Diaz), works in a pet store and crowds their cramped apartment with its denizens, including a brash parrot and a chimp named Elijah (she's been taking him to a chimp shrink). Wearing no makeup and frumpily dressed, with wide, blank eyes and big, frizzed hair, Lotte has a vaguely tropical, gone-native look. Just as Craig is more intensely connected to his puppet world than to the people world, Lotte is emotionally of-a-piece with her pets (she brings Elijah into their bed for consoling).

Up until this point, we've been witnessing a fractured romantic farce in which both romancers are essentially wooing themselves. But Jonze and Kaufman move way beyond the formalities of genre; the film progresses in a series of riffs and spirals, each one wilder than the one before, and yet it's all highly controlled, deadpan. The twenty-nine-year-old Jonze (whose real name is Adam Spiegel, of the Spiegel catalog family) is perhaps the best of the music-video and TV-commercial directors, but he doesn't go in for a lot of whiz-bang gyrations here; he understands how the film's transcendent strangeness is best served straight up.

What follows is a daisy chain of loopy linkages. Here's a taste: Craig takes a job as an entry-level filing clerk on floor seven and a half of a Manhattan office building, with ceilings so low that employees walk beneath them crookbacked. Craig's boss (Orson Bean) is a hale-looking 105-year-old who survives on carrot juice; Maxine (Catherine Keener), a snappish fellow employee, draws out Craig's lust and throws it back at him, unrequited. Then Craig discovers, behind a filing cabinet in his office, a portal which leads him, with a whoosh through its oozy dampness, straight into the head of John Malkovich. For precisely fifteen minutes he sees the world through the unsuspecting actor's eyes—reading his *Wall Street Journal*, munching his morning toast—before dropping rudely down to earth in a ditch beside the New Jersey Turnpike. Craig and Maxine seize the entrepreneurial moment—after hours they charge people two hundred dollars to "be" John Malkovich for fifteen minutes. Lotte gets in on the ride, too—she finds herself inside Malkovich as he makes love to Maxine, and falls for her, and she for Lotte, but only when Lotte is looking back at her through the eyes of the actor. All of which brings on Craig's jealousy—he decides he must inhabit Malkovich and dominate him the way he does his puppets.

The grandest joke in the movie is that, for the people who inhabit Malkovich, it's enough that they are inside him; it makes no difference if he's simply picking at some Chinese takeout from the fridge or ordering up bathroom mats from a catalog. Celebrity is all—even if, as with most of the people who are in for the ride, the specifics of the celebrity are fuzzy (no one seems to know the exact nature of Malkovich's credits). The vicariousness of life lived through another—which is the hallmark of our celebrity-obsessed age—is here rendered literally; even mundaneness is made to seem special when viewed through the eyes of a star. The famous are our portals into an enhanced nothingness, and we gladly go for it.

John Malkovich is the ideal actor to play, well, John Malkovich. His air of wayward distraction is aggressively creepy, his big, baldish head here has a puppetlike blockiness, and he looks like he might indeed have another pair of eyes inside his own. In fact, *every* actor in this movie (and they are all marvelous) appears to be inhabited. They contain a multitude of selves, like those Russian dolls-within-dolls. And yet, this flurry of inner identities—transgendered, transfixed, evanescent—feels right; it's how we see ourselves now, not as a single character but as a gallery of characters butting up against each other.

And the gallery is always up for grabs. When Malkovich, upon discovering what's going on, yells at Craig to seal up the portal because "It's my head," Craig responds, "It's my livelihood." Here, in a nutshell, is the postmodern condition: You no longer own your mind. And yet the movie doesn't stop there, for what is acting—what is all art—but a form of vicarious byplay? The audience sees through the eyes of the artist and, whether it be for fifteen minutes or fifteen hours, co-opts the artist's way of seeing. The metaphor of the movie ultimately collapses in upon itself: Jonze and Kaufman condemn the way the culture invades our heads, but their film is itself a portal into their own minds. For the artist, for the audience, there is no way to escape being a voyeur.

I hope I'm not making *Being John Malkovich* out to be some kind of philosophy seminar in camouflage, but, like Craig, it "raises issues," and I don't see why they should be downplayed just because the movie is such an abracadabra joyride. It couldn't come at a better time, both in terms of the zeitgeist it's lancing and in terms of the film industry, which needs all the replenishing it can get. It's the most impressive debut movie I've seen in years.

(New York, 1999)

Adaptation

Like *Being John Malkovich*, the first collaboration between director Spike Jonze and screenwriter Charlie Kaufman, their new movie, *Adaptation*, is spellbindingly original. At a time when even the sharpest Hollywood talents tend to play it safe, this film is almost an affront. It's as if the filmmakers were saying to us, "Movies don't have to be bad just because Hollywood makes it so difficult to be good." The movie business has never been more afraid of risk, and *Adaptation* is, among many other things, a comedy about that very problem. It's about the despair of an artist trying to be passionate about what he does in a bottom-line era that's anything but. Paradoxically, it's also about the miseries of having creative freedom, when there is no one to blame but yourself for what you come up with.

Kaufman is not only the movie's screenwriter but also its chief protagonist. The way this came about has become part of *Adaptation*'s wacky lore. Initially, Kaufman was hired to adapt Susan Orlean's nonfiction book *The Orchid Thief*, a marvelously meandering meditation on orchids and the mania for collecting them that focused on a South Florida trickster named John Laroche. (Orlean is played by Meryl Streep, Laroche by Chris Cooper.) Kaufman couldn't come up with a way to adapt the book as a conventional drama, so he ended up writing a movie about a screenwriter—"himself"—who can't figure out a way to adapt *The Orchid Thief* and ends up inserting himself into his own script.

What's more, Charlie has a twin brother named Donald. Both roles are played, in a real tour de force, by Nicolas Cage, in two of the slyest and most intuitive performances he's given in years. Donald camps out in Charlie's barely furnished Hollywood home and wants to be a screenwriter, too. (The screenplay for *Adaptation* is officially credited to the two brothers, for that hall-of-mirrors effect.) The brothers may look identical, but temperamentally they couldn't be farther apart. Donald is a loutish swinger whose script is a crass piece of commercialism about a serial killer with multiple personalities (its title: *The Three*). Sorry-faced Charlie runs himself down mercilessly and gets clammy around pretty women. He's the opposite of a Hollywood slickster, but the success of *Being John Malkovich*—we are shown staged flashbacks of the making of that film, with many of its original cast and crew reassembled—has made him "hot." Charlie's agent (Ron Livingston), a foulmouthed shark, admiringly calls him "the king of crazy shit." The producer (Tilda Swinton) of the *Orchid Thief* project tells him over lunch that she'd love to have a portal into his brain (shades of *Being John Malkovich*). Charlie would like nothing more than a portal into anyone's world but his own; he thinks his decision to place himself inside his own script is pathetic.

What makes the film so bizarrely touching is that Charlie is a *soulful* kvetch. Like everything else for him, screenwriting is intensely personal, and since his life maunders aimlessly, he can't understand why his screenplays shouldn't also; he doesn't think he needs conflicts and character arcs and all the other necessities of the trade espoused by screenwriting gurus like Robert McKee, the real-life script-seminar potentate played here by a bellowing Brian Cox. Donald swears by McKee, but Charlie despises what he deems the unnaturalness of McKee's commandments. And yet Charlie (not to mention the real-life Kaufman) is smart enough to admit that the McKees of the world have something to teach him: If you can figure out the logic of a story, maybe you can find the logic of your own life.

Adaptation zooms around in time, going as far back as the bubbling beginnings of the planet, with zippy little visual essays on Darwin and orchids. Susan Orlean, the Manhattan-based *New Yorker* writer, is also a protagonist, and her tagging-along with Laroche through the Everglades in search of rare orchids is her own swampy attempt at finding something to be passionate about. After a career of tightly controlled performances, Meryl Streep seems totally replenished in this film; maybe the heat and the languor got to her, but she's never been more sensually open than she is here. She seems to be in a perpetual state of awed discombobulation. (She has a great moment when, stoned on some plant powder Laroche has sent her, she imitates a dial tone.) In a way, Susan is a soul mate for Charlie, who is mightily disconnected, too; and yet, until the end, he never gets up the gumption to meet her. The closest he comes is chickening out when he finds himself in an elevator with her. Donald eventually ends up posing as Charlie to interview her.

Charlie can't help fantasizing about Susan, though. *Adaptation* gets at the way we build erotic scenarios around the authors we read and how we imagine their real lives to be. In *The Orchid Thief,* Susan the reporter and Laroche, her subject, are chaste acquaintances, but in *Adaptation* they become lovers. It makes sense, too. Laroche is skanky and missing his front teeth, but Chris Cooper gives him such a cunning vitality that you can see how he might crumble the defenses of someone like Susan, who, without being fully aware of it, is looking to be exalted by ardor. That's what Charlie is looking for, too, and the fact that he is trying to find it in, of all places, the movie business is what gives the film its wraparound wit and also its heavy air of regret. Only the ending falters (it did in *Being John Malkovich*, too). Jonze and Kaufman engineer the kind of shotgun melodramatics they otherwise deride, and even though this irony is probably intentional, emotionally it doesn't work at all.

Still, few recent movies have conveyed so forcefully how people can feel shut out by their own lack of passion, how they yearn to end the emptiness. *Adaptation* is full of defeatism: Charlie the nut-brain artist flounders while his brother's laughable high-concept script sells for a fortune. And yet the movie itself is proof that something new and triumphantly self-invented can still come out of the studios. Like the wild orchid, *Adaptation* is a marvel of adaptation, entwined with its hothouse environment and yet stunningly unique.

(*New York*, 2002)

RICHARD LINKLATER
Waking Life

Richard Linklater's *Waking Life* is an astounding, one-of-a-kind movie. A live-action film shot and edited on digital video, it was then "painted over" by more than thirty computer-graphics artists under the supervision of art director Bob Sabiston, and the result has a shimmering sinuosity. That's entirely appropriate for a movie about consciousness and dream states and how we apprehend reality. A nameless young man, played by Wiley Wiggins, passes through a linked series of vignettes in which people, singly or in groups, offer up their philosophical ramblings and pensées. As with the boy, we are never sure what is real and what is a dream. The imagery may pulsate, but the dialogue track is recorded straightforwardly, without artifice, and the clash between eye and ear is highly evocative and unsettling. Watching this film is like inhabiting two planes of emotion simultaneously, one soaring, the other down-to-earth. We're pulled in opposite directions, and yet, as both an intellectual and sensual experience, it all adds up. Or, to be more exact, the disarray of moods and ideas in this film forms its own kind of completeness. Linklater doesn't attempt to tie anything up, because life can't be tied up. Like any card-carrying postmodernist, he has a profound respect for ambiguity.

I realize this may sound like a snooze, or, worse, a pretentious snooze. It's anything but. If there was ever a film that made ontological exploration fun, this is it. Linklater uses a tango music track, and you can see why—with its split-second way of turning the corner on emotions, from the giddy to the tragic and back again, the sound of tango has the same sensual pliability as filmed animation. *Waking Life* revels in the chaos of conceits and of dreams, but in the process of taking itself very seriously, it also has a frisky, self-deprecating side. (In one scene, a band of men declares that they are "all theory and no action.") Linklater is like some brainy philosophy grad student who sees both the fervor and the whimsy in all this conceptualizing. For a movie that is so metaphysics-minded, it has an almost tender acceptance of how people can be bollixed by their own high-flown ruminations. It also has an awareness of how ideas can madden people and rip them out of their senses; a monologue of a jailed, vengeful man, his head a red bulb of hate, is particularly terrifying.

The mood of impassioned, questioning sympathy in *Waking Life* is similar to Godard's in his films from the sixties and seventies, especially *La Chinoise,* with its agitating intellectual renegades. Linklater didn't write his screenplay, exactly; for the most part, he shaped and orchestrated the self-scripted discourse of his separate characters, each chosen for their oddball passions. (Ethan Hawke and Julie Delpy, from Linklater's *Before Sunrise,* and Speed Levitch, the motormouth real-life tour guide from the documentary *The Cruise,* all turn up, but most of the other performers, including Linklater himself, are non-actors.) At one point, somebody tells the boy, "Your life is yours to create," and that's the spirit of the movie, too; Linklater and his animators appear to be whipping up the experience right before our eyes (although, in fact, it took about 250 hours of animation work to create each minute of film).

There's an awed wonderment at the core of *Waking Life,* not only for what it means to be wide-eyed but also for the properties of film itself. Much has been made by film theoreticians of the dreamlike nature of moviegoing, and most of the time this talk is just babble; if anything, we watch movies, good ones anyway, in a state of *heightened* consciousness. But Linklater is right in believing that, in the way movies are put together, their sense of time and place and memory mimic the nonlinear jumble of how our minds work. At least that's how *Waking Life* works. Its young visionary, who seems to be living inside a lucid dream, is the viewer's counterpart. Like him, we find ourselves fighting our way out of false awakenings. *Waking Life* may have been shot initially in a live-action format, but it needed the shape-shifting fluency of animation to bring out its essence. After you've finished watching it, you can't imagine it being done any other way.

(New York, 2001)

POSTSCRIPT

With *Slacker, Waking Life, The School of Rock,* the sublime young-love duet of *Before Sunrise* and *Before Sunset,* and the life-in-the-theater mini-classic *Me and Orson Welles,* Linklater has shown himself to be the most versatile and highly gifted director of his generation.

TODD FIELD

In the Bedroom

In the Bedroom, starring Tom Wilkinson and Sissy Spacek as parents coping with the murder of their son, is a lousy title for a wonderful movie. Adapted from the Andre Dubus short story "Killings"—a far better and more appropriate title—it unfolds with cumulative power. The narrative has all the contours of a classic revenge fantasy, but until the end we're too caught up in the human details and psychological nuances to register its inevitability. Pulled deeply inside the puzzlement and grief of Matt and Ruth Fowler, we see the world as they do; we're brought step by step, without our conscious assent, to the edge of a precipice that was waiting there all along.

Todd Field, who co-wrote the script with Rob Festinger, is an actor (*Ruby in Paradise, Eyes Wide Shut*) making his directorial debut, and he keeps the film squarely focused on the performers—which in this case is doubly rewarding since the performers are so uniformly good. It's rare to see a movie that serves acting in this way, without a lot of hocus-pocus camerawork and overwrought close-ups. Field keeps his distance from the players, allowing them to work up their dramatic moments in what resembles real time. They seem like actual, flawed human beings, and their fate matters to us. When Matt, a doctor in a Maine fishing town, moves into action against his son's killer (William Mapother), out on bail, our identification with the father is almost unbearable; if this man, so companionable and fair-minded, can be twisted toward such a retribution, then he could just as well stand in for all of us. It is not the violence of the already violent that is truly shocking—the real horror lies in watching *decent* people driven to mayhem.

Not that the Fowlers are sentimentalized. Part of what makes them seem so close to us is the ambiguity of their good intentions. Their boy Frank (Nick Stahl), at the beginning of the movie, has been having a summertime romance with Natalie (Marisa Tomei), a woman at least a decade older with two small boys. Ruth doesn't like the look of it: Natalie, living by herself, is not yet divorced from her husband, and she doesn't fit into Ruth's conventional notions of her son's future. Frank is a gifted architecture student on his way to college, and Natalie, bearing the comforts of a ready-made family, is, as Ruth sees it, a dangerous detour. Making matters worse for Ruth is the fact that Matt likes having Natalie around; he eyes her admiringly, taking pleasure in his boy's success with her, which he perhaps imagines as his own.

Matt and Frank are very close. We can see their shared delight in each other during a marvelous lobstering scene, as well as in any number of other, more covert and unspoken moments. Ruth, who keeps her home immaculately appointed, as if it were a fortress of domesticity, is more controlling with her son than Matt is; perhaps she resents the bond he has with his father. When Frank is murdered by Natalie's estranged husband—the murder, typical of Field's principled reticence, happens off-camera—Ruth's resentments boil over. "Frank died for your fantasy piece of ass," she cries out to her husband, who stands convicted and bewildered. Natalie, approaching Ruth for forgiveness, is slapped—that slap makes the screen vibrate. Sissy Spacek is as good as she can be here. The control that Ruth has exerted over her life has come apart, horribly, and she suffers for it as she makes others suffer. You can't pity her, because she doesn't invite pity; there's almost a nobility in the way this woman holds on to her rage, which is all she's got to get her through her grief.

Matt lives a different kind of hell. His way of surviving his son's murder is to stifle his mournfulness. Ruth pleads with him to stop acting like nothing happened, and she's not wrong to do so. But Matt has further to travel to reach his vehemence. When he begins to take tentative measures to root out the killer he is convinced will get off easy, it's almost as if he's separating himself in two, coolly observing himself play out his retribution. Tom Wilkinson gives Matt the look of a man entirely fixated by an idea; once this good doctor takes up the role of avenger, he acquires the cast-iron control that had been Ruth's. He becomes her surrogate, her savior.

The brief Andre Dubus story that this film fills out has a far more focused rage. It's a harrowing fable about the limits and bounties of Christian salvation—although the religiosity is all implicit—and Dubus gives everything a fairly lurid overlay, a brackish dread. Dubus saw the murders as the playing out of larger forces. Field, who was friends with Dubus up until his death in 1999, doesn't share the writer's Catholic presentiments or his ravaged masculine code; he's a much less complicated artist. But in his own straight-ahead way, he is pursuing the same issues of faith as

Dubus was. He's made a thriller about what we are capable of in the name of hatred—and of love.

(New York, 2001)

PAUL THOMAS ANDERSON

Boogie Nights

Writer-director Paul Thomas Anderson's *Boogie Nights* opens with a sinuous, breathlessly extended tracking shot that swoops us into a San Fernando Valley disco and then does a curlicue around a succession of faces. In the discotheque's low-lit luminescence, these people pop out like jack o' lanterns. They have the look of trashy royalty—exalted and debased.

It's 1977, the height of the disco era, and the royalty we glimpse are players from the porno-film world. Anderson takes a while to let us discover this. He wants us to feel the thump and swoon inside the disco the way Scorsese wanted us to feel the hellish intoxication in the early strip-bar scene in *Mean Streets*.

Anderson doesn't draw on the same Catholic tensions as Scorsese, but this two-and-a-half-hour porno-world epic finally offers up its own biblical-style retribution and forgiveness. It's a deeply divided film—hugely ambitious and uneven, with sequences that seem to point to a new, comically flagrant movie sexuality and others that drag one into the funky muddle of the dreariest dopehead downers from the seventies.

In its most basic outline, *Boogie Nights* is a rags-to-riches-to-rags saga—Horatio Alger as studmuffin gone bad. Eddie Adams (Mark Wahlberg) starts out washing dishes in that Valley disco and ends up as Dirk Diggler, porno's premier male star. His mentor is producer-director Jack Horner (Burt Reynolds), who first approaches Eddie in the dishroom by saying, "I got a feeling underneath those jeans is something wonderful waiting to come out." This may sound like a proposition, but it's strictly business. Later, for a look-see, Eddie unzips himself for the Colonel (Robert Ridgely), Jack's financier. In the porno world, sex organs are a commodity.

But sex is also sex, if you care to think about it that way. One of the those who does is Jack's associate Little Bill (William H. Macy), who continually walks in on his wife (real-life porno star Nina Hartley) being drilled by a succession of guys. What's funny, and odd, about Little Bill is that, unlike everybody else in his community, he actually *feels* the sting of sex—jealousy, rage, betrayal. There's a disconnect between the life he leads and the life he films.

For Eddie, his sexual equipment is his gift, his "blessing." A high-school dropout who lives with his milquetoast father and shrewish mother (Joanna Gleason) until he escapes into the porno film world, Eddie has an unstinting innocence. Even his ambition is innocent; he says he wants to be a "big, bright, shining star." He buys a fancy home and then stocks it with ceiling mirrors and leopard-print bedspreads. He can't tell real silver from fake. And yet we're meant to connect with his need to "find" himself by becoming a star. For Anderson, the indignity of working in the porno industry is not really an indignity at all. Porno, after all, is a business like any other, and, unlike most businesses, at least its corruptions are up front. What's important is that, for its players, the porno world provides a theater for self-fulfillment.

The misfits and the marginalized in *Boogie Nights* look after each other by creating their own family. The earth mother in this galaxy is Amber Waves (Julianne Moore), the amber-haired porno star who lives with Jack in his baronial Valley spread and tends to his flock, which also includes Buck (Don Cheadle), who is forever remaking his "image," and Maurice (Luis Guzman), who manages the disco.

Amber is locked in a wearying custody battle with her ex-husband (John Doe) over her son. She also is heavily into cocaine and, acting almost as a caregiver, introduces Eddie to coke. (It's what sends him into a downward spiral in the eighties.) Earlier, she appears with Eddie in his first on-camera sex scene, and she's a caregiver there, too. (It's a kick in this scene watching a great actress play a bad actress.) Amber ministers motherly advice to Eddie as they get it on.

What does Jack think when he watches them together? Anderson charges the moment with so many crosscurrents that you don't know whether to laugh or applaud or avert your eyes. On some level, Jack must feel outraged—after all, his partner is being damn well serviced by his protégé right before his eyes. But Jack has a higher calling. He wants his films to be "right and true." He wants the raincoat brigadiers to remain in the theaters for his movies until the end, not just until they've gotten off. For Jack, Eddie isn't just a gold mine; he's an artist, an artist of sex.

Reynolds has the right silver-fox look to play this porno pasha. He gives Jack an air of ceremonial cool. This cool operates even when he's auditioning sex players, as in the scene where Eddie and the bounteous Rollergirl (the extraordinary Heather Graham), who always keeps her roller skates on, couple on his couch. Jack looks on, lights a good cigar, and sinks into his own cozy dreamtime. He's a connoisseur of the primal act. Reynolds in this film cuts way back on his usual shtick, and the result is his best work in decades. He doesn't condescend to his character. Jack may be deluded—everyone in the film is deluded, especially Amber, who passes along her coke as if it were a peace pipe—but the delusions fuel hope.

Anderson captures the pretensions of the porno world—the way, especially in the seventies, the business catered to respectability. I covered the annual Adult Film Association awards bash at the Palladium on Sunset Boulevard for the *Los Angeles Herald Examiner* in the early eighties, and I was always amazed at what an alternate-universe Oscars show it was—complete with musical selections performed by porno stars from the five nominated songs, and clips, none of them X-rated, from the best "performances." Performers no longer active in hardcore, such as Georgina Spelvin, were feted with lifetime achievement awards as if they were Helen Hayes.

But Anderson doesn't just capture the pretensions of this world. He also falls for them. And that's where the film loses its edge. Only twenty-six, Anderson may barely have been out of his short pants for the time period covered by *Boogie Nights*, but he's still buzzed by that era's touchy-feely mantra. He buys into the cult of "creativity" that makes someone like Jack or Eddie an artist simply because he desires personal "fulfillment." When we see the trailer for a movie partnering Eddie and his buddy Reed (John C. Reilly) as Starsky and Hutch-style erotic action heroes, the results are laughably bad. And yet Jack thinks this is his finest work, and we're not meant to giggle at him. He may not be a real artist, but he has the artistic impulse, and, in true seventies style, that's enough to lift him into the pantheon.

Anderson makes a big deal about the shift that came to porn in the seventies: It went from being shot on film—where one could be an "artist"—to video. It's a shift Jack at first rejects, in a scene with the underworldly overlord Floyd Gondolli (Philip Baker Hall) that seems modeled on the Mafia powwow in *The Godfather* where Don Corleone rejects dealing drugs. Jack also rejects the use of amateur sex players instead of professionals. When he finally relents, it's as if a moment had passed into history—the moment when artists hoping to do something momentous in hardcore were beaten back into hackdom.

This is more than misplaced nostalgia. It is, alas, the crux of the movie. This sentimentalizing of porn is a disservice to porn—it tries to "legitimize" what by its nature is illegitimate. It also misses the commercial opportunism and legal maneuvering that were at the heart of the porno world's courting of the mainstream audience and press. The dream of artists in the seventies to make truly heightened erotic movies was carried forward by *Last Tango in Paris*, not *The Devil in Miss Jones*. It's a dream that has for the most part been jettisoned in an era when most studios and theater chains contractually ban NC-17-rated movies. Even *Boogie Nights* is rated R.

But even if we existed in an era more hospitable to sexual exploration on film, I don't think Anderson would approve. He may be moony about the swinging seventies, but he also thinks it's payback time for all that swinging. *Boogie Nights* is a lot more wiggy and heated about this payback than, say, *The Ice Storm*, which looks back to a community of seventies suburban libertines as if they were the Village of the Damned. (Their blood runs cold.) But the agenda is the same: You have to be punished for all that fooling around.

Anderson sets up his portrait of the porno world so that, when the drugs and violence kick in, we register the downfall of innocence. But the innocence is rigged. Anderson is very careful, for example, not to show Jack having sex with anyone; no casting couch sessions for him. Amber and Rollergirl are like mother and daughter, though in the actual porno world they would no doubt be called upon to have sex together—which would have made for a blacker and truer picture. Anderson also doesn't raise the specter of AIDS or, except ever-so-lightly, Mob involvement. If he *did* allow for these things, his one-happy-family scenario would collapse.

After his spectacular rise to glory, Eddie the innocent crashes and burns with a vengeance. And so does the film. The trajectory is a familiar one from the cycle of seventies druggie movies. This is a kind of nostalgia we don't need—who wants to be put through that deadhead *Panic in Needle Park* dreariness again? Eddie begins to resemble a porno version of the dissolute Jake LaMotta in *Raging Bull*, complete with the speech-in-the-dressing-room-mirror scene. Like Jake, he needs to come clean and roust his manhood. But when Eddie is finally reborn, it's as an innocent once again. He has his family waiting for him.

In most of the many recent—and mostly bad—movies about families, ranging from *The Ice Storm* and *A Thousand Acres* to *The Myth of Fingerprints* and *The House of Yes*, dysfunction is the norm. These films attempt to break apart the myths of familial togetherness.

Anderson, however, still sees the family as a source of salvation. He recognizes that, for all our cynicism, we still want to see it that way too, and so, in place of the old sugarcoated Ozzie and Harriet myths, he offers up a new one—a family of porno helpmates who form an ideal of togetherness. What could be farther from Ozzie and Harriet and yet so close? The family that makes sex films together stays together. *Boogie Nights* is one of the most traditional movies around.

(New Times, 1997)

SOFIA COPPOLA

Lost in Translation

I hope it will not be taken as a backhanded compliment if I say that Sofia Coppola's *Lost in Translation* is the best movie about jet lag ever made. Bill Murray plays Bob Harris, an over-the-hill movie star who is in Tokyo to pick up some easy money filming commercials for Suntory whiskey. Entombed in the ultrasleek Park Hyatt, unable to sleep, he frequents the hotel's low-lit bars and listens numbly to the lounge acts. He has no use for the Tokyo hubbub and ventures outside only at his peril. He looks like the undead.

The real world keeps intruding, though. Bob's wife repeatedly faxes him from L.A. with needling queries about home redecoration. Another hotel guest, Charlotte (Scarlett Johansson), who is accompanying her frenetically busy fashion-photographer husband (Giovanni Ribisi), strikes up a tentative friendship with him based on their shared grogginess. She brings Bob into the clubs and pachinko parlors and karaoke bars, and gradually this deeply unhappy man begins to unwind. He and Charlotte aren't lovers in any physical sense, but they enjoy the novelty of each other's company. They know that this is one of those far-flung friendships that will last only for the length of their stay, and it's sweeter (and more unsettling) for being so.

Coppola both wrote and directed, and there's a surpassing hopelessness to her scenes. She accomplishes the difficult feat of showing people being bored out of their skulls in such a way that we are never bored watching them. She does this by creating such empathy for Bob and Charlotte that our identification with them is almost total. Coppola has hit on a metaphor for modern alienation that is so mundane it's funny—she transforms the dark night of the soul into one big cryptlike luxury hotel. It's no wonder that when Bob decides to make a run for it, he acts as if he's planning a prison break.

Bill Murray has become an actor of extraordinary range over the years. It would have been easy for him to play Bob as a gaga jerk, but he never once succumbs to revue-sketch antics—not even when he belts out an Elvis Costello song in a karaoke bar. Murray conveys Bob's tiredness at what he has become, which surely predates his arrival in Tokyo. He takes no pleasure in being recognized by American tourists, or in seeing himself in movies or commercials on Japanese TV. He's settled into the kind of career where fame is essentially an annuity—and an annoyance. When, in a hilarious but also unexpectedly touching scene, he poses for his Suntory spot and feigns Sinatra-like insouciance, we can see how far from cool he has become.

When Bob is with Charlotte, he doesn't act younger than his years. He is exactly who is he supposed to be: a jaded man momentarily brought out of himself. He has no illusions that this is anything but a spree. He has a scene in which he talks to Charlotte about the difficulties of his marriage and his sustaining love for his children that has tremendous resonance for her; he is letting her know that one doesn't really get wiser as one gets older, just more temperate. Charlotte's own marriage is a disappointment to her, and she spends part of her time in Tokyo frequenting Buddhist temples, or taking part in flower ceremonies, trying to fill a void. None of this really works for her, but Bob's honesty, which is keyed to his weariness, does the trick. In the movies these days, it seems that as soon as an actress hits her twenties, she becomes a snuggle-bunny. It's a pleasure to see a performer who plays a young woman with smarts and substance.

Coppola allows for the strangeness in these people's lives. She doesn't try to "understand" them in any conventional sense. Nor does she try to fit herself into the Tokyo landscape; the movie, which was shot by Lance Acord in lustrous nocturnal tones, presents Japan as an outsider might see it, without apology. The night-worlds both within the hotel and without are equally odd and forbidding. Everything seems hushed—suspended in time—and yet there is always the sense of violence about to break loose. In Japan, the most extreme delicacy goes hand in hand with garishness, and Coppola offers up both for our delectation. It's a heady, hallucinatory combo. Bob and Charlotte would be dazed even if they got as much sleep as Rip Van Winkle.

(New York, 2003)

DAVID O. RUSSELL

Three Kings

Set during the Persian Gulf War, *Three Kings* begins in March 1991, just as the official cease-fire is announced. The soldiers at an American base camp in Iraq ring in the good news by boozing and whooping it up, but the spectacle has its ludicrous side: These ground troops, after all, have been cooling their heels for weeks while the war has been fought mostly from the air, high-tech-style. They're celebrating a triumph they didn't really contribute to as combatants, and, as soon becomes clear, the triumph is equivocal at best.

Writer-director David O. Russell piles on the ironies and sick jokes: we are reminded that many of the Iraqis fighting the Americans were trained earlier by the CIA to fight Iran; the battles being fought rack up predominantly civilian and not military casualties; beleaguered, defenseless Kuwait is chockablock with cell phones and Rolls-Royces, which the Iraqis regard as spoils of war. Iraqi rebels looking to George Bush for aid in ousting Saddam instead find themselves twisting in the wind.

Russell works on our nerve endings, seemingly intent on outdoing *The Road Warrior*. With his cinematographer, Newton Thomas Sigel, he's devised a bleached-out look for the film, especially in its early sections, that has a corrosive effect on our eyeballs; no beauty is allowed to filter into the flat Iraqi desert terrain, or into anywhere else, either. Russell throws in shock cuts and heads exploded by gunfire and close-ups of a wounded soldier's infected innards. He wants us to know that war—even an apparently absurdist war such as this one—is hell.

The action is carried forward by the film's four main protagonists—Special forces captain Archie Gates (George Clooney), a square-jawed cynic who's set to retire into civilianhood in a few weeks; sergeant Troy Barlow (Mark Wahlberg), with a wife and newborn baby back in Detroit; staff sergeant chief Elgin (Ice Cube), an airport baggage handler when not on active duty who believes Jesus protects him in the field; and private Conrad Vig (Spike Jonze), a Southern hick who didn't have a day job back home and looks up to Barlow. When a map to the hiding place of millions in gold bullion stolen from the Kuwaitis by Saddam is literally fished out of a prisoner's ass, these four, led by Gates, go AWOL to make the score, leaving camp at dusk and planning to be back by lunch. Predictably, things foul up, and they quickly become what Gates, especially, never intended: rescuers of Iraqi villagers set upon by their own troops.

Whacked-out and hyperkinetic as Russell tries to be, he still opts in the end for the most timeworn cynic-with-a-heart-of-gold clichés. Gates, for example, makes a big show early on of sticking up for No. 1, but his transformation into putty-tat is pretty pro forma. We're meant to recognize how the wigginess of the war maneuvers all four men into being the unlikeliest of heroes.

But since Russell never really allows us to develop a closeness to these men, it's difficult to get worked up about their exploits, even though they're on-screen practically nonstop and we see them get shot and tortured. After a while, they blend into the blasted landscapes teeming with insurgents and predators—except for Clooney, who's entertainingly hale.

Russell is caught in a conceptual bind that he never really figures his way out of: How to make an anti-heroic war movie with real heroes. His solution, in effect, is to have it both ways. He avoids standard-issue movie-star iconography but, storywise, makes a beeline for bleeding-heart humanitarianism. And so, the film, charged-up and smart as it often is, comes across as something of a con. Russell isn't just dramatizing the facts and the disgraces of the Gulf War but also using the war as a way to jazz up his own hokum. (In a stylistically very different way, this is what Terrence Malick did to World War II in *The Thin Red Line,* which aestheticized combat into a graduate-level course in metaphysics.) Hokum works best when it's presented unjazzed, like Rick in *Casablanca* coming down with a last-minute case of good-guy-itis.

One reason you can tell that Russell isn't functioning as an enraged, politically committed artist is that the violence in the movie doesn't deepen our responses to the people who are suffering it; the film begins with a head-exploding splat, and the splats that follow are mostly more of the same, except bigger and louder. Are the adrenaline-rush stylistics and the hip attitudinizing in this film—its mix of snicker and slobber—a "cool" new-style response to war? Movies about World War II and Vietnam have been straightforward or hallucinatory, political or apolitical, but rarely have they seemed as flip or as flashy as this one. Even *M*A*S*H,* which was set in Korea, kept its high jinks rooted in gallantry; Elliott Gould and Donald Sutherland could roust the military brass because they were great surgeons and they saved lives. Unlike Vietnam or Korea or World War II, the Gulf War is the first full-scale American conflict that the majority of today's moviegoing audience actually lived through; and it was, for them, a remote-control war, a video-game war. Not coincidentally, perhaps, there's something remote-controlled and rock-video-ish about *Three Kings,* and that may be enough to turn it into a hit.

The Gulf War was billed in this country as the exorcism of Vietnam—a point duly noted in *Three Kings*—but the Vietnam War didn't carry much meaning to the generation born after it. The Gulf War probably doesn't carry much jingoistic meaning for that generation either, especially since Saddam is still in power. (That fact gives the soldiers' exploits in *Three Kings* an existential kick.) Maybe the war would have meant more to people if they actually saw its human toll. But the real suffering that transpired in the Persian Gulf was mostly kept away from

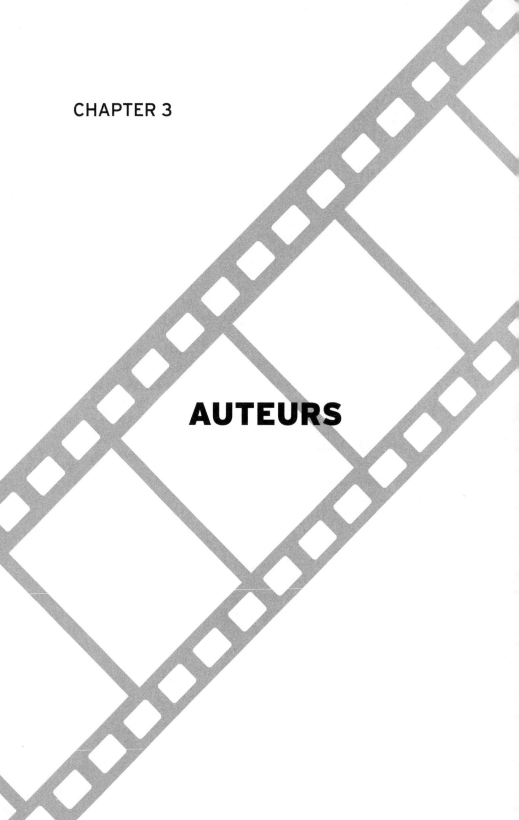

CHAPTER 3

AUTEURS

CURTIS HANSON

L.A. Confidential

The fifties-era Los Angeles of *L.A. Confidential* is Noir Central. Its denizens are tattooed in shadow; the play of light and dark in the streets, the police stations, the morgues, is fetishistic. The post-war L.A. touted in the travelogues and billboards is a boomtown, but what we actually see is unsettling: a city of the future infested by people with only a past.

Like the best noir crime thrillers, *L.A. Confidential*, directed by Curtis Hanson and very loosely based on the 1990 James Ellroy novel, suggests a menace even greater than the one we are presented with. It's been a long time since we've had sordidness this ripe in the movies. Hanson and his cinematographer, Dante Spinotti, understand why we allow ourselves to be taken in by noir—it sexes up our own worst suspicions about how the world works.

With a cast of more than 100 characters, Ellroy's novel is a sprawling overload of plots and subplots. The overabundance has an obsessive, almost punitive quality, as if the L.A. horror could no longer be contained within the confines of a single narrative. Pulp noir is, almost by definition, a slick genre, but Ellroy's book is a rare thing—a noir *epic*. If you stand back from its jumbled panorama, it comes together like one of those compressed 3-D images that suddenly snap into focus if you stare at them long enough.

Hanson and his co-screenwriter, Brian Helgeland, have hooked into Ellroy's depraved, moody-blues mind-set and tricked out a story line from his welter of happenings. The movie is still a dense thicket of subterfuges and wrong-way turns, but at least it's negotiable.

Besides, confusions are a part of noir. We don't look to these movies for handy resolutions, and the films that wrap things up for us are often the least resonant. Hanson makes this mistake at the end of *L.A. Confidential*, but otherwise he demonstrates that every safe exit is really a trap door. The result is perhaps the best noir crime movie since *Chinatown*—not that, aside from *Devil in a Blue Dress*, there has been much competition.

The assumption in noir has always been that appearances are *not* deceiving. If you're fat, you're gross; if you're a woman, you're no good; if you're rich, you're sleazy. It's a reactionary genre—or it would be except for the strain of sentimentality that runs through it. (Think of Raymond Chandler's Philip Marlowe—the white knight of the dark streets.)

The key to *L.A. Confidential*—what makes it different—is that just about everybody in it *isn't* what he or she seems. Sometimes the characters are even *worse* than you imagined; sometimes they show off a valor and a rue that spin you around. The mysteries to be solved in *L.A. Confidential* aren't only whodunits. The flip-flops of character are mysteries, too. We never are sure how people will act in this film, and that unease is part of its texture.

Ed Exley (Guy Pearce), when we first see him, is a Los Angeles police officer on the make for a higher rank. College-educated, the son of a decorated cop killed on the job, Exley, with his wire-rim glasses and pursed, polished features, is almost comically straight-arrow. But there's a connivance built into his uprightness, which he uses as leverage to get what he wants. In a police force rife with corruption, Exley accommodates himself to his image-conscious higher-ups as a do-gooder—a poster boy. When a number of his fellow cops brutalize some Mexicans brought to the police station on Christmas Eve, Exley alone rats on his comrades—and wangles a promotion for it. He's not wrong to rat. The cops—spearheaded by Dick Stensland (Graham Beckel), along with his partner, Bud White (Russell Crowe), and Jack Vincennes (Kevin Spacey)—behaved like racist thugs. But Exley uses the ugly incident as an *opportunity*, knowing full well he'll be shunned, or worse, by his fellow officers. He doesn't care; he doesn't really want to be liked by them anyway.

It's to the film's credit that Exley's apple-polishing is given its due. So is the cynicism and sense of betrayal from the other cops. We don't see much more of Stensland except his corpse, but White the bully-boy turns soulful and becomes Exley's antagonist. Taken by Captain Dudley Smith (the marvelous James Cromwell) as a strong arm on crime raids, White inevitably is drawn into a collision course with the golden boy. It's as if he and Exley were fated to square off.

Vincennes is the most jaded of the cops. Dressed nattily—he wears his finery the way a lizard wears its skin—he makes side money setting up Hollywood busts for Sid Hudgeons (Danny DeVito), the yowly editor of a tabloid magazine called *Hush-Hush*. Vincennes also works as an adviser to the television series *Badge of Honor*, which portrays the LAPD as shining warriors. He values his sleekness because it camouflages the scumminess of his operation. But he also values the scumminess; it confirms his wisdom about how rotten things are. Vincennes fancies himself a connoisseur of the vile.

What gives Spacey's performance its edge—its greatness—is that finally, we can see how little this connoisseurship means to him. Inside the sleek cynicism is a weariness with what he has become. When Vincennes is given an opportunity by Exley to right a wrong he perpetrated—a Hollywood bust turned murder—he jumps at it. His chance for redemption transforms him. It's as if the real person—guileless and decent—has melted away the mask.

Perhaps the reason Vincennes comes across as the most layered of the film's characters is because his take on things—detached yet impassioned—matches Hanson's. When Vincennes is at his sleekest, it's as if everything he speaks issues from an echo chamber of irony; he's supremely facetious. And Hanson directs the action in the same double-edged way. Underneath the cool-cucumber flipness, he's terribly engaged.

He realizes you can't direct a fifties crime noir as if we were still living in the fifties. When the police chief (John Mahnon) talks up the LAPD as a "great force in a great city," it's balanced by his directive to the cops regarding some black suspects in a brutal mass murder. For their apprehension he urges "all available force," and, to his credit, Exley gags at the euphemism. He mutters to himself, "Why not just put a bounty on them?"

Noir, for all its up-from-the-streets atmosphere, is situated in a pulpy never-neverland where everything we see and hear seems encoded yet explicit. The emphasis in *L.A. Confidential* on the racism and corruption of the LAPD grounds it. We could be witnessing the origins of an outrage that is still with us. When White, the self-styled avenger of battered women, shoots a rapist and then makes the shooting look like self-defense, we feel unclean watching the fix—even though our outrage matches White's. We're privy to an obscenity, and Hanson makes us feel our own complicity in it.

In fact, throughout *L.A. Confidential* we feel implicated in the luridness of what we're watching. That's one of the dirty pleasures of noir. Hanson has shuffled through these shadows before. His script for the almost unknown 1979 Elliott Gould thriller, *The Silent Partner*, was a marvel of malice. Despite some questionable casting involving the likes of Steve Guttenberg and James Spader, Hanson's third and fourth features as a director, *The Bedroom Window* and *Bad Influence*, were expertly creepy neo-noirs.

The casting in *L.A. Confidential* is mostly first-rate—though a little of DeVito's smirky bombast goes a long way—and the creepiness is more masterfully stage-managed than ever. Hanson has finally come into his own. A former movie critic, he seems to be playing out in this film his own fantasia on the noirs that formed him. When we follow the trail of blood in the Nite Owl Coffee Shop—the murder trail that leads to the black suspects—Hanson intensifies our dread drop by drop. It's as if an Edward Hopper all-night diner had blurred into a charnel house.

At the same time, Hanson is reaching for a more sentimental and valorous conception of the noir thriller than we are accustomed to in the movies. It's his way of recasting the genre by making it less reactionary. And so, in place of the standard-issue noir vamp who drives men to their doom, we get Kim Basinger's Lynn Bracken—the whore with the heart of gold. Lynn is a prize filly in the stable of pimp-financier Pierce Patchett (David Strathairn), who runs a house of prostitution featuring women surgically altered to look like movie stars. (Such a ring actually existed in Hollywood.) Lynn is the Veronica Lake stand-in, and Bud White falls for her. He lets her know she's *better*-looking than Veronica Lake—that's how we first know he loves her.

In his squad car, in the rain, he watches her from afar. Much later on, feeling jilted, he slaps her in the rain. (What would noir be without rain?) Lynn is the bright angel of noir who replaces the vamp, and it doesn't quite work. She's such an ethereal goddess that you crave some poison in the mix—something slutty and indefensible. Basinger has the right vanilla parfait look—she's certainly a pulpmaster's wet dream—but she's given things to say like, "Bud can't hide the good inside of him." And we're meant to agree with her.

Transforming a noir vamp into a touchy-feely angel of mercy isn't much of a bonus; noir shouldn't be this soggy and righteous. When someone like Jack Vincennes fights to reclaim his goodness, we can at least recognize the smarm it came out of. Lynn, though, is untainted from the get-go.

What this all means, I suspect, is that Hanson is much better at malice than virtue. He can't make the scenes with Lynn come alive because they're cream-filled with good intentions. It's the same creaminess that mars the film's ending. (The book's fade-out is vaguely similar but far less smug.) In a way, Hanson is a victim of his own success here: He's so good at nastiness that the counterbalancing sweetness pales in comparison.

He's not always at his best on the dark side, either. A scene involving the strong-arming of the D.A. (Ron Rifkin) is poorly staged, and there are a few too many cutesy-ironic touches, like the shot of Vincennes under a movie marquee for *The Bad and the Beautiful*.

But Hanson understands in his bones what draws us to this netherworld: We want to know where the bodies are buried. In one particularly startling sequence we actually find out—White crawls under a house and pulls up a rotting corpse. He becomes the Ulysses of noir. He's reached the rot that noir tries to slick up and glamorize.

The three lead cops in *L.A. Confidential* react to depravity; they have a conscience. Hanson wants to give us a richer sense of character than the standard noirs, and, by the end, his cops have earned their chops. The blood on Exley's face no longer looks decorative and out of place, as it did in the beginning. It looks like it belongs there—it's a part of his story. *L.A. Confidential* is about a war within the police ranks, and it's also a film at war with itself. Hanson craves the lurid shock of pulp, but he also wants to go beyond pulp. With his smarts and his almost tragic sense of the consequences of vice, he just about gets there.

(New Times, 1997)

Wonder Boys

As the novelist and creative-writing professor Grady Tripp in the terrific new comedy *Wonder Boys*, Michael Douglas has a shaggy, scraggly look, as if he's spent way too many nights fully dressed in a sleeping bag. Who would believe Douglas could look like a blood brother to Michael J. Pollard? Grady's dishevelment isn't the affectation of a prima donna scribe. It's just the way he is. He's a rarity in his circumscribed world of bookish academia—a man without vanity. Tenured at a Pittsburgh university, with one award-winning novel behind him and nothing published in the seven years since, Grady has seen his authorial life and his real life blur into a muddle. He has no trouble writing; he has trouble *not* writing. The voluminous single-spaced pages for his new novel are heaped about his home, with no end in sight. His life, like his manuscript, is an unedited digression. And yet Grady the wayfarer is bemused enough to realize that maybe his life isn't just the raw material for his art, but the artwork itself.

I don't think I've ever seen another American comedy that mixed rue and slapstick and sentiment in quite this way. Curtis Hanson, who directed from a delicately rendered script by Steve Kloves based on the 1995 novel by Michael Chabon, is the artist Grady would be if he were able to pare things down and make each detail count. There's a richness of tone, of emotion, in this film; the imbroglio of Grady's life is rendered lucidly and lyrically. The film begins with the revelation that Grady's wife has left him that morning and goes on from there to his sodden, heartfelt attempts to convince his pregnant lover, the university's married chancellor (Frances McDormand), that she was always his first choice. The film's long, wintry weekend is improbably magical; it seems to be taking place inside a snow globe that's been shaken up, with the lives of its inhabitants as flurried as the falling flakes.

Wonder Boys is a shaggy-dog story that is also a coming-of-age story. (The soundtrack, with artists like Neil Young and Bob Dylan, gives that shagginess a pedigree.) It doesn't matter that Grady is coming of age at fifty—he's a late bloomer. The film's biggest jest is that, when it comes to emotional maturity, age doesn't matter; if anything, the students that we are introduced to are more grounded than the adults. The notion that we understand who we truly are as we get older is a canard that Hanson mirthfully, and mercifully, explodes. The screw-ups in town cut across all age barriers. And yet, as ramshackle and addled as these people are, they are all, without their full awareness, searching for purpose in their lives. The search itself is funny, but the longing that propels it goes very deep.

Grady's most gifted student, James Leer (Tobey Maguire), seems at first to be a prize creepo, but his steady-state stare and odd, pinched comportment provide him with a tactical advantage in the human comedy; he puts everybody else off guard. Maguire gives James the "choked little powder-soft voice" that Chabon described in the novel, and it's a marvelous instrument. James is a junior con man who lies about his past and a lot more, but he's also an original. Unlike Grady, whose celebrated novel made James want to be a writer, he's actually completed the book he's been working on; and according to Grady's editor, Terry Crabtree (Robert Downey Jr.), who shows up with a transvestite consort (Michael Cavadias) in tow to attend the annual campus literary weekend, it's remarkable.

One of the beautiful things about *Wonder Boys* is the way Hanson lets the relationship between Grady and James find its own level; the former phenom takes under his broken wing the imminent one, and there's a wistfulness in the gesture. Grady's exasperated, prideful connection to James mimics the rituals of fatherhood. Grady sees in James the peculiarity he favors in himself, and he plays on it. James starts out not wanting to lose control of his emotions, but Grady, who likes his weed and has periodic blackout spells, shows him, by his own example, another way to live. They have a contrapuntal, moonstruck comradeship.

This film that does so much to heckle the literary life is nevertheless high on the excesses of that life. It's a movie in love with words and the textures of words, and what they might mean for the people who live by them. Hanson captures the preening pretensions of academia, the rivalries between the professors and the populist, best-selling interlopers; he reveals the skid marks on the tenure track. The academics and writers that we see are tweaked by their chosen métier. They know that being in and of the world of books gives them dispensation to be madcap. They become their own best protagonists.

The cast is superb across the board, but at the center of it all is Michael Douglas, who has never seemed as relaxed and generous. His Grady is a counterculture artifact, more holdout than sellout. The marijuana

fumes he swathes himself in are like incense; they perfume his disappointments. Grady fears that his books, maybe *all* books, don't mean anything
to anybody anymore, and for all his blurriness, it's a legitimate fear. But he
gropes his way to higher ground by the end. He discovers that his writing
isn't all that he is, and, of course, he becomes a better writer for it.

(New York, 2000)

MIKE LEIGH

Secrets and Lies

I am not among those merry legions who consider Mike Leigh's new film,
Secrets and Lies, a masterpiece. Still, given what else is out there right
now, it'll do. It has deeply felt passages, an eloquent sunny-sorrowful
tone, and freewheeling actors who tickle and abrade each other's nerve
endings. Leigh doesn't condescend to us, and so we feel complimented—
grateful. *Secrets and Lies* is too draggy and repetitive, but the small-scale
lives of its people are enlarged by Leigh's feeling for the lyrical possibilities in the everyday.

For those familiar with his work—not just his three recent theatrical
features (*Naked*, the wonderful *Life Is Sweet*, and *High Hopes*) but also his
television movies for the BBC and his plays—*Secrets and Lies* plays like a
Leigh compendium. It's got bleakness and class-consciousness and kitchen-sink comedy-drama and laughing-through-tears family squabbling
and double-basses mournfully sawing away on the soundtrack.

But what will probably make it Leigh's first mass-audience hit in
this country is its core situation: the reunion of Hortense (Marianne
Jean-Baptiste), who was given up for adoption at birth and who is black,
with her white biological mother Cynthia (Brenda Blethyn). It's hearts-
and-flowers time in the Land of Leigh. Audiences can feel that they're
taking part in something classy and nutritious and still have a good cry.

If they do cry, they'll be in fast company with the people on the
screen—particularly Cynthia, who spends most of the movie halfway between a sniffle and a wail. Cynthia's perpetual state of near-collapse has

its comic-horror side, and Leigh keeps her travails center-stage. He likes her wallop. (Leigh used Blethyn in a similar manner in his superb 1980 TV film *Grown-Ups*, where she was the deranged chatterbox who upends a bourgeois household.) It takes a while to realize Cynthia's caterwauling and clinginess are her way of coping.

One of the things Cynthia has to cope with is her rejection by her surly, chain-smoking daughter Roxanne (Claire Rushbrook), a sanitation worker who shares her apartment; Cynthia is also on the outs with her photographer brother, Maurice (Timothy Spall), and his tightly wound, upwardly mobile wife, Monica (Phyllis Logan), whom she holds responsible for the rift. With no man in her life and a drudge factory job, Cynthia is ripe for deliverance.

With her adoptive parents gone—the film opens with her mum's funeral—Hortense is ripe for deliverance, too. She decides to seek out her birth mother. The scene where she phones the shocked, boozy Cynthia and persuades her to get together, followed by their reunion in a train station tearoom, are small miracles of engaged byplay. Hortense was shocked when she first found out through a social services agency that her birth mother was white; now it's Cynthia's turn to be shocked. (At fifteen, she never saw the baby she gave up, and she had forgotten all about her liaison with a black man.) Cynthia and Hortense initially look funny together: The mother's big-boned whiteness doesn't jibe with her daughter's dark luster. More than that, Cynthia's shrill working-class twang and daffy patter clash with Hortense's soft-spoken poise.

Leigh doesn't milk the women's differences, though, and—it's an indication of his taste and intelligence—he doesn't play up any newfound similarities either. (A Hollywood hack would have them comparing ear lobes and pinkies.) We experience the connections between the two women at the same moment they do; improbably, inevitably, they become friends, and, Leigh is saying, maybe that is the best you can hope for.

In reaching out for family, Hortense gets caught up in the upsets and subterfuges of Cynthia's inner circle. Although for most of the movie her existence is kept secret from the rest of the family—only Maurice and his wife know Cynthia's history, anyway—Hortense has a dawning awareness of the mess she's coming into. She may be new on the scene, but the feuds that pull on Cynthia go way back. Leigh doesn't blame anybody. There are no villains. He keeps everybody spinning in their own intersecting orbits, and the film could easily twirl off into a half-dozen equally revelatory realms.

When, for example, Maurice is snapping his studio portraits, we're treated to a quick montage of humankind. As the people pose, we seem to be watching entire lives in microcosm—a boxer snarling for the lens; a mother with her triplet daughters; a gaggle of barristers; a pudgy, giggly lady in see-through frills; a tense, unhappy Middle Eastern couple; a beauty consultant who has lost her job because her face has been scarred in a car accident. Any one of these posings, we feel, could become its own movie. Leigh is unusual in that he's both a gifted miniaturist and a champion of the long form.

Maurice makes his living making people look good—trying to make them smile—so his own unsmiling family circle must count for him as a personal failure. Maurice has a roly-poly hedgehog look—he could be a character from *The Wind in the Willows*—but there's something overly righteous about him. When Cynthia embraces him in the room of their late father and weeps, he stands there baffled and unmoved. He seems to have sealed himself off from some great hurt, but he overvalues his own self-importance. After an unexpected visit in his studio from a resentful, dissolute photographer friend (Ron Cook), he remarks to his wife, "There but for the grace of God go I," and his words ring hollow because he's too eager to claim victory for himself. He's trying to look good by elevating himself above this sour, sodden man, and it only reduces him in our eyes.

Leigh is often spoken of in hushed tones as an "original," and there's some truth to this. At least his working methods are original to the commercial world of moviemaking; he fashions his films from a series of long-term improvisatory rehearsals in which his actors work up situations that eventually are scripted and lead to a theme—a story. The actors are kept in the dark about the big picture; often only upon seeing the finished film do they realize what Leigh was up to. The point of all this hush-hush hoo-ha is supposedly a freer and more immediate experience for the actors and for us.

Without downplaying the artistic advantages of using the medium in such an intuitive way, I would suggest that the same effects have been achieved by film artists with fixed shooting schedules and prepared scripts not worked up through improvs. Is what Leigh does any richer than what, say, Renoir or Ray or De Sica or Bergman came up with? His working methods are not so very different from how most gifted writer-directors operate—it's just that he brings his actors into the creative process a lot sooner. (He also seeks financing without a script or even a "concept," which rules out Hollywood, though I suspect some American independent cartel will be eager to take a chance on him now.)

All the exultation over Leigh's even-handed methods neglects the fact that, in his own freeform way, he is often working up his own skewed political agenda. I could barely make it through *Naked*, an anti-Thatcher-ish piece of glorioso glumness starring rubber-mouthed David Thewlis as an outlaw rapist and gutter poet. (Antiheroes should not be so obscenely self-regarding.) In *High Hopes*, as well as in such TV films as the 1978 *Who's Who*, Leigh has caricatured the upwardly mobile middle classes, as well as the twitty upper classes, with as much venom as any agitprop Marxist politico.

Although *Secrets and Lies* is a much more plangent and fair-minded movie, it still carries whiffs of class condescension in the scenes involving Maurice's wife Monica, whose upward-bound middle-classness is ultimately viewed as a strident substitute for her inability to have children. Mummy love is real big in Leigh's new film, and he sentimentalizes its healing powers with all the brio of a Hollywood romantic. (He's just not nearly as obvious about it.)

When he accepted Cannes's Palme d'Or for *Secrets and Lies* last year, Leigh, in a speech of excruciating humility, told his audience he made movies "about people, love, relationships, caring, real life—all the things that are important." Leigh's films are best when they are not trying to be Important, when he just lets his characters play out the grotesque funniness of their lives. (I'm thinking of his 1975 TV film *Nuts in May* and *Grown-Ups* and *Life Is Sweet* and the best parts of *Secrets and Lies*.) Leigh is a post-"kitchen-sink" social realist who brings to the kitchen the saving grace of comedy—which in his movies almost always issues from pain. (That's why his films are often saddest when they're funniest.)

The more Leigh bears down on his political agenda, the more he classifies his lives of quiet and not-so-quiet desperation, the phonier his movies seem (like *Naked*). If Leigh is serious about reaching for a more genuine and humane social realism, he doesn't need to punch up class differences. The differences in England are already manifest.

At least Leigh doesn't patronize the working and lower-middle classes; it's when he moves up the social register that things get iffy. He's too honest and exuberant an artist to indulge in the "little people" stuff that pocks so many films about the Common Folk. Neither does he glorify their drudgery or, like his compatriot Ken Loach, mistake drabness for reality. The Angry Young Man of the late fifties and early sixties has been washed down the kitchen sink. In his place Leigh gives us the Simpering Young Man (except he's not so young any more, and more often than not he's a she). Leigh's saving grace is also the saving grace of English drama: a love of eccentricity. At his best he uses eccentricity as a way into the soul. He and his actors are alive to the refreshments of the unexpected.

When Hortense suddenly pulls a funny face in front of Cynthia at their second meeting, it's a great moment because it's the first time they really laugh together. That funny face tells us Hortense is her mother's long-lost child regained.

(New Times, 1996)

Topsy-Turvy

Mike Leigh's *Topsy-Turvy* is a rich tribute to the theater and theater people. It's about how Gilbert and Sullivan's *The Mikado* came to be produced, but one never thinks of it as a stuffy biopic, or even, for all its plush period bric-a-brac, as a costume drama. Leigh and his players have such a tender and sympathetic understanding of this late-Victorian era that the pastness before our eyes shades into the present; we need no interpreter to make emotional sense of what we see. The artists' observations and intuitions bring us very deep into the drama.

The surprise here, of course, is that Leigh attempted this project at all; he's essentially a chronicler of the messiness of the modern-day lower-middle classes. The confinements of historical biography and Victorian decor do not, at first blush, jibe with his self-styled "organic" way of working, in which he brings the cast together for many months to improvise character detail and dialogue before the cameras roll. Leigh is a freestyle martinet—he sets up a long-term way to explore the emotional depths of his material that must be tremendously liberating for performers, and yet all the while he's shaping and beveling everything, and when he's finally filming, he's no friendlier to ad-libbing than, say, Cecil B. DeMille was. Leigh is often overpraised, I think, for his method. Plenty of filmmakers have elicited from actors the same high degree of psychological nuance without requiring them to live a commune-like existence in which their characters' biographies from birth are minutely recorded and picked over. There are moments in Mike Leigh's movies—I'm thinking especially of *Naked*—when I'd have been grateful for a lot *less* character analysis. The inherent danger in Leigh's technique is overindulgence. In movies, sometimes—oftentimes—you don't really want to know everything about a person. Just like in real life.

The rigors of making a period film, and of sticking relatively close to the facts, probably helped cauterize some of Leigh's usual excesses. Ironically, what should by all rights be his most reined-in film seems instead one of his freest. The freedom shows up in Leigh's love for this milieu—for what Gilbert and Sullivan conjure up for him. He is, above all else, a man of the theater, and he has the true theater lover's passion for the giddy reaches of drama—not only high emotion, but low burlesque. That last term is crucial, because it's what W. S. Gilbert, played extraordinarily well here by Jim Broadbent, rails against and tries to deny as he defends what he does to Allan Corduner's equally extraordinary Arthur Sullivan, who longs to write grand opera, not comic operetta. The *topsy-turvy* of the title, derived from a negative review of *Princess Ida* in the London *Times*, refers to the upside-down clickety-clack cleverness of Gilbert's plots, and it's both a disparagement and a tribute. The beauty of Gilbert and Sullivan's art, which is also its mystery, is that, gloriously minor, it's more redolent and lasting than many works regarded as major.*

Unlike a lot of movies about artists that skimp on their art, *Topsy-Turvy* really gives us an earful and an eyeful. Especially once *The Mikado* is in rehearsal, we're never far away from Gilbert and Sullivan's words and music, and this gives the film a continual lilt. Leigh and his longtime

---

* In his essay collection *I Have Landed*, Stephen Jay Gould, taking issue with this sentence, wrote, "But we will never gain a decent understanding of excellence if we continue to use this standard distinction between major and minor forms of art as our primary taxonomic device." Perhaps. Or maybe I should have sliced the taxonomy even finer and introduced the distinctions major-minor and minor-major.

cinematographer, Dick Pope, shoot the Savoyards up close, so we can see their sweat and makeup, and that helps make intimate what might otherwise resemble a series of production numbers. The performers, all of whom do their own singing, are playing characters who both fulfill our need for theatrical caricature and move beyond it. And so, for example, Timothy Spall's Richard Temple, who plays the Mikado, is a glorious stage diva who, when his Mikado's song is cut by Gilbert, reveals beneath the vamping a hurt man's pathos. Gilbert himself is a maze of contrariness, resolutely confident and mortally stung by his limitations. On the occasion of his opening-night *Mikado* triumph, he confesses to his wife, Kitty (Lesley Manville), that "there is something inherently disappointing about success," and he means it. Leigh doesn't play out the sobbiness of moments like these; he just touches on the sadness and moves on.

Though the film runs nearly three hours, it gets better as it goes along. The quirks and peccadilloes of its people, which may at first seem like cute bits, open into a deeper mood. Kitty may appear to be the archetypal "understanding" wife of a genius-autocrat, but she is pained by her separateness from her husband's emotional life, and when, near the end, she suggests to him a scenario for a new opera, it's something mad and surreal—an encoded way of passing along to her husband her hurt. The drinking problem of one of the Savoyards, Leonora (Shirley Henderson), which initially seems like an affectation, tears into her fresh beauty (it's like watching a rose petal famish from drought). Leigh gives her the final scene in the film, alone onstage singing "The Sun Whose Rays Are All Ablaze," and it's like his benediction for her, and for all who are fragile like her.

Sullivan comes across at first like a suave libertine, but he has an overcast look. After *The Mikado* has opened, his mistress, Fanny Ronalds (Eleanor David), tells him, as he lies ill in bed, that he lights up the world, and that he can't help it. Sullivan, who composes some of his sweetest music while plagued by bad kidneys, doesn't fully approve of his airy gift; it lacks the seriousness of high art, and so, for him, his renown is a kind of gentle mockery.

With all this, I've rarely seen a movie that brought out more of the affirming joys of a life in the theater. Sullivan conducting *The Mikado* can't hold back his bliss; it overrides everything that pulls him down. Gilbert, directing the cast, is in his eminent domain; the martinet has become patriarch, wit, father-confessor, God. He lives for nothing higher.

The players onstage are transformed, too; their vivacity represents their finest dream of themselves. *Topsy-Turvy* delivers an even larger dream: the theater as life's apotheosis.

(*New York*, 1999)

STANLEY KUBRICK
Full Metal Jacket

Stanley Kubrick has a visionary genius rep that transforms each of his movies into an event. Even the duds, like *Barry Lyndon* and *The Shining* are events—they're oracular bad movies. *Full Metal Jacket*, his first film in seven years, has been even more anticipated than usual for a Kubrick film. After all, it's Kubrick on Vietnam. But audiences expecting some sort of grand summing-up from the "2001" guy are bound to feel gypped. Whatever else *Full Metal Jacket* may be, it's not the ultimate Vietnam movie. And the fact that Kubrick couldn't pull it off—may not have wanted to—is perhaps the "statement" that some people have been looking for in vain. The movie's limitations seem not only Kubrick's; they seem to belong to the Vietnam experience itself, to our inability to come to terms with what it was all about. The only grand-scale emotion that arises from the film, as from most Vietnam movies and journals, is a furious nihilism.

Kubrick's post-*Dr. Strangelove* style—imperious, numbing, protracted—has the stamp of the definitive. In *Full Metal Jacket*, that style is at its most muscular and Olympian. The movie is structured in three acts, and the drama in each of the sections is, for Kubrick, small-scale; we watch raw marine recruits turn into killing machines after eight weeks in a South Carolina boot camp, then follow a few of them to Vietnam, where we witness a bloody skirmish in Hue at the height of the Tet Offensive in 1968. But because Kubrick has such an all-seeing-eye approach to filmmaking, these sequences don't have a small-scale *feel*. They're meant to be paradigms of wartime experience.

Kubrick, however, may have invested too much in his own myth (again). His scenes don't really provide the shocks of recognition that might shake their familiarity from other war movies; they don't give rise to a new emotional experience. The opening section, in the training camp, is in many ways the most familiar. (It's also the most effective.) The first shot of the recruits having their heads shaved, one after the other, like sheared sheep, is a taunt. It's a funny, archetypal boot camp scene, but the dead-on, unwavering camera placement is a tip-off that we're about to witness the systematic dismantling of these boys' personalities.

For a while, the marine recruits are a blur. Kubrick doesn't often go out of his way to particularize anybody, and even when he does, there's little psychological probing. He gives you just enough to push the story forward. (And, as it turns out, there's not much of a story.) In the initial lineup with the brass-lunged D.I. (Lee Ermey), Private Joker (Matthew Modine) emerges as ornery but respectful; the roly-poly Private Pyle (Vincent D'Onofrio), trying valiantly to suppress a grin, is pegged as a troublemaker. He's not, at least not intentionally; he's just not remotely marine material. Until he shows everyone up at target practice. Pyle, who's forced by the D.I. to waddle in lock-step in his undies and suck his thumb, is an innocent caught up in war-game psychosis. When he starts talking to his rifle, we know he'll soon go over the edge; and Kubrick draws out the inevitable, like a conductor working up the slow movement of a Mahler symphony. He's such a magisterial sadist.

Private Joker is the movie's chief continuous character, but the boot-camp sequences are shaped as Pyle's story. We're supposed to see that Joker couldn't help him; that the war games went out of control, as the real war will soon reveal itself to be out of control. The blank white South Carolina skies look anonymous, irradiated, post-apocalyptic, just as the skies in Vietnam will. (This movie should be called *Apocalypse Then*.) Kubrick wants us to recognize the dehumanization in this boot camp, and its matchup to the horrors that follow. He shows us the marines during an inspection lineup, immobile, arms outstretched, palms down—in the bright white light, they could be upright corpses. But Kubrick's technique is itself dehumanizing. He doesn't have the lowdown gumption or the passion to show us the true horror in this killer factory. Pyle's fate—which is the precursor of many of his cohorts' and tormentors' fates—has no sorrow in it, no pity. He's turned into a beastie: his final leer is like Malcolm McDowell's in *A Clockwork Orange*.

When Joker is assigned to Vietnam as a "reporter" for *Stars and*

Stripes, we expect him to carry the rest of the film. But he's barely a presence in the movie, even though he's on-screen most of the time and provides intermittent voice-over narration. He wears a peace symbol on his uniform and the scrawl "Born to Kill" on his helmet; he likes to do mock-parody imitations of John Wayne. He's a joker, all right, but who's the joke on? Matthew Modine gives a straightforward, unfussy performance, but he's playing an intellectualized role: Joker's pacifist-warrior blows Everyman smoke rings. Some of the more crudely drawn characters in the company, like Adam Baldwin's gung-ho racist Animal Mother, come across more strongly—by default.

There's an interview scene with Animal's company shortly before the Tet Offensive that's like a cynic's point-blank précis of the soldiers' attitudes toward the war. What comes out is that, practically to a man, none of them believe Washington's high-flown rhetoric about rescuing the South Vietnamese. In fact, the soldiers have more respect for the NVA and the Viet Cong than the Vietnamese they're supposedly defending— and who, in their eyes, show them no respect. ("We're fighting the wrong gooks," Animal says.) Kubrick, and his co-screenwriters Michael Herr (*Dispatches*) and Gustav Hasford (from whose novel *The Short-Timers* the film was adapted), hardly show us any Vietnamese at all.

Kubrick is presumably outraged by the Americans' xenophobia, but because the only Vietnamese he characterizes are hookers, he tends to reinforce his soldiers' worst attitudes. Once again, as in *Platoon*, we're in Faceless Enemy Land. And, when we finally do see the face of the enemy up close, the image is part of a polemic. The enemy is unmasked and destroyed so that our stand-in, Joker, can learn one of life's bitter lessons.

The long, drawn-out battle for the city of Hue that closes the film is different from any other Vietnam War movie scene. The setting, for once, isn't a jungle, it's more like a bombed-out urban ghetto. The sequence doesn't function on a much more exalted level than a good WWII combat scene, but at least Kubrick delineates the action sharply. His imagery does justice to Gustav Hasford's severest prose, and to Michael Herr's descriptions in *Dispatches*, where he describes Saigon during the Offensive as "so stark that, in an odd way, it was invigorating. The trees along the main streets looked like they'd been struck by lightning, and it became unusually, uncomfortably cold, one more piece of freak luck in a place where nothing was in its season."

Kubrick should have co-opted more of Herr's jive hallucinatory qualities. This movie is too damn *planned*. The rigor in *Full Metal Jacket* isn't really an artist's rigor, it's an authoritarian's. Kubrick is trying to make a movie about madness and chaos, but he won't give in to the chaos. He's still trying to rack up his neat little points about how nobody on our side believed in the war, about how the war morally destroyed even those who, like Joker, had the humanity and the wits to see through America's hypocrisy in Vietnam. It's not that these points aren't worth making, but Kubrick is so manipulative about making them that the movie ends up feeling rigged. Maybe that's why the ending has no cumulative force; we're watching the working out of a schema.

And there's another problem. We're supposed to be with the half-baked Joker at the end, as he parades his new fearlessness, chanting made-up words to the *Mickey Mouse Club* theme song. But, although Kubrick may not recognize it, the image that lingers in this movie comes just before—the face of a mortally wounded Vietnamese woman sniper, praying for death. That image suggests the totality of war's dehumanization. Except for this moment, Kubrick doesn't really include the ruined, ravaged Vietnamese in his schema. If there is ever to be such a thing as the "ultimate" Vietnam War movie, it will have to include the tragedy of the Vietnamese as well. Kubrick gives us half a tragedy.

(*Los Angeles Herald Examiner*, 1987)

Eyes Wide Shut

Eyes Wide Shut is being billed as more than a movie, more than even a Tom-Cruise-and-Nicole-Kidman movie. It's a Stanley Kubrick movie, which means, if his rep holds, that it's supposed to somehow intuit what's going on in our innermost lives and divine a millennial mood we may not yet even be aware of. The film is poised to be an epochal pop-cultural event, an art blockbuster. And since it's Kubrick's last, the genius-visionary mystique machine has been turned on by the media full-blast. *Eyes Wide Shut* is going to be read or, more to the point, misread as some kind of valedictory. But Kubrick never intended for this film to be his last—he was, for example, famously caught up in preparations for a movie about artificial intelligence. Besides, for a director whose themes were as churningly repetitive as Kubrick's, there can be no proper valedictory because the moment of serene repose never arrives.

It is this quality of personal obsession that makes *Eyes Wide Shut* such a hammerlock of an experience. It's a powerful movie without always, or often, being a very good one; watching it is a bit like being inside the twistings and conniptions of a control freak who longs to lose control, only to pull back tighter than ever. The oracular power often attributed to Kubrick's films from at least *A Clockwork Orange* on is keyed to the playing and replaying of a few themes and variations on paranoia and depravity. For all the vaunted bigness of his movies, they're not very symphonic—there are too few notes for that.

It's perhaps no coincidence that Kubrick punctuates the *Eyes Wide Shut* soundtrack with repeated earsplitting strikes of a single piano key whenever things get particularly deranged. The derangement starts early. Dr. William Harford (Cruise) and his wife, Alice (Kidman), segue from their swank Central Park West apartment to a pre-Christmas party at even swankier digs—an eerie aerie belonging to one of William's wealthy patients (Sydney Pollack) that resembles something out of *The Shining*. The coruscated moldings and gleaming amber interiors are infernally luxurious; the Christmas-tree bulbs are like warning lights. Alice finds herself dancing with an aging Hungarian roué (Sky Dumont) who has a desiccated line of patter; he quotes Ovid to her and invites her to check out the sculpture garden with him. She demurs, waving her wedding ring as if it were a talisman. But the film's vampiric tone has been set—we're watching a movie about sex as the Other.

The tone is amplified when William, having been courted by two leggy models, is called upon to revive a nude woman who has OD'd in his host's private quarters. Her pristine body is photographed like carrion before the feast. At home afterward, Alice and William get stoned in their crimson-sheeted bed after which she accuses him of party-time infidelity. He jokingly brings up the roué, and then she drops the bombshell—a reverie she had of being deeply smitten and willingly borne away forever from her husband and young daughter by a handsome naval officer she spied during the family's Cape Cod summer vacation. William listens to her rapt monologue with eyes wide open—Kidman gives a harrowing rendition—and the screen-filling close-up of him that Kubrick bestows is a doozy; this naif looks positively poleaxed.

The Harfords, it would seem, are not the sort of couple who get turned on by one another's erotic indiscretions. That would make for a different movie. This one—written by Kubrick and Frederic Raphael and closely patterned on the 1926 Arthur Schnitzler Freudian fantasia novella *Dream Story*—is about the damning effect of carnal urges. William may be the shining prince of the Upper West Side who flashes his medical ID card as if it were a sheriff's badge; he may have women slavering all over him. No matter. Alice offers up her reverie and William looks into the chasm, where he imagines Alice and the officer locked in lust. (The couplings he fantasizes are rendered in a radioactive-looking black-and-white.) He moves into a night world that encompasses both the ratty Village apartment of a sweet-souled hooker (Vinessa Shaw) and, later, an elaborate masked ball in a forbidding Long Island mansion. It's erotics high and low, and Kubrick seems to be making the tired old point that upper-class sex is more decadent than the lower varieties.

Coming a little more than halfway through this two-and-a-half-hour movie, the masque is the film's centerpiece, and it's around this time that things start to get really, if unintentionally, silly. The way Kubrick stages the scene, it's like the Vanderbilt mansion meets Hef's place. Guys in gargoyle masks stride through echoey amphitheaters in caped costumes and monk duds, chanting and acting all incantatory, while masked women mince about buck naked and lead men away to some unspecified delectation. William glides goggle-eyed through the rutting tableaux, and who can blame him? (A few digitized figures were inserted into the scene to block the view and secure the film's R rating.) It's quite possible that Kubrick never saw a lot of the tony blue-movie schlock that this sequence conjures up, but he arrives at the same place anyway. Who would have believed Stanley Kubrick as a deluxe Radley Metzger?

Kubrick is perhaps the least sensual of all the major directors, and so, when it was announced, however sketchily, that he would be making a movie about carnal knowledge, skepticism yielded to curiosity. Maybe he could do for humping what he once did for nuclear proliferation and space travel? But Kubrick can't give us the pleasures of the illicit in *Eyes Wide Shut,* only the terrors; and without those pleasures, what is there for the good doctor to be drawn into or renounce? (In the movie's archetypal scene, William on a house call is lured by an amorous patient while a corpse rests in full view.) For all its supersophisticated stylistics, the film basically issues from a zone of bourgeois complacency. The message is: Play around, get in trouble.

But it goes deeper than that. Alice's indiscretions are reveries; William's are bona fide. The film is a male fantasy of how women's imagined urges can destroy you just as if they were real. ("No dream is just a dream," William says at the end.) Kubrick's view of females is double-edged—with their sexual capacity, their instinct for infidelity, their aphrodisia, they are the annihilators of male contentment. And yet there are women in *Eyes Wide Shut,* like that sweet-souled prostitute, who are a balm; at the masked ball, an enigmatic siren offers herself up to save William's life, sacrificing herself to redeem his transgressions. So men are a party to annihilation, too. *Eyes Wide Shut* just might be the most elaborate male mea culpa ever committed to film.

Still, none of the personal destructions on view resonate, because the movie seems to be populated by the soulless. The dead—the corpses and cadavers—are of a piece with the undead. The casting of Cruise and Kidman, movie stars who give off a chilly fortitude, is all too perfect. Kubrick brings out the alabaster whiteness in their skin; he bathes them in blue light. Their acting, except for Kidman's monologue and a few racked moments from Cruise, is overdeliberate; they seem not so much directed as commandeered.

Kubrick wasn't able to relinquish his customary iron grip over his material and move into more perilous and mellifluous realms of desire. William's dreamlike passage has the force of an obsession, but it's Kubrick's, not William's. Kubrick's passion, finally, is not for letting go but for holding on. It's an understandable response—a human response, especially as one gets older—and so there is a poignancy to it. But the only overwhelming emotion I felt from *Eyes Wide Shut* had nothing to do with the movie, really. What I experienced was a sadness that, with this last film of Kubrick's, there will be no others, and a vision, which certainly had its triumphs, has been taken away.

(New York, 1999)

Stanley Kubrick:
An Appreciation

American artists are supposed to be voluptuously engaged with the world. The crabbed, cloistered types are okay for the Europeans, but we want our geniuses to go fifteen rounds with the zeitgeist. Stanley Kubrick, who died at seventy on March 7, 1999, was a king-size anomaly in the genius-artist annals. He was an American—Bronx-born, no less— who lived out his last four decades in England. Notoriously reclusive, he nevertheless made movies—especially *Dr. Strangelove, 2001: A Space Odyssey*, and *A Clockwork Orange*—that functioned as tuning forks for an entire generation. His films picked up the vibrations in the national static, and so he was dubbed a seer, even when, as in *2001*, it wasn't at all clear what he was seeing. Just what was that black slab supposed to symbolize anyway? Was the Star Child really *meant* to look like Keir Dullea, or was it just a lucky coincidence that Keir Dullea looked like a fetus?

Maybe obfuscation was the point—with his unprecedented freedom from studio interference and his commandant's temperament, Kubrick was the control freak as guru, yet he allowed his audiences to design their own meanings from his movies. And so *Dr. Strangelove* could be discussed with equal conviction as an antiwar screed or as a great big nihilistic cackle for people who really *had* learned to stop worrying and love the bomb. *2001* became the ultimate head-trip movie because it made everybody think they were dreaming their own trip right alongside Kubrick's—it made you think you were a guru, too. *A Clockwork Orange* was framed as a freaky indictment of totalitarian thuggery, but Kubrick made the savagery in it the most delicious item on the menu.

For much of his career, Kubrick was hailed for the fierce misanthropy of his vision. But the true misanthrope still connects to the idea of human possibilities, if only to reject it, whereas Kubrick, at least post-*Strangelove*, was enraged by the realization that human beings aren't as perfectible as machines. (One of his aborted projects, along with a Napoleon epic that would have starred Jack Nicholson, was a movie about artificial intelligence called *AI*.) He had the distinctly modern gift of making hardware seem oracular. Sensuality for him would not be found in coital couplings but rather in the sweet lubrications of high tech. What you feel close to in his later movies is not the people but the production design, the tracking shots, the fanatic detailing, the doomy abstractions. There is more sex in the docking of the spaceships in *2001* than in all the rest of his oeuvre. His just-completed final film, *Eyes Wide Shut*, starring Tom Cruise and Nicole Kidman, is rumored to be intensely erotic. May I eat my words.*

Movie directors often become famous for the films that set them apart from mere mortals. The Fellini who made *La Dolce Vita* and *Satyricon* and all those other apocalyptic orgies is the certified genius-visionary, but the Fellini who made *I Vitelloni* and *La Strada* and *Nights of Cabiria* is the true artist. Kubrick is perhaps the greatest exemplar in movies of the director as oracle, but some of his prophesying—like *Barry Lyndon* and *The Shining* and *Full Metal Jacket*—is smoke and mirrors. The Kubrick I love is the early one—the prodigy who made the crackerjack caper *The Killing*; the scarily intense pacifist World War I movie *Paths of Glory*; the stirring *Spartacus*, still the best of the Roman epics; and the two greatest and most original larks of the sixties, *Lolita* and *Dr. Strangelove*. *Lolita* is like a compendium of everything that had been done in comedy up to that time: a screwball romantic farce crossed with slapstick tragedy and presided over by Peter Sellers's hepcat scattershot torments. *Dr. Strangelove* may be the lead-in to Kubrick's subsequent dystopian funk, but it's the funniest dystopia on record, with some kind of classic scene going on every minute. Kubrick's mystique should not be allowed to obscure the great and good work he did when he was being just a plain old artist-entertainer.

(*New York*, 1999)

ALFRED HITCHCOCK

Rear Window

Alfred Hitchcock's *Rear Window*, which is being re-released in a marvelously restored print supervised by Robert Harris and James Katz, features James Stewart as the cinema's most famous Peeping Tom and is often described as the ultimate movie about voyeurism. Since watching a movie

---

* I didn't; see the review above.

is, in itself, a form of voyeurism, Hitchcock's film has also been called the ultimate movie about moviegoing. There may be some truth to this, but, like so much academic Hitchcock criticism, it doesn't really describe our feelings when we watch the movie; it doesn't convey our sheer enjoyment.

For much of his career, Hitchcock was categorized as a "mere" entertainer—the master of suspense. Then along came the *Cahiers du Cinema* crowd and the Brits to tell us that Hitchcock was the supreme Catholic artist for our age of anxiety and a rival to Poe and Baudelaire. This revisionism was, I think, overscaled, but I remain sympathetic to its intent; more riches, after all, are camouflaged by popular entertainment than by most of what passes for high art. With Hitchcock there was always, even in his most minor entertainments, a residue of fear, of dread, that was more expressive and unsettling than, strictly speaking, it needed to be. Perhaps more than any other director, Hitchcock controlled down to the minutest detail the environment of his moviescape; and yet the great theme of his best movies is the horror visited upon us by a loss of control. The extreme manipulation in Hitchcock's films, the sense we have that he has already anticipated our every response, can seem coldly calculating, but it probably helps to recognize that, deep down, he was just as frightened as we were.

Rear Window, which was released by Paramount Pictures in 1954, is perhaps the clearest example of a Hitchcock movie that functions on dual levels—it's both mousetrap and abyss. Contrast this with *Vertigo* (1958), also restored a number of years back by Harris and Katz, in which the mousetrap, for perhaps the only time in Hitchcock's career, is entirely gone, and what we get instead is pure, obsessive trance. *Vertigo* is a great walkabout of a movie, with delirium at its core. What disturbs viewers about it is that Hitchcock is supposed to be the director who makes us all, at least for the time that we are in the theater, a little crazy, and yet in this film the moviemaker himself seems unmoored. In *Rear Window,* Hitchcock never lets himself go like that, but the movie has a morbid, spectral atmosphere that links it with that later work, and Stewart's performance is almost a warm-up for what he would accomplish in *Vertigo*. In both films, his characters dally with a suspicion that ultimately engulfs.

Stewart's Jefferies in *Rear Window* is a news photographer laid up in his Greenwich Village apartment with his leg in a cast, the result of an on-the-job mishap. Peering into the windows of his neighbors across the

courtyard, he begins to imagine—first as diversion, then as obsession—
that a white-haired, barrel-chested salesman, Lars Thorwald (Raymond
Burr), has murdered his ailing wife and disposed of her body in pieces.
Jefferies's amateur sleuthing impresses no one at first, not his smart-aleck
nurse, Stella (Thelma Ritter), or his police-detective friend, Tom (Wen-
dell Corey), or his marriage-minded high-society girlfriend, Lisa (Grace
Kelly), who makes her first real appearance in the movie as a luminous
profile sliding with sensuous slowness into a kiss with the dozing invalid.
Jefferies, who can't get himself to commit to her, complains that Lisa is
"too perfect," and, actually, she is. (That was always the problem with
Grace Kelly.) But Hitchcock understood that dry ice can sting, too. The
blonde ice queens who often were his heroines embodied his aesthetic:
tight control on the surface and smolderings underneath.

Rear Window has a ghastly, comic subtext: Jefferies's obsession with
the supposed murder is also a projection of his own desire to be rid of Lisa
and her gold-plated ministrations. (She does things like ordering up to his
apartment dinner and champagne from "21.") Virtually the entire movie
is shot from Jefferies's vantage point inside his cramped apartment, and
the people who pass through it often register as intrusions. They distract
Jefferies from the real show going on across the courtyard—the summertime mini-dramas glimpsed through unshaded windows involving not
only Thorwald but a childless couple doting on a pet dog, a flirtatious
dancer, newlyweds, a sculptor, a composer, and a sad spinster who sets the
dinner table for two and eats alone. These window-framed vignettes are
trite, perhaps deliberately so, but they offer up a quintessentially urban
phenomenon. In the city, every window is a portal into an incomplete-
ly understood story. (*Psycho,* remember, opens with the camera's entry
into a randomly chosen window.) Hitchcock captures our compulsion
to transform our surroundings into a narrative, a cyclorama, not only for
our amusement but for our sanity.

He also recognizes how much we want the worst to happen. Like
Jefferies, we want the murder to be real. If it isn't, then we are merely voy-
eurs, and that's too sordid to contemplate. Even if it *is* real, even if we turn
out to be saviors instead of peepers, there's still a sordidness about the en-
terprise. If you break into people's carefully constructed worlds, you can
expect to come undone, too. Jefferies puts Lisa and, ultimately, himself in
mortal danger, and yet the most plaintive and powerful moment in the

movie comes when Thorwald confronts Jefferies in his apartment and cries out, "What do you want from me?" In the world of *Rear Window,* even murderers are entitled to a little privacy.

(*New York*, 2000)

ISTVÁN SZABÓ

Sunshine

István Szabó's highly uneven *Sunshine*, starring Ralph Fiennes in three separate roles, is an epic romance encompassing several generations of a Hungarian Jewish family as well as most of the twentieth century and its attendant political horrors. Szabó's script originally ran some 600 pages; the version that's on the screen, written in collaboration with the American playwright Israel Horovitz, lasts three hours. The results are schematic yet sprawling. We're watching the playing-out of a thesis, which could be summarized as *You can never escape your roots*, but along the way Szabó demonstrates the kind of grand-scale ambition one still sees in novels but rarely sees anymore in the movies. What I am speaking of here is *conceptual* ambition, not the bigger-is-better pomp and pageantry that most filmmakers mistake for breadth.

You certainly feel like you've experienced something when *Sunshine* ends. But what, exactly? Szabó's specialty, notably in films like *Mephisto* and *Colonel Redl*, both starring Klaus Maria Brandauer, is dramatizing the bloody confluence of politics and matters of the heart. He is a fatalist who believes that history plays out our destinies. And yet he is drawn to the ways in which people fight the inevitability of their fates. He's drawn to decadence too; the most memorable moments in his movies are not the humanist ones but, instead, those passages in which the screen is wormy with terror and corruption.

The Sonnenscheins (the name means "sunshine" in German) are the family whose destiny is being played out. Emmanuel (David de Keyser), the patriarch, created the family fortune with the marketing of an herbal health tonic; his advice to his two sons, Ignatz (Fiennes) and Gustave

(James Frain), is to "take nothing on trust, see everything for yourself." Gustave, in love with Ignatz's wife, Valerie (Jennifer Ehle), a first cousin raised within the family, becomes a firebrand physician who rails against the reigning Austro-Hungarian monarchy; Ignatz becomes a judge and staunch defender of the empire. With his father's blessing, he changes his surname from the Jewish-sounding Sonnenschein to Sors, an acceptably Hungarian appellation. Neglecting his wife, who despises his accommo-dationist cravings, Ignatz is a caricature of middle-class respectability, a poseur whose pose has become the man.

His son, Adam (Fiennes), an even fiercer assimilator, grows up into a lawyer and champion fencer who converts to Catholicism in order to compete at the highest levels. A gold-medalist at the 1936 Olympics in Berlin, he ultimately is done in by the fascist forces he refused to foresee. Adam's young son, Ivan (later played by Fiennes), who narrates the film, watches as his father is tortured and murdered before his eyes in a con-centration camp, and survives to revenge himself as a communist—be-fore falling victim to yet another strain of totalitarianism.

Szabó carefully sets up the three characters played by Fiennes to rep-resent the phases of a man's life: Ignatz wants power, Adam glory, Ivan redemption. He gives each of them a distinct look, too, as a beard gives way to a mustache and ultimately to a more sunken, sallow countenance. Casting Fiennes in all these roles is something of a stunt, but at the most basic level of our not confusing one man with the other, he brings it off. Missing, however, is the spellbinding performance that would unify this behemoth of a movie. Szabó's films require not only heroic protagonists but heroic actors to play them, someone like Klaus Maria Brandauer. (What has happened to him?) Fiennes's soulfulness can be wearying. He's too elegantly refined, too effete, too Dirk Bogarde-ish to carry the day. His resonant blankness doesn't allow us to see behind the mask, and in roles like these, that's a near-fatal flaw.

The meanings of this movie seemed coerced rather than arrived at. If we are meant to interpret *Sunshine* as a cautionary tale about the dangers of denying one's roots, we come face-to-face with the realization that for the Sonnenscheins, it ultimately mattered little to their survival wheth-er they declared themselves Jews. Would a scenario in which Ignatz and Adam embraced their Jewishness have resulted in a far different fate? Name change or no, Hitler and Stalin were still waiting in the wings. In one unsubtle scene, Ivan is asked why no one among the thousands of prisoners was moved to save his father when there were only three officers in command. At times, Szabó seems to be implying that his characters' accommodations brought on the dictators. The family, starting with Emmanuel, is never shown to be terribly rooted in Jewish tradition anyway. That may be part of the point, but we are being asked to mourn a lost cultural bond that has never been fully established for us.

There's something uncomfortably punitive about the way Szabó frames this story. Ignatz's wife, now a wise old matriarch (played radiantly by Rosemary Harris, Jennifer Ehle's mother), speaks of the family's fate as a Jewish fate. Is the assimilationist dream of wanting to belong such a grievous malady? And if one takes the larger view that many of these people have indelibly compromised their individuality, then why do they yet seem so individual?

For all its scope and intermittent power, *Sunshine* ultimately seems like a family squabble that Szabó has politicized into epic proportions. The brother-vs.-brother infighting, the messing-around with each other's wives, the affairs and recriminations and capitulations would be just as likely to occur in Boise as in Budapest. Inflating their importance by presenting them against the backdrop of the Holocaust and the Gulag in the end deflates them. Whenever Szabó inserts documentary clips of the Jewish ghetto, or the Hungarian uprising of 1956, the acted-out drama is vastly diminished by comparison. Conceptual epics are wonderful things, but the concept here is as deficient as the curative powers of the Sonnenschein-family tonic.

(New York, 2000)

NEIL JORDAN

Michael Collins

Neil Jordan's *Michael Collins* opens with Collins's trusted aide Joe O'Reilly (Ian Hart) speaking of his departed leader: "He never did what anyone expected." But, in fact, Collins (Liam Neeson) does pretty much what is expected of a movie hero: he fills the screen with noble bluster; he aches for freedom; he fights heroically. When he believes the time has come to segue from war to peace, he's the noblest of peacemakers. Collins—the Irish guerrilla tactician and anti-British warrior who died in 1922, just two months short of his thirty-second birthday, at the hands of the Irish Republican Army—is a martyr-in-motion. The film is his (belated) canonization.

Jordan has wanted to make a movie about Collins—"the Big Fella," as he was called—since he first began directing movies in the early eighties. From a purely technical point of view, it's probably a good thing he waited this long; his movie-making skills have never been sleeker. As a piece of period craftsmanship, *Michael Collins* is phenomenally successful. Using mostly Dublin locations, Jordan and his great cinematographer, Chris Menges, and production designer Anthony Pratt barrel us right into the action. The film is rigorously worked out yet impassioned; we don't get the feeling we're dawdling down memory lane. When Jordan uses actual black-and-white newsreel footage from the era, the effect isn't jarring because his recreations have the same gravity.

And yet instead of drawing us in, the romanticism of *Michael Collins* keeps us emotionally at bay. Jordan delivers a more conventional story than the great, wrenching material warrants. Even if you are unfamiliar with all the political intricacies of the Irish rebellion leading up to the Collins-engineered 1922 Irish Free State Treaty, which partitioned off the North, Jordan's hero-worshipping grandiloquence strikes a note that, while not altogether false, lacks resonance. Because blood still flows in Northern Ireland, we can't simply look at the film as a dirge from a bitter past. Inevitably, we also look to it for a grounding in the horrors of the present—as a way of understanding not only the historical roots of the Irish tragedy but also the psychology of political terrorism.

And it is in this realm—the psychology of violence—that Jordan's film falls the shortest. In effect, Jordan is saying that Collins is a force of history who stands outside the normal sway of psychological understanding. He's epic. How did Collins and his compatriots feel about the spillage of innocent blood? How charged up were they by their mayhem? Jordan breezes past this stuff and instead asks us to deify Collins as the true and neglected savior of his country. His glory is twofold: he's the architect of terrorist tactics that brought the British to the negotiating table; and he's the man who, in the cause of peace, stood up for the Irish Free State Treaty, which nevertheless set off a civil war.

The thrust of Jordan's view of Collins is that the Big Fella would not have condoned the violence of today's provisional IRA This is how Jordan attempts to create a mass-audience hero out of a genius of tactical terrorism whose methods remain all too close to home today. But who can say what Collins might have condoned now?

Jordan is enamored of the classic arc of Collins's life—the warrior renegade who reforms and is destroyed by his own renegades. It has a pleasing tragical quality. He's also enamored of Hollywood-style plot-making and grandstanding. (Parts of the film play like a thirties gangster shoot-'em-up.) Collins is set up in dramatic opposition to both Eamon de Valera (Alan Rickman), his mentor and the president of the renegade Irish Republic, and Harry Boland (Aidan Quinn), his closest friend and rival for the affections of Kitty Kiernan (Julia Roberts).

In Jordan's view, Collins is the shining knight to de Valera's prince of darkness. While Collins is a student of his people, the drawn-featured de Valera, who was known as "the Long Fella," is a student of Machiavelli. (What Jordan doesn't point up in a postscript, perhaps because it would lend comfort to the enemy, is that de Valera, who instigated the post-Treaty civil war supported by the IRA, ended up declaring the IRA illegal when it turned against him for failing to carry out his promise to establish an Irish republic that would include Northern Ireland.)

As for Harry, he's like one of those good-time/bad-time shoulder-punching buddies who shows up in Westerns opposite the stalwart hero. And, as in a lot of those Westerns, the buddies seem to be going through courtship rites. Harry and the Big Fella are the film's true romantic couple; by comparison, the scenes with Kitty are pro forma. When Harry ultimately sides with de Valera, Collins gives his chum his best scorned "Et tu, Brute?" look. Later, they grieve; Harry tells Collins, "I miss the old way it used to be," and Collins counters with, "We were too dangerous together." How can Kitty compete with all this manly mournfulness? She's the film's romantic relief, except there's no romance and no relief.

Jordan wants to create a tragic figure in Michael Collins, but he doesn't give us enough about him to sift through. When Collins says of the British, "I hate them for making hate necessary," we're meant to take him at his word. Wasn't there anything besides righteous virtue behind his wrath? (In real life, Collins liked to take a bite out of the ear of his defeated wrestling opponents.) Collins is converted into some kind of Irish Prometheus—which is also how the journalist Tim Pat Coogan depicts him in his massively researched Collins biography, *Michael Collins: The Man Who Made Ireland*. He is "humanized" for us by being reduced to a glorious naif—though in reality he wrote voluminously as well as voraciously reading Synge, Wilde, Yeats, Shaw. (In the film, Kitty remarks that he never writes letters to her—which is pretty funny if you know that an entire volume of their correspondence is in print.)

Collins is such a grand-scale character that we never even get a sense of the sheer arduous dailiness of his life—the way he bicycled everywhere on his missions in his pinstripe suit without being recognized by the authorities. Despite all the valiant I-am-Spartacus moments, the sequence in which we feel closest to Collins, in which we understand best what he's fighting for, is a small one—entertaining Kitty and her family in their parlor, he spins out some Irish doggerel and then breaks into a song.

It's a charming, folkloric moment, and Neeson seems buoyed by the offhandedness of it. He isn't weighed down by the importance of what he's doing. Neeson is one of the few actors who has the dynamism to carry epic movies; but, as in *Schindler's List*, he plays his heroes on—at best—two levels, when three or four are called for. Except Jordan isn't calling for any more levels. Neeson plays Collins the way Jordan sees him—righteously, innocently. Neeson can be great fun to watch, but if he doesn't perk up a bit he's going to end up in deadweight Harrison Ford territory.

The character with the most crosshatches is Rickman's de Valera. Despite his positioning as the scapegoat of the piece, de Valera comes across as such a complex figure that he takes over the movie whenever he's onscreen. He's like a full-bodied wraith; and, whether writing letters from prison or seated at the head of his banquet table of assassins, he has the luminous, slightly deranged look of the true revolutionary. He hauls his humorlessness around with him like an anchor. (In real life, de Valera, not surprisingly, lived into his nineties. Bile is a great preservative.)

Compared to an overblown, hero-hugging mess such as *Braveheart*, *Michael Collins* is a work of art. Jordan has a rare talent for creating hushed nocturnal landscapes. The moody-blues night town scenes in

Michael Collins have his distinctively lyrical horror-movie feel, and he sets up a sense of free-floating menace. You never know when someone's going to get it in the face. But all this artfulness can also seem like an evasion, a way to etherealize the subject. Jordan is impassioned about the *idea* of making a movie about Michael Collins, but when he gets right down to it he settles for the same old hero's halo. Collins was betrayed by so many people in his life—did Jordan think that lifting the halo would constitute yet another act of betrayal?

(New Times, 1996)

SATYAJIT RAY
The Home and the World

The imagery in the new Satyajit Ray film, *The Home and the World*, set in 1907 during the British partitioning of Bengal, has a plangent beauty that's suffused with the ancient. The yellows are the color of holy-book parchment, the greens and reds and blues in the drawing rooms and bedrooms seem burnished by time; they stand out with the clarity of fairytale illuminations. The colors in this movie seem drawn from an India that is slowly slipping from our eyes, and yet it is this India—this antiquity—that gives the imagery its extraordinary, mystical resonance. The glow comes from deep inside.

More than any other director, Satyajit Ray is aware of the talismanic power in the ordinary. It's not just the people in his film who carry mythic overtones; so do the objects—the chairs, tables, rugs, clothing. They carry an emotional weight out of all proportion to their placement on-screen. A mystical collusion exists between the people in *The Home and the World* and the ornamental finery with which they surround themselves. Bimala (Swatilekha Chatterjee), the young wife of an East Bengal maharajah (Victor Banerjee), moves with the slow and sensual, fated sweep of ritual. When she opens her closet and runs her fingers through her saris, she's dipping into a magic box, and her dark hands blend with the burnished golds and reds like oil paints.

Married to Banerjee's Nikhil for ten years, Bimala is a traditional Indian wife, satisfied in her ritualized seclusion from the outside world (purdah). Since her arranged wedding, she has never moved beyond her husband's quarters in the country estate where he is landlord; she has never mixed with his friends or associates. Bimala is pampered, but she doesn't have the plush narcissism of a housebound queen. She's ample, yet ethereal, and her face is suffused with the beauty of the classic Indian heroines. Nikhil adores her; a Hindu and a liberal, he encourages her to learn to speak and sing English, meet his friends, move about the estate. The movie is adapted from a 1919 Rabindranath Tagore novel, and Nikhil incarnates one of the great poet-philosopher's credos: "The broad mind is not afraid of accepting truth from all sources." Nikhil accepts those sources as a privilege of life.

When Sandip (Soumitra Chatterjee), a college friend of Nikhil's, arrives at the estate, Nikhil arranges for him to meet his wife for the first time, after only hearing her praises sung for ten years. Sandip is a political firebrand who stirs audiences with his ringing, cadenced speeches denouncing the British colonial policy of divide and rule that will split Bengal into two rival administrative units of Hindus and Muslims. He leads his followers in the cheer "Hail, Motherland!" and promotes the boycotting of foreign-made goods among the estate's poverty-stricken Muslim tenants—even though no adequate, cheaply priced Indian substitutes for these goods exist. (That's one of many reasons why Nikhil opposes Sandip's tactics.)

Nikhil's motivation in introducing Sandip to Bimala is, on the surface, impeccable: he wants his wife to break out of purdah. But we sense Nikhil's deeper motive. How can he be sure his wife truly loves him if she has never been exposed to other men? He prizes Bimala, but the unreality of his situation gnaws at him; he suspects his bliss may be counterfeit. And so he introduces Bimala to Sandip even though (or, rather, precisely because) Sandip is a galvanizing presence and a known womanizer. Sandip is everything Nikhil believes himself not to be.

Is Nikhil also unconsciously inflaming some private urge for self-destruction here? Perhaps, and that possibility gives the movie a darker psychological tone. But if Nikhil's selflessness is tinged with masochism, it also has an element of awe. There's a dazzle in his eyes as he introduces Bimala to Sandip; to be preferred by his wife in the face of such temptation will surely send him into a state of grace. Nikhil is looking for both confirmation and benediction in his marriage.

Ray shows us Bimala's unfolding entrancement with the outside world, which, to Nikhil's despair, comes to be personified by Sandip. Bimala watches Sandip's torch-lit orations through a lattice, her face striped in shadow, and she's stirred—without fully realizing it. Even though Ray is spiritually, and politically, in sympathy with Nikhil (as Tagore also was), he doesn't deny Bimala's wonder. When she walks for the first time through the doors that lead into another part of the estate, where Sandip awaits, Ray shows us her passage in a slight slow motion that mythologizes the moment; the hallway, with its gimcrack ornamentation, seems bright and candied, like a gingerbread house.

It's a child's storybook tableau, and because we perceive the passage through Bimala's wonderstruck eyes, the tableau is entirely appropriate. Ray moves us through the film with a trenchancy that makes each scene a revelation. The Tagore novel was written in a diary format, with each of the principals contributing his or her story in sections. Ray achieves a similar result on film by shifting the film's viewpoint among the three players, so that we indulge the sympathies of each in turn. The actors are so extraordinary that the sympathy never wavers. Their melancholy is almost a state of grace. With their great generosity, Swatilekha Chatterjee and Victor Banerjee (Dr. Aziz in *A Passage to India*) and Soumitra Chatterjee (a Ray veteran) are the ideal actors for Ray, who is among the most humanely compassionate—humanely *fair*—of directors.

So was Jean Renoir, who encouraged Ray as a young man about to embark on his first film: *Pather Panchali*. Renoir's oft-quoted response to those who asked him why his movies never contained villains was: "Everyone has his reasons." And so it is with Ray as well. It would have been easy to portray Sandip as a viper, but Ray understands his posturings (which is not the same thing as endorsing them). We see how Sandip bedazzles Bimala and, in so doing, bedazzles himself—the mark of a true narcissist.

We also see through him, with such clarity that he achieves the clownish poignance of a posturer who, finally, cannot live up to his own fantasy image. He's right to appeal to Indian nationalism but wrong (and obnoxiously self-serving) in his methods. When the poor reject his plea to stop buying foreign goods, he resorts to terrorism—sinking boats, torching crops. Because Nikhil is Sandip's friend, the poor, with their ancient, enraged faces, believe he is equally responsible. Sandip puts his friend's life in danger, but neither he nor the poor understand Nikhil's true gambit. Nikhil can't even ask Sandip to leave, because he knows his wife (or his wife's heart—same thing) would follow. His life is bound up totally with his love for his wife, and he demonstrates this in a final act of supreme romanticism—which is, of course, an act of supreme folly.

Like so many of Ray's films, *The Home and the World* can be viewed as a meditation on the mysteries of women. When Bimala is together with Sandip and Nikhil for the first time, Sandip flatters her with high-flown prattle about women's intuition. And yet Ray is in awe of women himself. For him, women are ineffably linked to the pull of the past; they glow with an aureole of antiquity. Ray shows us India as a palimpsest—the past is everywhere in the present. And women personify this past-in-the-presentness; they emblematize Ray's vision of life.

When she's viewed in this way, it's not surprising that Bimala, as simple as she appears, is nevertheless resonant with mystery. Sandip, with his virile beard and hortatory beguilements, is the male as posturer—the man whose mystery turns out to be that he has no mystery. Nikhil, on the other hand, has a fine-drawn beauty and a highly delicate sensitivity, as if his soul were embossed with gold leaf. In the movie's terms, he has a feminized spirituality (for Ray, that phrase would be redundant). Nikhil has the "women's intuition" that Sandip applauds in Bimala, and what he intuits about his wife drives him to despair.

At the end, Nikhil and Bimala face each other with an intensity that appears to merge them. They are more than husband and wife at this point; they're soulmates in the most transcendent of senses. When he leaves her in the night to meet the furious mobs, Bimala's soul is halved, and in the final harrowing close-ups of her ruined face, each slight shift is like a rent in the heavens.

(*Los Angeles Herald Examiner*, 1985)

POSTSCRIPT

In 2008, under the auspices of a U.S. State Department cultural outreach program, I spent two weeks in India, my first time, lecturing on Satyajit

Ray at the Kolkata Film Festival and some local schools. It soon became clear to me that the past-in-the-presentness I wrote about in *The Home and the World* is the defining essence not only of Ray's films but also of his homeland. I realized that my love for Ray's films is inseparable from a love for India itself.

MARTIN SCORSESE

Overview

Why do so many people think it was such an impossible stretch for Martin Scorsese to make *The Age of Innocence*? Did they think he would turn New York's Old Order in Edith Wharton's novel into a congregation of mooks? Did the cynics anticipate dialogue along the lines of, "You talkin' to me—*Countess*?" As distant and decorous as some of us find the film, it's still a movie made by a director who has been obsessed for most of his career with the ways social ritual clamps down on people. The same director who made *Raging Bull* made *Alice Doesn't Live Here Anymore*. The further back you go with Scorsese's films, the less perplexing *The Age of Innocence* seems.

I caught my first Scorsese film during spring break of 1972, in a fleabag Forty-Second Street theater on the bottom half of a double bill with a movie called, if I remember correctly, *1,000 Convicts and a Woman*. The film *Boxcar Bertha* was an American International Pictures cheapie starring David Carradine and Barbara Hershey. I went to see it because, through the college movie-nut grapevine, I had heard promising things about Scorsese's NYU film school student shorts and his 1968 feature, *Who's That Knocking at My Door?* And so I ascended to the theater's garbage-y balcony to "discover"—at least for myself—a new genius.

In those days, far more so than today, many of the most promising young directors sprang from schlock. (Today the tendency is to go from schlock to more schlock.) *Boxcar Bertha* was no masterpiece—more like a hillbilly *Bonnie and Clyde* retread—but it was such a smashing piece of direction that I left the theater convinced I had just seen the greatest terrible movie ever made. The kinetic passion of the moviemaking was so far in advance of the threadbare production that the effect was almost parodistic—as if, say, Orson Welles had given his all to a Gene Autry singing-cowboy feature. Here was a director with talent to burn. The fear, of course, was that, given the way Hollywood ruins talent, it would end up burning itself out on mindless programmers.

There's a story recounted in David Ehrenstein's book, *The Scorsese Picture*, about how Scorsese ran *Boxcar Bertha* for his close friend John Cassavetes, who took the director aside afterward and said, "Now that you've made a piece of shit, why don't you make a movie about something you really *care* about?" Scorsese's next film, *Mean Streets*, was so deeply personal that it made you feel as if you had tranced right into the director's own mindscape of guilt and retribution. For film critics like myself who had been following Scorsese even a little bit, *Mean Streets* was a whopping case of promises fulfilled. For emerging filmmakers, it was the key movie of its generation—the one great example of how a feature-length American movie made on a shoestring could nevertheless express a film artist's deepest torments.

Scorsese's career from *Mean Streets* to *The Age of Innocence* is emblematic of the ways in which an artist of his generation has twisted and turned in order to hold onto a piece of himself as the industry began an inexorable slide away from the freedoms that gave rise to films like *Mean Streets*. Thematically, he's moved out of the hothouse and into the parlor but, with the exception of *The Color of Money*, he's never made a film—not even his great rock documentary, *The Last Waltz*—that didn't seemed ballasted by personal obsession.

Obsessiveness is what's missing from the new generation of young independent filmmakers—including Quentin Tarantino (*Reservoir Dogs*) and Nick Gomez (*Laws of Gravity*)—who have assumed the impromptu in-your-face attitudes of Scorsese's early, great work but without his complexity or explosive urgency. Their movies are *all* attitude. *Mean Streets*, after all, wasn't only about a bunch of Italian-American guys riffing and slamming each other; *Taxi Driver* wasn't simply a squalid freak show. These films had a sense of mission that came out of a very real sense of Catholic sin and redemption. (It has been noted perhaps once too often that Scorsese trained for the priesthood.)

The depth of feeling in Scorsese's strongest films, which also, at its best, include *Raging Bull*, and even in his ardent misfires like *The Last Temptation of Christ* and commercial jobs like *Cape Fear*, is essentially religious (and, often, blackly comic). The hotfoot in his movies comes from hellfire.

Scorsese threw over the academic notion that a filmmaker must somehow "resolve" his conflicts in order to make a successful movie. With Scorsese, the conflict *is* the movie; the dramas are personal exorcisms that never end. Scorsese has always been one of the least sentimental of filmmakers—he doesn't deliquesce his raging bulls into pools of pathos. His movies, good and bad, are chocked with unremitting obsessives: Johnny Boy in *Mean Streets*, Travis Bickle in *Taxi Driver*, Jake La Motta in *Raging Bull*, Rupert Pupkin in *The King of Comedy*, Jesus in *The Last Temptation of Christ*, Tommy in *GoodFellas*, Cady in *Cape Fear*.

These avengers are there to shake out the demons from the film's "good" characters. Harvey Keitel's Charlie in *Mean Streets* says of De Niro's crazy Johnny Boy, "Who'll help him if I don't?" But it is Charlie and not Johnny Boy who holds his hand over a flame to experience the torments of damnation. Johnny Boy is Charlie demonized, and Charlie is drawn to him as he is drawn to the flame.

De Niro is at the center of so many of Scorsese's films because he is a genius at monomania—and monomania is the engine that, for good or ill, keeps these films on track. Scorsese needs these maniacs to balance out (and tempt) the people who are struggling to do right by their lives. (Every Passion Play needs its devil.) De Niro is singular among great actors in that, unlike, say Brando or Pacino, his characters don't have a whole lot of layering. With Brando, we are always aware of the emotional possibilities open to his characters. With De Niro, those possibilities have long ago been shut down—if they ever existed. What De Niro does at his best, as in *Taxi Driver*, is to get so deeply inside the shadings of a single emotion—a single fixation—that the chasm he opens up is like a highway to hell.

Obsessiveness can run dry, though. *Raging Bull* tapped out the vein. There was no further place for Scorsese to go into unyieldingness after Jake La Motta martyred himself in a wash of blood and battered his brains to the strains of Mascagni's *Cavalleria rusticana*. What seemed resonant and trance-like in that film, or in *Taxi Driver*, seemed merely spooky and one-note in a film like *The King of Comedy* and *Cape Fear*, or *GoodFellas*.

There was a pro forma quality to the horrors of *Cape Fear*. De Niro and Scorsese worked up a scare but they didn't yank anything new out of themselves. *GoodFellas* skimmed the surface of its horrors, too, zipping from one grotesque burlesque to the next, featuring at its core a blank—Ray Liotta's Henry Hill—surrounded by a bevy of other blanks. It was a zombietown gangster film with a chuckling facetious tone, but its cartoonishness made it scrumptious for audiences who prefer their monomanias lo-cal.

Scorsese must have recognized the need to move away from this torched terrain and renew himself, and that is perhaps why he alighted on *The Age of Innocence*. It brings him into the comforts of classicism, but it retains his lifelong theme of the individual crossed with society. He's trying to feel his way into society's upper reaches instead of its lower depths but the principle remains the same. What thematic difference is there, finally, between the scene in *GoodFellas* where Henry Hill asks a favor of the local *capo*, and the scene in *The Age of Innocence* where the well-born Archers ask the blue-blood van der Leydens to intercede in the matter of their cousin the countess?

Daniel Day-Lewis's Newland Archer isn't the usual Scorsese protagonist, though. He's a reactive hero—a man of tentativeness and breeding. And he is perhaps a reason *The Age of Innocence* feels a little hollow at its core. Newland is a bit of an asparagus; we don't feel his desperation at being closed off from his beloved and locked into the horrors of a predictable life.

Instead, the movie's center shifts to the countess because, as Michelle Pfeiffer plays her, she has the woebegone gravity of someone haunted by the predicaments of her class. Her beauty is a bit blurry and wan, as if she were already dissolving into a memento mori before her lover's eyes. Pfeiffer perfectly captures what Edith Wharton described as "Madame Olenska's mysterious faculty of suggesting tragic and moving possibilities outside the daily run of experience."

Scorsese, along with Francis Coppola, George Lucas, Steven Spielberg, Brian De Palma, and many others, was in the vanguard of the first generation of American filmmakers to come out of the film schools. They took up film not only as a means to "personal" expression but also as a way of commenting on—and thereby making their own—the films that formed them. They regarded the movies of their childhood and adolescence as a shared mythology. The references in their movies to other movies was as personal a gesture as the references to their own lives.

And yet the films like *Mean Streets* and *Taxi Driver* that made Scorsese's reputation implicitly rejected much of his cherished Hollywood legacy. They came out of a different, more underground tradition, bounded by the work of directors like Cassavetes and Shirley Clarke. He could follow up *Mean Streets* with a shaggy, crowd-pleasing romantic comedy like *Alice Doesn't Live Here Anymore*, as if to show his affection for the old studio tradition. But Scorsese's rejection/embrace of Hollywood came through most pointedly in his big forties musical *New York, New York*, which was as elaborately staged as anything by Vincente Minnelli but as dark, in places, as anything in *Taxi Driver*. Flawed, harrowing, it was an anti-musical that revealed Scorsese's need to go beyond Hollywood's happy-ending artifices even as he clasped them.

And wasn't *The Last Temptation of Christ* an anti-biblical epic? And wasn't *Raging Bull* a glove in the face of every other Hollywood boxing movie? As Scorsese's career has developed, his movie sources have been increasingly aboveground—he's gone from Cassavetes to DeMille, so to speak. But the subversive intent has always been there. What's different about *The Age of Innocence* is that, of his films, it's the least subversive of its sources. It summons up Visconti's *The Leopard* and Welles's *The Magnificent Ambersons* in tribute, not contention.

Is it unfair to ask for more steam heat from Scorsese? Classicism is perhaps best left to those, like Merchant Ivory, who share its temperament. There's a studied quality to *The Age of Innocence*—it's not an intuitive piece of work. (And it's not as deeply funny as Wharton, either.) But it's an honorable piece of work, an attempt by one of our finest filmmakers to extend his sensibility into the sorrowful reaches of classic, highborn drama. In a modern Hollywood preoccupied with mindless melodrama, this sort of film may be one of the few ways in which audiences can be made to feel they have experienced "art." What Scorsese has demonstrated throughout his career is that there are other, more challenging and vehement ways to experience art.

(*Los Angeles Times*, 1993)

POSTSCRIPT

Scorsese's second film following *The Age of Innocence*, coming after *Casino*, was the Dalai Lama drama *Kundun*. Somewhat inert as narrative, *Kundun* was nevertheless an extraordinary stretch—with its ritualism and its patterned palette and its stillnesses, it represented a whole new way of seeing for Scorsese. And a new way of feeling, too—a kind of contemplative delirium. *Kundun* was a heroic achievement for a filmmaker so far along in his career, and its commercial failure may have pushed him back into the safety zone of films like *Bringing Out the Dead*. It was around the time of *Gangs of New York* that I began to wish—still do—that he would just chill out and make something dinky and droll. He was caught in a conceptual bind in that film; he wanted to make a movie that was hyberbolic, almost hallucinatory, in its historical perceptions, and yet—except for Daniel Day-Lewis's Bill the butcher, who strode about like some kind of Kabuki arachnid in stovepipe hat and waistcoat—realistic in human terms. *The Aviator*, with its egregious miscasting of Scorsese fave Leonardo DiCaprio as Howard Hughes, was an arrant bid for an Oscar, which he finally won for *The Departed*—not much of a departure, although it was fun and better than the other post-*Mean Streets* goombah fests from Scorsese Inc., not to mention that Val Lewton movie with elephantiasis, *Shutter Island*. The 3-D *Hugo*, echoing *Kundun* in its affinity for childhood wonderment, had its entrancements, but I found it a deeply impersonal personal movie. Its cinema magician hero, Georges Melies, seemed worlds away from the idols who actually formed Scorsese's artistry: Cassavetes, Clarke, Anthony Mann, Elia Kazan, and all the rest.

THE COEN BROTHERS

Overview

A friend of mine once described the films of Joel and Ethan Coen as the movie equivalent of eye-catching curios you stare at in an antique shop without ever wanting them in your home, and I know what he means.

Their latest film, *The Hudsucker Proxy*, set in 1958 but often deliberately evoking the thirties, is a forty-million-dollar curio. As gewgaws go, it's monumental, a ship-in-a-bottle in full launch.

Of course, the detailing in their films, starting with their first, the low-budget, wacked-out Texas Gothic *Blood Simple*, was always scrupulously applied. It's just that now there's more appliqué to play with.

Through five films, which also include *Raising Arizona, Miller's Crossing,* and *Barton Fink*, the Coens have managed to make movies that don't look like anybody else's, even though they draw unapologetically from all over. (Several of their movies, like *Barton Fink* and *Hudsucker Proxy*, revolve around the ambiguities of authorship.) The paradox of the Coens' films is that they seem both one-of-a-kind and derivative, personal and impersonal. They draw on our memories of other movies not in order to evoke the same feelings in us but to distance us from those feelings. The Coens—like Kubrick, they are artists as control freaks—want us to know they're in control.

Their movies may be one-of-a-kind, but is it a kind you can warm up to? The dissociation one feels watching the Coens' films—particularly the most recent three—comes not so much from the gap between form and content as between form and feeling. This gap, like everything else in their films, is intentional. The Coens like to send you out of the theater with a postmodernist chill.

Given the amount of gluey sentimentality in most Hollywood movies, the wise-alecky frostiness of the Coens' films is something to be reckoned with. At least they don't slobber all over you. Technically the films are ambitious, so chockablock with references to old movies and myth that they ought to come with illuminated skeleton keys so audiences can follow along in the dark. But emotionally the films don't aim high. Often what you're left with, as in *Blood Simple* or *Barton Fink*, is a parched giggle.

From the very start, with *Blood Simple*, it was the "knowingness" of the Coens that endeared them to critics and movie producers. *Blood Simple* was a gory pulp melodrama with corpses buried alive and a heroine in peril in the final reel. But it was also a kind of critique of the form. The fancy camera moves, like the celebrated one in which the camera glides along the length of the bar and then lifts up over a napping drunk, were a way of placing the screen action within quotation marks.

The fanciness didn't serve any *artistic* agenda really; it didn't attempt to alter our way of seeing but instead tried to flatter it. (That's why movie-wise people loved the film.) When Jean-Luc Godard used movies tricks and quotes in his sixties films, he did it to break through to new subject matter, new states of political awareness. The Coens simply want us to know they've seen the same movies we have.

Raising Arizona, the Coens' next film, was breakneck where *Blood Simple* was deliberately laggard. If the dialogue in *Blood Simple* was paced Pinter-slow—for that extra-special mock-ponderous effect—the banter in *Raising Arizona* was positively hopping. The film featured those two world-class jaw-boners, Holly Hunter and Nicolas Cage, as a childless couple who, in desperation, swipe a quintuplet. Until the film skidded off-road with a warthog *Road Warrior* fantasia, it was amusingly mad-cap. (The sight of Cage fleeing a convenience store hold-up with a box of Huggies wedged under his armpit was a great yuppie era joke.)

But in a sequence like the one where the placid baby quint is left un-attended in the middle of the highway, or toted along for a bank robbery, the film also betrayed the Coens' penchant for giggly heartlessness. They outsmarted themselves on this movie. Playing to the audience's movie-in-spired anticipations as avidly as any action-movie hack, they didn't allow for where we might draw the line in our suspension of disbelief. (The film was a modest hit anyway, their only one.)

In *Miller's Crossing*, in which Gabriel Byrne played a gangland henchman who inexplicably offers himself up as sacrificial avenger out of loyalty to the boss who abused him, the Coens chucked their lickety-split cartoonishness and instead sunk deeply into the goo of mythic serious-ness. It was a gangster art piece set in 1929 in an unnamed city—gang-ster films, of course, should *never* be set in unnamed cities. Hermetically sealed off from any origins except old movies, *Miller's Crossing* was the closest the Coens have come to standard sentimentality. Maybe that's why it's so nerveless—they couldn't muster any conviction for those old Hollywood crime movie conventions because they live on the flip side of those conventions.

With *Barton Fink*, the Coens seemed crouched inside a private vi-sion that always threatened but never quite succeeded in going public. (It had some of the same humid, congealed tricksterism as the worst of Da-vid Lynch.) John Turturro's Barton, a Broadway playwright with a prole-tarian hit on his hands à la Clifford Odets, drags his heels to Hollywood to work on a Wallace Beery wrestling picture. He checks into a faded dump of a hotel where he befriends a burbly tenant who turns out to be a mass murderer, and inexorably unravels. Barton is passionate about the life of the mind and ends up toting a severed head in a box. (So much for the mind's life.)

The Coens deliberately made Barton a pointy-headed object of pathos; his ravings about creating "a new theater of and about the common man" are made to sound sickly and condescending. It's a cruel caricature but the cruelty is partly self-inflicted. Barton may represent the Coens' worst image of themselves. Opposite him is the studio head who has his own rant: "We need some heart in motion pictures." To Barton he wheedles, "Can you make us laugh, can you make us cry?" He's the crude Philistine voice of the Coens' harshest critics, and we're meant to side with him (sort of). But since his criticisms anticipate and preempt our own, the Coens manage to one-up the audience anyway.

The Coens were onto something bigger and more interesting and self-examining in *Barton Fink* than they were able to fully develop. Barton's blather about the Common Man turns to ashes before that Man's worst-possible-case embodiment, next-door neighbor Madman Mundt—and Mundt, played with proletarian heft by John Goodman, is metaphorically linked to Hitler, who also invoked the masses. The one good idea nearly buried beneath the hallucinatory gimcracks of this movie is that common-man playwrights like Barton Fink—like Odets and all the rest—are too touched by innocence and idealism and fellow feeling to recognize the true depravity inside the masses. They're sentimentalists presiding over their own undoing.

The script for *The Hudsucker Proxy* had been worked on by the Coens, along with Sam Raimi, since the *Blood Simple* days. (Movie trivia alert: Cage in *Raising Arizona* can be glimpsed for a second wearing a Hudsucker Industries work uniform.) It's their most cynical opus yet, and cynicism on this elaborate a scale really sours the atmosphere.

Tim Robbins plays Norville Barnes, a hayseed from Muncie, Indiana, working in the gargantuan, nightmarish Manhattan mail room of Hudsucker Industries, when suddenly he's installed as the company president. It's a Machiavellian ploy by the firm's board to avoid a public takeover by shaking investor confidence and allowing them to buy a controlling interest. But Norville, fresh-faced and oblivious, stymies the fix by getting the company to market his pet project—which turns out to be the Hula-Hoop. But this is not a success story, exactly; it all flashes back from Norville about to jump from the forty-fourth floor of the Hudsucker building on New Year's Eve.

It's a neo-Capra fairy tale—the borrowings from *Meet John Doe* in particular are legion—but with Capra's plump populism turned inside out. That might not seem like such a bad reversal except that, compared to the Coens' empty cackle, Capra's we-the-people balladeering at least had a hearty ring. Capra on some level believed in his boosterism.

The Coens believe only in their own thin cynicism. They condemn Norville as a lucky schnook in a schnooky world where you can be No. 1 only by creating useless fads for all the other schnooks out there—for, you know, we the people. Norville's comedown (or his comeback, for that matter) has no power or despair, because we are never allowed to glimpse any emotional possibilities in him. He's a puppet on a string—a plummeting puppet. And the Coens are puppetmasters.

At a time when even the most talented American independent filmmakers, like Gus Van Sant and Richard Linklater, are fiddling with anomie, the Coens' boisterous blankness can seem almost rousing. But only in a cynic's paradise could their designed-to-the-teeth exercises in nattering flapdoodle metaphysics satisfy our appetite for high style. Even Terry Gilliam, whose elephantiasis of style is even more unfortunate than the Coens', puts real passion into his panoramas. The Coens, by comparison, keep a smart, tight cool. They're the perfect postmodernists for a race of androids.

(*Los Angeles Times*, 1994)

POSTSCRIPT

The Coens' *Fargo* followed *Hudsucker Proxy* and remains their most celebrated film, though not by me. Except for Frances McDormand's pregnant police chief, all the characters in *Fargo* were freeze-dried joke butts. The film was cooked in a climate where whomping the "lower classes" was on the rise. Along with Alexander Payne's *Citizen Ruth* from the same year, where we were invited to chortle at antiabortion activists because they live in a crummy neighborhood near a noisy airport, *Fargo* represented fallout from the PC wars.

For me, the Coens' best film, far and away, is *No Country For Old Men*, a near-masterpiece (see page 454). *True Grit,* which severely tamped down the brothers' trademark nasty nihilsm, was perhaps not coincidentally their most commercially successful movie.

BERNARDO BERTOLUCCI

The Last Emperor

As a film artist, Bernardo Bertolucci is such a voluptuary that the subject of his new film, *The Last Emperor*, sounds almost too ecstatically good to be true, too rich. With close to ninety of its 160 minutes set inside China's Forbidden City, this epic about Pu Yi, the last imperial ruler of China, has enough grand-scale exotica to keep Bertolucci—and us—in a constant delirium

When this film really sings, it's as if Bertolucci had tapped the well-spring of cinema and, ecstatic, discovered the eroticism at its essence. Not that *The Last Emperor* is *Last Tango in Paris*. There's almost no overt eroticism in the film, but Bertolucci's ardor for the deep and sensual look of things fills every frame. He's a true pantheist; his bodyscapes and land-scapes have the same vibrant, fervid lyricism.

Pu Yi was three years old when, in 1908, he was installed as Lord of Ten Thousand Years by his great aunt, the Lucretia Borgia-like empress dowager Tzu I, who died within two days. (She's like a cross between Dickens's Miss Havisham and Jabba the Hut.) Forced to abdicate four years later with the first Republic of Sun Yat-Sen, Pu Yi remained locked inside the Forbidden City in the center of Beijing for twelve years—a figurehead deity surrounded by servants and eunuchs and a fortune in annual allowance.

The sequences inside the Forbidden City have the luster of fairytale enchantments, with the reds and violets and yellows glowing like pages from an illuminated manuscript. When little Pu Yi first enters his throne room in the Hall of Supreme Harmony, with its immense carved stone

Buddhas and golden dragons, it's as if he had gusted into a Manchu Oz. The dying empress on her giant bed at the far end of the hall has a fetid, decayed luxuriousness.

The weight of the ancient hangs in every corner of this city—a most extraordinary prison. Pu Yi rules it in a kind of cuckoo charade. His eunuchs and attendants kow-tow to his every whim; his bedroom, the scene of his wedding night to seventeen-year-old Wan Jung (Joan Chen), is lined top to bottom with small golden Buddhas. (On that unconsummated first night, invisible courtesans remove the couple's clothing layer by layer; the sheer *sound* of fabric against fabric has never seemed so erotic.)

With virtually no contact to the world outside the city's walls, except for the presence of his Scottish tutor (played by Peter O'Toole in all his brittle, storky magnificence), Pu Yi seems as illusory as a hologram inside a make-believe castle. He's a figment of a dynasty that no longer has any worldly function except a symbolic one, and even that is shorn away when Pu Yi, in 1924, is ordered by a warlord's troops to quit the Imperial Palace in an hour.

The abruptness of Pu Yi's exile is preceded by some of Bertolucci's most sweeping and caressing camera work. He turns us into voluptaries, too; we're ripe for the acres and acres of sweet, liquid, legend-tinged opulence that glides before our eyes. This is more than a triumph of production values. What you get from the Forbidden City sequences is something like a whiff from the center of the mystery. Working in a culture completely alien to him, Bertolucci raids it for its resonances. He *embraces* its unknowability.

If you've read any of Pu Yi's childhood diaries, published as *The Last Manchu*, you can see how Bertolucci has used the text as a fairytale source book. He's not interested in making a historical tract. What excites him, what has always excited him, is the spooky dualism of personality. An early film, *Partner*, was derived from Dostoevsky's *The Double*. In *The Conformist*, Jean-Louis Trintignant tried to normalize himself behind a mask of fascist aristocracy; in *Last Tango in Paris*, Marlon Brando's Paul, in his sexual trysts, tried to erase himself into anonymity.

Pu Yi is an extension of this effacement. He's a "deity" and yet he is all too insignificantly mortal. He's a living relic of a vanished dynasty. Exiled from the palace to Tienstin, where he carries on like a Western playboy and calls himself Henry, and then to Manchuria, where the Japanese set him up as a puppet ruler, he tries to regain his emperorship. Pu Yi is like one-half of a split image trying to once again become whole. Instead, captured by the communists after World War II, sent for nine years to a Maoist "re-education" camp, he spends his last years as a gardener in the Botanical Gardens of Beijing—an ordinary citizen. His anonymity is complete. He has become the Ultimate Conformist. He also seems wholly human for the first time—happy.

The largeness of this story resides in Pu Yi's insignificance against the vast, rolling backdrop of history. It's a mock ironic epic with something of a Kafka kick to it. But Bertolucci is also in love with finality and fatalism—it's no accident that two of his films begin with "Last"—and that limits his emotional involvement with Pu Yi. For all its delectations, *The Last Emperor* is a cool experience in many ways. (The convention of having Chinese characters who for the most part speak English also undercuts the exotica.)

The emotion in this film comes through in the opulent visionary tableaux, which are as astonishing as anything ever put on film. But Pu Yi is distanced from us, and Bertolucci is content to keep his distance. He begins the film in the re-education camp, and flashes back, just so we know how Pu Yi will end up—the film is one long inexorable slide into enforced anonymity. Bertolucci uses the foreignness of the culture to license his own hands-off approach to Pu Yi.

There's no attempt at a psychological portrait; it's as if Pu Yi was a concoction of fabulists, a creature pre-psychological, pre-sexual, hence timeless. And so we don't get more than the nuances of what it must have been like to grow up friendless, treated as a god; we don't get the dislocations of Pu Yi's life outside the palace, only his mania for imperial restoration. John Lone's performance is striking, mesmerizing, but it's essentially a series of almost Kabuki-style postures and congealments of mood. (Its closest equivalent is probably Nikolai Cherkassov's Ivan in Eisenstein's *Ivan the Terrible*, a film which, in its frieze-frozen audacity, has had its influence on this one.)

It's also surprising that the man who made *1900*, which concluded with a grand-scale peasants' hoedown under a giant red flag, declined to bring out more of the political flavor of Pu Yi's story. Maoism, like the factionalism that preceded it, is treated as so much show-trial pageantry. Particularly in its second half, the movie becomes a bit too edgy and truncated for the ceremoniousness that preceded it. (This may be because the theatrical version is one hour and twenty minutes shorter than its projected "video" cut.)

The political machinations of the Japanese are presented flash-card-style, and Pu Yi's Manchurian ancestry never quite comes into focus for us. You'd have a tough time figuring it out from this movie, but the Chinese considered the Manchu alien rulers, which must have made Pu Yi feel like an internal exile in his own country even before he abdicated.

And yet, the film does work up a rising wave of emotion at the end, when Pu Yi, now an old man, reenters the Imperial Palace and sneaks back onto his golden throne. He's reconnected to his childhood; the double-image has finally joined. I thought back to little Pu Yi scampering through a billowing golden curtain to the thousands awaiting his coronation; racing as a teenager across the city's tile embankments, unable to escape his confinement. The black jest of Pu Yi's story is the confinement that was his curse and was also the key to his glory, for only by being closed off from the world could he pretend godliness.

I had thought the operative image in *The Last Emperor* was Pu Yi standing, expelled, before the great crimson doors of his palace, his eyes blanked by sunglasses. I'm left instead with the image of the old emperor once again in his throne. For Bertolucci, Pu Yi's implacability isn't something to be delved into; the mystery *is* the man. In the end, that mysteriousness takes on the dimensions of a deep and sad and ancient story, and our distance from this man becomes both infinite and infinitesimal.

(*Los Angeles Herald Examiner*, 1987)

POSTSCRIPT

I had occasion to interview Bertolucci the day after *The Last Emperor* swept the Academy Awards with nine Oscars out of nine nominations, including ones for best picture and director. I wrote at the time:

> He seemed dazed by the adulation, glancing periodically at the two gleaming gold weights on his hotel coffee table as if they were tribal totems. Unlike *Last Tango in Paris* or even *The Conformist*, *The Last Emperor* is the sort of film that Hollywood can

abide. It's the work of a sensualist, but this time the eroticism is not ferocious. It's a work of political imagination, but the politics have a faint watercolor wash—vanishing-ink Marxism. *The Last Emperor* is an extraordinary visionary achievement, but Hollywood has no trouble enclosing it in the same continuum with Cecil B. DeMille and *Dr. Zhivago* and *The Winds of War*. "There is something I've been told by more than one executive," says Bertolucci. "They say, 'We like this movie because it reminds us of the real reason we are doing our job.'"

Like Godard and many other great iconoclastic European directors, Bertolucci has a surprisingly swoony relationship to Hollywood movies. When he talks about Hollywood now, he has an innocence that can't be faked—he looks at the smog-banks above the Hollywood Hills and sees Golden Age spirits. Like his young hero Fabrizio in *Before the Revolution*, Bertolucci finally has a taste for the blandishments of royalty, of life lived before the revolution. And, like Godard, his longest-standing vessel of worship has turned out to be not the radical left but the great god Cinema. Bertolucci can't be accused of being co-opted by Hollywood because, in a sense, Hollywood—its larger-than-life ardor and romance—has always been the radioactivity in his artist's veins. *The Conformist* was haunted by Bogart; *1900* by *Gone With the Wind*.

Stealing Beauty

Can it be that the director who did so much for butter in *Last Tango in Paris* has fashioned a dewy ode to virginity? *Stealing Beauty* would be an odd elixir coming from most directors; from Bernardo Bertolucci, it's almost perverse. And yet it's consistent with the central nostalgia in his movies: a longing for life lived before the upheavals of sex and loss, before the corruption of innocence.

In *Stealing Beauty*, nineteen-year-old Lucy (Liv Tyler), summering in a Tuscany villa hosted by close friends of her late mother, is an American innocent deflowered. Eventually. Bertolucci and his screenwriter, novelist Susan Minot, are in thrall to Lucy's maidenhood. And maidenhead. They've joined the sensibility of romance schlock fiction with a lament for blasted bourgeois lives. It's Harlequin Chekhov.

The blasted lives belong mostly to the villa's oldsters, the ones whose flowers were plucked long ago. Lucy's hosts—Ian Grayson (Donal McCann) and his wife, Diana (Sinead Cusack)—are Irish expatriates whose edgy moodiness clashes with the rhapsodic Tuscan backdrops. A sculptor who carves out his wood portraits with a buzz saw and frets energetically, Ian is captivated by Lucy's soon-to-be-stolen beauty. Alex (Jeremy Irons), a dying playwright dribbling away to nothingness, sees Lucy as a kind of angelic IV. Her virginity and its impending loss—who will be the lucky guy?—fascinate him. They become confidantes, soul mates. Not lovers, though. To ease the pain, she presents him with a joint wrapped in red ribbon; he vaporizes worldly wisdom. He tells her, "There is nothing more transporting than sex."

With a little rejiggering, *Stealing Beauty* might have been a nifty carnal comedy—an American waif, coyly unaware of her own luster, sends an entire Italian villa's inhabitants into a froth. But Bertolucci and Minot are too gaga for comedy. Their sustained note of regret is that Lucy cannot remain forever "pure." (Where are the great comedies that could be made about this sexlessly sexy era? Where are the great comic actors who might do for this period what, say, the early Woody Allen did for the post-Freudian generation?)

I've mentioned Chekhov, but perhaps the *Emmanuelle* movies are truer forebears. *Stealing Beauty* is too tony for soft porn, but it has all the prerequisites: a dreamy, gauzy glaze; an obsession with young virgins and their deflowering, including one near-rape scene and numerous near seductions; a "wise" old mentor for our nymphet; a few scenes with her listening, tremblingly, to other couples rutting; a chic party sequence with gamboling satyrs and lanky Eurotrash androgynes; a frisson of incestuous stirrings; snatches of Mozart on the soundtrack.

In films like *The Conformist* and *Last Tango in Paris*, Bertolucci drove more deeply into the farrago of lust than any other great director ever has. (*Last Tango* held out the promise that film artists would finally be able to confront the rawness and shock of sexual emotion with the same power employed by writers like Mailer and D. H. Lawrence and Henry

Miller.) If Bertolucci has mellowed, that's his right, but, at fifty-six, isn't it a bit early for him to be acting autumnal? Besides, the mellowness in this movie seems inauthentic and self-serving. The look-but-don't-touch celebration of gorgeous Lucy comes across as a testament to how sensitive *we* are; our lust for her is all gussied up with "adoration," as she remains a girlish, vapid cipher. Bertolucci is so high on her virginity he never penetrates her recesses, either.

What a great joke on us all—as we close out the nineties, the newest candidate for Hollywood sex goddess is . . . a virgin. It should come as no surprise that this is the latest stop on Hollywood's retroliner. Difficult as it is in the AIDS era to comfortably champion s-e-x, you can still eroticize its absence. Technically, you don't even need to be a virgin—you can play the spunky, sweet-souled girl-next-door and reap the benefits. You can be Sandra Bullock.

Paralleling this movie maidenliness is its equally retro counterpart— the glamour puss who appears to have barreled in from a forties to fifties time warp. Right now, there doesn't seem to be much middle ground in film between the innocent child-woman and the camp vamp. Both operate in an arena where sex has been made essentially unreal. Our supermodels—many of whom are getting into movies—could not have been born into a more welcoming era. Sexual glamour, when it shows up on-screen now, almost always comes across as a taunt, a put-on—as if life were one long catwalk. It's not just pre-*Casino* Sharon Stone and Madonna and Pamela Lee and the divas of *Waiting to Exhale* and the girls of *Showgirls* I'm thinking of here. There's also Demi Moore, with her industrial-strength libidinousness, and Nicole Kidman, with her hard, prom-queen casing. Linda Fiorentino in *The Last Seduction* is a man-trap vamp with a low-slung drone; Mira Sorvino in *Mighty Aphrodite* is a high-pitched porno cutie with a bouffant for brains. So many of these Hollywood glamour pusses have been acting like drag queens, nobody should be shocked by the success of *The Birdcage*. After all, why shouldn't men get into the act, too?

And what bodes for Liv Tyler? She's also viewable this month in *Heavy*, a lugubrious drizzle of a movie, in which she plays a sweet-natured waitress who captures the secret heart of her flabby, sweet-natured boss. (He's not heavy, he's my voyeur.) But it's *Stealing Beauty* that could put her over the top. For the teen crowd who knows her for her cover-girl looks, Pantene shampoo commercials and Aerosmith video—cavorting with gal-pal Alicia Silverstone while driving buffed men batty—she could become the class act in the romper room. (Upcoming are roles in features directed by Tom Hanks and Woody Allen.) For adults, Tyler could function, for a while, as a kind of quasi-jailbait fantasy—which basically is how she is presented in Bertolucci's latest. Her appeal—and this is what may make her a star—is her seemingly unpremeditated mix of maiden and siren.

It's a fortuitous combo for today's films; she fuses the two most popular female "looks" into a single airbrushed image. Tyler is not yet a terribly adept actress, but she doesn't really need to be. (Although, if she is going to continue working with great directors, it couldn't hurt.) When she appeared a few years back in Bruce Beresford's *Silent Fall*—a botched, fascinating thriller that practically no one saw—she had a lush, sultry, forties-movie-starlet quality that other filmmakers have not been able to capture. Maybe it's because they've been too high-minded. Time's a-wastin'. Doesn't Gen X deserve its very own Ava Gardner?

(*Los Angeles*, 1996)

POSTSCRIPT

The key sex-themed movie of this era was Steven Soderbergh's 1989 *Sex, Lies, and Videotape*, with its impotent video voyeur as hero. The orgasm—glory of the Beats, the hippies' latchkey to liberation, the feminists' Valhalla—was demystified in that film. It was about sex as power play, as denial, as metaphor. Sex as sex was disdained. The film appeared to have been made by a hip scold, and its ecstatic reception suggested that perhaps AIDS-freaked audiences were primed for a scolding. Still, the movie was more retro than nouveau—after all, the traditional sex scene in American movies, unlike, say, its racier European or Japanese counterparts, has often been keyed to a denial of explicitness. The famous erotic moments in American film, like Burt Lancaster and Deborah Kerr embracing in the waves in *From Here to Eternity*, or Elizabeth Taylor and Montgomery Clift mating their profiles in *A Place in the Sun*, are relatively chaste, and frequently in black and white—our fantasies color them in. Americans seem to need a bit of grandiloquence in their sex scenes if they are to be "classic"; they need an overarching romanticism that is, deliberately, old-fashioned. The grandiloquence serves a dual purpose: it distances us by exaggeration, but by matching up with our fantasies, it also draws us closer to the passion. It's this push-pull that provides the erotic intoxication in many a great American film romance. The subtext keeps rubbing up against the text. Of course, in modern American movies especially, the real eroticism, alas, is in the camera stylistics, in the almost fetishistic detailing, in the seductions of high-tech gimcrackery. The hollows and curves of a jet or motorcar, the sheen of a power player's executive boardroom, are riper than any flesh.

FRANCIS FORD COPPOLA

Overview

I'm more ambivalent about Francis Ford Coppola than about any other filmmaker.

He's responsible for the *Godfather* movies, which I consider the greatest American epics of the sound era, and yet he's also responsible for the bombastic *Apocalypse Now*, that jungle-fever jamboree, and *One From the Heart*, with its computerized passion and Kool-Aid colorations.

In his public pronouncements, he's sharply attacked the corrupt narrow-mindedness of the studios—and rightly so. But he's also said, "I think we're at the point now where art and technology are the same thing." He's cast himself as the Merlin of movies, but he sounds more like Wernher von Braun; he talks about *One From the Heart* in space-age jargon that makes one expect to see, at the very least, the cinematic equivalent of Sputnik. I'm convinced that his Zoetrope Studios is a noble, if misguided, experiment—I've been pulling for Coppola to become Hollywood's first artist-mogul. Instead, he's been carrying on more like a genius-blowhard.

First, I'd like to deal with the blowhard. Probably no contemporary filmmaker has provoked more printer's ink, and, Coppola's statements about the "decadent" press to the contrary, most of it has been favorable, often fawning. He's granted exhaustive interviews to most of the major newspapers and magazines, and most of the interviewers have been content to sit back and print Coppola's dissertations unchallenged. And he's as garrulous as a barnstorming politician. If Superman was able to leap tall buildings in a single bound, Coppola is able to reconcile Goethe, bunraku puppet shows, Consciousness Replacement, and David Begelman in a single breath.

Coppola reserves a special ire for movie critics. He's furious that the press chose to review *One From the Heart* on the basis of the previews he staged in New York and Westwood. As a matter of fact, in his position I would have been displeased, too—*if,* as he stated, the preview version was a work in progress. That's why I held up my review of the movie until I saw Coppola's "final" cut, which turned out to be virtually identical to the version I saw in Westwood. Is it naive to suggest that Coppola's displeasure with the critics has less to do with their reviewing a preview print than with their generally less-than-stellar response?

Take the strange case of Pauline Kael, for example. In a 1975 *Playboy* interview, when asked which critics he admired, Coppola mentioned her first: "When she writes about a film, she does it in depth. When I make a bad picture, I expect her to blast me higher than a kite, and I'll be grateful for that." This came after *The Godfather Part II* was released to raves. Cut to Kael's in-depth put-down of *One From the Heart* in the *New Yorker*. Cut to a February 9 *Los Angeles Times* interview with Coppola: "I'm insulted she reviewed *One From the Heart* [based on the preview]. Everyone knows Pauline has been struggling to maintain her level among the critics." In a February 10 *Washington Post* interview, he added: "Pauline liked *The Godfather* because she's into power." Some gratitude.

Then there's the way Coppola presented *One From the Heart* to the public. On the one hand, it was talked up as his homespun valentine to all the "little people" out there—all those pure-of-heart dreamers who, Coppola implies, are a breed apart from the cynical, impure-of-heart journalists. On the other hand, *One From the Heart* was supposed to be some sort of revolutionary cinematic breakthrough, a movie like no other. It's as if the film he was describing was a rocket launch, but one lit by a single wooden match.

I wonder if Coppola is aware of his condescension when he talks about the audience for his film. (If he really felt a kinship with the pure of heart, then why are the dreamers in *One From the Heart* so paltry and dumb-faced?) He's using the same "little people" pitch that Frank Capra and Samuel Goldwyn, among so many other film potentates, perfected years ago. The only difference is, Coppola's pitch is double-edged—his flattery of simple souls also functions as a karate chop to the press. In interviews, Coppola sounds like those movie producers who point to the huge grosses of films like *The Towering Inferno* and chortle about how out of touch critics are with their audience. The fact is, *One From the Heart* is a box-office flop; if anything, the response to it has been more positive in the press than it has been in the theaters, if one considers ticket sales. In light of Coppola's fickleness, how long will it be before he turns his little people into H. L. Mencken's "booboisie"?

As for the vaunted space-age technology that Coppola utilized in *One From the Heart*, I'm no visionary, but I have a hard time getting worked up about it as an *artistic* tool—which is how Coppola wants us to perceive it. For one thing, most of the supposed "innovations" in *One From the Heart*—the scrim-divided imagery, the sets used to convey the characters' emotional states, and so on—have been around, in one form or another, practically since the beginnings of film (and theater, too). The movie's primary innovations are strictly video/electronic—a director operating from a sound control vehicle such as the one Coppola used in *One From the Heart* can, by utilizing video cassettes, connecting recorders, and other devices, achieve a greater fluidity in the filmmaking process and thereby cut by at least two-thirds the cost and time it takes to complete a film. At least that's the theory. *One From the Heart* took just about as long to make as any standard movie, but the delays may have been caused by first-time kinks. But must we swallow the notion that all this gadgetry portends an *artistic* revolution? The impulse and intuition that goes into creating a work of art derive from the same mysterious source it always did—the mind. Pretending that advanced technology will revolutionize movie art is a bit like claiming that the invention of the electric typewriter resulted in better writers.

If the man behind all this grandstanding and folderol was some no-talent Mr. Wizard, this article could end right here. But here's where my ambivalence comes in.

Coppola is no fraud. He's made at least three great films (I include *The Conversation* with the *Godfather* movies). Around the time that Coppola made *The Godfather Part II*, he became a sort of hero for me.

Here was a director who used the freedom from studio interference that *The Godfather*'s success brought him to create a sequel that was even richer and more uncompromising. He demonstrated that it was possible for a great artist to work at the height of his powers inside the Hollywood factories; that great art and big box office were not, as so many of us had cynically assumed, mutually exclusive. It's a lesson that can't be demonstrated often enough.

When, in March of 1980, Coppola purchased Hollywood General Studios and converted it into Zoetrope Studios, with a roster of contract players and writers and directors and technicians, my feeling was: *Who better to revolutionize the movie industry than Coppola?* He was an artist who beat Hollywood at its own game—he wheeled and dealed like a mogul in order to turn out films like *The Godfather*, or sponsor such films as Carroll Ballard's great, lyrical *The Black Stallion*. (Ballard, one of the most gifted American filmmakers, had tried unsuccessfully for over twelve years to secure backing for his first feature film before Coppola, an old UCLA film school classmate, came to his aid.)

Now, in a marvelous act of subversion, Coppola was setting up camp in enemy territory, so to speak, and giving creative opportunities to some of the brightest young talents in the movie business: Caleb Deschanel, David Lynch, and Scott Bartlett, as well as Jean-Luc Godard, Wim Wenders, and many lesser-known names. Together with George Lucas, Coppola intervened with Alan Ladd Jr. at Twentieth Century-Fox to financially bail out a new film by one of Coppola's idols, Akira Kurosawa. He helped refurbish and distribute Abel Gance's silent 1927 classic *Napoleon*, and, with his promotional savvy, created one of the year's unlikeliest media events.

As it turns out, Coppola wasn't the mogul that he perhaps thought he was; creative and financial mismanagement have all but sunk Zoetrope. But the dream of a studio as an extended family of artists dedicated to making unconventional, handmade films is a good dream. The problem is, as Robert Altman also discovered with his own short-lived studio, Lions Gate, you have to have the films to subsidize that dream.

In the November 25, 1974, issue of *Newsweek*, Coppola was quoted as saying, "I'm at a Y in the road. One path is to become a manager and an executive who brings about great changes. On the other hand, there's a very private notion to put my energy into developing as a writer and an artist." What seems to have happened since is that Coppola has straddled both paths. If he has misjudged his abilities as a mogul, I think he's misjudged his abilities as an artist even more. He's cast himself as an innovator—a visionary—and yet his great work has been solidly grounded in the old-fashioned narrative tradition. Whenever he's tried to move outside that tradition—in *The Rain People, Apocalypse Now,* and *One From the Heart*—he's foundered terribly. He's a great classical director who has disdain for classical forms. He identifies with a true visionary like Abel Gance, and he also identifies with the martyrdom of visionaries. It's no accident, I think, that Coppola's pet project for almost ten years has been a movie about Preston Tucker, the forties automobile inventor who designed a cheap, beautiful, revolutionarily engineered car and was subsequently branded as a crackpot and destroyed by the major auto companies.

Like D. W. Griffith and Orson Welles before him, Francis Coppola is in the tradition of American film artists who think big. But, in recent years, Coppola appears to have confused big thinking with genuine artistry—he has elephantiasis of the imagination. When he waxes ecstatic about the likelihood of inducing 3-D holographic movies into the brain, he skirts self-parody. "It seems clear," he said in *Rolling Stone*, "that someday in the near future it will be possible to put *One From the Heart* directly into your mind!" (Good grief!) It would be nice to dismiss all this talk as idle blather, but *One From the Heart* really *does* look like a movie made by a man who has come to believe that "art and technology are the same thing." I keep thinking back to what Eleanor Coppola wrote about her husband in *Notes*, her diary of the *Apocalypse Now* ordeal:

> Lately Francis has been talking about his fears . . . His fear that he can't write. That his greatest success has come from adapting someone else's writing. My guess is that when he gives up, when he concludes he is not the kind of novelist or playwright he dreamed of being as a young boy, he will know what kind of a writer he is and it will be more right for him than anything he could have imagined.

I believe that will happen when Coppola stifles the technocrat in himself and allows the artist to once again come through. For the sake of movies and movie-makers everywhere, may that time be soon.

(*Los Angeles Herald Examiner*, 1982)

POSTSCRIPT

In the many years since this was written, Coppola has never come close to matching the first two *Godfather* films (although I rate *Apocalypse Now* somewhat higher now—in retrospect, I think it captured the freak-out phantasmagoria of that war in a way that none of the other, more conventional Vietnam movies did). He stopped directing altogether for ten years, only to return in 2007 with *Youth Without Youth* and, later on, *Tetro*—exactly the kind of disjunctive, "experimental" movies he values as art and many of us deem high-toned malarkey. (*Twixt*, his barely released latest film, is low-toned malarkey.) Instead of accepting his fate as a great classical filmmaker, he still wants to be taken as a "visionary." He touts his marginal new films by knocking his revered old ones. His latest line is that *The Godfather Part II* was unnecessary. Maybe we should just be grateful to Coppola for having made two of the greatest films ever made and leave it at that—even if he can't.

SPIKE LEE

Bamboozled

Bamboozled, the latest cri de coeur from Spike Lee, is about a frustrated black television writer, Pierre Delacroix (Damon Wayans), who ends up creating a new program for his network—a variety-act minstrel show set on a plantation and featuring black performers in blackface. Despite protests, the show—featuring Manray (Savion Glover), a formerly homeless tap dancer who is dubbed "Mantan" after the pop-eyed black comic Mantan Moreland, and titled *Mantan: The New Millennium Minstrel Show*—is a winner. Blackface, worn by all races, becomes the new national rage. Delacroix's boss, Dunwitty (Michael Rapaport), a vice president of the lagging Continental Network System, is ecstatic. Even President Clinton is shown watching the show and chortling.

Lee loads up his movie with so many hot buttons that the film resembles a compendium of all his previous provocations. It's the Compleat Spike Lee. If dunning and baiting and chastising and lecturing were all it took to create a powerful experience in the movies, then *Bamboozled* would be a masterpiece. It's far from that, although clearly the intention here was to be more than a movie anyway. Lee wants *Bamboozled* to be a call to action: *Stop the minstrelsy in our popular culture.*

The new minstrelsy, as alluded to in the film, shows up most readily on television, which is where Delacroix, the sole black writer on his network's staff, has been toiling without success. Delacroix believes the black middle class has not been given a chance to sample anything more than race-demeaning monkeyshines. His own shot-down ideas, which include a show about a black headmaster in an Eastern boarding school, don't sound so great, either, which may or may not be intentional. The implication here is that Delacroix, Harvard-educated and with a phony, pseudo-cultured accent, is a man out of touch with his blackness. And yet in the beginning, he remains angry enough to stick it to his white bosses. His pitch for the televised minstrel show describes it as satire; he talks about digging deep into his own pain, but what he really aims to prove is that the networks don't want to see blacks on TV unless they are buffoons.

This motive is blended in with another—Delacroix believes that by viewing something so offensive and racist, the country will wake up and move on to a better place. Of course, things don't work out that way, and he becomes an official advocate of the show's success and a self-hating sellout. His assistant, Sloan (Jada Pinkett Smith), goes along for the ride for a while but is aghast at what her boss has wrought; her brother Big Black Africa (Mos Def), who heads the rap group Mau Maus, is outraged enough to take up arms. (The group's final ambush by the police is meant to conjure the most notorious NYPD shootings of African Americans.)

Lee shot *Bamboozled* in digital video using multiple cameras, and it has the hepped-up quality of an exposé. Some of its tactics are lifted directly from *Network,* which also slammed viewers with self-righteousness and berated us for the soullessness of our appetites. Lee is a great hater. His distaste for Delacroix is so pronounced that the man never comes across as a tragic figure or much of anything else except a puppet. Even his education is held against him. (Maybe while he was at Harvard he should have taken a class with Henry Louis Gates Jr., who has written admiringly of Lee's movies.)

The real hero of the film is Delacroix's father, Junebug (Paul Mooney), a racy comic reduced to playing ghetto dives because, as he explains it, he had too much integrity to allow himself to be neutered by Hollywood. No sellout, he. Lee sees this neutering specifically in racial terms, but of course television is an equal-opportunity ball-buster. It is also, on occasion, a place for great comics, including black comics, to shine. Lee isn't terribly specific about what current shows, or movie stars, he believes are causing all the problems. He exhibits a more generalized anger, and in a climate where black movie stars and comics, despite ongoing injustices, have never been more popular with a wider range of audiences, that anger has its hollow side. The excitement and the craziness in pop culture right now have a lot to do with the ways racial categories in entertainment, which used to be pretty clear-cut, are now so jumbled. The racial divide is no longer Grand Canyonesque, but Lee wants us to know it's all a sham. At times, it appears that what's really riling him is not that black culture has, in his view, been minstrelized for public consumption but that so many whites are mixing it up with that culture.

A less punitive filmmaker might see something liberating or flattering or even comic in this state of affairs; movies and TV and hip-hop have turned a vast swatch of white kids into a nation of White Negroes. Lee shows us white people in *Bamboozled,* most pointedly Dunwitty, who think they're real soul brothers or sisters, and we're supposed to regard most of them with utter scorn. And Lee makes it easy for us to do so, since more often than not their hypocrisies are right on the surface. The *Amos 'n' Andy*-loving Dunwitty, whose office is plastered with photos of black sports greats and who has a black wife, tells Delacroix, "I'm more of a nigger than you are." His media consultant, a Yale Ph.D. in African American studies whose parents marched with Dr. King in Selma, proffers slick advice about how to buy the NAACP's complaisance regarding the minstrel show. The consultant's name is Myrna Goldfarb, and Dunwitty, who says "mazel tov" and jokes about the size of his nose, is clearly also meant to be a member of the tribe. What is this scapegoating doing in a movie that claims to promote fairness?

The film never makes it believable to us that blackface could become a national craze, or that critics would champion the minstrel show as groundbreaking. Does the show's runaway success mean that it's being interpreted by audiences and commentators as subversive satire designed to wake America up? Or does it mean, as Delacroix's disapproving mother laments to her prodigal son, that "a coon is a coon"? The latter, I think. The pickets against the show are led by the Reverend Al Sharpton and Johnnie Cochran, and they are not deluded men. The notion of a craze for blackface serves the film's hysteria about populism run amok in the liberal atmosphere of the new millennium. The film's model is not only *Network* but *A Face in the Crowd*, in which a guitar-picking corn-pone con man, Andy Griffith's Lonesome Rhodes, becomes a television celebrity and bamboozles the nation with his homespun charm. (Lee's movie is dedicated to Budd Schulberg, that film's screenwriter.) Savion Glover's Mantan is like a more innocent version of Lonesome—innocent, that is, until Sloan and his minstrel partner, Womack (Tommy Davidson), wise him up about how demeaning his success is. Sloan offers up little mini-tutorials in the history of minstrelsy; she confronts Delacroix with a videotape compilation of atrocious racial stereotypes from the history of film and television and shouts, "Look at what you contributed to!"

As awful as many of these images are, there is another side to this tragedy that *Bamboozled* is unconcerned with: the ways in which black entertainers, even in the most cruelly stereotypical of roles, often managed to steal the show anyway with their wiles and timing and spirit and beauty. Who could not have eyes for Bill "Bojangles" Robinson, even if he was hoofing with Shirley Temple? Poor Mantan Moreland and Hattie McDaniel and all the rest are made to take the rap in this movie for contributing to a legacy of racist degradation. One would think, given what they were up against, that a bit more sympathy might be shown to these people. But sympathy doesn't have much truck in *Bamboozled,* where rancor takes the place of argument and outrage is palmed off as art.

(New York, 2000)

WARREN BEATTY

Bulworth

It's the tail end of the 1996 California primary election campaign and incumbent Democratic senator Jay Bulworth (Warren Beatty) is having a nervous breakdown. Sleepless for days, famished, he channel-surfs aimlessly in the darkness of his office. In a rare moment of lucidity, he has an inspiration. He arranges to have a hit man assassinate him.

Suddenly freed from the need to plump for re-election, and expecting the hit to come at any moment, Bulworth sets out on the campaign trail with abandon. Delirious but happy, he says exactly what's on his mind—a big no-no in politics, where honesty is not always the best policy.

Framed as a farce, *Bulworth* begins with this premise and gets stranger and stranger. Unavoidably, because of the way Beatty—who not only stars but also serves as director, co-producer, and co-screenwriter (with Jeremy Pikser)—encourages the connection between himself and Bulworth, the film takes on the trappings of a personal manifesto. Bulworth is described in the film as an "old liberal wine poured into a new bottle," and that describes Beatty here as well. He's a liberal movie icon—the director of *Reds*—trying to air his gripes and passions about America without coming across as a fossil. His farce isn't as daring as he thinks it is, but it's a fascinating spectacle anyway. When, early in the proceedings, Bulworth veers off the campaign trail and starts rapping in a South Central L.A. club, it's like watching a sixties Stanley Kramer message movie spliced into a hip-hop fever dream. It may not be good, but it sure is different.

Is Beatty trying to commercialize his message-mongering by appealing to urban black audiences? Probably not. After all, since when have black ticket buyers been sure-fire hit makers? Beatty's courting of that audience might seem crass, but what's really going on here is that he's playing out a hallowed, white-liberal fantasy of being as black as any soul brother.

Taking it upon himself to stand up for all of America's dispossessed, Bulworth soon targets insurance companies, HMOs, television, Hollywood, the conglomerate-owned news media—you name it. As the film lurches along, we get nicked with a steady stream of homilies: "He that pays the piper does the show," and "What we used to call America is going down the drain," or, my favorite, "Everybody's got to keep screwing everybody until we're all the same color." Now that's what I call sexual politics.

There's a hectic quality to the movie, as if Beatty was afraid we weren't going to get the joke—or the message. It takes a while to get a fix on what he's up to. In the beginning, Bulworth is portrayed as a hypocrite who, in order to get re-elected, retreats from his liberal principles. His campaign spots have him saying things like, "I believe in a hand up, not a handout." He's not even a neocon—he's a pseudo neocon. The framed photos in Bulworth's office of him with black civil rights leaders and Bobby Kennedy tell the whole sad then-and-now story.

Speaking in a black church in South Central, Bulworth chucks his standard stump speech, which always begins with "We stand at the doorstep of a new millennium," and tells an increasingly hostile audience about how his promises of federal funding for the inner cities have been just a politics-as-usual sham. Moving on to a Beverly Hills fundraiser, he castigates the Hollywood elite for its garbage-y movies and, between chomps on crab cake hors d'oeuvres, tosses out a crack about the Jewishness of the industry.

At this point, we're apparently supposed to regard Bulworth as a screw-loose vulgarian, and yet Beatty is already nudging us to accept the senator's ravings as higher truths. Even his name, Bullworth, is metaphoric: his bull has worth. The sick joke at the heart of the movie is that in politics it takes a loony to level with us. Bulworth alone is unfettered enough to tell it like it is. Beatty plays into the widespread paranoia that do-gooder politicians are hypocritical toward the poor and that Hollywood is a toxic-waste dump.

With all its hip-hop and jive, *Bulworth* may seem new-style, but it's actually proferring a populism that Frank Capra would have loved. In a movie such as *Meet John Doe*, Capra gave us his archetypal citizen-politician: a guileless Gary Cooper who was such a hayseed that he couldn't help but talk straight. Beatty is harvesting that same old Capracorn, but in place of the hayseed innocent he gives us the guy who is so much the politician that it deranges him. His only therapy is to spew the truth.

Bulworth's pronouncements quickly pass from quasi-objectionable to right-on. By the time he shows up at all all-white church in Pasadena, we've already seen him spend the night as a whacked-out rap master in a hip-hop club, lusting after the beautiful, imperious Nina (Halle Berry), who commends him for his candidness and leads him on. Now that he's a soul man, there's no stopping him. He tries to get the hit against him canceled. He unloads bombshells in the white church about the true nature of politics: "The name of our game is 'Let's Make a Deal.'" (Stop the presses.) Two black girls (Michele Morgan and Ariyan Johnson) who hitch a joyride on his campaign wagon shake up the congregation's starched white choir. Presumably the problem with America is we just don't know how to get down.

Even though Beatty has Bulworth say that "poor white people and poor black people have more in common with each other than with rich people," the only poor we see are blacks. No poor whites. For that matter, no poor Latinos—and this in Los Angeles, no less. But though Beatty celebrates soul as the salvation of the nation, he doesn't have much feeling for the new hip-hop culture. He's playing an uncool, sixty-ish white guy, and indeed his direction comes across like the work of just such a dude.

His idealized view of black power also leads him into some unintentionally laughable terrain. He introduces the character L. D. (Don Cheadle), a South Central dope king who employs a band of gun-toting preteens. They threaten Bulworth on their mean streets, and he counters by buying them ice cream cones, which they gratefully lap up. How cuddly. A police car swings by, and a white racist cop spews epithets until, like an avenging angel, Bulworth steps in. Later, L. D. lectures the senator on the reality of ghetto life. His little soldiers, you see, are taking part in the "only growth center open to them." With no job and no education, what's a young man to do? Bulworth takes note.

In moments such as these Beatty isn't that far from the mindset of *Shaft* and *Superfly*, which often had pimps and pushers performing double duty as truth-tellers and victims of "the system." (At one point, Beatty actually shows us a movie marquee featuring *Superfly*.) But those movies were at least aware of their own hypocrisy. Beatty is almost touchingly naive. Make ice cream, not Uzis.

There's also a high volume of radical chic pumping through Beatty's bleeding heart. He is, for example, still moony about the Black Panthers. Bulworth's love for Nina is sealed when she tells him that "Huey Newton fed the kids on my block." It's as if Bulworth can embrace her beauty only if it's backed by the proper pedigree. His hots for her are guilt-free. Nina tells him at the end, "You my nigga," and she means it as the highest compliment. What a lucky guy. Not only is Bulworth the healer of races, but he's still babe-worthy. (Young black audiences watching Bulworth and Nina clutch each other may take a less charitable view of their union.)

The political fantasies in Bulworth extend beyond race. When the senator's invectives air on national television, he turns into a folk hero. No less a deity than Larry King informs us that America wants Bulworth not just for senator but for president.

But the movie overvalues Bulworth's straight talk. Hasn't Beatty been listening to American political dialogue in the past decade? This fanfare-for-the-common-man/down-with-big-business rap is indistinguishable from the patter that passes for populism these days from the right, left, and center. Even Ross Perot and Steve Forbes get away with it. When Bulworth tells us that "the rich are getting richer," and that corporations lock out free speech, he may be preaching from the heart but he's hardly breaking any new ground. Bulworth is supposed to be about the power of truth in politics, but it's so tone-deaf to the way the game is played that it becomes something it never intended: a movie about a con artist who finds a new con.

(*New Times*, 1998)

GEORGE LUCAS

Overview

The arrival of *Return of the Jedi*, the third film in the *Star Wars* trilogy, is being hailed as more than just an important cinematic event. Even before its official release this Wednesday, it's being written about in magazines and discussed on television in terms normally reserved for a major sociopolitical happening—and, in a way, that's appropriate.

George Lucas, the movie's producer and the creator of the *Star Wars* series, is a major pop-commercial force in the country—perhaps *the* major force. Almost every movie he has produced—not only the *Star Wars* series but *American Graffiti* and *Raiders of the Lost Ark* as well—has resulted in a magic mountain of fads and spinoffs and merchandising tie-ins. He's influenced the way an entire generation looks at movies, and he's also influenced what that generation expects movies to be. Even his detractors can't deny that fact.

Lucas has produced four of the most popular movies ever made; only his cohort, Steven Spielberg, can claim a similar achievement. It's natural, then, that we should look to *Jedi* for something more than entertainment, although the movie's only goal is to entertain. We look to it as the work of a visionary capitalist—the cinematic equivalent of, say, the Epcot Center.

But as a piece of moviemaking—of myth-making—there's nothing visionary about *Return of the Jedi*. It delivers the goods, all right; it whooshes across misty moons and desert planets with a full cargo of Wookies and Yodas and Jabbas and Vaders and Ewoks. Luke and Han and Leia and Lando are still in tow, and R2-D2 and C-3P0 still perform their squeak-and-squawk duet. We find out the answers to all the questions left hanging in hyperspace in *The Empire Strikes Back*. Will Luke Skywalker finally become a Jedi knight? Will Han Solo be freed from his carbonite sarcophagus? Is Darth Vader really Luke's father? Will the Rebels defeat the Empire at last?

Still, despite all the intergalactic hoopla, it's a surprisingly perfunctory experience. It's been two and a half years since *Empire*, and unless you're a die-hard *Star Wars* cultist, these questions may not be burning for you. And, as directed by Richard Marquand, *Jedi* doesn't make us burn to find out the answers, either. The movie exists almost solely on a special effects and gadgetry level; emotionally, it's as blank as Darth Vader's visage. This time around, the toys have taken over the toy store.

Perhaps this explains why the actors in the film seem so glum—they know they can't hope to compete with the voluminous blobs and fur balls and serpentoids that surround them. For actors, performing in a science-fantasy film must be a special sort of hell—they're almost inevitably upstaged by the hardware. In *Jedi*, when Mark Hamill confronts Jabba the Hutt, when Carrie Fisher's Princess Leia dallies with a teddy-bear-like Ewok, you can see their dismay. Without any strong character to play or any good lines to spout, how can they hope to compete? Even Harrison Ford, normally a rousing presence, seems bummed out.

If there has been almost no human depth to any of the science-fantasy classics, like *2001* and *Forbidden Planet* and *Star Wars*, that's largely because the filmmakers haven't thought in those terms; for them, emotional depth and science-fantasy may be mutually exclusive. But the one big exception to this rule was *Empire*, and so it's doubly disappointing that *Jedi* doesn't do justice to *Empire*'s legacy. It's almost as if Lucas and Marquand regarded the riches of that movie as a fluke—an aberration of the genre.

(In *Time*'s cover story on *Jedi*, Marquand derides Irvin Kershner, the director of *Empire*, as carelessly straying from the true faith. That's like complaining that Sam Peckinpah didn't turn out *Gunsmoke* instead of *The Wild Bunch*. Kershner, probably the most prodigiously versatile director in America, was, I think, primarily responsible for *Empire*'s greatness. He transformed the pop-comics graphics of *Star Wars* into rich, sinister compositions. It was like opening up the Sunday cartoon pages to *Prince Valiant* and finding instead the imagery of Bosch or Dore. Luke's rite of passage into Jedi-hood, his discovery that Darth Vader may be his father, had an emotional resonance unlike any other science-fantasy film. *Empire* was more than an agglomeration of Lucas's storybook fantasies; it was an homage to the whole history of movies—to the marvels that movies can provide.)

In *Jedi*, the characters run a distant second to the action, and the visuals are clean and uninspired—they don't look imagined, they look programmed. The story whizzes by without pause. It seems that the Empire has a new space station under construction that will be even deadlier than its previous base, the Death Star. For Luke to destroy it, he must first rescue Han from Jabba the Hutt, a goopy monster who resembles a mating of Sydney Greenstreet and a ton of Jell-O. Then he must reassemble the Rebel starfleet into one vast attack squadron. But the Empire has installed a power plant on the moon of Endor and, unless the shield it generates can be destroyed, the fleet is doomed. Then there's the dark side of the Force to contend with. The Emperor (Ian McDiarmid) forces a showdown between Luke and Darth Vader, hoping that the boy will emerge victorious—and become his newest ally in evil. The story's resolution wraps up the trilogy.

Scrunched inside the 500-plus special effects are some imaginative moments. Jabba and his Huttites are an impressively disgusting array of squish-and-slime creatures—there's something almost Fellini-esque about their gloppy grotesquerie. The Ewoks are a cute breed, I suppose, and I'm sure it won't be long before they're elbowing E.T. on toy-store shelves around the world. There's a speed-bike chase between the Empire's storm troopers and the Rebels that's as exciting as any pursuit ever filmed. It's a kinesthetic whiz-bang—you feel like you're zooming through the center of the screen.

But in many ways, *Jedi* lacks the spirit of the first two *Star Wars* films and, in this science-fantasy genre, spirit is everything. (Nothing is more vacuous than an accumulation of special effects—remember *The Black Hole*?) Yoda and Chewbacca and Obi-Wan Kenobi are hardly given anything to do. Yoda's passing, which should have been a magical moment, barely registers. The light-saber duel between Luke and Darth Vader is only adequately staged; when Vader is finally unhelmeted, the only surprise is in how unsurprising he looks—he might be Uncle Fester from *The Addams Family*. And the Emperor, whose face we *do* see from the start, doesn't carry the requisite almighty malevolence. If the Emperor of the Empire can't make us quake in our spaceboots, who can?

Lucas doesn't have the emotional commitment to this material that he had the first two times out. How else can one explain the short shrift he gives to Luke and Co.? Han and Leia hardly bicker at all this time around—did they perhaps attend an intergalactic consciousness-raiser in the intervening years? There's no simplicity in this film, nothing like that great comic moment in *Empire* when Han clonks the short-circuited console of his spaceship and it lights up. The action in *Jedi*, except for that speed-bike chase scene, isn't something to revel in; there's no exhilaration in the special effects—they come off like diversionary tactics. There are supposed to be six more episodes in the *Star Wars* saga, but I doubt Lucas will want to take it that far. It's time for him to create another storybook epic, in another time and another galaxy, far far away from this one. Better yet, it's time for him to cool out.

In Hollywood, if you produce enough smash hits, it's inevitable that you will be regarded as a genius—a seer. Because Lucas is the most commercially successful filmmaker in movie history, he is by now solidly ensconced in the genius category, even though he has made no such claims for himself. (He's as unprepossessing as Francis Coppola is flamboyant.) If Lucas has a genius—and I think he does—it's a genius for knowing where all the pop-cultural loot is buried. With the exception of *The Empire Strikes Back*, all of his big hits have been recycled versions of earlier movies and modes. But the recycling is generally deft enough to give audiences both the reassurance of old pleasures and the glitter of the new.

A movie like *American Graffiti* didn't strike new attitudes; it simply reflected a hankering for the old fifties attitudes of its audience. It was a piece of commercialized nostalgia, but nostalgia without cynicism. Until *Jedi*, it was this lack of cynicism that redeemed Lucas's ardent commercialism. *Jedi* looks like it was made to sell toys.

Lucas is one of the rare filmmakers whose private fantasies are in complete sync with popular junk fantasies. (To an extent, the same thing is true for Steven Spielberg, although Spielberg has a gift for transforming junk into poetry.) When he calls *American Graffiti* and *Star Wars* his "personal" films, he really means it. For Lucas, there's no difference between the authentic and the counterfeit. *Star Wars* was both highly entertaining and without a trace of genuine originality. You could pick out the swipes at once—Robby the Robot from *Forbidden Planet*, the little robots from *Silent Running*, the triumphal scene from *Triumph of the Will*, portions of the plot line of Kurosawa's *Hidden Fortress*, *The Wizard of Oz*, and *The Searchers*, and so on. Everything in that movie had an antecedent. *Raiders of the Lost Ark*, which Lucas conceived and produced and Spielberg directed, was one long cliffhanger—a traffic jam of Saturday afternoon serials. Lucas and Spielberg just kept pinging their B- and Z-movie escapades at us like spitballs. *Raiders*, like *Jedi*, was all escapade and no spirit, and that's the trap that Lucas's brand of moviemaking naturally falls into. That may also explain his movies' vast popularity. There's nothing to digest because everything has already been pre-digested. It's the perfect diet for the video game generation.

Unlike such contemporaries as Spielberg, Coppola, Brian De Palma, and Martin Scorsese, Lucas never worked on low-grade schlock as a way of getting to make the movies that really mattered to him. From the start, with *THX 1138*, he's made only those projects that presumably he cared about. And yet, with the exception of *Empire*, he's taken fewer creative chances than any other major filmmaker in his position. He has been quoted as saying: "I know what I liked as a kid and I still like it." That's his credo. But he hasn't brought a child's sensibility to his movies; that is to say, he hasn't brought a child's wonderment to movies. The simplicity of soul that might result in an *E.T.* is not a part of his makeup.

There's no reason why fantasy films can't have as much richness and vigor and depth as any other type of film. (To use an analogy from drama, is Shakespeare's *The Tempest*—the inspiration, by the way, for *Forbidden Planet*—a lesser achievement than, say, *Romeo and Juliet* or *Macbeth*?) It all depends on how it's done. The problem is, fantasy films, to be truly fantastic, require an imaginative range that's beyond the reach of most filmmakers. Lucas has more of a range and a reach than most, but *Jedi* is his Waterloo. The movie is a demonstration of the limitations of a pop-comic sensibility. There's no imaginative fervor to bind it together for us. It's a myth without a vision.

(*Los Angeles Herald Examiner*, 1983)

POSTSCRIPT

Obviously, I was wrong about Lucas dropping the franchise. (For good measure, in 2012 he sold Lucasfilm Ltd. to the Walt Disney Company, which plans to churn out new *Star Wars* movies every two or three years starting in 2015.) For a good laugh, you might go back and reference the inevitable 1999 *Time* cover story on *Star Wars: Episode 1—The Phantom Menace*, featuring a conversation between Bill Moyers and Lucas on the "true theology" of *Star Wars*. Both guys invoke heavy dudes like Dante and Milton to explain dark side bad guy Darth Maul's scare appeal, while, in another part of the magazine, Iain McCaig, who conceptualized him, cites Bozo the Clown as a chief inspiration. It doesn't take much to start a religion.

JAMES CAMERON

Titanic

If one is in a biblical frame of mind, the sinking of the White Star Line's R.M.S. *Titanic* about four hundred miles off the southern coast of Newfoundland in 1912 could well be characterized as an act of divine one-upsmanship. The 46,328-ton "ship of dreams" was struck down on its maiden voyage from Southhampton because mortals should not presume to blithely conquer the sea. Unsinkable? Ha!

If one is in a Hollywood frame of mind—in other words, vengeful, envious, anxious—the James Cameron film *Titanic* should also be struck down, because mere mortal film directors should not presume to run up a tab of over $200 million to make a movie that could be described as "Romeo and Juliet get dunked."

But hubris in Hollywood comes with the territory. And sometimes the gods smile. For all its bulk and blather, *Titanic* is no disaster. It's closer to being a great big romantic cornball success. The film makes it safely into port courtesy of its co-stars, Leonardo DiCaprio and Kate Winslet, and its sheer golly-gee monumentality.

Movie spectaculars are often anything but. *Speed 2: Cruise Control*, for example, cost $160 million, which is about $160 million too much. *Titanic* at least lets you know you're watching a movie—or, to be exact, a movie-movie, the kind you responded to as a kid when you sat wide-eyed in the front row and couldn't even follow the plot but it didn't matter.

Cameron, who also wrote the screenplay, seems to have conceived *Titanic* in precisely these googly-eyed terms, which is both the film's triumph and limitation. As a piece of storytelling, it's almost as easy to read as a grade-school primer; even toddlers shouldn't have trouble following the action. But one doesn't necessarily look to a movie like this for complexity. Cameron's script is all splash and swoon—it serves up the pleasures of the obvious. The people aboard the *Titanic* are instantly pegged for us, and they stay that way; they're either greedy or good-natured or craven or valiant. Ambiguity and subtlety are strangers to this film. They're about as welcome as icebergs.

The *Titanic* disaster is one of those epochal events that allows everybody to derive from it their own meaning, their own "spin." Just recently there's been a gargantuan Tony-award-winning Broadway musical, *Titanic*, and a spectral, delicate novel, *Every Man For Himself*, by Beryl Bainbridge. Close to a dozen movies have already been made about the *Titanic*, and the most famous of them, the 1958 British *A Night to Remember*, is, in its stiff-upper-lip rectitide, at the opposite end emotionally from Cameron's film.

Cameron's "spin" is a most familiar one. With its strict demarcations of first-class, second-class, and steerage, the *Titanic* was a floating—or sinking—microcosm of stratified privilege. Of its approximately two thousand passengers, the seven hundred or so survivors were overwhelmingly from first-class. Cameron pushes the class inequities with an almost Marxist zeal; at times we could be watching a blockbuster Hollywood version of vintage Soviet realism. Almost without exception, the rich in this film are effete rotters and scoundrels, while the working class are bursting with the life force. The wealthy represent the vanishing, Edwardian order of things, while the immigrant poor are the frontier spirit of the future.

And yet the class "analysis" in this movie isn't really political at all. It exists to set up the film's star-crossed romance. Poor boy gets rich girl—it's the oldest romantic ploy in the playbook. Jack Dawson (DiCaprio), a footloose, tousle-haired scamp who has made his living for the past two years sketching on the streets of Paris, looks up from steerage deck at a first-class vision of loveliness—Winslet's Rose DeWitt Bukater, a society girl who is returning to Philadelphia with her mother Ruth (Frances Fisher) and filthy rich snob fiancé Cal Hockley (Billy Zane). Jack wins his steerage ticket in a last-minute dockside card game in Southhampton, and yet, he seems more at home on the great ocean liner than Rose, who walks around entrapped in a gilded cage.

She is, of course, looking for a way out of her loveless betrothal. When Jack later saves her from jumping overboard in despair, she recognizes in this golden-haired Romeo her true paramour. He tolerates a dinner with her condescending consorts in first class—it's her prize for rescuing her—and then smuggles her into a steerage hoedown where she boozes and stomps it up. (Those poor people really know how to party!) Jack even teaches her to spit—which means you can expect the scene where Rose defends Jack's honor by spitting in the face of a rich prig.

But just in case you think she's slumming, we also discover Jack has the soul of an artist. When he sketches Rose nude in the privacy of her stateroom, he's making love to her. It's a thrilling scene because it's both intensely erotic and pristine; Jack and Rose are like blushing cherubim. When they do actually make love later, it's something of a let-down—they've already done it.

The romantic scenes in *Titanic* are extravagantly affecting, and this is a tribute not only to Cameron but also to his co-stars. When we see Jack and Rose tightly embracing on the ship's prow as the Titanic sweeps headlong through the ocean, it recalls the scene in *Superman* where the

Man of Steel flies Lois Lane through Manhattan's night sky. Sequences like these are experienced by audiences as a collective swoon. They're schlock raised to the level of schlock poetry, and sometimes that's more boffo than the real thing.

It's popular to call Cameron an action-hardware auteur, but he's always had a ripe, almost fervid romantic streak. In his underwater epic *The Abyss*, which was partly inspired by the first movies brought back from the ocean floor of the sunken *Titanic*, there's a sequence in which Ed Harris attempts to rescue a drowned Mary Elizabeth Mastrantonio that is almost frighteningly rapturous. That's the same effect he's trying for in *Titanic*, a movie in which the rapture comes from the beauty and the innocence of its lovers, and the fright from what we know must befall them. The huge doom awaiting them gives their love an operatic poignancy.

DiCaprio has an intuitive grace before the camera—he would have been marvelous in silent films—and the high polish of his features makes him seem anointed. Jack is a romantic's vision of working-class youth, and you accept his supremacy as the natural order of things. He gives flesh to this sentimental fantasy of the bright and shining poor. DiCaprio has just the right temperature for this film; if he were swarthier, he'd be competing with the ship, and if he were fey, he'd disappear. He never lets the *Titanic* get the better of him, and, considering its size, that's saying something.

Winslet at first seems stocky and unconvincing opposite DiCaprio. She's playing the sleeping beauty who needs to be awakened by the prole prince's kiss, but it's not until she returns his ardor that Winslet really shines. In her initial scenes with the first-class crowd, her snooty society mannerisms seem actressy, but alone with DiCaprio, skimming the winds or locked in icy waters, she matches his resplendent charm. Her features become softer; she's like a maiden in a cameo from an Edwardian locket. On-screen, DiCaprio and Winslet have the kind of innocence that can't be faked. This is a behemoth of a movie, with its near-actual-sized *Titanic* replica sitting in a tank of seventeen million gallons of seawater, and gazillions of special effects. DiCaprio and Winslet provide the human touch—and the ethereal touch—to keep the whole shebang afloat.

It's a good thing, too, since Jack and Rose are just about the only featured characters in the movie. Cameron doesn't have a very *layered* imagination. Usually these shipboard dramas are chockablock with subplots and supporting players. *The Poseidon Adventure*, for example, was practically a variety show for every B-list actor in Hollywood. *Titanic*, by contrast, is almost eerily empty of incidentals; just about everything that happens is keyed to the lovers' romantic predicament. Kathy Bates has a funny turn as the sashaying, new-moneyed "Unsinkable" Molly Brown—she calls out to John Jacob Astor by yelling, "Hey Astor!"—and David Warner is creepy as Cal's lethal manservant. But Cameron cares only about his lovebirds; he may be working on a humongous scale, but essentially he's a miniaturist here. He doesn't even play up the suspense of how the *Titanic* might have been saved. He doesn't outline the circumstances—the unheeded radio dispatches, or the push by the ship company's managing director to break an Atlantic-crossing speed record—that contributed to its destruction. He accepts the entire catastrophe as a piece of romantic fatalism.

Until the end, even the framing device Cameron introduces seems secondary: a fortune-hunting salvager played by Bill Paxton attempts to bring up from the *Titanic* wreck a fabled diamond, the "Heart of the Ocean," which, we soon discover, may have belonged to a survivor, the 102-year-old Rose (played by Gloria Stuart, in her eighties, who acted with Jimmy Cagney). But these salvage sequences were filmed in actual *Titanic* wreckage, and they have a documentary power that goes beyond the make-believe. We look at a chandelier floating in the fathoms, or the remains of a stateroom, and it's as if an old sad story had been resurrected before our eyes—or had never really gone away. And Stuart's luminous ancient beauty matches exactly what Walter Lord wrote of the survivors in his 1955 book *A Night to Remember*: "It is almost as though, having come through this supreme ordeal, they easily surmounted everything else and are now growing old with calm, tranquil grace."

Great film artists—from D. W. Griffith on—have been drawn to the colossal. But in modern-day Hollywood the logistics and the commercial concessions involved in making a super-spectacle just about preclude any sustained artistry. *Titanic* is far from a work of art, but it may be the best we can expect now from the studios in their continuing, insane game of my-budget-is-bigger-than-yours. It's a powerfully ersatz experience, but at least it's powerful. There's a lot to like here—at three hours and fourteen minutes, the film takes longer to watch than the *Titanic* took to sink.

(New Times, 1997)

WOODY ALLEN
Everyone Says I Love You

World governments may topple, stock markets may soar and crash, deadly viruses may mantle the globe, but one constant remains: Woody Allen still hankers for a Cole Porter-ized New York. You have to be a deep-dish romantic, or else a blinkered snoot—or maybe both—to persist in such a demonstration. We tend to associate the obsessions of movie directors with more lurid fare: Oliver Stone and conspiracies; Sam Peckinpah and violence; Spike Lee and race. In its own small-scale way, Allen's obsession is just as fervid. He dramatizes the lives of well-to-do Upper East Siders as melancholic extensions of the pop-show tunes of the thirties and forties.

When his movies are really lilting along, this pop dream can seem a choice confection. When they're just getting by, you begin to resent the tony, sanitized self-infatuation of it all. Woody Allen movies work best when you're having too much fun to notice there's no garbage on the streets, no subways, no black people, no noise. You have to be a true obsessive to keep Manhattan this time-warped.

In *Everyone Says I Love You*, Allen keeps his warp speed constant. It's a charmingly inconsequential musical romance—Allen's first—with numbers drawn from Porter, Rodgers and Hart, Bert Kalmar, and Harry Ruby, and many others. Not only Manhattan gets the Woodman treatment here; Venice and Paris come across as pop fantasylands, too (not much of a stretch there).

Allen plays Joe, a novelist who lives most of the year in Paris. His daughter, DJ (Natasha Lyonne), the film's narrator, is a redheaded teen who lives in Upper East Side splendor with her mother, Steffi (Goldie Hawn), stepdad Bob (Alan Alda), and Bob's children, Lane (Gaby Hoffmann), Laura (Natalie Portman), and Scott (Lukas Haas). Another half sister, Skylar (Drew Barrymore), is engaged to Holden (Edward Norton), a milquetoast lawyer in her father's firm who begins the film serenading her along Fifth Avenue with "Just You, Just Me."

Throughout the movie, Allen doesn't make a big deal about the musical conventions. He just lets the actors casually break into song and sometimes dance, and this could be off-putting for audiences who don't connect with the romantic traditions that inspire Allen. Since most of the performers, excepting Alda and Hawn, can't—at least in any professional sense—sing, the effect is sometimes like movie stars' amateur night.

But Allen means it this way, I think. He's after something besides homage here—something closer, in a much more simplistic way, to what Dennis Potter achieved in *The Singing Detective* and *Pennies from Heaven*, or perhaps what Jacques Demy brought off in *The Umbrellas of Cherbourg*. He's after the lift you get from pop; he wants to show how pop can turn the workaday into something romantic, even impassioned. The charming ditties and croon swoons on the soundtrack express more of these people's lives than they can express themselves. Their amateurishness is central to their appeal. It testifies to their heartfelt sincerity.

The problem with Allen's agenda is that, for the most part, the pop standards coming out of his actors' mouths don't quite jibe with their minds. The songs derive from a different era, a different mood. Norton singing "Just You, Just Me" or "My Baby Just Cares for Me" is a stunt in more ways than one; he seems cut off from his vocalizing because we can't really connect this type of music with this type of guy. (The Lettermen or the Swingle Singers would seem to be more his style.) Norton is essentially a stand-in for a junior-league Woody Allen. It's significant that Norton even *acts* like Allen—he has the same flustered mannerisms and hectic line readings. Usually it's the actresses in Allen's movies—especially Mia Farrow and Diane Keaton and Julie Hagerty—who have been encouraged to ape him. He's branching out.

Allen is aware that the songs don't match up with the actors—most of them, anyway. But for him this incongruity is proof of how far we have fallen. He's saying that these great old standards don't have to come to us—we have to come to them. They're timeless, we're evanescent. Allen's nostalgia is cast-iron. And he doesn't brook competitors. Despite all the teenagers in this film, we hear nothing of *their* music except for a swatch of rap—inserted condescendingly, of course. It's not enough that he pays tribute to his pop inspirations—he has to have disdain for everybody else's.

Would this film be much different without the musical numbers? *Pennies from Heaven*, for example, is inconceivable without its songs, even though, from a strictly narrative standpoint, it didn't need them.

But *Everyone Says I Love You* would probably have come across in much the same way without the music—except that the numbers italicize the tissue-paper plot and help buy it off. Without the music and dance numbers the film might seem disposable, though it kind of is anyway.

That's not all bad. Allen usually overreaches when he tries to be Ingmar Bergman—the closer he moves from Stockholm to Tin Pan Alley, the lighter his touch. And, unfettered, he pulls off some deft comedy here. When Joe takes DJ on a vacation to Venice, she spots an American, Julia Roberts's Von, who she thinks would be perfect for him. And DJ has an edge—the mother of one of her friends in New York is a psychiatrist who has been treating Von, and, for sport, the girls have been listening in on her intimacies.

DJ tells Joe all the things he needs to know to woo Von—from her favorite vacation spots to her G-spots. Allen turns an analysand's paranoid fantasy into a parody of how lovers know each other. Joe feels guilty about what he's doing, but he's too smitten to stop. Von is so amazed at his insight that she's smitten, too. An art historian unhappily married to a self-infatuated actor, she's found her white knight in the unlikely guise of a spindly nervous wreck. The high comedy in their scenes together is that she's so gaga at his simpatico she never registers what a bumbling worrywart he is. He patters on about Tintoretto, but all this blissed-out woman hears is a humming sound. He might as well be spouting nonsense verse—which he sort of is anyway. Roberts is lovely in the part. Delusion becomes her.

There are other bonuses in the cast. Alda is sharply funny as the patriarch Bob who can't seem to control anyone in his orbit. The key to his performance is that Bob doesn't really mind the lack of control. His daughters exasperate him; he wants to clonk his son for subscribing to *National Review*; his addled, live-in father (Patrick Cranshaw) thinks the Giants are still playing at the Polo Grounds; his wife, Steffi, born of money, overdoes the liberal socialite routine. In the funniest subplot, Skylar falls in love with a paroled ex-con, hilariously played by a furtive, feral Tim Roth, who was released through Steffi's bleeding-heart ministrations. But through it all, Bob loves the messy family feeling of it all. It gives his life—and the film—a buzz.

After the hideous way in which Goldie Hawn came across in *The First Wives Club*—all shrill and collagen-lipped—she bounces back. Steffi may have all the accoutrements of an Upper East Side princess, but her liberal do-gooder side is genuine. She really believes the best of *everybody*, even ex-cons on the make, and it's both the source of her comedy and her saving grace. Hawn isn't just doing a comic routine here; it's a full-out performance. Her scenes at the end with Allen by the Seine, or at a party where everyone dresses up as Groucho Marx, are marred by the kind of dreary you-always-made-me-laugh dialogue that the rest of the film scrupulously avoids. But Hawn brings some real feeling to the confabs anyway. It takes a rare actress to make fun of who she's playing and still make you care powerfully about her.

I don't think Allen has any illusions about rejuvenating the movie musical form; this maiden voyage is also a swan song. It's a song he doesn't mind; it expresses the masochistic side of him that says we can no longer get our romantic impulses from pop culture. Except, of course, *his* pop culture.

(*New Times*, 1996)

Wild Man Blues

In Barbara Kopple's new documentary *Wild Man Blues*, we follow Woody Allen around Europe on a whirlwind concert tour with his New Orleans jazz band. He's kvetching from the get-go. "I would rather be bitten by a dog than fly to Paris," he announces mid-air, then mellows on the Champs-Elysées by complimenting the gray weather. "I don't like sun," he declares. Who but Woody Allen would praise Paris for its drizzliness?

Even though *Wild Man Blues* is framed as a "candid" view of Allen, clearly he's playing up—or is it down?—to the camera. He's so closed-off that probably there was no way Kopple could have caught him with his guard down. He's too hyperaware of his shtick. The result seems less like a revealing look at the "real" Woody Allen—whatever that is—and more like a species of movie directed by Allen himself. He's been quoted as saying the film "depicted my personal life with an accuracy and wit that even made me laugh." If Kopple had made a film that *disturbed* him, that would have been even better.

It's a sly notion to capture Allen off-the-cuff—talking not about art and Freud and Ingmar Bergman but, as it is here, clarinets and jazz legend Sidney Bechet and how seasick he gets in a gondola. Kopple was clearly hoping for a sideways glimpse that would add up to a full portrait. But, as it turns out, we don't feel like we've learned anything new about him—at least nothing we haven't already learned from his movies. And because the Woody Allen in this film is so all-of-a-piece with the Woody Allen in his own films, we don't really trust *Wild Man Blues*. It's too pat. It plays up the idea that the person and the persona are the same thing, and, psychologically, that doesn't ring true—even though Allen has made a career fostering that very notion. Even when his private life went public a few years back—with his famous troubles with Mia Farrow and his eventual marriage to Farrow's adopted daughter Soon-Yi Previn—there was still the perception that we were witnessing a particularly tabloid-y Woody Allen movie. People want to believe that, in his movies and his life, Woody Allen is "Woody Allen."

And that's pretty much what he—and Kopple—give us in *Wild Man Blues*. It caters to our childlike wish that in reality, all movie personalities are indeed the way they come across on-screen. The larger-than-life aspects of the screen image turn us all into supplicants before the altar of stardom. And Woody Allen's star rose at a time—the mid-to-late-sixties—when stand-up and improvisatory performers were indeed working their own lives into their acts—not in the Henny Youngman or Bill Cosby manner but on a deeper, more psychodramatic level. We were encouraged to recognize the real-life aspects of their art—the stuff that made performers such as Allen, or Richard Pryor, so new-style funny.

But the narcissism in back of this approach has often gotten the better of Allen the filmmaker. Even when he supposedly flays his "real" self for public consumption in his latest film *Deconstructing Harry*, he's still enraptured by his own turmoil. (*This* must be the real connection Allen feels with his beloved Bergman.) *Deconstructing Harry* may have been warts-and-all, but its implicit message was: Love my warts.

In *Wild Man Blues*, we observe Allen traipsing with his band through Milan, Vienna, Rome, Bologna, London, Madrid, Paris, Turin, and Venice, and yet it's all a blur to him because he's not really taking anything in—and not just because of the tour's whirlwind pace, either. Since Kopple and her cinematographer Tom Hurwitz reportedly followed Allen and Soon-Yi around eighteen hours a day, we wonder why we never see them really mixing it up with the locals, or seeing the sights. Allen doesn't even mix it up with his own musicians, or know all their names.

For all his vaunted above-the-Hollywood-fray airs, Allen here comes across as not that much different from a typical movie or rock star who just barges through the territory in a capsule of self-containment. His connection to what he sees is surprisingly show-biz—at one point he says he can't be in Rome without thinking of *La Dolce Vita*. Kopple chimes in at this point by throwing some Nino Rota music on the soundtrack—to reinforce the notion that, for Allen, Italy is a Felliniscape. But this music sets up the wrong, jaunty tone. It cutesies up Allen's creepy inwardness.

It's fascinating to watch Allen playing clarinet in the film's many concert sessions because it's clear he's a control-freak trying—ever so slightly—to limber up. Clarinetists tend to be controlling types anyway, but the New Orleans style encourages looseness and improvisation—the sort of thing Allen once brought to his comedy routines. As a player he's not bad; to the extent that he can look happy, he even seems vaguely pleased with himself as he tootles before his adoring audiences. (He's smart enough to know they're there to see him, not to hear his music; he's also smart enough to remark that the same people who traipse out to his concerts don't always turn out for his films.) But unlike most jazz performers—even the ones, like, say Thelonious Monk or Miles Davis, who seemed transfixed by an inner beat—Allen doesn't appear to pull anything special from his audience. He's playing not *to* them but *at* them, and he doesn't really mix it up with his audience either, except at official functions where he seems—natch—uncomfortable.

Where he seems most *comfortable* is in hotel rooms, grousing with Soon-Yi and complaining about the paparazzi or the service. It's hilarious seeing Allen in Madrid complaining about the tastelessness of the hotel's Spanish omelet—it's like a prime joke in one of his movies. But after awhile our disaffection sets in here, too, because it's hard to connect with somebody who acts like Milan's regal Principe di Savoia is basically a Motel 6. Wandering the swank suites in his-and-her matching white bathrobes, Woody and Soon-Yi come across like youth hostelers who won the lottery—and don't care.

Soon-Yi has often been portrayed in the press as a bit dopey, but she's the heroine of *Wild Man Blues*—the control freak's controller. She chides her husband for not going out of his way to compliment his band, and she's right. She turns out not to have seen *Annie Hall* (!) but she *has* seen *Interiors*—and thinks it "long and tedious." (She's right about that, too.) Soon-Yi doesn't seem to be in awe of Allen, or even turned on to him; she's more like one of those attentive girl Fridays that powerful men often attract. As it's presented to us, there's an element of playact in their marriage; it has a rehearsed easygoingness which doesn't seem particularly put on for the cameras. They're like a comedy act but, even though he's old enough to be her grandfather, they don't really play up the generation gap. That's probably because you get the impression Allen in his sixties isn't far removed from Allen in his teens or twenties. He was *born* a kvetch, but he loves being pampered for his miseries. When he catches a "classic head cold" at the end of his concert tour, he's swaddled in hotel bedding while Soon-Yi tends to him—a Jewish prince in clover.

After the tour, Kopple springs a surprise on us: Allen pays a visit to his parents in Manhattan, and suddenly the film turns into a massive Freudian jest. His father, at ninety-six, has a full head of hair but not quite all his marbles; his mother, who looks a lot like Allen in drag, bemoans the fact that her son isn't married to a Jewish girl. Soon-Yi is present and says nothing, but Allen mutters into the camera, "This is truly the lunch from hell." It's a marvelous sequence even though it seems staged for our benefit—Allen's mother has her son's crack comic timing. When you hear her sigh about how her boy studied tap-dancing and singing but "never pursued" those interests, you feel like you're right at the root of Allen's neurosis. This family stuff is so stereotypically obvious that your first thought is: *Why has Allen needed therapy all these years to figure out why he's so screwed up?* Your second thought is: *He'll never get out of therapy.*

(*New Times*, 1998)

INGMAR BERGMAN

Overview

Ingmar Bergman has always been a tease when it comes to farewells. As far back as 1966, with the release of *Persona*, he delivered a speech entitled "Each Film Is My Last." When he announced in 1983 that *Fanny and Alexander* would *really* be his last, everybody assumed it was just another one of his Swedish jokes. Maybe so, but the punch line has been a long time coming. True, he made *After the Rehearsal* for television a year after *Fanny and Alexander*. But then, if you don't count a handful of televised stage performances—silence. At last he has a new movie, *Saraband*, also made for television and completed in 2002, when the director was eighty-four. The punch line may have fallen on deaf ears; with no new bona fide Bergman movie for decades, the current generation of filmgoers has come to regard him, if at all, as a relic. Even many of his older admirers, who grew up with *The Seventh Seal* and *Wild Strawberries*, have all but forgotten him. They long ago passed through their "Bergman phase." Some are surprised to hear he is still alive.

In fact, during his fadeaway from the screen, Bergman has written a number of screenplays for others, a novel, and a memoir, and remained quite busy as a stage director. And *Saraband*, which reunites Johan (Erland Josephson) and Marianne (Liv Ullman), the divorced couple from the 1973 *Scenes From a Marriage*, is a potent blast of Bergmaniana. It doesn't have the tempered air of a valedictory. Watching the film was, for me, like revisiting a foreign country I remembered fervently but hadn't been back to in a very long time. When one of the characters, Johan's woebegone son Henrik, proclaims, "Sometimes I think an incredible punishment is waiting for me," I beamed. Bergman's back!

And yet, there is a Rip Van Winkle aspect to his reappearance. *Saraband* is the work of an artist who, in terms of his lifelong creative obsessions, has never really been away. But the world has changed around him since his "retirement," and what people are looking for in movies may have changed, too. Bergman is undeniably one of the great directors but he has always stood for more than the sum of his films. From the first, he was regarded not simply as a movie director but as a visionary who grappled with the Big Questions of God and Man. His symbol-thick films were drenched in the night sweats of mortal torment. He was the kind of artist we had been brought up to believe was the real deal; he suffered for our souls.

We no longer regard artists, certainly not movie artists, as seers. We do not look to them for spiritual instruction. (Bloggers have become our new seers.) Bergman himself resisted such a role; in interviews over the years, he often seems almost comically obtuse about his intentions. Typical is an exchange from an interview with John Simon, who reasonably postulates that *Persona* is "really about how a person who feels empty, depleted, and sick gets back into life again by using another person," to which Bergman responds that the film is "a tension, a situation, something that has happened and passed, and beyond that I don't know."

It is, of course, a truism that artists are often their own worst explainers. And surely Bergman is being coy here, just as he was when he once likened himself to one of the anonymous artisans who built the Chartres Cathedral. But he's also being honest. No filmmaker who works as close to the knife edge of intuition as he does can hope to deliver movies with the thesis-like comprehensiveness and lucidity that his international admirers claim for him. (His movies are so impeccably crafted that it's easy to assume his thinking is equally rigorous.) And yet it is also abundantly true that, more so than with any other director, Bergman can be discussed in the same terms that (for better or worse) we reserve for a great literary artist. His visual language is voluminous, his themes upper case, and his fixations have a pedigree going back to Strindberg, Ibsen, Kierkegaard.

It was this appeal, in fact, that initially accounted for much of Bergman's attraction among American post-war literati who normally wouldn't be caught dead admitting that the movies could be an art form. Lionel Trilling, for example, reviewing a collection of Bergman's screenplays in 1960, even went so far as to confess that, although the director was "the only contemporary maker of films who figures in the mind of the public as a creative artist in his own right," he himself hadn't actually seen any of his films. Bergman didn't catch on exclusively with the aesthetes; his films also carried a seal of approval for the many middle-class patrons looking for a little intellectual "betterment." For all these audiences, Bergman made it reputable to like movies—or at least *his* movies. By comparison, attending a typical Hollywood film was like slinking into a theater wearing a raincoat.

Bergman ascended at just the right cultural moment for his myth to take root. Film theorists were advancing the auteur theory, which posited that the director was the "author" of his films. The expanding art-house audience in the mid-to-late-fifties, still recoiling from the horrors of war, was highly receptive to Bergman's brand of existential dread (and to the ministrations of psychoanalysis, which was also in the dread business). His movies were discussed as allegories about the soul's progression through an uncomprehending universe. Many of his most celebrated films through the mid-sixties were explicitly religious. In *The Seventh Seal*, Max von Sydow, a medieval knight (and prototypical modern man) famously plays chess with Death and cries out, "I want knowledge, not belief." *The Virgin Spring*, also set in the Middle Ages, is about a father who seeks to understand God's plan in the rape and murder of his daughter. Bergman's father was a severe Lutheran minister—he would punish his son by locking him in the closet—and one doesn't have to be a strict Freudian to see how fundamentally this upbringing affects the films.

Bergman has always downplayed the orthodoxy of his art. In the preface to his collected screenplays he says that for him, "religious problems do not take place on the emotional level but on an intellectual one." But what powerfully disturbs audiences about his movies isn't the sophisticated theology, it's the awe and fear at their core. Bergman transmutes religious stories into sinister fairy tales full of foreboding. Later on, when he had completed the trilogy of *Through a Glass Darkly*, *Winter Light*, and *The Silence*, the movies became less religioso but no less convulsive. *Persona*, *Shame*, *Cries and Whispers*, and *Autumn Sonata*, among many others, are still about the need for belief, the futility of belief, but this time the agonies are more secular. While God cools off on the sidelines, man and woman, parent and child, are center stage—often quite literally at each other's throats.

No matter how clotted with symbolism Bergman's films are, he never loses sight of his audience. Unlike another modern master, Godard, whose films have often resembled private affairs, Bergman is very much a showman in a venerable theatrical tradition. The rap against him has always been that angst in his shtick, which is one reason he is so ripe for parody. (Before he decided to *become* Ingmar Bergman, Woody Allen would send him up all the time.) But genius is not as malleable as talent, and it is the rare great artist who has not howled at the same moon for an entire career. What makes Bergman's particular career so unusual is that, unlike almost any other writer-director, he has been free to make personal movies since the very beginning. With unprecedented, conspiratorial intimacy, his great stock company of actors (Von Sydow, Ullmann, Josephson, Bibi Andersson, Harriet Andersson, Gunnar Bjornstrand, Ingrid Thulin, and others) incarnate his torments. The "real" world rarely collides with his own. When, for example, in *Persona*, he flashed images of the Warsaw ghetto or a Buddhist Vietnam War protester in flames, it was as if his antennae had suddenly picked up static from outer space. (That's not where he belongs; he's an inner space kind of guy.) With few exceptions, Bergman has never even ventured outside of Sweden, and many of his most famous films, especially the later ones, are chamber dramas for a handful of actors.

Few filmmakers have directed as many shattering performances as Bergman, or photographed them more expressively. Or been as preternaturally attuned to the psyches of women. The focal point of his movies is the human countenance in all its infinite masquerades. (One reason he loves filming monologues is because they allow him to zero in on the face in motion.) The old saw that filmmakers should avoid utilizing too many close-ups does not apply in Bergman's case—we can never get our fill of the faces in his movies because their mysteries always lie just beyond our comprehension. The most famous image from *Persona*, the merged profiles of Bibi Andersson and Liv Ullmann, made that mystery manifest. But dozens of other images are just as spookily ineffable as this one. There is no more resonant leave-taking in movies than the final shot of Victor Sjostrom's aged physician in *Wild Strawberries*, his head on the pillow after a long odyssey, as he turns into a revenant before our eyes.

Bergman's obsession with death is also an obsession with life—for what is being taken away. The rapture in *Smiles of a Summer Night* and *The Magic Flute*, or in the festive scenes from *Fanny and Alexander*, is the flip side to his doominess, and every bit as piercing. When the patriarch in *Fanny* closes out the film by exhorting his brood to "be happy while we are happy and take pleasure in the little world," he is speaking the bliss of common sense. Bergman was criticized for collapsing into bourgeois sentimentality, but after all the abysses he's spelunked, who had a better right to tout delight?

Besides, *Saraband*, which may indeed be his swan song, undoes the sentiment. It's set in a world where there is, at best, a nostalgia for happiness. Marianne and Johan, several times divorced, have not seen each other for thirty years. She surprises him with a visit to his summer lake cottage and they clasp hands, but they are only going through the motions and soon Marianne understands she has made a big mistake. Johan's estranged sixty-one-year-old music professor son Henrik (Borje Ahlstedt), by an earlier marriage, lives on the property with his nineteen-year-old cellist daughter Karin (Julia Dufvenius), with whom he shares a harrowing, quasi-incestuous relationship. In *Scenes From a Marriage*, Marianne and Johan were essentially the whole show. Here the progeny take over and their hatreds constitute a foul legacy. Marianne is the watcher in this passion play; Johan thinks he is already dead, which is how his son would like him. Henrik has the rumply, contented contours of a burgher, but when his venom rises he becomes a basilisk, and *Saraband* turns into the most unsettling of horror movies.

Sex is at the root of everything for Bergman, which is why even his most metaphysical voyagings seem mysteriously, unmistakably carnal. The sheer texture of flesh carries a charge in his films. In *Scenes*, the couple's emotional and sometimes physical violence was overwhelmingly sexual in nature. A saraband could be defined as an erotic dance for two, and in Bergman's new film, their dance has frozen in place. Sex no longer has the power to inflame them. In seeking out Johan, almost twenty years her senior, Marianne did not anticipate that he is beyond caring. She was trying to recapture herself as she was in her thirties, full of possibilities and game at another go-round. She's still game, but she knows now that there is no consolation to be found in her past with Johan, and this realization is both her tragedy and triumph. She has been jolted out of her final illusion, and the freeing up is redemptive. It's as if Bergman has placed a balm on her.

Saraband can be looked at as a movie about Marianne's aging and, in a sense, it's about Bergman's aging, too. As is often true of late works by movie directors, it has a pared down simplicity. (Think of Huston's *The Dead* or Bunuel's *That Obscure Object of Desire*.) But Bergman has most often been at peace when he is closed up with his camera and a few intense performers. Stylistically, there is nothing new about *Saraband*. What *is* new is that, at a time when so many filmmakers avoid the most atrocious realms of human experience, Bergman continues to hang tough. That's his heroism. That's why he still matters.

(Los Angeles Times, 2005)

ROBERT ALTMAN

Overview

Robert Altman, who receives an honorary Academy Award tonight, is perhaps the most American of directors. But his Americanness is of a special sort and doesn't really connect up to any tradition except his own.

Many movie directors, of course, have been comprehended as quintessentially home-grown artists. John Ford gave the Western landscape an elegiac purity; John Huston's best movies, like Hemingway's best prose, had a virile grace; Frank Capra manufactured populist fables; Sam Peckinpah's sweat-soaked world was riven by elemental forces of loyalty and betrayal. Howard Hawks's America overflowed with toughs who loved to talk; Preston Sturges, who adored jabber every bit as much as Hawks, served up a gaggle of archetypal eccentrics.

But Altman, who has ranged as widely as any of these directors across the American panorama, is a more mysterious and allusive artist. He is renowned for the buzzing expansiveness of his stories, the crisscrossed plots and people, but what strikes home most of all in this sprawl is a terrible sense of aloneness. In film after film, from *McCabe and Mrs. Miller* and *The Long Goodbye* to *Nashville* and *Short Cuts*, the human tumult masks a solitude. If being an American means being rooted to the land, to a tradition, a community, then it also means being forever in fear of dispossession. Altman understands this better than any other filmmaker. It's what gives even his rowdiest comic escapades their bite of woe.

In *Nashville*, for example, the freeflowing madcap pageant is studded with moments when we are brought shudderingly close to the privacies of the soul, as in the scene showing Ronee Blakley's breakdown on the stage of the Opry Belle, or Gwen Welles's forlorn striptease in a smoke-filled hall of hecklers, or Keenan Wynn receiving the news of his wife's death in the hospital just at the moment when a chatty, unknowing soldier sidles over to him. In the bar lounge sequence where Lily Tomlin is mesmerized by Keith Carradine singing "I'm Easy," she looks stricken by her own unbidden desire.

Altman once said, "Human behavior, filled with all its mystery and inspiration, has always fascinated me." To capture what he can of this mystery, he developed an extraordinarily supple technique capable of registering the subtlest flinches of emotion. His elliptical style allows us the pleasure (or at least the illusion) of discovering a movie for ourselves, without all the packaging and predictability that most directors go in for. (Sometimes however, as in most of 3 *Women* and all of *Quintet*, the ellipses swamp the movie.) His aural tracks pick up the halting, run-on gabble of people as they really sound. His cameras, seemingly on the fly, seize the small moments that are, in fact, the big moments—to take one example out of a thousand, the glance that Julie Christie's madam in *McCabe and Mrs. Miller* gets from Shelley Duvall's mail-order bride right after her husband dies and she knows the next stop is the whore house. Nothing is inconsequential, Altman seems to be saying in his movies, because everything has human weight if you know what to look for.

One of the reasons why his films can seem so cavalier to audiences is because his humanism is unsentimental. For him, sentimentality is just another false piety. Altman is not simply being a curmudgeon—he's intuiting his way to something more genuine. It makes sense that he has made a career out of subverting traditional genres: the war movie (*M*A*S*H*); the Western (*McCabe and Mrs. Miller*); the private eye film (*The Long Goodbye*); the musical (*Nashville*); the biopic (*Vincent and Theo*); the documentary (*Tanner '88*); the classic whodunit (*Gosford Park*); and so on. Genres can be a form of false piety, too.

Vincent and Theo, starring Tim Roth, is probably the most uncompromising movie ever made about an artist (and one of Altman's few films set outside America). One might expect this fanatically independent director, who has fought his way in and out of Hollywood for most of his working life, to covet the great painter's miseries. But no homilies are proferred here. Art may be Van Gogh's religion, but clearly Altman sees it as too high a price to pay. The Van Gogh of this movie is an artist not because of his madness but in spite of it. There is a livid, discordant quality to the film. When Van Gogh ventures alone into the fields to paint, the clacking of birds and insects is a beckoning malevolence. For Van Gogh, life is bedlam, and Altman, who surely must see this as a cautionary tale, recoils from the horror even as he appears to press into it.

Altman has had one of the most improbable careers in movie history. Starting out as a director for a dozen years of episodic TV shows like *Sugarfoot* and *Whirlybirds*, he broke through in his mid-forties with *M*A*S*H* and *McCabe and Mrs. Miller* and never looked back. It was as if all those years of hackwork had jolted him into innovation.

There is an almost ineffable sense of liberation to his films from the seventies. *McCabe and Mrs. Miller* has the visionary thrill of a Western entirely reimagined—its brutality bleeds through a palette as delicate as the wash of a Japanese screen painting. *The Long Goodbye*, which casts Elliott Gould as a new-style Philip Marlowe in a groggy, funkytown L.A that Altman captured better than anyone else, is a deliriously lyrical tragicomedy about being valiant in an unvaliant world. Altman seems to be trying out in it everything he knows about life and about moviemaking. In formal terms, it comes closer to pure jazz that any mainstream movie ever has. Certainly Gould, with his mumbled riffs and lanky lope, was never better. (Actors love Altman, perhaps because he has the good sense to be stupefied by what they are able to do.)

Later in the decade, after a six-year run of amazements that also included *California Split* and his masterpiece set in the Depression, *Thieves Like Us*, Altman lost his way for a time. Because of the bad box office on *Buffalo Bill and the Indians*, he was dropped by Dino De Laurentiis from *Ragtime*, instantly making that proposed version of E. L. Doctorow's novel a prime candidate for the Greatest Movie Never Made. The congregations in *A Wedding* and *A Perfect Couple* and the barely released *Health* were unfizzy—Altman Lite. The zoomy camerawork never seemed to zoom in on anything interesting and one longed for the babble to subside.

But then, following the debacle of *Popeye*, this improvisatory maverick who favored screenplays as mere blueprints confounded everybody by decamping from Hollywood and directing a series of letter-perfect stage adaptations of plays by David Rabe, Sam Shepard, and Christopher Durang. The results were doubly confounding, since in at least two instances—Donald Freed and Arnold Stone's *Secret Honor*, with Philip Baker Hall delivering a psychotic rant as a walled-in, post-Watergate Richard Nixon, and Ed Graczyk's mood-memory play *Come Back to the Five and*

Dime, Jimmy Dean, Jimmy Dean—Altman was at his most cinematically inventive. The faces of the actresses in that film, including Sandy Dennis, Cher, Karen Black, and Marta Heflin, have a silent-movie-star luminosity, a frailty. The pathos of death is in their fine-drawn features.

Altman confounded everybody again when, at the age of sixty-seven, he pranced back into Hollywood with *The Player*, a poison dart dipped in the nectar of sweet revenge. The film, adapted from Michael Tolkin's novel, plays extremely well as a black comedy about the film business but it's also about something deeper—it's Altman's death knell for his profession. The murder of the screenwriter by Tim Robbins's studio executive, which he gets away with scot free, stands in for the murder of movie art in modern Hollywood. The paradox, of course, is that Altman's movie is itself a work of art.

The Hollywood of *The Player* is as emblematically American as the Nashville of *Nashville*. Both are fiefdoms ruled by fear and glamour and populated by people who have a tense, wall-eyed watchfulness. They never seem to sleep. Altman has always had an almost anthropological avidity for rooting around inside a culture, which is another way of saying that, despite his penchant at times for drawing attention to the fact that the movie we are watching is indeed a movie, he has an impulse for the truth. His antennae are set to catch the vibrations in the zeitgeist. *Nashville*, coming off of the assassinations and Watergate and Vietnam, is one of the funniest movies ever made and also one of the scariest; it makes you feel in your marrow the derangement of American life. You sense that something bad is going to happen in that movie long before it actually does.

I have emphasized this darker aspect of Altman's career because the great hectic humor in his movies is so self-evident and because he has so often been written about as some kind of professional party-giver—an exalted maker of festive confabs. This kind of treatment may be a backhanded tribute to the sheer enjoyableness of his best films, but it doesn't begin to get at why he is so important.

If we sometimes feel in this country that we are caught up in an Altman movie in which we are onstage all the time and everyone is pointing a camera at everyone else, it is because he has given us a way of seeing that is eerily in tune with the times. He recognizes better than any other filmmaker how our lives have become commodified and corrupted by a society in which everything is for sale. The overheated jamboree of *Nash-*

ville and the banal apocalypse of the Raymond Carver-derived *Short Cuts* are all of a piece with the paranoid ferocity of *Secret Honor* and the vampirish *The Player*. They all jam together as one vast vision of an America stewing in its own juices.

These movies carry a furious sense of loss. It is in his two finest films set in the America past—*McCabe and Mrs. Miller*, with Warren Beatty's brash frontier dreamer, and *Thieves Like Us*, with Keith Carradine and Shelley Duvall as doomed Depression lovebirds—that Altman's full sorrow shines forth. Both films are elegies for innocence. Watching them is like gazing at a family photo album of loved ones long ago passed away.

Altman has never won an Oscar for directing a movie, though he's been nominated five times (for *M*A*S*H*, his only big hit, and for *Nashville*, *The Player*, *Short Cuts*, and *Gosford Park*). He has said of Hollywood, "They make shoes, I make gloves." Back in the seventies he was quoted as saying, "Sometimes I feel like little Eva running across the ice with the dogs yapping at my ass. Maybe the reason I'm doing all this is so I can get a lot done before they catch up with me." Tonight, at eighty-one, with a new movie based on Garrison Keillor's *Prairie Home Companion* set to open in the summer, the director gets to call off the dogs in front of half a billion people. It's a twist that could only happen in an Altman movie.

(Los Angeles Times, 2006)

The Player

If you had to construct the ultimate Hollywood movie, would it include a scene in which a couple of screenwriters pitch a project that's a cross between *Pretty Woman* and *Out of Africa*? Would your ear be tickled by a lexicon of insider lingo, or a whisper of roman à clef? Would famous movie celebrities pop up playing themselves as famous celebrities? Would it be about killings—particularly, box-office killings?

All this is in Robert Altman's *The Player*. In fact, a complete catalog of Hollywood-movie paraphernalia is on view, complete with movie-colony in-jokes for the "knowing." (Those *Pretty Woman/Out of Africa* pitchsters are played by Patricia Resnick and Joan Tewksbury, both of whom have written movies for Altman.)

But Altman has never been content merely to work within a genre when he could radicalize it instead. *M*A*S*H* was a war movie for counterculture hipsters; *McCabe and Mrs. Miller* was a Western with a core of poetic longing; *The Long Goodbye* was an updated Raymond Chandler private-eye thriller with a forlorn, galumphing Philip Marlowe at its center.

Is it any surprise, then, that *The Player* up-ends the Hollywood movie genre in the process of fulfilling it? It's the ultimate Hollywood movie because it seems to be about not only Hollywood but also itself. It's about how insanely difficult it has become for movie artists to get into the position to make a movie as good as *The Player*.

Altman's outsider-insider status, buffed and beveled to a fine point through years of Hollywood exile, is the perfect weapon for the job. *The Player* is an Altman party without the party hats. Its studio execs and screenwriters and movie stars are imperially self-enclosed. They're hyper-aware of the high stakes they are playing for; the more powerful they are, the more cooled-out they seem.

Altman had the intuitively right inspiration to fashion this modern Hollywood fable as a farce, but a slow-motion farce in which all the participants have a dreamy, underwater velocity. The piranhas swim in the same golden bowl as the tropical fish, and in a certain light, they're just as alluring. But what makes *The Player* a great Hollywood movie is that Altman and his screenwriter, Michael Tolkin (adapting his 1988 novel), aren't just spear-fishermen here. They're pulled in by Hollywood's lethal cool, by the mysteriousness of it, and so are we.

The classic Hollywood movies of the past have usually been wised-up hatchet jobs with a deep feeling for past glories, like Billy Wilder's *Sunset Boulevard,* or brightly decorated valentines like *Singin' in the Rain.* Even when the acid etched deep, as in Vincente Minnelli's *The Bad and the Beautiful,* the film itself certified Hollywood's supremacy; we were nudged to acknowledge that a corrupt studio system was the price one paid for movie magic—that corruption was even a necessary ingredient in the sorcerer's mix. The film implicitly asks us: "How bad can Hollywood be if a movie like *The Bad and the Beautiful* can come out of it?" It's the same question raised by *The Player*.

And the answer, of course, is: very bad. The magic we observe in *The*

Player, as befitting the modern corporate-conglomerate movie era, is all in the Hollywood rituals, not in the movies that come out of them. We don't even get to see any actual movie-making. It's as if the films didn't matter. All that counts is the deal, the "pitch."

The gallows humor in this farce is that *all* human transaction has been reduced to the pitch. The wheedling, anxious, fervid tone adopted by the screenwriters hawking their wares to producers is the same tone one hears in the movie between friends and lovers and enemies in the hubbub of the Hollywood parties or in the bistros or the hot tubs. Altman's overlapping sound techniques have never seemed more appropriate. He understands how, in the Hollywood party circuit, you have to keep your radar tuned to the babble of incriminating frequencies across the room. You never know if your career may be filtering through those squashed syllables.

And yet one of the ways we can sense Altman's disgust with this milieu is that, for the most part, his soundtrack is eerily, uncharacteristically empty. The jovial chorus of voices familiar from most of his other films has been replaced by a cryptlike creepiness in which the players at the very top measure out their words with a wary calm. Being garrulous isn't merely uncool. It's unsafe.

The Hollywood honchos in the film have concocted for themselves a hermetic theme park of a life. Even the desert getaway they favor resembles a movie set; the impossibly beautiful couple swimming languorously in the hot springs grotto could be a pair of movie stars. Or they could be movie-star look-alikes. In the shadows, does it really matter?

The theme park is wired by rumor, and as one of the players says in the film, "the rumors are always true." There's a vacuum-packed predictability to the place because so little outside the Land of the Deal is allowed to intrude. Names like "Julia Roberts" and "Bruce Willis" are invoked like mantras. The studio executives' almost mystical belief in formula plots is all of a piece with their formula lives.

That's why the film's chief player—Griffin Mill, the studio exec played by Tim Robbins—is so unnerved when murder complicates his own plot line. He's a whiz at figuring out where a writer's pitch is leading, but he can't figure out what will happen to his own life. And yet he's not so far gone that he doesn't find his predicament weirdly entertaining. (That's why he's the movie's hero.) In a way, Mill's murder rap gives him a status, a gravity that certifies his high-stakes brinkmanship.

In Hollywood, serious players are privileged to commit serious crimes, and murder is way up there—even worse than going $20 million over budget on a film.

Mill even takes up with the girlfriend of the murdered man—an ice princess played by Greta Scacchi, who matches up with his chilly cool. Scacchi's character superficially resembles one of those neurasthenic waifs, like Maria in Joan Didion's *Play It As It Lays*, who used to populate Hollywood novels of the seventies. But this waif has more steel; she'll survive. She's the modern power player's ideal mate—an alter ego.

The new Hollywood that Altman shows us still carries the vapor trails of the old. The studio's inner sanctums are deep-toned and Old World, as if the legendary moguls still hovered inside them. Movie posters from classic and Grade-B crime thrillers from the thirties and forties cover the walls. This piece of running-gag art direction is one of Altman's pop jests, but it also serves to point up the difference between the raw, tabloid force of those films and the blandness of our own.

Altman's attitude toward Golden Age Hollywood is cautiously sentimental. He recognizes that his artist's iconoclasm would not have thrived in those years either, but he can still respond to the fervor of that period. At least back then the totalitarians in charge loved the movies.

The Golden Age moguls saw the moviegoing audience in their own outsize image. With new-style producers like Mill, the joke is that they *have* no image, no contours. Mill has the baby-fatted look of a TV-generation potentate; his gaze has a built-in short attention span. His colorlessness is emblematic of Hollywood's approach to audiences. What need is there for a producer with a strong, fully formed personality when he can't act on his riskiest intuitions? The movies are not really being made to satisfy people, they're made to satisfy a checklist of demographic pre-sale requirements. Is it any wonder that the new generation of movie executives all have the same sleek look of powerful, prefab anonymity? (A witness fails to pick Mill out in a police lineup because of that anonymity.) It's a more Armani-ized version of the current, preferred look in American business culture, and *The Player* makes us aware of how cleanly and antiseptically Hollywood fits into that culture right now. Despite its deep-down wit and its off-center movie-star cameos, *The Player* is unspeakably sad and unsettling because Altman doesn't hold out a prayer that any art can come out of all this.

The irony, of course, is that Altman has made a movie that's supremely deft and pleasurable. As if to taunt his detractors, he even "tells a story" this time, and he does a better job of it than the hacks who have been getting work when he couldn't. (He still can't get the financing to make his long-held dream project *L.A. Shortcuts*.) Altman might be saying to us, "You see how easy this is?"

But his flourishes have a Pyrrhic quality. And so, although *The Player* has been hailed as Altman's triumphant re-entry into Hollywood, emotionally and stylistically it feels more like a leave-taking.

As a state of mind, "Hollywood" has always been a magical aerie for people all over the world; its movies have shaped our fantasies to such an extent that they literally influence the way we dream. What we get in *The Player* is a dreamless community where power-mongering has obliterated art, though not big profits. You don't have to work in the movie business, or even see a lot of movies, to tune into the message. Altman likes to deal in archetypes. His Hollywood, an American archetype if ever there was one, stands in for a much larger spiritual brutalization.

In the usual Hollywood novel, the screenwriter hero is portrayed as a wronged artist mauled by the studio brass; the book is his revenge. Tolkin put a backspin on this formula when he wrote his novel, with its producer antihero. In the movie, Altman and Tolkin extend the spin. There are no holdouts for artistic integrity in their Hollywood, not even among the writers—the corruption is total. They've caught devastatingly well how, in order to score in the new Hollywood, screenwriters have glommed onto the producers' market-research attitudes while the producers, in their most expansive moments, fancy themselves creators—artists. The screenwriters in *The Player* are enraged not because they are not allowed to function as artists but because they are not being asked to sell out. Or perhaps they don't have the talent to sell out.

The real murder in *The Player* is the murder of the art of film, and Altman indicts the audience right along with the Hollywood sahibs up on the screen. The connection between murder and power in this film seeps into your bones. In Hollywoodspeak, a good movie is a movie that makes money; a bad movie is a movie that doesn't. Altman's outrage at this equation is fiercely moral. He recognizes the continuum between this kind of thinking and the scene late in the film in which Mill, dazed by the crime he is caught up in, hears the murdered man's woman say cryptically to him: "If you don't suffer, maybe it isn't a crime."

It's a crime that is revenged in the perfect Hollywood manner. Everyone—the guilty and the innocent, the murderer and the provocateur, the sharpies and the stupes—comes out ahead. No one is so loathsome that you might not need them for your career. Besides, what's a little murder between players?

(Los Angeles Times, 1992)

MICHAEL MANN

The Insider

The Insider begins with a man, *60 Minutes* producer Lowell Bergman (Al Pacino), being whisked blindfolded in a car to a secret powwow with an Islamic terrorist. Bergman is there to set the stage for a forthcoming interview with Mike Wallace (Christopher Plummer), and he's in his element; boasting of the "integrity" of *60 Minutes,* he's a muckraking freewheeler par excellence. When Wallace finally comes on the scene, Bergman pampers and cajoles him as if he were a diva. The film appears to be saying: Forget the Hezbollah, this guy can handle *Mike Wallace.*

The real terrorist in the film is, of course, Big Tobacco; this prologue in Lebanon is like a featherweight preliminary bout before the main bone-crusher event. Early on, Bergman's stage-managing is intercut with unrelated scenes depicting the abrupt departure of Jeffrey Wigand (Russell Crowe) as chief of research at Brown & Williamson, the nation's third-largest tobacco company. (Wigand was fired as a probable consequence of his outspoken in-house concerns about the product's health risks.) Like gunslingers at high noon, these two men are fated to meet—except, of course, they end up slinging for the same side. Bergman at first is interested in Wigand's expertise in deciphering a load of clandestine tobacco-related documents, but he quickly sizes up the racked, somnolent scientist as the "ultimate insider" who can, with careful coaxing, deliver a whopping scoop for CBS and, incidentally, become the point man in the war against the tobacco industry. (He became the key witness in legal action taken by seven states seeking reimbursement of Medicaid expenses for smoking-related illnesses.)

With its big, gleaming righteousness and gangster-movie undertow, *The Insider* is like an elongated cross between *Silkwood* or *All the President's Men* and the sort of hyperbolic, noirish stylefests peculiar to its director, Michael Mann (*Thief, Heat,* TV's *Miami Vice*). As a filmmaker, he's a lot like Lowell Bergman here—driven and messianic, and hammy. The fact-based story he's telling, derived primarily from Marie Brenner's 1996 *Vanity Fair* piece "The Man Who Knew Too Much," is essentially in the standard ripped-from-the-headlines glamorama-Hollywood-thriller mode, but he gives it a doomy largeness. We're on a holy crusade here, with a full house of tormented souls and ogres and ordinary people made extraordinary by a higher calling.

As substantial a subject as Big Tobacco is for *The Insider,* the lying and evasions of Brown & Williamson aren't its real meat. Neither is the humiliating backdown of *60 Minutes,* which initially nixed the full airing of a damning interview between Wallace and Wigand for fear of being massively sued by B&W—and also, perhaps, for fear of derailing an impending sale of CBS to Westinghouse. (The interview finally aired on February 4, 1996, after much of Wigand's testimony was already a matter of public record following a suit against the tobacco companies, and after the *New York Times* and *Wall Street Journal* had detailed the cave-in at CBS.) The film's real subject, instead, is how the stakes have become so high in modern corporate culture that the whistleblowers end up playing by the same rules as the ones being whistled at. They all kowtow to the same greenback god.

Except for a chosen few, of course. Bergman rages against his superiors at CBS to get the incriminating interview aired while Wigand, his life a scary funk of harassment and recrimination, is left twisting in the wind. These two are portrayed as temperamentally opposite yet united by a passion for payback. Bergman, his hair blow-dry-shaggy in a most uncorporate way, still trails fumes of his counterculture past as a writer for *Ramparts*; he's the last best hope of his generation, and when the creator and executive producer of *60 Minutes,* Don Hewitt (Philip Baker Hall), accuses him of being a "fanatic, an anarchist," the sanctification is complete. Bergman is enough of a political animal to respect compromise, but his vainglory is that, when the screws are put to him, he refuses to back down.

Mann and his co-screenwriter, Eric Roth, are so busy propping up Bergman as an authentic hero out of his time that about halfway through this 155-minute movie, they lose sight of Wigand's story, which, at least the way it's been done here, is more emotionally complex, if less flamboyant. Al Pacino gives a real showboat performance, with full-body shimmies and burning stares and foursquare speeches, and Mann makes everything even more florid by positioning the actor against wide-screen, Valhalla-size backdrops as the overwrought soundtrack swells. (In one dark-lit long shot, Bergman stands knee-high in the ocean as he converses with a distraught Wigand on his cell phone.)

By contrast, Wigand is a stolid sufferer for much of the movie, but Russell Crowe gives him a seething core. With his hair lightened and thinned for the role, and a paunch added, Crowe is hardly recognizable from the bully-boy cop he played in *L. A. Confidential.* Wigand may have believed himself to be a man of science who could devise a "safe" cigarette, but he also wasn't above self-aggrandizement; as Marie Brenner wrote, "It is conceivable that B&W had sized Wigand up psychologically. He surely appeared to be highly ambitious, money-hungry, a potential captive to the firm." What gives *The Insider* its power, despite all the glossiness and excess, is that Wigand's dispossession and retribution come across as a key drama for our corporate-circus times. For Wigand, the price of reform is catastrophic. Testifying against B&W, he enters a night-world where his family is endangered and everything becomes commodified, including himself; he's a potential ratings-grabber for CBS until the network figures out it has more to lose than to gain from his appearance. Even iron-faced Mike Wallace—splendidly played by Plummer, with each syllable honed to a cutting edge—doesn't stand up for him. (Later, according to the film, Wallace sees the light.)

At one point, Bergman tells Wigand, "We're running out of heroes. Guys like you are in short supply," and the line has a hollow ring because it seems to come out of a movie about old-style heroism, and what we have with Wigand is something new. (Bergman's heroics, as depicted here, *are* something old.) Wigand's rage at B&W is more about pride than about doing good; if the company, after terminating him, hadn't insulted him by pressing for a more severe confidentiality agreement, he probably would have clammed up forever. Wigand as a hero feels right to us, more contemporaneous, precisely because, for a long time, he *doesn't* act on principle. He acts on pique and fear and gall. And yet he seems stunned—hollowed out—by his betrayal at the hands of B&W, and then again by CBS. This ultimate insider becomes the ultimate outsider. We're accustomed to the bland facelessness of the Corporate Man, but this film gives that anonymity a darker twist; when the first, bowdlerized *60 Minutes* show is aired, Wigand sees himself being sound-bited on TV with his face blanked out and his voice patterns disguised. What should be his coming-out party is instead a sick joke, a further retreat into nowhere.

It's a good thing Wigand isn't a conventional, come-to-the-rescue hero in *The Insider,* because, although Michael Mann tries for a victory dance, there's ultimately little cause for cheer. A few good men here got out with their honor intact, but Big Tobacco is still Big. In September, the Justice Department, after five years and millions of dollars spent, acknowledged that its criminal investigation of the tobacco industry was closed, opting instead for a civil lawsuit accusing the companies of racketeering and fraud. "It was a case," a Justice Department official was quoted in the *Times* as saying, "that the criminal division decided it was not likely to win." This is the real-world backdrop against which the righteous theatrics of *The Insider* play themselves out. It's a world in which there are many whistleblowers, and yet the tune remains pretty much the same.

(*New York*, 2000)

ROBERT ZEMECKIS

Contact

A lot of ink has been shed in the press lately about the "seriousness" of the new Robert Zemeckis film *Contact*, starring Jodie Foster as an astronomer who receives humankind's first extraterrestrial message. *Forrest Gump* made Zemeckis a guru; now he's being primed as a philosopher king. Is it rude to suggest that the high-mindedness of *Contact*—the deepthink about science and religion and the soullessness of modern society—isn't on a much more elevated plane than most science-fantasy books and movies?

Just about every piece of sci-fi has its mite of "meaning." In fact, you'd be hard-pressed to find a sci-fi movie—even *Attack of the Crab Monsters*—that doesn't work the Is God Out There? angle. *Contact* is being applauded because it presumes to rise above its origins, when, in fact, its origins are all of a piece with its pretensions.

And *Contact* sure is pretentious. It doesn't deliver on the deepthink, and it lacks the charge of good, honest pulp. It's schlock without the schlock.

The 1985 Carl Sagan novel upon which the film is loosely based started out as a movie treatment. But unlike most such treatments-turned-bestsellers—Erich Segal's *Love Story* is the classic example—you can't really spot an impending movie in the book. It's too chunky with data, and it barely registers a romance.

With his principled skepticism and his genius for popularizing science, Sagan certainly was a force for good in the world, but—bless his heart—he wasn't much of a pulpster or sentimentalist. In creating his heroine, Dr. Eleanor "Ellie" Arroway, he attempted to sanction his own high-flying fantasies within the comfy camouflage of fiction. But Sagan didn't have the novelist's skills or breadth of insight to bring Ellie and the book's many other characters to rousing, full-blooded life. What excited him was the science—the arguments about its purpose—and his characters were mouthpieces in the maelstrom.

Clunky as it is, what still comes through in the book is the spiritedness of the scientist's quest—though in writing *Contact*, Sagan may not have recognized that his imaginative reach was far greater in his nonfiction books and television specials. Still, in whatever form it took, we can still respond to Sagan's ecstatic commingling with the universe.

That's the kind of ardor you might expect to find in the movie version of *Contact*, which until his death drew on the participation of Sagan and his wife and collaborator, Ann Druyan. But the *Contact* filmmakers—Zemeckis and his screenwriters James V. Hart and Michael Goldenberg—are gassy with uplift. They provide the sob sister sentimentalities and sermonettes that Sagan was too smart, or too clueless, to include. The filmmakers don't build on the intelligence in the book; they tenderize it. *Contact* is a movie about intelligence that doesn't credit the audience with having much of it.

The film opens with a creaky prologue in which little Ellie, whose mother died in childbirth, loses her indulgent beloved father. We're primed to recognize that this orphaned girl-scientist, whose father taught her to use a CB radio, is reaching out to the stars as a way to reach out to her parents. It's the kind of soggy psychologizing that condescends to us—as if without this bit of "heart" we couldn't appreciate Ellie's intellectual quest. Her resilient skepticism—her unbelief in God—clearly exists to be overturned in the same way that, say, pacifists in war movies end up fighting for the cause. What we are meant to think is: Ellie doesn't want to believe in God, because she can't comprehend why he would take away her parents. We know she'll come around, at least partway. *Contact* is bound to get kudos for being "daring" enough to feature an upfront unbeliever as its hero, but the dare is never really taken up.

Ellie's counterpart, in one of the weirdest roles in recent movies, is the religious scholar and White House spiritual advisor Palmer Joss (Matthew McConaughey), whom she first meets while listening for extraterrestrial messages in Puerto Rico. He shows up looking shaggy and hip—less Billy Graham than Bruce Springsteen—and you think maybe he's a carny con artist. But, no, he's an angel of mercy. He does manage to score on the first date, but that's okay, because, you see, he's in love with Ellie and she with him, except that she can't bear the closeness and sprints from his bed and his life before things get too sweaty. (If the filmmakers had any sense of fun, they would have had Ellie the Unbeliever cry out, "Oh, God!" in the throes of passion.)

Years later Palmer reappears, groomed and telegenic, hawking on the talk shows his book *Losing Faith: A Search for Meaning in Modern Life*—and danged if we *still* aren't supposed to take this guy seriously. By this time Ellie is en route to her biggest coup—she will turn the world on its head by verifying that the rhythmic sonic squawks picked up by vast radio telescopes in New Mexico are in fact extraterrestrial messages. (They sound rather like a synthesized *Rite of Spring*.)

What would any of us really do if we were contacted by extraterrestrials? It's a lofty question. *Contact* brings it back down to earth with a thud by undercutting the awe with blather from government agency types such as National Security Advisor Michael Kitz (James Woods) and especially from Palmer, who still looks like he's on the make for Ellie. Their God-Exists-Does-Not-Does-Too byplay begins to resemble a weird mating dance between a hunky fundamentalist and a tight-ass libertarian. McConaughey, understandably, doesn't have a clue how to play Palmer, but he sure plays him atrociously.

Just about everybody in the cast comes across badly. As Ellie's mentor David Drumlin, Tom Skerritt is saddled playing a standard villain part; all he's missing is a silky mustache to twirl. Drumlin takes credit for Ellie's coups and even vies with her to be the first person sent into space to meet the aliens. (Those sonic squawks are encrypted blueprints for building a spaceship to their source, the planet Vega.) As a White House advisor, Angela Bassett looks poleaxed as the concept of prime numbers is explained to her; she carries herself with the rigidity of a grade-B player in a grade-Z sci-fi thriller. James Woods, especially when he's grilling Ellie in a Capitol Hill hearing, seems to be modeling himself on Senator Joseph McCarthy. He doesn't have his heart in the theatrics, though—he's frivolously feral. John Hurt turns up as a reclusive, bald-pated weirdo billionaire who funds Ellie's lift-off to Vega. He's like a cross between Dr. No and Howard Hughes. (He's also one of the few sympathetic characters in the movie—leave it to Hollywood to deify a venture capitalist every time.)

And then there's Jodie Foster. You can see why she was cast as Ellie— very few actresses can project intelligence as pointedly as she can. Foster is trying to get inside Ellie's rage for discovery without softening her for us. The problem is, Ellie *could* use a little softening. With her lips clamped and her jaw set, she's like a walking migraine. If her face were pulled any tighter, she'd be a skull. Foster's abrasive, unyielding performance confronts the current notion that women can score with audiences only if they play nice. Julia Roberts's career may have spooked a lot of actresses—smile and the world is yours, scowl and you lose it all. Foster has never played that game. She goes her own way, the way Bette Davis did, and, as in *The Accused* or *The Silence of the Lambs*, she can be powerful when she's playing a character fighting through her anguish with her smarts.

But Ellie—anguished, smart—also needs to be a romantic, and Foster fights that with every inch of her being. That's partly because she doesn't want to stoop to easy pleasures, but I think it's also because, as an actress, Foster lacks the expansiveness of soul that would make this woman come alive for us. She's much better at holding in than letting go.

The movie audience for independent and foreign films—what used to be called the art-house audience when there were still art houses—has often been taken in by the appearance of seriousness. (Ingmar Bergman played the science vs. faith game when Zemeckis was still in diapers.) *Contact* represents the mass-audience version of gulling the audience with high importance. It appears to be saying a lot—but what? When Palmer, who, unlike Ellie, never wavers in his beliefs, says to her, "Our goal is the same—the pursuit of the truth," he's just offering a sop to the audience. (We wouldn't want to alienate any truth-seeking ticket buyers, would we?) And when Ellie tells some school-kid scientists at the end to "keep searching for your own answers," it's more sop. After all, we've just been through two and a half hours of derring-do during which all manner of scurvy scientists and politicians have indeed been searching for their own answers. Has it improved their souls? *Contact*, for all its high-mindedness, isn't really about mind at all. It's about being pure-in-heart enough to be mushy-brained.

Isn't this the same formula that worked for Zemeckis in *Forrest Gump*? Forrest was the simpleton whose purity-of-essence trumped the worldly malcontents in his midst. Ellie is as smart as Forrest was stunted, but they are equal in the end in being sweet-souled. In *Contact*, as in *Forrest Gump*, there's something suspect about braininess. Intelligence, it's implied, keeps you from truly *feeling*.

This is an odd implication coming from a movie about scientists, but it fits right in with the popular mood. For Hale-Bopped audiences feeling crunched by the technology that was supposed to make them happier, *Contact* is here to tell you it's going to be all right. The aliens beckoning us turn out to be as sweet as Forrest Gump and as wise as Yoda. Just keep searching for your own answers, and don't sweat the millennium.

(*New Times*, 1997)

POSTSCRIPT

Contact provoked an uproar from the White House over the film's unauthorized use of Clinton press conference clips in which he appears to be acting in the movie while talking about space aliens. The hoo-ha obscured a central point: Hollywood doesn't feel it *needs* to ask the White House for authorization. It answers to a higher power—Robert Zemeckis.

ROMAN POLANSKI

The Pianist

The Pianist is based on the memoirs of Polish musician Wladyslaw Szpilman, who survived the Warsaw ghetto, and it's Roman Polanski's strongest and most personally felt movie. This should not come as a great surprise, since as a child Polanski survived the Kraków Ghetto and lost family members in the Holocaust. The real surprise is that the horrors on display in *The Pianist* are presented matter-of-factly—which of course makes them seem even more horrific. We are not accustomed to such reserve in a movie about the Holocaust, and especially not in a Polanski movie, where the violence has often been close to Grand Guignol. But in this film he is trying to be devastatingly true to his emotions, and so there is no need for hyperbole. At times, the tension between the unwavering directness of his technique and the anguish that is behind it is almost unbearable. When we see a Nazi soldier casually shoot a Jewish girl in the head for asking an innocent question, or when we see soldiers throw an old man in a wheelchair over a balcony, we are staring into an everyday inferno.

Szpilman, who is played with feral grace by Adrien Brody, survived it; alone among his family, he managed to escape from the ghetto and hide out in Warsaw until the war's end. We first see him in 1939, not quite thirty, playing Chopin during a radio broadcast interrupted by German bombing. Near the end, we see him playing the same nocturne in the radio station that had once been shelled. It's as if his story had come full circle, except that he is crying now and savoring each note the way he savored each morsel of food in captivity. Halfway through the movie, there's a great, brief scene where Szpilman is hidden away in a Warsaw apartment and unable to touch its piano for fear of alerting the neighbors to his presence. The silent agony that ensues is one of the most powerful expressions of spiritual denial I've ever seen in a film. Szpilman's artistry is not sentimentalized; we are never made to feel that he stayed alive because of it. Mostly he survived on luck and gumption. But Polanski recognizes the soul-deep power that music held for Szpilman, and his playing in the end is both an anthem of renewal and a lament.

Polanski doesn't sentimentalize the Jews, either. The Jewish police employed by the Germans in the ghetto are shown to be almost as ruthless as their overseers, and some of the underground operatives turn out to be scoundrels. In his memoir, which was published in 1946 under the title *Death of a City* and soon banned by the Communists, Szpilman wrote that his experience shattered his belief in the "solidarity of the Jews." No doubt some people will regard the divulging of that experience as a betrayal, but Polanski honors the Jews of Warsaw by not romanticizing them; besides, there are many acts of extraordinary generosity and courage in *The Pianist*. They are just as inexplicable as the depravities.

Although he engages in some minor arms smuggling, Szpilman himself is not especially brave or virtuous. He is not the kind of conventional hero—or anti-hero, for that matter—a movie such as this would seem to require. He's a watcher, a reactor, and yet his recessiveness has metaphorical power; Szpilman is like a wraith witnessing the ruin of his beloved city and its people. (*The Pianist* is, among others things, a eulogy for Warsaw.) When he is finally driven out of his hiding places and wanders the blasted streets, the imagery goes beyond starkness into the surreal—we might be looking at a lunar landscape by De Chirico.

The most remarkable aspect of Szpilman's memoir is that it was written so close to the time of the events described and yet is full of poise and equanimity. There is no ache for revenge in his book, and there is none in Polanski's film, either. Szpilman lived out his days in Poland as a celebrated pianist and composer of popular songs and children's music, dying in 2000. Polanski, whose notorious and harrowing life is well-known, had not, until this movie, filmed in Poland in forty years. And yet these two men, who might appear from their lives and works to be temperamentally unalike, share a distaste for special pleading or bathos. In *The Pianist*, suffering is seen with such clarity that its relief becomes a balm of the greatest magnitude. It's the relief we get when Szpilman plays the piano again, or merely makes it through another day. In moments like these, we are confronted with the significance, the momentousness, of the ordinary.

(*New York*, 2002)

POSTSCRIPT

After his vastly underrated *Oliver Twist*, which made clear for the first time in the movies why Dostoevsky admired Dickens, Polanski made the acclaimed *The Ghost Writer*, which reinforced his reputation, however qualifiedly, as Hitchcock's heir. Hitchcock turned audience manipulation into gamesmanship, and we enjoyed being gamed. It meant Hitchcock thought enough of our smarts to try confounding them. His relationship with his audience is based on an essentially English sense of wryness and propriety. Even in the savagery of *Psycho*, there is a sense in which he is toying with our frights; there's wit in the blood. The black joke in that film is how it overturns our conventional scary-movie expectations and becomes truly gruesome.

Polanski's horrors come out of a different tradition, more Eastern European, from Hitchcock's. His gamesmanship is closer to blood sport. Like Hitchcock's, Polanski's audience-response manuevers have sometimes been interpreted as a sign of artistry when they're often just high-end gimmickry. But, also like Hitchcock, Polanski is a special case. His best movies have a way of blurring the line—which is mostly artificial anyway—between the manipulations of a fright master and those of an artist. The dread that pervades, say, *Chinatown*, or *The Ghost Writer*, or even the middling *Frantic*, which is almost intolerably anxiety-provoking for its first, seemingly uneventful half hour or so, goes beyond pulpishness into richer realms of unease. These films are saying that while the stories we are watching are unhinged and full of fear, the real world in which they are created is even more so. (Inevitably, if unfairly, we regard Polanski's harrowing life and his movies as all of a piece.) The existential dislocation is total. Movies are not just movies; they're emissaries of a deeper disorder.

BOB FOSSE

Star 80

No Hollywood/Broadway director is more obsessively entranced with the allure of show-biz sleaze than Bob Fosse. In movie after movie (*Sweet*

Charity, *Cabaret*, *Lenny*, and *All That Jazz*) and show after show (*Pippin*, *Chicago*, *Dancin'*), he's cast himself as the purveyor of the dirty truth about show business, which he views as a metaphor for life—"Life is a cabaret." He's a gleeful, scabrous emcee, much like Joel Grey in *Cabaret*; he's tickled by the flames of perdition. *Star 80*, his latest movie, is, in some ways, the archetypal Fosse project, although it's far from his best.

In films like *Lenny* and *All That Jazz*, he dealt with the scumminess of success; in *Star 80*, he's dealing with a low-rent hustler, Paul Snider (Eric Roberts), and his "discovery," Dorothy Stratten (Mariel Hemingway), whose greatest fame was as the 1980 *Playboy* Playmate of the Year. Their lives are presented as even more representative of the American-dream-turned-nightmare than Lenny Bruce's. It's precisely *because* Snider and Stratten were second-raters that their story (based in part on Teresa Carpenter's *Village Voice* piece "Death of a Playmate") attracts Fosse—that, and, of course, the garish way that story ended, with Snider's shotgun murder of Stratten before he turned the gun on himself.

Snider had been a two-bit promoter and pimp in Vancouver in 1978 when he first met Dorothy, eighteen and blond and virginal, working in a Dairy Queen. Floored by her untrammelled beauty and knowing a good thing when he saw it, he snowed her with gifts and compliments. He didn't pimp Dorothy; that was small-time stuff compared to what he ultimately envisioned for her—a *Playboy* centerfold and Hollywood stardom. He was probably also in love with her but, in the movie's terms, that love was inseparable from usage; he loved her because of the goodies her beauty would bring them both. As he says to Dorothy's mother (Carroll Baker) when he's trying to convince her to sign the *Playboy* photo-release forms, "Together we could *be* somebody."

Even if you weren't already familiar with the details of this story, Fosse doesn't leave any doubt where it will lead. In fact, the entire movie flashes back from the charnel bedroom, with a close-up of the blood-smeared Snider, snarling and panting. The movie is toned up with gothic fatalism; because we know what's in store for Dorothy, her beauty and innocence carry a double-edge—we know it will be destroyed.

But Fosse doesn't seem much interested in Dorothy as a character. *Star 80* isn't her movie, it's Snider's, in the same way that Scorsese's *Taxi Driver* belonged to De Niro's Travis Bickle. It's a portrait not of the destroyed but of the destroyer. And Eric Roberts gets into the role with almost as much intensity as De Niro brought to his blocked, feral loner. It's an amazing, career-stretching performance. His Snider is like a before-and-after blend of the guy who gets sand kicked in his face with the bully who does the kicking. He builds up his lightweight frame with barbells and rehearses his come ons in the mirror (just like Travis Bickle did). His mustache and sideburns are real, but they look pasted on—like his smile. When he takes Dorothy out to a fancy restaurant on their first date and springs a topaz ring on her, he's in his element; it's like opening night after the dress rehearsal. Snider is so careful to make the right, slick impression that even his diction has been honed. His enunciation is almost brutally precise, as if he was terrified that any rogue wimpiness might emerge.

The most original sequences in the movie involve Snider's attempts to use his small-time huckster's savvy in big-time Hollywood. He may have been a floozie's rajah in Vancouver but, in Tinseltown, he's a speck. The real rajah of the piece is Hugh Hefner (Cliff Robertson), who lords it over the Playboy Mansion in his silk pajamas and gives Dorothy a fatherly lecture on how *Playboy* is more than a magazine, it's "a family." Snider's attempts to ingratiate himself with "Hef" (he quotes passages from the *Playboy* philosophy) are pathetic, and yet there's more genuine feeling behind those attempts than in anything else in the movie. We can feel Dorothy slipping away from him and into the gauzy glare of Hollywood, and he's helpless against the juggernaut. Even after he moves to Los Angeles and marries her, he can't hold onto her. When Snider hires a private investigator (Josh Mostel) and discovers that Dorothy has been having an affair, her first, with the director (Roger Rees) of her first big movie, Snider is half-crazed. He's like a trigger waiting to be pulled. She has become more than a meal-ticket to him; more than his passport to the Playboy Mansion. She is, in a sense, his idealized vision of himself. That's why, when he finally kills her, he must also kill himself.

Snider hates what he loves the most—wealth and celebrity—because he can't really have them. And so does Fosse, except that he's in love/hate not with dreams of beauty and megabucks but with smarm. Fosse can't distance himself from Snider, which gives the movie its obsessiveness but also its shallowness. He doesn't see the contradiction at the heart of the movie—that Snider wasn't an anomaly in this world, he was simply a smaller-scaled version of the big boys. When Snider, without Dorothy as his chaperone, is refused admittance to the mansion, that's supposed to be his mini-downfall—a prelude to horror. The implication is that if only Snider had been allowed entrance into the inner-circle, everything would have been all right. He would have turned out okay—like Hef.

The movie indicts Snider for his designs on Dorothy—it even indicts him for his tacky, lounge-lizardly clothes. (There is, however, one conspicuous omission: the bejeweled Star of David that Snider wore around his neck has been replaced by a gold dollar-sign.) But, except for Snider, the movie is incongruously easy on practically everybody. Aram Nicholas, the director with whom Dorothy has the affair, is such a sympathetic good-guy that the idea that he might have a few designs of his own on Dorothy is unconscionable. (Aram is based on Peter Bogdanovich, who directed Stratten in her only big movie, *They All Laughed*.) Didn't it occur to Fosse that a movie director might be just as inclined as a husband to idealize a beautiful actress, or use her to bolster a sagging career?

Hefner gets off even easier. To start with, he's played by Cliff Robertson, perhaps best known as JFK in *PT 109*. (It's rumored that Fosse's first choice for the role was Harry Dean Stanton, an actor with a genius for playing grungy slickers. Did Fosse lose his nerve, or did *Playboy* exert some control over the production in exchange for the right to use its name?) There's no indication in this movie that Hefner regarded Dorothy as his own passport to movie fame. Hefner may have had his sultan's pick of the Playmate litter, but the Hollywood establishment has always regarded him as something of an interloper—a big-budget Paul Snider. None of the movies he financed have been box-office bonanzas; even worse, none of his bunnies have ever made it in a big way in the movies. With Stratten, who had a bit of genuine dazzlement on the screen, he must have seen himself as a star-maker—at last. But the movie doesn't get into any of these areas. It's so careful not to ascribe ulterior motives to anyone (except Snider) that it seems lobotomized—or else just plain dishonest.

And what about Dorothy? As Mariel Hemingway plays her, she's simply a beautiful blank. She's such an innocent that she isn't even aware of the effect she has on men—there's no coquetry in her. Hemingway's innocence has been exploited in the movies before (in *Lipstick*, she was sexually abused by a Paul Snider-type character; in *Personal Best*, her love affair with a fellow female pentathlete was presented as a wonderment—a sexual rite of passage). In *Star 80*, Hemingway has a frisky loveliness, but we never know what's going on inside her head, perhaps because Fosse doesn't think it's important for us to know. She's in the movie to be victimized. The movie never suggests, of course, that she might have willingly complied in her victimization.

Star 80 is a powerfully uncomfortable experience, and it's not easy to shake off. But a lot of our discomfort comes from the queasy collusion that we sense between Fosse and Snider, who is presented as something more than a case study—he's more like an alter-ego (in much the same way that Roy Scheider was in *All That Jazz*—he rehearsed in front of mirrors, too). Dorothy Stratten's tragedy has been tricked up and distorted by Fosse in order to provide him with another "personal" sex-and-sleaze extravaganza, and he's hired Ingmar Bergman's cameraman, Sven Nykvist, to give it all a "class" look. When she was alive, Stratten was talked up by her publicists as a possible Marilyn Monroe for the eighties. In a way, that's what she's become; she's the latest martyr in the movie-land merry-go-round. Besides Teresa Carpenter's highly commendable *Village Voice* piece, and a subsequent, lengthy *Playboy* rebuttal, her story has already been used as the basis for a TV movie starring Jamie Lee Curtis; Peter Bogdanovich has written a memoir about her which is due out shortly; and *Playboy*, in an act of supreme brazenness, is coming full circle with a pictorial on Hemingway as Dorothy in the January issue. (Hemingway had her breasts surgically enlarged for the role.) The Dorothy Stratten story has become a cottage-industry; it appeals to show-biz doomsayers like Fosse because it's a confirmation of rottenness. But Fosse doesn't transcend the rot. *Star 80* is a classic example of a movie that exemplifies what it attacks.

(*Los Angeles Herald Examiner*, 1983)

BAZ LUHRMANN

Moulin Rouge

Baz Luhrmann's *Moulin Rouge* is being trumpeted by its creator as not merely a musical but, indeed, the Second Coming of the musical. Luhrmann is not a shy auteur; his previous film, starring Leonardo DiCaprio and Claire Danes and set in a kind of alternative-rock-video Miami Beach, was titled *William Shakespeare's Romeo + Juliet*, but although the Bard's words were bandied about, it might more accurately have been called *Baz Luhrmann's Romeo + Juliet*. I spent the entire movie fighting off the youth-pandering psychedelia in a vain attempt to locate the language, the performances.

The film isn't just in-your-face; it's also in your mouth, ears, nose, and arse. Luhrmann strips the play for action and bombast—not the smartest approach to this material—and fractures the speeches into sound bites. Sometimes it's difficult to hear the lines at all, what with the all the explosions and the jacked-up soundtrack featuring such groups as Garbage, Everclear, and the Butthole Surfers. When, near the end, Juliet says to her beloved, "O, think'st thou we shall ever meet again?" and Romeo responds with "I doubt it not," I didn't catch the "not." Some Romeo.

You can't even say that Luhrmann came up with a "concept." He's stocked the film with a cross-generational parade of costumes and architectural styles, but he has no comprehension of the play as play. The liberties he takes with Shakespeare seems motivated exclusively by expediency and commercial calculation. When, for example, he deprives us of a final reconciliation between the Montagues and the Capulets, it's not because he's pushing a fatalistic vision—he just wants to end things with a bang. Earlier, he has Romeo look up at the revived Juliet before expiring so we can catch the full effect of the boy's botched timing. Luhrmann must think there's no point in Romeo dying if Juliet isn't there to watch it.

In *Moulin Rouge,* which is set in the Montmartre section of fin-de-siècle Paris, Luhrmann is once again in attack mode; he may think he's resuscitating the musical genre, but it's more like he's stomping it.

Christian (Ewan McGregor) is the doomed poet who narrates his sad, *Camille*-like tale of how he lost the love of the courtesan Satine (Nicole Kidman), the star of the celebrated dance hall Moulin Rouge. We first see Satine descend from the hall's ceiling by trapeze as she proceeds to wow the ravenous crowd with "Diamonds Are a Girl's Best Friend" and "Material Girl." The tone is set: flagrant neo-kitsch. And this is one of the film's *milder* episodes. Luhrmann is a student of Busby Berkeley at his most high-fructose, as well as the tutti-frutti tradition of Bombay musicals, with their berserk wriggling and instantaneous breaking-into-song. He makes one long for the relative sedateness of the Ken Russell who made *Tommy*. Luhrmann hauls in everything from Rodgers and Hammerstein to "Nature Boy" to "Roxanne" to LaBelle's "Lady Marmalade," and the songs tend to segue into one another, medley-style. It's like being trapped inside a fever dream of Oscar-night production numbers.

Although McGregor and Kidman do their own singing, they appear vaguely disembodied when they warble—not so much because of technical difficulties but because the emotions don't seem to be emanating from the person. Christian and Satine are meant to be pop archetypes, and so is everybody else in the movie, including Jim Broadbent, bobbing about in an inflated suit as the nightclub's impresario, Harold Zidler, and Richard Roxburgh's Duke, with his twitchy mustache and his penny-dreadful designs on Satine. John Leguizamo plays Toulouse-Lautrec, sans paintbrush, as the Elmer Fudd-sounding ringleader of a gaggle of bohos. None of these characters resonates even as an archetype because Luhrmann is too busy trying to ram them down our throats. Fellini at his most orgiastic never gave us so many lurid close-ups of grease-painted cavorters and plug-uglies. And this is a movie that pretends to be making some kind of fashion statement! Even Nicole Kidman has a fright-night pallor: dark-rimmed eyes, fire-truck-red lips, bone-white complexion—all this *before* she gets consumption.

Luhrmann can't be criticized for not achieving what he set out to do. *Moulin Rouge* has the awful completeness of a fully realized bum vision. How could anybody who seriously wanted to revive the movie musical be so tone-deaf to the reasons why we love musicals in the first place? His movie is reminiscent of those bygone behemoth attempts to revive silent slapstick comedy, such as *It's a Mad Mad Mad Mad World*, in which an overload of antics replaced inspiration. *Moulin Rouge* references just about every splashy forties musical ever made, plus quite a few others, but what's missing is the simplicity of spirit that gave the best musicals their transcendence. There's been a lot of blather over the years about how the movie musical is a dead genre, deader than the Western or the private-eye picture. We are supposed to be a culture that has lost its innocence; we can no longer sanction watching people suddenly break into heartfelt song. And meanwhile, music videos are the lifeblood of MTV, and on Broadway, *The Producers* is beginning to dwarf Fort Knox. (It will probably come full circle and end up as a movie.*) Two of the greatest musicals ever filmed, *Yentl* and *Pennies From Heaven*, came out in the eighties, which is not exactly the Ice Age. If not much has been done in the movies since then, surely that is more a consequence of commercial cowardice than of audience antipathy. There is certainly no lack of singing stars from the worlds of rock and rap or Broadway or cabaret.

Luhrmann is not wrong in believing that new ways have to be dreamed up to connect the musical with a new moviegoing generation, but what he's done in *Moulin Rouge* is to scavenge all the old ways and then turn up the heat, burning away any honest feeling. He gives you way too much of what you didn't really want in the first place: soulless high jinks. Jim Broadbent's impresario is fond of saying "The show must go on," but must it go on and on and on?

(New York, 2001)

TERRENCE MALICK

Overview

Like some fleeting cosmological phenomenon, the appearance of a new Terrence Malick movie always seems to augur a shift in the Hollywood heavens—or at least that portion of heaven inhabited by cloudborne cineastes. Now that Stanley Kubrick has passed on, Malick is the undisputed recluse/auteur of the film business, the director that the most movie people would most like to work with, if only they could find him.

The New World, his new film about John Smith and Pocahontas and the Jamestown colony, is only his fourth in thirty-two years. That's the kind of statistic of which mystiques are made, and Malick's has held up surprisingly well. The question is: Why?

I think the answer has more to do with the *idea* of Terrence Malick than with the overall quality of his films. At sixty-two, he is one of the

---

* It did, alas.

most gifted directors of his generation, though even his most ardent en-
thusiasts concede that he has yet to make his *Citizen Kane*. But Malick
remains the sole poster boy from that seventies era when it was still possible for idiosyncratic artists in Hollywood to make in their own way the
projects they truly cared about.

The directors he started out with, like Coppola and De Palma and
Scorsese and Spielberg, long ago entered the mainstream, but here is
Malick in *The New World*, making very much the same kind of lacework
movie he might have made in 1974, the year of his *Badlands* debut. He's
been called the J. D. Salinger of movies, but Rip Van Winkle is closer to
the mark.

The seventies, of course, was also the era when Hollywood directors
were at their most self-infatuated. But not all the peacocks were poseurs.
The good and great movies from that era—ranging from *Mean Streets*
and the *Godfather* films to *McCabe and Mrs. Miller* and *Carrie*—represented a triumph of artistic, not narcissistic, sensibility. They were made
by directors with a new way of seeing, which was, in essence, a new way
of imagining.

This is what many of us miss most from American movies now—a
visual daring which is at one with a daring conception. This lack is felt
even in the so-called independent realm, which has been singularly unad-
venturous cinematographically and dramatically. Even a film as distinctly
and personally shaped as *The Squid and the Whale* is nothing much to
look at.

If there is a modern-day equivalent to the superstar auteurs of
Malick's generation, it would be Quentin Tarantino, and this is largely
because, unlike most of the interchangeable functionaries and music video mavens making studio movies right now, his films are flagrantly his
own. His relish for the sheer effrontery of movie-making links him to
the seventies, even though beneath all the swagger in his films is simply
more swagger. The vogue in this country for the Hong Kong director
Wong Kar-Wai is part of the same signature-style syndrome. Emotionally, his movies are a dreamier and more ambiguously melancholy version
of 1950 Hollywood kitsch à la Douglas Sirk, but all that pretty patterning sure gives your eyes a show.

Malick may seem an odd duck in this current movie climate, but then
again, he has never quite fit in anywhere. Unlike his contemporaries, he

has never really drawn on popular sources of entertainment, even though movies like *Badlands* and *The Thin Red Line*, at least thematically, have a long Hollywood lineage. Scorsese and Coppola may have been inspired by Visconti and Fellini, but their most obvious antecedents early on were American crime melodramas; De Palma raided Hitchcock; Bogdanovich raided Hawks and Ford.

Malick, by contrast, although he was part of the first wave of film school graduates in the early seventies, didn't seem to be reacting to or against anything in either the Old or the New Hollywood. He was a high-culture guy in a mass-culture medium—a Rhodes Scholar who once translated Heidegger—and he didn't seek to overwhelm us with pyrotechnics. He was offering us a look into his own private dreamscape.

The signposts in this dreamscape have remained remarkably consistent from movie to movie, whether he is filming the Dakota Badlands or *Days of Heaven*'s Texas Panhandle, or Guadacanal or Jamestown. His great theme is the despoiling of Eden. "How did this horror enter the world?" asks a soldier in *The Thin Red Line* as guts spray the supernal vistas.

For Malick, nature's beauty, which he captures using only natural light, is defined by the depravity that will always seek to undo it. His films, which have been graced by the long-time collaboration of his production designer Jack Fisk and the cinematography of such masters as Nestor Almendros, Haskell Wexler, and John Toll, are filled with breathtaking close-ups of animals and birds and insects—creatures that are elementally connected to the terrors in the wild.

He tends to film his people in the same way, as exalted specimens in the cosmic laboratory. This is why there are few memorable performances in his movies—he is more interested in actors for their sculptural and spiritual qualities than in what they can bring to bear psychologically. Sometimes he comes up very short; Richard Gere in *Days of Heaven* and Q'orianka Kilcher as Pocahontas in *The New World* are prettified blanks, while Colin Ferrell's Captain John Smith isn't even pretty.

Nature is a riddle for Malick, a rune that, if it only could be decoded, would yield up the secret of why we are placed on this earth. (An early, aborted project of his was an epic about the creation of the planet, no less.) Because he is always divining the ineffable, his movies can sometimes seem absurdly highflown and, from a real-world standpoint, insubstantial. He makes movies about sociopathic serial murderers, the agrarian poor, a major war theater in the Pacific and America's founding colony, and yet there is hardly any direct political engagement to these films at all.

Not that some people haven't tried to find it anyway. *Badlands*, for example, was misinterpreted by a number of critics as an elitist snob's attack on the soullessness of a mass culture that would turn wayward youth into killers and even media heroes. But Malick, who grew up in Oklahoma and Texas, wasn't mounting a cultural attack on rural hickdom. The Badlands in that great, spooky movie, which I think is easily his best, are entirely metaphorical; the wide open spaces are maddening because they isolate and distill our own worst impulses. Nature is forever putting our souls in jeopardy.

In *Days of Heaven*, Malick is similarly unconcerned with the socio-political class consciousness ostensibly at its core. The film, which despite its extraordinary picturesqueness seems more than ever to me an hors d'oeuvres tray posing as a full meal, exists primarily to showcase the climactic biblical-style conflagration of the landowner's wheat fields— the light that nature, in all its awakened cruelty, sends off. In *The Thin Red Line*, which came twenty years after *Days of Heaven*, the strategies of war and the bearing of the soldiers pale beside the Rousseau-like idylls of Jim Caviezel (warming up to play Jesus?) cavorting with the uncorrupted Melanesians. For Malick, being AWOL is a state of grace.

The Native Americans in *The New World* are equally uncorrupted. Pocahontas certainly is—she's practically a woodland nymph. Despite his super-sophistication, Malick has a deeply childlike conception of innocence. This must be why his films, which are sensual in an almost pantheistic way, are nevertheless without a carnal dimension. There is no sex in his movies, not even in *Badlands* or *Days of Heaven*. Sex occupies a baser realm than the rarified one he inhabits. The real action for Malick is all in the head, in his characters' inner musings that crowd the soundtrack. A major problem with *The New World* is that, despite its visual ravishments and convincing note of woe, its people don't seem to have much going on between the ears (or, as I say, the legs).

Malick's films may not always live up to his mystique but it would be a major blow if he were to take another decade-long siesta. The freedom he incarnates as an artist is not something deserving only of nostalgia for a bygone era. What about our own era? Something is lost in a culture when artists are not allowed to make fools of themselves, because foolishness is often the flip side of greatness. Despite all the floss in his films, Malick has had his share of that, too. He has dedicated his life to his own exalted idea of beauty, where even the tiniest dabs of creation have oracular power, and he has given us images, like the torched house in *Badlands* or the long shot of the train in black silhouette against a powder-blue sky in *Days of Heaven*, that will resonate for as long as there are movies.

The best passages in Malick's films are all about paradise lost. His own career, with its inexplicable absences, represents another kind of loss. But he is still among us and his way of seeing is worth championing in these machine-tooled times.

(Los Angeles Times, 2006)

POSTSCRIPT

I've cooled some on Malick since I wrote this. His overpraised artwork *The Tree of Life* had far more foolishness than greatness. Framed as a movie about a troubled Texas family in the mid-fifties, it was a cinematic hit list of metaphysical imponderables complete with vast, gleaming recreations of the birth and death of the cosmos, solar nebulae, Ligeti, Berlioz, and Brahms, the Book of Job, dinosaurs, protozoa, and more flowing magma than you can shake a stick at. (It was like one of those old New York World's Fair family-of-man documentaries gone beserk.) By coupling all this primeval hoo-ha with a singular family tragedy, Malick was attempting to demonstrate the oneness of the universe, I suppose, but never has a human drama seemed punier in the scheme of things. His next film, *To the Wonder*, reportedly premiered to boos at the 2012 Venice Film Festival, which I thought promising. But it's a dud—a passionless passion play that plays like the B-side of *The Tree of Life*. Ben Affleck, whose role mostly consists of him wandering around dazed and near-mute in flat landscapes, was quoted, rightly, as saying the film makes *The Tree of Life* look like *Transformers*. Malick has another film, starring, among others, Ryan Gosling and Cate Blanchett, ready to roll. Making up for lost time, he's become the hardest-working man in show business.

BRIAN DE PALMA

Overview

"Nothing stays buried forever," says a cop in the new Brian De Palma thriller *The Black Dahlia*. This basic rule of homicide investigation also applies to De Palma's career. One of his very first movies was called *Murder à la Mod*, and the murders have continued almost unabated ever since. So have the exhumations.

In De Palma's House of Pain, corpses have a way of springing back to life, if only in fever dreams. In *Carrie*, Sissy Spacek's blood-soaked prom queen exerts her revenge from beyond the grave—or, to be more exact, from inside it. At the end of *Blow Out*, Nancy Allen's throttled death scream, recorded on a surveillance tape, pulls apart the psyche of the man who failed to save her, a sound recordist for cheapie horror movies played by John Travolta. At the end of *Casualties of War*, a slaughtered Vietnamese girl, or her lookalike, beckons Michael J. Fox's Eriksson, the man who failed to save her. In movie after movie, De Palma keeps returning to the scene of the crime—he digs up his obsessions and buries them and hauls them up again.

At sixty-six, De Palma has been at it a long time, since the mid-sixties. While the other major directors of his generation—Steven Spielberg, Martin Scorsese, Francis Ford Coppola—have ranged high and low, De Palma keeps hitting the same groove. Like Hitchcock, to whom he has often been compared, and not always favorably, his name represents a brand.

For all that, the dread he parlays has never quite devolved into shtick because, even in a film as roundly slammed and wildly unsatisfactory as *The Black Dahlia*, there are moments when his ecstatic love of filmmaking comes through. But his ardor can be a mixed blessing. De Palma's technique alone can hold you, but sometimes we must ask: Technique in the service of what?

In the mid-eighties he said in an interview, "I don't start with an idea about content. I start with a visual image." In the same interview, he said, "I'm interested in motion, sometimes violent motions, because they work aesthetically in film."

But surely this patter about pure cinema is a decoy. A sports film, for example, offers abundant opportunities for dynamic movement, and yet De Palma has never attempted one of those. As a rule, things really get rolling for him when his camera tracks are slicked with fresh blood. The fact that the blood most often belongs to women, who are perceived as prey, or that sex is often the lure for violence in his films, fouls the air.

In *Dressed to Kill*, probably his most controversial movie, an unhappily married woman played by Angie Dickinson has a hot tryst with a dark stranger and gets sliced to death in an elevator for her troubles. The camerawork throughout all this is—no other word for it—gorgeous. It's an emblematic sequence for De Palma and the sickest of jokes—sex, even good sex, can only end badly.

Despite the super-sophistication of his technique, in essence De Palma's movies express, at least for men in the audience, how sex was experienced as an adolescent. An early adolescent. They capture the rage and mortification, the guilt, the tingle of voyeurism. In *Carrie*, the slo-mo glide through the girl's locker room that opens the movie is every boy's porno fantasia.

One of the most unnerving things about De Palma's films, even more so than their eruptive, gargoyle terror, is the suggestion that these adolescent anxieties are naggingly ever-present. The tyranny of sexual desire, woman as the Other—for most men, these fears still fly. And because De Palma came of age as an artist in an consciousness-raising era when the women's movement was in full swing, he has always been the whipping boy of those who flaunt their liberal bona fides. It was predictable that *Femme Fatale*, his most recent movie before *The Black Dahlia*, would be cheered by his detractors, many of whom believe he is the ungodly creation of his greatest champion, Pauline Kael. Aside from being his best movie in years, it also showcased a rare species for De Palma—the sexually in-control female hero, the pansexual praying mantis.

Equally unnerving in his movies is the cackle often underscoring the terrors. In a De Palma movie, the worst-possible-case scenario is almost always the only scenario, and there's a kind of ghastly comic justice in that. Carrie isn't just humiliated at her prom, she's doused in pig's blood. In return, she incinerates her classmates.

In one of his early, revue-sketch movies, *Hi, Mom!*, De Palma stages a sequence that, for sheer satiric audacity, is unmatched by anything else of that era. A gaggle of white, liberal, middle-class theatergoers attend an off-off-Broadway happening called *Be Black, Baby* in which African-American militants, in whiteface, paint the audience members' faces black and proceed to school them in what it's like to be black. They're terrorized, brutalized; there's even a rape. When it's all over, the dazed but grateful playgoers give the evening high marks. "It really makes you stop and think," says one.

In his early prime, De Palma was singled out for opprobrium, it seemed, because he did extremely well what the schlock horror meisters, with their scantily clad victims and bogeymen, did badly. He was also, as the draft-dodger comedy *Greetings* and *Hi, Mom!* and the rock-horror jape *Phantom of the Paradise* showed, closer to the Zap Comix ethos than is generally recognized. (The peep-art porno maven played by Allen Garfield in *Hi, Mom!* could have stepped right out of the pages of Zap.) Like R. Crumb, with his pageant of brazen racial and sexual stereotypes, De Palma was unapologetically upfront about the lurid inappropriateness of his fantasy life.

Unlike Crumb, he doesn't always make it clear if he is "commenting" on those gonzo stereotypes or buying into them. Probably a little of both. But he is a much more calculating artist than Crumb, who is so entranced by his own perversities that he can't quite imagine anyone being shocked by them. De Palma, by contrast, always has his public in mind. The diabolical streak in his thrillers comes from the fact that he is not as shocked as we are about what he is showing us. And boy, does he want us to know it.

And yet there is much more to De Palma than puppetmastery, just as there was with Hitchcock, who suffered a similar criticism. The adverse comparisons to Hitchcock have for the most part been unfair. While it's true that the distinction between rip-off and homage is sometimes stretched a bit thin in De Palma's films—*Body Double*, that bargain bin *Rear Window*, comes to mind—the whole feeling tone of his movies is much more voluptuous and surreal and malign. With Hitchcock, no matter how garish he gets, even in *Psycho*, we are still in the hands of someone who regards the murder genre as a bad-mannered branch of British etiquette. The horror thriller, for him, represents an aesthetic conundrum to be worked out.

De Palma's thrillers, at least as a point of origin, are more temperamentally aligned with cheapo exploitation pictures and pulp fiction. His effrontery is that he can, sometimes, as in *Carrie* or *The Fury*, with its psychokinetic soulmates, make art from dross.

What happens to De Palma in these films is similar to what happens to Hitchcock in a film like *Vertigo*. The scaffolding of plot and logic fall away, and the movie seems to slide into a fugue state. It becomes almost suffocatingly personal. The real point of comparison between Hitchcock and De Palma may be this—the extreme rigor of their technique masks a deep derangement.

De Palma's movies are best when they spook him, too—when they inhabit his private places. He can turn out a highly slick entertainment like *Scarface*, *The Untouchables*, or *Carlito's Way*, and you can enjoy them without once believing they mean much of anything to the director. (It must tickle the creator of *Be Black, Baby* to know that *Scarface* has become a gangsta touchstone.)

Blow Out, often regarded as his masterpiece, is marred by an overreliance on penny dreadful plot twists once John Lithgow's bull goose loony appears on the scene. But it's still amazing. Of all De Palma's movies, it's the one that cuts closest to the bone. Travolta's performance may be a big reason. Playing the sound effects technician who accidentally witnesses a political assassination and can't save the girl he loves from its annihilating consequences, he is atrociously responsive to the director's torment. De Palma's movies are often riddled with dualities and doppelgangers, but in *Blow Out*, it is Travolta and De Palma who are in deep communion.

Filmed in his hometown of Philadelphia, the movie released something intensely private in him. The murders are often shot from very high up, from a vulture's perspective, as if to anatomize the obscenity. De Palma was a teenage physics whiz and several of his movies, especially *Dressed to Kill*, feature geeky boy geniuses. Piecing together the truth of the assassination from bits of sound and picture, Travolta's Jack is a kind of scientist, too, but the upshot of the movie is that in the end, science can't help you. The irrational will always trump the rational.

Some of the most powerful, and powerfully violent, American movies ever made—such as *Bonnie and Clyde* and *The Wild Bunch* and the *Godfather* films—are personally felt on a very deep level, and yet also seem to have a purchase on the zeitgeist. They express a national mood. De Palma's films are not like that. (Neither are the films of David Lynch, another fabulist of his own innerscape.) Even *Casualties of War*, which is based on the true account of the rape and murder of a Vietnamese girl by an American patrol, is less a movie about that war than it is a grandscale re-enactment of De Palma's recurring nightmare—the torture of not being able to rescue a loved one. The scene in which the girl is torn from her family for a little "portable R & R" is the most powerful sequence he has ever shot because for once, there is nothing standing between us and the horror, no cackles, no sleight of hand, no baroque frissons.

I do not mean to slight those ingredients. Back in 1978, coming off of *Carrie* and *The Fury*, De Palma said, "I imagine that in the next ten or twenty years I'll start moving into more intellectually complicated things." In fact, those films were plenty complicated; the insistently Catholic sense of dread in *Carrie*, with its almost hallucinatory imaginings of the wages of sin, is far more complex than most of what passes in the movies for "intellectual." One of the reasons that the arbiters of critical taste have not always given De Palma his due as an artist is because he has worked predominantly in disreputable genres.

But there is a case to made against De Palma for other reasons. His apprehension of the night doesn't allow much daylight to seep through. If Steven Spielberg in his *E.T.* and *Close Encounters of the Third Kind* days was our chief purveyor of transcendental goodness, De Palma's MO has been almost unrelentingly Manichean, with the dark side hogging all the glory. (Be black, baby, indeed.) As *The Black Dahlia* makes clear, a complacency has worked its way into De Palma's heart of darkness. The movie seems anestheticized by its own aura of menace.

Six years ago, De Palma made *Mission to Mars*, which alone among his films is supernally hopeful and was almost universally panned. Were the critics maybe expecting *Invaders From Mars*? Making his way in Hollywood through four decades, De Palma has had to try for the big score just like everybody else. *Mission: Impossible* was his penance for the debacle of *Bonfire of the Vanities*, and *The Black Dahlia* looks like an attempt to revive the De Palma brand. Compared to the overheated gore-o-ramas of David Fincher and Quentin Tarantino, his two most conspicuous acolytes, De Palma seems almost like a classic now. He's imprisoned by his own legend, but I'm betting he has the Houdini moves to escape and astonish us—astonish himself—once again. For a director who prizes resurrections, that would be the neatest trick of all.

(*Los Angeles Times*, 2006)

CHAPTER 4

STEVEN SPIELBERG

Overview

Steven Spielberg, who at twenty-two was hired by Universal to a long-term contract, started out his career as the teacher's pet of the Movie Brat generation. With the unveiling of his first Indiana Jones escapade in nineteen years today at Cannes, he's proferring yet another polished apple.

It's been something of a class reunion lately. Francis Coppola made his first film in ten years, *Youth Without Youth*, a muddled mood-memory fantasia that attempted to recapitulate the handmade approach of his *Rain People* days. Martin Scorsese brought out his Rolling Stones documentary *Shine a Light*, which harkened back to his apprenticeship as editor of rock documentaries like *Woodstock*. Brian De Palma made his Iraqi docu-thingamajig *Redacted*, which, in its shape-shifty experimentalism, recalled his earliest, French New Wave-influenced movies like *The Wedding Party* and *Hi, Mom!*

And now Spielberg is set to deliver the biggest blast from the past. *Indiana Jones and the Kingdom of the Crystal Skull* is not exactly the movie you might expect to follow *Munich*. But then again, he once shuttled between *Schindler's List* and *Jurassic Park*. Of his contemporaries, Spielberg has probably undergone the greatest sea change throughout his career. The *Indiana Jones* franchise, like the *Jurassic Park* movies, are a palate cleanser for him—a cackle in between epic kvells. For this teacher's pet, the class syllabus changed a long time ago.

The directors of Spielberg's generation who came up in the late sixties and early seventies, many of them film-school-trained, were the first in America to push their encyclopedic passion for movies right into the forefront of their work. Their rebellion against Old Hollywood was essentially a pose, since directors like John Ford, Howard Hawks, and

Frank Capra were mainstays of their mindscapes. Old movies functioned for these filmmakers as primary experiences—touchstones of inspiration—in the same way that poetry or literature might have functioned for an earlier generation of artists.

Not all of the movie references were drawn from favorite Hollywood films. De Palma had his Godard phase before he entered his Hitchcock phase; Coppola drew heavily on Visconti's *The Leopard* (for *The Godfather*) and Antonioni's *Blow-Up* (for *The Conversation*). Scorsese's *Mean Streets* is bloodbrother to Fellini's *I Vitelloni* and owes a debt to the scruffy free-form spirit of the John Cassavetes indies. Even George Lucas, in his chilly debut feature *THX 1138*, piled on the art-house references to Jean Cocteau (*Blood of a Poet*) and Carl Theodore Dreyer (*The Passion of Joan of Arc*).

Spielberg, however, came from a somewhat different place. He never officially attended a major film school. His heroes were the big-picture guys like David Lean and Stanley Kubrick, or versatile old studio hands like Michael Curtiz and Victor Fleming—directors who could be counted on to deliver a reliable commercial entertainment (and sometimes more than that). While many of his seventies confederates, who also were to include such directors as Terrence Malick, Jonathan Demme, and Philip Kaufman, were attempting to work outside the industry, or subvert it from within through sheer force of artistry, Spielberg was directing episodes of *Night Gallery* and *Marcus Welby, M.D.* and then moving on to sharks and flying saucers.

In the more "serious" film circles, his prodigious filmmaking skills were held against him as proof that he lacked substance. Even Pauline Kael, his most ardent critical champion early on, wrote of his uncommonly touching first feature *The Sugarland Express*: "Maybe Spielberg loves action and comedy and speed so much that he really doesn't care if a movie has anything else in it. I can't tell if he has any mind, or even a strong personality, but then a lot of good movie-makers have got by without being profound."

And of course, as Spielberg began to rake in the riches, this was held against him, too. It has always been a truism of popular culture, no more so than in the seventies, that artistry and commercial success are mutually exclusive. And where exceptions to this rule were made, as in the case of the *Godfather* films, it was because they were recognized as gangster films in name only. They were really about the corruption of the American dream. Spielberg's early movies are rife with broken families and intimations of child abandonment, but they are glittery baubles when placed beside the dungeonlike Coppola and Scorsese pictures (especially the *Godfather* films, *Mean Streets*, *Taxi Driver*, and *Raging Bull*) with their floridly Catholic sense of sin and redemption. Spielberg, by comparison, at least up through *The Color Purple*, specialized in uplift, in the exaltation of the American dream. He himself became its personification.

Spielberg's "personality" does indeed come through loud and clear in those early films—*Sugarland Express*, *Jaws*, *Close Encounters of the Third Kind*, and *E.T.*—because of his delight, which we share, in how preposterously wizardly he is. Spielberg's genius was not simply to think like his audience—any good hack can do that—but to *be* his audience. His aesthetic instincts and his commercial instincts were twinned, and not in a calculating way, either—at least not until *Raiders of the Lost Ark*, which is when his large-scale entertainments, followed by the two *Indiana Jones* sequels and the *Jurassic Park* movies, turned into corporate theme parks themselves.

The career trajectory of Hollywood directors before the seventies typically followed the winding path from unpretentious to "prestigious" (i.e. Oscar-worthy). Take, for example, George Stevens, who went from *Alice Adams*, *Swing Time*, *Gunga Din*, and *The More the Merrier* to *A Place in the Sun*, *Giant*, *The Diary of Anne Frank*, and *The Greatest Story Ever Told*. Most of the seventies directors did their best to avoid this syndrome, or at least held out for as long as they could. Coppola's *Apocalypse Now*, a deranged movie about a deranged war, could never have been mistaken for a respectable war epic. Scorsese's biblical movie was *The Last Temptation of Christ*.

But Spielberg, being the most attuned of his generation to the mojo of Hollywood, was naturally the director who most wholeheartedly fell into the prestige trap. Whatever their merits, and in some cases they are considerable, films like *The Color Purple*, *Empire of the Sun*, *Schindler's List*, *Amistad*, *Saving Private Ryan*, and *Munich* are all deeply conventional in terms of how the world is comprehended. Some of these films may be better made, or, in the case of *Schindler's List*, more richly felt than their Old Hollywood counterparts. But all are afflicted with a kind of transcendent Stanley Kramerism. We are made to understand that moral lessons are being imparted and that, in the end, tomorrow will somehow be a better day.

And yet, Spielberg's career trajectory is by no means simple, for in the wake of *Saving Private Ryan*, he made two consecutive films, as well as a third several years later, that in many ways upend his beloved early work. *A.I.*, which was originally developed by Stanley Kubrick, is the dark side of *E.T.*, and *War of the Worlds* is the anti-*Close Encounters of the Third Kind*. The Philip K. Dick-derived *Minority Report*, which has no antecedent in Spielberg's career, is a scabrous freakout. None of these films are over-whelmingly successful—they're more fascinating as psychodrama than as drama. But they demonstrate, much more so than his "prestige" entries do, how spooked Spielberg's mind-set had become since he closed *Close Encounters* with a stirring snatch of "When You Wish Upon A Star."

In *Close Encounters*, aliens from outer space are benevolent emissaries who descend from the heavens in a dazzling cathedral glow and belt out boom tones of peace and love. In *War of the Worlds*, the aliens are arachnoid horrors who erupt from underground. Their call to arms is a bellicose bellow. The skies may have roiled in *Close Encounters* and Richard Dreyfuss's Roy might have made too much of his mashed potatoes, but we were never in any doubt that benevolence was upon us.

In *War of the Worlds*, the aliens initially are mistaken for terrorists. The film is, I suppose, Spielberg's post-9/11 movie, but even without 9/11 he might eventually have made his way to this scorched terrain. *A.I.*, which was made four years earlier, is about a robot boy who yearns to be human in order to win back the love of the flesh and blood mother who abandoned him, and for most of the way it's frighteningly creepy. *Minority Report*, about a future where cops, guided by all-seeing "pre-cogs," arrest killers before their crimes are committed, is a ghastly fusion of sci-fi and noir.

Some audiences, still wishing upon a star, experienced these films as intimate betrayals. And yet they cut the closest to his psyche. *Minority Report* specializes in shots of severed eyeballs—it's practically a motif. The most visually dynamic director of his generation wants to know what's it's like to fly blind. That's what repels him—and attracts him. "Right now I'm experimenting," Spielberg said at the time of *Minority Report*. "I'm trying things that challenge me, I'm striking out in all directions, trying to discover myself in my fifties."

For a director of conscience who can make his camera do anything, the realization that he has it in him to inspire absolute dread must be supremely unsettling. (I'm not thinking of *Jaws,* which was comic-book dread.) What surely must prey upon Spielberg as he gets older are not the bliss-outs he is uniquely capable of creating, but the horrors. The Normandy Beach landing in *Saving Private Ryan* goes way beyond the usual technical exercise; it's a fury against the flesh. In *Minority Report,* Tom Cruise's John Anderton, the chief of the Department of Pre-Crime in the District of Columbia, stands before a floating computer interface and, arms waving like an impresario, whisks around its mid-air crime scene visuals. It's a nightmare representation of the director as puppetmaster, and it comes with a kicker: Anderton, whose mind is a mausoleum of horrific images, is himself a murderer-to-be.

The filmmakers of Spielberg's generation wanted to take over Hollywood and change the face of an art form. And for a brief period, until the blockbuster syndrome kicked in in the mid-seventies, they did just that. Along with Lucas, Spielberg is often blamed for shutting down the renaissance, as if without *Jaws* and *Star Wars*, it would never have occurred to anybody in Hollywood to come up with high concepts and saturation marketing. "I hate Spielberg," a young filmmaker told me at a movie festival recently when he heard I was going to be writing about him. "He killed the indie film." And then he added, "But I loved *Jaws.*"

Spielberg has long been in a position to pretty much direct or produce whatever he wants. This makes him the only kind of auteur Hollywood truly understands. (Forget the Lubitsch touch—it's the Midas touch that makes the studio chiefs slobber.) He's taken more creative chances than any other director of close to his clout. Early films like *E.T.* and *Close Encounters* were experienced by audiences all over the world as invocations to a more ecstatic life. Plus they were playful and goofy. But there was no safety net for *Schindler's List*, and neither was there one for *Amistad* or *A.I.*

This doesn't mean Spielberg gets a free pass. Some of the cottages in his cottage industry have all the allure of McMansions. He has yet to make a movie that revels in the commonplace; for him, the ordinary is always (yawn) a springboard to magic. He has never made a movie with more than a trace of carnality. His world view is cut-rate Manichean— darks and lights and not much gray in between. It's a pity he shelved his plans to make a movie about his childhood idol, Charles Lindbergh, the all-American aviator and Fascist sympathizer. Now there's a character who would have put Spielberg to the test. Instead, he's gearing up to make *Lincoln* with Liam Neeson, which sounds like a snooze. And *Jurassic 4* is on the radar.

Spielberg is still the teacher's pet of his class, but the difference is that now he owns the schoolhouse. Maybe for a while he should try being a truant.

(Los Angeles Times, 2008)

POSTSCRIPT

Indiana Jones and the Kingdom of the Crystal Skull was a thrill-less thrill ride. Spielberg is still planning to make *Jurassic 4*. *The Adventures of Tintin* transferred his mania for graphic storytelling into the realm of motion-capture 3-D, but the results were mostly second-tier *Raiders*-style derring-do. In *War Horse*, with its picture-book imagery derived from David Lean and John Ford, he milked each scene for maximum memorability. The results were gigantic and generic. *Lincoln*, starring Daniel Day-Lewis, was respectable in a Golden Age of Hollywood sort of way, but I wish it had been more daring both as a piece of filmmaking and as an evocation of history. Lincoln's complicated attitudes toward slavery and the emancipation of blacks are streamlined and cleaned up for popular consumption. The film is best when it is at its most allusive. As I wrote in the *Christian Science Monitor*:

> Spielberg's films have often, if indirectly, been about the consequences of absent fathers on a family. There are times in *Lincoln* when our not-always-entirely-honest Abe is, in a sense, absent to himself. In some of the film's most mysteriously moving sequences, he appears while in mixed company to suddenly waft into some dark and private precinct. When Spielberg allows these silences—when for example, he simply shows us Lincoln slowly sauntering away from us down an unpeopled corridor—the film achieves a spooky eminence. Suddenly it becomes more than a history lesson, however well-crafted and

researched. It becomes a meditation on the unknowability of great men, of all men.

Indiana Jones and the Temple of Doom

For its first twenty minutes or so, I was convinced that *Indiana Jones and the Temple of Doom* was going to be deliriously enjoyable entertainment. (It's set in 1935, a year before *Raiders of the Lost Ark*, so I suppose it's a "prequel.") We initially see Harrison Ford's Indiana in a white dinner jacket, in a fancy Shanghai nightclub, as he barters with three Chinese meanies—they'll give him the antidote to the poison he just drank in exchange for the walnut-sized diamond in his coat pocket. In the ensuing tussle, both the diamond and the antidote vial go skittering across the floor, along with practically everyone else in the nightclub. Bales of balloons and spilled ice cubes confound the search; so does a gold-digger chanteuse named Willie (Kate Capshaw), who opens the film in a sequin-encrusted gown warbling Cole Porter's "Anything Goes" in Mandarin against a chintzy-musical production-number backdrop. The action swivels and swirls with such breakneck finesse that it's both great action-adventure filmmaking and a great satire of action-adventure movies. We laugh at the majestically facile pyrotechnics. Steven Spielberg, who directed this George Lucas production from a script by Willard Huyck and Gloria Katz, knows how to make an action scene snap, crackle, and pop, with each shot lasting not a millisecond longer than necessary. (His editor here is the wizardly Michael Kahn.) When Indy and Willie tumble out of the nightclub and into the jitney of Indy's sidekick, a twelve-year-old Chinese orphan nicknamed Short Round (Ke Huy Quan), the chase is on, and it speeds along for ten minutes in an unbroken arc with the help of a pilotless plane, an inflatable river raft, raging rapids, and steep cliffs, before finally setting down in an impoverished Indian village.

That's when the film gets into trouble. Up until this point, the movie has a breathless ease; the filmmakers have crammed a half-dozen classic perilous escape-and-chase scenes into such a short time span that we giggle at the sheer improbability of the feat. The opening number—"Anything Goes"—is certainly appropriate to the action, and we look forward to more of it. We look forward to seeing how Spielberg will top himself. But the action bogs down fairly early on; except for a rollercoaster-ride scene in a mine-shaft near the end, Spielberg never does equal his opening. But he certainly tries to, and the way he goes about it is perversely wrongheaded. Instead of the whiz-bang free-spiritedness of the intro, Spielberg settles into a story that's replete with crushings, whippings, maimings, torchings, and gougings. And he *lingers* on this material. It's as if all of his filmmaker's energy had turned mean-spirited and bilious.

This movie is not a "darker" version of *Raiders of the Lost Ark*; it does not, as some have been saying, bear the same relationship to *Raiders* that *The Empire Strikes Back* had to *Star Wars*. *Empire*, directed by Irvin Kershner, had a fullness of feeling that raised emotion to almost mythic heights. It was a great piece of magical filmmaking. But *Indiana Jones* is simply another piffle—only it's a poisonous piffle. There's less concentration on Indiana Jones's character quirks, less humor, and even less romantic spirit than in *Raiders*—that is to say, there's hardly any romance at all. That lack of spirit made the first film exhausting after a while; watching it was like watching a feature-length trailer. But at least *Raiders moved*; it covered a dizzying number of locations. *Indiana* stays put in the Temple of Doom for most of the movie and, after a while, you don't really care whether Mola Ram or Chattar Lal or the other Kali cult villains get offed or not. You don't even care whether the Indian children who have been beaten and imprisoned in the temple are saved. You just want *out*.

The liberation of these children, who have been stolen by the malevolent neighboring denizens of the Palace of Pankot from that impoverished Indian village, is ostensibly the movie's driving force. Even though Indiana claims he's only interested in recovering the village's sacred stone from the palace's temple, it's the recovery of the children that fuels his mission. Before he sets out on elephants to the palace, along with the reluctant, pampered Willie and the feisty Short Round, there's a scene that clinches Indiana's resolve. At night, the withered potentates of the village tell him that ever since their sacred stone and their children were stolen, nothing grows in the soil anymore. The place is like an Indian, death-rattled version of Hamelin after the Pied Piper lured all the children away. And then a starving Indian boy—an escapee, apparently, from the Temple of Doom—staggers onto the scene and collapses in Indy's arms. It's a strong sequence, but I also couldn't help wondering—how did they make that poor boy look so convincingly emaciated? Was he starved for the role, or was he already starving? It's indicative of the movie's numbing, literal-minded horrors that such a question is even raised.

Even if one accepts this movie's percussive, brutal techniques, it really doesn't work on its own terms. Indiana Jones wasn't exactly a hero-for-the-ages in *Raiders*, but here, he's not given much more to do than scowl and look raggedy (except for that white-suited entrance in Shanghai, where he out-debonairs 007). Harrison Ford, like Spielberg, seems to have channeled his energies into something sourish and nasty this time out—maybe that was the only way he could troop through yet another of these kiddie escapades and still keep his self-respect. Ford must realize that this movie really isn't designed for actors, and he's too good (and too unrecognized) an actor not to feel the constraint. So he plays Indiana sullen and nasty. With his battered, dusty fedora and ripped brown leather jacket, Indy is a bit like Fred C. Dobbs in *The Treasure of Sierra Madre*, right down to the sneaky glint of psychopathology in the eyes. With a little limbering up, Clint Eastwood could have played this role.

Raymond Chandler once said that he had a foolproof prescription for holding his readers' attention—whenever the story flagged, he'd throw in a dead body. In a way, the Chandler principle is at work in *Indiana Jones*. When Indiana and his cohorts have dinner in the palace, which is presided over by a boy rajah, the feast is live snakes, eyeball soup, chilled monkey brains. When Indiana finds a hidden passageway into the Temple of Doom, it's not unsurprising that Spielberg festoons the darkness with spikes and skeletons and every imaginable variety of creepy-crawler. When Indiana observes from afar a sacrificial rite in the Temple of Doom, we get close-ups of a man's heart being ripped out by the hands of a high-priest; then the man, still alive, is pinioned inside a mechanical cage and slowly lowered into a molten vortex. Later on, there are scenes of the chained Indian children being flogged; when Willie and Indiana are captured, we get to go through the heart-wrenching, char-broiled stuff all over again.

The "light" touches in this film are so infrequent that they almost feel like sops to the audience: Indiana whisking his beloved fedora at the last second out from under a descending wall of spikes; a contentious bedroom bartering scene between Indiana and Willie, as close as this film comes to romantic high spirits (they sleep in separate bedrooms in the palace, and, in her silk pj's, she bets him that it won't be five minutes before he's knocking down her door); a few moments between Indiana and Short Round (marvelously played by little Ke Huy Quan), whose New York Giants cap is as indispensable to him as Indy's fedora. (Short Round, incidentally, is an homage to the boy of the same name in Samuel Fuller's *China Gate*.) These moments aren't necessarily any better executed than the brutal material, but at least they have a whiff of human emotion to them. They freshen up the fetid air inside the palace.

As fairy tales go, *Indiana Jones* isn't necessarily much more brutal than some of the great Grimm stories, or even parts of Disney's *Bambi* and *Dumbo*, for that matter. And I don't doubt that some teenagers will gulp down the violence with the same thirst that they, and older audiences, display for slash-and-splatter movies. But that doesn't necessarily justify what the filmmakers have perpetrated here. Aside from the fact that most of the under-ten crowd will probably (as the movie ads warn) find this PG-rated film "too intense," it is, I think, irresponsible to cook up such a cauldron of violence for young audiences—or old audiences, for that matter.* (I gather adults aren't supposed to find hearts being pulled out of chests "too intense.") If you argue that fairy tales are inherently violent (as they often are), and that, as long as things end happily, violence in fairy tales can actually be cathartic (as some child psychologists do argue), then what is there to prevent filmmakers like Spielberg and Lucas from perpetrating even more vicious movies with a clean conscience? They are using the fairy-tale trappings of *Indiana Jones* as a license to kill—so to speak.

And *Indiana Jones* isn't even a good fairy tale. Its imagery and terrors don't have the force of the unconscious behind them; they're machine-tooled, which makes them seem even more calculatedly sadistic, since they don't appear to issue from human anguish. (The violence in this movie isn't so much scary as disgusting; as a comparison of *E.T.* and *Poltergeist* also bears out, Spielberg is much better at childhood wonderment than childhood fright.) In a good fairy tale, villainy has its attractions, goodness has its luster; but in *Indiana Jones*, Indy is a disgruntled misfit and Kate Capshaw, with her goldilocked resemblance to Mariette

---

* The outcry from this film was instrumental in the creation of the new PG-13 rating.

Hartley and Cathy Lee Crosby, is TV-bland and too eighties for this thirties setting. The villains aren't attractive, they're just baldpated ogres. As
Bruno Bettelheim has written, a classic fairy tale is structured so as to
give a child a way of understanding himself through the painful progress
of the story. A child looks to a fairy tale, however subconsciously, for a
clue to the meaning of life. In *Indiana Jones*, Short Round is in the movie
to give kids someone to identify with, but it's not his movie—it's not his
story. The best that can be said for Short Round, in fairy-tale terms, is
that he ultimately survives because of his love for Indiana. But a child
looking at this film for more than fun-house carnage is going to be very
disappointed. Has Steven Spielberg joined the dark side of the Force?

(*Los Angeles Herald Examiner*, 1984)

The Color Purple

The Color Purple is supposed to be Steven Spielberg's Big One. After a
decade of making audiences by the millions duck spears and sharks and
killer trucks and goblins and UFOs, after a nonpareil career as a won-
der-boy conjurer, he's decided to make a movie about adults, and not *just*
adults—*black* adults. Poor people. In the Deep South. His source material, Alice Walker's prize-winning, highly acclaimed 1982 novel, *The Color
Purple*, is his latchkey to grown-up respectability.

In Hollywood, respectability and awards go hand in hand, or, to be
more precise, fist in glove. Spielberg is the most commercially successful
film director ever, but the one jewel missing in his crown is an Oscar for
best director. (He wasn't even nominated for *Jaws*.)

The Color Purple is ostensibly about the ordeal of being a black woman in the South in the first half of this century. But the movie is really
about winning awards. Every scene is slicked up to be a stunner, no stop is
left unpulled, no camera move is left untracked. What's missing is a deep,
resounding reason to have made this film *for its own sweet self*.

The Color Purple is, after all, a modest story (so was *Sounder*). It's
emotionally complex, but in ways that have nothing to do with Spielberg's grandstanding. The film may get to the blubberers in the audience,

but there's something vital missing in this movie—a trace of genuine feeling, perhaps?

Alice Walker's short novel is mostly structured as a series of letters written by Celie, an illiterate black woman, to God and, later on, to her younger sister, Nettie, from whom she was separated in her teens and who, it is later revealed, became a missionary in Africa. (Nettie's letters to Celie fill out the rest of the book.)

Celie's down-home vernacular has a poetic lilt that keeps you reading. The book may be overextended and drenched in sisterhood-is-beautiful sloganeering, but it has an emotional core: Celie the battened-down ugly-duckling survivor with her huge capacity for love.

Without Celie's words to carry you into her thoughts, the movie, despite the occasional voice-over narration, lacks a vital center. As played by Whoopi Goldberg, in her screen debut, Celie is a heroine to whom everything *happens*. For a long time she seems not just ignorant and abused, but genuinely stunted. This may be Spielberg's political point—oppression infantilizes—but we don't get too many of the little tip-offs that might tell us this woman actually harbors a cagey, formidable mind. That's what's so funny about the book—Celie may come off like an ignorant dumbbell, but she knows what's what, and then some. She has a bead on everybody.

Whoopi Goldberg has a marvelous face, with surprising depths and hollows. The clear, sad eyes don't go with the scrunched, naughty kid's grin that sometimes breaks through; neither does the spooky sensuality of her low, rough voice. (Spielberg, who has found fame as the movie's foremost man/child, may have been attracted to these contrary qualities in her.)

I've seen Goldberg's one-woman Broadway show on HBO, and it's clear that she is immensely talented, that she carries around almost as many characters close to her heart as Richard Pryor. She gives the only remarkable performance in this movie. But we don't get to see too many emotions play across her face in *The Color Purple*. We don't even get to *see* much of her face; it's often hung low, deadened by the movie's beanbag approach to her character. Celie is the sorrowing sister of us all, but Spielberg doesn't give her enough nerve endings or smarts to draw us to her.

When the movie begins, Celie, sexually abused by her father—she bore him two children, which he quickly sold—is married off to Albert

(Danny Glover), a brutish widower with four kids who treats her like a rag mop. Albert is hot for Nettie (Akosua Busia), who joins Celie for a while to escape her father's advances. When she refuses Albert—in the umpteenth knee-to-the-groin sequence this year—he banishes her from Celie's life forever in a real soundtrack sweller of a scene. (Quincy Jones's prestige-picture score is like aural elevator shoes.) Albert spends most of his time loafing while Celie works his land, pack-horse style; the only thing he gets worked up about is Shug Avery (Margaret Avery), a sassy blues singer whom his father forbade him to marry.

When Albert brings a soused Shug back home to live with him, Celie isn't miffed; after all, she doesn't love Albert. She's mesmerized by this woman; she combs her hair and bathes her and carries her bags. And Shug, almost alone among the people in the movie, recognizes Celie's worth. In one of the few emotionally affecting scenes in the film, Shug, back on her feet and belting out the blues in a local dive, sings a tribute to Celie, and we can see Celie's face beneath her old woman's hat melt into a deep, stunned happiness.

Celie falls in love with Shug. In the novel, that love is consummated, but Spielberg keeps things patty-cake ambiguous—he doesn't want to alienate audiences with any distaff dalliance. Celie and Shug do a lot of dressing up and giggling together. This non-sexual affair might have worked if Spielberg had made it clear that Celie's love for Shug was, in a sense, a transference of her unrequited love for Nettie. But once Nettie is gone from the movie, we don't sense Celie's abiding love for her, or her faith that she still exists out there somewhere. (Celie doesn't find out about the Africa missionary stuff until much later, when she and Shug discover that Albert's been hiding Nettie's letters to her for years.)

We also don't feel Celie's love for Shug, even though that love is supposed to be central to the movie. But how *can* it be when that love is so watered down? What does Celie think about having Shug shacked up with Albert in her own house? No anger, no jealousy comes into play; Shug doesn't seem too concerned, either.

It's typical of *The Color Purple* that no one acts on his or her emotions in a way that makes psychological sense. Albert's children, who must be aware of their father's brutalization of Celie, are virtually uncharacterized; they're tiny-tot decor. When Celie finds out about Nettie's hidden letters, she strops a razor in preparation for shaving the blithely unaware

Albert, and you expect her to slit his throat—or at least have it out with him. Instead, Spielberg turns the scene into an anticlimactic downer. (He intercuts between the shave and scenes in Africa involving the ritual scarring of native children. The crosscutting is flashy and, typically, makes not a tad of sense.) The real payoff comes later on, when it no longer carries a charge. When Celie discovers near the end that the father who raped her was, in fact, only her stepfather, there should be rage—and horror—at that revelation, too.

What these scenes demonstrate is that Spielberg can't connect with the explosiveness of someone who carries around a gutbucket of rage inside her. He can connect only with the abiding love. But without the hatred that goes with the love, Celie's story—the whole story of blacks in this country—is defused.

It's true that Spielberg allows himself an assortment of villains in this film—namely, all male blacks and all whites—but the portrayals are so lacking in real rage that they seem whittled down and cartoony. He can't totally tap into Alice Walker's polemic of hate—which is maybe just as well. What remains of her conception in the film is still obnoxious. Her novel is, among other things, a hate letter to male oppression—specifically, black male oppression. And that includes African males—the patriarchal conspiracy is total. Black men in this movie are apparently not victims of racism. They are males before they're black, and that maleness indicts them. *The Color Purple* may be the first film where black men in the audience will want to slink out of the theater with the same anonymity whites sought at the black exploitation films a decade ago.

Celie is a feminist precursor; she wears a bloody bandanna around her head during forced coitus like a red badge of courage. And she finally receives her redemption through sisterhood; Shug, Nettie, Celie's daughter-in-law, Sofia (Oprah Winfrey), and the aspiring singer Squeak (Rae Dawn Chong) all lean into the wind like the prows of boats waiting to be swept into the clouds.

Some artists are capable of creating "children's" stories and drawing on the full range of adult emotions in a way they might not have been able to do in a more "adult" setting. Spielberg may be just such an artist. There's far more depth of feeling in *E.T.* than there is in *The Color Purple*. He also has a great comic sense, but Oscar-itis has sapped it. Has there ever been a movie with so many blacks in the cast that was this unjoyous?

If Spielberg thinks his people are too pained to laugh and whoop it up, not just in honky-tonks but in their mundane day-to-day lives, he doesn't know what black survival is all about.

Spielberg doesn't extend his imagination in *The Color Purple*, and it exposes him. He hasn't lived long enough in the right places to put this story across. In the end, all that's missing from the huggy-kissy happy-ending tableau is a shot of Uncle Remus and Brer Rabbit hopping toward the horizon.

(*Los Angeles Herald Examiner*, 1985)

Why the *Schindler's List* Backlash?

Schindler's List has won the best picture award from all three major film critics' societies, so it's not surprising a backlash should set in. Highly acclaimed movies usually inspire counterinsurgencies, and sometimes the back talk is even justified; critics groups, along with the Academy of Motion Picture Arts and Sciences, have a way of favoring the safe and respectable over the innovative and the disreputable. But the *Schindler's List* backlash is somewhat unique for appearing to be less a corrective to the overpraise than a cry of betrayal.

It's one thing to argue that *Schindler's List* is something less than a masterpiece. I would concur in that. As powerful as it is, it's a bit too buffed and noble, it doesn't have the clarifying transcendence of great art.

But the outrage goes deeper. What the naysayers are saying is that Steven Spielberg has, in the words of the *Village Voice*'s Jim Hoberman, "Spielbergized" the Holocaust. He's made "a feel-good entertainment about the ultimate feel-bad experience of the twentieth century." Hoberman—who at least has the distinction, along with the *New Republic*'s Leon Wieseltier, of writing the film's best knock—also writes: "The poster of a father grasping a child's hand is not the only aspect of *Schindler's List* that recalls *E.T.*"

Frank Rich, in the *New York Times*, refers to the scene where Oskar Schindler "gives a sentimental speech to the Jewish factory workers he saved, and they look up at him awe-struck, as if he were the levitating mother ship in *Close Encounters of the Third Kind*." (Wieseltier's piece is titled "Close Encounters of the Nazi Kind.") Excepting Ben Kingsley's Jewish accountant, Rich describes the other Jewish characters as "generic"—"as forgettable as the chorus in a touring company of *Fiddler on the Roof* or, for that matter, the human dino-fodder of *Jurassic Park*."

One would like to put these critics to the test—if it could be rigged to show that an unremarked young American or British director had made *Schindler's List*, would the references to the mother ship in *Close Encounters* or *E.T.* spring so readily to mind? One of the real-life Schindler survivors said of Schindler, "He was our everything, our mother, our father, our savior," and her remark is representative. This closing moment in the movie is appropriately full of awe because so were the Jews in the presence of the man who finally saved them.

Can anybody look at this film and seriously assume Spielberg invested the same emotional energy in characterizing its Jewish protagonists as he did in knocking over the screamers in *Jurassic Park*? Rich wishes that the Schindler Jews were as "individually and intimately dramatized as Anne Frank or even Meryl Streep's *Sophie*," but, of course, Anne Frank is symbolic if any human being ever was, and, as long as we're overcorrecting, Sophie the Auschwitz survivor was Gentile, not Jewish.

This "generic" rap against the Jews in *Schindler's List* doesn't allow for its many piercing moments of human loss. How can it be said that the Jewish maid of the mad Nazi Amon Goeth is just a generic blur? Her hair-trigger terror around Goeth, her shuddering self-will, is entirely specific to her predicament. When the Jewish servant boy of Goeth is at first "pardoned" for failing to remove a bathtub ring and then, almost as an afterthought, shot in the back, the moment is casually horrific. Like so much in the film, the death belongs to the individual but it has a collective horror. There's no way to dramatize the Holocaust without invoking this collectivity; each death assumes millions.

Behind these criticisms may lie the deeper conviction that the Holocaust should not be dramatized at all—by anybody; that, however, one does so is a disservice, an obscenity. This is not a new concept. Jonathan Kirsch, in his pan of *Schindler's List* in the *Jewish Journal*, quotes Theodor Adorno: "After Auschwitz, to write a poem is barbaric." That may be so, but isn't it also essential? And can one rule out dramatizations of the Holocaust as somehow beyond the grasp of art without also ruling out *all* dramatizations of life's horrors? Is *Schindler's List* any less defensible than, say, *Gettysburg*?

Kirsch compares the scene in the film where a trainload of women are mistakenly routed to Auschwitz to *The Perils of Pauline*. Fearing they will be gassed, the women are shaved and herded into the showers. But they are not gassed. Hoberman calls the sequence, with its "thriller suspense and last-minute rescue," the film's "nadir." So now Spielberg's narrative gifts—the same gifts that brought him to the preeminent position to make a Holocaust movie, in black-and-white, in Hollywood—are being held against him. (Charles Dickens employed suspense and last-minute rescues for emotional effect too. Why the double standard?)

The sequence in question actually happened—it's there in the Thomas Keneally book from which it's adapted—but its expansion in the movie is denounced as a way of giving aid and comfort to the enemy. "Why," asks Kirsch, "did [Spielberg] play out an elaborate scene in which the fundamental premise of the Holocaust deniers—no gas chambers actually existed—is played out in vivid and explicit detail?"

But Spielberg doesn't deny their existence. As Kirsch himself notes, in the next scene we see the ashes from a crematory wafting into the night sky. Is there anyone who can watch this shower scene—which expresses the redemptive miracle these women experienced as "Schindler Jews"—in the context of the entire movie and believe Auschwitz was anything but a charnel house?

Well, the Holocaust-deniers could. But why frame your movie to refute them when logic plays no part in their thinking anyway? *Schindler's List* may deal with a monumental insanity but it should not be faulted for speaking to the sane.

Spielberg comes out of a popular tradition of movie-making that binds audiences with shared emotions—whether it be uplift or terror. There have been great renderings of the Holocaust—ranging from the documentaries *Night and Fog* and *Shoah* to Primo Levi's *Survival in Auschwitz* and Art Spiegelman's *Maus*—that were not pitched for the mass audience. Spielberg, however, at his best, is a popular entertainer with a gift—a genius—for moving audiences simply and directly. (At his worst he's a nerveless enchanter.) There is nothing esoteric or ruminative about *Schindler's List*. Like Keneally's extraordinary book, the film works up its power by an inexorable accumulation of events that adds up to a complete vision of hell.

Spielberg's popularized technique in this film is there to make us see *more* of that vision, not less. And he doesn't popularize indiscriminately. We are never made to understand why Oskar Schindler, the Nazi war profiteer, risked his life to save more than 1,200 Jews; there is no defining *Aha!* moment that accounts for his heroism. It's a mystery, and Spielberg, like Keneally, honors that mystery by refusing to "explain" it. He also doesn't try to "explain" Amon Goeth, for to do so would be to "explain" the vicious riddle of Nazism—a riddle far greater than Schindler's.

Writing of the film in the Jewish daily newspaper the *Forward*, Ilene Rosenzweig says, "Given a chance to project to the world an image of Jewish life. Hollywood's undisputed box-office king chooses one of humiliation and death." In a commentary on the film in the *Times*, Rabbi Eli Hecht wrote, "I am sick and tired of this generation identifying Judaism with suffering."

In other words, it is bad PR to express the sufferings of the Jewish people; better to forget. This is a dreamland concoction far more dangerous and denying than anything Spielberg is accused of. (And, in this age of ethnic cleansing, it also implies the lessons of the Holocaust only apply to Jews.) As one *Times* reader wrote in response to the rabbi's piece, "Does Rabbi Hecht propose that, as Jews, we let Passover and Purim rest along with the Holocaust?"

Should *Never Again* become *Never Mind*?

It's also considered bad PR for a movie about the Holocaust to feature a non-Jew. "Unafraid to accentuate the positive," writes Hoberman, "*Schindler's List* necessarily focuses on Gentiles." Rosenzweig writes, "A reluctant Christian rescuer is a curious choice for Hollywood's definitive Holocaust hero."

This is an argument based on the needs of propaganda, not drama. Schindler saved over 1,200 Jewish lives, and the survivors' offspring account for many thousands more; he was honored as a Righteous Gentile in Jerusalem's Yad Vashem Holocaust Museum. The concept of the Righteous Gentile in Rabbinic literature predates Maimonides—it needs no defense now.

Rosenzweig sums up *Schindler's List* as a "feel good movie of Christian redemption and Jewish defeat." But this assumes that Schindler's fate and the fate of the Jews were not entwined; that their redemption was not mutual. Is it blasphemous to suggest that one can feel happiness at the end of a Holocaust movie if, in the end, thousands of Jews are saved? Their rescue does not deny the fate of the six million who were not rescued. Quite the contrary; *Schindler's List* derives its power precisely from how abjectly exceptional its story is. The most damning criticism made against the film is that it gussies up the Holocaust by framing it as a scenario of salvation. But lives *were* saved. They, too, deserve—even require—memorialization.

(Los Angeles Times, 1993)

Amistad

Steven Spielberg's *Amistad* is being given the Big Picture treatment—*Schindler's List* Big, not *Jurassic Park* Big. Last week's *Newsweek* featured the film on its cover, calling it "Spielberg's controversial new movie," even though it had not yet been released and the only "controversy" was a legal one about alleged cribbing by the screenwriter David Franzoni from the similarly themed novel *Echo of Lions*.

In fact, Spielberg's film—about the 1839 revolt of fifty-three Africans aboard the Spanish slave ship *La Amistad* and their subsequent capture and trials in America—is designed to be *un*controversial. It's not a work of great imagination or depth or historical feeling; except in its harrowing depiction of the Middle Passage, it doesn't try to offer up a view of race or slavery that might powerfully challenge audiences, particularly white audiences, to examine their consciences.

What it does instead is straightforwardly recreate an incendiary and relatively unremarked episode in American history, in which the captured Africans' cause is taken up by abolitionists and finally argued successfully by ex-president John Quincy Adams (Anthony Hopkins) before the Supreme Court. *Amistad* is not, by Hollywood standards, as hokey as most historical dramas but it's still squarely in the Hollywood-historical camp. Lavishly produced, it has a rehearsed dignity, as if it were intended as a super-duper high school history curriculum teaching aid.

The one bit of real daring in the film is its opening: Joseph Cinque

(West African actor Djimon Hounsou), the name given by the Spanish to an abducted Mende rice farmer enslaved aboard *La Amistad*, works loose his shackles and leads a revolt against the white Spaniards. It's clear what's going on even if we have not yet been primed as to why; horrifying as the scene is, it exists in a righteous, comprehensible framework. And yet Cinque, photographed against a thunder-and-lightning night sky, his teeth bared, is a monster unleashed—and that's the point. Cinque here is a white man's nightmare of the avenging savage, and Spielberg doesn't deny the bloodlust of the moment, or the revulsion and estrangement audiences of any color may feel in watching it.

This sense of dislocation is what's missing from most racial dramas, especially historical ones. So much is made of how we are all brothers under the skin that we never get to experience the strangeness and alienation that also is part of the picture. Herman Melville's great short novel *Benito Cereno*, which also was about a slave ship revolt, is the great American text of the horror of racial separateness, and it would probably be too incendiary to film even today (though John Huston and others, including Philip Noyce, wanted to). Early on in *Amistad*, Spielberg ventures into *Benito Cereno*-style choppy waters only to paddle into the shallows of the civics lesson. Shackles are transformed into laurel wreaths.

The drama is set in motion when the mutinous Africans, set off from Cuba and numbering thirty-nine survivors, are captured off the coast of Long Island and transferred to a prison in New London, Connecticut, a state where, unlike New York, slavery is still legal. Battle lines are drawn immediately. The abolitionists, headed up by the evangelical Lewis Tappan (Stellan Skarsgård) and scrappy property lawyer Roger Baldwin (Matthew McConaughey) and ex-slave Theodore Joadson (Morgan Freeman) face off in the lower courts against the government prosecutor William S. Holabird (Pete Postlethwaite) and the Martin Van Buren administration secretary of state John Forsyth (David Paymer).

Cranky and infirm, Adams resists the implorings of the abolitionists until Van Buren (Nigel Hawthorne), up for re-election and fearing the loss of the Southern states, overturns the lower courts and appoints a new and supposedly more sympathetic judge—to no ultimate avail. Adams's argument for the Africans' freedom, which actually took in some four and a half hours of dense legalisms, is reduced to a grandstanding monologue before the Supreme Court in which he invokes the spirit of the Founding Fathers (including his own father, John Adams) and receives for his troubles the hearty handclasp of a grateful Cinque. It's black chief/white chief time.

Spielberg and Franzoni (with a hefty uncredited assist from *Schindler's List* screenwriter Steve Zaillian) work their way through the maze of pressure tactics both sides employed. It's to their credit that the various legal maneuvers—the early attempt by the abolitionists, for example, to characterize the Africans not as slaves but as "stolen goods"—come across without a lot of dumbing down. And yet what is missing from the film is the almost hallucinatory jumble of legal complications and wranglings that the Africans' trials engendered, and the way those complications heatedly divided the country. The problem with *Amistad* is that, in attempting to render its events lucidly, it loses the drama in what was inherently a legal, ethical, and political crazyquilt.

The point of Spielberg's populist approach, of course, is that it *was* all quite simple: the *Amistad* case was about justice. Obviously. But so, in a sense, was the Civil War, and yet if one were to unclutter the issues of that war the richness of its drama would be lost. The *Amistad* case was a prelude to that war; its crazyquilt is cut from the same zigzag weave.

What's downplayed in *Amistad* is the extent to which the Africans' trials were a crucible for the country's attitudes toward slavery. (The world's attitudes as well—Spain and Britain were also key participants.) Supporters of the Africans were careful to avoid the fire-and-brimstone trappings of abolitionism, hoping to bring moderates to the cause through a concerted appeal to moral decency. The timing was right. As Howard Jones writes in his superb, densely detailed *Mutiny on the Amistad*, "Cinque and his companions could not have known, but . . . the nation was experiencing a widespread reform movement that, on the surface at least, exalted the common man and emphasized equality of opportunity."

The Africans were an ideal test case for trying out abolitionist sentiments because, shackled, they posed no real threat; there were even among them three young girls. They didn't want to overrun the United States, they merely wanted their freedom—to return to Africa. The lack of threat allowed anti-slavery sympathizers to feel both righteous and paternalistic.

Spielberg tries mightily to avoid seeming paternalistic in *Amistad* by introducing the character of Freeman's Joadson, who unfortunately is given almost nothing to do except stand around and be black. (It's a waste of a great actor.) Most of the white characters, even the Africans' defenders, seem in varying degrees craven and compromised. Tappan, for example, is revealed as a closet racist when he ponders the notion of martyring the Africans to help the cause. Baldwin is played (in too "modern" a fashion) by McConaughey as a righteous opportunist with granny glasses, which is rather a slur on the actual Baldwin, a staunch anti-slavery advocate right out of law school who, according to Jones, had in 1831 confronted an angry mob resisting his attempt to build a black training school near Yale College.

On the other side, Van Buren, no supporter of the Africans, is rendered daffily—he is last seen in defeat, his sideburns tufted and his eyes vacant, tuning his harp with a tiny tinkly bell.

Even Adams, for all his creaky dignity, is padded out with silly bits of business—like tending to his prize African violets. (Get it?) It wouldn't do to show Adams from the start as a man of unwavering principle; first we must see him reject the abolitionists' repeated pleas to enter the fray. Adams in reality was a trusted adviser from the start, and his reluctance to fully join in had mostly to do with his infirmities. In *Amistad*, his crotchety coyness has an unintended effect on us; it looks as if he waited out the Africans' cause until it entered the big time—the Supreme Court. He's an opportunist, too.

Adams's big speech before the Court gives Hopkins a fine hammy opportunity, and he delivers in his patented over-under-playing style. (Forty years ago the role would have gone to Spencer Tracy.) It's an effective scene but also somewhat dishonest—Adams invokes the Founding Fathers in his anti-slavery spiel without remarking that many of them were also slave owners. We're not meant to notice the omission. In civics lesson movies, the first casualty is irony.

Cinque and the other Africans are ennobled; their (subtitled) speech, their chants, their rituals, are far more passionate than the prattle of the whites. Although Spielberg shows how Africans themselves participated in the slave trade, he still pushes the notion that Cinque and his band are representative of a more wholly spiritual and evolved man. (Hounsou, with his large presence and rich-grained voice, looks the part of a natural prince.) When the Africans' lower court victory is overturned, Cinque can't understand why the white American system of justice "*al-*

most works." He wails, "What kind of place is this?" Did no one in his homeland ever welsh on a deal?

In a way, Spielberg is attempting to cast himself as the modern-day prototype of the white reformers in his movie. He, too, exalts "the common man." He may see it as his mission now, after *Schindler's List,* to use his unprecedented power in Hollywood to redress grievous wrongs and make the world a better place. (That is, when he's not making thrill-ride movies.) It's an admirable impulse, but it's the impulse of a politician, not an artist, though the two occasionally coincide.

One such occasion in *Amistad* is the depiction of the Middle Passage. The obscenity of what we're watching—in which black bodies are fed to the sea and mothers silently jump overboard with their babies— is matched by our realization that a mainstream Hollywood movie has never really depicted this Passage before. That's an obscenity, too. Normally when he goes into his righteous reformer's mode, Spielberg betrays his sharpest filmmaker's instincts. Not here. *Amistad* is itself a movie in shackles. Stylistically, it's staid—weighted with import. But in his depiction of the slave ship transit, Spielberg throws off the shackles. Be thankful for large favors.

(*New Times*, 1997)

A.I. Artificial Intelligence

A.I. Artificial Intelligence, which stars Haley Joel Osment as a robot boy who longs to be human, is officially billed as a Steven Spielberg movie, but for more than twenty years Stanley Kubrick had been developing the project. At one time, he wanted Spielberg to direct it. The finished product is a synthesis of Kubrick's vaunted imperiousness and Spielberg's dreamland pop. It's one of the weirdest achievements in film history; temperamentally, Spielberg and Kubrick are such polar opposites that *A.I.* has the moment-to-moment effect of being completely at odds with itself. Spielberg is able to duplicate precisely not only the grandiose and abstracted look of Kubrick's post-*Strangelove* movies but also their subzero emotional temperature; at the same time, he's fussing up the film with a vast storehouse of references to his own movies, most specifically *E.T.* He's trying to pump hot sentiment into the deep freeze.

The results are alternately emotionally wrenching, unsatisfying, and bewildering. How could they not be? *A.I.* bears strong evidence of the darker, kinkier, and more unforgiving Kubrick movie it might have been, but at almost every opportunity Spielberg, who also wrote the script, softens Kubrick's misanthropy. Maybe this tenderizing is all for the best—we don't need to see *Robo Eyes Wide Shut.* But since the Kubrick material also has the effect of denaturing Spielberg, nothing true-blue comes through from either filmmaker. Spielberg isn't liberated by Kubrick; he's reined in by him. *A.I.* is not so much an homage as it is a kind of hocus-pocus channeling of the Master's themes and tropes and camera moves, which are then super-imposed onto Spielberg's own.

The movie is set in a sterile future in which natural resources have been severely depleted and the birth rate is strictly regulated. Mechanical robots, acting as helpmates to humans and called mechas, are omnipresent. (Brian Aldiss's 1969 short story *Supertoys Last All Summer Long* was the film's initial inspiration.) Martin (Jake Thomas), the mortally ill son of Henry and Monica Swinton (Sam Robards and Frances O'Connor), has been cryogenically frozen until a cure can be found. Henry is an employee at Cybertronics Manufacturing, where its resident visionary, Professor Hobby (William Hurt), has developed the first child robot, David (Osment), whose capacity to love and be loved is unique. Henry brings David home to his grieving wife as a surprise gift; both parents are cautioned that once emotional imprinting takes place between them and their mecha, there is no turning back except to relegate David to the scrap heap. Following a family flare-up, David's odyssey to avoid that fate takes him into a nightmarish, carnival-like underworld of renegade robots who are chased and despised by the humans they nearly outnumber. With his mechanical teddy bear in tow, he takes up with the preening Gigolo Joe (Jude Law), who has been programmed to service flesh-and-blood women. Joe is creepy and yet, in his desire to please, touchingly lifelike. He clicks his heels like Ray Bolger; he cricks his neck and out comes "I Only Have Eyes for You."

One of the curiosities of *A.I.* is that the robots are arguably less androidlike than the humans, although with Haley Joel Osment it's hard to tell—he seems preternatural no matter what role he's playing. (William

Hurt is another one who always manages to seem zoned out.) There's a good sick joke in the notion that the robots are more human than the humans they are aching to be, but Spielberg doesn't seem to be in on it. David's Pinocchio-like quest to be flesh and blood and win back the love of his mother is played straight, even though Mom, despite her smiles and teariness, is a stiff. (David's unnurturing father is a standard Spielbergian distant dad.) *A.I.* makes a big deal about how we humans have lost the capacity to love in a society in which technology has displaced emotion. But its own capacity for emotion—with a few exceptions, such as a devastatingly sad scene with David pining for transcendence at the bottom of the ocean—seems forced rather than genuinely felt. This is what happens when you try to will a classic into being. Spielberg is grappling with a modern dilemma—technology versus heart—that deep down he doesn't buy into. It may have been true for Kubrick that humans are becoming more and more machinelike, but, dystopian scold that he was, this alarming development would have been, if anything, cause for celebration (or at least a black Mass). Spielberg, by contrast, has always had an almost beatific approach to technology—that approach is what gave *Close Encounters of the Third Kind* and *E.T.* their supernal glow. Spielberg isn't afraid of the future; on the contrary, he wants to be its ringmaster.

Is it any wonder, with all these crossed circuits, that *A.I.* is such a mishmashed fable? Fables need to be magically simple. Early in the movie, David's father cautions his wife that since David was created for love, he might also be capable of hate. This is a Kubrickian conceit. And yet David, despite at one point inadvertently endangering his family, is shown to be a sainted child without a speck of malevolence. Spielberg bathes him in a nimbus that would make Pinocchio warp with envy. David's love for his mother, as it's played out, is another example of brackish material making its way through Spielberg's cosmic car wash. With Mommy finally all to himself, David tucks her in and sleeps contentedly beside her and makes her coffee just the way she likes it. It's a boy's Oedipal fantasy served up without irony. Who could have predicted that "When You Wish Upon a Star" would come to *this?* Doesn't Spielberg recognize that this clash of the pre-Freudian with the postapocalyptic is just plain nutty?

With *Schindler's List* and *Amistad* and *Saving Private Ryan* behind him, Spielberg has certainly earned the right to create a dark *E.T.* Ex-

CHAPTER 5

ABOUT ACTING, STAR ACTORS, AND ACTING STARS

Acting in the Seventies

Offscreen, in interviews and on the talk shows, some of America's most enduringly successful actors seem wised-up, dispirited. They're more cynical than their counterparts of a few generations ago. Typically, these actors are middle-aged men who made it in the fifties and sixties and are still snug in the saddle, riding into a new decade. The notion that acting is not a fit occupation for a grown man has been around a long time, but it's become almost a daily refrain on the talk-show circuit.

Actors like Robert Redford, George C. Scott, Marlon Brando, and Paul Newman publicly regard their acting as a necessary evil—it allows them the luxury of doing what really "matters" in their lives (politics, car-racing, ecology, etc.). Their faces grin back at us from the all-star blockbuster movie posters like prize heads on a big-game hunter's trophy wall. The hunters' names may change from year to year (Joe Levine, Sir Lew Grade, Dino De Laurentiis, Irwin Allen, the Salkinds) but it's the same old floating crap game, with the same stars dealing from the same cold deck.

The successful middle-aged actor's cynicism rampant today can't all be blamed on male menopause; it has a lot to do with the increasing scarcity of movies being made, the scarcity of good roles. There were fewer than a hundred major studio projects released last year (with approximately the same number from independents); during the same time the pool of "bankable" actors—actors with the name value to get a movie financed—has become a puddle. Formula plots in Hollywood have given way to formula financing. "It doesn't matter what the movie's about," goes the conventional wisdom. "Just get Charles Bronson or Steve McQueen and the rest will take care of itself."

But even the concept of star financing seems to have fallen through partway. Charles Bronson has been on a losing streak for the last few years (Lord knows, it has nothing to do with his acting; if anything, it's improved). Steve McQueen's crack at Ibsen, *An Enemy of the People*, remains in the can after a year; Paul Newman's last two—*Buffalo Bill and the Indians* and *Slapshot*—were box-office disappointments; so were Liza Minnelli's (*A Matter of Time* and *New York, New York*); Jack Nicholson's name didn't do much for *The Passenger* or *Missouri Breaks* or *Going South*; and George Segal and Elliott Gould have been in enough gobblers in the last five years to last each of them a lifetime. Instead of opening up the floodgates for the gifted but "unbankable," this trend seems to have made narrow-minded producers even narrower. In five years, the annual number of studio-financed films will be down to seven, and they will all star Barbra Streisand.

The open cynicism of the Newmans and the Scotts and the Brandos is a front for their creative frustrations. The proof is, when they have a decent role, they give it all they've got: Scott in *The Hospital* and *Islands in the Stream* (and, on Broadway, in *Death of a Salesman*); Newman in *Buffalo Bill and the Indians* and *Slapshot*; Brando in *Last Tango in Paris*. These performances represent what is probably the best work of their careers. James Cagney and Cary Grant gave almost a lifetime of pleasure to audiences, but they were probably right to quit when they did; they were turning into less spry versions of what we always loved them for, and mealy-mouthed old-codger roles seemed just around the corner. Even if old age had made them deeper actors, I'm not sure that would have been what anyone wanted. (I like Cary Grant in *None But the Lonely Heart*, his "best" performance, but I love him in *North By Northwest*.)

But, after *Last Tango in Paris*, who would wish Marlon Brando into comfortable retirement? He may be aging to look ravaged, bloated, but he still has his danger. Even in the stills for *Apocalypse Now*, he carries more force than most actors do on-screen. George C. Scott will soon be seen in Paul Schrader's *Hardcore*—no piece of fluff; Paul Newman, despite the commercial failure of *Buffalo Bill*, has already finished another movie for Robert Altman (*Quintet*). It's not the good roles that make these actors openly cynical—it's the humiliating work and the interminable wait in-between. How horrible it would be for us all if one day these actors decided it wasn't worth the wait. Hollywood hasn't made it difficult for them to be actors (a star can always get work), but it's made it difficult for them to be artists. Laurence Olivier, the greatest actor of the century, wasn't "bankable" until just recently. And what has he been starring in? *Sleuth, Marathon Man*, cameos in *The Seven-Percent Solution* and *A Bridge Too Far, The Betsy*, and *The Boys From Brazil*. The big-game hunters like to have Olivier around; he gives their junk class.

Against all odds, Olivier is *still* terrific in these films, but other actors wade through a steady stream of junk without much effect at all. It's becoming painful to watch George Segal. *Fun With Dick and Jane* was bad enough, but *The Duchess and the Dirtwater Fox* and *Who's Killing the Great Chefs of Europe?* What made Segal so interesting a few years back— in movies like *Born to Win, Loving, Where's Poppa?, Blume in Love*, and *California Split*—was the suggestion of pain inside his funny faces. Movies used to have one sustained tone throughout—funny or scary, upbeat, downbeat—but some of the best movies of seventies—the films of Scorsese, De Palma, Altman, and others—are a deliberate jumble of disparate tones. Segal's actor's compression of sweet and funny and slapstick-sad seemed to make him the ideal new movie star. He could express torment in a new way: he incarnated the emotionalism of the most progressive movies of the seventies. But the only torment Segal expresses now is the torment of a gifted actor getting rich off his own profligacy. How long will it be before he's entombed in a Hollywood Square?

Elliott Gould's record is even worse. After *The Long Goodbye*, his career seemed ready to take off again but, except for *California Split*, there's been *I Will, I Will, For Now; Whiffs*, a real stinker about germ warfare; a dumb cameo in *A Bridge Too Far; Matilda*, a "comedy" about a boxing kangaroo; and *Capricorn One*. It's hard to believe now that he was the number-one movie idol on college campuses in the early seventies. Gould had a goofy athleticism in his early roles (*Bob & Carol & Ted & Alice, M*A*S*H*); he was grungy yet hip, and that appealed to students who saw themselves not only as bedraggled odd-men-out but as *winners*. Gould—like Woody Allen—was a winner who looked like a loser. Curled up inside the slouch and the loose jaw and the glassy eyes was a demon ready to spring, and when it did there was rage upon the whole straight, uptight world. Gould seems to have slipped away from his own wild Twilight Zone, where he always did his hottest work, and joined that straight, uptight world. He acts willfully spaced out now, as if his vacancy could somehow float him above the awfulness of his recent movies and spare him shame.

In poignant contrast to these tired, hang-dog, going-through-the-motions, star-stoned trips is the work of young actors like Jeff Bridges, Richard Dreyfuss, Sissy Spacek, Harvey Keitel, John Travolta, Nick Nolte, and Gary Busey. What a collection of faces! Each new movie generation has its stars who repudiate the glossy image of those stars who came before them—and in turn become glossified. One can't help but wonder whether it will be any different with these new kids in town. Or will they all George Segal-ize in ten years? (Perhaps Segal himself will revitalize, the way Brando did in the late sixties after a string of tired performances in dreadful movies.) There is probably more red-hot acting talent in American movies and television now than at any other time in our history. And, for most of these actors, their victories are the same old Hollywood victories of redeeming, through sheer talent, a counterfeit conception. What would *Somebody Killed Her Husband* be without Jeff Bridges? *The Goodbye Girl* without Richard Dreyfuss? *The Buddy Holly Story* without Gary Busey? Busey doesn't impersonate Buddy Holly, he actively inhabits his spirit; he doesn't keep a respectful actor's distance from his character and so, like Bridges, Travolta, De Niro, and others, he seems possessed on-screen. (So did Sissy Spacek in *Carrie*. She looked like what came out of the Serpent's Egg.)

Some of the best actors work the least, and not always by choice. Blythe Danner's television performance in *Eccentricities of a Nightingale* is one of the finest on film but, except for *Lovin' Molly*, the only starring role she's had in the movies has been opposite Peter Fonda in *Futureworld*, and that was three years ago. For those of us not close enough to New York catch their stage work, there's been nothing from Lenny Baker or Ellen Greene since *Next Stop, Greenwich Village*. Why has Ronee Blakely appeared (and briefly) in only one Hollywood movie since *Nashville*? Shelley Duvall was terrific in *Bernice Bobs Her Hair* on television and in Altman's *3 Women*; she was even terrific playing a psychotic in a *Baretta* episode a few seasons ago. Don't performances like these *mean* anything to producers?

Everybody knows movies have become primarily a young person's entertainment (the vast majority of audiences are under thirty); but it's only recently that the problems of youth have become the main dramatic mode in movies. Character and conflict are expressed in coming-of-age terms. The tribal rituals of adolescents, and those just a bit older, have all the Hollywood juices now. An occasional *An Unmarried Woman* will lure adults into the triplex, but the other two screens will feature *Grease* or *Saturday Night Fever*. This is yet more bad news for the George C. Scotts and the Paul Newmans—who wants to see them play *parents*?— but it means that young actors have a chance to connect with prime moviegoers in a more vital way than ever before. Or does it?

I had large reservations about James Bridges's recent movie *September 30, 1955*, a period drama about an Arkansas college kid's infatuation with James Dean, but it made me wonder—is it conceivable that a movie star today could have the impact on American youth that James Dean had on kids in the fifties? Dean is often spoken of as the last "real" star, the last movie actor to work his way into the collective national psyche. There's some truth in this. The Rebel Without a Cause was like a searing wound across the face of fifties movies. The directors and writers of movies like *The Wild One* and *Rebel Without a Cause* may have tried to sentimentalize their rebels, make them part of a social "problem," but the presence of Dean and Brando was far more troubling, more *enigmatic* than the pulpy movies they figured in. There was something going on in a James Dean movie that often had very little to do with the movie itself; two of the three movies he made before he died—*East of Eden* and *Giant*—were set in the rural American past, and yet young urban audiences identified intensely with them. They identified with Dean's torment— and with his narcissism.

The Rebel Without a Cause may have been symptomatic of a national ailment—postwar youth stuck in the Eisenhower limbo between Korea and Vietnam, in a conservative society that had no way to deal with or absorb their anger—but, in movie terms, their problems were almost always simplified to the problems of growing up in a broken home. In the sixties and early seventies most of the new movie misfits had doting parents (when they were mentioned at all), the broken home became society at large, and psychic rebellion turned inward. Movies like Dennis Hopper's *Easy Rider* and Bob Rafelson's *Five Easy Pieces* expressed a prevailing mood; they summed it all up for a generation that felt stifled by traditional culture and unwanted by the status quo. The movies' advice was to escape, but where to? Disaffected Americans—in Hopper's and Rafelson's terms, the "best" Americans, the ones who were in the best position to view the country's inner sickness—found themselves on the edge of a society that did not recognize or want them. Audiences felt protective toward James Dean, because he was really looking for love, but no one felt protective toward the counterculture movie antiheroes that followed a decade later. Audiences identified less with a particular movie star (Jack Nicholson, Dustin Hoffman, et al) than with the malaise he represented. This might not have happened if a star had come along with Dean's instinct to go for the emotional jugular, but, in any case, movies didn't rock the senses of the counterculture in the sixties. Rock music did. Stars like Dylan, Joplin, and Hendrix had an immediacy that was missing in American movies until very recently, and now the immediacy tends to come less from a particular star than from the obsessive visions of directors like Coppola, Scorsese, and Altman.

One of the real tragedies of American pop culture is that moviemakers did so little with the rock stars of the sixties. (It's almost as great a movie tragedy as the criminal, ongoing waste of black acting talent.) These stars might have invigorated movies and created a whole new audience. Instead, a great portion of that audience may have been lost to movies forever. They *did* turn out for *American Graffiti*, one of the last big predisco youth hits, but the atmosphere inside the theater was like a raucous high-school reunion. Significantly, *American Graffiti* was one of the few youth hits which did not strike new attitudes with its audience. Or rather, its new attitudes were simply a hankering for the old fifties attitudes of its audiences—commercialized nostalgia. (The movie seemed to be saying, "Look at how poignant we were!" Really, we weren't all that poignant.) *American Graffiti* was the most inevitable movie of 1973; the fifties finally became a period for the generation that grew up with James Dean. (The year the film takes place, 1962, wasn't conceptually part of the sixties at all, just closing out of the fifties.) The James Dean character in the film, Paul Le Mat's John Milner, the JD with a heart of gold, demonstrated how precious the rebel without a cause had become. The swagger of delinquency became a put-on and violence (like the wrecking of the police car by the local toughs) became slapstick.

In her 1964 essay "Notes on Camp," Susan Sontag wrote:

> Things are campy not when they become old—but when we become less involved in them, and can enjoy, instead of being

frustrated by, the failure of the attempt. But the effect of time is unpredictable. Maybe Method acting (James Dean, Rod Steiger, Warren Beatty) will seem as camp someday as Ruby Keeler does now . . . and maybe not.

But it's not only failure that has the potential for camp, it's also success as defined by values that we no longer share. There's a tendency among filmgoers my age (twenty-seven), and a generation older, to approach Dean or Brando revivals with trepidation. What if all that once meant so much to us now seems laughably camp? But it's been my experience that such revivals hold up quite well. James Dean movies, despite their large inadequacies, come alive whenever he's on-screen because he upped the emotional stakes so high. He gave the loss of love tragic overtones, and his acting rhythm—chaotic, fragmentary, driven—moved us kinesthetically. Dean didn't have the technical *simplicity* of most great actors; he fussed and carried on, he dripped narcissism. But even when his self-indulgence was awful you felt protective, which meant you *cared*. Part of this protection grew from the fact that it was often difficult to separate Dean's acting from what we knew about his offscreen life. His personas on-screen and off merged, which, in Method terms, made him the compleat actor. No other actor of his generation, not even Brando or Clift, and certainly few actors before him, gave us the overwhelming impression that if he didn't break through to the fundament of his feelings, he would go crazy. Dean's inarticulateness seemed more eloquent than the rhythmed, polished acting of his predecessors. For better or worse, he made them seem phony. His death at twenty-four, in an automobile accident, was the capper to his legend—Dean, the flaming angel of his generation, finally flew over the cliff he was heading for all along.

If Dean had survived, he might have grown as an actor (like Brando in *Last Tango*) but, given the changing times and the commerce of the film business, his legend probably would have been fatally compromised. I once asked Nicholas Ray, the director of *Rebel Without a Cause*, what Dean might have become had he lived. His answer: "A tired movie director." That statement probably reveals more about Ray than Dean, but it confirms our own suspicions about the inappropriateness of the rebel persona—perhaps *any* galvanizing persona—in the confused modern world of movies. Norman Mailer has written: "Part of the crisis of the twentieth century is that nothing like a coherent view of personality is able to prevail. We live in every concept of human motivation and they are all at odds." Until recently, this did not really apply to most movie stars, many of whom, like Gary Cooper, Bette Davis, and Clark Gable, had unambiguous movie personas. To paraphrase Mailer, their legend survived because they were *comprehensible*.

We may be entering a new movie-acting age now, where Mailer's crisis situation does indeed apply; that is, in the absence of the comprehensible core of character that an actor's star persona thrives on, the actor himself, not tied into concept of character, may become the real star. Robert De Niro, for example, is a star despite the fact that he has absolutely no categorizable persona. In the fifties, De Niro might have been in the rebel front line, but his spooky transformataions from role to role now, his newly stamped spirit each time out, seem to fit in with the uncategorizable seventies. In the same way, no one talks, except in verbal shorthand, about "the new Al Pacino movie." What is there to link *The Godfather* I and II, *Serpico*, *Scarecrow*, *Dog Day Afternoon*, and *Bobby Deerfield*?

It was easier to build star roles in the days when actors were more of a known quantity, when the motivations for their actions could be fit into a neat dramatic system. One of the reasons there aren't more women stars right now (there's certainly no shortage of good actresses) is because the popular values that might have formed a base for a female star persona in the past are outdated, or at least in flux. It's perhaps no accident that the two biggest female stars—Barbra Streisand and Liza Minnelli—have scored their biggest hits in stylized period pieces (*Funny Girl*, *Cabaret*) while their softer, more contemporary roles in movies like *Up the Sandbox* and *New York, New York* (the sexual dynamics of the latter were modern even if the period wasn't) have been rather bewilderingly received. Jill Clayburgh's performance as Erica, the bereft wife in Paul Mazursky's *An Unmarried Woman*, doesn't have the clarity of a star performance (probably because her life situation, by definition, lacked clarity); but Erica may be the closest thing to a movie heroine of the seventies that we're likely to get.

I love watching Cagney or Bogart in their custom-fit roles, but on a deeper level I don't really believe in their characters *as people* the way I believe Al Pacino in *Dog Day Afternoon* or Robert De Niro in *Taxi Driver*. The tailoring of roles to fit performers is, among other things, a form of protection—the lesions of character are never exposed, the mysteries of personality are minimized. Some actors, of course, go to the tailor regularly. One of the big reasons Clint Eastwood is so extraordinarily popular is that, in the midst of this maelstrom, he's one of the few stars around who *stands for something*. What he stands for—ostensibly, the traditional four-square conservative virtues—may be almost beside the point. Or could it be that Eastwood is so popular with young, liberal, college audiences because he certifies their reactionary fantasies? (I certainly hope not.) Eastwood's lean, wolfish face and fighting trim make him a suitable-looking hero for both urban-contemporary and Western law-and-order fantasies. He's pared down—ideologically and physically—for action.

Audiences love Clint Eastwood's uncomplicatedness, the "pure" pleasure of his heroism in a world where Good and Evil are as carefully delineated as the colored bars in a Mondrian. And they love the humor of his deadpan in such a world. But, although Eastwood is always cast as the hero, unlike actors like Richard Harris and Sean Connery, he doesn't have a heroic presence. He also doesn't have the humor to kid the made-to-order heroism of his roles, like Burt Reynolds. Or, more exactly, he doesn't feel the *need* to kid his heroism because he's still a believer. The political climate in this country isn't as divisive as it was in *Dirty Harry*'s heyday, when a homicidal maniac could be portrayed as a hippie with a peace-sign belt buckle. The embarrassment of Eastwood's last cop movie, *The Gauntlet*, was that he was still lambasting Hell's Angels and Easy Riders; someone should have told him to turn his clock ahead. Dirty Harry has been left out in the cold in the Carter era, and my guess is that Eastwood's cop will operate in an increasingly political vacuum in the future. The ads for *The Gauntlet* were already uniquely "elemental" for this urban-cop genre—Eastwood is standing stalwart like Thor against the forces of evil while his lady lashes herself to his trunk like a frightened gazelle. Was Warner Brothers trying to pretest *Conan*? If Eastwood's new "comedy," *Every Which Way But Loose*—that hop-head *Hee-Haw*—is any indication, he may have decided to throw in his badge altogether.

Could the recent proliferation of newspapers and magazines and television shows devoted entirely to stardom be symptomatic of the uncategorizability of most of the few who really are stars? In the lightheaded formats of these shows and journals, it's simpler to deal with pseudo-stars—there's no friction of thought involved. Suzanne Somers and Cheryl Ladd and Farrah Fawcett-Majors represent spic-and-span sex—sex as plastic—and so it's easy to promote them as celebrities. Celebrity is their true sexual attraction. It's harder to know what to do with an Al Pacino or a Robert De Niro. Rejection of commercial usage is built right into these actors. The avidity of the public for show-biz icons has created a circus-like atmosphere in the media, and it's becoming almost impossible for a serious actor to pass through it unscathed. An older actor like Burt Reynolds solves the problem by playing the fool—the stud sellout cackling at his own improbable good fortune. Serious younger actors are afraid of the media juggernaut; on the talk shows, you can see them listening to themselves, trying not to drone on like the successful, rich wax-statue of an actor sitting next to them. These older stars rarely stay on the talk shows for long; they leave, amidst tumultuous applause, to tape a *Dean Martin Celebrity Roast*—the younger actor's vision of hell. It's hard to lift oneself above the media juggernaut but, if you don't, you get steamrolled. In recent times, the only group of performers who have played the media game and thrived creatively are the comics; and that may only be because so much contemporary comedy is so media and show-biz oriented. (The *Saturday Night Live* bunch are like surfers making fun of the wave that is carrying them along.) Maybe it's always been that way, but the new crop of comedians (along with precursors like Carol Burnett) are perhaps the first to create entire careers around the notion that an immersion in pop culture will drive you nuts. And that nuttiness is what makes them hip.

In show biz terms, and as a form of American consciousness in general, hip used to mean black. Now what seems to have happened is that hip has lost its racial accoutrements (if it hasn't, then surely it must be moving toward middle-class white). Hip is no longer where you're from, it's where you're coming from, so to speak. And the hippest performers in movies and television now are the comics who seem to operate out of their own unchartable craziness. These new comedians have the same immediacy for young audiences that rock stars had for kids in the sixties. (*Rolling Stone* has more cover stories on yockers than rockers these days.) After years of "socially conscious" humor, savage humor, the street satire of sixties radicalism, what we have now is the humor of personal idiosyncrasy—grounded in pop culture—and the two progenitors of the new hip are Lily Tomlin and Richard Pryor.

Crazies in the movies and television used to be on the periphery of the action. Now they're the coming order, heading for the center of the action. They're not even crazy, exactly—they're screwloose visionaries. The lament of Lily Tomlin's loony UFO watcher in Tomlin's Broadway show *Appearing Nitely* is the melancholic motto of the new hip: "In this world, if you don't have evidence, you're nothing." That's because, in straight society, tangible evidence is all. *Appearing Nitely* was advertised as a one-woman show, but has there ever been an actress with as many different comic personalities as Lily Tomlin? What's so awe-inspiring and frightening about her is that she doesn't slip in and out of her characters in the simple way that, say, a mime shifts faces with a wipe of the hand. She, too, seems possessed on-screen. In *The Late Show*, she got so far inside her Hollywood weirdo role that what might have been conceived as a comic turn became almost soulful.

Richard Pryor is probably the most gifted stand-up comic in America, but he's been mostly hamstrung in the movies. Pryor and Tomlin—true soulmates—can get together on one of her television specials and swing off each other's zigzag syncopations like a fine jazz duo. Pryor's bugged-out, hallucinatory quality, his ambiguity, is enough to make the tube's eye blink. (A sound engineer trying to lay in canned laughter over a Pryor television performance would be befuddled, because the comic rhythms are so offbeat.)

Obscenity is Richard Pryor's comic propulsion and, onstage, in front of a live audience, he really cooks in a way he can't on television. Pryor's nightclub humor is more savage and racially oriented than the other hip comics, but he isn't really lashing out at Whitey (that's small potatoes); he's battling private demons. Without obscenity, Pryor's whole character is defused. This is partly what's wrong with him in the movies. The roles he's been getting—except for *Blue Collar*—are too silly to accommodate his demons. They don't have the substance for obscenity, and so they don't mean anything to him. He can be ingratiating, with the audience rapport of a devil, in films like *The Bingo Long Traveling All-Stars and Motor Kings* and *Silver Streak*, but when it comes time for some serious acting, he closes himself off. He wears his zonked baby face like an opaque mask throughout most of a movie like *Greased Lightning*. Maybe one of the reasons he could be taken seriously as an *actor* in *Blue Collar*, a movie where he plays a Detroit auto worker who sells out to the white bosses, is because he wanted his fans to know—he wanted *himself* to know—that he was only acting. He had to create a character and so, acting a man unlike himself, Pryor, paradoxically, appears unfettered on-screen for perhaps the first time.

It's one of the characteristics of the new hip comics—not just Pryor and Tomlin but Steve Martin, Chevy Chase, Martin Mull, the *Saturday Night Live* bunch, Andy Kaufman, Robin Williams—that they are constantly *on*, constantly in character. They don't even crack up in the middle of one of their own skits to show they're only fooling. They're too *obsessed* to crack up. They represent craziness without sentimentality. Their comic personalities are woven around the put-on, and improvisation becomes a way of scrounging for idiosyncrasies that will, hopefully, connect with their audience. Young people who don't personally identify with these comics still connect with their craziness.

Woody Allen, who may be the closest equivalent to a movie cult hero among young audiences in the seventies that James Dean was in the fifties, inspires a much closer personal identification. His craziness is really sanity—that's what's so funny about it. We can feel the frustrations it comes out of. Woody may look like a schlemiel, but he's got his pride; he may hesitate on his way to the bedroom, but—the point is made in every movie—he's good in bed. ("I'm thin but fun.") Woody's flip absurdism fits right in with the new hip comics; his sentimentality, his obsessive New York Jewishness, link him with an earlier set of comics, even those just a bit earlier, like Robert Klein.

He can draw on the same depths of feeling that Lily Tomlin can, but he's not as spacy as she is. Woody is a hip comic with, at bottom, square values. That dichotomy may have accounted for the huge across-the-board appeal of *Annie Hall*, which was, after all, a traditional love story. For the first time, people started to take a Woody Allen film *personally*.

The lack of sentiment in the new hip comedians is a form of distancing, like those adolescents who make fun of everything to avoid getting serious. The "*Saturday Night Live*" crew are not satirists exactly—that would imply a point of view. They're more like equal opportunity gagsters (Gilda Radner is the only regular whom one can take to heart, and that may have less to do with her material than with a certain sweetness and simplicity). Their routines are the brightest regular comedy on television, but watching the show can be a cool experience; the put-on isn't a very endearing technique. Now that the counterculture has grown up and melted into the Establishment, it's hard to know whom to trust (clothes and hair aren't the symbols they used to be). The new comics don't want to appear square, so they put *everyone* on—that way they don't leave themselves open. Their often straight-laced appearance is symptomatic of this: It's a fake-out. Dan Aykroyd and Jane Curtin could be the couple in the suburban tract home next door; Steve Martin, with his white three-piece suit and silver-toned hair, looks like a smiley, clean-cut junior accountant; Chevy Chase might be the bright young Republican hopeful in a Democratic district—until they open their mouths. "Never trust anyone over thirty" has changed to "Never trust anyone." These performers are digging for the comic possibilities in the paranoia.

There's one more point that should be made. Many of these comics are—of all things—sexy. They're obsessed and they think well of themselves—they're narcissists, and narcissism is the new sex appeal in the movies. That's why the ad for the new Lily Tomlin-John Travolta disaster *Moment by Moment*, is so unintentionally funny. The ad shows Travolta and Tomlin—in huge profile—looking adoringly into each other's eyes. They share such a facial resemblance that they might be melting at their own mirror images. Lily Tomlin is hilarious in her one-woman show; she's also a turn-on. Her sexual radiation is inner-directed; her sleek, calisthenic movements are self-caresses. She's not only the most original comic presence in the movies, she's almost the most ambiguous new sexual presence—and the two are perhaps not as far apart as one might imagine.

(*Los Angeles Herald Examiner*, 1979)

MARLON BRANDO

An Appreciation

The obits and appreciations of Marlon Brando, who died at eighty on July 2, emphasized his torn T-shirt iconography and his Don Corleone. That's not surprising. In addition to his incomparable gifts as an actor, Brando had the quite rare ability, which goes beyond talent or even luck, to embody, many times, a national mood. Stanley Kowalski in *A Streetcar*

Named Desire, Terry Malloy in *On the Waterfront*, the biker in *The Wild One*—these portrayals emblematized, and galvanized, the post-war misfit youth generation. As the Godfather, Brando had the grave politeness of a killer patriarch who knows in his bones the down and dirty ways of the world. The most powerful movies of the Vietnam era had a tragic, illusionless dimension; Vito Corleone was the American immigrant success story turned nightmare. These icons, it must be noted, were also romanticized—Terry Malloy may have sold out his promise but not, in the end, his soul; and the Godfather was the protector we might all wish for. The romanticism, of course, was essential to the iconography; it made it possible for us to thrill to everything that was disreputable in these men without sinking into the tar pits of total despair.

But to commemorate Brando as some kind of exalted trademark of the rebellious fifties or the ravaged seventies is to vastly diminish his achievement, because there is so much more to these performances than sociology. He was far too protean to stand pat as the emblem of anything. When Terry Malloy said, "I coulda been a contender," he may have been speaking for all our dashed dreams, but he is also irreducibly that boxer in the backseat of that cab. Brando ushered into the movies the present-tense immediacy of the Method, but his best performances (and even most of his minor ones) go way beyond theatrical technique; what you get from Brando in *On the Waterfront*, or as the furiously desolate Paul in *Last Tango in Paris*, is a quality of human observation and intuition equal to a great novelist's.

Brando once called acting "the least mysterious of all crafts," but he showed it to be the most mysterious, because with him it didn't seem like a craft at all—it was more like a conjuration. Most actors work on one level only. Their emotions have no backstory—rage is simply rage, cheer is cheering. A very good actor can work a few more levels in, a great actor a few more. And then there is Brando, whose every gesture, every quaver is thick with the infinite inner chaos of his characters. In his very first movie, *The Men*, in which he plays a paraplegic vet, there's a scene where he leaves the hospital to be with his bride on their wedding night, and his knee begins to shake uncontrollably as he sits in his wheelchair. His new wife, played by Teresa Wright, recoils slightly, though she's seen this before, and the look on Brando's face, with its impasto of scorn and rage and woe, is so horrifying that he looks like a man whose life has been hauled out and murdered right in front of his eyes. His silent scream is deafening.

Brando could be equally eloquent in roles in which the character's turmoil was deeply, spookily submerged. As Major Penderton in John Huston's *Reflections in a Golden Eye*, adapted from a Carson McCullers's novel, he played a man whose homosexuality is so repressed that it has become an incubus. Trailing the handsome soldier on whom he's fixated, the major might be sleepwalking. The uncomprehending thrill of this brief, soft pursuit has placed him in a trance. Near the end, when he looks into a mirror and rubs cold cream onto his waxy, immobile face in expectation of his suitor's arrival, the self-hypnosis is horrifyingly complete.

I've chosen examples from two lesser known Brando movies because too much of what was written and spoken about him at his death emphasized his greatest hits. (The Huston film, astonishingly, was barely mentioned anywhere, and denigrated when it was.) There are other revelations—his sadistic caretaker in *The Nightcomers*, which was fashioned as a prequel to Henry James's *Turn of the Screw*, and which he made a year before his comeback in *The Godfather*; his American Nazi Party chief George Lincoln Rockwell in *Roots II*, with his wary menace and bonhomie. Just because Brando did not have the glorious career we wanted for him should not blind us to all that he did accomplish.

And yet, the trajectory of his life in the movies—from *The Men* right through to the lucrative cameos in mostly second-rate films that closed out his final decades—has an all too familiar arc common to those unfortunate enough to be geniuses in Hollywood. Buster Keaton comes to mind, and of course, Orson Welles, who like Brando swelled into a cartoon of himself. But it would be a mistake—another form of romanticism—to pin the damages of Brando's career on the heartless commercialism of the movie business. For in the end it was Brando who had the power, as few actors have ever had, to fulfill himself as an artist. (He was only forty-eight when he made *The Godfather*.) In the sixties, after the debacle of *Mutiny on the Bounty*, Brando's commercial stock dropped, and so for a time, did his inspiration, in clinkers like *Morituri* and *The Appaloosa*. But if sixties-era Hollywood—perhaps its blandest era—could offer virtually nothing to incite our greatest actor, he might have ventured overseas, as Burt Lancaster did in Visconti's *The Leopard*. (Visconti desperately wanted to work with Brando, as did David Lean and many others.) After *Last Tango in Paris*, when he was at his most bankable since his early years and coming off probably the finest performance ever given in movies, Brando sat out the rest of the seventies except for small roles in *Superman*, *The Missouri Breaks*, and *Apocalpyse Now*.

The seventies in Hollywood—with all its creative ferment and risk-taking—was tailor-made for Brando. Instead, it was left to his spiritual progeny—Pacino and De Niro and the rest—to carry the torch. *Last Tango in Paris* was the last leading role Brando would ever play—by choice. Should we have been surprised? After all, he never set foot onstage again after his triumph in *Streetcar* in 1947. Renunciation for Brando was a form of effrontery—he let it be known that acting even at his highest level was, in his words, "an empty and useless profession." The gods must have had a good laugh when they created this man; he despised what he did, and no one did it better.

(New York, 2004)

NICK NOLTE

As Tom Wingo in *The Prince of Tides*, Nick Nolte is playing a character who is trying to close himself off from his own pain. "I was a champion at keeping secrets," he says, but he isn't really. Tom may have the thickened look of a superannuated golden-boy jock, and he may sport his Southernness like a medallion. But his hulky jauntiness can't disguise the stricken look behind his eyes, or the way his face slackens into an aghast mask when the sorrows cut too deep. The truth is that Tom is very bad at keeping secrets, and it's a measure of how extraordinary Nolte's performance is that we pick up on this the first moment we see him.

Nolte has often been extraordinary, but his work in *The Prince of Tides* may finally give him the full recognition he deserves. He's currently also on view in *Cape Fear* playing a terrorized lawyer, but it's a far less free-wheeling and resonant performance. *Cape Fear* is emblematic of all the times he has been used by directors as a cog in the machinery. *The Prince of Tides* is a culmination of the best work Nolte has done in the movies.

One of the reasons his work has tended to be overlooked until now is that, unlike so many actors who specialize in playing misfits, Nolte doesn't go in for a lot of beetle-browed, flibbertigibbet, scratch-and-grunt Methodology. When he plays an over-the-hill football player in *North Dallas Forty* or a besieged Vietnam vet in *Who'll Stop the Rain*, or a scraggly bum in *Down and Out in Beverly Hills*, he's so far inside these characters that we never spot the technique in back of the performance. Everything he does seems completely in character, almost pre-consciously so. You don't register the outriggings of mannerism, the rehearsed pauses and studied glances. His acting seems to derive from an intense physicality; he provides a link between acting and athleticism. He has a superb athlete's awe for the eloquence of body language. No other actor is as good with the sheer utensils of his trade. Take two of his best performances—the shaggy Expressionist artist in Martin Scorsese's *Life Lessons* mixes his paints as if they were lifeblood; the photojournalist in *Under Fire* works his cameras as an extension of his torso.

This physical expressiveness, especially in someone as beefy as Nolte, can provide moments of revelation that the punier actors can't approach. When his characters are in conflict, their agonies take on a larger-than-life proportion; it's as if his body were contorted against itself. In American movies, actors of Nolte's bulk are generally not employed for their subtleties. They're cast as loamy salt-of-the-earth types, lunkhead rampagers, heavies. Actors like Stallone or Schwarzenegger may sometimes play heroic characters, but they don't really have a heroic presence; they can't incarnate heroism, and they don't have the performing equipment to show its contradictions. That's why they can so easily lampoon their own image—it was never that rich to begin with.

The heroic presence conveyed by Nolte is much more in line with actors like Sean Connery or Richard Harris who, in their performances, appear to have a purchase on something larger than themselves. Their agonies and triumphs move us kinesthetically, and their emotions are a majestic and heightened version of our own.

There are other actors out there, like Ed Harris and Fred Ward, who are capable of rooting out the sensitivities in common-man misfits. But no one is quite like Nolte in the way he manages to be both larger-than-life and down-to-earth. He's a rarity—a believable Everyman. And the reason he's believable is because he works from the inside out, from the gut; physical honesty is equated with emotional honesty. There's no gaseous we-the-people agenda inflating his persona—he can't even be said to *have* a persona. When someone like Kevin Costner goes into his Everyman routine, the flat, toneless diction and dampened energies and impassive handsomeness are meant to summon up a Gary Cooper-like mystique. It's the mystique of the Westerner, and it can be fearfully boring. (Costner is best when he's throwing tantrums.) Why do so many actors think it's all-American to be muted? Is the theory perhaps that the strong-and-silent types have the best propulsion to sweep stealth-like into the byways of the small-town psyche?

Nolte doesn't play these laconic games. He brings his characters—his convicts, vets, hobos, shutterbugs, football players—to rip-roaring life. You would never think of them as all-American archetypes, even though, in a sense, that's what they are. They contain a crazy-quilt of possibilities, which is why, when they mutate from one guise to another, like Jerry in *Down and Out in Beverly Hills* going from his tramp rags to his Rodeo Drive duds, the transformation seems magically right. We can see how it all fits together.

The unity that he brings to his roles is often enough to unify his movies. He gives them a core of meaning. As Lee Umstetter, the paroled lifer in *Weeds* who tours with his own theatrical troupe of ex-cons, Nolte shows us how performance has sustained him behind bars and again on the outside. When he's performing his self-written part, wearing bright white makeup and strung out hair like some sort of gonzo Kabuki, he's an amazing actor playing a not very good one. But Lee's avidity for acting overrides his meager abilities. His acting is his salvation. Onstage, he clicks off his wary con's radar and exults in his own uncensored self.

One of the reasons Nolte made such a bang-up impression when he debuted on television in 1975 in *Rich Man, Poor Man* is that he was almost too strong, too unruly for the small screen. But that show's miniseries format at least suited his power; his Tom Jordache had the kind of novelistic complexities that deserved an extended run. Watching that show, it was clear that Nolte was a born movie actor (though it had taken him more than a dozen years of knocking around regional theater to make it to the screen). His first feature film of consequence, *The Deep*, came a little more than a year later, and it remains his worst—not necessarily because the film was dreadful but because his character was an unadulterated beefcake and Nolte seemed content to play him that way. It's the performance of an actor bound for a routine career as a moving target in a shooting gallery.

Nolte has never made that mistake again, although he's been indifferent in films like *Another 48 Hrs.*, where he looked miserable lugging his carcass through the tumult while Eddie Murphy dithered in his own zone of self-adoration. When Nolte doesn't put himself into his work, his staunch reserves of feeling turn to marble; he's block-like, transfixed. And we can feel betrayed, because Nolte is one of the few modern actors who have demonstrated a depth of emotion playing the kinds of characters who are usually given short, disdainful shrift in the movies—the jocks and good ol' boys, the kind of guys who look at home sullenly nursing a beer in a low-lit topless go-go joint. He can make us ashamed of taking these guys for granted, of thinking we already knew everything about them. There's an egalitarianism about Nolte's best acting; he doesn't condescend to his characters (or to us). He can discover the emotional possibilities in them because he hasn't closed himself off—he's not after the quick fix, the caricature, the snobberies confirmed.

Nolte is less effective when he tries for a ferocious, bad-guy malevolence, as with his corrupt, walrus-mustached cop in *Q & A*. At a time when some of the most acclaimed actors, like Robert De Niro and Anthony Hopkins, are connecting with audiences by turning themselves into specialists of the grotesque—the human equivalent of moray eels—Nolte brings a companionable and hearty presence to the "normal" range. And he brings to his characters a note of regret, too, of missed chances.

It's conceivable that if Nolte had scored in movies a decade earlier than he did, when he was still in his mid-twenties, he might have gone on to a routine career in action films and clobber comedies. But what makes his performances in films like *North Dallas Forty* and *Who'll Stop the Rain* so moving is the undercurrent of loss, of being irrevocably past one's prime. (It's this sense of loss that connects Nolte to some of Brando's work—the sense of time and corruption robbing you of the chance to be a contender.) Desperation has made these men ardent. The over-the-hill wide receiver recognizes the corruption of his sport; the Vietnam vet accepts the brutalities of his drug smuggling. And yet these are hard-core romantics—both characters radiate a core of decency and sacrifice themselves for a friend, for an ideal.

Nolte takes the romanticism of his role in *The Prince of Tides* all the way; that's why it's the culmination of his work to date. Without him, the film might have devolved into high-flown camp (some of it is anyway, particularly the shampoo commercial-style love scenes he shares with Barbra Streisand in the last half hour). The "sensitive man" stuff in *The Prince of Tides* could perhaps work only with an actor of Nolte's bearing; his Tom Wingo may not realize it, but he's already attained the manhood he aches for. His marriage is a shambles, his twin sister has attempted suicide. Everything about the performance reveals Tom's desperation.

There's a forced theatricality about him. In his sessions with his sister's New York psychiatrist, played by Streisand, he cultivates his Southern charm with an over-deliberate swagger—it's as if he were constructing the armature of his own sanity. When he's playing with his two young daughters, the frolicking is a bit too carefree—Tom is idealizing the childhood he wished he had. And when he's emotionally challenged, he often retreats into his own childlike cocoon, which makes his hurt only more transparent. Tom is so physically emotive that when he moves into his own hushed space, his stillness can seem a little creepy and self-mesmerized, as if he were trying to block out all bad memory and will his own amnesia.

He can't do it, of course, but we respond to the pain behind the attempt. For Nolte, Tom's heroism is in his final breakthrough to feeling, and that's the heroism of the performance, too.

(*Los Angeles Times,* 1991)

POSTSCRIPT

Despite his best efforts to convince us otherwise—his infamous DUI mug shot, his tropism for indifferent material—Nolte can still be remarkable, as in *Affliction* and *The Golden Bowl* (see pages 510 and 487, respectively).

Hollywood's Lost Generation of Women

In *Pretty Woman*, Julia Roberts plays a minty-fresh hooker who finds true love with her wealthy john. In *Miami Blues*, Jennifer Jason Leigh's hooker is a perky, girl-next-door type who yearns for homespun married bliss with a psychopathic trick. In *Last Exit to Brooklyn*, Jason Leigh is a tough-tender streetwalker who lures unsuspecting galoots to their doom.

What does it say about Hollywood that, of all the roles being offered actresses right now, these three are probably the juiciest? Women are such an endangered species in the movies that the vamp has become high concept.

There have probably never been as many gifted actresses in America as there are right now, but their gifts have been allowed to flourish almost exclusively in the theater or on television. Onstage, performers like Mercedes Ruehl (*Other People's Money*) and Joan Allen (*Burn This*) and Patti LuPone (*Evita*) are electrifying. On television, you watch Annette O'Toole in *The Kennedys of Massachusetts* in a state of rapt admiration. When these same actresses show up in films, it's likely to be in scrunched-up bit roles: Ruehl had a dismally strait-laced cameo as a sympathetic shrink in *Crazy People*; LuPone was shoehorned into *Driving Miss Daisy*; Allen was an extended blip on the screen in such films as *Tucker* and *In Country*. O'Toole was harrowing as a distraught wife in *Love at Large*—for all of her ten (count 'em) minutes of screen time.

Even the actresses well-known—honored—for their past film work are likely nowadays to be playing blurry back-ups to the male lead. In *Bird on a Wire*, Goldie Hawn appears to have entered a booty-shaking contest with Mel Gibson. (Worse, she loses the contest.) Barbra Streisand and Bette Midler are the female stars with the greatest clout, but Streisand is just now about to begin filming her first film in three years, and Midler has turned into a weepy self-parody. Even her silly, wiggly walks lack spring.

It's heartbreaking to scan the pool of great (or potentially great) actresses out there—not just the famous ones, like Jessica Lange and Debra Winger and Michelle Pfeiffer, but the scores of the less renowned—Maria Conchita Alonso, Bridget Fonda, Joan Cusack, Joan Chen, Pamela

Reed, Lena Olin, Natasha Richardson, Anjelica Huston, Christine Lahti, Dianne Wiest, Laurie Metcalfe, Ellen Barkin, Kathy Bates—to mention only a handful. The embarrassment in this embarrassment of riches is that these actresses, all primed for major careers, are entombed in Hollywood's development-deal dungeons. An entire generation of female performers is being squelched by an industry that finds no percentage in accommodating their talents. And by repeatedly going buddy-buddy or solo, an entire generation of male performers is being squelched, too.

Things were not always this bad. Until the past several decades, women were as integral to the movies as men; female stars were as hallowed as their male counterparts. Lillian Gish and Richard Barthelmess were equally revered. Greta Garbo hogged as much of the glory as John Gilbert. The goddesses, like Joan Crawford and Lana Turner, were, in their heyday, as big a box-office draw as the gods, like Gable and Bogart. Their salaries were commensurate, too; money is always a tip-off to what Hollywood thinks of you. The roles of Hollywood's Golden Age goddesses may not have been any more complex or advanced than the roles offered today's top stars (although many of them were), but at least there were far more of them, and the characterizations, because they were designed to fulfill people's fantasies, meant something special to audiences.

The old studio system was responsible for many travesties, but most of the memorable movie goddesses, from Garbo and Dietrich through Gardner and Monroe, were creations of that system. The studio's stable of writers and directors and cinematographers and costume designers were allowed to work up intensely creative partnerships with performers. The studio machinery was geared up for the long run of an actor's career. Aging beauties were eased into more "realistic" roles.

Today, an actress who has passed unrecognized into her thirties stands almost no chance of making it, because in that age bracket the roles just aren't there for her to be discovered. And even the actresses who do achieve success in their twenties and thirties often find they've been put out to pasture later on. The vital female stars of only a decade or so ago, like Jill Clayburgh and Ellen Burstyn and Cicely Tyson, are, for all intents and purposes, in a state of involuntary semi-retirement from the movies. Like their younger counterparts, the ones without movie work, they reserve their occasional successes these days for the stage or TV. It's as if their movie careers never happened.

The free-agency of the current, post-studio-system era has not been kind to the creation of movie stars. Left to their own devices, many stars choose projects that are almost comically wrong for them (like Jane Fonda's spinster *gringa* in *Old Gringo*, or Dustin Hoffman as Sean Connery's son in *Family Business*). But male stars at least have a surplus of decent roles to fight over, since virtually all of the "important" movies, and most of the unimportant ones, are written expressly for them. With women, what's left after Meryl Streep goes shopping?

The movie business is increasingly being driven by the blockbuster mentality, and blockbusters are almost always action epics in which women are relegated to a status position somewhere between the hardware and the special effects. The true partnership in these films is between man and machine. The production costs are rising—*Total Recall* and *Die Hard 2*, for example, both reportedly around $60 million. At a time when foreign markets are becoming almost as lucrative as domestic ones, it makes commercial sense to stock these films with American stars who have international appeal. And that invariably means male action heroes. Don't count on seeing *Batwoman* any time soon (particularly after the smashing success of *Supergirl*).

For women in the movies, their heroism is reserved almost entirely for the emotional arena, where the triumphs are less photogenic—i.e. less saleable. Occasionally you get something like Sigourney Weaver as an intergalactic Mother Courage battling aliens, but most female action heroines are simply women recast in standard male scenarios, like the lady cops of *Blue Steel* and *Impulse*.

The scant supply of meaningful roles for women isn't only a product of the blockbuster mentality; it's equally linked to Hollywood's avoidance of what is disparagingly referred to as "women's issues." The conflicts of contemporary women don't fit neatly into the standard Hollywood story lines, and in today's Hollywood, neatness counts. The disarray of modern relationships is confusing and threatening—that is to say, uncommercial—to studio heads. And these days, with the demise of most of the small independent companies, the studios are practically the only game in town. Since the new conflicts are not readily marketable, and the old conflicts, in a contemporary setting at least, are moldy, the studio solution has been to can the conflicts altogether.

On television, where projects can move into production faster and where there is less at stake commercially than in the movies, one is much more likely to see honest depictions of women's emotional lives, even the messier aspects; one is also much more likely to see, especially in the never-never-land of the soaps, the kind of old-fashioned romantic scenarios that thrived in the forties and fifties. There's something for everyone, and if the TV shows are no good, there's still the great old romantic movies on view on cable TV, a spectral reminder of what once was.

It's no accident that virtually the only movies to offer full-scale roles for women these days are the ones either set in the past, like *Enemies: A Love Story* and *Dangerous Liaisons* and *Driving Miss Daisy*, or else in some dream-time present, like *The Fabulous Baker Boys*, which draws on our romantic notions about the past as filtered through the movies. The pastness of these movies functions as a kind of shield from contemporary concerns, and yet, because many of them feature a real avidity for sexual and emotional conflict, they seem more alive, more in the present tense, than many of the contemporary movies. (*Enemies*, set in 1949, is a lot more vital than, say, the modern-day *Stanley and Iris* or *Stella*, both of which might have emerged from the thirties.)

The truly contemporary movies that attempt to show off "modern" conflicts often end up schizzy and retrograde. *Baby Boom* proffered an impossible fantasy; it said women could be CEOs and homemakers and land Mr. Right, all at the same time. *Working Girl* featured a heroine, Melanie Griffith's Tess, who was both ditz and whiz—she reaches the top because of her business smarts but also, although the film doesn't point it up, because (unbeknown to her) she sleeps with the right guy.

Of course, the weirdest hybrid fantasy around is the aforementioned *Pretty Woman*. If you bother to take this retooled *Pygmalion* seriously, you might balk at the dubiousness of its dual protagonists: Julia Roberts's Vivian, the happy hooker with a heart of gold, and Richard Gere's corporate raider with a heart of gold. Clichés old and new, both crocks. The film is a smash hit, but it's also provoked more vehemence from moviegoers I've heard from than any other current film I can recall. It confirms a dirty little truth: retrograde fantasies still hold sway.

Vivian could have been something else besides a prostitute and the film would still have fulfilled its fairy-tale aspirations. And yet, in the current movie climate, it makes perfect sense that she is one. The film solves the problem of how to create a modern romantic relationship by making it strictly cash and carry (at first). The film is like a reversal of those gold-digger comedies where Marilyn Monroe cajoled the Corporate Man into loving his millions—in order, of course, to lavish them on her. In *Pretty Woman*, Vivian shames her john into looking beyond his millions (while still reaping their benefits). *Pretty Woman* functions as a warped Prince Charming fantasy for women while, for upscale men, it offers the reassuring life lesson that women aren't just after them for their money.

I don't mean to imply that actresses should only play "politically correct" parts. As a matter of fact, most roles worth playing are politically *in*correct. Who would argue with Jane Fonda's performance in *Klute*? Or, for that matter, with Julia Roberts's amazing work in *Pretty Woman*, or Jennifer Jason Leigh's in *her* two current films. But the sudden influx of these roles is, I think, part of a long-term industry-wide retreat from feminist concerns. At the root of these concerns is the old male bugaboo: Can women be trusted—as business associates, as sex partners, wives? As equals? The answer usually takes the form these days of a brutal put-down. The implication of a film like *Pretty Woman* is that Vivian is a hooker not because of degraded economic necessity but because she chooses to be one—because she *deserves* to be one.

In the immediate post-World War II era, women who had entered the work force during the war found themselves cast out and replaced by returning veterans. Hollywood responded to the problem by concocting fantasy goddesses—the pneumatic, walking, talking pin-ups who reached their apotheosis in Marilyn Monroe. Their cheesecake glamour, totally without threat, was a kind of antidote to the anxieties of the times.

In today's sexually confused society, Hollywood's response to feminism can't be as blithely concocted as in those va-va-va-voom days. As a result, there are very few, if any, "pure" sex sirens on-screen today, certainly none who are major stars (Madonna probably comes closest). Male stars, because their appeal is more simplified and comprehensible, have even taken over the pin-up function from women. The latest films of Mel Gibson and Tom Cruise and Eddie Murphy practically dispense with female co-stars altogether. They're self-infatuated swoon-a-thons.

The dynamism of many of Hollywood's legendary actresses, like Bette Davis and Katharine Hepburn and Barbara Stanwyck, carried a threat even when their roles didn't. Oftentimes men, even more so than women, responded to these actresses; they wanted more of a challenge from their female stars than did the women in the audience.

But the only dynamic, threatening women in the movies right now are the crazies. Their conflicts may develop from a realistic base, like Glenn Close's spurned avenger in *Fatal Attraction* or Kathleen Turner's miserably unhappy wife in *The War of the Roses*, but invariably these characters spin off into a self-immolating, horror-flick rage. Even a "role-model" heroine like Sigourney Weaver's Dian Fossey in *Gorillas in the Mist* is made to seem inhumanly obsessed with her mission. Her heroism comes across as lunacy.

Everybody recognizes that the movies reflect shifting attitudes in society, but that doesn't mean that those attitudes automatically show up in the movies. At least not right away. There's a built-in time lag in the way Hollywood confronts social upheavals—look at how long it took to get Vietnam on the screen—and never more so than in these dog days of the bottom line. Hollywood's solution to the "woman problem" may yet result in a compensatory avalanche of strong, complex, smart, funny female portrayals. In the meantime, this waiting game is excruciating.

(*Los Angeles Times*, 1990)

DEBRA WINGER

It's a blessing to see Debra Winger in two major movie releases at the same time. She's stronger in *A Dangerous Woman* than in *Shadowlands*, but that hardly seems to matter. What's important is that one of the best movie actresses around is once again connecting with audiences.

Not that she's been away, exactly—she didn't pull a Julia Roberts-style disappearing act the past two years. But the two films she appeared in during that time didn't acknowledge her gifts—worse, *she* didn't seem to acknowledge them.

She had a dingbat supporting role in *Wilder Napalm*, released earlier last year but completed in 1991, a black comedy about two pyrokinetic brothers that resembled a Sam Shepard play on Thorazine. *Leap of Faith*, though it had a career-stretching performance by Steve Martin, again relegated Winger to a sideline attraction. She barely had the screen time to locate her character, much less develop it. And before those films, there *was* a two-year disappearing act after *The Sheltering Sky*. In that dry-gulch period, she walked off *A League of Their Own* and Alan Pakula's *Significant Other*.

All of Winger's walking, of course, only reinforced her rep for being "difficult"—a frequent slam against strong-willed actresses. (When Bruce Willis or Alec Baldwin do this sort of thing, they're just being guys.) But some difficulties are worth it. Show business needs its sacred monsters. The scandal of Winger's career has not been her temperamentalness but, rather, the reluctance or the failure on the part of most of our finest filmmakers to fashion great roles for her.

For Winger may be that peculiarly American phenomenon—a great actress who has yet to appear in a great movie (and precious few good ones). She's also had the misfortune to give two of her best performances in movies that practically no one saw: *Mike's Murder* and *Everybody Wins*, both of which, to compound the misfortune, were drastically recut.

After Winger appeared in *Terms of Endearment* in 1983, she was the hottest young actress in Hollywood, with two hits, *An Officer and a Gentleman* and *Urban Cowboy*, already behind her. She hasn't had a hit since, and yet there's a recognition when she's on-screen that hers is the kind of talent that unifies audiences in simple, direct ways.

This is not the only way to connect with audiences or to be a star, but, compared to the glossy etherealness of many female stars, Winger's directness really clears the air.

Winger started out in films like *French Postcards* and *Thank God It's Friday* and on television as Wonder Woman's kid sister Drusilla, but her breakthrough came in 1980 with *Urban Cowboy*. She lent some flavor to that canned corn. As Sissy, whose marriage to John Travolta's Bud skids into a quick U-turn, Winger made it seem as though this woman's upsets were frighteningly vital. There's nothing showy or anecdotal about her work in this film.

Everybody remembers the moment when Sissy bucks the mechanical bull at Gilley's Kama Sutra-style, but the real payoff to that scene comes right after Bud, who has witnessed everything, clomps out of the bar furious and humiliated. We see a look of humiliation on Sissy's face that matches his. She can't bear to hurt him and yet she just did, willfully and unsparingly. Winger gives us all this in close-up, in a few heart-stopping seconds.

The reason Winger's sexually heightened scenes are often so resonant, so talked about, is for precisely this sort of insight. She gives sex an
emotional charge. In *An Officer and a Gentleman*, her brief, notorious
coupling with Richard Gere has a heated, everyday sensuality; they look
like real people enjoying each other's bodies, not just a couple of pumping
movie stars. That scene in *An Officer and a Gentleman* may have helped
to make it the Make-Out Movie of its year, but its power comes from
what it represents for Winger's Paula—it's a confirmation (she thinks)
of her man's love. And because Paula has already shown us how much in
need of love she really is, the scene is, in the truest sense, a consummation.

Winger can fill out a rigged fairy tale like *An Officer and a Gentleman* and make it seem almost real because she doesn't play up Paula as a
working-class ditz; this woman's sexual longing is part of a deeper longing,
and Winger doesn't sentimentalize it (even when the script does). Most
working-class women who appear in our movies might as well be carrying
a placard—"Look at Me, I'm Underprivileged." But for Winger, in movies
like *An Officer and a Gentleman* and *Urban Cowboy*, being working class is
just a part of who she is, neither a defect nor a badge of honor.

She was also the truest thing in *Terms of Endearment*, with its sitcom
Norman Rockwell-ish vistas of the middle class, and its dying Camille
finale. Winger played up the knockabout comedy of mundane bliss and
misfortune; her scenes with her philandering husband, whom she loves
anyway despite herself, or with her dotty mother, her milquetoast lover,
her rapscallion children, are like illuminated pages in a family album.

Winger has a gift for sanity in this movie that turns her trials into a
kind of communion with us. We know people just like her—we *are* her.
It's the most difficult kind of heroic performance because it confers on an
ordinary character an unstressed specialness.

Winger's defining characteristic as an actress is a fluid, radiating intelligence and an almost ecumenical respect for emotional truth. This
explains how she can present a woman who might otherwise seem mundane and give her a rich buzzing inner life. The bank teller hooked on a
low-level drug dealer in *Mike's Murder* or the flippy floozie in *Everybody
Wins* might seem depressingly retro were it not for Winger's capacity to
give each woman her due.

She can show you how these women, against their reason (or unreason), might be pulled into sordidness by men, and how they might hang on. In *Mike's Murder*, for example, her Betty is excluded from the bewildering object of her own passion. She gets drawn into the outlaw world of her cryptic lover after his murder because she wants to know what happened not only to him but to herself. They have a phone sex scene, that, for her, is practically a deflowering; in bed with him, she's beyond the reach of caution. Her serene languor when she's with him transports her. When she looks at Mike's photo at the end of the film and smiles, it's like watching the lifting of a fever dream.

In *Everybody Wins*, Winger commandeers what is otherwise a pretty terrible movie by sheer force of talent. Perhaps only an actress who radiates intelligence can play so well a character whose intelligence is deranged. In terms of character, the film is like the flipside of *Mike's Murder*; Winger plays a woman with a lurid, possibly apocryphal background who lures a decent man into unthinking ardor. Angela Crispini is the kind of role that, with a less gifted actress, might have turned into a multiple-personality tour de force—in other words, the kind of performance you want to avoid. But the split personalities in this film seem so richly lived-in that, individually, they could each sustain their own movie. What unifies Angela in all her guises is self-exhibitionism. She's turning herself on, horrifying herself, and it's as if Angela is not really there except as witness to the spectacle.

Angela's voice can swing from unctuous breathy sincerity—the voice of a radio pop psychologist perhaps—to something scabrous and overenunciated, as if she were clamping down on her words to anchor her fear. Her moods may swing but within each mood she's rapt, flush. She melodramatizes her life in order to give it form—in order to make it comprehensible to herself.

In *A Dangerous Woman*, she plays a woman, Martha, who also seems shattered by some kind of inner trauma but, unlike Angela, she is completely guileless. Where Angela was flamboyant and ferociously sexual, Martha seems stunted, childlike. She has an almost animal reaction to fear, and to happiness, too. And yet the most moving moments in the performance are when Martha is caught in the blur between the two. Her childlike looks are so poignant because you can see the adult trying to come through.

When she is kissed by the handyman who has moved into town, Martha ranges from blissed out to freaked out; Winger gives you ten emotions in a glance. When we see her later, she's still carrying an electrostatic charge from the clinch. Martha's clompy grace, her tight, imperious smiles when she's scared, her shorn quality when she tries to make herself over for the handyman—all of these things come from deep inside the actor's art. This role could have devolved into the "town screwball," but Winger gets inside her skin. It's her way of conferring her blessing on Martha.

She's impressive in *Shadowlands*, too, although the role is too inspirational and constricting for her. As Joy Gresham, the unhappily married American poet whose correspondence with C. S. Lewis leads to a friendship and then to love, Winger is used for her brusque forthrightness; like Martha, she speaks the truth. Most of the movie is given over to the ways in which Lewis is brought out of his comfy cocoon and delivered for the first time since childhood into the real world of pain and loss and love. Joy is not required to go through a comparable register of revelations, but Winger undercuts the role's sacrificial angel aspects by showing us Joy as an essentially lonely woman beneath all the cant. Her provocations of Lewis have a twinge of rage in them.

Winger's appearances in these two films are heartening because they show she's still challenged by acting. She's almost always chosen her roles on the basis of risk, and even when the risk hasn't paid off, as in *Betrayed*, or in *The Sheltering Sky*, where she seemed wan and disembodied, you could respect the fact that she wasn't just plunking herself into a pool of froth. As *Legal Eagles* demonstrated, she couldn't have made a go of it in conventional vehicles anyway. Without the opportunity to employ her fine-edged instincts in that film, she seemed dank and characterless beside the fluffed golden glamour of Robert Redford and Daryl Hannah. Even her marvelous, raspy, honking voice, with its squeaks and blats and deep-toned murmurs, seemed juiceless.

Winger's career is bound up in challenge in more ways than one. She also represents a challenge to Hollywood. Here, after all, is an actress who requires great roles at a time when most roles for women are dinky and ornamental and when women pushing forty are lucky to get *anything* to play. Hollywood has never been very accommodating to actresses like Winger of strong artistic conviction. And Hollywood has never needed them more than now.

(*Los Angeles Times*, 1994)

POSTSCRIPT

A year after this was written, Winger, publicly drubbing the state of movies, famously walked away from the acting business and only somewhat recently, with *Rachel Getting Married*, took on a movie role, albeit a small one, worthy of her. Her presence, as always, remains a guarantor of dramatic truth.

JESSICA LANGE

Blue Sky

Jessica Lange's acting in *Blue Sky* leaves you awestruck. It's a great performance. Because the film, which was shot in 1990, is just now being released—it's yet another foundling from the pre-bankrupt Orion Pictures era—its appearance is like a gift.

It's an especially welcome gift, because Lange hasn't been acting much in the movies lately. (She'll appear in *Losing Isaiah* in November.) She starred on TV in 1992 in *O Pioneers!* and, later that year, on Broadway as Blanche DuBois in *A Streetcar Named Desire*. But her two most recent movies are *Cape Fear* and *Night and the City*.

You have to wonder how it is that Lange could give the performance she gave in *Blue Sky*—it's probably her best, even better than her Frances Farmer in *Frances* or her Patsy Cline in *Sweet Dreams*—and keep away from the cameras for so long. The lack of good roles for actresses is no excuse. Lange is the kind of actress film artists write great roles *for*.

Lange's role in *Blue Sky* as Carly, a manic-depressive army wife, is, at least superficially, one of those life-force sexpot vamps who periodically turn up in the movies in order to reduce stalwart men to foaming fumblers. She's conceived as a sort of cross between a Tennessee Williams hothouse violet—a deranged, damaged maiden—and a late-fifties/early-sixties glamorpuss in the Marilyn Monroe style. (The action is set in 1962.)

Part of what Lange accomplishes with Carly is to demonstrate how close in neurotic temperament these two female incarnations really are.

They both rise and fall on the fragilities of beauty. The loss of beauty—or at least its illusion—becomes the loss of self.

Carly knows she is still beautiful, and she exults in her own good fortune. She sashays with the humor of a woman who believes herself blessed—the gods must want her to entertain them, too. Carly models her look on the reigning movie queens: Monroe, Elizabeth Taylor, Bardot. She has seized on movie-star glamour for its power to transpose her life into a swoony, scandalous fantasy. The irony is that Carly is an original—the more she mimics her fanzine idols, the more she emerges in all her ravaged singularity. When she's manic, she's too much for herself—too ferociously pent-up and passionate—and that's exactly the state she craves. She needs the fix of delirium.

She's a trial to her two daughters, who indulge her episodes with a mixture of horror and annoyance. (They're like abused seraphim.) She's a trial to her husband, Hank, an army radiation scientist, played by Tommy Lee Jones, who decided a long time ago just to love her unconditionally. (The felt, underplayed graciousness of his performance helps make Lange's possible. And, of course, few directors could work more wonders with actors than Tony Richardson—this was his last film.)

But, on some essential level, Carly's deliriums have so much more romantic feeling, so much more danger, than anything else in her family's life that she has become indispensable to their will. She's a maddening creature in full swoon but, when she's in a generous mood, she transforms their dullish life into a high-spirited casbah. (The black comedy of the piece is that Carly makes her husband and children miserable so she can commiserate with them in their misery and make them whole.)

Carly's high spirits lift her way off the ground, but she can't stay up there forever. It's when she comes down with a crash that she terrifies. When Hank—partly because of Carly's take-it-all-off high jinks—is transferred at the start of the film from Hawaii to a military base in Alabama, Carly's sensual, dolled-up funniness inflames to a full-scale rage. Her baby talk and sweet smiles, so transparently protective, burn away, and she flees her run-down new home until Hank tracks her down in a supply store like a cornered animal.

"I can see that radiation just coming off you," she wails at Hank, who talks her down with an infinitely comforting patience. He rescues her again, and, yet again, she will betray him. But as he approaches her in this scene, Carly's eyes shine in admiration for her rescuer. The harridan has turned into a supplicant.

Carly's rages are scary because they don't have the self-dramatizing play-act quality of her swoony, rapt episodes. When she's dancing her flamenco for a bunch of wide-eyed soldiers at the base in Hawaii, or even when she's just dancing sinuously by herself, she has a dreamy, comic quality that lets us know she's in on her own self-delusion. She plays to an audience, even if that audience is herself. (In a sense, the role is all about the illusionary, crazy-making art of acting.)

But, when she feels trapped and cornered, her voice drops from a hushed Southern breathiness to a hard, low-slung rasp. (The vocal shifts are reminiscent of Vivien Leigh's Blanche in the movie version of *Streetcar*.) Her movements becomes jagged. She's not self-dramatizing in these moments; there's no bravura, no studied self-awareness, nothing to distance her (or us) from her pain.

You can see why she avoids the pain—it strips away her camouflage and leaves her ragged and illusionless. When she's high, she's hellbent to stay that way. She has a split-second sensuality; she can turn it on in an instant, before the despair crowds in. When she thinks Hank is losing his love for her, she sits up at night while he sleeps; when he wakes up and sees her, she asks him if he still loves her and then, before he can answer, advances upon him like an uncoiled dream walker.

As the distressed Frances Farmer in *Frances*, Lange sometimes had the lurid, scary, powder-burned look of a figure in a Weegee photograph. In *Blue Sky*, Lange's Carly, at low ebb, sometimes has the bereft, denuded look of a woman in an Edward Hopper painting. Carly can appear so languorously sad—it's not the way we want to see her. (Sadness doesn't make her soulful; it saps her.)

You can almost forgive her hurtful sprees—like the way she carries on with the base commander in full view of everybody—because it's her way of murdering despair. Carly's seductions hurt everyone around her, but, for her, they're not quite real. She doesn't *want* to be "real." She wants to retreat into her own movie-glamour authenticity, and the men she seduces are just play-actors in her pageant.

Carly ends up a heroine by rescuing Hank from a nasty military double-cross. After saving her so many times, she saves him. It's a supreme act of love, and Lange has prepared us for Carly's strength by already showing us, in flashes, the depth of that love and the mettle in her mania. Without this last-inning righteousness, Carly might seem too overpoweringly deluded, too neurotically "womanly" for modern audiences. But she'd be a great character even without this final triumph. Her greatness is in not holding anything back.

The real heroism in *Blue Sky* is the way Jessica Lange doesn't hold anything back. She has so much to give. It's a fierce display.

(Los Angeles Times, 1992)

TOM CRUISE

Top Gun

Don Simpson and Jerry Bruckheimer, the designer-movie mavens who produced *Flashdance* and *Beverly Hills Cop*, have pitched their penchant for high concept *very* high this time out—into the stratosphere. Their new concoction, *Top Gun*, is about world-class jet-fighter pilots, and at least one-fourth of the movie takes place above the clouds. Too bad the entire movie wasn't airborne; whenever the story touches down, it falls apart in the hand like thousand-year-old parchment.

This is the sort of miserably conceived movie, written by Jim Cash and Jack Epps Jr. and directed by Tony Scott, that could have been redeemed only by star power of the highest wattage. Movie stars can sometimes create their own independent drama with a film; their creative tensions, their allure, become the real subject of the movie. But *Top Gun* has Tom Cruise, as "Maverick" Mitchell, the cockpit joy boy who makes it into the navy's elite Fighter Weapons School at San Diego's Miramar Naval Air Station. Cruise doesn't hold the screen like a movie star, although, to a portion of the teen audience, he certainly passes for a star nowadays. He strikes designer-jeans poses and his blank, fixated stare and teeth-baring smile makes him seem as flat and despiritualized as a Sunset Strip billboard portrait. (A friend suggested the film be retitled *Top Gum*.) Cruise wasn't bad in *Risky Business*; his adolescent gallivanting suited him. But *Top Gun* calls for a mesmeric hell-raiser, someone with a radioactive core of danger. "When I first saw you, you were larger than life," smitten astrophysicist Charlotte "Charlie" Blackwood (Kelly McGillis) divulges to him late in the movie. How's that again?

Maverick is supposed to be the kind of nonconforming aerialist who both rankles the military and represents its highest hope. He doesn't fly by the rules, he's a menace to his co-top gunners in their joint maneuvers, but he's still the kind of guy you'd want in a pinch when the MiGs start firing at your tail. It's a variation on Gordon Liddy's Watergate poser: "If you were in a sinking ship, would you want me in the boat with you or John Dean?" (How about neither?) Maverick comes from a flying background—his father, shot down over Vietnam in ignominious, still-classified circumstances, was a daredevil, too. (The boy's top-gun instructor, played by a brush-cut Tom Skerritt, flew on many missions with him.) So it's in the boy's blood to redeem his father's name and prove he's the best. (*An Officer and a Gentleman*, anyone?)

His chief competition in the Fighter School, "Iceman" (Val Kilmer), derides Maverick's showboating. No matter. This guy "feels the need for speed." The film is full of the kind of pushing-the-edge-of-the-envelope jargon that recalls far happier days aloft in *The Right Stuff*. The characters talk about "pulling Gs" and "yanking and banking," but don't be gulled into mistaking this stuff for "authenticity." This is, after all, the kind of movie where an international incident with the Russians is concocted just so the hero can feel good about himself at the end. (I wouldn't trust its research on non-military matters, either. At one point, Maverick, listening to Otis Redding's 1968 recording of "(Sittin' On) The Dock of the Bay," recalls how his parents used to listen to the song when he was a kid. But his father was killed in 1965. Welcome to the Twilight Zone.)

The script for this movie could have been spliced together with taffeta and Krazy Glue. Charlie the astrophysicist comes on like a savvy smart cookie, but as soon as she gets googly-eyed for her pupil, she might as well be an air-headed *hausfrau*. The filmmakers have no faith in this woman's brains; she's in the movie to pull some Gs in the romance department, although Maverick seems more interested in beating out Iceman for the top gun best-flier plaque. That's where the real romantic juices are. The filmmakers seem to know it, too. McGillis doesn't click with Cruise; her passion for him resembles plain old lust, but it's fobbed off on us as true love. The filmmakers dutifully wedge in a few titillation scenes: Maverick shows up shirtless in the elevator with Charlie, in a scene that looks tacked on after the film was already shot. (McGillis's hair doesn't match her hair in rest of the movie.) Then there's the obligatory bedding-down scene, which appears to have been photographed through turquoise lacquer.

The aerial scenes are where the movie's real coupling takes place. They're kinesthetic in an abstract way, since you're never quite sure who's attacking whom, or from where or why. (It wouldn't have killed the filmmakers to explain what a MiG is. Some in the audience thought our boys were firing at "Micks"—the IRA is coming.) The confusion in the sky is typical of the movie, which specializes in anything-for-effect image clusters thrummed to a rock beat. Even an airmen's volleyball game is edited into a clatter of soaring-ball and beefcake shots. There are a few good moments from Anthony Edwards's "Goose"—Maverick's easygoing radar intercept buddy—and the film's notion that top gunners are spiritual cousins of rock stars is intriguing. But it's also commercially calculating, and the calculation in *Top Gun* is so ruthless and relentless that it's like a slap in the face to the audience.

The Top Gun school was supposedly created in the late sixties because the American fighter pilots' kill ratio—the ratio of shot-down American planes to the enemy's—has been in decline since World War II. The rock-star joy boys in *Top Gun*, loop-de-looping in their $35-million-apiece F-14 Tomcats, are portrayed as America's finest. They're Right Stuff guys. But the movie never gets into how these guys cope with peacetime. Wouldn't they secretly itch for a confrontation with the enemy just to demonstrate their skills in a real-life situation? The movie never digs into the paradox of warriors whose lives are geared for a war that may never come. That's why the filmmakers cook up a MiG fracas at the end; they can't bear to see all that training go to waste. And so we watch enemy planes being incinerated in the air, video-game style, as the audience applauds each kill.

Don Simpson has been quoted as saying that he and his partner "simply love movies, and we want to make the kind of movies that you can see on a Saturday night with a Coke and a box of popcorn." In other words, movie-movies. But even kick-up-your-heels date-night movies have to deliver. Simpson and Bruckheimer are wizards of a small, slickster's domain, where studio market research has been sleeked into an aesthetic style, and previous hits are tarted up and recycled. (Simpson was head of production for Paramount when its *An Officer and a Gentleman* was in production.) *Top Gun* doesn't provide the emotional satisfactions of anything as basic as a coherent plot, a good love story, believable characterizations. (When, for example, Maverick finds out the truth about his father, the moment is tossed away like a used spark plug.) It's directed not by dramatic instinct but by board-room fiat. *Top Gun*, by itself, isn't worth blowing a gasket over, but it's symptomatic of the sort of current commercial thinking that believes all you have to give a young audience now to create a hit is a star and a soundtrack album and a checklist of pre-approved elements (like jingoism and snazzy duds). Never mind if they add up to nothing; never mind if this demeans the audience and leaves them with nothing memorable they can take home from the theater. Except, perhaps, the taste of Coke and popcorn.

(*Los Angeles Herald Examiner*, 1986)

POSTSCRIPT

Cruise has loosened up as an actor over the years—I'm thinking particularly of *Jerry Maguire* and *Magnolia*—and yet there's something strenuous about his soulfulness; he turns everything, even repose, into calisthenics. It's not enough that he's a great big movie star (though not as big as he once was); he has to be taken as something more, the CEO of his own destiny.

AL PACINO

Looking for Richard

Looking for Richard is Al Pacino's shaggy, nutty, wheedling documentary about a staging of Shakespeare's *Richard III* and the art of performance. Filmed between jobs over a period of several years, it shows us Pacino in a flurry of guises. We see him as Richard, of course, but also as "himself"—which most often turns out to be a scraggly, bearded roustabout.

For movie and theater audiences accustomed to watching Pacino's dagger stare and cloaked intensity, the actor in this movie is something else again—he's bumptious and glib and more than a little wacky. With his baseball cap turned around and his mouth motoring, he's like a Bardic, superannuated Dead End Kid. He draws his viewers and his cast of well-known actors—and even people off the street—into an extended bull session about Shakespeare: How can you explain his power? How do you read his lines meaningfully? Pacino has already played Richard three times on the stage, so *Richard III* is his focus—though he opens and closes the film with a passage from *The Tempest* and keeps hauling in references to *Hamlet*, usually to its disadvantage, as if he was downgrading a competing brand. (We are told that *Richard III* is the most performed of Shakespeare's plays. Take *that*, Prince of Denmark.)

The snippets and occasional extended scenes from *Richard III* were staged in full costume for the film and feature some big-ticket names: Kevin Spacey as Buckingham, Alec Baldwin as Clarence, Winona Ryder as Lady Anne, Aidan Quinn as Richmond, Estelle Parsons as Queen Margaret, Kevin Conway as Hastings. Pacino interviews Kevin Kline, Kenneth Branagh, Rosemary Harris, Vanessa Redgrave, Peter Brook, John Gielgud, Derek Jacobi, and James Earl Jones.

Accompanied by his cohort and confidant, Frederic Kimball, who "cowrote" the film and functions as a kind of Falstaffian Ed McMahon, Pacino makes his way pilgrimage-style to Stratford to visit the Bard's birthplace and to the reconstructed Globe Theatre in London. He takes his cameras into the South Bronx; into The Cloisters, a medieval museum in Manhattan where he also did some filming; and into Lincoln Center, where, unbelievably, two cops throw him out for lacking a movie permit. Are New York's Finest still pissed about *Serpico*? (Pacino handles the roust with abrasive panache.)

The movie is about Shakespeare, but even more it's about Pacino's bewildered passion for acting. He's like a junkie celebrating the maddening glory of his fix. It's not just the craft of performance that turns him on, it's the whole dizzy realm of the actor's life. For Pacino, life is what you do to work yourself up to a performance. Time spent away from the stage or the cameras is downtime—unless it's grist for acting. Pacino has said in interviews that he subscribes to the philosophy of Karl Wallenda of the Flying Wallendas that you are only living if you're "on the wire." For

Pacino, acting is a high-flying tightrope act, and the highest flying is on the stage, in Shakespeare.

Which is not to say that *Looking for Richard* is rich with insights into Pacino's working methods. Like most American actors, including most great ones, he's inarticulate about what he does. To some extent, he's even pleased with this state of affairs—you can see in the way he yowls and rambles about Richard that he prizes his own "primitiveness." Actors enjoy elucidating their craft, yet, at the same time, they don't really want to know how they do what they do. They want to preserve the mystery because in that mystery is the sense of discovery that makes great acting possible. Actors, particularly those trained in the Method, love to jawbone with each other about every nook and cranny of their characterizations, but most of it is just patter. You might expect novelists, for example, to be able to articulate the essence of what they do, but for actors we have lesser expectations. It may be that the kinesthetic nature of acting, with its connections to the subconscious and the mysteries of personality and mimicry, make it inexplicable to most of its practitioners.

In *Looking for Richard*, the British actors and directors interviewed are invariably more articulate than their American counterparts, and yet their repeated point is that Brits often lose the sense of their performance by overanalyzing. Peter Brook talks about how the British doing Shakespeare are so concerned to speak the lines mellifluously that they lose the passion behind the lines. Vanessa Redgrave makes the point that the iambic pentameter rhythms in Shakespeare should not be strictly enforced: "You must find the iambic pentameter of the soul. Should you find that reality, all the rest will fall into place."

When Pacino is casting about with his fellow actors for "ideas" on how to play *Richard III*, he reminds you of every drawn-out theater-study experience you had to endure in high school or college. The inadvertent comedy in *Looking for Richard* is that some of the finest actors around, such as Pacino and Spacey, don't really have that much more to bring to the party than a slumming theater arts grad student.

You see Pacino whipping himself into shape for the role and you think, *What good can come of this?* And then, when you see him playing Richard, some of it is indeed overwrought and underdone. But some of it, such as his wooing of Lady Anne or his speech that begins, "I am so far in blood . . . ," is great, and you realize that a lot of Pacino's jet-powered ditheriness is what he uses to achieve liftoff. It's what he finally clears away in order to effect a sense of tense repose in his acting. The irony in *Looking for Richard* is that we're looking at the flibbertigibbety well-springs of an actor who has achieved prominence through the force of his stillnesses—most notably in the *Godfather* movies.

But the highwire haywire aspect of Pacino's personality can sometimes be his redemption as an actor. Those zonked stillnesses of his in such films as *Bobby Deerfield* or *Cruising* can be murder, whereas in *Dog Day Afternoon* Pacino's high-flying act seems to express everything he can do as an actor. It's probably his best performance and, on the evidence of *Looking for Richard*, also the one closest to his temperament. Of course, he doesn't always score when he's flying high; as the mayor in *City Hall*, I thought, his grand-standing was none too grand. But Pacino takes risks that pay off. And he wants to be seen as a risk-taker—that's one of the reasons he made *Looking for Richard*. The subtext of the film is: "I may be a movie star, but I am serious about what I do."

For Pacino, that seriousness takes the form of theater work. There is still a cultural snobbery loose in the land that says stage actors are superior to movie actors, and Pacino plays into that snobbery. He may not be aware that his finest acting has been not on the stage but on film. (He's currently starring in Eugene O'Neill's one-man show *Hughie* on Broadway.) I've seen him several times onstage, most memorably on Broadway in *American Buffalo*, and he's been powerful. But I would suggest that Pacino's particular brooding brand of greatness requires a larger arena than the proscenium arch. Onstage, his force can seem blocky and undifferentiated, but in the movies, especially in close-up, he can really take you on a soul dive.

In *Looking for Richard*, Pacino is on a quest for "the meaning of Shakespeare in our lives." He goes up to people on the street, asks them about his plays, and for the most part gets foggy responses. He explains to anyone who will listen the ways in which the Bard can be made accessible to general audiences. But Pacino's mission here, I think, is as misplaced as all those commentators who try to make Hamlet or Romeo and Juliet or Othello resonate for us by making their agonies "relevant." (Othello/O. J. was a big fave last year.) Shakespeare experienced in this way becomes a kind of magisterial guidance counselor. The reduction of his plays to the standard contours of grand passion—as a way to inveigle bored audiences unresponsive to the beauties of language—is patronizing. (Film adaptations of *Twelfth Night, Hamlet*, and an updated *Romeo and Juliet* will all be out by year's end. The honors English field trip brigade must be on red alert.)

Pacino reconciles his love for Shakespeare with the popular artist's dream of Shakespeare for the masses. And it's a good dream. But the masses today aren't the masses of the Globe Theatre. Like it or not, the greatness of Shakespeare's language will never be accessible to the vast majority of the mass audience—or the high-art minority audience, either. Pacino approaches Shakespeare on the most melodramatic and straightforward of levels because that's how he makes sense of his performance. He needs to think melodrama in order to get at drama.

But if we are to base our discussion of Shakespeare on how "exciting" and "relevant" he is to our lives, we are vastly diminishing him. Pacino—not as an actor, but as a proselytizer for Shakespeare—is as fussy and well-meaning and misguided as those teachers who encouraged us to find parallels between *Romeo and Juliet* and our senior prom.

(*New Times*, 1996)

RICHARD PRYOR

Jo Jo Dancer, Your Life Is Calling

Not many film artists have had Richard Pryor's opportunity, in *Jo Jo Dancer, Your Life Is Calling,* to make a self-directed, self-starring, semi-autobiographical movie. It's a genre that includes Chaplin's *Limelight* and Francois Truffaut's *Day for Night* and not many others. But, unlike Chaplin and Truffaut, Pryor, who also co-wrote and produced, has never directed before; he's trying to make sense out of his bruised, hallucinatory life, and he's striking connections in the dark that may be apparent only to him. I don't think *Jo Jo Dancer* is a very good movie, but it has its fascinations—at least for Pryor fans. Watching it is like overhearing the patter of a close friend coming out of a delirium. The movie lets you know what Pryor values most in his life. It's clear that being a rich and powerful movie star who can make the whole world laugh isn't anywhere near the top of his list.

What he appears to value most is surviving. As is the case with many ex-alcoholics and ex-junkies, the triumph of simply getting through the day, and the day after, without succumbing to personal demons, has become the core of his existence. Pryor's demons are still his propulsion, but his strength comes from overpowering them—in an infinite series of tiny, and not so tiny, self-confrontations. *Jo Jo Dancer* is yet another self-confrontation; it has the pull of a movie that Pryor *had* to make (as he has admitted in interviews). Playing a world-famous comic and junkie named Jo Jo Dancer, he opens the film with his near-immolation following a free-basing accident, and throughout the movie he cuts repeatedly to his charred, mummified body in the hospital bed. Pryor wants to rub our noses in the horror of his self-destructiveness; he also wants to defuse that horror by showing us so many pop-eyed, ghastly close-ups that it eventually will lose its force. The movie is an exorcism, with Pryor playing both demon and exorcist.

Pryor's last two stand-up performance films—*Richard Pryor Live on the Sunset Strip* and *Richard Pryor Here and Now*—were made after his 1980 accident. The subtext of those films was that, without his trademark "crazy" anger, he would lose his antic, dangerous comic spirit and turn into a heartwarming, family-entertainment comedian—a stringier Bill Cosby. Pryor said he couldn't "hate" anymore; he feared the newfound balm he offered audiences would waft them away from the furious center of his art. He must have been thinking: *Why should audiences accept my revivalist Mr. Clean act when they can get lowdown with Eddie Murphy?* Pryor may have harbored the fear that it was not himself that audiences responded to, but his shocks. And without the shocks, he felt defrocked in their eyes.

This fear is, I think, unfounded. Even at full strength, Pryor's act never divided audiences; it unified them as ringsiders in the human comedy. But Pryor most likely doesn't see things that way, and his doubts give *Jo Jo Dancer* its woozy poignancy. Pryor truly wants be liked. That, rather than making people laugh, has become his highest ambition. (Audience acceptance would certify his abstinence.) But Pryor doesn't have the directorial smarts to mute and stylize his heartbreak; he doesn't have the faintest notion of how to work up a *Terms of Endearment*-style bawlfest. And that's probably just as well; the sentimentality and special-pleading and self-basting in *Jo Jo Dancer* are offered to the audience without mediation, as a heap of unsorted emotion. This artlessness comes partially from incompetence but also because Pryor doesn't see the *need* for art in a movie about his life. Pryor probably regards *Jo Jo Dancer* as his most "honest" achievement, because it's not glitzed by artifice—or belly laughs.

The "honesty" in *Jo Jo Dancer* is nevertheless highly self-serving, although Pryor is such a *sympathetic* tormented soul that the movie never seems like an obnoxious ego-wallow. (It ought to.) After the free-basing scene, the movie flashes back to Jo Jo/Pryor's childhood, where little Jo Jo (played by the delightful, camera-ready E'Lon Cox) is being raised in his family-owned Midwestern brothel. You may feel you could forgive a kid anything who grew up staring at his hooker mother through a keyhole, but the brothel scenes don't have a traumatic tone—they're closer to the homey, convivial whorehouse scenes in *Pretty Baby*. But when Jo Jo's mother (Diahne Abbott) tells him, "I have nothing to give you, I gave you everything I had," you realize you're being set up for Dickensian heartbreak. What follows—the teenage Jo Jo's banishment from his father's house—is an extension of that heartbreak, and so are the scenes with Jo Jo and his one true friend, his grandmother (the wonderful Carmen McRae), and also the road-to-celebrity scenes with Jo Jo and his various wives. Jo Jo's descent into drugs and alcoholism is partly explained by the influence of sinister Hollywood smoothies with coke-spoon smiles; the reasons for the breakups of Jo Jo's many marriages are also suspiciously face-saving. His first wife fakes being pregnant to tie the knot and won't stand by him in his quest for a show-biz career. His second wife (Barbara Williams), who is white, sends the marriage into the dumper by sidling into group sex at a druggie party that the couple reluctantly attends. ("But I thought that's what you *wanted*," she mews to her devastated Pagliacci.) His third wife (Debbie Allen) philanders.

These scenes almost completely miss out on the sort of impacted hostilities and tensions, racial and otherwise, that must have accompanied their real-life counterparts (judging from Pryor's monologues in his stand-up movies, not to mention the lurid leaks in the press). They have an almost childlike naiveté; they cast Jo Jo as a poor put-upon soul—he's the Little Tramp contending with bigger tramps. Jo Jo is supposed to be a comic rebel, but you'd never know where his rebellion came from. Jo Jo's inflammatory reputation as a stand-up comic doesn't connect with anything that we see in his life, and so it just seems like shtick. But Pryor, except for some wonderful scenes in a mob-owned rat-trap early in Jo Jo's career, doesn't bother to show us much of Jo Jo's performing power at all. (These scenes feature a great team: Paula Kelly, Art Evans, and Billy Eckstine.) Pryor doesn't seem to care about Jo Jo's artistry. In fact, on some level, you get the feeling he *condemns* it, since it was Jo Jo's gifts that got him into the Kleig-lit arena that allowed him to self-destruct.

A perverse sort of masochism is at work in *Jo Jo Dancer*. Pryor doesn't want us to jive on Jo Jo's talents. He gives us a marvelous pantomime of a baby being born, and a bizarre drag number, but not much else. Jo Jo's rise to glory is glossed over in a montage scene that deliberately trashes his performer's rhythm. Since Jo Jo was not happy while he was making others happy, we're supposed to regard his routines with disdain. We're not meant to enjoy the show, we're meant to pull a lesson out of it, the way Scrooge, guided through his life, was meant to understand how he became what he was—in order to shape up.

The ghosts who guided Scrooge are replaced in *Jo Jo Dancer* by Jo Jo's spiritlike alter ego, which wafts out of his charred body in the opening scenes and sticks by him for the rest of the movie. This spirit keeps nudging Jo Jo (and us) with tiny take-heed warnings; he's a surprisingly humorless conscience. What really pulls *Jo Jo Dancer* down is this moralistic game plan. We're meant to look at Jo Jo's life not in terms of the pleasure he gave himself and others, but rather in terms of the tremendous toll that that pleasure took. And because so much of that toll is presented as Jo Jo's victimization, the movie has a sickly "Why me?" tone.

Richard Pryor, in his stand-up routines, is a great, unsparing artist. In *Here and Now*, shot mostly in the French Quarter, he sidles into an extended take-off on a junkie—from shoot-up to euphoria to nod-out—that's one of the most extraordinary and self-lacerating pieces of acting I've ever seen. All the frights and rage and desperation of his years of addiction are compacted into this tragic little vignette. We see him strung-out, eyes closed, his needle-pocked arm limp and enlarged at his side, his bent body arched like a weeping willow, his mouth obscenely agape. He registers the bone-chill of true terror.

In *Jo Jo Dancer*, you want to respond to his truth-baring, even if it's on his own terms. But there's no character to hang onto in this movie, just snippets of personality. Onstage, Pryor is a genius at instantly seizing the essence of his characterizations, whether it be a bawling baby or a wino or an opium pipe. But he has no distance from himself here; he can't comprehend his own life, and for that reason, he can't dramatize it. He seems to know this, too. The garbled sequences and ellipses in this movie are on display, as if Pryor was hoping the audience could pull together his life for him in a way that he couldn't do for himself. If Pryor truly were devoid of his demons, he might indeed be able to dramatize his life, the way an old soldier can turn battles into anecdotes. But *Jo Jo Dancer* is the work of a man still caught up in the battle.

(*Los Angeles Herald Examiner*, 1986)

EDDIE MURPHY

Overview

Does Eddie Murphy know how good he is as the soulful R & B singer James "Thunder" Early in *Dreamgirls*? Playing a shimmying satyr on the skids, he seems almost aghast at his prowess. It's the performance of his career—a great performance. He has stunned even his most ardent fans, many of whom believed he didn't have it in him to be a "real" actor, let alone an Oscar nominee.

And yet this is the man who can be seen in the same multiplex playing, among other characters in *Norbit,* a voluminous Gorgon overflowing her garter.

"Eddie Murphy as you love to see him!" run the newspaper ads for *Norbit.* But how exactly do we love to see Eddie Murphy? As big momma? A nebbishy twit, perhaps? How about the megaplump Professor Klump or a Beverly Hills cop? As Donkey in *Shrek*? As, God forbid, Dr. Dolittle?

Consistency is not a charge you could ever level at Murphy. But those who see him as a first-time genius in *Dreamgirls* must not have been paying attention. He has often been undervalued as an actor because, for the most part, he has been best in slapstick burlesques such as *Bowfinger* or *The Nutty Professor* (a performance for which, to its credit, the National

Society of Film Critics in 1996 awarded him best actor). Bottom line—great actors are not supposed to make fart jokes.

But even if one grants Murphy his glories in these films, his career, despite his pick of the litter, is slathered with simply dreadful stuff. What do we expect of Eddie Murphy? To put the question more directly, what does he expect of himself? He is one of the most commercially successful actors in history and also one of the most confounding.

When Murphy arrived on the scene in 1980 as a member of *Saturday Night Live,* he was, as an African American, the recipient of two warring traditions: the credit-to-his-race Sidney Poitier syndrome, which was on the downswing, and the so-called blaxploitation cycle, with its Shafts and Superflys.

Murphy, nineteen when he began the show, took a swing at both. He parodied Gumby, Buckwheat, Jesse Jackson, pimps, black power ranters. He was pompadoured James Brown dipping his toe in a hot tub and shrieking, "Hot tub!" Murphy almost singlehandedly kept *SNL* alive in the early eighties.

He could make you feel like you were in collusion with his down and dirtiest impulses, and he went further into brambly territory than the rest of the cast. But ultimately, he was all about role-playing as a performance statement, not as a political statement. For him, the black-white divide was just a variation on the doubleness that divides all comics—the chasm between how they see themselves and how others perceive them.

Unavoidably, however, Murphy incorporated into his routines the wish fulfillment fantasies of not only blacks in the audience but whites, too, who enjoyed having the racial tables reversed. He became an instant movie star with *48 Hrs.* and *Trading Places* in large degree because he was so much smarter and more flagrantly funny than his white counterparts. Still pretty much a revue-sketch comic, he barely gave Nick Nolte and Dan Aykroyd the time of day in these films. He was a cocky monologuist, all mouth.

By the time he made *Beverly Hills Cop,* it was clear that Murphy also fancied himself a Stallone-style action hero. Whenever he went into his lawman routine, he froze up and lost his specialness. For the first time in his career, a scene was stolen clean away from him—by, fittingly, a comic, Bronson Pinchot.

As the diminished sequels to *48 Hrs.* and *Beverly Hills Cop* ticked by—as well as lucrative but unmemorable fare like *Harlem Nights* (where he, as co-writer-producer-director, cut his co-star and idol Richard Pryor off at the knees), *Coming to America, Boomerang, Vampire in Brooklyn*—a lot of people wondered why Murphy wasn't making the earth move in his films the way he once did in television. He was no longer a rock star, he was just another movie star.

To some extent, this was an unfair expectation, for how many corrosive comic actors have ever triumphed for long over the homogenizing effects of Hollywood? Most of Murphy's *SNL* colleagues (Chevy Chase being only the most conspicuous example) lost their edge in the movies and became entrapped in the muck of family entertainment. But there were also rare exceptions, like Aykroyd, especially in *Driving Miss Daisy,* and Bill Murray, who developed into far more accomplished, far more mysteriously gifted movie performers. When you see Murray get inside his spooky silences and open himself up in *Lost in Translation,* you realize you're watching a transformation that is at the very heart of acting.

It took a while for Murphy to achieve this kind of audacity and come into his own as an actor. Because he came out of stand-up and sketch comedy, he learned early on to coast on attitude; there was little continuity of character in his performances. In *Trading Places,* for example, we never see in the successful businessman the foul-mouthed vagrant he once was. It's like watching two different actors.

But then there is *Bowfinger,* where he plays, among other roles, a relentlessly paranoid movie star who is clearly a ruthless send-up of himself and his very public problems, or *Life,* where he plays with total authenticity a convict who ages forty years in the course of the movie, or *The Nutty Professor,* where the pairing of decorous, fat-suited Sherman Klump and his testosterone-fueled alter ego, Buddy Love, defines the yin and yang of Murphy's career (and also of African-American personas in show business).

It's one of the most startling comic performances on film, right up there with Steve Martin in *All of Me.* With his brown jacket and bow tie, his chuckling low voice and Oliver Hardy-like gracefulness of movement, Klump is determinedly old school. Murphy has a deep-down affection for this man. His Buddy Love, on the other hand, with his bodytight duds, hyperventilated hyena laugh and propulsive patter, is Murphy's nightmare unveiling of his own inner imp. As is often the case with Murphy at his best—or even much lower down, as in *Norbit*—what at first seems like blatant racial caricature turns out to be much more complex and emotionally nuanced.

As James "Thunder" Early in *Dreamgirls*, Murphy hasn't split himself in two—or three or five. He is playing a man who is triumphantly, tragically himself. He is also playing, for the first time in his career, an artist, and perhaps this explains the ferocity and despair with which he attacks the role. Early is an ecstatic entertainer self-immolating in his own spotlight; the sheer sexual pleasure of performing has rarely been so well expressed.

This is why, to protest his new, sanitized self, Early drops his pants onstage in exulant protest. This is why, when he gets the word that his soul sound won't cut it anymore, he shuts down right before our eyes. He pulls out the heroin and prepares for dreamland and the ravaged look in his eyes tells us he's not coming back. This is not Early's final scene in the movie but it should be. It's his poisoned valedictory.

Murphy is totally exposed in this film—there are no fat suits to act as a poultice.

Sometimes actors reach so far inside themselves that they are left bewildered by what they have brought forth. This performance as James "Thunder" Early is the latest, and most confounding, chapter in our long and complicated relationship with Eddie Murphy. He is only forty-five. May the complications increase.*

(*Los Angeles Times*, 2007)

Harlem Nights

Harlem Nights is the first movie to costar Eddie Murphy and Richard Pryor. Watching the sorry, unfunny mess that has resulted is like witnessing a highly touted heavyweight title bout that inexplicably turns into a pat-a-cake session between cruiserweights. Even those of us who have

---

* They haven't, as films like *Meet Dave, Imagine That, A Thousand Words, Tower Heist* ad nauseum confirm. Murphy is the hit man of his own career.

just about given up on Murphy hoped the pairing with Pryor would snap him to attention. But it's been a long stretch since either Murphy *or* Pryor has thrilled audiences with anything more than their star power.

There was a time—say, seven or eight years ago—when such a confab would have raised the rafters. Murphy began his four-year stint at *Saturday Night Live* during the 1980–1981 season, and his appearances on that show, with his impersonations of pimps, jailbirds, Gumby, Buckwheat, and Bill Cosby, are his comic high points. Pryor, of course, had a thriving if uneven movie career in the early eighties. His glory, however, was his stand-up comedy films, particularly the 1978 *Richard Pryor Live in Concert* and the 1982 *Richard Pryor Live on the Sunset Strip*. They were the movies in which Richard Pryor could be Richard Pryor.

In the intervening years, Murphy has become a major movie star largely at the expense of what made him a TV star. He's moved away from the quicksilver, revue-sketch humor and the edgy playfulness of his *Saturday Night Live* days and turned himself into a commodity. His comic facetiousness has turned stone-cold. Whereas he once professed his idol to be Richard Pryor, his movies suggest another deity: Sylvester Stallone.

Murphy is a movie star because his films make fortunes, but is there anything stellar about his work as a thirties nightclub dandy in *Harlem Nights,* a movie in which his character's homicidal streak is played for cheap laughs? Is there anything anointed about his work in films like *Beverly Hills Cop II* (a movie originally intended for Stallone) or *The Golden Child* or *Coming to America?* His reprehensible 1986 stand-up comedy film *Raw,* which begins when, leather-suited, he strides onstage amid hoopla more appropriate to the Second Coming, represents his "purest" expression to date; in it, his free-floating hostilities descend on women, gays, whites, blacks—take your pick. *Raw* was a real potpourri of hate. To review it was to leave the domain of criticism for psychiatry.

Stardom can sometimes enlarge an actor's possibilities and bring out what was nascent, and best, in his talents. The reverse seems to have happened to Murphy. In *Saturday Night Live*, he was part of an ensemble; he was challenged by the other performers. In his movies, starting with his first (and still best) film, *48 Hrs.,* where he costarred with Nick Nolte, Murphy has essentially been performing solo. He works with such crackerjack precision that sometimes he doesn't need anybody else around; he can be his own most appreciative audience.

But Murphy desperately needs to be challenged in the movies. Yet, given the fact that he controls them so completely—he is writer, director, and executive producer of *Harlem Nights*—how will that ever happen? His clout has allowed his worst instincts to come through.

Richard Pryor is playing his surrogate father in his new film, but there's an element of condescension in the casting. Pryor is positioned as Murphy's wise and cautious mentor, an elder statesman. It's the kind of "tribute" that's indistinguishable from neutering.

If Eddie Murphy's star power has allowed him all too successfully to tincture his films with the poison of his stand-up-comedy attitudes, then Richard Pryor has the opposite problem. His box-office clout has allowed him the opportunity to make a series of marginal movies with virtually no connection to his great stand-up persona. In films ranging from *The Toy* to *Bustin' Loose* to *Brewster's Millions,* Pryor has opted for the cushiony comforts of family entertainment. With his pick of writers, directors, and costars, he has willingly led himself into creative oblivion. It's as if Lenny Bruce walked into a movie career playing a Muppet.

It's never been easy for a volatile talent to score in the movies; the commercial demands of the business are invariably at odds with true subversiveness. But Pryor has the kind of control that might have preserved his rawness on film, not only in his concert movies, but in his dramatic films, too. The cuddliness of his screen image is a sick joke; it might seem like a put-on if only Pryor showed some sign that he was in on the con. But he's resignedly bland in his movies; anything malign or threatening has been bleached out.

With an artist as troubled and complicated as Pryor, it's difficult to assign motivation. Does a film like *Bustin' Loose,* where he plays a good-natured grump to a busload of kids, represent what Pryor thinks the movies deserve? Does he think such movies represent what *he* deserves? He has never quite given up entirely. Bad as it was, his 1986 autobiographical film *Jo Jo Dancer, Your Life Is Calling,* which he also directed, was at least an attempt to scour the treacle from his image. In films like the 1972 *Lady Sings the Blues,* where he played Piano Man to Diana Ross's Billie Holiday, the 1978 *Blue Collar,* where he played an autoworker, and the 1981 *Some Kind of Hero,* where he played a POW returning from Vietnam, he gave indications of wanting to do more as an actor than just make nice. For years there was talk that he was preparing a film biography of Charlie Parker.

The problem may be that Pryor believes that, in order to quell his demons, he can't draw on anything in his life that means anything to him. In *Live on the Sunset Strip,* talking about his recuperation after his free-basing accident, he says, "Maybe I ain't funny anymore. Maybe I ain't angry at nothing for real in my heart." But the triumph of that performance was that Pryor demonstrated he *could* be an artist without working up a fount of rage. Pryor has been funnier than he was in that film, but he was never as mysteriously moving, or as fragile.

Actually, Pryor has always been mischaracterized as an incendiary comic. He was never really a social-activist crusader; his stand-up riffs exposed racism, but his humor was deeply personal, screwed up, aloof. The Get Whitey agenda of the early seventies never quite played for Pryor as it did for other black comics and actors because Pryor was after private demons, not white demons. His landscape was ultimately interior. He could split himself into an entire gallery of characters: winos, junkies, hustlers, movie executives, ex-wives. He could animate inanimate objects, like, most memorably, his cocaine pipe in *Live on the Sunset Strip*. The only thing Pryor can't play is normal, and that, ironically, is what he's set out to be in movie after movie.

The history of black performers in the movie business is such a trail of waste and despair that the ascension of Eddie Murphy and Richard Pryor has symbolic value out of all proportion to their actual achievement. With few exceptions, black actors have only been accepted as stars when they were comics.

This must explain some of Eddie Murphy's rage. Deprived in his early movies of any love interest with his white female costars, straitened into situations where he played the black sidekick joker to white actors, he has overcompensated by shunting his creative energies into a makeover that probably means a lot more to him than it does to audiences. His attempts to promote himself as a stud action-hero with a curdling cruel humor must function as a kind of retribution for him. For some of us, it's a punishment.

(*Los Angeles Times,* 1989)

WILL FERRELL

In this Apatovian Age of the Big Baby comedy, Will Ferrell is the undisputed avatar. He plays seriously self-absorbed characters who do not have much self to absorb. He is also, obliviously, a tantrum-throwing tease. In movie after movie, and, before that, on *Saturday Night Live,* he bares his midriff, he displays the ringlets of his fuzzy-wuzzy chest. Can no one stop this man from mooning? From streaking?

In his new comedy, *Semi-Pro,* set in the seventies when hair was big, he plays Jackie Moon, a one-hit-wonder whose single, "Love Me Sexy," allows him to own, coach, and play power forward for the Flint, Michigan, Tropics of the American Basketball Association. Like his recent movies, *Talladega Nights: The Ballad of Ricky Bobby* and *Blades of Glory,* it's slipshod slapstick punctuated by bursts of inspired nuttiness. Moon's mantra is "Everybody love everybody," but by the time the season plays out he's wrestled a bear, partaken of the latest in dumpster cuisine and chewed out a ref with unprintable spew.

All of which is typical of Ferrell. His specialty is to flip flop between the passive and aggressive polarities of his characters. That's why he was so good as George W. Bush—he never forgot that Mr. Mission Accomplished had once been a male cheerleader. (Ferrell, of course, played a cheerleader on *SNL.*) Often Ferrell's placid cluelessness is just bubble wrap for the beast within. The default position for all men, he seems to be saying, is to behave badly. (The reason he makes so many sports movies must be because he views athletics as the cauldron of blowhard masculinity). The more straight-arrow Ferrell is, the more avidly we crave his fits. His ordinariness, his sweatered middle-class whiteness, is a setup. You can be sure that, soon enough, he'll bawl—or hurl.

And yet there's an innate sweetness to Ferrell even when he's on the rampage, and this is what separates him from, say, John Belushi or Bill Murray, two earlier *SNL* alumni who tilled the same scorched earth. Those guys meant business, hostility was their root and branch, but the anger in Ferrell's characters is like a fever that flares and then, just as mysteriously, lifts. The reason he's so good as the elf in *Elf* is because he didn't need to fake the innocence. When he downs a gallon of Coke in one swig and lets out an interminable, industrial-strength burp, he's no slobbo, just a big kid.

Ferrell captures the fatuousness that is every man's downfall. His most memorable characters on *Saturday Night Live* were the ones that gave that fatuity free rein. Playing along with Chris Kattan as one half of the party-hopping, body-jerking Butabi brothers—a role he later repeated with mixed results in his first starring movie *A Night at the Roxbury*—he was like a Bizarro Planet version of John Travolta's Tony Manero from *Saturday Night Fever*. With his thatched hair parted up the middle and his bright white teeth and blank Roswell alien eyes, he seemed pole-axed by hottie overload.

His hot-tubbing, sangria-sipping swinger on *SNL* looked like a debauched apostle. His Robert Goulet behaved as if all the world was his lounge. As James Lipton, the host of *Inside the Actor's Studio*, Ferrell looked like the second stage of the Wolfman. (He is often at his most deranged when he sports a fake beard or mustache—it brings out the Paleolithic in him). He nails Lipton's oleaginous persona, his sepulchral, Master Thespian intonations. We are made to understand that, no matter the wattage of the guest, Lipton is the true star.

Ferrell is also a marvelous physical comic—another reason, perhaps, why so many of his movies center on sports. He's not wonderful in the way that, say, Steve Martin is, or Jim Carrey. Martin at his best has a gyroscopic aplomb; he finesses gravity. Carrey is a human Slinky. Ferrell's virtuosity is clunkier. While Carrey appears to have no bones, Ferrell is all torso and kneecaps and elbows. His bigness—he's six foot three—gives him a daffy discombobulation. Striding buck naked through the suburban streets in *Old School* (perhaps his best comedy), or Lutzing across the ice in *Blades in of Glory*, he moves like a mildly inebriated llama.

It's no news that comics yearn to display their inner Pagliacci and Ferrell is no exception. In *Live from New York*, the 2002 oral history of *Saturday Night Live*, he was interviewed after he ended his seven-year stint. "My dream of all dreams," he said, "would be to do what Tom Hanks or Jim Carrey have been able to do—make the transition somewhere down the line from doing comedy to dramatic parts in the movies."

This he has done—sort of. In the little-seen *Winter Passing*, he played a supporting role as a spacey former guitarist of a Christian rock group called Punching Pilate who quit the ensemble when it "went all ska." It's the sort of part he might once have worked up as an *SNL* skit but he was affecting in it. The spaciness came out of a hurt and not the usual void. He's also touching as a lovelorn out of work actor in Woody Allen's comedy-drama *Melinda and Melinda,* but he was fitted with Woodyisms that didn't sound right coming out of his mouth. *Stranger Than Fiction,* where he plays a tax man who discovers he's a character in an author's novel, was a depresso meta-drama that used Ferrell's big blankness as a placard for angst. (At least in Carrey's meta-movie, *Eternal Sunshine of the Spotless Mind,* the misery was energized).

You can't really fault Ferrell for wanting to secure the occasional day pass from Team Apatow. And yet films like *Old School* and *Kicking and Screaming* and *Anchorman: The Legend of Ron Burgundy* did occasionally scale the hyperventilated heights of his best *SNL* work. Unlike his "serious" films, they don't feel like diminutions of his appeal. As with so many *SNL* stars before him, Ferrell is caught in a bind—repeat yourself and rake in a pasha's riches or stretch yourself and, as they say in politics, risk alienating your base.

But what if Ferrell's dumb comedies were smarter? What if he stretched himself in ways that, instead of blanking himself out, deepened and complicated what we already love about him? Eddie Murphy was able to do it, and Bill Murray and Steve Martin, but not many others. Ferrell, especially among the younger set, has phenomenal audience rapport—he helped launch the highly successful comedy website FunnyOrDie.com last year—and that should count for something as he attempts to move beyond his revue-sketch roots. (It may be that, in the future, the comics who thrive will be the ones who come across best as digitized miniatures.)

The saving grace of the Apatow movies and their ilk, the thing that cauterizes the raunch, is that the women in them are always wise to the men—they've got their number. Ferrell has often worked well with strong women, such as Zooey Deschanel in *Elf* or, when he's not being a zombie, Maggie Gyllenhaal in *Stranger Than Fiction.* They bring out in him a yielding, beseeching quality. As he moves into his forties, Ferrell's creative salvation could be the romantic comedy, and I can think of a few directors—like Richard Linklater, or the Alexander Payne who made *Sideways*—who could take the romance in directions that we, and Farrell, might never have imagined.

Here's something I can imagine right now: Ferrell playing Bush in his final hours in the Oval Office. And wouldn't you kill to see him in a comedy sketch as Daniel Day-Lewis in *There Will Be Blood*? No doubt the pants would come off.

I'm all for Ferrell as Everyman, but in the process, let's not lose sight of Everyjerk. Let's not throw out the Big Baby with the bath water.

(*Los Angeles Times*, 2008)

POSTSCRIPT

This was written before such ineffably awful movies as *Land of the Lost* and *The Campaign*. Ferrell's career, despite the occasional oddball foray like *Everything Must Go* and *Casa de mi Padre,* could use a lot more cowbell.

ROBERT DE NIRO

American movies have rarely been worse, but the acting in them has rarely been better. What this means is that the acting is often the only reason to stay with a film. It also means that most good actors end up playing out their careers in third-rate material.

But what about an actor like Robert De Niro, who has the power to pick his own projects and even heads his own production company, Tribeca Films? Did he really need to play his umpteenth stalker-psycho in *The Fan*? Forget about what a performance like this does for *us*. What does it do for *him*?

As the baseball fanatic obsessed with Wesley Snipes's superstar San Francisco Giants slugger, De Niro is scrunched and obdurate, with nasty-nutty eyes. He's done this sort of thing so many times he seems to be literally doing it in his sleep. His cracked wacko grin has about as much menace as a plastic Halloween pumpkin. De Niro draws on our memories of him in *Taxi Driver* (where he was great) and *The King of Comedy, Cape Fear,* and *This Boy's Life* (where he wasn't).

Actually, De Niro hasn't been great in quite a while, though critics still reflexively refer to him as our premier actor. To be fair, it's not as if he has only taken on projects like *The Fan*. It just seems that way. He pokes around periodically as a nice guy in the movies, but De Niro "nice"—in such movies as *Falling in Love, Stanley and Iris, Awakenings,* and *A Bronx Tale*—is often De Niro neutered.

He'll star in two other films this year—Barry Levinson's *Sleepers* and the Broadway comedy adaptation *Marvin's Room*—and perhaps they will allow him the latitude to do something new in the movies for a change.* The most promising thing they have going for them is that they are not directed by Martin Scorsese. But wait—Scorsese has announced plans to make the Richard Pryor story. Can we expect to see De Niro in his most challenging role yet?

Of course the De Niro-Scorsese partnership resulted early on in some extraordinary work. As Johnny Boy in *Mean Streets,* Travis Bickle in *Taxi Driver,* Jimmy Doyle in *New York, New York,* and Jake La Motta in *Raging Bull,* De Niro was more than Scorsese's leading man—he was the director's demon seed. They brought out in each other a feral, operatic hipsterism; they merged improvisation and the Method and the revue sketch with lapsed Catholicism to create a new and alarmingly comic sense of dread. De Niro's acting, like Scorsese's direction, seemed to erupt right in front of us. You came out of a movie like *Mean Streets* or *Taxi Driver*—even more so than in *Raging Bull*—feeling as if you had been ringside at a live event.

But that was all a long time ago—*Raging Bull,* the last collaboration I liked, was 1980. They don't do anything for each other any more. The animus has lost its animation. Did the critics who chided De Niro in *Casino* for retreading his work in *Goodfellas* forget that the *Goodfellas* performance was a retread, too? De Niro doesn't descend into the spooky crawl spaces of character that made him such an original presence in his seventies films. Few know the difference. But De Niro must. Could it be that playing Rupert Pupkin in *The King of Comedy* convinced him that he could coast on acclaim by blanking himself out? As an actor, his idea of playing soul-dead is being brain-dead.

But the dead-headedness isn't reserved only for his stalkers and psychos and goombahs. It's there as the Oliver Sacks patient in *Awakenings,* where he uses his character's unreachableness to dim effect; it's there in

---

* They didn't.

Guilty by Suspicion, as a blacklisted screenwriter who rats; it's there as the nighttown hustler in *Night and the City.* Directing himself in *A Bronx Tale,* he played up his lumpy prole side, which already proved a big yawn in films like *Stanley and Iris.* De Niro isn't cut out to play Everyman— even at half speed, he's too wily and furtive about the eyes. An actor like Tom Hanks can do it because there's something cushiony and nonthreatening about him. His ordinariness, as in *Apollo 13* or *Forrest Gump,* is the launching pad for his sanctification. And because Hanks conveys an essential decency, he can play the heroic common man and get away with it.

De Niro doesn't have that same simplicity; when he relaxes into ordinariness, he effaces himself because he's not drawing on anything that means anything to him. His saving grace is that he can't quite sink into mush with a straight face. He crooks his grin, and the jig is up.

De Niro, right from the start, was a special case. Although he was compared to the early Brando and to Pacino, with whom he's often erroneously lumped, De Niro was the strangest cat in the petting zoo. He didn't have Brando's emotional muscularity; with Brando you could see moment by moment how his characters struggled to shape to their passions. Pacino, though he has his own blank streak, has something of this quality, too—a spirited emotionalism that lets you know what his characters are going through.

But De Niro has always had a cauterized, closed-off quality; he's not the sort of actor who carries you along by eliciting a sympathetic response. His best performances—not just in the early Scorsese films but also as the young Vito Corleone in *The Godfather Part II* and, to a lesser degree, as the Jewish mobster in Sergio Leone's *Once Upon a Time in America* and as Irving Thalberg in *The Last Tycoon*—all feature characters with a cold spot where their heart ought to be. So what is it that makes his unreachableness as, say, Travis Bickle in *Taxi Driver* so much more eloquent than his blankness in a movie like *Cape Fear* or *The Fan*?

The answer is that in *Taxi Driver* De Niro willed himself into such fierce psychological vibration with Travis that what ended up on the screen had an almost unbearable purity. He didn't go in for the usual tricks and feints that actors work up to let us know they're playing bad guys; he avoided the paraphernalia of performance that would seek to "explain" Travis for us. This was a daring, modern approach to acting—and yet it was clearly acting, not psychodrama. Later on—it starts to show up in

Raging Bull—De Niro began to erase the line between acting and behaving. He rolled out his performances without attaching any depth charges to them, and so what we ended up with was soulless mimicry.

De Niro's appearance last year in Michael Mann's *Heat* was billed as the movie equivalent of the Thrilla in Manila—De Niro and Pacino acting opposite each other for the first time! But after the big buildup, all we got was a single scene in a diner (unless you count the shootout at the end). De Niro wasn't bad in *Heat*—his blankness at least had some intensity this time out. Playing a professional crook, he had the wariness of someone prepared to walk out on his fly-by-night life at any moment and never look back.

But the strong-silent enigmatic stuff De Niro was called upon to do in *Heat* derived from the French noir *policiers,* and, proficient as he was, he seemed as caged by the conception as his crook was caged by fate. He brooded till the cows came home. So did Pacino. Their big scene together turned into a real broodathon—it was more like a stunt than a collaboration. *Frankenstein Meets the Wolf Man.* They didn't draw the scene out into anything memorable; maybe they were trying for Dostoyevsky, but what we got was tony tough-guy-ism.*

De Niro at his best collapsed the standard Hollywood tough-guy persona, and he did it, not coincidentally, in the wake of the Vietnam War. He brought out the psychotic potential in the American man of action in a way no American movie star had dared since Humphrey Bogart in *The Treasure of the Sierra Madre.* Like many of the best directors of that era—not just Scorsese but Coppola and De Palma and Peckinpah—he gave violence its complicated, crazy-making due. If De Niro could put that complicatedness back into his acting—if he could once again play out the true warp and woof of rage—he might also put some of the sting back into our violence-themed movies. But he's older now, and probably the rage has burned off. If he must persist in playing nutcases, shouldn't he at least make the self-parody intentional?

(*New Times,* 1996)

---

* They appeared together full-time, to nobody's advantage, in *Righteous Kill.*

POSTSCRIPT

Subsequently, in such movies as *Analyze This* and *Meet the Parents* and their sequels, De Niro did indeed make the self-parody intentional, and found a whole new and younger audience. But it was in the comedies *Wag the Dog,* playing a political fixer, and the Hollywood satire *What Just Happened?,* both directed by Barry Levinson, that he once again displayed the shaggy, farcical gifts he revealed very early in his career, especially in Brian De Palma's revue-sketch *Hi, Mom!*

SYLVESTER STALLONE
Rambo

The posters for *Rambo* that have been proliferating like kudzu across the urban landscape feature a blurry black-and-white rendering of our hero's iconic mug. It's a pop abstraction—part Che Guevara, part Jesus, part FBI's Ten Most Wanted List. The posters are telling us: he's back and, boy, do we ever need him.

This Rambo redux makes sense in a post-9/11 world where nobody in Hollywood seems willing to invent new-style heroes to match up with new-style villains. The Iraq-themed movies, in particular, have been conspicuously, even necessarily, anti-heroic. Enter John J. Rambo. Officially, he is not fighting Al Qaeda—he's embroiled upriver in the Burmese civil war rescuing medical missionaries. But we all know who the Burmese are standing in for. (By the way, did nobody tell the filmmakers that Burma is now called Myanmar—or is *Myanmar* too much of a mouthful for Rambo?)

I'm not surprised that Sylvester Stallone revived Rambo. Like the *Rocky* series, the *Rambo* franchise, which has huge global appeal, is his annuity. But I was initially puzzled about who the audience for this film would be. It's tough enough getting boomers out of the house to see anything these days let alone another movie about a galoot with a bowie knife as big as the Ritz. And their children? Without any emotional connection to Stallone or any first-hand memories of Vietnam, wouldn't they be even less likely to bite?

As it turns out, no. The film did respectable business in its first weekend—half the audience was younger than twenty-five, two-thirds was male—and there is talk now of a fifth *Rambo*. (Stallone also wants to revive the *Death Wish* franchise. Oy.)

I saw the film on its opening night in a mostly filled theater where every splatter was greeted with whoops. This R-rated *Rambo* is almost obscenely graphic. (Memo to the MPAA ratings board: Exactly how violent does a movie from a reputable distributor have to be to get slapped with an NC-17?) Stallone opens his pulp fantasia with actual documentary footage of Burmese corpses, which is a bit like asking for butter on your popcorn and getting blood instead. Soon enough Rambo arrives and we get all too realistically staged shots of exploding heads, limbs, bellies. Whenever his scowl hit the screen, the audience went wild, knowing that carnage cannot be very far away. (If Stallone and Mel Gibson ever decide to collaborate on something, send in the clowns.)

The audiences lapping up this stuff aren't ghouls—they fell silent, for example, when the real-life atrocity footage came on. They're simply reacting to the film as a species of video game, and their rebel yells feel more honest than the "serious" political overlay Stallone periodically injects into the mayhem. "He's a beast," one admiring twentysomething viewer told me afterwards, adding that he liked Rambo because as a kid he saw the earlier installments with his father. It's all about bonding.

Could Rambo be the Tony Bennett of the new movie generation? His retro-ness has become his pedigree. Of course, in both his Rocky and Rambo incarnations, Stallone has always been blatantly retro. The *Rocky* movies draw heavily on Depression-era tropes; the *Rambo* narratives are positively primeval. (With his no-tech skills and half-Indian blood, Rambo is as elemental as Tarzan, if not as talkative.)

Unlike other aging stars (such as Bruce Willis) attempting to revive their action franchises, Stallone, in *Rambo,* doesn't try to tamp down the toll of the years. (He didn't in *Rocky Balboa* either, which accounted for its sweetness and may have been the key to its commercial success.) Stallone is a bit like the latterday John Wayne, who also put his gruff weariness on display. But Wayne, in films like *Rooster Cogburn,* consciously cartooned his own image, while Stallone in his Rambo mode is still playing it straight. And this squareness may be one reason why his audience still find him authentic—a classic.

But the Rambo character, who was originally conceived at a time when Hollywood was cuckoo for Joseph Campbell, has always been surprisingly shape-shifty. His myth mutates with the times. The novelist David Morrell, who created the Rambo character, once described his gameplan: "Take some hippie off the street and make him the fastest gun in the West." In 1982's *First Blood,* John Rambo, the long-haired drifter and Congressional Medal of Honor winner, is harassed by the local cops and proceeds to tear up half of the Pacific Northwest. Cornered at the end, he wails against the ingrates who welcomed him back from Vietnam with cries of "babykiller." You've got to hand it to Stallone—he co-opted the peacenik hippie martyrdom of films like *Easy Rider*, even as he trashed them.

In 1985's *Rambo: First Blood Part II,* he is sent on a recon mission to locate American POWS in Vietnam—which plays out as a symbolic redo of the war—and asks, "Do we get to win this time?" His special ire is reserved not for the Vietcong he encounters (they run like ninnies) or their Russian overlords (funny accents). The real enemies are the bureaucratic stooges in Washington who still don't want him to win. This time his closing wail is: "All I want is for my country to love me as much as I love it."

The next installment, 1988's *Rambo III,* has our man living as a handyman in a Thai monastery, except for the occasional out of town smackdown, when the call comes to once again go up against the Russkies, this time in Afghanistan. (Rambo is nothing if not a Cold Warrior.) Stampeding through an orgy of explosions, Rambo has ample time to display his scarred torso—his stigmata. His captured mentor, Richard Crenna's Colonel Sam Trautman, berates the Russians for fighting a war with a people who would "rather die than be slaves to a defeating army." Mujahedin and Vietcong—soulmates.

Twenty years later, in *Rambo,* the truth is out. Speaking to himself and to a band of mercenaries, he says, "You didn't kill for you country, you killed for yourself." For Stallone, being true to your essence is everything. The message of *Rocky Balboa* was "fighters fight." That's also the message of *Rambo.* With his uncanny instinct for riding the zeitgeist, Stallone may have lucked out yet again.

"War is in your blood" is Rambo's rallying cry. In a terrorized modern world where the battle lines are constantly being redrawn or can't even be found—where the tortured and the torturers are sometimes interchangeable—Rambo's meathead existentialism at least has the ring of a convenient truth. Fighters fight. And aging action icons make sequels. Maybe in the next go-round Rambo and Rocky can team up to save the world. Suggested title: *Apocalypse Yo.*

(Los Angeles Times, 2008)

BUSTER KEATON

When I saw *The Unknown Chaplin,* the 1986 Kevin Brownlow-Derek Gill documentary on Charlie Chaplin, my first response to this great work was a companionable one: I wished they might do the same thing for Buster Keaton.

Keaton is no longer the almost-forgotten artist he was from the thirties until the early fifties, before he was resurrected by James Agee and the French and the British and movie-lovers with long memories. He's no longer on the endangered species list of great American film artists. But Keaton's films don't show up in the repertory houses and museums and college film societies with anything like Chaplin's frequency.

Yes, Keaton's reputation is secure, but for a new generation of filmgoers and filmmakers, it's mostly based on history-book hearsay. And so the appearance of Brownlow and Gill's three-hour *American Masters* documentary *Buster Keaton: A Hard Act to Follow* represents more than an answered prayer of mine.

The show also has the potential to re-launch Keaton in the public imagination and, more to the point, in public theaters. In the movie world, accessibility is all. With few exceptions, Keaton's films have everything going for them except accessibility, and that's an aesthetic crime comparable to, say, warehousing Mark Twain's works in a rare books collection for the chosen few.

A Hard Act to Follow doesn't contain the wealth of recently discovered outtakes and home movies that turned *The Unknown Chaplin* into a full-scale artist's sketchbook-on-film. We saw how Chaplin developed his ideas over the years, from house-party whims to studio-set improvs to finished sequences that will forever resonate on the screen as if they just *happened*—once and for all time.

Keaton's work has the same miraculous, in-the-moment beauty, but the documentary evidence of how the tortuous was transformed into the instantaneous is not so plentiful with him as it was with Chaplin.

The most detailed documentation in *A Hard Act to Follow* has to do with Keaton's decline; the rare footage, the excerpts from the sound shorts and features, the TV clips and candid interviews, increase with his years. As a result, the Keaton film has a fullness, a roundedness, that the Chaplin documentary, which didn't go beyond the silent years, lacks. The Chaplin film was about a career. The Keaton movie ends up being about a life.

In its contours, it's a classic American artist's life; that is to say, it's an American tragedy. The last words in the documentary come from Keaton, saying, near the end of his life: "Well, it was a great life. Sure it was." He sounds as if he means it, but there's a rummy's regret in that flat, gravelly, resounding monotone. By all accounts, Keaton was the most accommodating and gentlest of men. Even at the end of his life, he didn't have it in him to lash out. Instead, he lashed inward; he drank away his timing, his instincts, his mettle.

But he must have known that his downfall was not entirely self-induced. Did he recognize by the end how precious he was to movie-lovers, and to the art of film? Did he exact his revenge on the thirties movie bosses who broke him by surviving to see his work applauded by a new generation?

For the one thing that Keaton was adamant about to the end was his art. Not that he saw himself in such highfalutin terms. He once said, "No man can be a genius in slap shoes and a flat hat." But he had an orneriness about his work that belied an artist's pride.

There's a marvelous home-movie sequence in *A Hard Act to Follow* where we see him refuse to throw out a gag in one of his last films, the Canadian featurette *The Railrodder,* because he is absolutely convinced of its *rightness*. Actually, the director has been trying to nix the gag because of its potential danger to Keaton, but Keaton won't hear of it. Fearlessness was part of his artist's pride, too. (The scene was eventually filmed, triumphantly.)

Keaton's great period lasted scarcely six years, from 1923 to 1929. These are the years when he made for his own production company such films as *Our Hospitality, Sherlock Jr., The Navigator, Seven Chances, The General, College,* and *Steamboat Bill Jr.* It's one of the most flabbergastingly productive stretches in film history, cut short by a studio system that could no longer indulge his independence. (Talkies were not the problem; of all the great silent comedians' voices, Keaton's matched up best with his silent persona.) His film work began with Fatty Arbuckle shorts in 1919, after a childhood spent in a family vaudeville act, and no doubt his tutoring in the world of medicine shows and vaudeville contributed to the fecundity of his ideas when he entered movies.

But Keaton was not at all unique among performers in coming to film from the scruffier precincts of the stage. What *is* unique in his work, from the very first film he directed, is a way of seeing, a vision, that owes almost nothing to his origins. (In *The General,* this accidental Dadaist had an eye as spacious and as open to grief as Matthew Brady's.) The concatenation of gags in his films owes more to engineering than to vaudeville, but the gagsmanship comes out of a world view that was as resolutely fixed as Keaton's great mournful emblem of a face.

The physical universe in a Keaton movie is always an obstacle course to Buster. Sometimes it works for him, sometimes it's exasperatingly contrary. The real challenges in a Keaton film are not between Buster and other people (usually meddlers) but between Buster and other objects (usually whirling). His great deadpan is the visual obbligato that underscores everything.

The deadpan, which was actually quite alive, is the focus of the whirligig. Keaton's relationship with the animate and inanimate world is not, however, one of antagonism; it's more like a collusion among respectful, dueling spirits. The collapsed houses and lumbering locomotives and ghostly, vagrant schooners and runaway boulders in his movies are impelled by the same animus as Keaton—it's the most natural thing in the world for him to go up against them, or to use their gravity to right his own balance.

The visual clarity of Keaton's style is integral to this vision. After all, in a world of warring gravities, it's essential to see the battlefield. The precision of Keaton's style is functional—it allows us to see the landscape uncluttered—but it also represents the orderliness toward which all the disarray in Keaton's films aspires. The stark simplicity of Keaton's great-est films—*Sherlock Jr., The Navigator, The General,* and *Steamboat Bill Jr.* (which Charles Riesner directed)—has an almost surreal exactness. It was atrociously important to Keaton that this world operate according to the rules—that there be no fakery in the shots. The whirligig had to obey all the physical laws, and we had to *see* those laws in operation.

"Comedy is serious business," Keaton once said (presaging the words of his closest modern equivalent, Steve Martin, and his "Comedy is not pretty"). What he meant was that one must respect the naturalness of the terrain, and its ability to yield up not just laughs but magic. His genius for thinking up "natural" gags was co-existent with his respect for the laws that governed those gags. He could no more cheat nature on-screen than he could break into an ear-to-ear grin.

In a film like *Steamboat Bill Jr.,* the physical gags, like Keaton hop-ping up into the slanting wind at the end, are so perfectly connived that they're peerless—they work their way into areas so calibrated yet dream-like that, at their essence, they are not, strictly speaking, funny. They're mysteriously beautiful. And equally beautiful is the spirit behind those gags. That's why so many of the famous sequences in that film, like the facade of a house falling over Buster, framing him in the rectangle of a window, don't work when they're duplicated—i.e. ripped off—in other movies, or TV. That beautiful spirit is missing.

At the beginning and at the end of his career, Keaton's face was a clas-sic. James Agee wrote that Keaton's face in his silent films ranked "almost with Lincoln's as an early American archetype." And the face he present-ed at the end, from the drivel of the *Beach Blanket Bingo* movies to the more high-toned drivel of Samuel Beckett's *Film,* was archetypal as well.

It was the face of a slap-shoed, flat-hatted vaudevillian turned soul-ful; it was a face that told us there was more resonance in the comic's art, more ghostliness, than you might ever have imagined. In the movies, his sorrowful bewilderment gave his extraordinary handsomeness a spiritu-ality that, at bottom, was not comic—or meant to be.

When sorrow ceases to be mysterious, it becomes pathos—that's what separates good Keaton from bad Chaplin. Keaton never really asked for love in his movies but we in the audience felt protective anyway. Only the girls in his movies immediately perceive his innate grace and sensitiv-ity. Keaton's athleticism was funny and fraught with pratfalls, but it was

CHAPTER 6

SOME MASTERPIECES

The Night of the Hunter

As a teenager in the late sixties, I first saw *The Night of the Hunter* not inside the hushed precincts of a New York revival house but, instead, on commercial-interrupted television. Wedged between the hawking of wares, the film was still flabbergasting. Not only had I never seen another film like it, I had never *imagined* anything like it. Subsequently, in art houses and film societies, I gave myself an education in the great movies of the past; the film's visual influences—especially, and quite consciously, D. W. Griffith, silent German Expressionism, and *The Magnificent Ambersons*—became increasingly obvious. But one of the great paradoxes of *The Night of the Hunter*, which is about a deranged preacher's pursuit of two young runaways in the Depression-era Ohio River backcountry, is that it recalls so many other movies and yet is one-of-a-kind. Charles Laughton, whose only directorial effort was this, tapped into the feeling tone of Griffith's pastoralism; he slipped inside the sinister, chiaroscuroed lubricity of the early Lang and Murnau movies. He gave the aestheticism of those movies a new lease on life and a new appalling comic tone, too—perhaps the most disturbing and original aspect of *The Night of the Hunter* is how deeply *funny*, in all senses of the word, this frightening story truly is. The movie can be seen not only as a kind of summation of what came before but also as a forerunner of what would come later, in the yin-yang tonal shifts and slapstick horror of such films as *The Manchurian Candidate* and *Lolita* and *Bonnie and Clyde* (which is also set in the Depression) and *Blue Velvet*. And so, we have another paradox: the movie is both recipient of a tradition and precursor of a new one.

A big reason *The Night of the Hunter* seems so fresh—even though it was shunned by the public upon its release in 1955—is because it lacks the well-oiled sameness of mood that even the most notable Hollywood movies of its time had. Its crazy-quilt emotionalism is much closer to how we experience the world now. Still, the extreme mood swings in *The Night of the Hunter* have always disrupted audiences, even its most fervid appreciators. The movie is amazingly soulful and yet, unless you get the hang of it, it can be baffling. When I saw the film at an evening tribute for its star, Robert Mitchum, not long before he died, some in the audience howled in all the "wrong" places, convinced that the preacher's high dudgeon and Laughton's storybook symbolism were flubs or, even worse, put-ons. But the howls, if I'm not reading too much into them, also carried an undercurrent of discomfort and perplexity. In the air that evening was at least the grudging realization that *The Night of the Hunter* was no ordinary movie, bad or otherwise. Those members of the audience who think they're smarter than this film always end up outsmarting themselves.

If you were to show *The Night of the Hunter* to an audience of children, I suspect it might be more easily grasped by them than by adults. It mixes the horrid and the peculiar in a way that kids intuitively understand. The Davis Grubb novel on which the film is based is highflown hillbilly Gothic, but Laughton recognized at its core the glowing radium of a resonant tale. (The script is credited to James Agee, and certainly the film is an emanation of his lifelong obsessions with myth and poverty and Christianity and childhood abandonment, as well as his love for artists such as Griffith; nevertheless, Laughton reportedly pared down or discarded much of what Agee gave him and went back to the book, where most of the film's dialogue, and even some of its imagery, comes from, though virtually none of its gallows humor.*) No other American movie

---

* Since this was written, Agee's 293-page first-draft screenplay, about double the size of the script published in *Agee on Film, Volume II,* was found in a box in a Manhattan brownstone belonging to the Agee family. As Jeffrey Couchman writes in his indispensible book *The Night of the Hunter: A Biography of a Film,* "Yet however diffuse the first draft is, Agee did the initial, difficult job of 'cracking the book'—finding a cinematic structure, selecting scenes to dramatize with sound and image, and drawing dialogue from Grubb's third-person narrative. Although Laughton had to make selections from Agee's mass of material, the first draft provided him with an overall plan—and many specific ideas—that guided him during revisions." Couchman argues for a shared credit between Agee and Laughton. Writing in *Written By,* the magazine of the Writer's Guild West, F. X. Feeney, who also read the first draft and defends Agee's sole screenplay credit, writes, "From start to finish, what Agee gave Laughton is an 'extended play' version in prose of the finished film." Plans to publish Agee's original script are apparently in the works. I can't wait.

has so intimately resembled an elaborate children's fable *as imagined by a child*. The look of the film—shot by *Ambersons'* Stanley Cortez—leaves the impression of something newly imprinted, as if everything were being seen through the eyes of a rapt cherub for the first time. There's an exaggerated purity to the imagery. The film's terrors are typically black; the enchantments are transcendant, starlit.

Mitchum's roving preacher, Harry Powell, is a false prophet whose falseness is instinctively sensed by children. (Most adults are taken in by him.) With L-O-V-E tattooed above his right knuckles, and H-A-T-E tattooed above his left, Powell is a vagrant demon; his pocket switchblade slices through his trousers when he's aroused. (If there is such a thing as Old Testament Freudian, Harry Powell personifies it.) His nemesis is Miss Rachel, played by Lillian Gish, a mother hen who gathers up foundlings and runaways and brings them into her home. Rachel is as immaculate as Harry is depraved; she lives by the Scriptures and knows them well enough to recognize when they are being fouled.

And yet nothing is as simple as it seems in *The Night of the Hunter*. The visuals are conceived in tones of jet black and pearl, but the film is far from schematic; the darkness and the light are always bleeding into each other. Rachel abhors Harry, but hearing him in the night intoning "Leaning on the Everlasting Arms," she joins in the singing even though she sits inside her house with a rifle in her lap to defend her brood against him. Harry is a trickster who seems to have entered into the story in order to test the spiritual mettle of the pure-in-heart, and those not so pure-in-heart, too. If the film has any literary antecedent, it would not be Davis Grubb's book, but rather Melville's *The Confidence-Man* or Twain's *The Man Who Corrupted Hadleyburg*, comic-horror texts with a sly, enraged comprehension of man's weakness and duplicity.

Serving time in a penitentiary at the start of the film, Harry finds himself sharing a cell with Ben Harper (Peter Graves), condemned to be executed for a robbery in which someone was killed. The stolen cash, as Ben tells it, was meant to feed his wife Willa (Shelley Winters) and their two children, Pearl (Sally Bruce), who is perhaps four or five, and John (Billy Chapin), who is around ten. Try as he might, Harry can't extract the hiding place of the money from Ben before he dies; but he makes it his business, when he's released from prison, to woo and marry Ben's widow. He loathes her wedding night advances, and she loathes herself for having made them. The shy, dutiful Willa vows to become the chaste woman Harry wants her to be, but her face at the torch-lit revival meeting where she proclaims her sins has a hideous carnal ferocity to it. (Perhaps *this* is the woman Harry wants.) Harry mesmerizes Willa into a brief life of terrible piety before finally dispatching her. *The Night of the Hunter* expresses the sheer terror that men can hold for women, and women for men. Willa and Harry are riven by more than the secret of where the money is hidden; they're separated from each other by something insuperably elemental between the sexes, a difference, in the movie's terms, almost of species. Harry's murder of Willa occurs off camera, but we see its aftermath: her submerged body resting in a rusted open convertible at the bottom of the lake, her long hair streaming out in an undercurrent thick with delicate water grass. It's an image to place beside Shakespeare's description of the drowned Ophelia.

Harry loves the orotundity he gives his syllables; there's fire and brimstone in the breath. When John and Pearl, stolen cash in tow, break away from him and race for the river, the low, strangly yowl he lets out is both shockingly funny and hair-raising—a bogeyman's aria. The children's flight from Harry, which ends with their rescue by Rachel, is one of the most supernally eerie sequences ever filmed. (Walter Schumann's buoyant, infernal score sets the movie's mood throughout.) The toylike boat that carries them along the moonlit Ohio is framed in the foreground by a succession of immense, looming close-ups of frogs and caged birds and spider webs and a pair of shivering rabbits. This is the extended sequence that makes some audiences groan, perhaps because it is so grandiloquently *obvious*; but I think its greatness lies precisely in its obviousness. Who, except curdled cynics, would reject the grandeur that comes from such an enhanced symbolism, which is no different in kind or in depth of lyric feeling from a fearful Bible story or a Grimm's fairy tale?

Mitchum had his greatest role in *The Night of the Hunter*, and it's his finest performance. His cunning and his torpor, which always carried a sadistic, sensual edge, achieve here a kind of apotheosis. He's more malevolently erotic in this film, with its storybook homilies and bejeweled night skies, than in any of his hothouse melodramas. Sex—the awareness of the temptations it can bring—etches through the imagery; it's what is held back and denied and still corrodes the screen. But it is the hatred of sex—Harry's hatred—that is the true corrosive in this film. He's twisted by his own abhorrence, and yet his writings are a form of self-stimulation. Harry's consmanship works so well (for a time) with Willa and her townspeople because, in their own way, they are just as aghast as Harry is at the pleasures of the flesh—and just as drawn to them, too. The reason Harry has made such a success of himself is because he shows up in a community ready-made for his handiwork.

Thus, the pastoralism of the Griffith films, which this town evokes, is undercut by Laughton even as it is being commemorated. He draws out the hysteria that was always present just below the surface of these sanctified rural tableaux. (The hysteria comes from fearing the loss of innocence.) It makes poetic sense that Laughton would cast Lillian Gish in *The Night of the Hunter*, not only because she was Griffith's greatest actress but also because, in such films as *Way Down East* and *Broken Blossoms* and *Orphans of the Storm*, she expressed both the luminescence of her virginal heroines and also their affrighted souls. In *The Night of the Hunter*, Rachel may be the savior of these orphans of the storm, but there is also the suggestion of a life once lived apart from the goodness she engenders. (She speaks cryptically of her estrangement from her son.) Rachel is a worthy adversary for Harry because, one feels, her purity has already been tested. She has seen enough of life to account for the Harry Powells of the world, while Harry has no real conception of purity except as something he must annihilate. And so, in a sense, the preacher is the true innocent in *The Night of the Hunter*; the L-O-V-E and H-A-T-E spelled out above his knuckles represent the breadth of his existence. He's untainted by complexity. Rachel, for all her motherly chipperiness, sees things whole. The waifs she raises are her bulwark against wickedness; she herself is a kind of idealized waif, gifted with worldly wisdom. (Has any actress ever looked more youthfully beautiful in old age than Lillian Gish?) Rachel proclaims that children are man at his strongest, that they will abide and endure. It's an affirmation that is also a plea. She's soliciting the fates for a reprieve from horror. *The Night of the Hunter* is a fable that passes from darkness to light, but we are left in no doubt that the wolf is forever at the door.

(*The A List*, 2002)

Time Out

Time Out, from the young French writer-director Laurent Cantet, is a hushed, small-scale masterpiece that inexorably moves into the shadowlands of tragedy. Vincent (Aurelian Recoing) is a bourgeois family man who, unbeknownst to his brood, has recently been fired from his position as a mid-level corporate consultant but still pretends to go to work each day. He dutifully calls his wife from his cell phone to tell her how the job is going and that he loves her; in reality, he spends his time driving the highways, sleeping in his car, sometimes overnight. Eventually, he invents a new job for himself that he claims takes him frequently to faraway Geneva, working to help Africa for the United Nations. In order to keep money coming in, he spins an investment scam and bilks several of his old friends and colleagues. Ultimately, Jean-Michel (Serge Livrozet, who looks a bit like Cocteau), a toothy, sixtyish hotel manager who is also a career thief, enlists him in smuggling fake designer goods into France. Vincent sinks further and further into a miasma of seediness and deception, and yet—this is the greatness of the film—he is never so alive as when he is tranced out by his own duplicity.

If all the movie were saying is that Vincent is another casualty of the corporate culture, it would not be so profoundly unsettling. Cantet confounds our expectations—instead of showing us a modern man who is bereft without the work that gave him his identity, Cantet gives us someone whose identity is *fulfilled* by the void. Vincent probably spends more man-hours contriving his double-life than he ever did at his real job; his illusory existence has more gravity, more vibrancy, than his comfy home life, complete with three children and doting parents and a wife, Muriel (the extraordinary Karin Viard), who suspects something is amiss but looks the other way. Muriel is a schoolteacher who had higher ambitions for herself, and, like her husband, she feels penned in by her middle-class routine. Her unspoken complicity in Vincent's deception is a folly that enables him to stoke her fantasies of success as well as his own. She's devastated by how closed-off he has become and yet she wants the lie to be true.

At one point, Vincent confesses to Jean-Michel that the only thing he really liked about his old job was the long road trips he made alone. We don't need to be told this, really; it's right there in Vincent's bright, glassy eyes when he drives with aimless purposefulness down the high-ways. Probably he is a man for whom being a husband and father was, at bottom, an alien existence—just one more entrapment. Vincent may strike a chord with contemporary audiences bent on seeing his predica-ment as a parable of corporate woes, but he's closer to a character out of a Hawthorne story (*Wakefield,* to be exact). The breach in his soul is what gives him his soulfulness. He presses on with his schemes and disappear-ances knowing full well that he is only buying time for himself, and there is a kind of madness in this. Aurelien Recoing is a celebrated French stage actor making his first major movie, and he gives Vincent an eerie, disaf-fected calm; he's playing a phantom made flesh.

Vincent feels real pain in scamming a hard-up friend who has sought him out, and he tries to make amends. But he operates in a world in which people unwittingly encourage his deceptions because they want their lives to be better. On some level, Vincent must feel that he is min-istering to their fates, as he is ministering to his own. He's delusional and starkly realistic at the same time, and Cantet doesn't try to psychoanalyze him; he recognizes that what motivates Vincent is probably unknowable. Certainly he is unknowable to himself. In the end, when he is found out and brought back into the life he once lived, he looks permanently riven. The big blank space inside has been revealed for all to see, and he can't sit comfortably in his own skin anymore. A job interviewer, impressed with him, asks Vincent if he is ready to take charge, and he answers, "I'm not scared." He's petrified.

(*New York*, 2001)

Au Revoir, Les Enfants

In Louis Malle's great *Au Revoir, Les Enfants,* based on incidents from his own childhood, the utter simplicity of his technique pulls us into the privacies of his experience. And because his subject—an eleven-year-old boy's recognition of the horrors of the adult world—is such a resonant one, the final effect of his bracing, unencumbered directness is over-whelming. Rarely have audiences' tears been more honestly wrung.

Malle has explained in interviews that the real-life events behind this film were his motivation for becoming a film director, that he wanted to make the film as his first but felt he could do the subject justice only now. (It's the first film he's directed in France in ten years.)

This probably explains why *Au Revoir, Les Enfants,* set in a provincial Catholic boarding school at the end of World War II, seems like a culmination of the themes Malle has dealt with in the past in movies like *Lacombe, Lucien* and *Murmur of the Heart.* Everything comes together in this film: bourgeois japery, Catholicism, mother love, guilt, and collaboration. And yet we never feel as if we're watching a compendium. Rather, we appear to be tapping into the source of Malle's inspiration. It's easy to understand why Malle considers this story the archetype for his artistry.

At the beginning of the film, eleven-year-old Julien (Gaspard Manesse) and his older brother, Francois (Stanislas Carre De Malberg), say goodbye to their mother after the Christmas holidays and take the train back to boarding school. There, a new boy, Jean Bonnet (Raphael Fejto), one of three new arrivals, is quartered in Julien's dormitory. Julien and his classmates don't make things easy for Bonnet—they taunt him at recess, call him "Easter Bonnet." The pranks have the usual cruel harmlessness of a boy's club initiation, but Bonnet doesn't seem at all interested in being initiated.

He's a loner in a special, unexpressed sort of way, a way that begins to seem exotic to Julien. Like his classmates, Julien is an upper-class kid with a smart sense of privilege; he's a pint-size custodian of his own good fortune. But Bonnet's sense of inner privilege seems more rooted—there's something else besides money at work here.

At first Julien resents Bonnet, who effortlessly challenges his academic superiority; Bonnet is a math whiz, a voracious reader—he's even an adept pianist. But there's nothing showoffy about Bonnet, and that probably rankles Julien most of all. In his boy's view of things, Bonnet is snubbing him by so matter-of-factly expressing his talents. It's as if Bonnet didn't care enough about his competition to flaunt his gifts.

Malle structures the movie as a kind of boy's-book detective story, but with an adult's perspective. Gradually it becomes clear to Julien that Bonnet, along with the two older new students, are Jews in hiding from the Gestapo. (Bonnet's real surname is Kippelstein.) Julien holds onto his little secret for a while, as if to warm himself with it. When he finally tips Bonnet off that he knows, the boys tussle, and the subject is never brought up again. Bonnet's remoteness, which the other children interpret as snobbishness, has a blanked-out, stupefied quality; he's trying to understand his intimate inclusion in the war's vast machinery of hate.

One reason Julien never brings up Bonnet's Jewishness again is that he doesn't really know what to *do* with the revelation. He knows nothing of the horrors lying in wait for the Jews, only that they are, somehow, marked as undesirables.

In one scene near the end, when Julien and Bonnet have become tentative, mutually respectful friends, Julien reads to Bonnet a hot passage from a contraband copy of *Arabian Nights*. For Julien, Bonnet's Jewishness is part of the same fantasy-world exotica. When Bonnet joins Julien and his mother and brother for dinner during parents' visiting day, Julien toys out loud with the misbegotten notion that his family may have a Jewish aunt. He's tickled by the subterfuge of being Jewish.

In that same restaurant scene, Malle stages a confrontation between some Vichy collaborators and an old gentleman, a regular customer eating alone at the table across from Julien who turns out to be Jewish. The collaborators are shouted down by the patrons, even by a table of German soldiers.

The sequence, like several other confrontations with "the enemy" in the film, has a deliberate clumsiness. The French collaborators are so primed to accommodate the Germans that they've become walking parodies of their captors—the Germans scoff at their absurdity. All the military maneuvers that intrude on the boys' cloistered world have the same dumb play-act frightfulness, as if the war outside were simply a more cumbersome, adult version of the school's color wars.

Julien is obviously meant to be Malle as a young boy, but the characterization is free of the moony nostalgia that tenderizes most artists' self-portraits. Gaspard Manesse is an extraordinary little actor, and his face is ideal for the role; you can see how his features are being shaped by his intelligence. There's an acuity, a principled defiance, in his look.

And a touch of vanity, too. When he clucks to himself in amazement, "I'm the only one in this school who thinks of death," we can laugh at his fatuousness. The true terror of death hasn't even hit him yet; he's just being fancy and self-absorbed.

Julien hints early on that he wants to become a priest, and one suspects it's because the Catholic Church appeals to his sense of privileged pomp. But also, it appeals to his decency—the same decency that eventually comes out in his friendship with Bonnet.

In one of the most remarkable scenes in the film, the school's headmaster, Father Jean (Philippe Morier-Genoud), delivers a sermon to the boys' assembled families, derived from St. Paul, about the necessity for Christian charity. (Some of the well-to-do parents storm out, feeling under attack.) Julien has absorbed the enlightenments of his teachers: it's no accident that the priests of *this* school chose to hide the Jews.

There's another remarkable scene in the film where the priests show Chaplin's silent short *The Immigrant* to the kids, with a live piano and violin accompaniment. The sequence goes on for a long time—too long, I thought at first. But Malle is right to keep the scene going. It's the only time in the film when all the boys' hopes, and the priests', are raised at once. It's the only time we see them unified by a common purity of feeling, and you want the moment to last forever, because you know it can't. It's the only time we see Bonnet laugh—this same boy who, later, when asked by Julien whether he's ever afraid, replies, "All the time."

This scene carries over into the rest of the film like a piano chord held by a pedal until it gradually fades away. The sequence fades into the terror of the final moments, when the Gestapo moves in. Malle is summoning up a nightmare for us piece by piece; the linkage of events has a nauseating inevitability. We can see in Julien's stricken, benumbed face that he will never forget what he is seeing, that he will spend his whole life trying to comprehend its horror. *Au Revoir, Les Enfants* is Malle's attempt to comprehend, and it's an epitaph, too. It ranks with the greatest films to come out of France since the war that spawned its sad story.

(*Los Angeles Herald Examiner*, 1987)

The Last Letter

Shot luminously in black and white, *The Last Letter* consists only of a performer—Catherine Samie, the legendary French stage actress and doyenne of the Comédie-Française—and a bare stage; no props, no score. And yet Samie is such an extraordinary camera subject, and her visual evocations are so rich, that the film seems densely inhabited. It's an epic of the imagination—a sixty-one-minute, subtitled monologue derived from a passage in Vasily Grossman's socialist-realist novel *Life and Fate* and directed by the great documentarian Frederick Wiseman in his first dramatic foray.

Samie is in deep communion with the camera. Her most fragile and nuanced emotions have a grave ferocity. Her hands have the lyric, spidery expressiveness that one often sees with great mimes or deaf performers, and she has the rare ability, through some mysterious inner transmutation, to make herself look ancient one moment and maidenly the next. Dressed simply in black, a Jewish star stitched to her dress, Samie is laying herself bare, and the effect is like watching one long catharsis of pain and woe and benediction. I felt like I was holding my breath from the film's first frame to its last.

Samie plays Anna Semionovna, a physician interned in 1941 in a Ukrainian ghetto that is about to be liquidated by the Nazis. Her monologue is a spoken letter to her scientist son, Vitya, who is safe outside enemy lines. (Grossman, who suffered under Stalin and worked as a mining engineer before becoming a writer, lost his mother to the Germans.) Anna knows she will never see Vitya again, and so this letter, which she intends to smuggle out of the camp, is her way of setting down how she would like to be remembered. It is also a way for her to comprehend her life and bear witness to it—a way to prepare herself, and her son, for her death. She talks about the small, incremental horrors that led to her internment and how, even now, when all hope is lost, there is hope. She describes the ragged, despicable behavior of the neighbors she thought were her friends but also mentions the rare, revivifying acts of astounding kindness. A recognition of her own mortality has sharpened her senses; whereas before she would look into the eyes of her patients and see cataracts, now she sees souls.

Wiseman had previously directed *The Last Letter* at the Comédie-Française and at the American Repertory Theatre, and he uses the camera to deepen the chiaroscuro effects he achieved onstage. The close-ups of Samie, with her helmet of thin white hair, are always held for precisely the right number of beats. Wiseman understands the phosphorescent power of her face and how, in intervals, we must turn away from it or be blinded. He has always had an unerringly musical sense of how to pace a sequence. The periodic shots of Anna fragmented in shadow against bare walls are like gentle punctuation. They are also metaphors—this woman, with her formidable, almost sculptural presence, is fading before our eyes. Anna is aware of her evanescence. As one who always identified herself much more as a Russian than as a Jew, she speaks of her sudden, startling love for "this world of proverbs and Sabbaths" that will soon disappear. She links her newfound tenderness for the Jewish people with Vitya; it is a reminder of her love for him.

Anna talks about how a son should always tell the truth to his mother, and now it is her turn to speak with ravishing honesty to her son. Her truth is her final gift to him. She asks his forgiveness for leaving his father; she confesses her fear of pain and of the panic that chills the heart. She wants her son's help and yet rejoices that he is safe and will not meet her fate. Before the war, Anna had consoled herself with the thought that one day she would tell Vitya of her life and all her mistakes and longings. Now she must die alone, and her words to her son are like a soft sacrament: "Be happy with those you love, those around you, those who have become more dear to you than your mother." *The Last Letter* is the saddest and most beautiful of lullabies.

(*New York*, 2003)

Blue Velvet

David Lynch's *Blue Velvet* is a great movie, and one of the rare American films of the past decade to make a difference in the medium. It gets into areas of dread and shock and torment that are so profoundly dislocating and dreamlike that, watching it, you feel as if you're coiled right up inside the vision of an artist with a live feed to the unconscious. The movie-making has a hushed, incantatory quality even when the action is rabid; Lynch's imagery is continuous with the unwakened states that most filmmakers (and audiences) censor. The movie has a stark, hallucinatory clarity. You think back on it as you would think back on a particularly fervid dream.

Blue Velvet, like most great movies, alters our way of seeing. Lynch's vision seems pulled by the very nature of the movie medium itself, which has always been co-existent with dream states. By making those states shockingly evident on film, Lynch risks disturbing audiences and, predictably, the people who don't like *Blue Velvet* don't just dislike it—they detest it. Still, that detestation may be one of the truest responses to the film.

Recent Hollywood movies, even the few good ones, look like they were made to be shaken off, and *Blue Velvet* isn't a movie you can shake off; it's actually more disturbing on a second viewing. A film that fuses sexual terror with murderous, bottomless-pit anxiety is so far from the easy-viewing fare we've been getting at the movies that *Blue Velvet* has the effect of a sick, black joke on an industry that has given up on the magic of movies. Lynch is saying that movies don't only have the capacity to coddle us; they also have the power to leave us aghast, not in the pop-gruesome way of the horror cheapies, but in the deeper way of artists, by drawing on our dark dreams and bringing them to a simmer.

The slowed-down opening images in *Blue Velvet*—the shots of yellow tulips, fire trucks, grade-schoolers crossing the street—glow with a heightened nostalgia. Not for long. Lynch quickly gives us the theme of the movie in miniature: a middle-aged man watering his lawn is suddenly stricken, clutching his throat in a paroxysm of pain before collapsing. The ratchety whir of warring insects takes over the soundtrack, as the camera scurries deep into the lawn's underbrush, with its battalions of festering horrors. We've been given a glimpse under nature's rock, and soon the glimpse will magnify—only the creatures will be bigger, life-sized. The human hellions in *Blue Velvet* will crawl out from under the rock of consciousness and take over the screen.

Jeffrey Beaumont (Kyle MacLachlan), the college-age son of the man who collapsed, returns to his Middle American hometown, Lumberton. He spends a sad, wordless session with his father in the hospital and then, cutting through a field on his way home, finds a detached ear in the grass. This ear, with its poetic associations from the Bunuel/Dali movies and the surrealist painters, is Jeffrey's latchkey into a mystery. He shows it to the town's police chief (George Dickerson) and, aided by the chief's teenage daughter Sandy (Laura Dern), tries to solve the enigma. In the course of his voyaging, he encounters a beautiful local nightclub chanteuse,

Dorothy Vallens (Isabella Rossellini), whose specialty is singing "Blue Velvet." He discovers that, in exchange for sexual favors, her husband and child are being held hostage by a maniac, Frank Booth (Dennis Hopper), and his scuzzy minions. Jeffrey's detective work becomes more and more obsessive. The netherworld he slips into has a sensual, trancelike pull on him; he's transfixed by the horrors of which men are capable—of which *he* is capable.

Blue Velvet is conceived as a poetic allegory. "Why are there people like Frank?" Jeffrey asks. Frank is everything that perverts goodness— he's malevolence incarnate. He's also Jeffrey's unadmitted animus. To save himself, and right the world, Jeffrey must destroy him. Lynch's poetics have a Freudian cast, but they're not doctrinaire; if they connect with any of the hallowed psychosexual totems, it's at their most basic level—at the same source of fear and anxiety that fairy tales draw on. Frank is Jeffrey's dark double, and his false father; when the boy is in the maniac's clutches, Frank is keyed up, seething. His favorite song is Roy Orbison's "In Dreams," which he carries on cassette; he smears lipstick on his face and mashes his face against Jeffrey's, spitting out, tonelessly, "In dreams I walk with you . . . in dreams you're mine." Frank's omnisexual ferocity is directed at Jeffrey, at Dorothy, at the whole world. The sour, sick fury of his impacted sexuality makes the screen tremble.

In the movie's centerpiece scene, Jeffrey hides in Dorothy's closet and, through the slats, watches Frank, enraged, inhale a gaseous stimulant through a face mask as he batters Dorothy while he copulates. Just before this scene, Dorothy had discovered the boy in her apartment (he was searching for clues) and, holding out a carving knife, orders him to strip. Swooning, she fondles him, knife poised. Lynch goes so far into depravity in this scene that you can't believe what you're watching; your jaw drops. Lynch gets deeper inside the scourge of sexual terror than any director ever has—the only comparison is with Bernardo Bertolucci's *Last Tango in Paris,* where the sexuality had an emotional violence that also stunned audiences into absolute silence. For Lynch, sex is the force that draws you into life's dark mystery, and at the pit of that mystery is horror. Frank and Dorothy call each other "Mommy" and "Daddy" in that apartment scene; what Jeffrey the voyeur witnesses is like a child's first frantic, uncomprehending glimpse of sex.

What makes such scenes so dreadful for audiences—the reason

some people will recoil from them and call the movie exploitative trash—is that Lynch has eroticized them. For Lynch, all fascinations contain a sexual secret. That certainly doesn't mean that he endorses what goes in this movie. If one feels compelled to look at an auto accident on the freeway, and receives a thrill up the spine, that doesn't mean one endorses auto accidents. Lynch doesn't attempt to deny the horrid fascination of what he shows us. Before he administers the antidote, he wants us to taste the poison.

Lynch has worked with the awful allure of rot in his previous films— *Eraserhead*, *The Elephant Man*, and *Dune*—but *Blue Velvet* carries his themes so far that it's almost a career apotheosis. It enlarges his obsessions. Dorothy's apartment has the same steady-state creepiness as the apartment in *Eraserhead*. (It even has the same radiator.) It's a chamber of horrors, with Jeffrey appearing in the corridors like a dreamwalker out of a Cocteau film. The apartment's colors, the mauves and deep greens, are lurid and mesmerizing—these colors still have some blood in them. Inside her apartment, Dorothy seems as trapped and transfixed by her fears as Jeffrey does, and they go at each other like co-conspirators in a mutual nightmare.

Compared to this world, Laura Dern's Sandy, and the whole straight-arrow Lumberton community, pale. Lynch doesn't have the same feeling for paradise as he does for hell, and the lack makes *Blue Velvet* a slightly lopsided allegory. Laura Dern, lovely as she is, should be more transcendent. So should Kyle MacLachlan—he's too blank to register Jeffrey's morbid stirrings. (MacLachlan, who resembles Lynch, functions as the director's alter ego; it's a stand-in role.) But Isabella Rossellini, with her big black wig and crimson lips, is a ripe, ravaged image. She seems to understand exactly what Lynch wants; her acting is a series of poetic moods. Dennis Hopper certainly knows what Lynch wants. From *Easy Rider* to *Apocalypse Now* to *Blue Velvet,* Hopper has epitomized the aberrant archetypes of each era. He gives one of the most infernal performances ever seen on film.

Blue Velvet comes out at a time when sex and violence in pop culture have come under increasing attack. The force of *Blue Velvet* is, in a way, a testament to what the bluenoses are attacking; it demonstrates the awful power in what the whole Reagan eighties culture is trying to deny. Lynch's movie is presumably contemporary, but he gives it a slightly wacky fifties

time-warp ambiance, as if to seal the correspondence between then and
now. And yet Lynch hankers for fifties tranquility. That's the irony of
Blue Velvet. He's a small-town regular guy except for one crucial thing:
he's got an incubus inside him that won't allow him to accept that tranquility. Like Jeffrey moving to Dorothy's noxious flame, he's compelled
to root out all the dirty little secrets.

(Los Angeles Herald Examiner, 1986)

Something Wild

Something Wild makes you feel wonderful, like a great piece of funky pop
music or a jazz riff that whisks you around corners you didn't even know
were there. It begins as a comedy and turns deadly serious, but you still
come out of the theater on a high, percolating. The director, Jonathan
Demme, has such a sympathetic embrace of wayward American lunacy
that you're grooved by how wild things are out there—how screw-loose
everybody is if you give them half a chance.

Among other things, *Something Wild* is probably the first film to
demonstrate that yuppies have soul—although not at first glance. Charlie Driggs (Jeff Daniels)—he's a company tax consultant—has just been
promoted to vice president. We first see him in a midtown Manhattan
diner where, for thrills, he sneaks out without paying the check. On the
street he's stopped by a woman from the diner, Lulu (Melanie Griffith),
who's on to him. Dressed in a slick black number and a drizzle of African
and American Indian jewelry, wigged in a jet-black pageboy like Louise
Brooks (whose most famous role was Lulu in *Pandora's Box*), she looks
like a nouveau Navajo. Before Charlie has a chance to argue, he's in her
ball-fringed convertible heading for a motel in Jersey.

Even after Lulu manacles Charlie to the bedpost, it's not clear what
this slutty Tinkerbell is after. Lulu's affectless deadpan and little-girl voice
is all-American creepy, but there's a sharp glint of sanity in her eyes. She's
like the embodiment of Charlie's shaggy escapist fantasies; he's flattered
by her attentions and wants to impress her with what a closet outlaw he
is. ("I channelled my rebellion into the mainstream," he tells Lulu in the

car, gloating with tiny self-satisfaction.)

There's no malevolence in Lulu, despite the S&M trappings and the pranks. (She calls Charlie's boss while he's shackled and puts him on the line.) She apparently knows exactly what turns Charlie on—not just sexually, but emotionally, too. She represents his filthiest fantasies, but sanitized, without the sting of true eroticism. When Lulu convinces Charlie to drive on with her to Pennsylvania and stay the night at her mother's house, we begin to recognize that Lulu is concocting a fantasy of her own. Dressed small-town conservative now, with blond hair, she introduces Charlie to her mother (Dana Preu) as her new husband and, later on, maintains the ruse at her high school's tenth reunion party. (A nice touch: her mother, without letting on to Lulu, sees right through her.) Charlie goes along with it—he's a little freaked about what he's gotten into, but he's also digging the subterfuge. He's tickled by his newfound capacity for lying.

Until the moment that Lulu runs into an old flame at her reunion, *Something Wild* is a lark. The movie captures the giddy exhilaration of jumping into a car and hitting the road—chucking it all. Demme, and his first-time screenwriter, E. Max Frye, show us roadside America, with its slush cones and all-night convenience stores and ragtag motels, better than any moviemaker ever has. The flimsy bric-a-brac is illuminated by the illicit; this is, after all, the territory you light out to when you want to escape, have affairs, change your identity. Demme puts reggae on the soundtrack, and pop-funk rhythms and rock, to enhance the allurement, the strangeness, the sexiness of the terrain. (The artists range from John Cale and David Byrne to the Feelies, who also appear in the reunion scene.)

The scariness of being cut off from your home base begins to creep into the movie when Lulu's flame, a recent ex-con, takes over the picture. Ray Sinclair (Ray Liotta) looks like a fifties hood—tattooed and brush-cut, with a muscle-man T-shirt and a smiley sneer. He's so far out of Charlie's world that it doesn't even occur to Charlie to be afraid of him; it's not until Ray holds up a convenience store and busts Charlie's nose, while Lulu looks on helplessly, that the jig is up. Holed up in a motel with Lulu and a nose-bleeding Charlie, Ray can't believe this doofus has actually had a go with his girl. But Ray doesn't see in Charlie what we do. His fantasies have been fermenting so rapidly on the road that he can't just drop the whole thing and go back to his vice presidency. The terrain that promised such illicit pleasure now becomes his nightmare, and he has to find his way out of it. He begins to trail Ray and the trapped, resigned Lulu (Audrey turns out to be her real name.) He's fired up to be a hero. All at once, his "real" life has turned counterfeit.

Demme has made slapstick comedies before, like *Crazy Mama*, and he's made revenge thrillers, like *Fighting Mad*. But he's never blended the two the way he has here. In a way, *Something Wild* is Demme's *Blue Velvet*. It has a similar scenario: a callow guy allows himself to be seduced into a hellish world dominated by a crazy. The difference is, Lynch's movie took its imagery from the abstractions of modern art; Demme works off pop culture—specifically, pop music. Lynch is interested in seeing just how far you can bring a movie image to stasis and still make it resonate; Demme gives his images a beat—a syncopation—that carries you along. The resonances sink in later. (Maybe that's why Demme's movies are always even better in the memory.)

The trio of lead performances in *Something Wild* is extraordinary. Melanie Griffith, who was so good in Brian De Palma's *Body Double,* isn't like anyone else on the screen today. Her Lulu is prematurely savvy—a tinkly-voiced bad girl with a wised-up matron's air. When she's held captive by Ray, her allurements vanish and we see the scared, hard-bitten woman underneath. Newcomer Ray Liotta (he's appeared in soaps and a few TV movies) creates the kind of powerhouse impression that major careers are based on. It's a classic debut performance—right up there with Richard Widmark in *Kiss of Death.* Charlie may not pick up on Ray's danger at first, but we sure do—this guy carries around with him the sour, impacted rage of a hoodlum who no longer connects with the straight world. All of his psychosexual webbing is with the underworld; he has a con's radar for people's soft spots, and he waits a while, for sport, before he moves in for the kill. And yet—and this is what makes Liotta's performance so original—Ray doesn't think of himself as a bad guy. He's simply going after what he thinks is rightfully his.

But it's Jeff Daniels's performance that the movie hinges on. He has to somehow convince us that the milquetoast Charlie of the opening scenes has the same potential for rage as Ray. Daniels's acting is so beautifully worked out that you never doubt what you're watching; his transition into brutality has a cockeyed inevitability. What's so frightening about *Something Wild* is that Demme uses our good-time feelings for Charlie as a set-up for the disturbances that follow. Trailing Ray and Lulu to Virginia, he's obsessed and humiliated, and it's both funny and awful to see him so murderously wound up. He's linked to Ray in a way we never thought possible, not just through his love for Lulu, but on a deeper, more primal level. Charlie isn't enhanced by violence, though, the way he might have been in a Peckinpah movie, and he doesn't work through it to sweet-tempered oblivion, the way David Lynch might have had it. Demme's humanism softens the script's territorial edge. Charlie isn't really better off for this joyride, he's just different. He has a capacity for horror now.

The black joke in *Something Wild* is that yuppies are only one step away from the abyss—just like everybody else. Their cushioned, moneyed world may seem infection-free, but only on the surface. Demme and Frye are using Charlie's yuppieness as a modern archetype, just as Ray's swagger is vintage fifties Hoodlum. The movie clashes these archetypes to get at something new in the ethos—the malice rattling inside the culture's complacency. *Something Wild* may be one of those rare American movies, like *Shoot the Moon* and *Blue Velvet* and some of Altman's work, that intuits more about what's going on in society than can possibly be known firsthand. For all its frolics, the movie is an apprehension of a coming storm.

(*Los Angeles Herald Examiner*, 1986)

The Wind Will Carry Us

The great Iranian director Abbas Kiarostami has said in an interview, "I immediately stop in front of a subject that invites me to contemplate it." He was referring to his work as a still photographer, but the same approach is evident in his films, and none more so than his newest, *The Wind Will Carry Us*. The terrain he offers up to us has a rough serenity; the ridged, rolling hills are monumental yet evanescent in their remoteness. Kiarostami is no mere picture-postcard portraitist. For him, the changeableness of landscapes, the way light and shadow play across them and colors deepen or pale, is a spiritual value. The invitation to contemplation that he talks about is really an invitation to bring our way of seeing into harmony with nature. The human drama in his new film is charged with the drama of the encompassing universe. It's all part of the same continuum.

As a film director, Kiarostami places himself among his audience; his imagery seems to open up its revelations to him at the same time as it unfolds for us. Most filmmakers do not invite us to collaborate in the visual experience; their vision is presented to us as a kind of proclamation, with all the inherent ambiguity in the imagery shaved away. Kiarostami, whose approach to nature must partly derive from Muslim culture (although it also seems pantheist), leaves the meanings open and various. The rich, slow deliberativeness of his style is in the tradition of directors like Yasujiro Ozu and Satyajit Ray, who also found great resonance in the communion between man and nature. With those directors, one often felt that a film of theirs consisting entirely of rivers or cloud formations or just empty rooms would still convey more of the eloquence of life's passage than an ordinary director's acted-out drama. So it is with Kiarostami. The introduction of people into his supernal tableaux does not alter his vision so much as it completes it.

In *The Wind Will Carry Us*, a producer from Tehran (Behzad Dourani), accompanied by a camera crew (whose faces are never shown), arrives in the remote mountain village of Siah Dareh in Iranian Kurdistan to record the impending ritual funeral ceremony of an ancient woman he has been told is near death. The villagers believe these men to be engineers intent on uncovering buried treasure from a local cemetery. With his jeans, unbuttoned shirt and sunglasses, and ever-present cell phone, the producer—no name for him is given—is a figure of some amusement in the valley. Whenever a call beeps, he charges in his Land Rover to higher ground in order to get proper reception; as the days stretch on and the old woman inexplicably improves, his crew threatens to mutiny. The producer doesn't have time for the villagers at first, except as potential co-conspirators. He befriends a young schoolboy, Farzad, in order to get the inside scoop on the old woman's health. He regards most of the locals as quaint artifacts of a vanished culture.

The community, however, is far from vanished, and it slowly elicits from the producer a vivid sympathy. Through poetry recitations he tries to draw out a young uneducated girl milking a cow in a cave; he tells her that "writing poetry has nothing to do with diplomas," and he means it. But Kiarostami isn't going for anything as simple as a back-to-nature idyll here. The villagers aren't some hazy, salt-of-the-earth conceit; they're a joking and savvy bunch, and their imbroglios, such as a scene involving a complaining waitress and her sullen male clients, are folkloric comedy sketches. (The contrast between the majesty of the natural surroundings and these petty flare-ups is a constant source of humor.) When the producer organizes a rescue operation for a local man who has been buried alive, the old doctor who arrives on his rickety, buzzy motorbike is not one to speak reverently of religion and the purported glories of the afterlife. "Prefer the present to these fine promises" is his choice advice.

Kiarostami preserves his outsider's view in *The Wind Will Carry Us* and, by doing so, brings the film even closer to us than if he had attempted to go native. There is much for the eye to take in: the harsh contrasts of weathered women in their black chadors against the village's piercingly bright white walls; the panoramas that look like pastel-tinged Ansel Adams vistas, but with layered bunches of color reminiscent of Morris Louis. Kiarostami has a sophisticated aesthetic sense that never fades into pure abstraction. His artifices are his way of moving deeply into the overwhelming mystery and emotion conjured up by this material. As with his old doctor here, Kiarostami's preference is for the present; he's ravished by the ineffableness of what he sees. The villagers are right—the producer is indeed looking for buried treasure. He doesn't find it in a local cemetery, though, but in the air and the people all around him in this dappled, murmurous valley.

(*New York*, 2000)

Kaos

Paolo and Vittorio Taviani's *Kaos* is easily the best movie I've seen so far this year. It's not like any other film except, perhaps, other Taviani brothers films, like *Padre Padrone* and *Night of the Shooting Stars*. Part fairy tale, part pagan romp, it's a rude, exuberant, animistic epic of magical realism. The movie draws so profoundly on so many of the generally untapped resources of film that its originality seems almost diabolic. Without consciously preparing us, the Tavianis strike one-of-a-kind images that are feral, lyrical, unspeakably moving.

Kaos isn't their greatest film—it's made up of four Pirandello stories, plus an epilogue and prologue, and two of the stories are tedious—but its finest moments are moving in ways that seem basic to film, to the power of film artists to pull you deep inside an image or a scene until you're nose to nose with sheer terror or sheer beauty. The Tavianis make no clear distinction between the two. They can show you a bright, full moon in the night sky, and it's so utterly fairy-tale gorgeous that it's terrifying. They can also show you a peasant raging and howling at that same moon, and his contortions are so grotesquely exuberant, so dancelike, that you register the rawness of his life force. Dance is integral to the Tavianis' characters; it possesses them, it's how they ritualize their joy, their demons. And primitiveness has a beauty in *Kaos* that's unlike anything we're used to seeing in the movies; it's primitiveness stripped of any salt-of-the-earth sentimentality. The visionary newness of this film is dizzying.

The howling-at-the-moon sequence, *Moonsickness,* is the second, and best, of the four stories, all of which are derived from a fifteen-volume collection of Pirandello tales, *Novelle Per Un Anno,* translated as *Stories for Every Day of the Year.* (The brief prologue also takes off from a story, *The Crow of Mizzaro.*) I've read three of the stories available in English translation, two of which Pirandello later dramatized, and they're remarkably different in spirit from his modernist plays (which were mostly written after the stories). Pirandello was a Sicilian who studied in Germany and spent most of his life in Rome; the stories that comprise *Kaos,* which are all set in turn-of-the-century Sicily, are like folk tales that a rapt child might have heard once and never forgotten, no matter how "sophisticated" or removed from his roots he became. The Tavianis seize the animus of these stories and improve them, fill them out.

With Pirandello, the Tavianis share a robust appetite for fantastical collisions with the "real world." Animals talk, the dead wing invisibly through the forests at night. But it was Pirandello's method to move in his fictions from the "civilized" to the unknown, which is where the fundament of his art truly resided. The Tavianis don't deal in such strict dichotomies. For them, the universe is an upturned planetarium of harrowing delights. The brittle Sicilian landscapes look as they did centuries ago. Antiquity bursts through the living. The unknown and the fantastical hypercharge everything.

In *Moonsickness,* for instance, we discover that the new husband (Claudio Bigagli) of a pretty, sloe-eyed bride (Enrica Maria Modugno), unbeknownst to her, turns into a raving loony every month during the full moon. How did this come about? He confesses ashamedly to her that when he was a baby, his peasant mother would leave him alone to look up, transfixed, at the night sky while she harvested the tall wheat. It doesn't logically follow from this that the baby should grow up to rave at the moon, like a werewolf, and yet the conceit seems magically apt for a Taviani movie. This episode is saying that nature gets into your blood and sets you off; it dazes and deranges. *Moonsickness* is the funniest, and the scariest, werewolf movie I've ever seen. The humor comes from the moon's bedazzlement, which is like the joke of the gods. The horror comes from the fact that the poor husband doesn't get the joke. He can't handle the *intensity* of the bedazzlement.

There's an added element to this tale that, like so much in the Tavianis' work, gives it an erotic depth charge. The wife, in order to protect herself against her husband during the next full moon, implores her mother and her handsome, adoring cousin (Massimo Bonetti) to stay the night with her, barricaded, while the husband roars outside. (The closest neighbors are miles away.) As night descends, the four characters—they're like co-conspirators, really—eat dinner outdoors, and the husband sends off a few premonitory whiffs of craziness. You can see that he enjoys tweaking his guests' fear; it's the only power this powerless man has. But when his wife and the cousin are alone in the dirt-floored bedroom, rippling with desire, he shrieks and rushes the barricades. It's like a primeval vaudeville sketch—the enraged cuckold is transformed into a monster. His howls crowd out his wife's moans.

The story that precedes this one, *The Other Son,* is harrowing in a more rugged, nuanced way. Fourteen years ago, the two sons of the now ravaged, dilapidated Mariagrazia (the great Margarita Lozano) left Sicily for America, where they settled in Sante Fe, never to be heard from again. The episode is about the mother's spirit-sustaining hope that her sons will return to her. She dictates letters to them, to be delivered by new emigrants from the village, and they're always the same; they're like incantations. But it turns out that Mariagrazia (who looks like a tumbleweed Anna Magnani—she's magnificent in her ravagement), has another son in the village whom she refuses to acknowledge despite his doting, sorrowful countenance.

Just when we think Mariagrazia is as batty as the villagers claim, she confides to a young doctor the reason she scurries away in rage and fear from her "good" son—the Other Son. And the reason is so dreadfully awful that it's like another joke of the gods—only the gods in this episode are crueler and more merciless than they will turn out to be in *Moonsickness*. We're filled with compassion for the bearded, woeful son; when he cries at his mother's rejection, the camera passes by a wall of stones, and the stones seem to be crying, too. But we're also repulsed. Mariagrazia's nightmare revelation has made us her confidant. Her furious features, when we last see them, have the strength of full-blown sanity behind them.

The last two stories in *Kaos*, *The Jar*, and *Requiem*, aren't up to these first two. *The Jar* is about a huge terra cotta jar belonging to the local *padrone* that mysteriously splits open one night, and how a local hump-backed artisan, hired to repair it with his miracle glue, ends up caught inside. The giant jar has an Arabian Nights fancifulness, and it's all mildly amusing, but the actors mug a lot and you long for the story to end. *Requiem,* which is about the attempt by some peasants to bury the patriarch of their clan on land they do not own, is even more laggard. It's the episode that, months from now, no one will remember from this film. (It does have one wonderful moment—when the peasants, in the woods at night, imitate the sounds in the brush and a rushing train. Suddenly we're in a Sicilian *Midsummer Night's Dream.*)

But the film's epilogue, *Colloquio con la Madre* (*Conversing with Mother*) is, for me, perhaps the most moving sequence in any Taviani brothers film. It opens with a shot of Luigi Pirandello (Omero Antonutti), whose tales we have just witnessed, fast asleep, his arm dangling abstractedly, on a train he is taking from Rome to Sicily, to which he is returning after many years following the news of his mother's death. He alights from the train in a daze; he thinks he may still be dreaming, and the smudged-charcoal sky and soft pastel landscapes certainly have the allurements of a dream. He is taken by carriage to his mother's old house, now vacant. (The carriage driver is the cousin, older now from *Moonsickness*. Luigi at first can't remember his name—he can't remember the name of one of his own "children.") Alone in the large sitting room, Luigi sees his mother reappear before him. It's as if we were seeing the scene through the eyes of the departed—shadows watching shadows.

He tells her that he can't remember a story she used to tell him about her girlhood and, as she recounts it to him, we see what she describes: the girl, her mother, and her brothers and sisters in a tartan fishing boat with a red sail, gusting toward Malta, where their father is in political exile. They rest for a spell on a white pumice island, and the girl, who is reluctant to leave her mother, is the last one to join her siblings and race up the powdered mountain and then down the slope into the azure sea.

We watch this reverie and suddenly we recognize why Luigi blocked it out. His mother left behind her mother in it, and now he must do the same. We're left with a long, lingering shot of the gaunt, elegant writer in the sitting room. He's alone now, bowed in memory. It's one of the greatest leave-takings in movies. *Kaos* opens with a quote from Pirandello: "I am a native son of chaos." By the end, he's an orphaned son, too.

(*Los Angeles Herald Examiner*, 1986)

The Makioka Sisters

Kon Ichikawa's *The Makioka Sisters* may just be the most beautiful-looking film I've ever seen. It's a ravishment of color and texture and flesh. I don't think there has ever been a movie this beautiful that was so meticulously controlled. Ichikawa shows us the patterning in a square inch of kimono, gives us the squeak of fabric shifting against fabric, shows us the architecture of a cherry blossom, skin that glows like pearl. The movie is such a nonstop sensual experience that you sit there from the first frame in a state of pure, beaming ecstasy.

I don't want to give the impression that *The Makioka Sisters* is simply a gorgeous exercise in style, devoid of human content. I'm not sure how he's done it, but Ichikawa, with his great cinematographer Kiyoshi Hasegawa, has given his characters a novelistic richness while also displaying them as poetic emanations. The women, the four Makioka sisters from Osaka, are so beautiful that they seem anointed; their brightly colored kimonos and lustrous skin are real jaw-droppers. This movie gives you such a feeling for the scintillation of flesh that it's not only a visual experience, it's a tactile experience, too. In an early scene, the youngest of the sisters, the headstrong Taeko (Yuko Kotegawa), sees the glowing, ivory-white bare shoulder of her second-oldest sister, Sachiko (Yoshiko Sakuma), as she dresses before a mirror. No other response is possible; Taeko reaches out to touch the flesh, as we do.

The movie, set in 1938, is adapted from a classic novel by Junichiro Tanizaki, whom Ichikawa has adapted before, in the more overtly erotic 1959 *Kagi* (*Odd Obsession*). Ichikawa has a direct pipeline to Tanizaki's way of seeing. This passage from Tanizaki's *Naomi*—his first important book, written in the twenties—could just as easily be a description of an image in *The Makioka Sisters*:

> Her [Naomi's] delicate skin, though still moist, was a pure vivid white . . . . Her face was glossy, as though a membrane of gelatin had been stretched across it. Only her eyebrows were still wet. Above them, on her forehead, the cloudless winter sky was reflected in pale blue through the window.

Imagine the visual and tactile beauty of this passage extended 140 minutes, and you have some idea of the experience of this movie. Ichikawa's feeling for the sheer sensuality of things gives the movie an eroticized shimmer. The film is about the fate of the four Makioka sisters, raised in wealth by their merchant father but now, their parents dead, their wealth depleted, struggling to maintain their dignity and social position. Tsuruko (Keiko Kishi), the oldest sister, is married to a banker (Juzo Itami, director of *Tampopo*) who made the pragmatic, unfavorable decision to sell the family shop in order to make ends meet. Now the offer of a promotion to a bank in Tokyo threatens to pull the family from its roots. Sachiko lives in the suburbs of Osaka with her docile husband, Teinosuke (Koji Ishizaka), and the two youngest sisters, Yukiko (Sayuri Yoshinaga), a beauty for whom the family is trying to find a respectable match, and Taeko, a doll-maker who, as tradition has it, is constrained from marrying until her older sister weds.

The four women are distinct and unique and yet, in some magical, unstressed way, sisters. (It's one of the most convincing sister acts in movie history.) Tsuruko is old enough to be the youngest girl's mother, and that's the role she unself-consciously assumes. Of the four, it is she who most registers the regret and sadness at how little the Makioka name means in an increasingly Westernized Japan on the brink of war. There's nothing haughty about Tsuruko's pride. She's so extraordinary a creature that that pride seems only just—her birthright. *All* of the Makioka sisters move in a kind of radiant swoon. They are not fully aware of their incandescence; it startles them, and they're humbled by its blessing.

A comic motif involves Yukiko's suitors—widowers, an expert in fish—and we look forward with glee to each meeting. Yukiko is the only sister who incarnates traditional Japanese female passivity (she won't even talk on the telephone). She is such a fairy-tale vision of femininity that she stuns each man she meets—they all want her. Her effect on men is comic, also poignant; the poor souls are mesmerized by their proximity to such purity. They know they may never pass this way again.

Taeko is Yukiko's opposite number. She smokes, wants to make her dolls in Paris, and sometimes wears Western clothes. She was involved in an elopement scandal with a jeweler's son five years ago; her taste in men is wayward. Taeko seems the most lost of the sisters; she's caught in the limbo between family tradition and Westernization. She makes a pain of herself because she feels neglected, but her dissolution can't erase the imprimatur of her beauty. Even on the skids, she has a high gloss.

In form, *The Makioka Sisters* is something of a tragedy, but it's not a weak-kneed tragedy. It offers a serene acceptance of life's disappointments, like that other great Japanese family tragedy, Yasujiro Ozu's *Tokyo Story*. And, like *Tokyo Story,* it has such a deep, resounding feeling for the textures of everyday life that you really don't think of the film as being a tragedy at all. *The Makioka Sisters* is an astounding, revivifying experience. It reaffirms beauty as an innate and indispensable quality of cinema.

(*Los Angeles Herald Examiner,* 1985)

Pretty Poison

"You are going into a very real and very tough world. It's got no place at all for fantasies."

This warning at the start of *Pretty Poison,* issued to Dennis Pitt

(Anthony Perkins) by his gruffly paternal case officer, Morton Azenauer (John Randolph), on the day of Dennis's discharge, is a confirmation of the young man's defenselessness. Dennis was institutionalized at fifteen for setting fire to his aunt's home with, unbeknownst to him, his aunt still inside it. He is out on his own now for the first time, and his parting joke to Azenauer—he says he'd prefer an interplanetary assignment to the factory job awaiting him—is not even a joke exactly. For Dennis, being out in the "very real" world is indeed a kind of science-fiction-style relocation. He's a stranger in a strange land. The tense, overrehearsed manner in which he speaks—even in casual conversation he appears to be reading from a teleprompter—is his way of reining in a barely concealed hysteria.

When we next see Dennis he is employed at a mill in western Massachusetts that dumps toxic chemicals into the Housatonic River. He girds himself to become an eco-terrorist. (You get the feeling he's less interested in saving the planet than in playacting the role of saboteur.) Having violated his parole, he is tracked down by Azenauer, who can't bring himself to dash Dennis's future. "I'm not going back," he yells to Azenauer. "This is my life, my one and only life."

Released in 1968 without advance press screenings, *Pretty Poison* sank at the box office but became an instant succès d'estime—and remains so to this day. The fact that the movie didn't roll out with the usual Hollywood hype may have worked to its advantage. Audiences feel more proprietary toward orphaned movies, especially B movies.

But *Pretty Poison*—it was the debut feature of director Noel Black and was written by Lorenzo Semple Jr., based on a novel by Stephen Geller—is something of a B-movie manqué. Despite its low-budget trappings and rudimentary murder plot, the film is, from a psychological standpoint, almost bewilderingly complex. Nothing is at it seems, starting with Perkins's performance, which only the unenlightened would deem a Norman Bates redo.

He was never better than he is in *Pretty Poison*. Whereas even his best previous (and subsequent) work was often jangled by tics and stammers almost to the point of self-caricature, here he moves beyond all that. Or rather, to be exact, he gives us a clear, wide view into the psycho-sexual underpinnings of his signature mannerisms. It's like looking at a two-dimensional portrait that, on closer inspection, suddenly snaps into 3-D. Perkins was sometimes accused of playing adults as if they were arrested adolescents, but here his characterization makes perfect sense. Dennis is locked inside the mindset of a traumatized fifteen-year-old. Throughout the film, Black gives us a series of meltingly lyrical long shots of Dennis stretching out his gangly legs and racing through town, and it's as if, in those brief moments, Dennis is unlocking himself. The sheer joy of physical release has made him ecstatic.

The pathos of *Pretty Poison* is that, despite his flippancies and junior G-man demeanor, Dennis is almost mordantly aware of his torments. They give him a greater appreciation of normality, and so he lives a kind of double life. Not entirely without cause, he imagines that the world conspires against him. Worse, he conspires against himself, and on some barely perceived level, he knows it. He aches to be happy. This is why he is smitten the moment he spots the goddessy blond high school senior Sue Ann Stepanek, played by Tuesday Weld. Dennis sees romance as his redemption, and he woos Sue Ann the only way he knows how—by pretending to be a covert CIA operative enlisting her in a secret mission to sabotage the mill.

Like Perkins, Weld carries her own baggage from previous films, but even in her sex kitten phase she had a sly knowingness about her allure. That's what she has here, too, except now her beauty is a deadly weapon. Sue Ann is the pretty poison. At the start of their courtship, Dennis involves her in his tricky, goofy missions; he can't believe his luck at landing a hometown sweetheart. But Sue Ann's blank prettiness masks a gargoyle. The black comedy of the piece is that the all-American Sue Ann turns out to be a great deal more disturbed than Dennis, the institutionalized arsonist.

He comes to realize this at the moment when, during a nighttime raid on the mill, the nightwatchman is injured and Sue Ann, with lascivious glee, finishes the old man off. Dennis looks at the dead man and all that secret agent artifice of his instantly burns off. What we see is a morbidly afraid boy. Sue Ann, however, is sexually high from the experience and consummates the moment with Dennis, whose best and worst fantasies are thus simultaneously fulfilled.

And yet, because he still clings to his reverie of Sue Ann as a "clean, true girl"—his words to Azenauer—he can't bear to see her as she is or admit he is afraid of her. He's stricken. After the long night, he goes by himself to a park and sits in a swing in the early dawn and seems horribly alone.

Sue Ann, of course, is not afraid of Dennis because she has no capacity for fear. Particularly on a second viewing of the film, it's clear that Sue Ann is on to Dennis very early. He's the patsy she has been looking for to eliminate her harpy mother (Beverly Garland). Sue Ann is like Barbara Stanwyck's black widow from *Double Idemnity* transplanted to the environs of Norman Rockwell. But she is not as overtly calculating as the standard noir vamp, and this is, finally, the most disturbing thing about her. She's a sun-kissed psychotic with a killer instinct so primordial it's practically unconscious with her. Her murders are like dream walks.

Dennis can't save himself because he can't shake off the blissful future he envisaged with Sue Ann. An added horror is that he comes to believe—wrongly, perhaps—that he was a goner long before he met her. The nightmare scenario he has entered into certifies his long-held self-image of personal depravity. He grows up in the end, though. He understands what has happened to him too late, but it is this understanding that rescues him even though he winds up behind bars. *Pretty Poison* is a coming-of-age movie about a kid who talks crazy to keep sane. The Dennis who looks out at us in the last scene is fiercely, desperately sane, and this newfound condition is both his glory and his prison.

(*The B List*, 2008)

Shoot the Moon

Shoot the Moon, starring Albert Finney and Diane Keaton, has so many emotional crosscurrents that the screen almost trembles. The movie mainlines pure feeling from its very first shot. It's about a hellish marriage and, at least on the surface, the plot is not that unfamiliar—we've seen this domestic discord before in scores of soap operas and "problem" plays. But Alan Parker, the director, and Bo Goldman, the screenwriter, take such a fresh view of a marital breakup that it's almost like watching this material on-screen for the first time.

George Dunlap (Finney) is a successful writer who, when the movie begins, can no longer abide his marriage. His face is sodden with blocked emotion; he's at the end of his rope, and the rope soon snaps—he leaves his family and moves in with his young girlfriend (Karen Allen). In the beginning his wife, Faith (Keaton), has the blowsy, beaten look of a woman who's trying to hold her life together and salvage her emotions while still taking care of four rambunctious daughters, ranging in age from perhaps five to thirteen. Sherry (Dana Hill), the oldest daughter, understands intuitively what's going on with her parents; she's hypersensitive to their torments, which she internalizes until her pain is as great as theirs. Sherry is trying to comprehend her parents as though they were adults who are responsible for their actions. What she is too young to realize is how pain can contort the behavior of adults into something childlike and irrational. George and Faith are no more in control of their feelings than their children, and yet their children look to them for comfort. That's the tragedy at the heart of the movie.

It's a tragedy in the most pastoral of settings. The Marin County countryside where the Dunlaps reside, in their spacious, old house, is startlingly verdant. The landscape is so beautiful that the unhappiness of its inhabitants is made to seem even more shocking than it would be in, say, an urban setting. If these people can't get sustenance from such beauty, then what can they get sustenance from? Throughout the film, Alan Parker isolates Faith and, particularly, George, in compositions set against the coastline and the hills. Whenever there's a downpour, the landscape seems to be weeping.

Unlike most marital breakup movies, *Shoot the Moon* doesn't ennoble suffering. Misery hasn't made George soulful—he looks racked. Even when he's with his girlfriend, his brow is a tight band of tension. Faith has more moods, more expressions. In an early scene, when she drives in silent misery with George to a book-awards dinner, her face looks as hard as a harridan's. (From certain angles, Diane Keaton resembles Garbo in one of those fugitive shots of her outside her New York apartment.) At other times, her face in the moonlight seems frosted. When, after George has left her, Faith invites to dinner the contractor who's building a tennis court on her property, she has the luminescence of a debutante. But Faith is hopeful without having much hope. She has a chummy, tentative affair with that contractor (Peter Weller), but she doesn't really put much store in it. She knows it isn't meant to last.

George is far less practical than Faith. Even though he is the one who breaks off the marriage, he can't quite accept what that means. Without being fully aware of it, he wants back in. He keeps returning to the scene of the crime, not just to see his children but to tempt Faith. When he realizes that she has not crumpled without him—that she has, in fact, taken a lover—he's both proud of her and maddened by her independence.

George doesn't take a very romantic view of his own suffering; it turns him into a violent rampager who, at one point, breaks into his house and crashes into his eldest daughter's bedroom in an attempt to see her against her wishes. But George does harbor certain romantic-masochistic fancies about being a writer. He feels a kinship with Jack London, whose burned-down home, now a historical landmark, he visits with his girlfriend and three of his daughters. George has led a privileged life, and he knows it. His wife has devoted her life to their children, leaving him pretty much free to ruminate. As the movie develops, we become aware of how guilty George feels for that privilege. That's really why he leaves—he can't handle either the guilt or the awe he feels for what Faith has done.

I hope all this doesn't imply that *Shoot the Moon* is some sort of feminist tract. It's far too complex and unsentimental for that. Alan Parker and Bo Goldman are scrupulously fair-minded—they give all the characters their due. The Marin County of this movie is the same stomping ground that Cyra McFadden ploughed in *Serial,* but, seen through artists' eyes this time, it's barely recognizable as such. Karen Allen as smiley Sandy, George's girlfriend, whose speech is awash in pop-therapy cant (she tells George, "You're my friend"), is viewed by the filmmakers with the same even-handedness as George and Faith. And the Dunlap children are perhaps the most unsentimentalized, and therefore the most realistic, children ever seen in a movie. (Besides the extraordinary Dana Hill, there's Viveka Davis, Tracey Gold, and Tina Yothers.) Except for Sherry, George's daughters are equal-opportunity ragamuffins—they give each of their parents countless chances to prove their love. They're surprisingly resilient—almost comically so. Their high-spiritedness has a slapstick energy that turns even the most brutal assaults, such as George's household rampage, into black comedy. (After the smoke clears, the youngest daughter, the red-headed Molly, asks her father if she can make him a hamburger with onions.)

Diane Keaton has often been a graceful, offhandedly funny performer but, except for moments in *Interiors* and *Reds,* she's never demonstrated as much depth as she does here. Every gesture is in character; every look has overtones. We can see in Faith not only the woman she has become but the girl she was when she married George—a little star-struck, perhaps, and eager for nurturing. Albert Finney's performance is not quite as translucent as Keaton's—we can't see as many emotional possibilities in it—but he's more than up to the role's demands. I think it's his finest performance on film. And on a smaller scale, Peter Weller's Frank matches him as the tennis-court contractor.

It's possible, I think, to view *Shoot the Moon* as a screwball comedy turned inside out. When George and Faith accidentally meet at a swank restaurant and create a scene, the episode is played for broad laughs. Alan Parker's staging here is maladroit, but the sequence works anyway; it carries us back to the pleasures of thirties screwball comedies even as the movie goes beyond those pleasures. Howard Hawks once said that he would only direct a tragedy if he saw no way to make it a comedy. Alan Parker and Bo Goldman have it both ways in *Shoot the Moon*. It's a sorrowful film, but it expresses the human comedy. Watching it, you're amazed at what love and lovelessness can do to people, how it can warp them into monsters and rag dolls and buffoons. This movie is saying the same things the screwball comedies were saying, only in a different key—it's saying that, on some essential level, human beings are bewilderingly inadequate to the demands of love. They can't handle it.

(*Los Angeles Herald Examiner*, 1982)

Hamsun

Jan Troell's *Hamsun*, starring Max Von Sydow, is easily the greatest film I've seen in years. It takes you as far out as you can go—to the limits of feeling. As a movie about a great and grievous artist made by an artist of equal rank, it is perhaps unique in film history. It's about the final seventeen years in the life of the Norwegian writer Knut Hamsun, winner of the 1920 Nobel Prize in Literature and, in his eighties, an ardent defender of Hitler. Hamsun went from being a national hero to a national disgrace. This film plays out the passion of his fall.

The Swedish director of the two-part masterpiece *The Emigrants* and *The New Land*, Troell has once again locked into a great, epic subject—the enigma of the artist who is also a fascist. He doesn't attempt to "solve" the enigma. The atrocious, beleaguered Hamsun, who died at ninety-two in 1952, was a supreme writer. His novels *Hunger, Mysteries,* and *Pan* are, in their jagged explorations of states of mind, among the greatest fiction of the twentieth century—though, in fact, they were all written in the 1890s. How could an artist so intimately connected to life and suffering also be a champion and a pawn of monsters? It's a paradox that goes to the heart of what it is to be a human being.

Most biographical movies lurch from high point to high point, but *Hamsun*, which was scripted by Per Olov Enquist, has a fated pull, as if we are watching the ritualistic playing out of some infinitely sad story. It begins with the news that Hitler is dead. With a mixture of pride and fear, Hamsun and his wife, Marie (the astonishing Danish actress Ghita Norby), also an ardent Nazi supporter, await their inevitable arrests for treason in the idyllic shelter of their country farm in Norholm. Despite their collusion, they seem isolated from each other.

We then move back nine years to 1936, and the roots of that isolation become manifest. In the fields of Norholm, Hamsun and Marie are caught up in a livid, harrowing fight which seems like the summation of a lifetime of bad blood. Twenty-three years her husband's junior, Marie seems dowdy yet ravaged; Hamsun, nearly deaf, his gait rickety, has a practiced, patriarchal air. Marie left the stage to marry him, and now she attacks him with a performer's vengeance: "Why did you take up thirty years of my life?" She's still an actress—she sees herself as a ruined innocent. "You've made me old," she says, and he responds, "Yes, we've made each other ugly."

This sequence, coming almost at the start of the movie, grabs you by the throat. It's like suddenly being thrust into an arena marked off by O'Neill or Strindberg (whom Hamsun knew and admired to the point of copying his bristly mustache). The hellishness of a bad marriage carries its own meaning. As this scene plays itself out, we recognize that the couple's hatred for each other binds them. This harrowing dance gives them life.

Despite his detestation of the theater, Hamsun is a species of actor himself. He is almost sadistically aware that, by his provocations and deprivations, he has given Marie her greatest role—the sorrowing wife of a national treasure.

Marie's induction into fascism comes about because Quisling (Sverre Anker Ousdal), the leader of the Norwegian Nazi Party, recognizes Marie's fierce need to enact an important role. After years playing Hamsun's wife and serving as the official mouthpiece at honorary events, Marie takes on a far larger role; she's wooed by Quisling into reading from Hamsun's agrarian epic *The Growth of the Soil* in rallies throughout Germany. Dressed in a brightly colored folk costume, flanked by crimson, swastika-emblazoned banners, she luxuriates in her showcase. And yet there is something deeply hardbitten about this woman—she knows she only has the spotlight because she is the proxy of a man she both reveres and detests.

Hamsun's family shares this same love/hate, and it tears them up. His children—two sons, Arild (Gard Eidsvold) and Tore (Eindride Eidsvold) and two daughters, Cecilia (Asa Soderling) and Ellinor (Anette Hoff, who might have stepped out of an Edvard Munch painting)—regard him with a mixture of awe and reproach. They pull at him, they want to matter in his life, and yet they also want to be apart from him.

Like the ritual warring between Hamsun and Marie, this dance between Hamsun and his grown-up sons and daughters has a primal, familiar horror. The children of a great artist have a particular burden; they must work their way out of the shadow that both glorifies and effaces them. For Hamsun, being a father means lording it over the manor. His patriarchy has epic force and, in its remoteness, an epic horror.

And also an epic banality. There is in Hamsun's conduct with his family a parallel with his outrageous embrace of National Socialism. Both are the work of an imperial crank. Hamsun's pro-Nazism—his belief that Norway would become the crown jewel in the New German Order—was the flipside of his longstanding and irrational hatred of the British. He was political in a peculiarly instinctual and childlike way.

In Hamsun's first and perhaps greatest book *Hunger*, we seem to be residing right inside the circuitry of a desperate man's mind; the first-person narrative has a shifting, frantic obsessiveness. Hamsun brought to his real-life political affiliations a similar quality of dreadful waywardness. He was a dabbler. There's a shimmering black comic moment in *Hamsun* when the writer meets with Terboven (Edgar Selge), Norway's vicious Reichskommissar, who compliments him on a particularly fragrant anti-Semitic passage from one of his newspaper screeds. Hamsun replies that he has no hatred for the Jews, and when Terboven asks if he's read *Mein Kampf,* Hamsun replies, "No, but I read the reviews."

Primarily because of his films with Ingmar Bergman, Von Sydow has become for the world the iconic Scandinavian—as iconic a personage, perhaps, as was the real-life Knut Hamsun in his glory and disgrace. The Scandinavians like a fine pitch of suffering in their iconography—they want their heroes to anguish mightily for them—and Von Sydow brings to anguish a great gravity. But his performances for Troell—in *The Emigrants, The New Land,* and *The Flight of the Eagle*—are every bit as good as his work with Bergman. Even better perhaps, since Troell brings out in him a more human-scaled plangency.

In *Hamsun,* Von Sydow gives what could well be the performance of a lifetime. He may be playing an enigma but he charges the role with a full-bodied comprehension of what age and pride and ruination can do to a man. His awesome understanding of character is a tribute to Hamsun, the great psychological novelist (who, ironically, closed himself off from self-understanding). And yet people looking for "answers" to Hamsun's personal and political pathologies won't find them in this film, because Troell and Von Sydow aren't looking for simple causations. There are no "Rosebuds" in *Hamsun.* But you can sense in Von Sydow's performance how this gruff, brittle dignitary might have taken up with the Nazis as a way to fire his flagging powers. Hamsun was a man who needed to work in the face of hostility; as a young writer he would give lecture tours denouncing Ibsen and Tolstoy. For his old age, what better furnace for opprobrium than Nazism?

There are two extended sequences in *Hamsun* in which Von Sydow is unsurpassed. The first is Hamsun's meeting with Hitler (Ernst Jacobi) in the Fuehrer's Alpine aerie. (Their dialogue together is based on actual transcripts.) Hamsun has engaged the meeting to protest Reichskommissar Terboven's brutality, but the much-touted confab goes disastrously wrong. Hitler wants to talk about art, and Hamsun, who has been feverishly rehearsing his words, wants only to secure Hitler's assurances. The old man's tactless desperation turns him into an enraged supplicant. When Hitler all at once turns on him in a fury it's as if Hamsun is mugged of his own reason. He seems horrifically foolish and endangered, and the bright Alpine air suddenly seems thick with a thousand invisible knives.

The second sequence is Hamsun's speech before the Norwegian court trying him for treason after the war. Kept away from public view by the authorities, confined to nursing homes and psychiatric wards, Hamsun is a wraith everyone expects to conveniently expire. But this unrepentant man who earlier had wished to die now lives only to defend himself.

Just before his defense, we see Hamsum viewing concentration camp footage and running aghast from the projection room. The horror of his allegiance has come home. Now, for his day in court, he puts up a decorous front, but his clipped words have no steel. He concludes by saying, "I am at peace with myself," and then sits down and closes his eyes, and we see no great peace. Hamsun is already separating his soul from his body. He has the look of a man burning in passage.

There is an awe in this film, and a horror, at what a human being is capable of. *Hamsun* is no apologia, but it is a supremely humanist indictment. In the end, the furies that have lashed out at the old man pass away. We seem to be watching the bejeweled closing to a dark fairy tale. This pastoralism is part of the story, too; it's the beauty at the heart of the enigma. Hamsun and Marie nestle together under a lush laburnum tree, and it's as if time itself is weeping. What Troell has given us in *Hamsun* is a benediction for man's bewildered fate.

(New Times, 1997)

CHAPTER 7

DOCUMENTARIES

When We Were Kings

In Norman Mailer's *The Fight,* his great book on the Muhammad Ali/ George Foreman Rumble in the Jungle, he begins by writing of Ali, "There is always the shock in seeing him again. Not *live* as in television but standing before you, looking his best. Then the World's Greatest Athlete is in danger of being our most beautiful man, and the vocabulary of Camp is doomed to appear. Women draw an *audible* breath. Men look *down.* They are reminded again of their lack of worth."

This may sound like hyperbole, but Mailer—like Ali—lives in the region where hyperbole can be transcendent. (It can also be bull.) Mailer's response to Ali in this passage is also our response to seeing him in *When We Were Kings,* Leon Gast's amazing documentary about the 1974 Zaire fight and the events surrounding it. The film is unabashed hero-worship, but Ali is so clearly a hero here that we don't feel swept away by gush. And because of what Ali has become—and George Foreman, too, with his fabulous newfound cuddliness—the movie is doubly poignant now. The documentary is, in essence, not much more than a record of what happened in Zaire, but it has been assembled with a real feeling for the historical moment. It's literally a blast from the past.

It's also something of a miracle because it almost didn't get made. (It recently captured awards from the Los Angeles, New York, and National societies of film critics for Best Documentary.) Gast, who had already directed documentaries about the Hell's Angels and the Grateful Dead, was initially hired to film the musical festivities surrounding the fight. He had in mind an African-American *Woodstock* complete with James Brown, B. B. King, the Jazz Crusaders, Bill Withers, and the Spinners. Then, four days before the fight was scheduled, a cut to Foreman's eye during a sparring session postponed the match for six weeks. Gast ended up training his cameras on Ali for much of that time, and what he came up with is the core of this movie.

It took almost twenty-three years to assemble. Returning broke from Zaire with 300,000 feet of celluloid—about a hundred hours—Gast spent the next fifteen years processing portions of the film as he was able to pay for it. After finally untangling legal rights and acquiring completion funds, Gast and his newfound partner, David Sonenberg, an influential music talent manager, made the decision to insert additional fight footage and archival clips. They brought in Taylor Hackford to shoot and edit into the film look-back interviews with, among others, Mailer and George Plimpton and Ali biographer Thomas Hauser.

Gast includes snatches of the musicians doing their thing, but for the most part *When We Were Kings* is a musical in form far more than in content. It's *shaped* like a musical—an opera, really—with arias of exhortation, massed choruses, and pomp. Gast knows how to syncopate the story; he gives it a pulse that makes it seem like the whole cavalcade of hype and holler is once again upon us.

Of course, we know how it all turned out—Ali, game but somewhat past his prime, stunned the world by knocking out the man most believed would demolish him. Gast builds our knowledge of the fight's outcome into the film's structure; there's a retrospective thrill in seeing how hot the tumult got. It's easy to forget now how genuine was the fear that Ali might be *killed* in the ring.

It's the fear that underscores everything we see—the interviews with the sports commentators and trainers and fight organizers, with Ali's giddy multitudinous African fans and even a worrywart Howard Cosell, who hyperbolizes about his concerns for Ali's safety. Mailer makes the point during an interview that Ali must have recognized in his most private moments that Foreman could pulverize him, and the perception lends an extra dimension to Ali's most hysterical rants against his challenger. He takes up the African cry *Ali boma ye*—which means "Ali, kill him"—and is so rapturously insistent in leading the charge that the effect is frightening. It's as if Ali were exorcising his own horrors right before our eyes.

Ali was attuned in a way Foreman wasn't to the *political* momentousness of the event. "From slave ship to championship" was how he billed the fight, and his back-to-Africa oratory resonated with the Zaireans, who revered him not so much because he was a great fighter but because he stood up to the American government and refused induction into the Vietnam War. "No Vietcong ever called me nigger" was his mantra in those years, and it made him a champion's champion for people who sized up the racist implications of that war.

Ali had to demonize Foreman in the eyes of Africans; it was his standard operating procedure to run down his opponents before any fight. But Ali was faced with a problem in Zaire—in a match between two great black boxers in the "homeland," how do you play up the racial angle? Ali was in fact much lighter-skinned than Foreman, but he castigates him as, in effect, white. "He's in my country," Ali says of Foreman, who had the misfortune to arrive in Zaire with his German shepherd—the very dog used by the Belgians to police the Congo.

Throughout *When We Were Kings*, Ali comes on like—in Gast's words—the Original Rapper. He successfully bleaches Foreman with his patter; he milks the press, the trainers, the camera crew. He says, "I'm not fighting for me, I'm fighting for black people who have no future." Ali is not only a boxer of genius, he's a politician of genius. I remembered being baffled by how wooden he was playing himself in *The Greatest*. But Ali—who has as much charisma as any movie star who ever lived—can come alive only by his own wit and instinct. To play a role in a movie, even if the role is himself, would mummify his genie.

When Ali lit the Olympic torch in Atlanta and we saw up-close the effects of his Parkinson's disease, the press covered the moment as if it were an unalloyed triumph. The commentators didn't allow for our mixed emotions, our rage even, for what Ali had become—possibly owing in large measure to his having taken so many blows to the head from such fighters as George Foreman while we cheered him on. Ali is a hero still, but in a more complicated way. His presence is both an inspiration and an admonition. *When We Were Kings* brings back the unimpeded joy we once felt in Ali's presence. It's a movie in a state of denial—magnificent, unapologetic denial.

(*New Times*, 1997)

Streetwise

The documentary *Streetwise* was shot using a new high-speed Kodak film and extremely sensitive radio mikes, and the result is a heightened realism that has the in-close observation and intensity of a dramatic film. We've never seen filmed-on-the-sly confrontations captured with quite this much verity before. As a result, the movie has a strange complexion—it seems to be staged. And, in a sense, it *is* staged. The nine Seattle street kids whose lives were filmed by the camera crew during a two-month shoot in 1983 play up to the camera; some of them have the instincts of improv performers, and they love to show off their down-and-dirty savvy. But the movie's steady, dispassionate gaze neutralizes the kids' antics. They can't help revealing themselves. They can't disguise how scared and unformed they are.

Streetwise has its origins in a July 1983 *Life* magazine story by photographer Mary Ellen Mark and staff writer Cheryl McCall. Titled "Streets of the Lost," it was a slick, unromanticized report from the front. Given the richness of the material, it's not surprising that McCall and Mark felt the need to go back to the streets with a camera crew and capture the subculture in a movie. Mark's husband, Martin Bell, a British cinematographer with several anthropological documentaries to his credit, returned with the women to Seattle in mid-August, and much of the filming was done on Pike Street, in Seattle's Tenderloin district.

At first, the movie seems haphazard, as we slide in and out of the lives of the street kids. But they gradually become familiar to us: there's Rat, a puny, malnourished, wily seventeen-year-old boy who wears a Yankee cap backward; Tiny, a fourteen-year-old prostitute with a hard-set jaw; DeWayne, an emaciated sixteen-year-old whose father is serving thirty years in the federal pen for robbery and arson; Shadow, eighteen, who gives blood for money, goes in for heavy tattooing and hair-dying, and considers himself not a pimp but a "playboy"; Kim, sixteen, an adoptee who has run away from her suburban parents and become a whore; Patty and Munchkin, seventeen and eighteen, a street couple; Shellie, thirteen, a runaway, sexually molested by her stepfather, who moves in with Patty and Munchkin and turns tricks to pay her way; and Lulu, nineteen, a tough lesbian who patrols the streets with a protective swagger—she boasts about how many runaways she's sent home.

The movie is something of a crash course in how to survive on the streets. Many of the kids live in abandoned apartments and flophouses and earn their money turning tricks, pimping, selling blood, cadging spare change. They're too young for government relief. They bathe in public restrooms, wash their clothes in laundromats, forage for food in garbage dumpsters. In one of the movie's lighter moments, Rat demonstrates a technique called "dumpster diving"—call a pizza joint from a pay phone, order a few pizzas with something unpopular on it, like pineapple, stick around at the pay phone for the verifying call-back, wait an hour, and then raid the dumpster behind the restaurant for the unclaimed pies.

What's extraordinary about these kids, however, is not their street savvy. (If they were so savvy, they wouldn't keep ending up in jail or detention centers—or worse.) The amazing thing is how they still manage to come off like kids. They're a weird combo—wised-up, hard-bitten cynics who look prematurely old, and yet have the sportive childishness and goofy, aloof dreams of pre-adolescents. Wizened by malnutrition, their features are tight and pasty and their eyes are deadened. And yet, as if to compensate for their enforced maturation, they often cavort and tumble like kids who are *younger* they are.

These children who have been mugged of their childhood don't show much remorse or anxiety; that would imply a perspective on their actions that, for the most part, they don't have. Kids like Rat and Tiny live continually in the moment, and that gives the movie a vivid, present-tense immediacy; when violence suddenly erupts on the street, it's not shocking—it's just part of the continuum we've been witnessing.

Rat talks about the parents he ran away from and how they're "a part of my past now." But he doesn't seem to have had any past—it's as remote as his future (he wants to be an air force pilot). Tiny, who lives with her alcoholic mother, never knew her father—for all she knows, she might have "dated" him without knowing it. When she's with her mother, there's a cuckoo quality to the pairing; we see Tiny pick out makeup with her mother from a mail-order kit, and it's a nice, homey tableau until you realize that Tiny will be using the cosmetics to doll up for her johns. Her mother, who looks like a bigger-boned duplicate of her daughter, knows Tiny is hooking but thinks it's "just a phase she's going through." The mother's massive self-delusion has carried over to the daughter. She probably no more believes her daughter is a prostitute than she believes herself to be an alcoholic. But you know where her real sympathies lie when Tiny, craving attention, asks her too many questions and the mother, in the next room with a bottle, barks out: "Don't bug me, I'm drinking." It's the most heartfelt statement we hear from Tiny's mother in the entire movie.

A moment like this captures the horror of addiction in a way that most fiction films never approach. And certainly there's more truth in the movie's view of streetwalking than in an exploitation film like *Angel*. Exploitation films have raided so many of the same subjects in this movie for so long that some people may think that *Streetwise* is more sensationalistic than it really is. They may quarrel with the way the filmmakers structure the film to lead up to the suicide of one of the kids. But, if I have one complaint about the film, it's that the filmmakers weren't unscrupulous *enough*. For the most part they don't romanticize the kids (although I could easily have done without the growly Tom Waits soundtrack, which tells us to "Take Care of All the Children"), but we don't have a wide-enough overview of what the kids are up to. Rat and some of his buddies carry guns, which they claim are only for self-defense. Is that really true? And, if it is true, for how long will it continue to be? There are a couple of scenes with social workers and doctors, but no interviews with the police, who might have given us an even more sordid (and unsympathetic) view of the life we're witnessing. There's no treatment of male prostitution.

In the *Life* piece, McCall wrote: "Boys do drugs to survive the humiliation of turning tricks, just to live with themselves." In the movie, we don't see the street kids shooting up, and, more important, we don't see them shooting up other kids. (If we did, we might not so easily condone their victimization.) The whole business of drug trafficking is downplayed in the movie in a way it wasn't in *Life*, and I'm not quite sure why—it couldn't have been because of legal constraints, when you consider that the movie crew managed to gain permission to film just about every nook and cranny in Seattle, including a coffin with the body of one of the kids.

Maybe one of the problems was the filmmakers' decision to let the kids themselves provide the narration. That technique gets you into their heads in a startlingly direct way, but it also closes us off from the information—the facts and figures—that this material cries out for. Documentaries have gotten such a bad name from the learning-lab horrors of our high-school days, which always seemed to be about the life cycles of the basic food groups, or from the propagandistic *March of Time* genre, that documentary filmmakers, following the lead of the recent Fred Wiseman, may have overcorrected. We never seem to find out enough about the *subjects* in modern documentaries; the difference between a richly detailed piece of impressionism and a gloss is not always clear, and *Streetwise* is no exception.

Still, it's a tribute to the film that it makes you want to know more. The movie is a real eye-opener, even though we might want our eyes opened even wider. And some of the movie's deficiencies may be inherent in the documentary form; it's possible that the full richness of this material can only be expressed in drama. *Streetwise* is the best movie I've seen on its subject, but it doesn't have the power or the depth of *Shoeshine* and *Pixote* and *The 400 Blows*. What you take away from the movie is a portrait of a spooky new underclass of child-drifters, and a couple of extraordinary scenes, like Rat's detention-cell farewell to Tiny, or De-Wayne's chain-smoking father, in prison, lovingly scolding his visiting son. At its best, *Streetwise* does justice to a great tragedy: the corruption of innocence. There aren't many movies around that can make that boast.

(*Los Angeles Herald Examiner*, 1985)

The Gleaners and I

"I like filming rot, leftovers, waste," Agnès Varda tells us in her documentary *The Gleaners and I*, a lyrically ramshackle essay about people, including Varda herself, who don't fit into society's cubbyholes. The "gleaners" in the title are all manner of folk who gather up castoffs, oddments, and curios from dumps and harvests, and Varda explicitly links them to the gatherers in paintings by Millet and Jules Breton.

Using a digital video camera, Varda films her present-day gleaners in urban and rural France as they forage and lollygag; she films herself, too, eating a ripe fig or offering up a close-up of her aged hands. (She notes, bemusedly, their "horror.") Her ostensible subject is an excuse for a larger one—how improvisation and art are inextricably linked. Her digressions—about her own life and the lives of her subjects—are the core of her craft. Playfulness leads to a wider, more intimate discovery. Filming the big trucks she passes on the highway, Varda talks about the magical largeness such vehicles once held for her as a child; a ragtag former trucker in an encampment of gypsies talks about a past life and the wife and children he is no longer able to see; a man scrounging for edibles turns out to have been a biology grad student who now teaches reading skills to mostly African immigrants in the shelter where he lives; a retired bricklayer stands before a momentous tower of junk he has, over the years, fashioned into something out of the *Arabian Nights*.

Varda is open to the surprise of the dailiness that surrounds her; every story, every whim takes her down another byway. Even her rest periods are resonant; at one point, her journey is held up by a flock of sheep crossing the road, and Varda says how much she likes it when animals block her way. For her, life is an accumulation of possibilities. "A clock without hands is my kind of thing," she tells us, referring to a curio, and indeed it is: There's a timelessness, an immanence to what she shows us. In truth, the animals blocking her way aren't blocking anything. They're a part of her path.

(Los Angeles Times, 2001)

Buena Vista Social Club

Many of the marvelous Cuban musicians and singers in Wim Wenders's wonderful documentary *Buena Vista Social Club* are well beyond sixty, but they don't see themselves as aged. Onstage, jamming together, or in smaller recording sessions, they have an aliveness that obliterates any concerns we might have about their frailty. It's not simply that music keeps these artists vital. It's as if they never grew old at all. I've never seen another movie that so clearly expresses the sensual sustenance that great folk culture provides its practitioners.

The film grew out of sessions with the artists in 1996 organized by the guitarist, composer, and record producer Ry Cooder; the album that resulted, called *Buena Vista Social Club* in honor of one of East Havana's long-gone music-and-dance emporiums, became a surprise best-seller worldwide, revitalizing many careers. In 1998, Wim Wenders, returning with Cooder to Havana, filmed the musicians as they recorded an album showcasing bolero singer Ibrahim Ferrer. During their days off, Wenders filmed them talking, informally, about their pasts.

The ninety-two-year-old guitar and *tres* player Compay Segundo, with his wide, lewd smile, and Ruben Gonzalez, the eighty-year-old jazz-and-mambo pianist whom Cooder once described as a Cuban cross between Thelonious Monk and Felix the Cat, seem to exist totally within the realm of their music. As with most folk artists, their sounds are inextricable from the anecdotage of their lives. Their stories, their histories, are all of a piece with the words they sing and the notes they play—with their lilt and whoop and glide. The performers are ecstatically comfortable in the spotlight and equally at ease away from it. The way they carry themselves offstage is gently stylized, as if, in sauntering down the streets or roaming about their cramped apartments, they were shimmying up to the fates. The graceful slow-motion swing of their movements is a kind of offering—a way of acknowledging the blessing that has been bestowed upon them by a life of music.

Ibrahim Ferrer, whom Cooder brought out of oblivion, says at one point, "We Cubans are very fortunate—we have learned to resist the good and the bad." This lyrical evenness of temperament shows up in his vocalizing, which seems beyond the injuries of infirmity or society's neglect. In his white jacket and white cap, the seventy-two-year-old Ferrer, with his soft speaking voice and beautiful, becalmed face, is a radiant icon of elegance. The implicit assumption behind his singing—it was the same with Nat "King" Cole—is that there is silk to be found in the jumble of the world. Ferrer's voice draws out a clean, silky line that's so pure it doesn't seem to be born of experience—it's just there, floating and seraphic. His sounds represent a dream of how we wish our drudgeries and defeats could be recomposed, transcended.

Wenders filmed the Cuban artists along with Cooder and Cooder's drummer son, Joachim, performing not only in Havana but also in concert in Amsterdam and, triumphantly, in Carnegie Hall. (It was the first time most of the Cubans had been to New York.) The best group number in the movie, Compay Segundo's "Chan Chan," is also its first; it has the slow stealth of a leopard's lope, and it seems to tune your entire body as you listen to it. Segundo—born Francisco Repilado and raised in Santiago—has a deep-down gladness, almost a mirth, when he plays guitar and sings. He's immensely tickled by the provocativeness—the presence of the carnal—in his tone. He's a great old bawd; his seductions are embracing, but there's some heavy fondling in the embrace.

The irony reflected by this movie is that, on the one hand, everybody who listens to the traditionally acoustic Afro-Cuban music is turned on by it—not just the musicians and recording engineers and audiences, but the people in the street. (At one point, the terrific bolero singer Omara Portuondo, the only female in the group, starts wailing, and a passerby, a middle-aged woman, joins in as if to do so were the most natural thing in the world.) And yet this is a minority music in Cuba, in the same way that jazz is in America. The neglect that these musicians fell into parallels what happened to many of our jazz and blues legends. Even before Communism's full flowering, many of their careers were on the wane, and Wenders is wise not to politicize their plight. Swooning right along with the rest of us, he's too carried away by the music for that.

We understand completely what Ry Cooder is talking about when he says he prepared his whole life to produce these artists—he first heard tapes of Cuban musicians back in the seventies and made a trip to Havana to hear more, but it wasn't until 1996 that he was able to return and make recordings. The music is a siren call for Cooder; when he joins in on the Buena Vista sessions, he's not being a bwana but insinuating himself into the music as an act of devotion. (His son Joachim, the drummer, in the course of just moving about the streets, seems to boogie with a perpetual beat, as if Cuba itself were one big jam session—a bay of gigs.)

Cooder is an exemplary artist-producer. He's mixed in the celebrated older Cuban musicians with some younger members of the group, such as the astonishing *laud* player Barbarito Torres, and, on bongos, Julienne Oviedo Sanchez, who also plays with the new-style big band NG La Banda. The result, although you would never think of it in such academic terms, is an anthology of Cuban musical styles. The mesh is perfect; it all goes together, and the beaming faces of the performers conferring joy on one another is itself a piece of music. "I'm under the spell of this," a wide-eyed Ibrahim Ferrer says as he walks down Fifth Avenue before his Carnegie Hall appearance. Watching this movie, I was spellbound, too. It sends you into a state of rapt, sexy, swinging awe.

(New York, 1999)

Stone Reader

In 1972, eighteen-year-old Mark Moskowitz, who has since become an acclaimed director of political spots and commercials, picked up *The Stones of Summer*, a well-reviewed book by first-time author Dow Mossman, and couldn't get into it. Twenty-five years later, he tried again, loved the book, and subsequently discovered that Mossman had vanished without publishing another word. With a diligence that only a true book nut can appreciate—there are Mark Moskowitzes crowding the narrow aisles of every used-book store in the country—he set out to discover what happened to Mossman. His film *Stone Reader* is a marvelous literary thriller that gets at the way books can stay with people forever. Moskowitz interviews a standout crew of commentators, including Robert Gottlieb, who talks about editing *Catch-22;* Frank Conroy, who presides over the Iowa Writers' Workshop, where Mossman once toiled on his novel; the literary critic John Seelye, who could pass for an old salt on the *Pequod*; and, most poignantly, Leslie Fiedler, who died two weeks ago, in what may well have been his last filmed appearance. They all look lit up by a love of literature.

Fiedler was especially intrigued by the spooky phenomenon of the one-shot novelist, and so is almost everyone else in the movie. (Harper Lee of *To Kill a Mockingbird* is practically the film's mascot.) The silences of gifted writers have many causes, but what's clear in *Stone Reader* is the plain fact that novel-writing is a soul-churning experience not to be entered into lightly. It's possible to make too much out of all this tortuousness; after all, lousy novels are probably just as agonizing to produce as great ones. Moskowitz understands this, but he also says at one point, "Reading is the only thing that keeps me sane." He subscribes to the cult of the novel, and I suspect that most people who will love this movie do, too. *The Stones of Summer* sounds like a terrific book, and I hope this film will get it re-issued by one of those rare enterprising souls in a publishing business increasingly inimical to risk.*

(*New York*, 2003)

---

* Barnes and Noble brought it out under its own imprimatur.

Domestic Violence

Frederick Wiseman's documentaries have a dramatic truth available almost nowhere else in movies right now. His new film, *Domestic Violence*, is one of his most affecting. It's primarily set in a shelter in Tampa, Florida, called the Spring, and from inside its institutional-white interior we observe caseworkers and abused women and children trying to make sense of their shared situation. The victims are alternately resilient, apologetic, enraged, aghast. From what we hear, it's possible that many of these women have never felt this free to open up. One after another, they break into arias of self-revelation and disgust. A middle-aged woman in a group-therapy session says, "I was told all my life that I wasn't worth anything," and laughs at her own gumption in finally being able to tell her story. But hysteria roils the good cheer; like so many of the other women we see, she moves with hair-trigger sensitivity from glee to tears.

It was never Wiseman's intention to provide anything like a cross section of the abused; for one thing, the residents of the Spring are mostly lower-middle-class and not highly educated, and we see no battered men. Still, what the film may lack in comprehensiveness it more than makes up for in depth of feeling. Regardless of how different we at first may believe we are from these people, Wiseman makes it clear we are not a class apart. In varying degrees, we *are* them. He doesn't categorize their torment, or what led to it; he demonstrates how the roots of domestic violence are as tangled as the mysteries of any family.

Although the cycles of abuse recounted in this film have a sickening repetitiveness, they never degenerate into case studies. The film puts us in the same position as the caseworkers; we strive to see these sufferers whole, unobscured by social-science cant. The cant is there, all right, but somehow, in context, it becomes something else, more complicated. These caseworkers, as well as the police officers Wiseman films on their patrols, use officialese to both control volatile situations and insulate themselves from the agony of what they're attempting to control. The jargon forms a protective shield that, in the end, doesn't really offer much protection at all; the horror bleeds through anyway.

Wiseman shot this three-and-a-quarter-hour film over a period of two months, and took more than a year to edit it. (Along with his companion piece, *Domestic Violence II*, which follows abuse cases through the courts system, it will be shown on PBS next year.) As is usual for Wiseman, the film's texture is novelistic rather than, as with most documentaries, slam-bang revelatory. There's no voice-over narration. The tone he provides is one of principled outrage. Avoiding any comforting resolutions, Wiseman offers up moments, some decisive, some desultory, from the lives of people who then pass from our sight. Along with his cinematographer, John Davey, he opens up human experience in a way that seems both caught-on-the-sly and primal. The camera's gaze is unwavering, as it must be, and it unifies the suffering that we see. What Wiseman doesn't show is often as powerful as what he does. In a closing scene, for example, he films two cops responding to a call made by a bare-chested, slightly inebriated man who wants the woman he shares his home with to leave. At first, the scene plays out as a routine, nonviolent domestic quarrel—the police eventually leave without making an arrest—and you wonder why Wiseman included it. Then the enormity of what will happen after the cops leave sinks in, and the helplessness of the woman onscreen is matched by our own.

Domestic violence has been exploited in numerous TV specials and "reality shows," but Wiseman lets the material breathe in a manner unique to the subject. At the shelter, he allows encounters between participants to play out in something like real time, and although this is a risky dramatic ploy, it makes sense here because tedium itself is part of the therapeutic process. He has too much respect for these people to simplify their condition, and his respect frees us to register a full range of emotional responses.

We can observe, for example, how many of the women try to both shamefacedly cover up their bruises and exhibit them as war wounds; we can see how the younger female victims are more voluble than many of their hardened older counterparts. Some of the women express fears that their children, having witnessed domestic violence from infancy, will in turn become violent. A few already have—in one black-comic interlude, caseworkers mull over what to do with a teenage boy at the shelter who is himself a batterer. The youngest children in *Domestic Violence*, playing happily in the nursery and participating in sing-alongs, have an uncomprehending fortitude; their crayon drawings, which express the mayhem they've seen as a kind of fairy-tale illustration, undercut the sunniness.

You look into these brimming, rapt faces and wonder if they're already lost.

Perhaps the saddest and yet most revivifying episode in the film involves a woman who checks herself into the shelter after fifty years of marriage. This decorous, fine-boned lady, with artfully applied makeup that covers her swelling, has a poignant frailty; she speaks to her caseworker in polite, apologetic tones as she recounts her miseries, and your heart goes out to her. I've rarely seen as much unalloyed bravery in a movie. For her and for the other women here who allowed their stories to be told, *Domestic Violence* commemorates that courage.

(New York, 2002)

Bright Leaves

Ross McElwee, the documentarian whose latest movie is *Bright Leaves,* has slowly but steadily built up one of the richest bodies of work in contemporary American film. Since the seventies, he has been making movies about his family and friends that are so emotionally complex and innovative that they redefine the parameters of cinematic autobiography, a notoriously self-indulgent genre. In his best-known documentary, *Sherman's March,* the woebegone director retraced General Sherman's Civil War route through the South and offered up indelible sketches of seven women he met along the way. (The film was subtitled, only partly as a put-on, *A Meditation on the Possibility of Romantic Love in the South During an Era of Nuclear Weapons Proliferation.*) In *Time Indefinite,* he married (finally) and became a father himself after the sudden death of his own.

In *Bright Leaves,* perhaps his best film, McElwee, a native North Carolinian living in Boston, returns to his roots for, as his wife says, his "periodic transfusion of southern-ness." There he meets a second cousin, a movie buff, who thinks that the middling 1950 Warner Bros. melodrama *Bright Leaf,* starring Gary Cooper as a nineteenth-century tobacco baron, was actually based on McElwee's great-grandfather John, who created the Bull Durham brand but ended up bankrupt after wrangling with the rival Duke clan. McElwee would like to believe that Hollywood inadvertently created this "surreal home movie reenacted by Hollywood stars." (It piques his appreciation of the absurd.) Leisurely yet philosophic, *Bright Leaves* is itself a species of home movie. Speaking off-camera in his ruminative drawl for most of the film, McElwee lays out his life as an ongoing narrative about mortality, using the Cooper film (which he shows clips from) as a jumping-off point for a meditation on his own family and its legacy, and the legacy of tobacco and its ills. His physician grandfather was a heavy smoker who died of cancer; his father and brother, also doctors, treated many cancer patients, some of whom are interviewed. His friend Charlen, a one-woman gabfest who has a recurring role in McElwee's movies, talks about her dying, chain-smoking sister.

Tobacco represents for McElwee a confounding family inheritance; he relates a dream in which the large leaves give off "almost a body heat." A nonsmoker for many years, he describes the erotic possibilities of lighting up, the "deadly, intimate" effect of someone else's smoke in your lungs. McElwee is unimpeachably honest about his own susceptibilities. Harrowing in its depiction of how tobacco can tear lives apart, *Bright Leaves* is nevertheless anything but a screed. At a time when the most celebrated and popular documentaries are politicized and nuance-free, McElwee refuses to indict anyone. His comprehension of human frailty is what makes him an artist.

McElwee is digressive in the best sense. He takes the time to discover what people are like when they are being themselves; he wants to know where their lives are taking them, what byways they are going down. The North Carolinians he captures—the teenage beauticians who giggle and smoke outside the shop, the amateur gospel singer who needs no prompting to rejoice in the next world, the aged hospital patients who, in their sickness, are trying to hang on to their dignity—make up an intensely American portrait gallery. As a filmmaker, McElwee is both a participant in their stories and alienated from them; he is forever the observer. And what he observes most of all is the continuum of the human experience— *Time Indefinite* could stand as the title for all his works. The very process of directing a movie has a trancelike effect on him. "When I'm looking through a viewfinder," he says, "time seems to stop." But there is something despairing in this admission, because he knows that, even on film, he can't hold onto what is dearest to him. Filmmaking becomes a way of

CHAPTER 8

ISSUES
(MOSTLY HOT-BUTTON)

Blood Sport:
Quentin Tarantino and *Kill Bill*

Even as a kid watching old Westerns on TV, I sensed something was not right. A guy—let's call him the good guy—pulls a gun on another guy and kills him. Very soon, the good guy re-enters the world of his friends, his family, he has a drink, a few laughs—life goes on. Killing another human being has about as much psychological impact on him as taking out the trash.

This is the template for most depictions of movie violence, and we may have moods when we desire nothing more explosive from movie-going than this guilt-free release—this lie. We fantasize that we could kill if we had to and survive with our souls unscathed. Movies are an unmatched medium for appealing to our most visceral and disreputable fantasies, and there may be a primal need to watch things blow up big. I wouldn't trust anyone who felt otherwise. It's when the real world—real emotion—intrudes on all this cartoon exaggeration that things get dicey. We are living through parlous times, and more and more I find myself in a state of disconnect between the disasters of war in the real world and the usual movie mayhem. Escapism is fine, but where are the films that capture, if only indirectly, the frights we are escaping *from*?

When it came out last year, *Kill Bill Vol. 1* set off a lot of the usual alarms about the soullessness of its violence. I didn't think the carnage, which was stylish in a martial-arts-flick/video-game sort of way, signaled the end of Western civilization, but there was one scene—a deadpan confrontation between Uma Thurman's avenging Bride and the four-year-old girl whose mother she has just murdered in her own kitchen—that was so cretinously unfeeling that it made me wonder if this director, who has made his reputation concocting scenes of extreme savagery, had ever actually witnessed one himself. Maybe he has, but to judge from his movies, his responses have been pulped and chop-sockied and put through the spaghetti-Western strainer.

As it turns out, *Kill Bill Vol. 2* isn't quite the bloodbath its predecessor was. In the first film, the pregnant Bride is left for dead in an El Paso chapel by the Deadly Viper Assassination Squad headed by her boss and lover, Bill (David Carradine). Revived, she begins methodically hunting down her assailants. In *Vol. 2*, she scratches off the final three names on her hit list: Bill's brother, Budd (Michael Madsen), a bouncer in a titty bar; Elle Driver (Daryl Hannah), a leggy blonde who sports an eyepatch—her one good eye will inevitably get plucked; and Bill, who plays a big bamboo flute and speaks in that somnambulant purr familiar from Carradine's *Kung Fu* days. The Bride, as always, has a sleek, almost synthesized look, as if she were computer-generated. En route to her final revenge, she gets pummeled, buried alive, shotgun-blasted.

Tarantino's outlaw-brat rep rests mainly on his dog-eat-dog unsentimentality—there are no good guys in his movies, only bad and worse. Surprisingly, *Vol. 2* is heavily fragranced with lengthy interludes about the enduring love between the Bride and Bill and about how she wanted to give up killing when she became pregnant. Since we already know from the conclusion of the first film that the Bride's baby has survived, the only real suspense—other than anticipating how Bill will get whacked—lies in waiting for the reunion of mother and daughter. It is here that Tarantino, just as in that kitchen scene from *Vol. 1*, reverts to his old, unfragrant self; another little girl, the Bride's this time, survives the murder of a loving parent without registering the slightest flicker of woe.

And it is right about here that my misgivings resurface. I don't mean to unduly target *Kill Bill Vol. 2*—it's certainly no worse than most of the blam-blam fare out there. But what I crave now are movies that speak to me in a different way about violence, that acknowledge the fact that real people are harmed.

The nature of warfare, or more precisely, the ways in which we have been allowed to see it, has altered our perception of violence. Hollywood movies about, say, World War II and Korea, were mostly sanitized, and they could get away with it because so much of the actual newsreel coverage of those wars was equally sanitized. Our access to the Iraq war, what with the Pentagon ban on shots of coffined soldiers, is in many ways equally sanitized, and far more troubling, since the blackout represents the triumph of the image-control machine over credibility.

But Vietnam was different. For most Americans, it was a televised war, and the battle images that poured into our living rooms had a gruesomeness that no movie could compete with. Although Hollywood didn't deal with Vietnam directly until years after the war ended, the movies of its era were far more blood-soaked than those that came before. The old tastefulness suddenly seemed inadequate—a sick joke.

Many of the best films I grew up with, when Vietnam was raging and the assassinations were still fresh, had a complicated comprehension of suffering and brutality: *Bonnie and Clyde*, *The Wild Bunch*, *Straw Dogs*, the *Godfather* films, *Taxi Driver*. Without being obvious about it, these movies issued from a place very deep inside the torn-up American psyche. They themselves were a species of violent act, provoking in audiences a full battery of fearful, often contradictory responses, a kind of exhilarated dread.

I am not arguing for a more in-your-face treatment of violence in our movies—as if that were the only way to render the subject honestly. The graphic bloodiness of these movies is not what made them memorable. We cared, in the widest sense, about, say, Travis Bickle, because his derangement had a human face—he was both startlingly close to us and unreachable. As Tarantino's movies demonstrate, overkill, when applied to people with all the weight of holograms, can anesthetize us to any real pain on-screen. The anesthesia I'm talking about is more than local; one reason so many of us felt jolted by the images from Fallujah is that they shocked us back to a time, the Vietnam era, when we were not insulated from such ghastliness.

The call here is not for more explicit violence—if that's even possible—but for a more explicit portrayal of the human consequences of violence. We are not entirely without these moments in our recent movies. Ron Shelton's uneven cop thriller *Dark Blue* had a ferocious subplot about the dementia of what happens *after* the trigger is pulled. Todd Field's *In the Bedroom* is about a father's revenge, which is made to seem inescapable, against his son's killer. It makes perfect emotional sense for this good man, this "good guy," to perpetrate his crime—this is why the movie is the deepest kind of horror story. And he isn't cleansed at the end, either; he's spooked—nullified—by the possibilities he has discovered in himself. And then there is *Mystic River*. It's a rich irony that Clint Eastwood, who has been associated for most of his career with screen characters who are, to put it mildly, unreflective about their own sadism, should have reinvented himself as one of Hollywood's more sensitive souls. The trauma of violence is the gist of *Mystic River*. It's a legacy without end.

For film artists to be true to the experience of violence, they must also be true to every other aspect of life. The search for that truth is inevitably part of a greater search for emotional authenticity. I've lost my sweet tooth for slice-and-dice escapism, and perhaps this is why I feel the need to see movies that don't simply glamorize or fetishize or supernaturalize brutality. The riven world with all its suffering seems matrix enough right now without investing a lot of time in *The Matrix*. And killing Bill seems irrelevant with so much real prey on the loose and ourselves caught in the crosshairs.

(New York, 2004)

Sexual Harassment/Sexual Politics: *Oleanna* and *Disclosure*

Earlier this year, many months before the appearance of *Oleanna* and *Disclosure,* a network news show asked me to come up with a list of movie clips for a segment on sexual harassment. What seemed like an easy request turned into a real head-scratcher. Almost without exception, the examples were of the giggly-smirky variety.

There are tons of movies where bosses pinch or ogle their secretaries, but it's always played as a joke. Even when it's not endorsed as a joke, it's a joke—like the "A Secretary Is Not a Toy" number from *How to Succeed in Business Without Really Trying.*

Did I hear you mention *The Apartment*? But, in that movie, Shirley MacLaine is genuinely in love with the boss.

Where are the movies that show the unwelcome lunge, the power play, the fear?

The arrival of *Oleanna* and *Disclosure* isn't exactly a case of the famine turning into a feast. It's still a famine out there. As far as I can tell, Hollywood has never made a serious mainstream movie specifically about the effects of sexual harassment against women in the workplace. (Hollywood movies, as opposed to TV, try to stay out of the workplace altogether—too "real.")

But now we've got two films that show us how men are harassed—by women. As evolutionary leaps go, it's a great sick joke. What can we expect next? A searing drama starring Arnold Schwarzenegger as a destitute welfare mother?

Right now, it's okay for Meryl Streep to be harassed on a river raft (in *The River Wild*) but not at the office. Given how few serious films are funded in Hollywood about women's lives, and given the honchos at most studios, it would be surprising if there were any films out now that *didn't* posit sexual harassment as male victimization.

What both *Oleanna* and *Disclosure* are about is not so much sexual harassment as the abuse of the charge of sexual harassment. In David Mamet's movie version of his two-character play, a somewhat supercilious professor up for tenure is dragooned by one of his flunking female students into a morass of false harassment and rape charges that scotch his tenure and ruin his career. He ends up physically assaulting her—he becomes the person he was falsely accused of being.

In *Disclosure,* starring Demi Moore and Michael Douglas and directed by Barry Levinson from the Michael Crichton bestseller, Tom Sanders, a married-with-children executive at a Seattle high-tech computer company, is preyed upon by Meredith Johnson, an old girlfriend from another division who has been promoted over him. She is now his boss. Meredith initiates a sexual encounter in her office; he breaks it off; she charges harassment; he countercharges. It's he-said-she-said time at the corporate O.K. Corral.

Both Mamet and Crichton—whose book was dubbed *Harassic Park* when it came out—have made a lot of noises in the press about how *balanced* their material is; how the hurts of men and women are given equal time. But what comes across in the play and the book and, now, in the movie adaptations, is essentially a rant against the destruction of male privilege. The destroyers are a frigid scold and a hothouse Circe.

How can we accept in *Oleanna* that both the professor (William H. Macy) and his student (Debra Eisenstadt) are equally culpable? Mamet may like the way that sounds, but his movie sure doesn't play that way. The student's charges are patently false—we can see that. And yet she somehow manages (offscreen) to persuade a tenure committee that she was harassed and raped; she blossoms from a frightened, insecure wall-flower to a full-throated feminist squadron leader backed by the muscle of her "group." It is only on a phony-mythic level that *Oleanna* evens the playing field. The professor may be innocent of his student's *specific* charges but he is guilty of the larger charge of male power-mongering; he's a patriarch. Collective guilt turns him into a bogeyman.

No sexual tension whatsoever exists between student and teacher; their face-off is all ideology and sloganeering. If there is any consummation at all, it's in the final provoked assault against the woman (which the audience is made to crave). Mamet turns the dissonance between men and women into a screech. Some balance.

In his afterword to *Disclosure,* Crichton admits that the "great majority of harassment claims are brought by women against men" and defends the use of a role-reversal story for its power "to examine aspects concealed by traditional responses and conventional rhetoric." Fair enough. Even if one pauses at the way Crichton in the book self-servingly overstates the statistics on female-to-male harassment in order to give us the heebie-jeebies, the subject is still fair game. But in place of our "traditional responses" Crichton has inserted his own traditional agenda. Once again, as in *Oleanna,* what is billed as a level (scorched-earth) playing field turns out to be a mirage.

Beneath all its reverse-field politically correct rhetoric, *Disclosure* basically is a puritan cautionary fable about a power-thwarted man who turns the tables on a predatory vamp. Meredith is a veritable T. rex of sex. Our first shot of her in the movie is a low-angle hubba-hubba glimpse of her gams. (Crichton was one of the film's producers.) It's odd—none of the Good women in the movie—Tom's wife, his lawyer, co-workers—are characterized as fully sexual beings. It's as if sex appeal was a malignancy.

Actually, Meredith really isn't sexual either; her lunges are power plays. In the novel, Crichton served up a full women's chorus of feminist ranters, including a vitriolic newspaper columnist who refuses to believe that women can oppress men, and Tom's very own wife, a lawyer who mouths the party line and can't take more time out for her children. Tom's lawyer, a Latino woman, is lethally effective and yet her strength is as chilling and steely as Meredith's.

The movie, scripted by Paul Attanasio, eliminates the columnist and ups the sympathy factor on the others but the only truly sympathetic woman is a starchy, fifty-something co-worker and mother who recognizes Tom's valuable contributions and lacks the asp of carnality. Her ambitiousness, unlike Meredith's, is acceptably prim. She gets her reward. Meredith, following in a long line of ruthless boss women in the movies, gets her comeuppance.

The movie initially shows us Tom in a few offhanded moments ogling a woman's rump or swatting his secretary's. But all this is innocent stuff. Basically Tom is no Oppressor. He's not even terribly ambitious—he expected to be promoted to Meredith's position but apparently didn't think he had to angle for it. He's naive enough to believe the corporate world is a meritocracy, and yet his naiveté is his saving grace. It sentimentalizes him.

Disclosure comes out at a time when man-bashing has become part of the tone of the culture—it has even achieved *Time* cover-story status (a sure sign that the tone is fading). By transforming the fears of men who see their power being eroded by ambitious women in an increasingly competitive job market into a species of victimization, Crichton has pulled off a real switcheroo; he's given Pale Males official minority status, with all the rights and privileges thereof.

Tom even gets to have sex (sort of) with Meredith—a woman much more exciting than his wife. And—here's the best part—he doesn't have to take any real responsibility for the sex. (First *Fatal Attraction,* then *Basic Instinct,* and now this. Michael Douglas must be royally pooped.) Tom's enforced submission is eroticized—this could be the first heterosexual male rape fantasy ever depicted in a mainstream Hollywood movie. But because Tom doesn't go all the way with the sex he feels secretly emasculated, feminized. He even has a bizarre dream where his boss—Meredith's mentor, played by Donald Sutherland—tries to soul-kiss him.

Tom is only righted when he does to Meredith figuratively what she does to him literally. He's been to the dungeons of the vamp goddess—the childless, familyless, castrating vamp—and returns victorious to the meadows of domesticity where his adoring wife and daughter await.

Who says you can't have it all?

The impasse between men and women has become big business. It sells magazines and books and movies like *Disclosure* and *Oleanna*. The hot field in science right now is evolutionary biology, which basically says that what keeps us apart is all in the genes. Maybe it is. Maybe men are wired from pre-birth to like the Three Stooges and women are wired to like *Fried Green Tomatoes*. But there's a defeatism about these findings that fits into the way we feel—if men and women are bio-genetically incapable of changing what keeps them at odds, then what's the use? *Vive la différence* went by the boards some time ago. Now it's more like *Vive la guerre*.

But are *Oleanna* and *Disclosure* the best bulletins from the battle-front that we can come up with? Both would be better if at least they acknowledged the author's real impulse, if they exploited all that messy male rage at what women hath wrought. What's bad about a movie like *Disclosure* isn't its glib, crass nastiness. That's what's *fun* about it. It's fun in the way that films noirs like *Double Indemnity* or the current *The Last Seduction* are. Hate is a turn-on in those films; the gunsmoke from the war between the sexes is their oxygen. No, what is bad about *Disclosure* are the constant irruptions of sanctimony, as if we were watching a civics lesson and not a ripping revenge fantasy. Why not just lay out all the demons and can the cant?

And maybe when this latest backlash fades we can actually have a movie about a woman who is sexually harassed by a man.

What a concept!

(*Los Angeles Times*, 1994)

Twisting in the Wind: Politics Left and Right

There's a new tone to movies now—the movies of the Reagan era—and you can sense it as surely as you could sense the rage and hopelessness in the Nixon-era films. There were no Vietnam films made during that Nixon period, but the war bled through its most important movies, such as *Bonnie and Clyde, The Wild Bunch, Deliverance,* and *The Godfather,* like ink through a blotter. The Watergate-era movies which followed, like *Serpico* and *Dog Day Afternoon,* had an exuberant, almost baroque fatalism. They were confirmations of corruption, and they captured the rot of the times in the same way that key movies before and after reflected the tenor of Kennedy and Johnson and Carter.

The new tone of the Reagan-era movies is there in a phenomenally successful bring-'em-back-alive pulper like *Rambo*. It's there in films as diverse as *Risky Business* and *Places in the Heart*. Both, in their own ways, are success stories about Americans—they're about getting ahead. And that's just what audiences want right now. They want to *root* for something, and the movie business has hoisted America as the rooting interest. The themes of the Reagan-era movies are all-of-a-piece with the slogans of the 1984 Reagan Presidential campaign. They're both saying America is back again, standing tall. We're winners. On the surface, the tone of these new movies is straightforward, and yet it's a paradox—it's both reactionary and populist. It's impossible to comprehend what's going on in the movies now without understanding what's been percolating in films, particularly on the left, in the last two decades. For the fact is the right has all the juices now, while the left has cut a tortuous path only to arrive at a cul-de-sac.

It was not always so. Back in the sixties and early seventies, the left was juiced by the Bomb and Vietnam, which were perceived as right-wing madness. The signature liberal response to that madness, at least in the movies of the last two decades, was a flamboyant nihilism typified by the Stanley Kubrick-Terry Southern *Dr. Strangelove,* appropriately subtitled *How I Learned to Stop Worrying and Love the Bomb*.

Strangelove was a giddy cackle of a movie that turned despair at any sort of constructive action into a new form of hip; it was less a call to sanity than a call to *insanity*—as a way of keeping sane. (It had an unquestionable influence on *M*A*S*H* five years later, as well as *The Right Stuff*.)

Easy Rider, which was also co-written by Terry Southern, was the progenitor of another form of liberal fatalism. It was a sentimental, masochistic jag and, much more than *Strangelove,* it set the tone for the most incendiary movies that were to follow. The movie played like a modern-day hippie Western, with motorbikes instead of steeds. The hippies, in the guise of Dennis Hopper and Peter Fonda's Captain America and their communal-family friends, were the true inheritors of the land, but they couldn't lay claim to that inheritance; the heartland was poisoned with rednecks. The stoned haze that surrounded Hopper and Fonda was a way of etherealizing them from the corruption of what America had become, just as cackling was the way to get up, up, and away in *Strangelove*. But at the heart of *Easy Rider* was the masochism that *nothing* would save the flower-power people. And so Captain America is finally blown away by a redneck's rifle.

As a piece of counterculture hopelessness, Arthur Penn's *Little Big Man*, adapted from the Thomas Berger novel, went much further than a movie like *Easy Rider*. Whereas *Easy Rider* said that America had become corrupt, *Little Big Man* reached back into the American past to demonstrate that we were *always* rotten; that racism and genocide were sewn into the Stars and Stripes. General Custer, with his flowing caramel hair and Vandyke, was portrayed as a loony monster, and the fife music that accompanied his Indian attacks was a chill dirge. It was a prime example of the liberal de-mythologizing of America—in order to expose what was supposed to be the dirty truth underneath. (Right-wing movies of the era, like *Patton*, sought to *re*-mythologize American history.)

Many of the period films of the era were about the rooting out of an indigenous racism. Sometimes, as in the case of Abraham Polonsky's Western, *Tell Them Willie Boy Is Here*, they were written by filmmakers who had made their reputations a generation earlier with less scabrous versions of the same message. (Polonsky, like Ring Lardner Jr., who wrote *M*A*S*H*, had been blacklisted in the fifties.) But, in the case of blacks in film, the impulse to reclaim the past opened up new areas of experience on the screen—at least in some cases. There was a split in the depiction of blacks; there were the blaxploitation films, like *Superfly* and *Shaft* (largely produced by whites), which threw the racism that white liberal filmmakers were decrying back in their faces. In the world of blaxploitation, whiteness was a disease, and no film was complete without its blue-eyed devil who was torched or pounded or impaled in the final reel.

But some black movies set in the past, like *Sounder* or *The Autobiography of Jane Pittman* or *Roots,* (the latter two for TV), didn't employ history as an ideological battering ram. Before them, most "serious" movies about blacks were liberal consciousness-raisers in the Stanley Kramer mold (*The Defiant Ones, Guess Who's Coming to Dinner*)—they generally posited superblacks (usually Sidney Poitier) against bigoted or uncomprehending whites, with the whites finally coming around to the realization that—hey—blacks were just the same as you and me. A movie like *Sounder,* however, about a black sharecropper family in the thirties, didn't try to be a trussed-up civics lesson—even though it had the effect of unifying audiences. It implied that the past could be depicted as something other than the progenitor of present corruption.

Coppola's *Godfather* films may have been about the corruption of America, but they were the first big films to imply that something precious had been corrupted—the little boy singing to himself in his cubicle in Ellis Island grows up to be the Vito Corleone whose son orders his own brother's murder.

Like *Sounder,* Coppola's movies were re-examinations of the past, free of the America-the-awful self-hatred that rent the screen in so many other movies of the period. They opened things up. Without them, a movie like Robert Altman's *Nashville,* which looked at the American flag and saw a crazy quilt, might never have been made.

At about the same time that filmmakers like Altman were looking at the crowds, others were looking at the loners at the edge of the crowd. (Altman, in fact, was capable of looking both ways—a lone gunman rounds out *Nashville.*) The impulse was the same—to find a clue to the American psyche, the American sickness. *Taxi Driver* and *Dog Day Afternoon* were both about characters who might have been marginalized in the movies a decade before. And there was no attempt to "explain" these characters. (The usual psychosexual explanations were glaringly inadequate.) A movie like *Little Big Man* was full of "answers"; these films were full of questions.

Some liberal moviemakers, in their frustration, searched for historical archetypes they could be comfortable with. Woody Guthrie was summoned for duty in *Bound For Glory,* Lillian Hellman was the star of *Julia,* and was portrayed by Jane Fonda, who was about to embark on a career playing women at the dawn of liberated consciousness. She became as much an emblem of bleeding-heart liberalism as Clint Eastwood was an emblem for bleeding heart (and head and legs and torso and every other body part) conservatism.

Still, there were a few contemporary forays. *All the President's Men* reclaimed a liberal archetype of the recent past—the crusading journalist who exposes government (i.e. right-wing) corruption. But if audiences were looking for a summing up of what the country had been through—a movie that would put Vietnam and Watergate behind them—*All the*

President's Men clearly wasn't it.

In very different ways, the three major Vietnam movies that were released around this time—*Coming Home, The Deer Hunter,* and *Apocalypse Now*—attempted that summation. But each cast the war in false terms; *Coming Home* was about Jane Fonda's liberalization, from being the dutiful wife of a Vietnam captain to the lover of an anti-war veteran. And since the husband was played by Bruce Dern, and the veteran by Jon Voight, her choice was preordained. The movie's final shot of Dern's suicidal scamper into the surf was a liberal wish-fulfillment fantasy—it was an obnoxious way to write off the right, just as Fonda's coming-of-age portrayal was a self-serving view of those middle-class women who lacked her enlightenment. The condescension was explicit.

The Deer Hunter approached Vietnam from the opposite direction. It celebrated the war as a boys'-book rite of passage; for the working-class steelworker buddies who fought in the war, Vietnam was less a political battleground than a testing-ground for the masculine-code. As pulpy and fraudulent and xenophobic as the movie was, *The Deer Hunter,* for its time, had something new going for it, although that "something new" was at least as old as the Hollywood Hills. It presented the common man as an exalted species—the spirit of America. He wasn't in the movie only to be liberalized in the final reel. Ultimately, the purpose of the Vietnam War in *The Deer Hunter* was to create a community of survivors, who gather in the end to sing "America the Beautiful." In the movie's macho ethic, the singing of the song isn't particularly jingoistic; it comes across more like a paean to comradeship.

Francis Coppola's *Apocalypse Now* was a hallucinatory jamboree, dark and dense and clotted with distemper and mythic meanderings. He seemed to be saying: *This war is too big for me or anybody else to deal with now. It's too soon to sum up. I can only offer you my pain and my bad dreams.*

The left-wing movies that came out around the same time, films like *Norma Rae* and *The China Syndrome,* were among the last hold-outs of the "issue-oriented" liberal advocacy movie; their upbeat endings were in contrast to the fatalism that has followed. But this fatalism is different from the *Easy Rider* variety—there's no sentimentality to it, no masochism. Defeatism is more like it.

Liberalism has been put on the defensive, and it hasn't put up much of a fight. The lack of galvanizing themes on the left was obvious during the 1984 presidential election, when Walter Mondale seemed to shift the thrust of his campaign weekly in an effort to discredit America's movie-star president and his movie-movie reassurances. The liberal bleeding heart has developed arteriosclerosis and movies register the faintness of the pulse. *Reds,* Warren Beatty's John Reed epic, felt like a mammoth apologia; *Absence of Malice* was widely hailed as a corrective to *All the President's Men,* which it was, although it overcorrected. *Daniel* turned the Rosenbergs case into an orgy of special-pleading. It was masochistic, but in an out-of-touch way—which a movie like *Easy Rider* never was. It never even claimed to be about the Rosenbergs specifically, and fudged the issue of whether the martyred couple were communist spies. In the end, *Daniel* was like most Hollywood social-problem pictures—it sat down to be counted. Even those films where one would have expected a note of triumph ended on a downbeat; Paul Newman recoups his honor and strikes a blow for the little guy at the end of *The Verdict,* but we're left with a final image of him alone in his office, bummed out by a bad romance. *Missing,* which attempted to implicate the CIA in the death of a young American in Allende's Chile, worked itself into a lather of accusatory anti-Americanism but then opted for a "*Z*"-style coda which explained that the implicated government officials were never brought to justice. In *Silkwood,* the fact that Karen Silkwood set in motion the successful shutdown of a dangerous nuclear-chemical plant was all but tossed off—the real message of the movie seemed to be that society's corruption has irradiated us all. Even the two big anti-nuke films of the past few years, *Testament* and *The Day After,* despite their pious, "progressive" overlay, pigged out on the fatalism that imbued so many of the films on the left. And what could be more fatalistic than a nuclear holocaust?

If most new movies from the left seem undynamic and unmoored, that's because, in dramatic terms at least, the left doesn't have the bedrock of core values that the right has. Having little patience for defeatism, audiences understandably look elsewhere. (Commercially speaking, the worst thing that's happened to liberal filmmakers is that their convictions lack entertainment value.) Then, too, most moviegoers today are in their twenties; they've been accultured to goofball romps and space-wars extravaganzas—movies that provide a quick fix. Because of the dominance of this audience, and its tremendous influence on what sort of films get made, most socially conscious material in the movies these days ends up

Aside from *The Right Stuff*, with its whiff of Strangelovian goofiness, the left isn't having much *fun* with the right these days. Fun isn't in the zeitgeist. *Deal of the Century*, a black comedy about U.S. arms shipments to the Third World, had the same sourish reactionary mind-set as what it was purportedly attacking. *The Survivors*, starring Robin Williams as a berserk survivalist in a right-wing military training-camp, had inspired moments, but it was equally fizzle and sizzle. With so little humor, you would hope that there would at least be more good muckraking documentaries around on the order of Barbara Kopple's 1977 *Harlan County, U.S.A.* But even many of the best documentarians these days (like George Nierenberg, who made *No Maps on My Taps* and *Say Amen, Somebody*) are increasingly depoliticized.

More often now, the tendency with movies on the left is to take potentially strong subjects and then let the air out of them. With all the problems facing the educational system today, *Teachers* has to *invent* a problem: one lead character turns out to be a teacher who's an escaped mental patient (and he's played by Richard Mulligan, the same actor who played Custer in *Little Big Man*). *Swing Shift*, about the women who were suddenly thrust into the assembly lines during WWII, looked like a commercial for a *Life* album about the home-front years. *The Big Chill*, about the reunion of a group of seven college anti-war activists from the sixties, breezed along on a jet stream of jabber that might have been written by a superannuated-hippie version of Neil Simon. In its hyprocrital two-step, *The Big Chill* implied that the sixties activists were never that serious to begin with, yet demonstrated that the only way for that generation to thrive in the eighties was to drop their social ideals. The movie was a celebration of sellout.

Other films, like *Country*, seem hard-hitting until you actually look at what you're being hit with. The Iowa family-farmers in the movie are suffering, but it's made to look as though none of them ever heard of a lawyer—they suffer without intelligent recourse. Even though U.S. farmers were battered by both Carter's Russian grain embargo and Reagan's Payment in Kind program, no farmers here talk politics. In fact, they hardly talk to each other at all—they've been muted by the movie's pioneer piety. (Following the Depression model, the poor aren't supposed to talk as much as the rich.) In the end, the movie's we-the-people-ism backfires, since the situation looks a lot bleaker for the farmers than you might guess from the tacked-on upbeat coda.

The Killing Fields is another movie that isn't quite what it appears to be. It's about the friendship in Cambodia between *New York Times* war correspondent Sydney Schanberg and Dith Pran, who assisted Schanberg and chose to stay with him when the Khmer Rouge took over his homeland, instead of flying to safety with his family. Pran saves Schanberg's life during the takeover; later, he's separated from Schanberg (who feels guilty at abandoning him) and survives years of imprisonment in Khmer Rouge camps.

On the surface, the movie appears to have all of its liberal credentials in order. Schanberg blames himself for Pran's decision to join him when he had a chance to evacuate and for not finding a way to save him from the Khmer Rouge. But, as portrayed in the movie (though not in Schanberg's original magazine piece from which the movie is derived), Schanberg's guilt has Great White Father overtones. (It doesn't help that none of the Cambodians' dialogue is translated for us. Didn't the filmmakers think their words were important?) In most of their scenes together, Pran comes across like a glorified coolie and Schanberg is often peremptory with him. And is it not implicity racist to make such an issue of Pran's staying behind with Schanberg, as if, without coercion, no Asian in his right mind could possibly share the same anything-for-a-story commitment that some of the Western reporters had? The filmmakers are doing more than dramatizing Schanberg's irrational guilt—they're giving it credence to lend their movie a dramatic center.

There are other areas of experience that left-wing filmmakers (and not only left-wing filmmakers) appear to have abdicated completely. You have to look far and wide these days to find a movie that features blacks in any sort of meaningful way. *The Cotton Club* trashed a great subject. *A Soldier's Story,* adapted by black writer Charles Fuller from his own play, is generally a powerful WWII movie about an all-black training-camp platoon torn apart by self-hatred. But it cops out in the final reel. The soldiers at the end strut off to war in Germany without a trace of irony; their victory march has the unfortunate effect of a cakewalk. Richard Pryor, except for his infrequent live-performance films, appears to regard his film work as a species of family entertainment; one of his latest ventures was a kiddie TV show. Prince is a potentially great screen star, and he's the first non-comic black performer in years to demonstrate cross-over appeal. But Prince is *sui generis*. The two most popular black stars right now are Mr. T—who looks like a cartoon of every white suburban grandmother's nightmare—and Eddie Murphy, who, in movie after movie, uses his blackness to out-white whites—i.e. make more money than them.

In contrast to the muddle on the left, the right seems hypercharged. Its energy comes from its dead-set certainty about the fundamentals of American life. What's important here is not so much that audiences truly believe in the God-country-family fundamentals, but that they *want* to believe. The fantasy has a greater pull than the reality, and what better arena to fantasize than the movies? It's no secret that many of the movies that stir audiences now draw on a reactionary militarism. (*Rambo* is only the latest in the line.) They feature Americans back in action. Even in defeat, we're victorious. *Taps,* a surprise hit a few years back, dealt with the bloody revolt of teenage cadets when they hear their military school is going to be shut down. *Blue Thunder,* supposedly about the defeat of a right-wing paramilitary conspiracy by an ace Vietnam-vet cop (Roy Scheider), turned instead into a glorification of destructo hardware; the conspirators' baby—the big Blue Thunder helicopter—stole the show. *An Officer and a Gentleman* gave us a misfit (Richard Gere) who is straightened out by the military—just as Tyrone Power and so many others were in the forties. Why, the military even teaches him to love.

There's certainly no ambiguity in the incipient racism (or, to put it more kindly, nationalism) at work in the recent Vietnam movies: *Uncommon Valor,* John Milius's *Red Dawn, First Blood,* and its sequel, *Rambo.* All of these films are righteous wish-fulfillment fantasies—we may not have won the war, they seem to be saying, but we'll sure as hell win the post-war. In *Uncommon Valor,* Gene Hackman, who believes his MIA son is still being held prisoner in Laos, organizes and trains a battalion of his son's Vietnam buddies and carries out a rescue mission. The film's attitudes towards the Vietnamese and Laotians were as crude as Hollywood's treatment of the Japanese in the WWII films. That's no accident—the movie was attempting to present the Vietnam War (in the guise of the post-war rescue operation) in the same clear-cut terms as a "popular" war like WWII. As right-wing fantasies go, *Uncommon Valor* was just about perfect; because the mission occurred *after* the real war, it wasn't weighted with messy questions of ideology, like "What were we doing there in the first place?" It gave the veterans a chance to win the war without any strings attached.

John Milius's *Red Dawn* was an even more extravagant right-wing fantasy. The movie supposes that the Russians, in concert with the Cubans and other stooge allies, stymie America's nuclear capability and invade the country, sneaking across the southern border. In an occupied town, some members of a local high-school football team—the Wolverines—escape to the woods and wage guerilla warfare on the invaders. These boys are your average all-American good-kid jocks: just the type, in Milius's worldview, who would drink deer's blood and kill Commies while, presumably, the good liberal townsfolk fall in line to be brainwashed. (Actually, in psychological terms, it's probably the rah-rah adolescents who would be the most attracted to the invaders' militarism.) In *Red Dawn,* we're once again fighting Vietnam to win. Milius folds the left-wing in upon itself; he sets up a foreign-invaders scenario that, on the surface, mirrors the American incursion into Vietnam. But instead of making the Americans the aggressors, he makes them the underdogs—he practically turns the Wolverines into the Viet Cong. And he has them pose in tableaux that co-opt the guerilla poster-art imagery of the sixties radical left. You can practically see Che Guevara peeking through the timber.*

In *First Blood,* Sylvester Stallone's John Rambo, a man-without-honor-in-his-own-country, is unjustly picked up (and roughed up) for vagrancy in a drizzly Pacific Northwest town, and goes on a one-man rampage; he takes to the hills and uses his Vietnam guerilla training to destroy the town before finally being captured. We're meant to identify with his fury just as surely as we were meant to sympathize with the anti-hero alienation of a Dean or a Brando.

First Blood was a rabble-rouser's idea of how to repatriate the Vietnam vet into the good graces of American society; it turned the psycho stereotype, which has plagued many movies dealing with such vets, into a dramatic plus—Rambo blew up that town because of our sins of neglect. In *Rambo,* our hero is sprung from a chain gang by his ex-Green Beret commander in order to perform a top-secret reconnaissance mission over

---

* In the unnecessary 2012 remake of *Red Dawn,* the bad guys are now North Koreans, although they were originally supposed to be Chinese until somebody figured out that the Chinese buy movie tickets.

Vietnam to locate possible American POWs. Right away, our suspicions are aroused—the bureaucrat in charge of the operation wants Rambo to only take *pictures* of the prison site in question. What's more, the guys in the briefing room pop open a bunch of Cokes but they *don't offer Rambo anything.*

When Rambo finally makes it to the prison, he finds ten half-starved American POWs. He spirits one of these men out of the jungle, but it turns out the Americans aren't overjoyed about the discovery; the mission, as it comes clear, was supposed to put the POW issue to rest back home by drawing a blank. Leave it to Rambo to leave egg on the face of those Washington wimps. What follows is like *The Terminator* with foliage. Rambo, left to die by the Americans and voluptuously tortured, blasts and scorches his way through the jungle, wiping out entire squadrons of gooks and Ruskies. He muscles through the underbrush with his quiver of explosive-tipped arrows and a jumbo-sized bowie knife that should send the *Soldier of Fortune* magazine subscribers in the audience into a swoon. There's even a scene in which a soldier actually shoots a rifle point-blank at Rambo's chest and—nothing happens. Righteousness has made him invulnerable. Isn't that what this whole reactionary wish-fulfillment genre is all about?

When Rambo is first approached about the reconnaissance mission, he asks the question: "Do we get to win this time?" What follows, of course, is a symbolic winning of the war. If you bother to take this film seriously on more than a Neanderthal search-and-destroy level, you might ask yourself whether you really want someone like John Rambo to be your symbolic martyr. Stallone is almost sub-verbal in this film, with deep-set, unblinking eyes; he's like a psychotic, feral child. But that's obviously not how we're supposed to regard Rambo; we're supposed to view him as wounded not by bullets but by America's indifference to the plight of the Vietnam veteran. ("I want for my country to love us as much as we love it," he says at the end, in his longest extended bit of dialogue.) He reclaims our national honor even though we're too liberalized (i.e. wimped out) to realize how much we need it.

A significant number of military experts now believe the Vietnam War was unwinnable except through the destruction of the entire country. But Rambo/Stallone apparently knows differently. He's also sure that there are still Americans being held in Vietnamese prison camps. That should help raise the hopes of all the families of MIAs out there who will see this film and have their agony inflamed. Is *Rambo* the work of a blistering patriot, or is it a cynical piece of demagogy? In Hollywood, it's often difficult to separate a filmmaker's commercial instincts from his true beliefs—success has a way of blurring the distinctions. What comes through finally in this film is not the fury of the righteous but the self-aggrandizement of a movie-star who has appropriated a few incendiary political symbols for his own deification.

The renascent nationalism in the movies parallels another movement—the re-establishment of the family. In the late sixties and seventies, movies about families were relatively rare compared to earlier eras. (That's another reason why *Sounder* seemed so special.) Movie families tended to be communal, like those in *Easy Rider* or *Billy Jack* or *The Wild Bunch,* or dynasties, like the Corleones in *The Godfather.* One would have thought that the momentum to change this would come from the right but, at least initially, it was movies like *Kramer vs. Kramer* and *Ordinary People*—movies conversant in neo-Freudianisms and the new liberal chic of male "parenting." Later on, there was the nuclear family in *Testament*—the sacrificial family. But there were also films like *Tender Mercies,* with its parched fundamentalism, where a family is shown to be a man's salvation. Or the extraordinary *Shoot the Moon,* where the family is both a man's salvation and destruction. The phenomenally successful *Terms of Endearment* was a revamping of the same laughing-through-tears family pieties tricked up with hip/funny dialogue and snazzy TV rhythms. And, of course, the whole family-farm-cycle series—*Places in the Heart, Country,* and *The River*—now demonstrates that liberal audiences don't *need* sarcasm and TV snazziness. They take their pieties straight.

The resurgence of the family in the movies is part of a larger conservative movement to reclaim the idealized values of an earlier era. The impulse to recapture the past has a different function now than it did in the *Little Big Man* days. History is being used for reaffirmation instead of accusation. In movies like *Places in the Heart* and *The Natural* and *Racing With the Moon* and *Swing Shift,* the past has a classic pictorialism—a stillness—that suggests a time when the country was becalmed with innocence.

These movies represent a new fusion. At first glance they seem to belong solidly in the liberal camp. But, although they may look like Carter, they've got Reagan innards. There is often a muted iridescence to these films, as if they came out of our collective good feelings about the American past. Even though *Places in the Heart* is set during the Depression, *Racing With the Moon* just before America's intervention in WWII, and *Swing Shift during* WWII, these movies are groggy with nostalgic uplift. That's one of the reasons why they seem so phony—they don't really connect with their subjects. They aren't even *about* their subjects, really—they're about Feeling Good Again.* In a movie like *Places in the Heart,* it's really beside the point to argue that a lot of things don't make psychological sense. Would Sally Field, whose husband has just been murdered by a drunken black kid, take in as a handyman a black vagrant who's just robbed her of her silverware? Well, in this movie she does, because her character's inner goodness can see right into the vagrant's inner goodness. *Places in the Heart* is a prime example of how populism functions in the movies nowadays. In the *real* Depression thirties, the populist films of Frank Capra and others were anti-big-business, anti-big-city, anti-big government and resoundingly pro-little-guy. The rich were broadly caricatured, the poor were ennobled. In the New Populism, big government is still out, and corruption is still tied to the big city (which explains why virtually all today's populist films are rural.) But big-business doesn't have such a bad rep now, and neither do the rich. *Places in the Heart* is least successful (on a dramatic level) in its scenes involving the mercenary banker who wants to foreclose Sally Field's farm—that is to say, when it tries to draw on Depression-era clichés that no longer jibe with the mood of the times. It's *most* successful when it does what some of the Depression populist films also did—when it merges the imagery of the social-realist left with the themes of the reactionary right.

Places in the Heart has all the accoutrements of liberal humanism, including the Good Black; it's even got Sally Field out there in the cotton fields picking right alongside the blacks. But the movie also has its Capracorn little-people side, and that's always had a phony, reactionary flavor. Sally Field, without any background in business or farming, hauls herself out of poverty by reaping the largest cotton crop of the season against seemingly insurmountable odds. The movie becomes a hymn to the pi-

---

* According to some who have seen it, Demme's original cut of *Swing Shift,* before Goldie Hawn messed with it, is considerably less groggy.

oneer spirit. It appears to be saying: *If everyone had been like Sally Field, there wouldn't have been any Depression casualties.*

The reactionary element in the movies may be renascent but, at least on an aesthetic level, few films from the right have much more going for them these days then pedal-to-the-metal forward thrust. A movie like *Red Dawn* is incapable of putting across the pictorial beauty of heroism. There hasn't been a good James Bond-style piece of cold warriorism in years. *Risky Business* puts an art-house glaze on its teen antics and adds a dollop of smug elitism. It could have been made for all those Ivy League bound teenagers who call up the financial-advice radio-talk shows nowadays inquiring about best-bet stock options. Right wing heroes like Clint Eastwood can't stick to what they do best—blowing people away. In *Tightrope,* Eastwood's last big film before *Pale Rider,* he plays a divorced New Orleans cop who tracks down the killer of a string of prostitutes— all of whom have serviced Eastwood. A lot of people, including many liberal critics, were impressed with this film; they seem to think that having Eastwood make it with a hooker makes him a "dark" character. (But, then again, Eastwood, with his direct-action, no-nonsense approach to corruption, has always been many a liberal film-goer's guilty pleasure; the almost complete lack of moral ambiguity in his universe gives his films a cartoonishness that makes them "safe" for liberals to cheer along with.) *Tightrope* is one of the few recent films from the right that has an erotic element, but the eroticism is a lead-weight tease. Showing us the cop's sexual dark side doesn't explain him at all—it's a detour pretending to be the main drag strip. That's probably because Eastwood's presence isn't really a function of his sexuality; it's a function of his politics. Whatever is churning inside his screen persona (and it's often hard to tell from his acting if there *is* an inside), it's got a lot more to do with vigilante justice than sexual peccadilloes.

One of the areas where films on the right have often succeeded, sometimes inadvertently, is in their depiction of the rubes and the rednecks and crackers—the sort of people that liberal filmmakers tend to either prettify or ennoble or ignore. You often get more of a sense of what's knocking around the wide open spaces from any old country-western clobber-comedy than you do from a movie like *Country.* But, here too, the right hasn't followed through. What you have too often is the Clint Eastwood/orangutan or Kenny Rogers six-pack sort of film—debased country. And the populist imagery in movies on the right is a far cry from John Ford. It reached its apotheosis in the Madison Avenue nativism of the Reagan campaign films, which, with their sunset-dappled farmhouses and amber waves of grain, looked, in selected stills, like *Places in the Heart.* They're both "selling" a way of life.

Until fairly recently, movies were twisting in the wind, trying to find a place to land. The aftermath of Vietnam and Watergate brought out a powerful confusion—in the movies and in the country—and not much art came out of that confusion. The miserable quality of the movies in the last eight years or so can be blamed on a lot of things, including the self-punishing practices of the studios, but it's also symptomatic of a more profound problem—the lack of strong themes in popular culture. After Vietnam and Watergate, there was a period of retraction. There were, of course, lots of good films, but so many of them weren't really *about* anything (or, if they were about anything, it was other movies). This vacuum made possible the success of the teen romps and the star-wars extravaganzas. (George Lucas couldn't have been born into a better generation for his talents.) In a way, the conflicts of the *Star Wars* films, with their cosmic battles between good and evil, was a comic strip response to the problem of finding basic themes again. And there were an unusual number of films, like *Greystoke* and *Never Cry Wolf* and *Iceman* and *Quest for Fire,* that seemed to be reaching back to the very beginnings of man for some fundament of feeling. Even movies like *E.T.* and the mermaid comedy *Splash* and *The Brother From Another Planet* and *Moscow on the Hudson* were about the elemental and the innocent. The implicit message of these movies seemed to be: if you want to come up with something new that will move audiences, you have to start from scratch.

With the New Populism and the New Patriotism, movies may have found a place to land—at least for a spell. There are strong vibrations of a new mood in films like *Places in the Heart* and *Red Dawn.* The crude heroism of the new bring-'em-back-alive-from-Vietnam movies, which besides *Rambo* include a string of highly successful low-grade Chuck Norris vehicles, is a form of elementalism, and so is the archetypal nostalgia of a movie like *The Natural* or *Racing With the Moon.* And, of course, the family/farm movies are "elemental," too; getting back to the land is their way of starting from scratch. But these films aren't only expressing a mood—they're pushing a mood. In the guise of unifying the mass audience, they're also banging the drum for reactionary values. These movies about the land (that never get their fingernails dirty) are a part of the cant of the old-fashioned. They want to return to a time that never was.

There's an undeniable power to the pull of an idealized past, and it would be smug to deny its force for those who seek the balm of a less complicated world. In some ways, we *all* seek that balm. In the movies, whatever moves people mightily is worth understanding; film critics often demean the power of movies by demeaning the movie-fed emotions of the mass audience. But that doesn't mean one has to endorse the movies that inspire those emotions. I would endorse films that once again embrace the contradictions in our society, for that's where the true artistic vitality lies. I'm thinking of a movie like *Melvin and Howard,* where Melvin Dummar and Howard Hughes—the yin and yang of the heartland—sit together in the front seat of Dummar's pickup singing "Bye Bye Blackbird." All the nutso contradictions in America are in that front seat. The problem with the movies now is that they don't admit the contradictions. They don't admit the jam-packed whirligig of this country. Pauline Kael has called movies our national theater. Crowd the stage, I say.

(*Los Angeles Herald Examiner*, 1984)

White Rage:
Falling Down

Targeting bad guys in the movies can be a tricky business. Problems set in once you get past cannibal shrinks and Freddy Krueger and homicidal movie executives. In a film industry where fomenting hate can be big business, the question of just who is safe to target is no idle issue.

Falling Down is a real rabble-rouser with an entire home-shopping network of hates, but it gets audiences high by keeping things ghastly-giddy in the "I'm as mad as hell, and I'm not going to take this anymore" mode.

The filmmakers work in their worst-possible-case stereotypes and then make us side with the guy taking pot shots. That's how the movie gets us to hate "politically sensitive" targets with impunity.

The scowling, buzz-cut targeter, played by Michael Douglas, is generally identified as D-FENS because that's what it says on the personalized license plate of the car he abandons at the start of the movie on a choked freeway in the downtown L.A. district.

An aerospace worker who was fired from his job a month before, he just wants to get across town to Venice to see his child on her birthday. But things keep getting in the way. At every one of his Stations of the Cross (pun intended), we're served up a fresh new outrage.

Heading the hit list are surly Korean merchants; Latino gangbangers; lying, cheating, homeless beggars; do-nothing construction workers. In case those targets seem too reactionary, we're offered as decoys neo-Nazi survivalists, country-club snobs and filthy rich doctors.

In a more ecumenical vein, we're given a back list of people who won't serve you breakfast at a fast-food joint during lunch hour, and guys who harass you to get off the pay phone. We're given traffic jams, smog, graffiti. There's a red-hot button for everyone to push.

Or almost everyone. For you only have to imagine what this movie might have been like if the lead had been played by, say, an enraged Asian, or a Latino, to recognize how rigged it really is. *Falling Down* isn't some all-purpose cry of disgust. It's the howl of a scared, white, urban middle-class man.

What's obnoxious about the movie is that, even though it sustains a tone of apocalyptic tomfoolery, it plumps for D-FENS's prejudices. (That tomfoolery is a decoy too; it helps soften us for the punch.) D-FENS may be a nut, the film is saying, but he's a necessary nut—"our" nut. He's a guerrilla in the political correctness wars; his scorched-earth trek across Los Angeles obeys no proprieties.

Movies like *Falling Down* don't get made unless the movie company—in this case, Warner Bros.—thinks these targets can be hit without penalty. The studio line is that this is a movie that is meant to make us aware of hate; but the whoops that the film carefully engineers from the audience at each kill and kapowie tell a different story.

The film's sheer overload of targets is in marked contrast to what we've been used to in movies for the past decade or so. Before then, in the period, for example, that stretched from roughly the late sixties to the mid-seventies, you could expect to see movies where hippies, Vietnam vets, black drug dealers, white drug dealers, bleeding-heart liberals, cops and the press were all regularly whacked.

Some of those films tried to explore what was churning us up, while some merely exploited our feelings of helplessness. But at least the bugaboos were out in the open.

Contrast this with the weak-tea movie scene of the past decade. The convergence of Reagan-Bush era feel-goodism and bottom-line don't-rock-the-boat studio management resulted in a generation of non-controversial films that never seemed to explicitly address our prejudices. What we got instead was subtext and symbolism, like the way the city, in movies like *Batman,* was made to stand in for all that was rotting and malevolent in society. Race issues had to wait for a new generation of black filmmakers working mostly outside the industry.

Falling Down is a last-minute whammy from the Reagan-Bush era that finally makes explicit the social divisiveness that was implicit in so many of the films from that period. And it's a return to some of the worst prejudice-baiting impulses of the seventies films, with none of their redeeming virtues. It's a smorgasbord *Death Wish.*

The film encourages audiences to groove on D-FENS's reprehensible actions by building into each one of them an audience-pleasing rationale. Shooting a man and plugging a pay phone are all experienced on the same level. This is how you turn a psycho into a sacrificial hero.

When, for example, D-FENS tears up a Korean grocery store because the owner won't give him change for a phone call without making a purchase, the rationale is that D-FENS is just standing up for his rights as a consumer. All the products in the store are over-priced, so he smashes them.

The Latino gang member he shoots point-blank went after him earlier with a switchblade and, later, an Uzi, because he wandered unknowingly onto the gang's turf. How was he to know?

The homeless guy who asks him for money—and is turned down flat—turns out to be a smarmy faker. The rich doctor whose home he trespasses is not, say, an emergency room physician or a cancer specialist but a plastic surgeon (read: Beverly Hills phony baloney). The bald neo-Nazi who runs an Army surplus store spews drool about Jews, gays, women. He gets his, too, just so that we know D-FENS isn't as bad as all *that*.

But notice who this film *doesn't* go after. Latinos and Koreans and neo-Nazis and fast-food operators are apparently fair game, but after that it gets a little touchy. We see conspicuously few black people, for example. Those that we do see, like the well-dressed crazed-with-grief man who pickets his bank because they won't give him a loan, or the chubby, polite kid who teaches D-FENS how to shoot a bazooka, are haloed. (Is it too cynical to suggest that the Korean merchant in this film was included as a sop to the animosities of the commercially imposing black audience? After all, middle-class whites do not have much truck with Korean merchants.)

The police, personified by an avuncular, thoughtful detective played by Robert Duvall, are on their best behavior. No police brutality in sight. (To balance out the score sheet, Duvall, of course, is given a sympathetic Latino partner, a woman.) In this land of Rodney King and L.A. police chief Daryl Gates, these omissions are weird blips in the hit parade. Could it be that the scourges behind this film came down with a case of cold—no, make that *frostbitten*—feet?

Even without seeing any prominent black faces, we get the point—Los Angeles is a melting-pot nightmare.

Even the ecosystem has rebelled. The air is molten with smog, the palm trees are choking. D-FENS is a white reactionary's fantasy hero because his targets are the minorities and immigrants who are trying to make their way into a society he finds himself excluded from. He served his country with distinction as a defense worker until he was cut loose; he kept an eye out for the Commies; his father won the Purple Heart in World War II. Is this the thanks he gets?

Falling Down is set up to show us that, in a mixed-race society where everybody is at each other's throats, middle-class whites have assumed minority status too; they have it as bad as everybody else now. And what the film attempts to do is to give its white audience license to stop feeling guilty and start getting angry.

From Bogart to James Dean, movie anti-heroes have traditionally been romanticized. Deep down they covet the society they pretend to reject. D-FENS, with his buzz cut and his nerdy pocket protector and thick glasses, is intentionally anti-romantic. He rejects the *idea* of society—or at least a mixed one.

He's the first rabble-rousing representative on film of the new "oppressed" white minority, though you can hear his nonstop voice on talk-radio bands from coast to coast. *Falling Down* has some of the same loony oomph as the far-right wing radio talk shows—it drowns you out by raising backlash to new heights of clamor. To the loudest goes the spoils.

"How did I get to be the bad guy?" asks D-FENS just before his final curtain. We in the audience, of course, know differently. After watching *Falling Down,* we know who the real bad guys are.

(Los Angeles Times, 1993)

Anti-Hero Worship: *Malcolm X*

Is it a coincidence that Superman died the same week the movie *Malcolm X* opened? In popular culture, styles of heroism have their cycles, and the square-jawed, lily-white, goody-two-shoes supra-human is currently out of the loop of fashion.

But Malcolm X has survived the gantlet of historical reassessment. A new generation responds to his principled rage precisely because he *isn't* lily white and goody-two-shoes. He's an antihero—a subverter of the white racist status quo—who, in the Spike Lee movie and in popular culture in general right now, has been sanctified with the legendary look of the traditional hero. American culture is essentially transformational; yesterday's firebrand is today's voice of reason.

Malcolm X comes out at a time when the movies are starved for heroes—which is another way of saying that the country is starved for them. One of the explicit themes of the recent Presidential campaign was the question of "character." Who could you trust to act properly "heroic" when the chips were down? George Bush's old-guard war-hero WASP Republicanism clashed with Bill Clinton's baby-boomer New Covenant. Leaving aside the matter of political truth or untruth in these poses, both were nevertheless presented as styles of heroism, and Clinton's proved the more marketable.

Heroism—a display of courage and nobility that appeals to the best in us—has been a sometime thing in our movies in part because the country has had no unifying vision. We tend to import our heroes nowadays: Lech Walesa, Nelson Mandela, Vaclav Havel, even Gorbachev. These men are linked with emergent and righteous national movements. (And they're far enough away from us to avoid our home-grown media scrutiny.) They testify to the force of national consciousness in creating popular heroes.

Our most iconic movie heroes, whatever one thinks of their personas, have always been linked to a four-square concept of what America is all about. John Wayne was two-fisted and rode hard and was never without a gun; Jimmy Stewart had his drawling, homespun rootedness; so did Henry Fonda and Gary Cooper. Humphrey Bogart was never so American as when he was an expatriate in *Casablanca*. The rebels without a cause, like James Dean or the young Brando, defined themselves by their opposition to a society they felt excluded from.

American movies have often been better—livelier and more fun—when they featured antiheroes. The rebels undercut the homiletics of standard-issue heroism; they spoke to our discontent and our cynicism, our sense of how things really were, to a far greater extent than the role-model types. But their discontent was, in itself, an act of heroism—they challenged the suffocating fitness of things.

Heroism and antiheroism thrive on a national sense of identity, a comprehensive core, a vision. Lacking these qualities in our national life, our movies have been bereft of the sorts of heroes who might connect up with us, even in opposition. We've been treated instead to a spate of antihero heroes, ranging from RoboCop to the Terminator to Batman, who operate out of a techno-pop-comic never-never-land.

There have been other movie hero sandwiches lately. In *Under Siege,* Steven Seagal's aikido moves have gone big-time patriotic. *JFK,* the most hero-worshiping American movie in years, offered up a deliriously idealized version of President Kennedy and a counter-myth about his assassination. We've been treated this year to musty neo-Capracorn, like *Hero,* and the dumb revisionism of the Columbus movies. We've retreated safely to a quasi-mythic past, as in *The Last of the Mohicans.* Heroism in our movies—as opposed to our TV shows, which often deal with the less action-oriented, "mundane" heroics of ordinary people, and which therefore provide virtually the only screen opportunities for female heroism—is almost exclusively the province of an idealized past or a cartoon present.

When the idealization works, as in Daniel Day-Lewis's full-out embodiment of Hawkeye in *Mohicans,* the results can be exhilarating. There are other modern actors who have a heroic dimension: Nick Nolte, Mel Gibson, Morgan Freeman, for example. Unlike, say, Tom Cruise, who is often a hero in his films by virtue of casting rather than presence, these actors express the tensions and contradictions that give heroism in the movies a human face.

We can, if we choose, scan the faces of an older generation of movie-star heroes, like Robert Redford and Paul Newman and Clint Eastwood. But the effect they provide is not satisfying in the same old ways. They evoke a more complicated response now; age has melancholized their features. The power with which Eastwood's *Unforgiven* moved audiences had its source in our response to Eastwood's deep-creased Westerner's face, a road map of time's passage—his and ours.

In the aftermath of the Vietnam War, the standard do-gooder action hero could no longer be taken straight in our movies; his heroics, fairly or not, took on a sinister, villainous cast. The cynical, tragic, hopeless tone that crept into our films in the wake of Vietnam was responsible for some of the greatest movies of the era: the *Godfather* films, *Taxi Driver,* and many others. But it also created a vacuum for the kind of traditional heroism that is one of the prime enjoyments of moviegoing.

It's no accident that this was the period in film history—the Toy Store Epoch—when George Lucas & Co., toting their well-thumbed copies of Joseph Campbell's *The Hero With a Thousand Faces,* began bombarding us with superhero jamborees; they provided us with heroes who were literally (and conveniently) out of this world. If heroism is what appeals to the best in us, then the subsequent Reagan-Bush reign, with its appeals to the mercenary in us, did not exalt the cause of heroism either. It has left us with a yearning for the possibilities of heroism cross-wired with a cynicism and a self-consciousness that will not allow for the possibilities of human greatness.

No doubt the problem is compounded by the ways in which celebrity has replaced heroism as the modern archetype of that greatness. In a mercenary culture, fame is its own reward. But fame, by these rules, is also fleeting. Our idea of the movie star—the new celebrity hero—is an agglomeration not only of that star's screen appearances but also of everything else we are made to know through the media about his off-screen life.

This media climate, which Daniel Boorstin first recognized in the mid-sixties in his book *The Image: A Guide to Pseudo-Events in America,* and which has reached its apotheosis today, has also made it difficult to recognize the "true" hero. Even when the heroes are acknowledged, the acknowledgment is in the same old celebrity-mongering terms, Gorbymania, anyone?

This is conspicuously the case with Malcolm X. The full force of media marketeering has been brought to bear on his life until its meaning is befogged in a welter of insignias and paraphernalia. The Spike Lee movie plays into this commercialization by making Malcolm a kind of smoothed-out storybook hero—he's sanctified by his martyrdom. *Malcolm X* is undoubtedly a significant sociological event. There has hardly ever been a big biographical film about a black hero who was not a sports or entertainment star. But the most startling thing about the movie— once one gets past the opening credits with the burning American flag forming the letter "X" and the Rodney King footage—is how purposefully unstartling it is. It is being widely compared to *Gandhi,* as if that were high praise indeed. Has everyone forgotten what a high-minded, Oscarized long sit that film was?

Malcolm X has rhetorical power. Denzel Washington captures Malcolm's cool ferocity as an orator, his fierce, scary sense of entitlement. But the film, except for its opening, doesn't really have an in-your-face immediacy. It's part of an older, softer, more conventional tradition of biographical enshrinement. Lee's portrait is almost entirely devoid of psychological dimension; perhaps he feels that a psychoanalytic view would demean black experience by particularizing it and separating it out from its historical context.(Or maybe he's just better at creating mouthpieces.) He draws on the *Autobiography of Malcolm X* almost exclusively, barring from his film any material from texts like the controversial, psychosexual 1990 Bruce Parry biography.

Except for childhood flashbacks, Malcolm's siblings, who were major influences throughout his life, have been eliminated. Lee doesn't really situate Malcolm's struggle in any larger framework—we don't get much sense of how his battles were a part of the total home-front scene of the fifties and sixties. We are shown Malcolm's progression from hustler and convict to the man he became, but the episodes are like a series of illuminated pages in a holy text. They are demonstrations, not explications, of his spiritual journey.

This approach might have gotten by in the Golden Age of the Biopic—the thirties and forties. (Except, of course, Hollywood would never have dreamed of making a movie about someone like Malcolm X back then.) But we require a fuller approach now, one that does justice both to our yearnings for a champion and our media-wise cynicism.

Would a movie that dealt with Malcolm's early racial and sexual fears, that got more deeply into his white-devil preachings within the Nation of Islam, that pointed up his anti-Semitism and his detestation of the civil rights movement and bourgeois blacks—would such a movie have upended his heroism? Or more likely, would it have dramatized his final dilemma, when he felt caught in a trap between the moderate and the militant? Would it have humanized him and defined his struggle so that we could feel the full resounding force of his evolution? The challenge in this tell-all age of celebrity heroism is to create a hero not only in spite of but *because* of the hero's failings—what he had to overcome.

If Malcolm X, almost alone among "contemporary" American heroes now, seems aligned with the likes of Walesa and Mandela, it is because he, too, is linked with a new generation's emergent and righteous national movement—a movement of black pride. That's why his presence, as contourless and spiritualized as it is in the film, still fills the screen. This is a lot to get from a movie and yet it's not enough. *Malcolm X* is much closer to political hagiography than political art.

Is the civics lesson worshipfulness of *Malcolm X* justifiable because so few films about black heroes are made? Is this what we can look forward to if movies are produced about the lives of, say, Martin Luther King or Paul Robeson? In light of the way his film has turned out, Spike Lee's contention that only a black director, namely himself, could do justice to Malcolm's life takes on an unexpected meaning. *Malcolm X* suggests that movies about black heroes are entitled to partake of the same big-picture piety and impersonality as the standard biopics about white heroes. Hasn't the previously provocative work of filmmakers like Lee himself rightly accustomed us to a more challenging standard?

(*Los Angeles Times*, 1992)

A Little Princess

What do you do when you've made one of the most magical family films ever made in this country—the kind of movie parents are supposedly clamoring for—and the families can't be convinced to come?

This must be the question that Warner Bros. and the people who made *A Little Princess* are asking themselves right now. They've done everything right; this adaptation of the Frances Hodgson Burnett classic about Sara Crewe, the ten-year-old "princess" who grew up in India and who changes the lives of everyone around her at Miss Minchin's School for Girls in New York, has the emotional depth and storybook splendor to stay with audiences forever—and not just young audiences, either. Like *The Red Balloon* or *The Black Stallion* or *E.T.,* it's the kind of film that could turn kids into movie lovers for life. (If only there were enough movies in their future to replenish that love!)

But if the commercial response to a film like *A Little Princess* is this tepid, what chance is there that other gifted filmmakers will be encouraged, not to mention financed, to also do it right? (*A Little Princess,* which opened May 10, has to date grossed around $5.4 million. By comparison, *Casper* in its first weekend grossed $22 million.)

Certainly the *critical* response has been everything the filmmakers could have hoped for. It's probably the best reviewed movie of the year. Still, a film about little darlings in a Victorian Gothic girls' boarding school in 1914 is a tough sell these days at the multiplex.

It wasn't always this way. If this film had been released in Hollywood in, say, the thirties (when the Shirley Temple version of this material was made) or even as recently as the seventies, it would have been cherished unapologetically by audiences. But today apologies apparently are in order. Much more so than ever before, the "family film" carries an air of disparagement.

It's become a ghettoized genre: G-rated pap for pokey preteens. Parents don't expect anything from these movies except a headache. The whole idea of a family in a theater experiencing together a movie that unifies their imaginations, and their love for movies, has degraded. We are now living in a time when family entertainment, in the form of interactive computer games and videos, has become a compartmentalized, isolating experience. It is the home, and not the theater, that has become the family's total entertainment center.

A film like *A Little Princess* doesn't fit into the turbocharged, Dolby-ized atmosphere of today's movie world. Which is not to say that it is without special favors. But, unlike most movies nowadays, it doesn't try to do everything for us except park our car. It doesn't try to rattle our bones or turn itself into a theme park or a toy store or a computer game. Have we lost faith in the sheer, radiant, ungizmo-ed *simplicity* of the film-going experience?

The people who made *A Little Princess*—the honor role includes director Alfonso Cuarón, screenwriters Richard LaGravenese and Elizabeth Chandler, producer Mark Johnson, production designer Bo Welch, cinematographer Emmanuel Lubezki, composer Patrick Doyle and editor Steve Weisberg—draw us into a state of heightened, imaginative complicity, as if we were dreaming right along with Sara in this girls' world.

The film has fantasy sequences set in a dream-book India that have a ravishing, antique prettiness, with blues and reds and yellows that seem freshly mined, and compositions that, in their sophisticated primitivism, look like leaves from Kipling's *Jungle Book* re-imagined by French painter Henri Rousseau.

In a sense, the film's entire world is fantastical—that's the core of its meaning. The filmmakers want us to perceive the fundament of magic in the everyday, and how that magic can sustain one's spirit. The motherless Sara's world away from India is as densely packed as the mythic landscape of Prince Rama and Princess Sita with which she captivates her school friends. The myth parallels her own separation from her father, who placed her for safekeeping in the school and is later presumed dead fighting in World War I.

The monster who abducts the princess has her counterpart in Eleanor Bron's Miss Minchin, a Dickensian scourge who casts Sara into the attic, making her a servant girl when she can no longer afford to be a student. Miss Minchin seems to bundle up the darkness about her. She's an emanation of the school's dank, deep green chambers. And the little girls who ultimately vanquish her are spunky, entranced cherubim; the big bow-knots in their hair always seem ready to fly apart from the force of their fantasias.

The Hollywood marketing juggernaut may have rolled right over *A*

Little Princess, which has no merchandising hook and no big stars in its cast (although, with any justice, Liesel Matthews, who plays Sara, should be a star). Kids bombarded by *Casper* trailers and *Casper* toy tie-ins naturally want to see *Casper*. Never mind that it's a cheesy, half-witted escapade. Kids want to be part of the pack, and so, perhaps, do the parents who take them. We all want to be winners now, piling into the top-grossing movies in order to be part of the action. And the media wants to be on top, too; when a film like *A Little Princess* doesn't immediately rack up the numbers, coverage dries up fast. So do available movie screens; exhibitors and distributors can't be bothered trying to build an audience for the film. No one wants to look uncool touting a "loser," especially one that's about little girls. Let the movie fend for itself in its video re-release.

If the juggernaut has rolled over *A Little Princess* it's only because audiences have lost the spirit of resistance. Hollywood can be indicted for many crimes but the indictment here is with people who claim to hunger for heartfelt, inspiring, nonviolent family fare and then, with *A Little Princess* around, line up for *Casper* and clobberfests like *Die Hard With a Vengeance* instead. Maybe a fall/winter release would have helped the film's chances but, if a movie of this quality can't find an audience in the late spring/summer, that's indictment enough.

A Little Princess is still around, though. Flattened by the juggernaut, it is yet possible, at least for a while longer, to pick yourself up off the Tarmac and enter into a resplendent realm. The magic of movies is still, fitfully, alive.

The question now is: Is the audience for it dead?

(*Los Angeles Times*, 1995)

The Innocence Game

It's Age of Innocence time at the movies. In film after film this summer we've been put through the same toddling paces. Forget the swank spies and overmuscled clobberers. We're being asked to crown a new movie hero—the pure-in-heart man-child Forrest Gump and all the purer-than-thou preteens and tots from kidpics like *Angels in the Outfield, North,*

Getting Even With Dad, and *Little Big League.*

What do these films have in common—aside from high glucose tolerance? The children (or child-men) in them all come from broken or dysfunctional homes, mostly without fathers. They're wiser than their parents, wiser than adult society. Their wisdom serves one cause only—to re-create a family for themselves. Errant fathers—the goblins of this genre—must be brought back into the fold or else replaced with a kindlier model.

We're accustomed to thinking of child-themed films in Victorian terms—as demonstrations that children can be rescued from their truancy. These new films reverse the terms. They're all about how the family can be rescued—by children.

Actually, the Romantic era is more appropriate to what's going on here than the Victorian. That era's idealization of the child was all-of-a-piece with its idealization of man in his basic state—childlike, at home among the bushes and the berries, untrammeled by the false refinements of city life. Infants and idiots were regarded as closest to nature; in their primitiveness was a purity that could be exalted above mere intellect. (Animals were considered primitive-pure too, which is perhaps why we're also seeing films about collies, seals and stallions.)

Forrest Gump—even the name has a vegetative, close-to-the-earth sound to it—has an IQ of seventy but he's supernally decent. Raised without a father by his aphorism-spouting mother, he passes through the key Boomer decades—the fifties through the early eighties—without registering the wrenches in public life. Vietnam, assassinations, Watergate—none of these sway him. (It's our fantasy of how we would like to have survived those years.) Forrest wants only the love of his lifelong, father-abused friend Jenny; he wants a family. We're supposed to applaud the bumpkinish divinity of his quest.

We're made to understand that it takes a child—a child-man—to explain to us what really matters in life. In an age of experts, Forrest is the wise man as simpleton, the straight arrow as holy fool. His innocence is like a balm for the turmoil of the past four decades. The film wants to turn us all into Gumps—it wants us to jog right alongside him as he sprints across America the Beautiful.

Even though Forrest's innocence exists in separation from the big bad world, the filmmakers aren't quite as innocent as their hero. They score reactionary points repeatedly as Forrest moves through the decades—none of that hippie-dippy, war-protesting, free-loving, drug-chugging stuff for him. (The film never makes a case for what corruptions the counterculture might have been reacting *against*.)

All these ills are what he must rescue Jenny *from*—he must bring her back to herself, to their childhood roots in Greenbow, Ala. The real idiots in *Forrest Gump* are the counterculture clowns and assassinating crazies who never had any innocence to lose. It's time to mend what they tore apart. Forrest is our Puritan knight errant for traditional values. Essentially sexless, he stands up for family, true love, small-town life, mothers, serving your country, winning the American Dream.

Expect to see Forrest Gump campaign stickers in the upcoming elections—for *both* parties. For it's the measure of the film's across-the-board success that it camouflages its politics as a kind of fuzzy nostalgic populism. It's flower power nineties style—Romanticism with a conservative core.

If *Forrest Gump* is a balm for lobotomized Boomers, the welter of kidpics this summer resembles a load of Boomer guilt. These films are the next stage in the recent male weepie cycle where hard-pressed yuppie dads finally reconnect with their families by locating the child within. In those films, ranging from *Regarding Henry* to *Hook,* children were essentially employed as peewee spirit guides; they were accessories to the adults' quest for goodness. In this summer's crop, it's the kids and not their parents who are center stage. Of course, the kids are all boys. Girls are eerily absent from these family sagas. Is this because girls still are not regarded as Leaders of Tomorrow? That's the downside of the traditional-values ploy—it delivers traditional prejudices.

The male weepie cycle was a reaction to the recession. It was a touchy-feely response to a time when overachievers became under-earners. With the recession receding, the new family film is less about parents coping with downsized expectations—they've learned to cope—and more about pint-sized sages bringing their errant parents back into the fold.

In *North,* for example, the boy's parents are such nattering, whiny careerists that he sues to find a new, caring pair. His trek takes him through a sitcom array of moms and dads from Texas to Hawaii to Ward Cleaverish suburbia before his real parents inexplicably defrost and celebrate their wonder boy. Like so many of the films in this cycle, *North* seems to be an expression of hurt and regret that all families aren't as peachy-keen as the ones in sitcoms. It's a sadness particular to Boomers.

Little boy North at least has parents he can rehabilitate. In most of the other films, the boys—a bland, virtuous lot—have to haul their fathers back onto the scene or else find new ones. In *Angels in the Outfield,* Roger the motherless angel-gazer rises above his uncaring biker dad and fetches himself a better one, the manager of the Angels, whose team his visions bring to glory. Roger teaches his new adoptive dad to believe in the miracle of love all over again. (Tellingly, the star of the original 1951 *Angels in the Outfield* was a girl, but don't despair. When Roger says his prayers at night he follows "amen" with "a-woman." This kid is more PC than God!)

In *Little Big League,* twelve-year-old fatherless Billy Heywood inherits ownership of the last-place Minnesota Twins, becomes its manager and teaches the ballplayers to love the game all over again. Even though love and not winning is the message here, the team—natch—wins the pennant. In the current Hollywood, if you're good you're a winner. (Forrest Gump became a war hero and millionaire.) Billy even has final say on who his new dad will be—he turns out to be his best big buddy and the Twins' captain. (Is there a preponderance of baseball-oriented kids films because baseball is perceived as being a game between fathers and sons?)

Even Macaulay Culkin is in the wisdom-dispensing business these days. (If there's a *Home Alone 3* he'll probably put his parents into therapy.) In *Getting Even With Dad,* Culkin's Timmy, motherless, is dumped by his aunt at the doorstep of his petty thief deadbeat father. Timmy hordes the cache from his father's recent heist and, in exchange for its return, blackmails Dad into showing him a fatherly good time at the ballpark, the aquarium, the museum. Dad comes around; he learns to love again. He even chooses his boy over his loot—a throwback to male-weepie-style sacrifice. And Timmy engineers a romance between Dad and the undercover cop who is trailing him. He'll be getting a new mom of his own choosing.

Children in society, as opposed to children in the movies, are currently afflicted with bad PR. On the talk shows, on magazine covers and Op-Ed pages, we're confronted with the phenomenon of the child as abused tyrant, prey to drugs, gangs, crime. Our idealized notions of childhood innocence don't jibe with the gang-banging Uzi-toters in the news. For those who can't see the Forrest Gump for the trees, this phenomenon can best be blamed on the breakup of the family, on welfare, on those pesky two-career households. In a particularly woozy moment you may even go so far as to blame it all on *Murphy Brown*, on Hollywood.

The current crop of kidpics resembles nothing so much as Hollywood's craven response to its own (supposed) culpability. They certainly don't look like movies that spring from any genuine childhood feeling; for one thing, the kids in them are all too goody-goody and role-modelly. (And, in fact, most of these movies have been flops with kids.) They elevate children at the expense of parents—fathers, mostly. It's a kind of penance on the part of adult filmmakers for past sins. Single motherhood, as opposed to absent fatherhood, is spared—that's a political hot potato. And notice that the settings are mostly white and middle-class, which helps eliminate poverty and racism from the family-misery equation.

The kids have a sense of entitlement. No children of rage here. (How appropriate that *The Little Rascals* should be made into a movie now, with its rainbow coalition of benign tots carousing in an L.A. paradise.) Uncynical, steely with self-esteem, they instruct their parents in how to love them in the way a family counselor might. The parents, or parent-figures, are rewarded in increments for the good they do their boys.

The innocence game isn't only being played for penance. There's also a pushy self-righteousness about these kidpics. The filmmakers are angling for merit badges in the moral crusade. Since no one in Hollywood is making children-oriented movies with any bite or realism, the way is open for message-mongering schlockmeisters to muck about in fantasyland.

But this business of turning kids into wise adults and adults into wayward kids only works when it's done with some snap—some naughtiness—instead of all this moral overload. If there's a road back to innocence, these films haven't found it.

(Los Angeles Times, 1994)

On the Pleasures and Dangers of Pulp: *Unlawful Entry*

In the vicious thriller *Unlawful Entry*, a deranged L.A. cop, played by Ray Liotta, fixates on the comfortably middle-class couple he is supposedly protecting—he terrorizes the husband and tries to make whoopee with the wife. In *Lethal Weapon 3,* Mel Gibson and Danny Glover are once again barreling through a crash-and-burn fest in gang-ridden L.A. In the Tom Clancy-derived *Patriot Games,* Annapolis history professor and CIA analyst Jack Ryan, played by Harrison Ford, goes *mano a mano* with a radical IRA splinter group.

These movies, as well as the recent *Basic Instinct* and *Cape Fear,* are ostensibly melodramas set in a thrill-seeker's fantasy land. Except that— darn the luck—the real world keeps intruding. L.A. cops, after all, aren't cyborgs and the IRA isn't composed of Klingons. These movies try to strong-arm us into a state of movie disbelief, but can we suspend disbelief so easily? More to the point, *should* we?

In pulp, the volatile subjects of drama—the conflicts of sex and race and class—are sensationalized and writ large. The question of how seriously we should take pulp is basic to our filmgoing experience right now, because, unavoidably, it constitutes just about everything we see. The disruptions these films provoke are routinely dismissed with the It's Only a Movie defense. Political correctness, so the defense goes, is taking all the fun out of melodrama, the whole point of which is to pit heroes against villains. The more "incorrect" the villainy the better. Lighten up. It's only a movie.

But sensationalistic material doesn't exist in some value-free zone. Or is it okay to be racist or misogynist in pulp entertainment—which is presumably manufactured for the unthinking masses—but not in "serious" high-toned fare? Movies are supposed to be the great democratic art form, but the sick joke of films like *Basic Instinct* and *Cape Fear* and *Unlawful Entry* is that they stir us up by drawing on our most reactionary sexual and racial fears and assumptions. They unify us by playing into our prejudices. Some democracy.

More maddening than all this exploitation, perhaps, is the filmmakers' *indifference* to social reality. The cartoon calisthenics of *Lethal Weapon 3,* for example, have no business being set amid the miseries of modern-day, crime-ridden L.A. By working in some heavy-duty gang-busting, the filmmakers are just camouflaging the buddy-buddy japery with a phony social consciousness—while continuing to juice the action.

What these filmmakers may not realize, or care about, is that we live at a time when it's not even possible to stage these cartoon shoot-'em-ups in real locations without the foolery ringing false. You can't use cities like New York and Los Angeles as cardboard cutout backdrops anymore because they're too overpowering, too resonant with urban horror stories. (The days of *Dragnet* are definitely over.)

That pulp can seem brainless and yet still carry political content should be obvious—certainly the notion has been recognized, and exploited, by politicos both on the right and the left. So why does it come as a shock to many people that a movie that wasn't directed by one of our two official hollerers, Oliver Stone or Spike Lee, can still plug into the political static? Not all movies with political content come on like manifestoes.

When a *Variety* reviewer, Joseph McBride, wrote last month that *Patriot Games* was "anti-Irish" and "fascistic," prompting a highly publicized rebuke from his own editor, many who read the review were surprised to discover that anybody might take Tom Clancy's pulp for anything more than a kick-back time-killer. Yet this film's melodrama is greased by its hero-worship toward the CIA and the British ruling class. (Those attitudes are toned down from the book which, incidentally, carries a praiseworthy blurb from that noted literary critic Caspar Weinberger.) You don't have to agree that *Patriot Games* is a fascistic movie to recognize that it's gummy with political labeling.

We may not always be consciously aware of what these movies are proffering; nor, for that matter, are their makers. But surely on a deeper level we—literally—get the picture. Pulp movies carry a charge precisely because they don't lay out all the meanings for us like the prestigious message movies do. They aren't weighted down with high-flown inspirationalism like *Gandhi*; they don't try to make you a better person. Instead, they deep-rub our prejudices and confusions, and this is often why the average thriller is more disturbing to us than its more "responsible" counterpart; it's less polite about muscling in on our fears. When a great piece of pulp comes along, like Don Siegel's *Dirty Harry* or Sam Peckinpah's *Straw Dogs,* it can really wipe you out because, from the first frame, your psyche is gripped in a submission hold that never lets up.

Unlawful Entry isn't great pulp; it's not even terrific. But it's a good example of how a thriller can raid the zeitgeist. We've seen this many times before, and with even more deliberation: *Dirty Harry,* with its tarnished knight battling a coddled-by-liberals psycho sporting a peace sign belt buckle, was a methodical reactionary fantasy; *Straw Dogs* was a take-no-prisoners demonstration of the territorial imperative. *Unlawful Entry* doesn't lay its cards on the table quite so blatantly as those films, but it's still dealing from a stacked deck.

On the surface, the film seems to be setting up Ray Liotta's Officer Pete as the latest in a line of monomaniacal revengers: a man-in-blue variation on Glenn Close in *Fatal Attraction* or Rebecca De Mornay's nanny in *The Hand That Rocks the Cradle.* As the film begins, Richard (Kurt Russell) and his wife Karen (Madeleine Stowe) are terrorized in their home by an intruder; as Richard watches helplessly, the intruder holds Karen at knife point before fleeing. When Pete and his partner arrive at the scene of the crime, we're give a "meaningful" close-up of Pete as he drinks in Karen's beauty. He supervises the installation of a security system; he takes Richard out on night patrol with him—macho buddies.

But Pete has a surprise. Alone in the squad car with Richard, he drives to a run-down apartment, bursts in on the intruder who terrorized Richard and his wife and then, when Richard refuses to do the honors, beats the suspect to a, well, pulp.

From this point on, Pete's psychopathology insinuates itself into every aspect of the couple's life, though, significantly, Karen is so mesmerized by Pete's cuckoo cooing that it takes her most of the movie to finally heed her husband's warnings.

The crack in this neat scenario is that Richard, not Pete, is the film's real target. He's portrayed as a species of wimp. A real estate developer of sorts—i.e. a yuppie softy—he's all too anxious to partake of Pete's derring-do. Until it gets too dangerous for him, that is—until it gets real. And the point is not very subtly made that he doesn't really satisfy his languorous wife, either.

With all the current concern about L.A. police brutality, this film wants us to know that, if you're white and middle-class, brutality is the price you pay for protection. If you're white and well off, your comforts are bought at the expense of poor blacks. Is it just a coincidence that the intruder who breaks in on Richard and Karen is a very dark-skinned black? (Pete, of course, is given a black partner; in Hollywood, and not only in Hollywood, racism and integration go hand in hand.) Pete may be a bad apple but Richard and Karen planted the seed. In a way, *Unlawful Entry* is as much a letter bomb for liberals as *Dirty Harry* was.

We've just been through a cycle of recession-era movies where lawyers and doctors and profiteers jettison their corporate achiever ways for the blandishments of family. Now this cycle may be moving into thornier terrain. In *Cape Fear,* a well-to-do lawyer, complete with bad marriage and wayward daughter, clashes with a bugaboo sexual terrorist who scorches the protections of the middle class.

The *Cape Fear* side of *Unlawful Entry* reaches beyond political sniping and into the primeval muck. Richard can't hold onto his woman because he's been softened by the very middle-class comforts he is now in danger of losing. Karen is portrayed as femininity incarnate; she's so maidenly that she seems perpetually in mid-swoon. Her trance-like (and unconsummated) confabs with Pete tell us that women really want the rough 'n' tough stuff and, what's more, *you can't really blame them.* Richard *deserves* to be terrorized. Only by besting Pete's brutality can he regain his manhood. In pulp, what is sexually reactionary and what is politically reactionary usually go hand in hand. *Unlawful Entry* is quite a handshake.

It's typical of pulp that it raises complicated concerns—the kind of concerns that are the stuff of real drama—and then uncomplicates them and makes them as easy to read as a tabloid headline. There's no suggestion that Pete's behavior is in any way connected to the practices of the Los Angeles police force; he's simply the bogeyman. It's a convenient demonization for audiences wary of the institutional abuses of the police. Just get rid of Pete and things will be fine.

Pulp has always been one of the preferred ways of transmitting "ideas" in American society; its crude vitality suits us even as it devalues debate. If the pulp that's currently making it into the theaters these days seems particularly crude, well, that's certainly in keeping with the national temper. The tone of political debate is itself pulped; the official solutions to urban despair are invariably of the law-and-order variety. The ways in which political candidates attempt to demonize each other is all-of-a-piece with the movie thrillers. The winning candidate is often the one who can co-opt from popular culture the most potent pulp symbols—stretching from Willie Horton to the yellow peril. Pulp movies *have* to be especially crude right now. They've got real competition.

(Los Angeles Times, 1992)

Paradise Lost?
The Truman Show

The Truman Show, starring Jim Carrey, is the zeitgeist movie of the hour. How could it not be? It's all about the omnipotence of television and how our lives seem scripted by some unseen force—a TV producer, perhaps? Zeitgeist movies, almost by definition, get written about not only by film critics but also by "pundits" and op-ed pontificators. And a movie that supposedly zeroes in on the way television has transformed our reality is a double bonus—it allows the media to carry on about the media.

Paramount Pictures, the film's releasing company, is certainly pushing the zeitgeist approach, with costly full-page reprints in major press outlets of a deep-think *Esquire* rave by David Thomson that calls it the "movie of the decade"—not to mention the verbiage in its own press kit, which tells us the film "reflects the hopes and anxieties that grip us all as the century lurches to a close." Jim Carrey as a poster boy for the millennium? Get used to it.

Truman Burbank (Carrey) is introduced to us as a hyperstraight insurance adjuster who lives in the peachy-keen town of Seahaven with his Clairol-blonde, hypersweet wife Meryl (Laura Linney). Everything about Truman's world is honeyed—it's like a fifties sitcom crossed with a Norman Rockwell townscape. It's all too good to be true, of course, and sure enough, it turns out to be a fabrication. Unknown to Truman as the film opens is that, from the moment of his birth, he has been the star of a twenty-four-hours-a-day TV show.

Seahaven is, in fact, an immense soundstage, and its inhabitants, excepting Truman, are all actors. Over the thirty years of Truman's existence, the number of cameras covertly trained on him has gone from one to 5,000. Virtually his entire life is documented from every angle. Seen around the world, with an audience in the billions, his TV show is the longest-running "real-life" soap-opera on the airwaves. And because Seahaven is an island and Truman has conveniently been made to have a fear of crossing water, he has never left his village. He doesn't know what everybody else knows about him. He's a star without the realization of his own stardom—which, of course, is the essence of his immense appeal.

The orchestrator of this opera is the television director Christof

(Ed Harris), who conceived the show and has become such a God-like manipulator that, for the unwitting Truman at least, he might as well *be* God. Christof—he has just that one name, like a cult leader or a Beverly Hills hairdresser—wears a beret and the intense, purposeful look of a messiah. He's demonic in his industriousness, and yet—you've got to admit it—he puts on a terrific show. And he genuinely loves Truman, in a way a puppeteer prizes his prime marionette.

The conflict comes when Truman, about a third of the way into the movie, finally figures out what's really going on. Comprehending the made-up nature of his life, he struggles to escape Seahaven.

Christof, ever the director-genius, even manages to turn Truman's attempts to flee into a ratings-grabber. And yet he doesn't want the show to climax; he doesn't want his star to break away even after it's clear Truman has found him out.

What probably makes this film resonate for the zeitgeisters is that Truman's realization of his own stardom is presented as *tragic*. He's an Everyman who realizes he's a Nowhere Man. Truman is, almost literally, a child of the media. Directed by Peter Weir from a screenplay by Andrew Niccol, *The Truman Show* is anything but a celebration of media-made culture. If it were, Truman's discovery would be not a tragedy but a triumph. Imagine! He doesn't just have fifteen minutes of fame, he's had thirty years of it! How ungrateful can you get?

From a strictly filmic point of view, *The Truman Show* is remarkable. Weir sets up Seahaven—actually a ninety-acre planned community on Florida's Gulf Coast—as the kind of storybook suburb so "perfect," it's surrealistic. An Australian with a penchant for delivering the cold creeps to audiences—*The Last Wave* is his most renowned excursion into high-toned heebie-jeebies—Weir understands fear. We've seen a variation on these twinkly suburbs before in, for example, the films of Steven Spielberg, especially *E.T.*, and in Robert Zemeckis's *Back to the Future* series. But those directors offered up their "model" communities with great affection. To a large degree, Spielberg and Zemeckis were formed by the fifties culture of straight-laced sitcoms; what they chose to present is not so much an accurate rendition of that era as a *nostalgia* for it. Like Truman, these directors are children of the media, but unlike him, they also control its expression. They're Truman on the inside, but on the outside they're Christof.

Weir, however, doesn't have any nostalgia for the fifties sitcom culture because, among other things, he never was a part of that *Ozzie and Harriet* generation. Neither, for that matter, was Niccol, the young screenwriter, who grew up in New Zealand. (He wrote and directed the highfalutin, futuristic *Gattaca*, which also was about a man escaping his destiny.) The film centers on a kind of leisure world of true-blue Americana, but there's a foreignness to what we see. Everything is so idealized that it's eerie.

That eeriness is basic to the movie's game plan. If there is a TV antecedent to *The Truman Show*, it's not *Ozzie and Harriet* but the Patrick McGoohan series *The Prisoner* and the messagey, Rod Serling-scripted *Twilight Zone* episodes. *The Truman Show* is a cautionary fable about the televisionization of life, but it draws on our own cozy familiarity with television.

Carrey is the perfect actor to play Truman because he has always seemed not quite flesh-and-bone. When he stretched like a slinky in *The Mask*, he was completely fulfilled as a performer; the Pepsodent smile exploded into a toothy terror, and he became larger-than-life. His elasticity gives him a rubberoid quality—he may be the closest thing to a human cartoon we've ever had in the movies. Carrey fits right into the spic-and-span spookiness of Seahaven because the community mirrors his own empty-shell screen persona. As a comic actor, Carrey plays off his (apparent) bright and shining normality. (It's what Steve Martin used to do.) His all-American, clean-cut features are a put-on. He's such a straight-arrow that he's a squiggly line.

I've always enjoyed Carrey in the movies, but there's something a bit unsettling about the way he turns himself into a curlicue. When Jerry Lewis, to whom he's often (inaccurately) compared, went into his rubber-man nutsiness, you weren't particularly jolted by the transformation because Lewis was pretty much zonked from the get-go. The same is true of a wild-man comic like Robin Williams, who starts out manic and just gets freakier the more he free-associates. Williams, in his manic mode, would have been the exact wrong actor to play Truman because Williams is the *comic* embodiment of what television can do to a person; he's like a great, big, buzzing squawk box pouring out the jumble from a thousand TV shows. Carrey's blandness—before he gets stretchy—is in some ways more suggestive of what television can do to you than Williams's fireworks displays.

Carrey incarnates the filmmakers' notions of the hollowness of TV. Truman only recognizes he has a soul when it becomes clear to him that, in effect, he's been robbed of it. He figures out that he was the first child to be legally adopted by a corporation, and that his parents, wife, and best friend (Noah Emmerich) are just actors hired to play their parts (like everybody else in Seahaven). And yet, on some level, these people really do care about Truman—more, perhaps, than they might if they were real friends and relatives. That's why the film is a horror comedy of a very peculiar sort. It doesn't set up its pretenders as malevolent beings. They're just doing their jobs.

Carrey must have recognized early in his career that there was something unsettling about his super clean-cut look. (He's a dead ringer for Darrin in *Bewitched*.) That's why he's always fiddling with it, stretching it. When he played the creepo in *The Cable Guy*, he turned off a lot of his usual audience because he wasn't playing nice. He was a cartoon, all right, but a dark one. The movie was a failure, commercially *and* critically, but it indicated Carrey was at least clued into what was disturbing about him.

He's the best thing about *The Truman Show*. He doesn't offer up evidence that he's about to deliver the definitive Hamlet of his generation, but what he does in this film is very subtle—he plays someone with all the heft of a hologram, then proceeds to give it weight. Even though we're way ahead of Truman every step of the way, and even though we're placed in the snooty position of looking askance at his middle-class banality, we never feel superior to *him*. That's a tribute to Carrey. With a less inventive actor in the part, we might have felt like we were watching a rube getting his comeuppance. We might have identified with Christof. There's still a hefty element of cruelty in the movie's agenda—we spend a lot of time watching Truman getting whacked by Fate—but Carrey brings us into a sympathy with the character. He doesn't make us squirm. Instead, we feel for him when he starts squirming.

So do the audiences watching his "show" in their living rooms and workplaces. They cheer him in his escape attempts and start up "Free Truman" rallies. It's not just that they love Truman; it's that his story has taken on the contours of high drama. It's an engineered scenario that has burst its bounds and become "real." His odyssey has everything—an Everyman hero, chases, suspense, "heart." (In a soppy subplot, Truman is provided with a girlfriend from his past who tries to wake him up to the artificial nature of his life.) And just in case his loyal fans want to relive earlier Truman life experiences, there's also the "Greatest Hits" videos.

The Truman Show gets glancingly into the way television series, especially "reality-based" ones, insinuate themselves into the dailiness of our lives. They become lifestyles for their audience. This is the function that movies used to serve in popular culture, but the intimacy of the TV medium is unbeatable—it brings people and events directly into our home and scales things down to a fine familiarity. In *Understanding Media,* Marshall McLuhan wrote, "The television audience participates in the inner life of the TV actor as fully as in the outer life of the movie star"—although most TV actors don't have much inner life.

Television also brings products directly into our lives. That's why it's such a great medium for the sell; the items put up for sale on-screen are, in a sense, *already* in our homes—they're right there, in our living rooms, gleaming back at us from the tube and waiting to be pulled in. *The Truman Show* makes this point rather too bluntly; all through Truman's televised life, we're privy to product plugs displayed front and center—beer labels, kitchen appliances, food brands. That's insidious, all right, but of course, in TV land, what's worse are the plugs you *don't* see coming.

The Truman Show comes along at a time when television is a particularly hot button to push. Everything from the O. J. Simpson extravaganza to the two Jerrys—Springer and Seinfeld—has been put forth by politicos as an example of how zombiefied we are by the box. If television—so the thinking goes—can unify the mass audience, then surely it also sets the woefully low tone for that audience's values. "Real" news has blurred into "real" events staged for the news—such as the recent incident in Los Angeles in which a man killed himself on the freeway for the delectation of the local eyewitness-news skycams. We've gone from thinking that television is a baby sitter, a timewaster, a magic carpet, a drug, to something far more unfathomed. In *The Truman Show,* television is like some mystical force—a death ray—that exists apart from its practitioners. Christof may be the deity of the piece, but ultimately he's only serving the force. Television is an alternate universe that has become our primary universe.

It might be useful to look back at the last movie to really lambaste the tube—the Paddy Chayefsky-scripted 1976 *Network,* which also zoomed through the zeitgeist. Like *The Truman Show*, *Network* provoked a lot of hand-wringing about the awfulness of television, but it was far more traditional in its attacks. Peter Finch's Howard Beale, the "Mad Prophet of the Airwaves," rallied his audiences against TV by delivering on-air sermons to his rapt followers.

Here's a sample:

> Television is not the truth. Television is a goddamn amusement park. It's a circus, a carnival, a traveling troupe of acrobats, storytellers, dancers, singers, jugglers, sideshow freaks, lion-tamers, football players. We're in the boredom-killing business so, if you want the truth, go to God, go to your guru, go to yourself because that's the only place you're going to find any truth.

Beale is in a long line of freaked-out movie messiahs who speak the "truth"—the latest incarnation is Warren Beatty's Senator Jay Bulworth in *Bulworth*, who lets it all hang out on television because he's too crazy to lie anymore and ends up a political hero and a sacrificial lamb. (Like Beale, he's finally assassinated for his troubles.) But Chayefsky also gives us William Holden's Max Schumacher, a deposed network news producer who doesn't need to be freaked to tell it like it is. His big kiss-off scene with Faye Dunaway's predatory child-of-the-media TV executive has "op-ed" stamped all over it. He calls her "television incarnate . . . indifferent to suffering, insensitive to joy." For her, he says, "all of life is reduced to the common rubble of banality. War, murder, death are the same as a bottle of beer." He tells her, "I'm real. You can't switch to another station."

The difference between *Network* and *The Truman Show* is that Chayefsky still had a soft spot for the good old days of television—presumably the so-called Fifties Golden Age, when he was writing original network dramas like *Marty*. There's a God hanging over *Network*, but it's not some Christof-like puppeteer—it's the spectre of Edward R. Murrow. Chayefsky's weepiness for the bygone greats kept him from totally trouncing the medium. It wasn't *television itself* that was the enemy, it was the people who had commandeered its power. He was partway to *The Truman Show* in that film when he has Beale say to his audience, "You're beginning to think the tube is reality and your own lives are unreal." In *The Truman Show*, the camouflage is complete. Christof says to an interviewer, "We accept the reality of the world we live in. It's as simple as that." But the movie's "reality" is created for the camera. You can run but you can't hide.

In its own mystic, ethereal way, *The Truman Show* is as dewy with sentimentality as *Network*. It says that the only person with the strength to fight back at the banalization of TV-induced life is the one man who is untainted by it—Truman the innocent. And, boy, is he innocent. There hasn't been a movie hero this wet behind the ears since Forrest Gump. He's practically infantilized. It's significant that Truman is never shown making love to his wife—it's difficult to imagine him doing so anyway. (The couple is childless.) If we are meant to identify with Truman, it's because he represents all of us before the fall—before we succumbed to television's siren song.

The Truman Show isn't saying anything that media critics haven't been complaining about for years. It's just saying it in a different, weirder key. TV has long been an all-purpose target for just about everything that's wrong with society. A movie that says it's all narcotizing and corrupt, that our lives have become indistinguishable from the shows we watch, is tonic for people looking for the easy way out. Even before its official release, the film has occasioned a lot of self-righteous posturing. After all, by pointing out the horrors of the tube, you are also implying that you are not fully taken in by them.

The film's take on television is rife with condescension—it's not so much holier-than-thou as holier-than-them. And yet, ironically, in order to be a hit, the film needs to connect with the very people to whom it condescends—for example, the planned-community, Middle American folks who look to a place like Seahaven for refuge. In general, the audiences for Truman, even when they are rallying him on, are shown to be a pretty lumpy lot. They are the consumers—the sponges—and they're fickle. When the Truman show finally goes off the air, they just want to know what else is on. Implicit in all this is a class bias that the filmmakers barely acknowledge. Usually when people talk about the ill effects of TV, what they often are really saying is that the mass audience is too stunted to ward off its whammies. Not so with us educated types. We know about stuff like post-modernism. We don't watch *The Jerry Springer Show* and the Home Shopping Network, we watch *Masterpiece Theatre*. We only watch the news for the news, not for the sensationalism. We can spot the ways in which television manipulates us.

But the real black comedy of media manipulation is that the marketeers and programmers use the so-called educated audience's cynicism about the process as part of the package. They *build in* our skepticism, so it's possible that such an audience is even more likely to be hoodwinked by TV's truth-and-reality games than the great unwashed. *The Truman Show* would have been a smarter and more accurate commentary if it wasn't so busy trying to flatter us about how smart we are. Really, we're not all that smart. Neither are the filmmakers. Their sappy version of a better life for Truman is right out of an old Frank Capra movie, and isn't on a much higher aesthetic plane than what they're attacking.

Hollywood movies don't often dabble in "ideas," so when one comes along, such as *The Truman Show*, it gets the state-of-the-union treatment. And yet I remember a movie from years back, Albert Brooks's 1979 *Real Life*, that said just about everything *The Truman Show* did and was a lot fizzier. Brooks played a pushy TV director who films a year-long documentary about a "real" family and ends up driving them and himself and everybody else crazy. The movie got into the wacked-out love/hate relationship we have with television—and the absurdity of making the "real" real.

Unlike *Real Life*, *The Truman Show* tries to educate us. Education is the essence of that deadweight genre, "the message movie," and despite its new-style flash, that's exactly the genre into which *The Truman Show* fits. The movie touches a nerve with people who feel guilty—but perhaps not *too* guilty—about soaking up tube time without actually *improving* themselves.

It touches another nerve as well. The omnipresence of the media has confirmed for many people a paranoid view of life. How can we keep track of all the nefarious conglomerate interconnections anymore? *The Truman Show*—financed by one of the world's largest corporate conglomerates—plays into a populist vogue that says we're all victims. Truman is our martyr. The film is a nightmare but an oddly comforting one. It absolves us of any responsibility to tune out the buzz—or turn off the tube. Probably most of us exiting *The Truman Show* will nod approvingly at its dire warnings, then go right home and switch on our favorite sitcom or tabloid talk show. And our souls will not perish in the process.

(*New Times*, 1998)

Pleasantville

In *Pleasantville*, two nineties teenagers from a broken suburban home are magically zapped by a Yoda-like television repairman (Don Knotts) into the black-and-white world of a fifties *Father Knows Best*-ish television sitcom, also called *Pleasantville*, which has spawned a cult following on cable TV. David (Tobey Maguire), smart and socially awkward, knows every bit of trivia about the show. He's smitten by the fifties—and not even the actual fifties but a pasty, idealized version of them. His twin sister, Jennifer (Reese Witherspoon), is a frisky crumpet. She's hooked on the here and now; that's where the action is.

It was bad enough when the doomsayers were indicting *The Jerry Springer Show* for hollowing out our souls. Now we've got to worry about Nick at Nite. What David and Jennifer discover in moving about the town of Pleasantville is that the ideal is not so ideal after all. Their brave new world is inhabited by dimensionless dweebs. Their Pleasantville parents, George (William H. Macy) and Betty (Joan Allen), are like Ozzie and Harriet with extra treacle. The high-school basketball star, Skip (Paul Walker), is strictly golly-gee. Chattering lassies and Brylcreemed boys swarm the screen.

It should all be nightmarish, but it isn't. Gary Ross, the screenwriter of *Dave* and (with Ann Spielberg) *Big,* making his directorial debut, isn't interested in doing a *Village of the Damned* number. The citizens of Pleasantville aren't hollow, exactly; they're more like empty vessels waiting to receive the light. Ross finds them poignant. Corseted by confectionary lives, they fumble toward freedom, and as they do, little smudges of color creep into their world. Some of these effects are quite lovely. Tears track down cheeks, leaving flesh tones in their glistening wake; flowers glow red and yellow in the pearly black-and-whiteness. For Ross, the goal is to get it all in color. That's his idea of a world viewed without blinders.

Which is not to say he's too starched for satire. He takes his share of potshots at these villagers. But his bent is one of messianic civic-mindedness—he's also dabbled in speechwriting for the Clinton administration—and he's on a mission here. He wants to do more than save souls. He wants to *invent* them. The un-people of Pleasantville learn that life is not always pleasant, and the realization humanizes them. Amen.

They learn that firemen exist to put out fires—not just to rescue treed cats. They experience a rain shower for the first time. They experience sex. They experience discrimination, too; the black-and-white townies heckle and pummel the "coloreds"—the people whose awakened emotions have literally turned them into living color—before the toughs, too, are transformed. The mayor (the late J. T. Walsh, in his last role) issues an official code of conduct that tries to turn back the clock. (Perry Como is in; Elvis on the jukebox is out.) Books, previously mere props filled with blank pages, are starting to fill up with words. We watch them heaped by angry demonstrators and torched. (Some of the titles: *Huckleberry Finn, The Catcher in the Rye.*)

Such ugliness, we are made to feel, is the price of freedom. But do we really need all this hoo-ha? Hauling in images of race brawls and book burnings collapses what might otherwise have been a frail, fragrant comedy about how our pop fantasies betray us. Yet even the theme of betrayal is suspect. Nobody—not even studio executives—actually mistakes *Father Knows Best* for the real world. Ross is subverting a discredited pop ideal. Worse, he wants to be hailed as a truth-teller for his troubles. *Pleasantville* is a prime piece of showbiz sentimentalism; it says that life isn't like Hollywood, yet its frame of reference is almost entirely Hollywood pap—and white, middle-class pap at that. It flatters itself that the peachy-keen sitcoms we sat through as kids—or that our kids sit through in cable-TV reruns—remain defining moments.

Ross wants us to break free from the deadening blandness of this communal upbringing. But his own imagination is often on the same mundane, fifties-sitcom plane. He doesn't bring anything into the mix that might truly jolt the agenda. We get no bulletins from the outside—no Korea, no HUAC, no nothing. The town's kids lap up Mark Twain all right, but we don't hear a thing about the outlawry of, say, Ginsberg or Kerouac or Mailer or Burroughs. The Elvis that we hear on the jukebox is doing "(Let Me Be Your) Teddy Bear"—Elvis at his coziest. Mr. Johnson (Jeff Daniels), the moonstruck soda jerk who pines to be an artist, has a yen for David's mom, Betty, and renders her nude. This is supposed to be shocking, taboo-busting, but his paint-by-the-numbers expressiveness is as cozy as "Teddy Bear." Even Jennifer, who heats up Skip with her grope-a-thons on Lovers' Lane, is chastened for our benefit. In the old movie tradition of bad-girls-gone-good, or sort of good, she ends up turning away from lust. Instead of coming out to play, she stays in her bedroom, claps on an unflattering pair of specs, and reads D. H. Lawrence. (Sublimation is all.)

There's a grandstanding, Capra-esque moment near the end of the movie when David, who has seen the light, exhorts the townspeople to embrace what is happening to them and not be afraid. Recognize the sexy and the dangerous, he sermonizes: "All these things are within yourself." This child of TV has come full circle. No more reruns for him. From now on, it's all first-run.

Is anybody likely to feel liberated watching this film? Ross wants change—just not too much. If he had followed the logic of his own conceit and allowed things to get *really* funky, *Pleasantville* might have turned into another *Twin Peaks*. David wants people to embrace within themselves the sexy and the dangerous, but the way Ross sets it up, there's no place for that sex and danger to thrive. The film pays lip service to emotional liberation without really allowing for its consequences. It's just a Norman Rockwell portrait with a somewhat racier palette. The actors, trying their damnedest to give their roles some lyricism, end up frozen on the canvas.

Pleasantville is the latest movie to thwack television for poisoning our marrow. After *The Truman Show*, everyone is probably sick of the whole discussion, but here we go again. What's up with all of this? It wasn't so long ago, after all, that Hollywood started churning out affectionate big-screen versions of old TV shows—everything from *The Addams Family* to *The Flintstones*. (The boomers running the studios are reliving their childhoods by fobbing off their favorite thumb-suckers on the rest of us.) Could *Pleasantville* and *The Truman Show* be Hollywood's make-nice response to the attacks leveled against it by politicos for befouling our minds with gratuitous sex and carnage? Publicly the moguls have groused, but privately there has been much wringing of hands. Don't forget—the flip side of Hollywood's errant crassness is an arrant social consciousness. Bigger even than winning the Nobel Peace Prize is copping the Jean Hersholt Humanitarian Award on Oscar night. *Pleasantville* scores well on this playing field; it's positively *clogged* with social consciousness. It wants to make us better citizens by pulling us out of the fantasy machine.

And it does so by turning itself into a massive mea culpa. The film is an apology for the ways in which show business mesmerizes us with false hope. It's saying that if we are disappointed by life, we should look to the shows we grew up on and pay heed. It takes a real movie-colony mind-set to root the world and its problems in the boiler room of the dream factory. Still, Ross could be onto something; maybe people soaked in pop culture are increasingly looking for an all-purpose pop-culture explanation for why everything has turned out so lousily. As explanations go, this sort of thing makes a superficial kind of sense, and it's more fun to play around with than Marxism or Freudianism or just about any other ism. Just think—you can watch *Ozzie and Harriet* reruns *and* bemoan the sick soul of America at the same time. Or you can take yourself to see *Pleasantville*.

(*New York*, 1998)

Passion Ploy:
The Passion of the Christ

Mel Gibson's *The Passion of the Christ* bears the same relation to other biblical epics as a charnel house does to your local deli. To say that it's the bloodiest story ever told is an understatement; rarely has so much red stuff flowed in *any* movie. To some extent, I was prepared; Gibson's *Braveheart*, in which he played thirteenth-century Scottish rebel William Wallace, ends with Wallace's interminably tortuous demise on the rack—a warm-up, both emotionally and stylistically, for Christ's martyrdom in *The Passion*. But, before the Crucifixion, we are treated, in fetishistic detail, to nearly two hours of scourging and flaying. By the time Jesus is nailed to the Cross, you may be too numb to care. No doubt Gibson intends all this gore as a testament to his uncompromising faith; he's compelled to show us the horrors that other Christ-themed movies downplay. But I didn't leave *The Passion*—which is about the last twelve hours in the life of Jesus, with dialogue delivered in Latin and Aramaic—believing I had witnessed a movie made by a man of great spiritual gifts. Gibson's fervor, it seems to me, belongs as much to the realm of sado-masochism as to Christian piety.

It isn't just the violence that is overplayed. There is so much creepy-Gothic Sturm and Drang in *The Passion* that at times it seems as if Clive Barker should get credit for the story along with Matthew, Mark, Luke, and John. Jesus is played by James Caviezel, who looks like a bearded, beatific Sam Waterston before his wounds render him unrecognizable. In the film's first scene, in Gethsemane, where Jesus has gone to pray after the Last Supper, we are introduced to a shape-shifting, androgynous Satan and a doomy, clamorous score more appropriate to *Pirates of the Caribbean*. After Jesus is brought before the Pharisees and accused by the high priest Caiaphas (Mattia Sbragia) of blasphemy for believing himself to be the Messiah, the movie becomes less Gothic and more like a religioso WrestleMania smackdown. The jeering Roman soldiers under the control of Pilate (Hristo Naumov Shopov), governor of Palestine, are so cartoonishly brutal that they seem to be firing themselves up to enter the steel cage. Big, broad strokes—that's Gibson's forte.

Pilate is the only character besides Jesus whom the film presents with any nuance; as PR for the prefect, *The Passion* could hardly be better. Going beyond what is written in the Gospels, not to mention what is in stark contrast to Roman histories of the era, this Pilate is torn about what to do with Jesus. Counseled by his wife (Claudia Gerini)—at one point, he asks her, "What is truth? Can you tell me?"—he tries to save Jesus from the Jewish mob; he even hands Jesus over to Herod (Luca de Dominicis) in the hope that the problem will just go away. This proves a dead end, since Herod, portrayed as a mincing queen, doesn't take the bait. ("Work a little miracle for me?" he coyly asks the would-be Messiah.) It turns out that this powerful prefect has no choice but to accede to the wishes of Caiaphas and the other rabbis—even though it was they who served Pilate, who had sole power to execute. The way Gibson and his co-screenwriter, Benedict Fitzgerald, tell it, Jesus is maneuvered to the Cross by high priests who prey upon Pilate's fear of Caesar's retribution should rebellion break out. The Romans inflict unimaginable agonies upon Jesus, but behind it all is Caiaphas's bland smirk; he doesn't get his hands dirty. Caiaphas even shows up for the main event at Golgotha, presumably to keep an eye on things—a detail that somehow got by all four apostles.

Is *The Passion* the work of an anti-Semite? Far be it for me to cast aspersions on such an ardent fan of those sons of Israel, Moe, Larry, and Curly. Still, in the September 15, 2003, *New Yorker*, Gibson claimed that "modern secular Judaism wants to blame the Holocaust on the Catholic

Church." He belongs to a splinter sect of Catholicism that rejects the Second Vatican Council, which reconciled Christians and Jews and said that "the Jews should not be presented as rejected or accursed by God, as if this followed from the Holy Scriptures."

The Passion is not about reconciliation. You might never get the idea from it that Pilate slaughtered Judeans by the thousands for sport. Still, as Passion plays go, the movie doesn't fulfill one's worst expectations. Gibson financed the $25 million film himself and is heavily promoting it as a vehicle for Christian outreach. He doesn't turn the Romans into "fall goys" (in the immortal words of the late Dwight Macdonald). But he is also careful to plunk into the story various Jews who are sympathetic to Jesus, including a few dissenters in the high priests' temple and a weeping young mother on the road to Golgotha.

Nevertheless, the engine of this movie is not passion but anger. When Gibson flashes back to the Sermon on the Mount, Jesus's words about loving those who hate you come across as oddly hollow, since there is so much unmitigated hate in the movie. Even the Pietà frieze near the end is curiously unfeeling. The horrors in *The Passion* cry out for vengeance, just as they did in Gibson's *Mad Max* and *Lethal Weapon* movies. The film ends with Christ's Resurrection. *Get thee behind me, Satan*!

It is, of course, unfair to expect Mel Gibson to give us an artistic expression of the Passion on par with, say, Bach's or Grünewald's. And I (almost) prefer his bloodbath to the prim reverence of a movie like George Stevens's *The Greatest Story Ever Told*, with cameos by everyone from John Wayne to Ed Wynn. But *The Passion*, as much because of its controversies as in spite of them, is likely to be seen all over the world by people thirsting for spiritual connection. The real damage will not, I think, be in the realm of Jewish-Christian relations, at least not in this country. Anti-Semites don't need an excuse to be anti-Semites. The damage will be to those who come to believe that Gibson's crimson tide, with its jacked-up excruciations, is synonymous with true religious feeling.

(New York, 2004)

Neo-Noir

Los Angeles is the city where you go to lose your past and create your future. It remains so despite the cataclysms of the past few years. It's Makeover City, which is probably why it's always been a Xanadu for con artists, and for artists, too—the distinction in L.A. is not always clear. It's a place where you feel as if you're on the lam even if you stay put for thirty years. You're on the lam but you still want to look good. The sunlight is an emollient; it makes you feel burnished, rich, favored.

Film noir, with all its poignant, wronged dupes and inky femmes fatales, has an enduring appeal in the movie capital. From before *Double Indemnity* right past *The Grifters*, it's a genre that is seemingly at odds with the city from which it slinks. If, in the popular imagination, sun-embossed Los Angeles is all future and no past, film noir is speckled with night creatures who are all past and no future.

Film noirs aren't set only in L.A., though it certainly helps. Noirs set in New York, like, say, *Sea of Love*, always seem redundant—the city is too menacing to act as a backdrop to the menace in the foreground. Noirs don't even have to be urban, though that helps too; their landscape for murder is best outfitted in concrete. The new cycle of contemporary rural noirs, like John Dahl's *Red Rock West* and, for the most part, *The Last Seduction*, are tart downers. Urban noirs set up the countryside as a moo-cow place of refuge—if only as a place to expire in peace. The rural variants close off even that possibility. Corruption has gummed up the hinterlands, too. There *is* no refuge.

But wherever noirs take place, just about all of them are concocted in L.A. They take place in an L.A. of the mind, where the streets are often rain-slicked and the after-hours action reaches toward dawn, where men wear trench coats and black jackets and black ties and women with high-maintenance black lipstick are armored in form-fitting sheaths.

The classic noir plot is about passion as descent—a hard-boiled softy is pulled down to his doom by a born-to-be-bad temptress. But noir is just as easily defined by its enameled fragments of style, its Kabuki. Noir is about guns pulled out of desk drawers, ceiling fans, blackmail photos, cigarettes, jukeboxes, shattered wedding photos, black widows, voice-over narration that sounds like it was recorded at 3:00 AM in an all-night diner, fingerprints, penthouses, a pair of eyes in a rearview mirror. The buzz of a motel sign is a clue to the mood. Noir is, finally, about being trapped, and the patterns of entrapment are depicted in near-abstract visuals. Characters are rendered as half-shadowed, almost sculptural forms; the glow of a street light through venetian blinds registers as ghostly prison bars on the sodden, aghast face peering through the window.

When noir becomes unmoored from its usual strictures it can still function as noir if the mood is voluptuous enough; *Batman* and *Blade Runner* and *The Crow* could qualify. Color noirs like *Chinatown*—or just about any noir made from the sixties onward—still partake of the darkness. There's something unseemly, almost fetishistic, about the play of light and dark. Characters are tattooed in shadow. Noir lives seem to be taking place in the interrogative glare of a police lamp.

In film noir, the subject proceeds from the look. Noir, in other words, is a species of fashion. Its characters are forever modeling in an infernal pageant about money, sex, and death. And perhaps noir is increasingly fashionable now because, as an antidote to the in-your-face tabloid horrors that push at us from all sides, we yearn for depravity with a bit of the moderne to it. We want the stuff of noir that's been co-opted by the scandal sheets and the talk shows and Court TV to be reclaimed by the conventions of forties pulp. We want it to be nasty *fun* again. Noir represents a safe retroism—antiqued by rules as rigorous as those of chivalric poetry—and it's stylish, too.

But fashions—in clothes or politics or pop—don't hang around for very long these days; everything is in a postmodern flip-flop. The Beats and the Atomic Age and hard rock and rap are cross-wired with forties sultriness and fifties va-va-voom. A glib neo-noir like Quentin Tarantino's *Pulp Fiction* heats up the jumble; it Mixmasters pierced body parts and Hawaiian shirts and Armani jackets and fifties diners and a soundtrack of surf hits and boomer faves. The short-attention-span generation has evolved its own aesthetic—impermanence is permanence.

Noir—traditional noir, anyway—attempts permanence another way, by reaching for the archetypal. (*Archetypal*, replacing *mythic*, has become the latest Hollywood buzzword.) Directors, particularly the younger, film-school set, don't know what to do with the times, so they retreat to timelessness. John Dahl remarked in an interview: "If someone watched *Red Rock West* and thought it was made ten or twenty years ago, I'd be thrilled." Timelessness is classic.

Los Angeles, with its prefab impermanence, is a city forever in search of the classic. In pop-culture terms, Hollywood movies have provided L.A. with its only hallowed text, and within it the film noir occupies pride of place. Noir isn't really so at odds with its city. They need each other. Where better to set off such sleek anomie than in the wonderland where, if you're lucky enough to hit with a script or get a record deal, if you land a series or get discovered, you can all at once vault your crummy life and become a pop pasha? Fast-track L.A. and film noirs both hinge on fate, but in the films the fate all runs downhill (everything always ends up worse than it started). Few noirs flatter the city. What we most often see are the back alleys and dingy offices and nondescript streets. The ocean is there only to remind us of the end of the line. Penthouses are aeries from which to view the glittering rot below. It's paradise nixed.

Noir may be a classic, but even classics have their season. The movie cycle, with its roots in the pulps, began in the early forties—*The Maltese Falcon* is the first celebrated example—and stretched unbroken through the mid-fifties, with brutal scaldathons like *The Big Heat* and *Kiss Me Deadly*. The genre's trademark expressionism was largely an imported pleasure; many of the best noir filmmakers, like Billy Wilder, Fritz Lang, Robert Siodmak, and Otto Preminger, were Austrian or German immigrants to Hollywood in the thirties. (There's a lot of Weimar in noir.) The term "film noir" is an imported pleasure, too, coined after World War II by Hollywood-steeped French film critics.

The cycle was set up in the late thirties, when Hollywood movies were still marinating in post-Depression funk and fatalism. Then the war years came along and pasted over the national scowl with patriotic bumper stickers. The postwar flourishing of noir was a rebuke to all the enforced uplift. In a world where edgy servicemen didn't really know the wives or girlfriends they were returning to (and vice versa), noir secured a terrain where men deeply distrusted women. In a climate where prosperity was suspect, noir assumed—Balzac was right—that behind every great fortune was a great crime.

The sixties and early seventies were a noir dry gulch. Those years thrived on a flamboyant, free-form alienation, whereas, in the best noirs, the alienation is encrypted in the style. Recently—with titles both famous and obscure, like *Bad Influence, Malice, Final Analysis, Basic Instinct, Body of Evidence, China Moon, Dream Lover,* and *Color of Night,* in addition to Dahl's films and Tarantino's first feature, *Reservoir Dogs*—noir has been on the upswing because of circumstances strikingly similar to those of its heyday. Post-Vietnam funk, Reagan-Bush feel-goodism, the smudging of sex roles, AIDS, the recession—a brewmaster for neo-noir could not hope for a yeastier mix for fear and loathing.

Noir, for all its taint and shadow play, is obsessed with purity. The fated noir hero, from Raymond Chandler on, has always carried a princely nimbus. But all that Philip Marlowe stuff ("who is not himself mean, who is neither tarnished nor afraid") has its reactionary side, too. In the current, raging sexual arena, noirs play out a man's worst wimpy self-image. For men, noirs feed the fear that you're not a tough guy but a taken guy. You're soft in the head. Women are beastly; their tears are vitriol. The men in noirs tend to be slack and damaged, but the femmes fatales—think of Kathleen Turner in *Body Heat* or Anjelica Huston in *The Grifters*—are intimidatingly sky-high goddesses. The noir femme fatale is Hollywood's response to the feminist rant about why there aren't stronger roles for women. The answer is: maybe sharky Hollywood producers don't care for strong women unless they're deadly. Besides, smart-cookie women have always loved noirs. The avenging vamp is far from their worst self-image—there's too much sex in it.

Noir is vehemently un-PC and anti-feel-good, and this is another clue to its enduring guilty-pleasure appeal. The guilt lies in our recognition that hate is a pretty exciting—a pretty sexy—emotion. Noir luxuriates in the effrontery of the obvious. If you look bad, you are bad. Dames are bad. Obesity is heinous; the rich are rotters. Noir cuts to the reactionary quick. (For all that, noir has always been one of the few genres that explicitly recognize, if only for the purposes of plot, the existence of a class system in America.) Its cast of characters is limited. Los Angeles is the great modern American melting pot, but, except for Tarantino, few of the neonoir filmmakers admit Latinos, blacks, or Asians into their movies (not even as bad guys). It's a convenient never-never land, like the Universal Citywalk, a mall where locals and tourists can dawdle and buy gew-gaws in a riot-free zone of totalitarian spic-and-span. How come no one has come up with NoirWorld?

In a way, Los Angeles already has its NoirWorld. It's right there in the cheap-chic neo-noir look on Melose Avenue and Hollywood Boulevard, in the coffee shops and in the burgeoning blues clubs. The cutting edge Xers of Hollywood are into a kind of fringy, baby-noir getup—lots of black and white and sunglasses.

How much of this look derives from films? Hollywood movies no longer are central to the lives of high-school and college kids in the way that, say *Saturday Night Fever* or *The Graduate* were. Rock and rap have almost entirely assumed this defining function. (For twentysomethings, it's much hipper now to rent an old black-and-white Hollywood movie than to see a big new one.) But a few of the flukier hits, from directors like David Lynch, Tim Burton, John Waters, and Gus Van Sant, still make a connection on the style level. They're fringe hits for the fringe-youth mass audience.

The neo-noir look on the L.A. streets is the uniform from the fringe hit *Reservoir Dogs*, with its gallery of clueless hommes fatales. Instead of the big shoulders and double-pleated pants from the forties, it's a late-fifties, early-sixties thing: high-buttoned black suit, black tie, white shirt, shades. The Xers sporting this style are noir's missing link. If there had been any noir heroes in the Kennedy era, they would have looked like this.

The look is anonymous, thrifty, and rebellious—but not *too* rebellious. After all, these Xers are less interested in tearing down the middle class than becoming it. So it's a black-and-white look that works high and low. You can go from thrift threads to Armani without ever having to warp your personal style.

The female Xers of Hollywood are caught up in a complementary noir-o-rama. The fifties lingerie look, the peignoirs and corsets and Wonderbras, plays off the contempo coffee-bar look, with its black nail polish, black lipstick, black jackets. Why, even hot young L.A. blondes are dyeing their hair black!

The over-inflated fatalism that was always the lifeblood of noir has seeped into the Xers. Feeling powerless, they convert black-and-white blankness into something alienating and hip. It's a taunt, a joke—the "empty" generation is flaunting its emptiness.

But these kids also care deeply how they come across; they connect with the adolescent romanticism inside their pose. And that's part of noir, too. It's all about caring while pretending not to. The baby-noir Xers are touchingly up-front about their anomie. They can't hide it so they turn it into an emblem. They've instinctively grasped the essence of L.A., which is also the essence of film noir. It's the place where your identity and your secret identity are joined.

(Esquire Gentleman, 1995)

Thelma and Louise

"You've always been crazy," says Susan Sarandon's Louise to Geena Davis's Thelma just after her friend holds up a convenience store. "This is just the first chance you've had to express yourself."

In a movie year not notable for its *oomph* and controversy, the new Ridley Scott film *Thelma and Louise,* written by Callie Khouri, has been riling up audiences into a love-it-or-hate-it lather. As rigged and goofy and problematic as it is, the film has struck an exposed nerve.

It starts out innocently enough. The two friends set out for a weekend fishing trip—Louise to escape her waitressing, Thelma her creep-o husband. It kicks into gear at a honky-tonk stop-over in Arkansas, where Louise fends off the attempted rape of her friend by offing the lout with a .38-caliber pistol. On the run across three states, they turn into self-styled feminist vigilantes.

Women are supposed to deplore violence in the movies, but a lot of women seem to be charged up by this film. Is it because the tables have turned? Could it be that violence is okay as long as the object of that violence is appropriately scummy? In *Thelma and Louise,* retribution is all.

Thelma and Louise isn't the only recent movie where women have been "expressing" themselves. In *Mortal Thoughts,* directed by Alan Rudolph and scripted by William Reilly and Claude Kerven, Demi Moore's Cynthia and Glenne Headly's Joyce are, like Thelma and Louise, best friends implicated in the murder of a creep—in this case Joyce's husband James, played by Bruce Willis at his burbliest. The new Blake Edwards comedy *Switch* begins with the drowning/shooting of a flagrant yuppie Romeo by his three on-a-string main squeezes.

Even the French cinema, where women are most often exhibited as demure objets d'art, has hit it big in this country with Luc Besson's *La*

Femme Nikita, where a feral beauty expends a fair amount of her screen time plugging holes into people. Hollywood is now talking about a remake.

Women do not often get the opportunity to project strength in the movies, or to be physically threatening. When they have any significant role at all—a rarity right now—it's more likely to occur within the boundaries of moral or emotional heroism, as embattled single mothers (*Men Don't Leave*) or courtroom lawyers (*Class Action* and *The Music Box*). But the more photogenic brands of heroism and anti-heroism—shoot-outs, firefights and destructo derbies—occupy most of the current action movies. And in these movies women have, at best, decorated the fringes of the frame.

When women have been allowed to demonstrate grit and physical courage, it is usually in cryptomale action roles, like Sigourney Weaver as the intergalactic big bad mama in *Aliens,* or Jamie Lee Curtis as the terrorized cop in *Blue Steel,* or, lower down the food chain, in Amazonian folderol like *Red Sonja.* Some of these movies get a comic charge from their take-no-prisoners femaleness, but there's something closed-off and stunt-like about the heroism they project. They probably satisfy men's fantasies far more than women's. Corseted and cartoonish, these heroines can toy with the male audience's unexpressed desire to be sexually overpowered, because men aren't required to take them "seriously" as women.

It's a sick joke that actresses can only assume dominant roles now by co-opting male action parts that, in many cases, aren't worth playing anyway. Where is the glory in being the female Arnold Schwarzenegger or Bruce Willis? The alternative for gutsy actresses is very often to play murderesses and vipers, like Anjelica Huston in *The Grifters,* Glenn Close in *Fatal Attraction* and Ellen Barkin in *Sea of Love.* As exciting as many of these performances are, they all derive from a pulpy, thriller mind-set where women are warped by their psychosexual tensions into *femme fatale* destroyers.

The other type of female destructiveness, as demonstrated in movies like *Sleeping With the Enemy* and *Silence of the Lambs,* comes in response to male psycho craziness. It's a standard-issue fun-house formula—the terrorized woman finally routs the bogeyman. The violence is eroticized, which is a dead giveaway as to what's really going in these movies. The pay-back is a form of sexual release, just as the action leading up to it is a weirdo form of foreplay.

One of the distinguishing characteristics of a new-style female marauder movie like *Thelma and Louise* is that the violence in it isn't eroticized. In this film, and, to a lesser extent, in *Mortal Thoughts,* what we're seeing is a sort of post-feminist howl. The expectations of feminism have gone bust, and in its place is a righteous, self-immolating fury. The women in these movies reinforce each other's rage toward men; they trade on the cruelty men have shown toward them. In the process, they willingly sacrifice themselves.

Movies like *Thelma and Louise* and *Mortal Thoughts* are pumped with feminist mythology and chockablock with macho straw men. Neither of these pictures has a single sympathetic male—well, just one, perhaps, played as a police investigator in both movies by Harvey Keitel. The Land of Louts game plan functions like fast-read feminism.

Most outlaw-on-the-run movies, especially the famous ones, like *Bonnie and Clyde* and *Badlands,* have also pushed a social agenda; they've tried to implicate America in the characters' moral sickness. It's part of the appeal (and the danger) of movies that so often these outlaws also end up glamorized. In *Thelma and Louise,* the glamour of the Davis-Sarandon pairing is part of the polemic; their ability to magnetize men is crucial to the film's storyline. They are also virtually the only women that we see of any significance, all the better to reinforce the us-against-them agenda.

The agenda is scrupulously detailed. Thelma's husband is a jerky crank, who, when he finally gets a call from his errant wife, is more interested in the football game on TV. Louise's boyfriend seems like a decent sort, but he doesn't recognize her pain, and ultimately he betrays her; the stud drifter (Brad Pitt) who gives Thelma the night of her life in a motel room ends up betraying her, too. Zipping down the interstate in Louise's green 1966 Thunderbird, the women keep crisscrossing a trucker who jiggles his tongue at them; they retaliate by leading him on and then nonchalantly blowing up his truck. (Freud would have a field day with the way that long sleek truck is photographed.) Staring down the muzzle of Louise's .38-caliber, a brusque highway patrolman who has flagged the women for speeding ends up a whimpering simp locked into the trunk of his squad car. Even the details you catch out of the corner of your eye are prejudicial, like the shot of the FBI man killing time by reading *Boudoir* magazine. (The shot isn't played for laughs.)

By setting the movie in Arkansas, Oklahoma, and Texas, the site of innumerable man's man Westerns, the filmmakers seem to be gleefully plunking the outlaw women down in enemy territory. By implication, the whole country is enemy territory; women aren't safe anywhere, not even in the wide open spaces. When Thelma wants to go to the police after Louise plugs her attacker, Louise can't believe her naiveté. "We don't live in that kind of world," she says, as if the police would actually believe her side of the story.

If the movie had been structured around Louise—wised-up, slightly blowzy, still branded by the ravages of her own rape years earlier—the movie would lack shock value. Louise we could expect violence from. But Thelma is deliberately presented to us as a fun-loving ditz, so her gun-toting transformation carries an extra measure of symbolism. Unlike Louise, Thelma is the kind of woman men are programmed to take advantage of; she blames herself for the ruckus she causes. If Thelma can strike back, the film is saying, then women's rage is total. She's plucked the last straw and set fire to it.

In *Thelma and Louise,* the women are in the driver's seat, and the men along the roadside are relegated to the kind of piddling cameos that the women used to inhabit. For those who respond to it at all, the film is being enjoyed as a rich joke at the expense of the male actioneers who rule Hollywood's roost. It's a sisterhood bash-a-thon.

But the film may not be as far removed from the "woman's film" genre as you might think. Like *Mortal Thoughts, Thelma and Louise* does not inhabit the decorous middle-class world of the classic woman's film, which means that the women's rejection of their surroundings can be more easily accepted by the mass audience; there are fewer material comforts at stake. And it's worth mentioning that Thelma and Louise are both conveniently childless.

Still, *Thelma and Louise* harbors some of the same sentimentalities as the weepies. Both scenarios exalt sacrifice. In the *Back Street* or *Stella Dallas* scenario, the woman sacrifices herself for her lover, her family, her child. In *Thelma and Louise,* the two women sacrifice themselves like winged angels for their freedom. Hounded by men literally to the edge of doom, they take flight.

Given the dinky, subordinate role of most actresses in our movies, and given their rage at being blockaded in their craft, a movie like *Thelma and Louise* was inevitable. It plugs into not only the anger and frustrations of women working in Hollywood, but also their larger frustrations in society.

But is this movie really something to celebrate as a trendsetter? *Thelma and Louise* is graced with the kinds of small details about women's lives lacking in male action movies, and that, as much as anything else, may account for its popularity with women. (Men can enjoy it as a masochistic joy ride.) But, as drama, it's just about as vague and negligent as any macho shoot-'em-up. The womens' descent into the outlaw life has no psychological horror; the film *commemorates* the fact that their anti-male mayhem turns them on. Imagine how different the film's tone would be if Thelma or Louise had accidentally plugged a woman.

Women have as much right to their road-movie shoot-'em-ups as men, but that doesn't negate the overheard comment of one woman as she left the theater after the screening: "I liked it, but women are different. Why not a different story?"

If the success of *Thelma and Louise* means we're in for a rash of female outlaw movies, that shouldn't be interpreted as a feminist step up, any more than the rash of pusher/pimp roles in the so-called black-exploitation movie era indicated an honest dramatic depiction of black life in America. If the only way a woman can light up the screen these days is with a .38-caliber pistol, isn't that just another form of subordination?

(*Los Angeles Times*, 1991)

The People vs. Larry Flynt

The People vs. Larry Flynt is a Hollywood rags-to-riches success story with a twist. The recipient of the American Dream is a pornographer who admits to losing his virginity at eleven to a chicken and is known for saying things such as, "A woman's vagina has as much personality as her face."

But Larry Flynt (Woody Harrelson) also won an important Supreme Court victory in 1988 expanding the reach of the First Amendment, which is presumably why a movie has been made about him. I say presumably because I don't think the film's wiseass jocularity reflects a deep concern for our free-speech rights. The director, Milos Forman, has been quoted as saying that the hero of the piece is the Supreme Court, not Flynt, but that's not how it comes across. When at one of his many obscenity trials Flynt says, "All I'm guilty of is bad taste," we're meant of giggle in agreement.

Flynt's saga is tailor-made for hipper-than-thou libertarians. As the head of the *Hustler* empire, he purveyed porn a full notch raunchier than *Playboy* or *Penthouse*, and, because he supposedly appealed to blue-collar readers—his crotch shots were wider and his cartoons grungier—he could be hailed as a porno populist. In fact, *Hustler* had a higher newsstand price than those magazines, with an average reader's income of $50,000—but hey, populism doesn't come cheap. When his obscenity trials started getting national attention, Flynt acquired a civil-libertarian cachet. He wrapped himself in the flag—literally, using it as a diaper in one of his trials—while also grabbing his crotch. It's the American way.

The People vs. Larry Flynt, which has a spotty, often sharp script by Scott Alexander and Larry Karaszewski, plays up the high-flying American-ness of Flynt's weirdo saga. Running moonshine as a boy in Kentucky, he graduated to running go-go dance joints in Cincinnati and parlayed a sleazoid newsletter into *Hustler*, which hit the big time when Flynt published paparazzi nudie shots of Jackie O. Over the years he spent $40 million defending himself against everybody from Charles Keating (James Cromwell) to Jerry Falwell (Richard Paul), whom Flynt riled in a mock Campari ad in *Hustler* that described how the Moral Majority leader lost his virginity in an outhouse—to his mother. (This was the free speech that the Supreme Court ultimately upheld in 1988.)

Flynt also hooked up with Althea Leasure (Courtney Love), a seventeen-year-old bisexual stripper in one of his Cincinnati clubs who went on to marry him and help manage his empire. When Flynt was shot by a fanatic outside a Georgia courthouse in 1978—rendering him wheelchair-bound for life—it was Althea's idea to put a photo spread of Flynt's wounds into *Hustler*. Althea and Larry both entered a pain-killer twilight zone; but, while he kicked his habit, she stayed hooked, contracted HIV, overdosed in her bath.

Consider Flynt's self-made pasha's privileges, his martyrdom at the hands of an assassin, his abiding love for Althea, his brief fling with born-again Christianity, his poster-boy status in the Free Speech wars—I mean, could you devise a better hero's résumé for the superannuated counterculture? Woody Harrelson plays Flynt like a wily hillbilly dizzy with his own lewd good fortune. At first he doesn't connect up with the "socially redeeming" side of his legal battles; he's a pornographer and proud of it. But Flynt slowly takes on the trappings of respectability; as time goes on, his raps about free speech become a shade less self-serving. The pitchman begins to believe his own pitch. Even his scuzziness acquires a righteous glow—"If they'll protect a scumbag like me," he announces after his Supreme Court victory, "then they'll protect all of you."

The film allows us to buy into Flynt's self-righteousness and still get our rocks off. In a way, what Forman and his screenwriters are doing is a new-style variation on the old DeMille biblical epic syndrome—tickle us with depravity and then denounce it. Only here they tickle us with raunchiness and then canonize it. *The People vs. Larry Flynt* is an Oliver Stone production, and it has the same two-faced gusto as some of the films he's directed himself. (No, see, we're not *glorifying* violence in *Natural Born Killers*, we're *condemning* it.) Actually, the film could use *more* gusto—if Stone had directed *Larry Flynt* it might have been a marvel of bad-taste outrageousness. Forman is a bit too tactful, too measured. He's making a movie about someone who lacks the ability to censor himself, but Forman doesn't pop his own id out of the genie's bottle. There's a square hipsterism at work in *Larry Flynt*. It's a movie about the *Hustler* king made by people who appear to have never taken a close look at *Hustler*. The choral strains that lilt the soundtrack during the closing credits are not intended ironically.

Neither is a sequence like the one in which Flynt stages a Fourth of July free speech rally and stands Patton-like before a huge American flag. Flynt is a blowhard joker in this sequence, but when we see a video montage of atrocities from the concentration camps, Vietnam, Klan lynchings, the film gets into black-comic areas it's too callow to handle. These images take us out of the movie. I realize a political point is being made here—in totalitarian states it's the pornographers who get rousted first. And Forman, whose parents died in the camps, surely understands the gravity of what he's showing us. But there's still something sleazy about the way Flynt co-opts these horrifying images in order to justify his good ol' boy raunch. The filmmakers, for libertarian reasons and because they admire his kick-ass style, are so solidly on Flynt's side that they don't think to scorch him for this stunt.

There's also something a little sleazy—hypocritical—about showing us glimpses of death camps but keeping us away from full-scale *Hustler* smut. Sony, the distributor of *Larry Flynt*, apparently doesn't share Flynt's quaint notion that sex sells—they don't risk an NC-17 rating. If we saw some of Flynt's more fetid handiwork, we might be less inclined to cheer him.

As Flynt's chief lawyer, Edward Norton stands in for us when he tells the porn king, "I don't particularly like what you do," adding, of course, "You represent something bigger." (A bigger paycheck for sure; $40 million in lawsuits make one hell of a meal ticket.) Later on we hear Flynt intone, "I would like to be remembered for something meaningful." Like this movie? (The real Flynt, looking as gelatinous as Jabba the Hut, has a cameo as a judge presiding over an early obscenity trial.) When *Larry Flynt* is in its low-down high-minded mode, it's like a Stanley Kramer socially conscious drama for pseudo-hipsters. The film is much better— much more original—when it embraces the looniness at the heart of this all-American saga.

There's a crackpot porno poetry, for example, in Flynt and Althea's courtship rites. She proposes to him in a postorgy hot tub, and they both have to reassure the other that marriage doesn't mean monogamy. It's a funhouse-mirror romance; love means never turning away multiple partners. Courtney Love brings out Althea's sly, slurry sensuality, the way she seems ready at any time to mount just about anything—animal, vegetable, or mineral. Later on, when she's in her drug haze and her hair resembles a rainbow mop, she vamps about Flynt's L.A. mansion like a sleepless Scheherazade.

Flynt's scenes with evangelist Ruth Carter Stapleton are another screw-loose high point. As played by Donna Hanover (the wife of New York City mayor Rudolph Giuliani!), Stapleton comes across as an ardent cipher. She tells Flynt, "We're both trying to release people from sexual repression," and you almost believe her. She's hypnotically vacuous. The filmmakers don't really take a position on whether they think Stapleton is a phony, but the joke is even funnier for that—Flynt the con artist is conned by a higher power. For a time he's born again, sort of—his mix of religion and porn in the pages of *Hustler* runs to stuff such as photo spreads of Adam and Eve.

Larry Flynt feels like tarted-up sixties vaudeville. That's both good and bad. Its sixties-style mix of sex and drugs and politics is livelier than what we're used to now, but like many of that era's gonzo extravaganzas, it runs out of steam. Irreverence only carries you so far. And so *Larry Flynt*, after a rollicking first hour, bogs down in Althea's extended druggie aria (Love's performance also bogs down). Flynt's repeated obscenity trials become a big bog too—it's like watching one of Lenny Bruce's later routines, when he tried to roust us with legalisms. Harrelson is fun in the beginning, in the strip joints, with his sky-blue suits and primped hair—he has a great lewd smile he never loses. But he doesn't have the stamina or the watchability to keep us hooked on Flynt through his many incarnations. He's a quick-change artist who keeps changing into the same suit.

If the best parts of the movie have a Terry Southern-ish flavor, that might be because Flynt is a character who might have sprung full-blown—so to speak—from Southern's fervid noggin in his peak *Blue Movie* period. And yet Southern seems like a classic right now. Obscenity has its time line; we've moved past the prurience in *Larry Flynt*. Compared to what's out there in, say, the cybersexual arena, Flynt's indiscretions pale. Time has fossilized him into a chic icon for slumming civil libertarians. The best sick joke in the movie is that we can now look back on his smut with nostalgia.

(*New Times*, 1996)

Captain Video

Video criticism parallels video art—both are in their infancy. It's not often that a new arena for reviewing opens up; for a critic such as myself, whose work has been self-limited primarily to dramatic and documentary feature films, the domain of video art is infuriating, bracing, nettlesome. Infuriating because so much of the material that I've seen is pokey, wan, arty in the worst eye-swimming, experimental-film sorts of ways;

bracing because even the worst of the work operates in an aesthetic zone that is as far removed from most narrative films as concrete poetry is from Elizabethan sonnets; nettlesome because a new critical vocabulary must be invented to accompany the new aesthetic.

Allow me to admit a few biases. I have never cared much for most of the video art I've seen. I've stayed away from it. The video screen is scaled to the intimacy of home furnishings; that intimacy—familiar yet chill—is basic to the medium's iconography, in the same way that the big screen is integral to the iconography of movies. I favor the larger-than-life, wrap-around qualities of film, the pictorial and aural richness. I also favor narrative film over avant-garde image-clustering—not that all video art tends towards abstraction. But most of what I've seen does. And the abstraction, while it can occasionally be exhilarating, is too often without emotional tone; the video artists have gone gizmo crazy, they're hammer-locked by their own technique. Video art has been given a bad name, and rightly so, by the sort of chi-chi experimentation that goes well with brie and white wine and mauve-walled art galleries and designer hair-dos. Video is cheap enough to produce, by feature film standards, and yet its very cheapness and accessibility has created a contradiction—video-making is within the financial reach of many, and yet, like most modern art, it's surrounded by a noxious aura of elitism.

Still, video presents a challenge to the film critic; it challenges his assumptions about the nature of the visual image, and how it can be manipulated. It challenges the critical territorial imperative that states that the only good and lasting work comes from the narrative tradition, that there may be ways for film to tingle an audience's soul that video can only approximate. It may not be fair to compare the plasticity of the film image to that of video. (It's like comparing hallucinations.) Video, at its best, represents a new way of seeing. Of that much I'm convinced. And I'm fascinated by the visual textures of video; by its colors. Video hues are often primary and incandescent, like deep-sea coral. They have an irradiated lustre. I've seen these colors before, in paintings by Magritte and Hockney and others, but not often in movies. The sounds in video are frequently as abrupt, partial, and abstract as the imagery. Words are broken down into notes, syllables; the familiar becomes privatized. The impulse behind this visual/aural abstractionism seems the same—to destroy all but the most essential components of sight and sound.

Many of the videos I've seen that have excited me, or enraged me, emphasize the medium's capacity for abstraction. Their scenarios and stratagems involve stylized movements, where the actors are reduced to blips and blurs and fragments of torsos, textures of skin, hair. The hues seem inner-charged—light does not seem to affect their tonality. Settings are often darkish, penned-in. The spoken voice verges on flat, tone-dead recitation—the voice "purified" of emotional levels. Of all visual forms, video, by virtue of its technology, seems the most capable of imprinting "real" life; the home-movie, to take the simplest example, has a present-tense quality that is freezing in its matter-of-factness. This quality may account for the video artist's desire to snap time in his work; to give the illusion of a *resonance* in time. Video is a domain where, because of the present-tenseness of the imagery, death seems impossible. It is always more shocking to see a violent act in video than on film, just as it is more puzzling to watch a deceased actor, or any now-deceased person, in video. One can't imagine that this person, so startlingly, so matter-of-factly *there*, no longer exists. The success of the video artists' struggle to re-shape their medium—their way of seeing—may have much to do with their sensitivity to video's damned present-tenseness; the sense that things are happening on the spot. These artists are attempting to void that currency in order to give the medium what can only be termed a tragic quality—one that can accommodate the dimensions of death.

Doug Hall's *Through the Room*, one of five short segments of his *Songs of the '80s,* might have been made in response to this problem; it works against the sheer immediacy of the video format by trying to create levels in time. Its temporal sense appears to issue from the center of a dream; long-takes and *longeurs* alternate with flash-cuts from parallel time-zones, flash-forwards that only acquire meaning when the video has ended. The video's final effect is a paradox: jumpy stasis. Its elements are spare and strikingly delineated, like pieces in a child's toy kit: a bone-white chair in what looks like a large, empty tenement lobby; a man in a rumpled suit, his hair shocked into vague, flame-like wings on either side of his head. First we see the empty lobby, then the flash of a chair, then milli-second cuts to a conflagration; the man appears, disappears in a blink, reappears in held, frozen poses, disappears, snaps into space again, cautiously approaches the chair, is zapped, reappears astride the chair, freezes in imploring, back-arching, positions in the corner of the lobby, as a major choral chord—a plea? an annunciation?—crescendoes on the soundtrack in irregular waves. Then a slow fade into a wide-open-plains vista; the white chair reappears, then the man, gazing into distraction, stationed like a sentry around the chair, is repositioned, in slow staccato symmetry, closer and closer to the horizon. Blank empty vista fades back into the empty lobby, then the chair pops into place; the man, seated, flames out, as he does a slow-curl of horror into oblivion.

This brief recounting of *Through the Room* can't avoid inadequacy. One of the problems of video criticism is that, as the work under consideration approaches abstraction, one's critical vocabulary becomes dependably less and less evocative. One might as well try with words to convey a piece of music. What's missing from these accounts is the tang of the event. The power of *Through the Room* comes directly from the very elements of film and video—the time-sense, the counter-point of image and sound—that are most indecipherable. And yet those elements are the soul of moving pictures; it's what makes the mundane inexplicable, haunting. Criticism is supposed to elucidate our feelings, to explain *why* we are moved in a certain way, or why we weren't, or how we could have been. But abstract video is, perhaps by nature, inexplicable. That doesn't mean it's above criticism but, rather, that it's at the heart of criticism, which finally is concerned with what can only be intimated. To be moved without consciously knowing why is maybe the profoundest emotion in the arts; a great artist, and that includes the few great video artists, mainlines that emotion. *Through the Room* is emotionally moving out of all proportion to what we are being shown. Even its clearest description—it's the story of a man who can't escape the fix of his obsession, and burns—doesn't quite capture its quality. But it comes close enough; it implies the tragedy that Doug Hall reaches for—the sense that something vital has perished.

Ed Emshwiller's *Skin Matrix* is a further explosion into abstraction. Emshwiller, first in film and now video, has been doing some of the most inventive work in the visual arts for over twenty years. His discovery of video has an ecstatic quality—unlike many video-makers, Emshwiller seems to be working in the field by choice, not necessity. *Skin Matrix* is one of the very few computer-generated videos that doesn't leave one feeling like a machine for watching it. Patterns of skin and beard, zig-zagged and thicketed, give way to faces cubed and sectioned, wiped horizontally by a rolling bar, fractured into a mosaic, then a sort of peeling wall-painting portrait—like a flaked face on the vulcanized walls of Pompeii, or, sometimes, a Mayan mask, with liquid eyes blinking in the deep-brown armature. The colors are like rich, phosphorescent acrylics. Emshwiller impinges his faces with textures of wood-grain, snow scapes that may be desert scapes, sea-stones, algae. The luminescence is ambiguous—these must be the colors of radioactive decay. That sense of decay, of something fundamental expiring, is what makes *Skin Matrix* moving. Although its style couldn't be more different from *Through the Room*, it shares that video's deep sense of loss.

Emshwiller is, however, far less fatalistic than Hall. He even gives us a final image, a blue phalanx soaring high above mountain ranges, that is ineffable—it's the image the video has been working up to, without our conscious awareness, all along. Emshwiller confronts aesthetic problems in his work that are central to video, especially computer-generated video. How does one create a work that is plangent and ambiguous and lyrical from techniques that seem to duplicate the inner coils of machine-think? Film has always been a medium born of the sophistication of science, but video takes that sophistication one step further; its computer-generated techniques represent the exposed circuitry of science. The hyper-precision of grid-lines and pulsing, expanding geometries is not what most of us have been led to believe art should be. It's joy-buzzer art—its highest station is to be rinky-dink. At least that's what bad practitioners have made it. But the excitement of the video arena is that its laws are in constant flux; artists change those laws as they go along. Emshwiller is working in the most exciting and dangerous area of video, because he risks being gizmoed into high-tech heaven. But his visual conceptions are so inventive that he flabbergasts you. And Emshwiller, at least in *Skin Matrix,* puts the human face at the center of his film. He's delirious with the possibilities of what can be done with faces, the way the Cubists must have been. There's an avidity in the way he devolves facial conformations into skeletal road-maps—he transposes eyes, lips, teeth, noses. Computer-generated video is potentially the least "representational" of mediums, but, by inserting his faces in *Skin Matrix,* Emshwiller sets up an aesthetic torque. The human factor keeps reasserting its primacy amidst the gimcrackery. His soundtrack is resonant with creepy-movie music, and no wonder. The video itself is haunted—by the human face.

(*Resolution: A Critique of Video Art*, LACE, 1986)

Kaboom Town:
L.A. Disaster Movies

The city of Los Angeles—more precisely, the state of mind that is La-La Land—is a big fat bullseye for just about anybody who has ever felt pulled down by age and defeat. L.A. mocks the luckless, the unloved, the unappreciated. It also mocks the successful, since one is constantly surrounded by people far more favored than oneself. L.A. is Mission Control for the dream factory, so it's no wonder Angelinos are enraged when their dreams go kablooey. City of Angels? Guess again. Those angels are furies.

The revivals featured in the "Los Angeles Destroys Itself" sidebar of the L.A. Film Festival—*Earthquake, Escape From L.A., Night of the Comet, Them!,* and *Miracle Mile*—are all disaster films of one sort or another. Not many of them are wonderful. The best is the little-seen *Miracle Mile,* a night-blooming doomsday thriller that, in one scene, offers up a quintessential ghastly-funny southland image—a fat rat plopping out of a palm tree.

The authentic L.A. disaster movie genre, in fact, is the film noir, where the acids of sin and revenge seep into the ground water and poison everything. The play of bright white and pitch black in a movie like *Double Idemnity* is a visual diagram of the sacred and profane, with the profane always winning out. These movies are saying, Don't let all that sunshine fool you—the soul of this city is dark, very dark.

One big reason the typical disaster movie, as opposed to the film noir, has never quite worked for L.A. is because, in the popular imagination, the city is already rotted out from the inside. Its demolition is redundant.

There is usually, and often inadvertently, a comic undertone to the L.A. disaster movie. There has to be some payback for all that fun in the sun and we get our kicks from figuring out who the victims will be, and in what order they will drop. (Usually minorities are the first to get offed, along with a token white star or two.) Characterization is kept to a soap-opera minimum. These are pawns, not people.

And then there are all those stilt homes and freeway curlicues just crying to come down. Compared to most great cities, L.A. is unmoored, pre-fabricated. The Botoxed, creaseless narcissists who incarnate La-La-

Land are also a species of fabrication. Bring them down, too. It's no accident that the archetypal dystopian L.A. movie is *Blade Runner,* where the replicants and the humans are virtually indistinguishable.

Movies are a popular medium and so it makes sense that Hollywood would draw on the hoariest L.A. stereotypes when visualizing its destruction: movie agents, like cockroaches, survive the apocalypse, brokering deals in the inferno; the L.A. Memorial Coliseum becomes the Roman Coliseum; the Hollywood Sign bursts into flame as if it were the Burning Bush. Workaday non-Hollywood types are not often given center stage in these films. Neither are the poor, particularly the non-white poor. The true L.A. disaster movie would be about illegal aliens, not aliens from outer space.

Although it's nothing more than smart-alecky shlock, John Carpenter's *Escape From L.A.,* set in 2013, is a useful compendium of I-Hate-L.A clichés and also the only movie in the current series that stirs the racial pot. In the aftermath of a 9.6 quake, the city, now an island, has become a deportation site for sinners—i.e. hookers, atheists, meat eaters, smokers. (What—no schlock filmmakers?) America's president, played by Cliff Robertson at his most walleyed, is a religious zealot who welcomes the earthquake as the fulfillment of Armageddon.

Meanwhile, a Che Guevara look-alike exiled on the island is orchestrating a Third World invasion of L.A. Is Carpenter buying into the notion of L.A. as Sin City or is he condemning it? Is he lampooning angry Third World immigrants or siding with their unrest? Who can say? He goes with whatever makes the biggest boom.

Decibel-wise, *Earthquake,* which will be shown in its original teeth-chattering Sensurround, is the loudest boom machine in the bunch. It's also the archetypal L.A. disaster movie, which is to say, it's both indispensible and awful. There's something oddly comforting— guilt-free—about watching an urban destructo orgy that will never be mistaken as a metaphor for 9/11. The opening moments serves up aerial shots of Los Angeles for our delectation—it's like a death tease. When the quake finally hits almost an hour into the movie, it looks like nothing so much as a snit fit orchestrated by God. "We should never have put up those forty-story monstrosities," bellows penitent architect Charlton Heston while plunging papier-mache girders pick off fleeing extras. (The horrific traffic snarl that ensues resembles any old afternoon on the 405 today.) The most seismic shock in the movie: Lorne Greene, seven years her senior, plays Ava Gardner's father.

The God of *Earthquake* could not have had much of a sense of humor. All that vehemence just so we could watch a gaggle of movie stars get flattened! In film after film, Los Angeles is incinerated Old Testament-style for our sins. Doesn't the diety have more pressing business? Maybe that old joke is true—what God really wants to do is direct. But why must he use L.A. as his backlot?

Actually, maybe God has moved on to other things. These movies haven't really been made about L.A. for over a decade. The featured films in the festival range from the mid-fifties to the mid-nineties—well past the heyday for disaster flicks. With the exception of flare-ups like *The Day After Tomorrow* or *Poseidon,* the genre, which is certainly not confined to L.A., faded largely because the films were too pricey to produce. The advent of CGI effects could usher in a new era, as it already has with, say, gladiator and pirate movies, except that 9/11 has taken all the fun out of it. L.A. has plenty of new disaster movie targets—the subway system, Walt Disney Concert Hall—but what mogul has the stomach to explode them?

The only earthquake in the movies right now is the simulated one beneath the Vegas casino in *Ocean's 13.* Charlton Heston dodging a boulder has been replaced by Al Gore at the lectern. Armageddon has gone global. In the disaster derby, L.A. is small potatoes.

(Los Angeles Times, 2007)

Moviegoing Manners: A Tale of Woe

There was a time, I think it was back in the Paleozoic era, when it was possible to go to a movie theater and hear more noise coming from the screen than from the audience. It was possible, once upon a time, to be lulled by the gentle snoring of one's seatmate. Today that same seat filler is likely to be bleating into a cell phone, or text messaging, or tweeting a friend, who is probably also in a movie theater.

Before I spin out this tale of woe, however, let me quickly insert a faint ray of hope—a recent *Los Angeles Times* report says that the National Association of Theater Owners, faced with an alarming slide in attendance, is looking into ways to jam cell phone signals, "eliminating the chance that dramatic silences will be interrupted by a 'My Humps' ring tone."

The movie-going experience, especially for those of us who are middle-aged enough to note the difference, has changed catastrophically in the past decade. People have brought their home-viewing habits into the theaters. Actually, it's worse than that—watching a movie at a multiplex is often a lot yappier and more aggravating than watching one at home, unless of course you live in a kennel.

I happen to be one of those people who don't like a whole lot of hub-hub, least of all inside a movie theater. Since I am a professional film critic and attend hundreds of screenings a year, this presents a distinct problem for me. Many of my screenings are for critics only, so you would think I have a comparatively easy time of it. Think again. The press, as we all know, is so well behaved.

There is one group, for example, whose identity I won't divulge except to say that they dispense Golden Globes every year, who are notorious for smuggling hot and spicy casseroles into screening rooms (often poorly ventilated) while pursuing a line of nonstop chatter in heavily accented English. Then there are all those critics who pull out their lighted pens at the drop of an insight.

But that's old school behavior. New school is bringing your laptop into the theater and typing your insights as you go along. If enough of these typists are in the theater, the collective sound is like a squadron of rats clacking across a linoleum floor.

Critics also enjoy impressing other critics by venting aloud for all to hear. One famous critic used to belt out an anguished sigh whenever she found a film too drippy; another regularly rocks the room with a laugh pitched somewhere between a croak and a whinny. At film festivals like Toronto and Cannes, the one-upsmanship often takes the form of instant mini-dissertations, as in "That tracking shot is so Tarkovskian!"

But at least all this obnoxiousness can be linked, however tenuously, to a love for movies. Worse is when the movie agents and buyers invade the screenings and, within minutes of sitting down, whip out their Blackberries to make a deal. They don't call it the movie *business* for nothing.

All things being equal—and they rarely are—I like to see movies with real people, as opposed to critics or Hollywood types. The atmosphere in the room is less rarified and the responses more honest. The bad news is, the atmosphere is also rowdier. And unlike at home, where you can tell your children or spouse or friends to can it and still stand a reasonably good chance of surviving, the multiplex is a cauldron of strangers who do not take kindly to instruction. Note what happens the next time you see one of those trailers telling everybody to please not talk during the movie. Everyone starts talking.

I used to have a prepared comment for the babblers who always seem to sit directly behind me. You know, the kind of people who feel duty-bound to provide a running commentary on the action to their partner, as in "Look, he's opening a door." I would turn around and ever so politely say, "Would you mind speaking a little louder? I can't hear you over the soundtrack?" But this proved to be too Zen for most people, some of whom actually *did* speak louder.

So now I do things differently. Rather than provoke confrontations, I simply scope out several empty alternate seats before I take my own. If the going gets rough, I switch. This does not work if the theater is packed, in which case you better hope that seated near you is one of those guardian angels with no compunction about shushing down the opposition.

But even when the talkers are compelled to quit it—not, I might add, by the ushers, since there aren't any—they find other ways to make their presence felt. People who are annoying in one way are usually annoying in many ways. Quieted down, these same patrons become foot jigglers or high-decibel whisperers. They rifle through their seemingly bottomless handbags for—what exactly? It always escapes me. Candy, swathed in the noisiest foil, is unwrapped. Popcorn is consumed kernel by kernel.

And of course, the quieted-down rarely stay quiet for very long. First-date couples are the worst—the guy is always trying to impress the girl with a patter of hogwash and she is too polite or intimidated to stop it. Generally speaking, the younger the viewer the more likely he or she is to jabber on and on, but there are numerous exceptions to this rule. Age has no dominion over manners.

Just look at the cellphone noise pollution epidemic. If you ask someone to keep quiet nowadays, you are likely to get back a look of genuine astonishment. People who are plugged into their own hum don't recognize your right to silence. What they recognize is their right not to be silent. It's democracy in action all right.

Not to put too fine a sociological point on it, but the epidemic of bad manners in the movies is part of a much larger swine flu gripping the land. What it all comes down to is this—there are few private zones in public spaces anymore. Restaurant reviews in many of the big city newspapers now rate the decibel level right along with the food and the service.

Maybe film critics should do the same thing for movie theaters. Not this critic, though. I've heard enough.

(The Christian Science Monitor, 2006)

Blackface: Robert Downey Jr. in the Tropics

What is going on in the zeitgeist when an African American is poised to become president and Robert Downey Jr. is in blackface? In the new comedy *Tropic Thunder,* Downey plays actor Kirk Lazarus, a Russell Crowe-ish Aussie who is cast as a black soldier in a blood-and-guts Vietnam War epic. Method Man that he is, Lazarus dyes his skin, mats his hair and revamps his voice into a guttural drawl that's equal parts plantation and blaxploitation. His flared sideburns might have been modeled on Jim Brown's in *100 Rifles.*

Ben Stiller co-wrote and directed *Tropic Thunder* and stars in it as a would-be war hero. He has said in interviews that Lazarus represents nothing more than a satirical swipe at overly intense actors, so let's start out by taking him at his word.

Viewed purely as performance, Downey's boundary-bending turn is an actor's holiday at the expense of actors—specifically, and self-mockingly, Downey himself, whose intensity, like Daniel Day-Lewis's, is notorious. *Tropic Thunder* opens with a faux trailer for an earlier Lazarus movie called *Satan's Alley,* in which Downey plays a smoldering monk in what looks like a cross between *In the Name of the Rose* and *Brokeback Mountain.* Desire has made him molten.

It takes a prodigiously gifted actor to lampoon himself and still wipe everybody else off the screen. Throughout the shoot, on-screen and off,

Lazarus never once falls out of character, not even with his scoffing black co-star (Brandon T. Jackson), who thinks this white dude is crazy. You can't help admiring his nutbrain dedication. In the acting biz, absurdity and genius are never far apart. If you doubt it, consider this—Lazarus's folly and Laurence Olivier's jet black Othello inhabit the same play-act continuum. Downey makes Lazarus both the butt and the paragon of his profession.

Downey—whose previous Great Moment in Racial Comedy was an improvised scene in James Toback's *Black and White,* in which he makes a pass at Mike Tyson and nearly gets pulverized for his troubles—knows how to capture the self-delusions of the anointed. Lazarus is a five-time Oscar winner who doesn't realize how far out his Method has taken him. (Neither did Dustin Hoffman's prima donna in *Tootsie.*) But he's quick to spot the exhibitionism of others.

Stiller's Tugg Speedman, for example, known for his action roles, is coming off a colossal flop in which he played all too realistically a mentally challenged hayseed named Simple Jack. Lazarus offers up to Tugg the cautionary example of Sean Penn, who went Oscarless in *I Am Sam.* "Never go full retard," he counsels. Of course, if Lazarus had been cast as Simple Jack, he would have gone full frontal lobotomy.

(Stiller's caricature, which has already drawn protests from more than half a dozen disabilities organizations, lacks the cutting edge of Downey's racial whammy. It's closer to goony, Farrelly brothers-style bad taste.)

Early in his career, Downey had a stint on *Saturday Night Live,* and his acting here, while far more sophisticated, is linked to those revue-sketch years. *SNL* has always specialized in skewering the outsize pretensions of the theatrically deluded. Think of Bill Murray's oleagineous lounge singer bending his voice to the theme from *Star Wars.* Or Jon Lovitz's Master Thespian molding each syllable for the ages. What made the routines so funny is that, on some level, these actors weren't kidding. Their mockery of ego was balled up inside their own egomania. Downey's Lazarus, with his free-form riffs on the peacockery of performing, fits right into this company.

So do his riffs on race, which have an even earlier pedigree. Downey's father, Robert Downey Sr., directed 1969's funky, acidulous *Putney Swope,* about a Black Power takeover of a lily-white Madison Avenue agency. A year later, in Brian De Palma's *Hi, Mom!,* black militants stage an off-off Broadway show called *Be Black, Baby,* during which, in white face, they force their white patrons to wear blackface and then proceed to terrorize them in order for them to better "understand" the black experience. The comic kicker comes at the end. Says one brutalized white guy, admiringly, about the evening: "It really makes you stop and think."

These underground movies, mostly forgotten now, nevertheless set the template for the scabrous racial vaudeville that morphed into the blaxploitation cycle right on up through rap. For white audiences, especially guilty liberals, the message in these movies was explicit: "We really *are* your worst nightmare."

Historically, white actors in blackface incarnated the cruelest of racial caricatures. (Even when Fred Astaire in *Swing Time* wore blackface in tribute to Bill Robinson, it was implicit that Bojangles could never star in such a film.) But one cannot talk about blackfaced white performers without at the same time summoning up the camouflages worn by black actors—worn, in many cases, in order to have any career at all. Throughout all too much of Hollywood's sorry history, particularly pre-Sidney Poitier, black performers, with no decent roles available to them, wore minstrel masks, too. They acted out the demeaning images whites set for them (and still, like Robinson himself, frequently managed to be more electric than their often starched-white counterparts). By the time the sixties counterculture came along, attitudes had shifted. Black minstrelsy became a put-on—a weapon. Be black, baby.

The weaponry, literally and figuratively, was even more apparent in the blaxploitation films, where the bad-guy white characters were often as demeaned and demonized as blacks once had been. (Typical was Rip Torn in *Slaughter* nattering the N-word as he goes up in flames.) The stoneface stud mask worn by the Shafts and the Superflys emblematized the worst-case fears of whites—fears of black sexuality, black payback. But selling fear can be lucrative, and fear, right up to the present time, carries its own cachet of cool. Is it any surprise that whites are the largest consumers of gangsta hip hop? Or that a too-cool-for-school director like Quentin Tarantino, the filmmaking embodiment of Norman Mailer's *White Negro,* should act as movieland's soul brother No. 1 by getting his groove on with *Pulp Fiction* and *Jackie Brown*? Despite, or perhaps because of, Obamamania, our so-called post-racial society has rarely been more race-conscious. (The brouhaha over the *New Yorker*'s Obama Bin

Laden cover is Exhibit A.) How all this will play out in terms of popular culture is anybody's guess, but the yin-yang is very heady.

For the only time in film history, for example, black actors can now be stars without first being "black." By this I mean, they can, like Will Smith or Denzel Washington, play just about anything without having to be racially typed. (Big exception: they still can't romance white women—the last taboo.)

On the other hand, there is Downey in *Tropic Thunder*, who rubs the audience's face in the fact that we are not remotely "over" race—or, to be precise, racism. Paradoxically, the zeitgeist that accounts for the ascendancy of Will Smith also makes Downey's performance possible. This is because the political correctness quotient tends to dip in less straitened times. Instead of being grossly offensive, Downey's Lazarus comes across as a daring racial jest. (The jest would have been even more daring if he had been American.) Whereas blackface once expressed the most cringe-worthy aspects of white racism, here it reveals the opposite—Lazarus's makeover shows up the arrant silliness of white fantasies of "blackness." The soldier he plays, Lincoln Osiris, is a patchwork derived not from life but from show-business, from blaxploitation films and *Benson* and *The Jeffersons*. He's the freak that results when whites attempt to forge a black identity from the spare parts of pop culture.

I don't want to make too great a case for *Tropic Thunder*, which pulls many more punches than it lands. But something new is going on whenever Downey is on-screen. He has the wit to recognize that, in this country right now, where Barack Obama's public appearances are covered in the press as theater, race is regarded as a species of performance art. He's the court jester in our national masquerade.

(*Los Angeles Times*, 2008)

On Male Weepies

The male weepie, a newly minted genre for the post-yuppie era, is in full flood. Consider: in *Regarding Henry,* a crass, hotshot lawyer played by Harrison Ford is wounded in the head, suffers almost total amnesia and, in his new life, realizes the error of his anything-for-success ways. He and his family end up making the supreme downwardly mobile sacrifice—they trade the Upper West Side for Greenwich Village.

William Hurt's crass, hotshot doctor in *The Doctor* literally gets a taste of his own medicine when he comes down with cancer of the larynx. His suffering is meant to tenderize him to the plight of others and make him a better healer.

In *Dying Young,* a well-to-do, highly educated cancer patient, played by Campbell Scott, finds true love in a seaside idyll with his down-to-earth, working-class nurse, Julia Roberts (!).

In *City Slickers,* which is ostensibly a comedy, a trio of male friends led by Billy Crystal go on a cattle-drive vacation that turns into a consciousness-raiser on the prairie.

Then there are the movies that, while not strictly speaking weepies, still turn the spigot—Mel Brooks's *Life Stinks* and the new Michael J. Fox comedy *Doc Hollywood.*

Even the Terminator is weepy these days. In *Terminator 2: Judgment Day,* our Austrian-accented cyborg sacrifices himself, and the last words spoken about him have the ring of benediction: "If a terminator can learn the meaning of a human life, we can too."

For a while, it looked like the only men making a grand-scale impression in the movies were the psychos—like the wise guys in *Goodfellas,* or Hannibal Lecter from *The Silence of the Lambs.* The men in the new male weepies are the reverse-image of the psychos; they implode not from rage but from "sensitivity."

We've been primed for these men for a while now. *Awakenings* was essentially a male weepie; *Dances With Wolves* was one too. It had many of the requisite requirements, including a martyred central male figure who chucks the cruelties of civilization for "the simpler life." Kevin Costner's Lieutenant Dunbar was a selfless sufferer—and we got to witness his selflessness in, by rough estimate, 469 adoring close-ups. Raging narcissism is the keystone of the male weepie.

The major precursor, however, is probably *Big,* where Tom Hanks played an eight-year-old in a grown-up's body. The film's measured, ungoofy style clued us in that it wasn't just a romp—it was a *parable.* It stumped for the spiritual benefits of being a child again. The new male weepies, keying into the current pop-psych-speak, are real big on "locating the child within yourself"—though most male execs don't seem to have any trouble locating that child. It's the humane adult they can't find.

In a male weepie like *Regarding Henry* or *T2,* the hero is led by a child to discover his innocence and, in effect, becomes a child himself. The alternative to the hard-driving power-mongering breadwinner is a kind of stunted, baffled, sexless creature. We've gone from Rambo to Rain Man.

Like most movie trends, the male weepie is a delayed reaction to long-term rumblings in society. It's actually a step behind; in popular culture now, the sort of male sensitivity-training represented by these films has been muscled aside by the likes of Robert Bly (author of *Iron John*) and Sam Keen (*Fire in the Belly: On Being a Man*), patriarch worshipers who sponsor retreats where middle-class achievers huddle in tepees, grab their tom-toms and get all atavistic.

Sometimes what's churning up the country never makes it into the movies at all; the studios, which thrive on formula, are scared off by anything they can't digest. Hollywood conspicuously ignored feminist outrage in the seventies and eighties, in much the same way that Vietnam was ignored for many years. But in this age of the recession, the downturn of the well-to-do has a Depression-era sentimentality that Hollywood, and many film critics, find irresistible. These movies give everyone a chance to plump their virtue.

Hollywood is never so much Hollywood as when it's thumping for the simple, humane life—for everything it isn't. (May one presume that the producers of these films will follow the advice of their movies and devote the remainder of their lives to good works?) Since most of the big breadwinner roles still go to male actors, it makes sense that many of these actors would mainline the new sentimentality by sucking in their cheeks and looking bereft. (How aptly named is William Hurt!) It's the kind of socially conscious star-trip that actors, and Oscar voters, adore.

The male weepie shares many of the same defining qualities as the female weepie, and it has the added commercial advantage these days of attracting a sizable female audience. Both genres are intimately keyed into middle-class values. Despair is usually recorded as a fall from affluence; the sanctity of home and hearth is nostalgically rendered; romantic transgressions are punished with a Puritan vigor. The tone of these films is often subdued and dewy, for that all-important "prestige" effect. Repeated close-ups of the trembling, suffering hero or heroine are stockpiled.

It should come as no great surprise that the women in these new movies are really no more invigorating or three-dimensional than in the usual Hollywood fare. Since the male weepie is essentially about the hero's narcissism, the wives and girlfriends appear primarily as helpers. They broker their men's new-found sensitivity. It's significant that very few of the male-female relationships in these films have a sexual edge. The women's ministrations are essentially motherly, as befitting their infantilized men. If the female weepie, with its cult of sacrifice, often reinforced the female audience's most masochistic side, the male weepie tells men not to worry if they fall. Someone will still be there to tuck them in at night.

The dream of chucking it all for a simpler life is rampant right now among superannuated yuppies, but the simple life in these movies still looks pretty flashy. No one takes a real financial bath—that downgrade from West Side penthouse to Village townhouse in *Regarding Henry* is about as bad as it gets. This have-your-cake-and-eat-it-too fantasyland quality is typical of the male weepie; just as what befalls the hero is often "accidental" (an unexpected affliction), so is the resolution equally fortuitous (the illness is stayed, the memory creeps back, justice prevails). The social background for these movies is rooted in Reagan-era, greed-is-good malfeasance but the movies themselves have no social reality. Weepies rarely do. And so it's probably irrelevant to point out that, of course, fancy apartments in the Village cost a fortune, or that famous surgeons are not likely to get routine patient treatment in their own hospital.

The hero's loss of traditional, career-related power in these films is accepted as a virtue. That's because power, as defined in movies like *The Doctor* and *Regarding Henry,* is perceived as a disease separating these men from their own best and most tender selves. It's a disease handed down from father to son; both movies point up how the father's work ethic was instilled in the boy. (Hurt's character is the son of a doctor; the father of Ford's character co-founded his law firm.) The lawyer played by Harrison Ford is shown to be a conniving workaholic who chews out his daughter, carries on an affair, has gaudy, expensive taste, and doesn't like showing affection in public (or, one presumes, in private). Why, he even *smokes.* The doctor drives around in a Mercedes, talks glibly to his patients on his car phone, and actively downplays the importance of a bedside manner. "A surgeon's job is to cut" is his credo.

The disaffection for power in these movies is deliberately, and offensively, simplistic. The implication is that, in the professional arena, absolute power corrupts absolutely. It's a convenient fantasy for a downwardly mobile era.

The psychosexual subtext of the greed-is-good eighties was that riches equalled virility. Lucre was the emollient of the soul. We passed through that decade as we might pass through a radioactive cloud, and now the most irradiated and soul-sick of its moneyed survivors—the shell-shocked, fallen-on-hard-times careerists—are starting to crowd our screens. In the new recessionary climate, the same Hollywood that used to glorify money and macho now glorifies their absence. In eighties terms, the men in these movies have been emasculated but that's not how we're meant to view them. Instead, their weepiness is sugarcoated in moral superiority. In the guise of a new sensitivity, the male weepies are simply glamorizing the loss of power. Its heroes have the glossy, martyred look of sainthood.

(Los Angeles Times, 1991)

Screen Test(osterone)

How many ways can a man be manly in the movies these days? The film historian Robert Sklar once wrote that "each generation exaggerates its own crises of masculinity." If this is true, we must be in a doozy of a crisis right now.

There hasn't been this much industrial-strength machismo, both as cause for celebration and denunciation, since the post-Vietnam Reagan eighties superhero heyday of Rambo and Gordon Gekko. Consider, for starters, that the *Superman* and *Die Hard* franchises, long dormant, were recently revived; a sequel to *Wall Street* is being readied; a new Indiana Jones movie is in the pipeline; and that, come January, Sylvester Stallone, having already revived Rocky, will once again be wearing the Rambo muscle suit. Not one to press his luck, Rambo will be touring Myanmar, not Baghdad.

I don't want to overplay the parallels between the Reagan and George W. Bush years, but might the backwash of a colossally unpopular war have something to do with the fact that so many of our movies are— how can I say this politely—atavistic?

On the far side of the blood-and-biceps *Beowulf,* consider the gallery of actors today who represent throwbacks to a relatively uncomplicated male mystique. When Russell Crowe or George Clooney are talked about or written about, the tone is often almost strenuously adulatory, as if they stood for an old-style Hollywood machismo that must be preserved at all costs. Crowe was on the cover of *Men's Journal* last month as "Our favorite S.O.B." A new Colorado magazine called *Shine* featured Clooney on its inaugural cover and inside announced that he "embodies the courageous John Wayne spirit of the Westerns" (which is probably the last thing Clooney wants to hear).

Still, it can be deeply satisfying to watch these actors preen. A little masculine confidence goes a long way in the movies and, in the right roles, these men remind you of what you loved about, say, Bogart or Mitchum or McQueen. Crowe can be sluggish and inchoate in a Depression-era retread like *Cinderella Man,* he can be thuddingly heroic in *Gladiator,* but at his best, in *L.A. Confidential* and *3:10 to Yuma* and, to a much lesser extent, in *American Gangster,* he has the bullyboy insolence of male privilege down pat.

Clooney, in particular, is associated in the public imagination with Golden Age Hollywood icons. In his self-deprecating savoir-faire he is seen as a burlier version of Cary Grant, while his Danny Ocean routine has some of the Sinatra finesse. In films such as *Syriana* and *Michael Clayton,* he plays the standard Bogart cynic turned do-gooder. It's easy to imagine Clooney fitting into any number of Hollywood classics, from *Casablanca* on down. (Clooney is a godsend to all those women who, during the pre-*Departed* reign of Leonardo DiCaprio, despaired of ever seeing a leading man on the screen who looked to be past the point of his first shave.)

But a retro-ness clings to Clooney that, especially for a younger generation, may ultimately work against him. He's a new movie star in an old mold as opposed to, say, Johnny Depp, who has a satyr's pansexual appeal and the shape-shifty genius to fully inhabit, even unify, mindscapes as disparate as Tim Burton's and Jerry Bruckheimer's. Depp is the most original male presence in the movies in large part because is the most original sexual presence.

By comparison, actors such as Clooney and Crowe, or Denzel Washington, rarely get to play out their sexual dynamism. Is it because Hollywood thinks there are no women who are their match? Despite their high whammo quotients these men have starred in alarmingly few romances, let alone erotic dramas, and that's a deprivation for us all. The Golden Age icons may have been men's men, but they were overwhelmingly defined by their maddening/ornery/blissful relations with women. The sullen gravitas of Clooney, Crowe, and Washington in *Michael Clayton* and *American Gangster* represents an overvaluation of the strong-and-silent mystique, and it reminds me of what Gore Vidal once wrote about the humorlessness of American society: "What other culture could have produced someone like Hemingway and *not* seen the joke?"

If atavism is truly your meat, you'll find it most blatantly on view in the brawnfest *300*, where Spartan beefcake enthusiastically disembowels wounded Iranians—oops, Persians—before expiring valorously at Thermopylae. It's there in *Beowulf*, where, thanks to motion-capture technology, the hulky, ovoid Ray Winstone is transformed into a warrior with miracle abs. Brad Pitt must be wondering why he spent all those months buffing up to play Achilles in *Troy*. No more is it necessary for an actor to put in quality time with a personal trainer. In the future, all the personal trainers in Hollywood will be CGI technicians.

These big-screen blam-pow epics tap the same market that caters to World Wrestling Federation smackdowns and male niche TV shows like *Lost* and *24* and all-testosterone-all-the-time cable channels like Spike TV. They appeal to men who tune out regular boxing but tune into extreme boxing. This he-man swagger, of course, takes in a lot more than the movies these days—it's also the preferred stance in our presidential politics, where the candidates who come out swinging get the most ink. (Now that *Invasion U.S.A.* eighties action star Chuck Norris is soldered to the Huckabee campaign, who's waiting in the wings? The Rock? The Hebrew Hammer?)

The "actors" in *300* and *Beowulf* fly the banner for a movie business that may one day rate the annual Comi-Con convention in San Diego as highly as Cannes. But they're not the only screen stars who seem like replicants these days. Matt Damon in the *Bourne* movies is a heat-seeking missile who incises his way into mayhem with an almost preternatural velocity. The new James Bond, as played by Daniel Craig, is a feral assassin who doesn't blink an eye while electroshocking himself back from the dead. Craig doesn't have the suaveness or the square-cut facial planes of his immediate predecessors (and that's a good thing). In the past, the Bond movies were never really about violence; they were about how stylish you could look while being violent. *Casino Royale* changed all that.

The nauseating uptick in carnage on display in *Saw IV* and all the rest is a low-rent manifestation of the same hyperviolent syndrome often found in big-ticket *Bourne*-style action pictures. In both instances, we are witnessing a worst-case scenario of male aggression—maleness and murderousness are twinned. (In the case of a lurid art film like *The Brave One,* Jodie Foster's Charles Bronson-ish vigilante is the Frankenstein monster created by male murderousness.)

It's easier to dismiss this scenario in the slasher cheapies, which were also quite big in the eighties, than in the more serious current fare. In many of the Iraq-themed films, the psycho soldier, so familiar from Vietnam-era movies, is once more a featured player. The traditional all-America good guy is the bad guy again. In the centerpiece to Brian De Palma's *Redacted,* which is based on a real incident, American soldiers in Samarra rape and murder a fifteen-year-old girl and her family. In Paul Haggis's *In the Valley of Elah,* also inspired by a true story, a recently returned American soldier who served in Iraq—the son of a Vietnam vet played by Tommy Lee Jones—is ultimately discovered to have been murdered by men in his own unit. In both movies, the perpetrators are portrayed as hollow-eyed thugs. The implication is clear—these men were zombified by an unjust war (or conversely, an unjust war attracted zombie recruits). Instead of going after the policy makers who put these men into that war, the filmmakers demonize the soldiers themselves.

If there is a more all-American male icon than the fighting soldier, it's the Westerner, and he, too, has undergone an extreme makeover. Traditionally Jesse James has been touted in the movies as a mythic hero in much the same way that he once was in the dime novels. In *The Assassination of Jesse James by the Coward Robert Ford,* Brad Pitt's Jesse is a sociopath whose antennae are tuned to the tiniest quavers of betrayal. His murders are swift and remorseless. In one sequence, seeking vengeance, he savagely beats an innocent boy. This Jesse James is one of the very first

casualties of the American fame industry and, as such, Pitt, who has a
sly knowingness in the role, is perfectly cast. The legendary Westerner
has been transformed into an icon deranged by his own celebrity. His
murderer, Casey Affleck's Robert Ford, is ultimately also annihilated by
his own notoriety.

Joel and Ethan Coen have said that in their *No Country For Old
Men*—which is set in Texas in 1980 but feels contemporary—the classic Westerner is split into three archetypes at war with one another. Josh
Brolin's hunter Llewelyn Moss is the scruffy Everyman who makes off
with somebody else's millions from a drug deal gone wrong; Javier Bar-
dem's Anton Chigurh, whose massive head looks like a carved chess piece
and whose weapon of choice is a cattle stun gun, is the sagebrush Terminator who pursues him. Tommy Lee Jones's Ed Tom Bell is the local sheriff who tracks them knowing full well that a new malevolence has entered
into the West that he cannot survive. Ed Tom Bell may be Old School but
Chigurh is Old Testament.

It's significant that even people who admire this movie feel cheated
by its fatalism. They want a happy ending. (Don't they know Cormac
McCarthy, who wrote the novel, doesn't do happy?) These are the same
folks who complained that the killer wasn't captured at the end of *Zodiac.*
Without Chigurh's rampant, unpunished depravity, which is so ghoulish
it's comic, the movie has no meaning. He represents the sheer animality
of male aggression. His triumph in this most masculine of genres certifies his ascendancy in a terrifying modern world where we no longer feel
protected.

A generation ago, in his *Eyes of Laura Mars* days, Tommy Lee Jones
himself might have been well cast as Chigurh. But with this movie, and
In the Valley of Elah, he's eased into a more sanctioned tradition—the
strong-silent man of principle. In both films, his weathered antiquity is
perceived as on the way out—and more necessary to America than ever.

The comedy of the horny brigade in the Judd Apatow films, of Sa-
cha Baron Cohen in *Borat,* or even the guys in *Wedding Crashers,* acts
as a fizzy chaser to the heavy bourbon of the big boys. (Vince Vaughn is
the opposite of the strong-silent type—he's weak and he never shuts up.)
Clooney in his movies may have all the right moves, he may look like there
was never a time when he didn't have them, but it is Steve Carell trying to
hold on to his virginity, or the buddies from *Superbad* desperately trying

to lose theirs, who capture the imagination of Geek Nation—which, it turns out, covers a large swath of the male population. Leaving aside the raunch factor, the men and boys in these movies are innocents—blood-brothers to Tom Hanks's Josh, the twelve-year-old thirty-year-old in *Big,* a key eighties movie about the wonders of arrested development. Not surprisingly, *Big* is being talked about for a remake.

In the end, there can't be all that much of a masculinity crisis in the movies if Clooney and Carell can co-exist in the same eco-system. There is, however, one species of men's movie that is largely AWOL, and it's the same one that flourished just before the primal heroics of the Reagan era took hold. Films as disparate as *Dog Day Afternoon, McCabe and Mrs. Miller, Deliverance,* and *Raging Bull* didn't rubberstamp the prevailing macho orthodoxies, they challenged and subverted and worried them. It's difficult to be a man, these films said, and by their willingness to embrace moral ambiguity, they honored that difficulty. At a time when we are at war and masculine force in the movies is being trumpeted or pilloried, I have a suggestion for Hollywood. Why not give Rambo a rest and revisit the realm of films like these instead?

(*Los Angeles Times,* 2007)

CHAPTER 9

COMEDIES (INTENTIONAL AND UNINTENTIONAL)

INTENTIONAL

Sideways

Sideways is the sweetest, funniest, most *humane* movie I've seen all year. I emphasize its humanity because most of what passes for comedy these days, whether it be low-concept or smarty-pants, is little more than gag-fests peopled by joke-bots. In the movies and on television, it's become hip to make comedies about nothing, à la *Seinfeld* and *Curb Your Enthusiasm*, or, in the case of *I Heart Huckabees*, everything—which might as well be nothing. Frosty facetiousness is the signature style of the new "intellectual" American jape, and until now, I would have lumped Alexander Payne—who directed *Sideways* and adapted it from a Rex Pickett novel with his partner, Jim Taylor—into a mix that includes such prodigious smart alecks as Paul Thomas Anderson, the Coen brothers, and David O. Russell. In his previous feature films, *Citizen Ruth, Election*, and particularly *About Schmidt*, all of which were set in his native Nebraska, Payne was keen on displaying his own superiority to his characters. His movies were vehicles for vengeance against the heartland. (No yokel, he.) But somewhere between his last film and his new one, Payne traded in his sarcasm for a soul. Maybe it has something to do with the fact that *Sideways* is set in the golden pastoral haze of California's Central Coast wine country. Or maybe it was just all that wine.

Paul Giamatti's Miles, a woebegone eighth-grade English teacher and would-be novelist, is the film's unlikely Pinot aficionado who sets off from L.A. on a wine-tasting trip with Jack (Thomas Haden Church), an old college friend and washed-up actor, the week before Jack's wedding. Miles is still sulking two years after his divorce from a woman he still pines for; Jack, who has large, rangy features and big hair and a surfer dude's deep drawl, aims to cheer him up by getting him laid—a cure-all that he also reserves for himself. (He calls this trip his "last week of freedom.") All the standard clichés are in place for a midlife-crisis, buddies-on-the-road movie, except that none of it plays out the way you'd expect. These guys may be an odd couple, but the mismatch makes psychological sense: Miles confers a connoisseurship on his friend, who doesn't read much and thinks all wines taste pretty much the same; Jack stokes Miles's id. If they had met as adults, they would probably not have connected, but college friendships are forged at a time when everyone is experimenting with who they are.

In each other's company, the experiment resumes. Miles and Jack knock about as if they were still late-stage adolescents. They're still figuring out who they want to be, which gives their strenuous efforts at happiness an added poignancy (and absurdity). We can see that Miles, who according to Jack has been "officially depressed for, like, two years," is more than just a glum shlub; he may not be able to get his book sold, but his love of language is as real as his love of the grape. When he talks about literature or his favorite wines, he isn't showing off. He's trying to live up to his own best image of himself, and he seems transported. In his own dim way, Jack understands this, which is why their friendship is more complicated than it appears. Jack is always telling the people they meet that Miles's book is being published, and he isn't being cruel—he's trying to inspire Miles to be the guy he was before the two-year tailspin (and also get him some action).

Miles has a wonderful monologue in which he rhapsodizes about the Pinot grape to a sympathetic waitress, Maya (an extraordinarily good Virginia Madsen). He calls it thin-skinned, temperamental, in need of constant care and attention. Of course, he is talking about himself. (Jack, by contrast, is a Cabernet that can grow anywhere and thrive even when neglected.) Miles is preternaturally sensitive to his own shortcomings. When Maya, who also knows her wine, leaves him an opening to make a pass, he lets the moment slide away, and his misery shines forth from his eyes like a death ray. Giamatti is letting us know that Miles's eloquence about wine may just be a fancy way of tarting up his drinking habit, his sadness. But he isn't simply replaying his Harvey Pekar from *American Splendor*. This is a whole other species of depresso—tender, enraged, rueful about what he has lost. At least Pekar was published.

One of the wonderful things about *Sideways* is that Payne gives its women equal standing (that's why it's not really a buddy movie). Maya is every bit as intricate as Miles—she has her own self-revealing monologue about how wine is "actually alive," gaining complexity until its inevitable decline. But she's blunter than he is. She tells him she loves wine because, when all is said and done, it "tastes so fucking good." Hard knocks haven't bruised her the way they have Miles; she's still in the game, going for a degree in horticulture and taking things as they come. Miles may be one of those things, but she doesn't press it—she respects his grief, and she's also a little wary of it.

Maya's friend Stephanie (Sandra Oh), a local wine pourer, is the film's freest spirit, and an ideal playmate for Jack. Their carnal romps, at least until Stephanie finds out Jack is engaged, are great lewd slapstick. Miles chastises his friend, but it's hard to argue with the guy's life force, which is so outsize it's comic. Jack has an actor's penchant for playing everything center stage; when he's recognized by a waitress for some crummy, long-ago soap-opera role, he acquires an imbecilic glow—he's in clover. (Soon after, he's in her bed.) Thomas Haden Church is known primarily for the inane sitcom *Wings*, so his performance here is a revelation—he gives depth to shallowness. Jack the satyr-narcissist is a figure of fun, but he harbors his own losses. That's why he plumps up every time he's noticed. He compensates for his show-business failure by converting the world into his very own playhouse.

Miles and Jack, in their own ways, are in awe of women—of their power to scramble a man's good sense. Miles's ex-wife, when we finally meet her, is no gorgon; she's decent and intelligent and still cares about him, only not enough. With Miles, declarations of faith are supposed to be forever. He can't abide the waywardness of affection, any more than he can abide someone who doesn't love Pinot. In *Sideways*, wine is much more than wine. It's a metaphor for the spirits that bring us to a reckoning with ourselves.

(*New York*, 2004)

Diner

If I had not been primed in advance, I would not have expected much from writer-director Barry Levinson's *Diner*. If there's one thing we don't need now it's another fifties rite-of-passage movie, complete with the obligatory buddy-buddyisms and a soundtrack of Golden Oldies. Levinson, who co-wrote . . . *And Justice For All* and *Inside Moves*, as well as, among other credits, *The Carol Burnett Show*, Mel Brooks's *High Anxiety* and *Silent Movie*, has in the past demonstrated a wacky, uneven flair. But nothing in his previous work gives any indication of the depth in *Diner*, which also marks his directorial debut. He's accomplished a minor miracle—a movie that, on the surface, is thoroughly familiar and yet, because of its artistry and perception, seems totally fresh.

The movie opens on Christmas night, 1959, in Baltimore. There's not a whole lot of plot; essentially, we follow for a few days the lives of five guys in their early twenties—ex-high-school buddies—as they try to come to terms with their encroaching adulthood. In conventional terms, nothing much "happens" in this movie. It's a multi-character study, and we quickly sort out the characters: there's Eddie (Steve Guttenberg), a fervid Colts fan who's about to get married (but first his wife must pass a football quiz!); Billy (Timothy Daly), Eddie's prospective best man, who, in town from grad school, discovers that his sort-of girlfriend Barbara, a local TV-studio engineer (Kathryn Dowling), is pregnant; Shrevie (Daniel Stern), who appears to prize his record collection more than his wife Beth (Ellen Barkin); Fenwick (Kevin Bacon), a hard-drinking college dropout on the bum from his upper-class family; and Boogie (Mickey Rourke, the arsonist in *Body Heat*), a soft-spoken ladies man and gambler who works in a beauty parlor—with his oily pompadour and smart jackets, he's like a hood-prince. (There's also a sixth character—Paul Reiser's Modell—who's used in his brief appearances as the group's comic foil.)

None of these characters are quite what they first appear to be. Eddie swaggers a lot, but he overdoes it; he has the fast, clipped speech of someone who's trying to fortify himself against uncertainties. Billy has a clean-cut handsomeness that bespeaks blandness, but he has surprising reserves of vehemence. In a strip-joint/bar with Eddie one night, he shouts down the lagging house band and then sprints up to the stage to pound out some boogie-woogie—it's as if Bobby Rydell turned into Jerry Lee Lewis. Fenwick at first comes across as a spoiled-brat goof-off with the scary, gruff voice of a premature alky but he, too, shows unexpected depths of feeling, as well as smarts (watching *College Bowl* on TV, he consistently blurts out the correct answers ahead of the Ivy League eggheads). Shrevie, the only married member of the group, is never at a loss for words with his friends, but he has nothing to say to his wife, or she to him. When Eddie, nervous about the upcoming wedding, talks to him about what married life is like, Shrevie comes across as small-spirited, unfeeling. He sees marriage in almost purely sexual terms—as a way of insuring regular nookie. And Shrevie is dispirited by that regularity. Domesticity depresses him.

Because he acts out, or pretends to act out, the boys' erotic fantasies, Boogie is the group's unspoken leader. Boogie, like the others, is more complex than he at first appears. He may be a smooth-talking con-man with women, but he's a *heartfelt* con-man; his soft-soothing patter is a clue to some essential tenderness. Of all the boys, he's the only one who is able to really talk to women, to level with them. "If you don't have good dreams, you have nightmares," he says, and he means it. At times, he has the blasted look of someone who's trying to shuffle off bad dreams but, when his life connects with his fantasies—when, for example, he spots a vision of loveliness cantering on her horse in the countryside—he has a satyr's gleam in his bright eyes. He's the most poetic character in the film because, despite all his bull, he's the most open to the emotional possibilities in life.

It's rare to see a movie where the friendships seem as real, as lived-in, as they do here. This is partly due to Levinson's reverberant script and direction, and partly a result of the fine ensemble acting. The performances are uniformly superlative. The actors have reimagined their roles, which on the surface seem so familiar from other movies, as completely as Levinson has. When the boys congregate at the shiny, art deco Falls Point Diner on the edge of town, we can see immediately why they're friends. Inside the diner, with its harsh, white light—like stage-lighting—they take turns being on; they're like a round-robin of stand-up (or sit-down) comics, and their actions crystallize their characters. Nothing that they do inside the diner is quite real—the affections and hostilities that fly through the air don't really lead anywhere. They're stage routines, and yet they provide a more heady interaction for the boys than anything on the outside (in the same way that many theatrical performers claim to be most alive when they're onstage.) When some real life butts into this bright fantasy world—when Eddie, alone with Boogie, drops the mournful news that he's a virgin—the moment cuts though the atmosphere like a shiv.

The world that the diner insulates these boys from is the last dregs of the fifties—a time when young men and women were beginning to really question their relationship to each other. What they're going through is a faint prelude to the social upheavals of the sixties; the people in *Diner* are the last shock troops of the old order. They accept the rigid social confines of their lives, but it doesn't sit too well with them. The women in this film feel excluded from the men's lives without really wanting to take part in their rituals; Eddie tells Billy that the two of them share secrets his future wife "will never know," but he says so with false bravado. These people are sensitive and intelligent enough to register, however subliminally, a sense of missed emotional connections. And, finally, that sense of loss is tragic. Even if they don't feel the loss, we do. The modern perspective that Levinson gives *Diner* makes it seem, despite its considerable humor, ineffably sad—even the soundtrack, with up-tempo standards like Elvis Presley's "Don't be Cruel" and Fats Domino's "Whole Lotta Loving," carries an echo of regret.

If the young men in this film believe that marriage primarily means missing out on things, that's because they don't know what to say to women. That's why Eddie puts his fiancee through a multiple-choice/true-false football quiz; if she passes, then they can marry and at least he'll have something to talk about with her. *Diner* gets at the psychological roots of buddy-buddyism. For a guy like Eddie or Shrevie, their lives will never have the vibrancy that it did before they were married; they can still hang out together, but it won't be the same. (Their slang word for a gorgeous woman is—revealingly—"death," as in "she's death.") Billy, who is meant, I think, to be a precursor of a "liberated" man—he actually thinks his girlfriend's TV-studio job has value—may have a more hopeful future. So may Boogie, if he's lucky. Fenwick seems primed for dissolution; so does Beth, as long as she's with Shrevie. *Diner* reveals its people for who they are and also what they will become. The perspective of time gives us a double-image. And, because the future of these people seems for the most part as muted and drained of color as the look of their present (as photographed by Peter Sova), we want to hold onto them while there's still some vitality left. After the movie has ended, the closing credits come on, and we hear again on the soundtrack for several minutes the joyful, animated voices of the guys in the diner, ribbing and taunting each other. At the screening I attended, no one got up to leave until the voices had faded away.

(*Los Angeles Herald Examiner*, 1982)

Roxanne

Roxanne is one of the most beautiful, elating romantic comedies ever made in this country. It makes you feel mysteriously, unreasonably happy, as if you were watching colors being added to a sunset. The glow from this film stays with you; it has a radiance like no other movie. Steve Martin, the writer-star, and his director, Fred Schepisi, create a cockeyed higgledy-piggledy universe that's as magically stylized as anything the great silent comedians came up with. The comedy comes out of the delicately illuminated setting, and the romance does, too. The movie is about the *rightness* of true love, and everything in nature—the quality of the light, the steep slope of the streets, the pure, wide mountain vistas—seems to conspire in the annunciation. We're watching a world where purity of feeling counts for as much as the purity of the glorious natural surroundings; a world where love—poetically, inevitably—will out.

By reworking Edmond Rostand's 1897 *Cyrano De Bergerac* to a Washington off-season ski resort, Steve Martin, playing the long-nosed town fire chief, C. D. Bales, courts disaster. Instead, the preposterousness of updating this glorious old warhorse works in the film's favor; it's part of the storybook charm. C. D. is the town's natural aristocrat; his off-kilter athleticism and courtly, self-absorbed quirkiness set him apart from his neighbors. He's like a more heightened version of eccentric. His long, tapered nose gives him a surreal handsomeness.

That nose is C. D.'s shame, but it's so much a part of who he is that he's unimaginable with anything smaller. A normal-sized nose would diminish him, make him seem less fantastic—in the same way that a smiling Buster Keaton would be a reduction of his character's poetic possibilities. The Keaton reference is central; no comic actor since the great Buster has been able to work up such an abundance of physical comedy. Martin works with such precision that there isn't a movement that doesn't contribute to what we know about C. D.; the sheer joy of physical release is in every skip and skedaddle.

C. D. is so deeply ashamed of his nose that he compensates by becoming a connoisseur of his fine points; he moves about in a state of fine-tuned, calisthenic rapture. He can shimmy up the side of a house to the roof in a few quick pull-ups. He walks up and down the slanty streets at gravity-defying angles; he's never quite on the same plane as anybody else, he's always just a bit askew from the horizon. C. D. *conspires* with gravity (as all the great silent comics did). He uses the loopiness of nature's forces to assert his specialness, and turns stunts into dream walks.

It's a measure of Martin's performance that he manages to give C. D. a romantic core, without pathos. In this movie's supernal setting, pathos would seem as jarringly out of place as a shout in a canyon. When C. D. first meets Roxanne (Daryl Hannah) he's flabbergasted, as we are, by her beauty. But we see his awe in small, self-revelatory ways. He doesn't work against the planes of his surroundings quite so much when he's around her. Roxanne moves in a lyrical sweep, and C. D. acquiesces in that movement. It's a way of romancing her, of keying into her cycles.

To C. D., Roxanne is a heavenly vision—the apotheosis of the beauty that surrounds him. (The whole town sparkles like an upturned planetarium; C. D. is its honorary moon man.) She's an astronomy student searching the skies for a new comet she believes is out there, waiting to be discovered. Closer to earth, she has eyes for one of C. D.'s new volunteer firemen, the hunky but painfully shy Chris (Rick Rossovich), who runs for cover whenever he gets close to Roxanne. Just as in *Cyrano*, she and Chris are brought together by the man who loves her most. C. D. is prevailed upon by Chris to ghostwrite love letters to her; then he prompts Chris's speeches to her under her balcony, finally taking over himself, shadowed from recognition. Roxanne is in love with C. D.—embodied by Chris. He's the go-between in the demolition of his own true love, and yet he keeps on going, writing reams of letters, devising speeches. When he's in love, even gravity seems to have lost its tug on C. D. He's comet-like, carried away by his ardor, his folly.

C. D.'s wooing of Roxanne, through Chris, is done almost entirely with language. Martin's script for *Roxanne* is in love with words and their power to entrance. C. D. is agile, and he can punch, too, but words are what carry him away. When a guy in a bar makes a dumb crack about his nose, C. D. one-ups the lout by improvising twenty proboscis put-downs in a row, in a heightened, exhilarated patter. (It's a variation on the most famous scene in *Cyrano*.) C. D.'s infatuation with language comes out of his most private precincts—when he's revved up, his speeches have the frantic, lickety-split velocity of a lonely man suddenly trumpeting his own inner dialogues for all to hear. His florid, triumphant love pronouncements are really a triumph of spirit, and that's where the real romance in *Roxanne* lies. What we immediately respond to in C. D. is what Roxanne finally responds to as well—not the beauty of his words so much as the beauty of the spirit behind those words.

This awareness of the primacy of the spirit makes *Roxanne* a deeply humane comedy. Schepisi and Martin embrace C. D. because they recognize his value; they recognize the beauty in his stumbly troupe of volunteer firemen, too. (The standout crew includes Michael J. Pollard, John Kapelos, Steve Mittleman, and Matt Lattanzi.) But it's not just the romantics and the outcasts that the filmmakers side with. They also confer their blessings on Chris by eventually pairing him off with a more suitable soul mate (Shandra Beri), a waitress-cutie for whom his lunky muteness is as enticing as C. D.'s verbal ravishments. All of the movie's characters are haloed by the filmmakers' good graces, and that includes Fred Willard's tin-horn town mayor, and Shelley Duvall's cafe owner—C. D.'s best friend. Schepisi, with the help of his great cinematographer, Ian Baker, creates a cuckoo, cloud-borne community, part Brigadoon, part Milkwood; its inhabitants are magical versions of the everyday. Everything seems anointed in this town, newly minted: the firemen's bumblings are like the beginnings of slapstick; the starry heavens are like the first big night sky you can remember looking up at as a kid; C. D.'s love for Roxanne is like the first love. The freshness of this world matches the freshness of Schepisi and Martin's vision. Like C. D., they're romancers, too. Their movie sends you into a swoon.

(*Los Angeles Herald Examiner*, 1987)

Mars Attacks!

Forget *Independence Day*. If you really want to see Earth get it, you can't do any better than Tim Burton's *Mars Attacks!* It's a destructo orgy orchestrated without any phony-baloney sanctimony about the fellowship of man—or spaceman.

Burton isn't interested in intergalactic amity; he's not even interested in preserving the Earth. He's like a precocious, nut-brained kid pumped with fifties sci-fi pulp. But he doesn't take his pulp straight. Burton turns inside out the tacky stalwart grandeur of such films as *The Day the Earth Stood Still* and *Earth vs. the Flying Saucers*. Part homage and part demolition job, *Mars Attacks!* is perhaps the funniest piece of giddy schlock heartlessness ever committed to film.

Pure id runs riot: movie stars get incinerated right along with the extras; Sarah Jessica Parker's head gets transplanted onto a Chihuahua's body; Martians morph into robotic *Playboy* babes with beehive 'dos and torpedo tits. Everything about *Mars Attacks!* is flagrantly lewd yet presexual—a preadolescent's fever dream. The real sex in this movie is in the wacko mayhem and the gorgeousness of the grotesquerie. It's a nonstop kitsch spritz.

Burton's fecund imagination is so free-ranging, it's eerie. Along with his screenwriter, Jonathan Gems, he draws not only on fifties sci-fi but on images from Cocteau, *Dr. Strangelove, The Bride of Frankenstein*, and pulp comic books and trading cards—including, of course, the 1962 Topps *Mars Attacks!* series, which was withdrawn from the market for being too lurid. He riffs on the seventies cycle of disaster epics such as *The Towering Inferno* and *Earthquake*.

The implicit joke behind those straight-faced disaster films was that destruction was a turn-on; in *Earthquake*, audiences grooved to L.A.'s collapse—it was biblical-style retribution for Sin City. In *Mars Attacks!* Burton brings the joke out into the open; he doesn't disguise his glee in blowing things up, and his main targets—Washington, DC, and Las Vegas—are eminently blow-up-able. They're America's yin and yang; the White House and the MGM Grand are the twin tepees of our national imagination.

Everybody gets it in *Mars Attacks!* (Everybody *deserves* to get it.) We first see a herd of cattle on fire stampeding through the Kansas heartland—it's a tip-off that the Martians have arrived. A credit sequence follows in which their saucers wheel through space like giant hubcaps while, on the soundtrack, the woozy sound of the theremin gives us cold creeps. Then we switch from the heartland to the Pentagon—commonly a reassuring trajectory in fifties sci-fi.

But the Washington honchos here are far from reassuring. President James Dale is played by eyebrow-flexing Jack Nicholson, who also plays the sequined Vegas real estate hustler Art Land—hustlers high and low. General Decker (Rod Steiger) is a bald-pated horror whose game plan for the impending Martian touchdown is simple: "Kill! Kill! Kill!" His opposite number, Paul Winfield's General Casey, sees the Martian arrival in the Arizona desert as a peace offering; he greets them with the intergalactic sign of the doughnut. The interminably pipe-puffing government scientist Donald Kessler (Pierce Brosnan) is so preternaturally calm he's practically an alien too. He's all intellect—all head—so when the Martians actually reduce him to a floating cranium, he's essentially the same guy. If, postdecapitation, he seems vaguely denuded, it's not because he's bodiless but because he's pipeless.

Depending on whether they swing to the Right or to the Left, sci-fi movies usually thump either for Pentagon power or we-the-people gumption. But Tim Burton is an equal-opportunity scourge. It's as if he read all those high-toned tracts on the "meaning" of fifties sci-fi flicks—how they were a metaphor for the Cold War and nuclear holocaust—and decided to diddle those theories every which way. You can't call *Mars Attacks!* reactionary sci-fi. True, the heartland masses, led by trailer-park patriarch Joe Don Baker, are mostly stunted yokels—but then, so are Washington's top brass. The Washington Monument building is just a goofball phallic symbol. The Martians snip it and tip it. *Mars Attacks!* is prepolitical in the same way it's presexual; it uses its emblems of force demonic kiddie-cartoon-style.

When Stanley Kubrick and Terry Southern lampooned the military in *Dr. Strangelove*, they did it with an overlay of jokey sophistication—it was supposed to be black comedy for "knowing" adults. Burton's visual fantasias—the way, for example, he turns Vegas into a fan dance of irradiated reds and blues and greens—are certainly sophisticated. But his sensibility isn't—at least not in the usual ways. He's making fun of fifties schlock sci-fi in *Mars Attacks!* but he's also deeply drawn to it; this is why he could make a movie such as *Ed Wood*, which enshrines schlock. (*Ed Wood*, of course, ends with Wood riding high and leaves off his life's sordid denouement into porno and alcoholism.) Success in the movie business hasn't made Burton "knowing." He's goofing on fifties schlock, but he's not "commenting" on it. To do that would be to disown the love he feels for it.

The love runs pretty deep, and the genuine scariness that sometimes arises from *Mars Attacks!* is keyed to just how deeply all this schlock has burrowed into Burton's brain. There are people who couldn't stomach Burton's *Beetlejuice* and *Batman* and, especially, *Edward Scissorhands*. The pop dementia on view seemed too unsettling; he set us up for a cartoon romp and then went all ghastly on us. Burton takes audiences farther out into the realms of pop-comic heebie-jeebies than any other director, but some audiences respond to him the way they more often respond to David Lynch. They want to know why this guy is dumping all his sicko stuff on us.

It's easy to be affronted by what Burton is doing in his movies because there *is* an element of cruelty in his relationship with the audience; there's a joy buzzer in his handshake. He wants to give us the willies because he's already got them—and he doesn't want to be alone with them. Better we should *all* be spooked.

The Martians in *Mars Attacks!* are a full grade scarier than we might expect from a sci-fi spoof. As designed by the wizards at Industrial Light and Magic, they're computer-generated gargoyles with big brains like curlicued blooms of tufa; their lidless bulging eyeballs and skull smiles are not remotely cute. When the Martians create a Playmate to heat up the president's libidinous press secretary Jerry Ross (Martin Short) and gain access to the White House, their creation (Lisa Marie) resembles the dream-walking undead in a film by Cocteau or Franju (specifically *Eyes Without a Face*). Her herky-jerky gyroscopic glide through the hallways of power is one scary-funny wiggle. Jerry is so smitten with her that he starts to move like her. When he pulls on her flesh, her cheek falls away (so does Jerry). This Martian Girl is a pinup nightmare—the wrath of plastic.

The Topps *Mars Attacks!* cards, painted by veteran pulp magazine artist Norm Saunders, were dandy little decals of luridness. The cards' titles—such as "Destroying a Dog," "Burning Flesh," and "Beast and the

Beauty"—were emblazoned on lascivious scenes of destruction backgrounded by blood-red skies. There's nothing spoofy about these cards. They may be gross-outs, but they sure are fervid.

Burton connects to the kid-stuff horror in the cards—they probably function for him like pieces of the Grail. He also feels affection for their frights. He wants us to know that the bluenoses were right—the cards *were* dangerous. In *Mars Attacks!* Burton, who started out as an animator, uses the cards' luridness as inspiration, but then he gooses us. *Mars Attacks!* is scary-funny in ways we haven't seen before—except perhaps in other Burton movies or in Peter Jackson's *Dead Alive*, which also goosed us with overkill.

The one character in the film who comes across as genuinely heroic—as opposed to mock-heroic—is Lukas Haas's Richie, the Kansas slacker who, helped inadvertently by his dotty grandmother (Sylvia Sidney), figures out a way to burst the Martians' brains. (Their craniums appear to be engorged with Prell.) It's perhaps no accident that Richie, with his shambling alertness and scraggly locks, resembles Burton. Richie brings out Burton's Boy Scout side. When, on a Kansas back road at night, a giant Martian robot clomps after the boy attempting to escape in his truck, we fear for him in a way we don't for anybody else in the movie.

How could we fear for anybody else? Burton's satiric point is that the humans are just as soulless and far-out as the Martians. They're too stunted to even react properly to the invasion; while the world is being incinerated, Vegas still packs 'em in and the White House is still giving tours. A TV reporter (Michael J. Fox) tries to wangle a Martian interview; he might be trying to score a celebrity. Tom Jones, who seems ageless enough to be an alien himself, continues to croon "It's Not Unusual" even when his backup singers turn out to be barking aliens.

The fifties sci-fi movie stalwarts, such as John Agar or Richard Carlson, were so deeply bland that they might as well have been androids. But their blandness wasn't intended satirically. In *Mars Attacks!* the more straight-arrow you are, like Pierce Brosnan's pipe puffer, the weirder—and more laughable—you seem. Burton casts Jim Brown as an ex-heavyweight boxing champ who, dressed as an Egyptian, works as a Vegas casino greeter; it's such a funny image, and Brown is so imperially blank, that you almost don't mind the fact that Burton hasn't really figured out what to *do* with him. (He ends up boxing the Martians—big wow.) Burton's clunkiness at least is in the service of a higher clunkiness.

It would be too bad if smart adults turned away from *Mars Attacks!* and left it to the smart kids. A lot of drippy movies are out there appealing to the Child Within; Burton's new film appeals to the Brat Within. Despite a few forced efforts at topicality and political jokesterism—like the scene in the White House in which the Reagan chandelier crushes Glenn Close, as the president's shrewish wife, or the way Paul Winfield recalls General Colin Powell—*Mars Attacks!* stays resolutely within its nuthouse campgrounds.

Fifties sci-fi movies may have been a skewed response to Cold War fears, but *Mars Attacks!* is a *post*-Cold War romp. The Russians don't even figure in it. And with no Commies around to target, Burton goes blooey and targets *everything*. We've come a long way. *Dr. Strangelove*, our greatest Cold War comedy, was, of course, subtitled *How I Learned to Stop Worrying and Love the Bomb*. In *Mars Attacks!* Burton has his Martians inhale a nuclear missile and get high on the radiation. You can't love the Bomb any more than that.

(New Times, 1996)

Man on the Moon

The pivotal moment in *Man on the Moon*, starring Jim Carrey as the late Andy Kaufman, comes when Andy tells his girlfriend, Lynne Margulies (Courtney Love), that she doesn't know the real him, and she responds, "There *isn't* a real you," and he says, "Oh, yeah, I forgot." Director Milos Forman and his screenwriters, Scott Alexander and Larry Karaszweski, have attempted to make a movie about a human nullity, and a fair amount of screen time is taken up with Kaufman's bizarre routines and shenanigans. He doesn't reveal himself onstage, and he doesn't offstage either; whether he's playing Latka Gravas on *Taxi* or the crumb-bum Vegas entertainer Tony Clifton, he never breaks character.

The usual Hollywood approach to celebrity bio is two-pronged: Freudian-ize and canonize. *Man on the Moon* goes heavy on the canonization—that's its major weakness—but it doesn't pretend to "explain"

Kaufman. No childhood trauma, no Rosebud, awaits our discovery. The movie assumes that performers are authentic only when they're performing, and so the Andy that Milos Forman gives us is always *on*. He needs to be entertained by audiences—by their cheers *and* jeers—at least as much as they need to be entertained by him.

What the movie doesn't explore is how Kaufman might have been deeply pained by his multiple-man mind-set, and it also doesn't suggest the cruelty behind some of his so-called performance art. When he refuses to play Latka for a clamorous college audience and, instead, submits the few of them who remain to a cover-to-cover, English-accented reading of *The Great Gatsby*, the scene is played as if he were asserting his right to be an artist and not just a sitcom personality. But when he wasn't taking them out for milk and cookies, Kaufman regularly rebuffed his audiences, and he didn't do it because he was protecting the purity of his gifts. He did it because he probably couldn't help himself, and because flop sweat for him was just as sweet as the nectar of adulation. Heckling was music to his ears; that's why he made such a big deal out of wrestling women in his self-created "intergender" championship matches. Strutting and playing the villain inside the ring, he could provoke a direct-action response from audiences even more effectively than in the comedy clubs. *Man on the Moon* makes the same mistake that Bob Fosse's *Lenny* made—it gives the abrasiveness of its subject a saintly glow.

Perhaps part of that glow exists because many of the people who were important to Kaufman's life and career—including George Shapiro, his agent; Bob Zmuda, his friend and writer; and Lynne Margulies, his girlfriend—acted as advisers and, in some cases, co-producers on the film as well as being depicted in it. A lot of the action has a scrubbed, authorized feel. Thus, when Shapiro, played as a lump of human kindness by Danny DeVito, first connects with Kaufman, he tells him, "You're insane, but you might also be brilliant." In a nightclub, Paul Giamatti's Zmuda plays the stooge to Andy's Tony Clifton, getting razzed before an unsuspecting audience and having a drink thrown in his face, and afterward it's all fun and games between them. We don't see how Zmuda might have reacted to this kind of usage, or what resentments or competitiveness may have been behind it. Courtney Love's Lynne first encounters Andy when she loses to him in one of his wrestling matches, but soon after she turns into a drab, devotional caregiver. Their relationship is depicted as a love match, but there's virtually no sexual dimension to Kaufman in this film; he's almost as infantilized as Pee-wee Herman.

Jim Carrey plays Kaufman onstage with an uncanny exactitude, but what are we watching exactly? He's doing more than mere impersonation, and yet Kaufman never comes to full-blooded life for us, any more than Carrey's Truman, another hologram of a person, did. When I did a brief interview with Kaufman in L.A. in the early eighties, I thought I was talking to somebody out of *The Manchurian Candidate*. There was a propulsive, gaga rhythm to his patter. I was hoping *Man on the Moon* would prove an enlightenment, but by conceiving of Kaufman as a holy hollow man who lived only through his guises, the filmmakers have deprived Carrey of the opportunity to go behind the comic's fixed blank stare. If there's no there there, why should he, or we, bother? The movie is intended as a celebration of Andy Kaufman, but it's the kind of celebration that denatures its subject. It's not the "real" man we're missing. We're missing a man, any man, period.

(New York, 2000)

Almost Famous

Cameron Crowe's *Almost Famous*, set mostly in 1973, is a blissfully sweet coming-of-age movie in which everyone, young and less young, comes of age. William Miller (Patrick Fugit), the fifteen-year-old budding rock journalist, is the film's centerpiece, and he's a wide-eyed munchkin savant, a cherub in the Dionysian circus of rock and roll. He's so virginal he's comic; roving groupies take one look at him and can't wait to deflower him en masse, for the sport of it. On assignment to cover the touring up-and-coming Led Zeppelin-ish band Stillwater for *Rolling Stone*, William becomes its unofficial mascot. Russell Hammond (Billy Crudup), the lead guitarist, has the requisite hippie Jesus look, and he sees in William not only an acolyte but, as the relationship deepens, a musical soul mate as well. What unites these two is the ecstasy of knowing just how deep-down good rock music can make you feel. A teenage rock journalist in the seventies before writing the book *Fast Times at Ridgemont High* and getting into movies, Crowe still feels this ecstasy in his bones, which is why his movie looks vibrantly alive instead of shimmering with that phony nostalgic haze common to period films set in that era. But Crowe is also honest enough to recognize how intricately bound our feelings for rock are to our zig-zag attitudes about sex and pomp and rebellion and cool. It's the rock lifestyle, as much as rock itself, that is being celebrated here.

Crowe sprinkles a pinch of powdered sugar on that lifestyle, but this approach is preferable to being subjected to the usual litany of overdoses and whoring. He does indeed bring some of this material into the movie, just enough to make us feel its sting, but he's not trying for an exposé. (What's left to expose, anyway?) His movie is like a souvenir of personal memories that have been candied by time. Crowe's films, especially his first two as a writer-director, *Say Anything . . .* and *Singles*, have always displayed an unyielding affection and longing for family, and what he finds in the rock world of *Almost Famous* is the greatest of extended families, an orgy of companionship. William's single mom, Elaine (Frances McDormand), who thinks rock and roll is a doomy siren's call, is the Mother Courage of the piece. She's already driven away William's sister Anita (Zooey Deschanel), who bequeaths her record collection to her brother. Then, for the first time in his life, William also leaves home, to follow Stillwater. Elaine is a monster but a very human one; in her own Gorgon-like way she cares deeply about her son, and she's certainly not wrong to worry about the drugs and the sex. But her defiance, which exhibits a comically overheated, rock-stars-have-kidnapped-my-son paranoia, is partly what eggs him on, and she knows it. William may be a cherub, but he's also a chip off the old block. His errantry is a backhanded tribute to his mom's mettle.

Early on, William acquires a mentor, the rock critic Lester Bangs (Philip Seymour Hoffman, who may be the best character actor in America). It is Bangs, with his gonzo's radar, who immediately perceives what lies ahead for the boy. "You cannot make friends with the rock stars," he tells him. "Friendship is the booze they feed you." And yet friendship is what William craves even more than reputation, even more than music. Crowe doesn't take a hard-line attitude toward all this; the movie is saying that some things are more important than journalism, at least to the journalist. The puff and glitz that some writers churn out may be murderous to their profession, but castigating those writers is not what this

movie is about. Who can fault William for "getting too close" to his subject? *Almost Famous* isn't about the making of a great rock scribe (which
Lester Bangs emphatically was). It's about how rock and roll messes you
up and brings you into a new relation with yourself. Besides, William
manages to deliver the goods—his story on Stillwater for *Rolling Stone*,
which both he and the band at first regard as a betrayal, is an uncensored
tribute to their shared spree.

Crowe brings out the emotional levels in William's odyssey. The boy's
almost palpable need for a father figure is fulfilled by the yin and yang of
Lester and Russell. Somehow William manages to reconcile himself to
both. Usually in movies it's the rock stars who are mythologized, but here
it is Lester the critic who gets the Yoda treatment, dispensing sage, scurrilous *pensées* over the phone from his platter-clogged apartment. Crowe,
who recently published a book of his affectionate, wide-eyed interviews
with his directing hero Billy Wilder, has an affinity for tenderizing deep-
dish cynics and outlaws: the Lester Bangs of this movie is a cautionary
guru who understands the rot and corruption of rock but still loves it
for its charge and its disposability; Russell Hammond assumes, uneasily,
the role of rock satyr. A gifted guitarist, he seems slightly baffled by the
writhings of his audience.

Russell may possess the onstage swagger of a star, but he looks to the
uplifted gaze of William to validate his cool. And he really loves music.
In the most serenely satisfying moment in the movie, Russell threatens
to leave the band after repeated clashes with the thin-skinned lead singer (Jason Lee). He's brought back into the fold when the group, aboard
their touring bus, joins in singing Elton John's "Tiny Dancer," tentatively
at first and finally at full throttle. Suddenly all is right with the world.
It's both a fantasy and a validation of how music can banish every bit of
badness from your life.

Crowe knows how to bring out the youthful ardor in his actors. Patrick Fugit has the most difficult role, because William is essentially an observer, a peacemaker. (As a writer-director, Crowe is a peacemaker, too;
he likes to bring people together.) William is the still center, or off-center,
of every scene in which he appears, but his recessiveness is intensely inquiring and likeable. Kate Hudson, playing Russell's chief groupie, Penny
Lane, is a swirl of concupiscence in faux-fur-collared coats and lace tank
tops. Hudson brings out the preternatural womanliness and pathos in

this girl, who can't be much older than William; she's wised-up already, and her baby fat is becoming hard-edged. Billy Crudup has been dubbed a star-in-waiting for so long that this film seems almost like a coronation. His performance may resemble a loose-limbed frolic, but it's also feral and intuitive and carries within it the remembered essence of every celebrated and not-so-celebrated rocker from that pivotal era. Crudup understands Russell's complicated position in William's life, which is why the final reconciliation between the two is such a beautifully conceived finale. It's just a simple grace note of a scene, but, like the entire movie, it has a soft, abiding resonance.

(New York, 2000)

UNINTENTIONAL

Under the Cherry Moon

For those who thought Prince's first film, *Purple Rain*, was the *Citizen Kane* of rock movies, I have urgent news: his second, *Under the Cherry Moon*, is no *Magnificent Ambersons.*

I'll say this much for His Purpleness—he may be culpable for turning out this nickel-plated disaster, but it's still more fascinating than most stinkeroos. Prince, after all, isn't doing roach motel commercials or booking passage on *The Love Boat*—at least not yet. He still has his screwy integrity, which includes releasing this movie in black and white (although it was reportedly shot in color) and splintering virtually every number on the soundtrack. (He seems to be saying, "No one's going to accuse *this* film of being a rock-album movie.") *Cherry Moon* is like a black ghetto kid's Deco fantasy of crashing white jet-set society. Playing a gigolo musician named Christopher, newly arrived on the French Riviera, Prince goes hog-wild for costumes. He first shows up in a glitter number that looks like newly molted snakeskin. From there, he moves on to a d'Artagnan frill-o-rama, and then a two-piece modified bellhop outfit—his belly button showing—complete with Cisco Kid hat and toreador pants. The

British heiress (Kristin Scott-Thomas) he's trying to wangle is also feath-
ered and behatted with enough designer finery to strangle Rodeo Drive.
In fact, there's so much Chanel-like costuming in this moony, villa-infest-
ed movie that you start having *Last Year at Marienbad* flashbacks.

The movie certainly has a look. The problem is, Prince, who directed, doesn't really know what to do with that look. He doesn't really
care, either—Essence of Showoff. He talks to himself a lot, but he's not
lonely, really—he's just paying tribute to his ego. He's self-infatuated in a
creepy, crepuscular sort of way; he loves looking hooded and sulphurous.
Prince's Cantinflas mustache and medallioned chest really wow 'em in
Antibes. All he has to do is tinkle a white piano and send off little Maria Montez smolder-glares, and before you know it, some rich socialite is
sending him mash notes on her cocktail napkins.

With his best buddy, Tricky (Jerome Benton), Christopher/Prince
crashes a couple of fancy-dress parties and puts the moves on everything
in sight. But the heiress he wants to make it with, Kristin Scott-Thomas's Mary Sharon, isn't encouraging—at first. She darts away from his
smoldering glances and falls in with a conga line; she takes trans-Atlantic
calls from her snit boyfriend (winner of the Worst Cary Grant Accent
Award). She and Christopher/Prince have shipboard fights; she calls him
a gigolo and he calls her a cabbage head. (Actually, Scott-Thomas looks
more like Marisa Berenson trying to look like Cher trying to look like
Claudette Colbert in *Cleopatra*.)

This So's-Your-Old-Man stuff doesn't last long, though. Mary Sharon falls for the way Chri—oh, forget it—*Prince* laps his lips at her and
spittles his hair. You can bet no one in that humidified villa of hers has
ever done *that* to her before. Besides, Prince falls for her, too. He's in
love with her—he wants to take her on a "trip to the moon" (presumably
cherry). He tells her, "With you I can be an honest man."

That's the pit in Prince's Cherry. He's really a pixie-softie at heart. He
takes Mary Sharon to the beach and smears himself onto her while can-
dles flicker, Harlequin-novel-style, in the background. He reads her his
poetry, such as it is. (It's like naughty Edward Lear.) When he's shot, he
gives her dying-Camille looks. The blood trickling down his chin looks
like mascara.

I don't want to make this movie sound more fun than it is. Prince
may be a rock potentate, but, as a director, he has a deadbeat, rhythmless

film sense. The sleek cinematography (by Michael Balhaus) is wrecked by framing that's always a few feet off kilter. (This style is known as Early Frank Perry.) The pauses between dialogue make Harold Pinter sound lickety-split. I wish this film *had* been a rock-album movie. At least then we could have heard the *Parade* LP complete. *Cherry Moon* will probably pack in the Prince fans for the first week or so, but after that, they're gonna have to sell off costumes in the lobby. Cut-rate.

(*Los Angeles Herald Examiner*, 1986)

Meet Joe Black

Suppose you were Death and you were visiting the mortal realm for the first time. What would you do for kicks? Maybe check out Graceland or take in the slopes at Aspen? Splurge at Barneys or cool out on the Côte d'Azur? Wouldn't you want to boogie? Wouldn't you want to feel *alive*?

The big cheese in *Meet Joe Black* doesn't think so. Joe (Brad Pitt) is Death personified, and he acts like death warmed over. He manifests himself in human form in order to mingle with mortals, but he doesn't look like he's having a lick of fun. Then again, *Meet Joe Black* isn't a comedy. Actually, it is, but the joke is on the filmmakers. Few movies in my lifetime have offered up so many inadvertent cues for audience wisecracks. The wisecracking is a form of self-preservation; if the film isn't going to entertain us, then we'd damn well better entertain ourselves.

This has been quite a month for ponderoso uplift at the movies—first *Beloved,* and now this. *Meet Joe Black* is like a Hallmark card with elephantiasis. Media tycoon William Parrish (Anthony Hopkins), to whom Death pays a visit, specializes in dispensing greeting-card-style wisdom. He counsels his marriageable physician daughter Susan (Claire Forlani) to hold out for the right guy: "I know it's a cornball thought, but love is passion, obsession. Forget yourself and listen to your heart." Forget the heart; is anybody listening to this dialogue (courtesy of four—count 'em—screenwriters: Ron Osborn, Jeff Reno, Kevin Wade, and Bo Goldman)? It *is* cornball; just because the filmmakers admit as much doesn't make it any less so. The director, Martin Brest, wants to be both a schlock-meister and a serious artiste. But in the *Titanic* era, corn is best served up without all this coy self-consciousness. *Titanic* piled on the hearts and flowers, but at least its death cruise had a schmaltzy monumentality. It was an ersatz romance with enough ardor to resemble the real thing. *Meet Joe Black,* which lasts almost as long as *Titanic,* doesn't have that kind of oomph; it's dour and shrouded, a lifeless romance about the value of life.

At the outset, Parrish is visited by Joe Black as the tycoon nears his sixty-fifth birthday and his family prepares a big celebration. It seems Joe is curious to take a look around before he brings Bill into the Great Beyond. He sets out his nonnegotiable offer: as long as Bill keeps things interesting, he's spared. Joe may be a bit of a sadist but—here's the surprise—he's also a virgin. Death, where is thy stinger?

He warms to Susan, but it takes her a while to reciprocate. She's confused, you see, because she met an identical sweet-talker the day before in a coffee shop and went all ga-ga over him; he's the same gent Joe later dispatched in a car accident so he could inhabit his body. Talk about the perils of dating in the big city! Joe has no memory of having met Susan, who thinks he's a mope compared to the brash guy he replaced. And yet there is something about him—perhaps it's that he looks like Brad Pitt?—that pulls her in.

Pitt can't seem to get a fix on how to play Death. You can't blame him; after all, it's not exactly a role you can research firsthand. Still, his Joe doesn't add up—one minute he's coolly sinister with Bill, the next he's as innocent and dopey as Lenny tending the rabbits in *Of Mice and Men.* He develops an appetite for peanut butter, and it's barely different from his appetite for Susan. It's all the same to him—at first. When Joe finally gets carnal with her, their lovemaking is depicted in that lyrically slowed-down way that lets you know sex is truly a beautiful thing. No hot monkey love for these two. Getting down with Death turns out to be the ultimate in safe sex.

Joe claims he's lingering for the lessons. "I chose you for your excellence and your ability to instruct," he tells Bill early on. But what it really looks like to us is that Death digs the good life—not just Bill's peanut butter (chunky) and daughter (smooth) but his sumptuous New York penthouse and Versailles-style country estate. It's depressing but true—Death is a social climber. The filmmakers, too, seem inordinately impressed by Bill's riches even as they pretend that money can't buy happiness. The camera slavers over the parquet floors with inlaid borders and the carved moldings on the door frames. Bill is the kind of CEO Hollywood can feel sanctimonious about—he's a bit gruff in the boardroom, perhaps, but he's a philosopher-king who runs a good, clean empire and cherishes his wife's memory and has a really classy art collection. When it looks like Joe might take the unsuspecting Susan along with them into the hereafter, Bill even stands up to the guy. He scolds Death!

The filmmakers have described *Meet Joe Black* as a "meditation on happiness," but it's more like a *Twilight Zone* episode played at the wrong speed (an early *Zone* in fact featured a very young and blond Robert Redford as Death). The film didn't need to be three hours. I can only surmise that Pitt's clout kept it at that length. If so, he did himself no favors. The camera lingers for what seems like aeons on his face, but nothing new is revealed, no depths, no hollows, no sparkle; he's just a blank glamour-puss. Forlani also gets the walleyed treatment, and she offers up two expressions: a suggestion of a smile (to indicate thought) and a slight squint (to indicate passion). Hopkins does best with his opportunities, but this is not, to put it mildly, one of his most exacting performances. After a while, you just want to bring on the hereafter and get done with it.

Why does Death bother to show up at all? In the 1934 movie *Death Takes a Holiday,* starring Fredric March, Death crossed the human threshold because he wanted to discover why people feared him. In *Meet Joe Black,* which lifts a few plot elements from that film, Death just wants his close-ups. The film isn't about mortality; it's about star wattage. Audiences can take great comfort in knowing that Death looks like Brad Pitt. But hey, folks, it's only a movie. Do not go gentle into that good night. And hang on to your peanut butter.

(*New York*, 1998)

The Messenger:
The Story of Joan of Arc

In *The Messenger: The Story of Joan of Arc*, we first glimpse the fabled warrior maiden as a young peasant sprite gamboling through multicolored fields. She also spends quality time in the confession booth badgering the local priest with her piety—he can't believe this little sprig has so much that she wants to be forgiven for. When the British invade Joan's village, she watches her older sister first murdered and *then* raped by a soldier in need of a shave and some heavy orthodonture. Is it any surprise Joan will grow up to defeat the English at Orléans? The only surprise here is her transformation from Pippi Longstocking look-alike to her adolescent in-carnation as runway model for the latest in fifteenth-century armorwear. As personified by Milla Jovovich, Joan is lanky and statuesque, with styl-ishly sheared hair and accented cheekbones. Her perfect teeth are whit-er-than-white. When it comes to dentistry, the French win this Hundred Years' War hands down.

Director Luc Besson, who never met a camera move he didn't like, is perhaps best known in this country for *La Femme Nikita*, and there's a lot of Nikita, who also looked like a supermodel, in this Joan. She's a righteous assassin prone to hissy-fit outbursts of remorse. (Apparently, it never dawned on her that people fighting a war actually get slaugh-tered.) The timing for Besson's take on Joan was inevitable: after George Bernard Shaw and Dreyer and Bresson (what a difference an "r" makes); after Jean Seberg and Maria Falconetti and Ingrid Bergman, the world is finally ready for Joan of Arc as the prototype of grrrl power (Joanie the Brit-slayer). Storming the British battlements at Orléans, she takes an arrow full in the chest and, retreating to safety, urges her warriors to press on. (This part of the spectacle could be called "Start the Revolution Without Me.") But then Joan plucks out the bloody thing and rejoins the fray. The battle scenes are in the *Braveheart* tradition—the score sounds like cannonballs trying to mate, while legions of armored and vo-luminously hairy bellowers clank to be free. In their verbal ripostes to the French, the British here are far from flowery. They respond to Joan's entreaties to yield to the Kingdom of Heaven with a hearty, "Go fuck yourself!" Historical accuracy can be so limiting, *n'est-ce pas*?

Besson and his co-screenwriter Andrew Birkin are offering up Joan as mystic, maiden, martyr (choose any one or combination). The maid-en part doesn't work because of Joan's high diva quotient; the martyr part is tempered by our desire, after listening to so much of Joan's ho-lier-than-thou yowling, to see her taste the flames and be done with it. The mystic part has potential, but Joan's visions are about on the level of a Björk music video, and Besson introduces a character known to Joan as the Conscience, who tests her faith, or something, but is impossible to take seriously because he's played by Dustin Hoffman in hooded robe and beard. Hoffman delivers his lines in a kind of dry, oracular patter; he could be Obi-Wan George Burns. I don't think Hoffman has ever been sillier, though he's not meant to be, exactly.

Contrast him with John Malkovich, playing Charles VII. With his dauphin's haircut and ceremonial duds, this king is a fruity fanatic, and Malkovich gives him a gaudiness that's the most entertaining thing in the movie. Watching the actor here, it occurred to me that the reason he was so perfectly cast in *Being John Malkovich*, where he spends some of his screen time inhabited by a woman, is that, as a performer, he projects in almost equal measure feyness and macho belligerence. With Malkovich, you may not always know what you're getting, but it all adds up. He's turned the omni-weirdness of his screen presence into a remarkably supple comic instrument capable of spanning centuries; whether he's appearing in the deadpan futurism of *Being John Malkovich* or the deadweight antics of *The Messenger*, Malkovich is oddly, absolutely *right*. He's just about the only reason to pace yourself through this movie, but maybe not reason enough. I suspect its audiences will be ahead of the British in sounding the retreat.

(*New York*, 1999)

Evita

A famous movie composer once told me a joke: Two songwriters are sitting around, and one of them says to the other, "I just saw the most amazing thing. A man fell off the roof of a building, hit a ledge, fell to the street, got winged by a bus, and run over by a car—and he's completely unhurt. What a lucky guy!"

"No, no, no," answers the other songwriter. "You know who's lucky? Andrew Lloyd Webber is lucky."

This preamble is by way of explaining that I've never gotten Webber either. I dutifully trudged off to *Phantom of the Opera* (great chandelier) and *Sunset Boulevard* (I prefer the movie), but with *Evita*, I got as far as the Patti LuPone-Mandy Patinkin cast album (great voices, weak material). Since *Evita* started out in 1976 as a concept album—it was staged two years later—my cultural loss would not appear to be total.

Well, you can run but you can't hide. Now there's *Evita*—the Movie. Starring Madonna. Soon to be followed by Evita—the Fashions. According to my press notes, writer-director Alan Parker (*Pink Floyd—The Wall*) submitted to Webber and his lyricist, Tim Rice, 146 changes to the original score—far fewer than Madonna's costume changes. Will the Madonna/Evita Power Glamour look take hold? Retailers are banking on peplum suits by Tahari, lace separates by Jill Stuart, tango dresses by Nicole Miller, and authentic Perón shoes by Salvatore Ferragamo. Be there or be square.

Evita has had so much prescreening buzz that the film itself seems like yet another excuse for more buzz. Will it make Madonna a movie star—finally? So many people want her to be one that this bellicose pseudo-opera might just do the trick. In the modern movie era, if you hit the right media buttons often enough you become a star almost by fiat. (Did you happen to catch Madonna's "diaries" in the November *Vanity Fair*?) The role of Evita is a starmaker all right, but Madonna, even when she's belting out numbers from the balcony, is curiously recessive. She's not bad when she's playing the early Eva—that is to say, when she's scrounging and sleeping her way to the top—but she's fairly blank when she has to look caring and devotional and toss baubles to the poor and expire like Camille. As an actress, Madonna has to work on her vulnerability more.

You sympathize with her, though; Parker surrounds her with so much totalitarian hoopla—*Triumph of the Will* with a beat—that it's amazing anybody could puncture his wall of sound. As Juan Perón, Jonathan Pryce doesn't even try; he seems sozzled by all the tumult. (With his teeth capped and his hair darkened, Pryce looks like a vampire on 'ludes.) Antonio Banderas, his hair shiny and full, is more Breck than Brecht. Glamourpusses plus proto-fascism—that's *Evita*'s formula for success.

(New Times, 1996)

CHAPTER 10

LITERARY AND THEATRICAL ADAPTATIONS

The Golden Bowl

With the release of the new Ismail Merchant and James Ivory adaptation of Henry James's *The Golden Bowl*, it bears repeating that their movies have long borne the criticism, at times unfair, of being *Masterpiece Theatre*-ish. (*The Remains of the Day*, for one, is far better than that.) Their films represent not only a body of work but a body of opinion about what movies should be: decorous, literate, preferably derived from the classics. As producers and directors, Merchant Ivory remain the leading practitioners of what used to be every studio chief's stock-in-trade, the prestige picture that wears its breeding on its sleeve and earns it creators awards and honorary degrees.

This type of movie fell out of fashion in the counterculture era and has never entirely regained its cachet. Rightly or wrongly—and I am of both minds on the subject—there is something vaguely suspect about the Merchant Ivory school of filmmaking. Too often the quality of the films is confused with the quality of their source material, as if a movie based on Henry James or E. M. Forster already had a leg up on greatness. But audiences, particularly those who have moved beyond the models of artistic excellence inculcated in high-school honors English class and on PBS, aren't so quick to be wowed by such a preening prestigiousness anymore; the model for what constitutes a great film has become more flexible, more keyed to popular culture than to high culture. (Popular culture has never been more debased, but that's another story.)

This is not to say that the old tradition of high-brow, classic-based filmmaking is always just a ruse to reap honors. Filmmakers of a certain stripe have always tried to do justice, even partial justice, to the great literature they love. You can accuse Merchant Ivory of flaunting their refinements, but nowhere in even their most waxen films do I detect a cold and cynical calculation. They genuinely believe they can animate these great books into great movies. It's a forgivable delusion given credence by the fact that, once in a very long while, a literary masterpiece actually *does* become a film masterpiece (David Lean's *Great Expectations*, for example). But that is the great exception. One can pretend to judge the quality of Merchant Ivory's *The Golden Bowl* without recourse to Henry James's novel, and perhaps that would be the decent thing to do; but if such a movie is expected to share in the reflected glory of its source, then surely it's fair to go back to the source.

With *The Golden Bowl*, Merchant Ivory, along with their longtime screenwriter Ruth Prawer Jhabvala, are tackling the James text that is his most maddeningly and illustriously indrawn. (Published in 1904, it was his last completed novel.) Its human interplay is ground into such a fine psychological powder that we appear to be in the presence of a race of people, or at least of an author, whose sensibility for shifts of mood and thought and strategy is so subtle and rarified as to sometimes seem beyond comprehension. With its winding, maniacally mellifluous sentences stretching on for half a page, the novel is all grand abstraction and allusion. The movie brings out the drama in the book by, in effect, making exterior everything in it that was interior. This represents almost a rebuke to James's art, and yet, since the movie medium has never been very good at conveying complex inner states of being, there probably wasn't any other way to adapt the book. But even on this explicit level, the movie doesn't live up to its own designs.

Set in England and Italy between 1903 and 1909, the film offers up a bankrupt Italian price, Amerigo (Jeremy Northam), his American bride, Maggie (Kate Beckinsale), Maggie's wealthy-tycoon father, Adam Verver (Nick Nolte), and Charlotte (Uma Thurman), who becomes Adam's wife while remaining Amerigo's lover and, tenuously, Maggie's friend. The deepest attachment in the film is supposed to exist between Maggie and her adored father (who is introduced as "America's first billionaire" in a rather crass attempt to link his story with our own era). That link explains why Maggie, when she sees her father's marriage jeopardized, as well as her own, snaps into action. But Kate Beckinsale doesn't express the blooming connivance of this prim woman, nor does Uma Thurman convey the stealthy wiles of someone veiled in sweet deception. Her Charlotte is an obvious temptress, which rather coarsens the drama. We end up waiting for the inevitable catfight.

The most persuasively human character turns out to be Adam Verver, and that's because Nick Nolte senses in this robber baron a touch of the artist—or at least a man with a genuine appreciation for art. Adam's vast collection, which he plans to house in an American museum he is constructing, isn't merely the spoils of war; it's the truest representation of his ideal self, of the *artiste* he would like to be. When he shows Charlotte his Raphael drawings, he handles them as if they were gold leaf. Adam carries around in him a plangent sorrow that's never really explained for us; it's just *there* in his fixed, faraway looks, as if the life being played out before him were all a thing of the past. What makes Nolte so much stronger than the other performers is precisely this sense of mysteriousness and indirection, which doesn't really correspond to the Adam Verver of the novel but certainly jibes with James's overall method. Everyone else in the movie is all too easy to read, but Adam Verver has a lyrical opacity that comes across as one actor's heartfelt tribute to the Master.

(*New York*, 2001)

Under the Volcano

John Huston has wanted to make a movie out of Malcolm Lowry's rambling, visionary, expressionist novel *Under the Volcano* for thirty years, and now that he's finally made it, he still doesn't have a movie. Of all the major postwar novels (*Volcano* was begun in 1938 and finally published in 1947), Lowry's is probably the least likely candidate for a successful film. Set on the eve of World War II in Cuernavaca on the Mexican Day of the Dead, it's about the last twenty-four hours in the life of alcoholic British ex-Consul Geoffrey Firmin (played in the film by Albert Finney). In the course of the day, Geoffrey's errant wife Yvonne (Jacqueline Bisset), who has been separated from him for a year and filed for divorce, returns to him; unable to bear the weight of this long-sought gift, Geoffrey spirals even further into self-destruction.

The semi-autobiographical novel takes place almost entirely inside Geoffrey's mind, and his whole life pours through the prose—his fears and philosophies and evasions and longings. His tragedy is both a specialized case—a boozer's apotheosis—and a symptom of a death-rattled, valueless world on the verge of a Fascist apocalypse. The reason this novel has been so difficult to adapt to the screen is that, if you eliminate its dense exfoliation of ideas and emotion and just stick to the story, you're left with a rather paltry plot. And that's exactly what John Huston and his screenwriter Guy Gallo are left with. They've reduced Lowry's novel to a maundering movie about a portentous drunk.

The film doesn't even function as an explanatory slide-show of the book. How could it? The movie medium is capable of a great many miracles, but explicating interior states of consciousness isn't one of them. To those unfamiliar with Lowry's novel, Huston's film will probably seem puzzling and a bit blank—there's obviously something "important" happening, but the movie rarely lets on what that might be. Guy Gallo's fidelity to the bare bones of the plot may seem like an intelligent choice, but it's also a classy form of uninspiration. (Probably the only way to make the novel work on film would be to completely rethink it—in the manner of, say, Robert Altman's *The Long Goodbye*.) But even if one accepts the film's surface fidelity, Huston's film skimps on the available opportunities.

He doesn't, for example, try to find a cinematic equivalent for Geoffrey's rich, subterranean moods; Gabriel Figueroa's cinematography is disappointingly glossy, and the Mexican symbology—such as the skeleton's Dance of Death that opens the movie—hits you over the head. (Anyone who has ever seen Eisenstein's documentary *Que Viva Mexico*, or even seen stills from it, will feel a distinct visual comedown in this film.) Huston's straight-ahead, unadorned style is temperamentally unsuited to Lowry's material; he can't—or doesn't want to—bring out the resonances in the landscapes, and the Mexican peasants look posed. Even though Yvonne's return to Cuernavaca is made memorable by Finney's acting in the scene (he has to look at her four times before he believes it's really her), Huston subsequently does nothing to make her wondrous; Bisset's beauty is supposed to be enough for us (her wan performance certainly doesn't help).

The third major character in the film, Geoffrey's half-brother Hugh (Anthony Andrews), who was Yvonne's lover and is staying temporarily with Geoffrey, registers even less; there's almost no sexual tension between Hugh and Yvonne. Hugh, who spent time with the Republicans in the Spanish Civil War and wears a cowboy hat most of the time, is supposed to represent the man-of-action pose that Geoffrey rejects. (At one point in the film Hugh shows off by jumping into a bullring and playing the matador.) But Hugh comes off as such a ninny that he's no match for Geoffrey even at his most sozzled. Despite Huston's long-term preoccupation with this project, there's no urgency in his film-making; his imagery doesn't have the force of obsession. Lowry's novel, paradoxically, is a much more cinematic experience than the film.

The Consul's self-destructive, self-dramatizing despair has many roots in the novel. In the movie, his despair seems primarily the result of a failed marriage; in other words, in its own quietly efficient way, Huston's *Under the Volcano* is a Hollywoodization of the story. (The movie's ad line reads: "One cannot live without love.") But the lost-love scenario doesn't explain why, when Yvonne returns (inexplicably) to Cuernavaca, eager to rehabilitate Geoffrey and take him out of Mexico, Geoffrey deliberately trashes their hopes. His action only makes sense if you understand Geoffrey's demons, and his demons are too expansive and nightmarish for the narrow confines of this movie. Huston shows us scenes from the book, such as Geoffrey's loop-the-loop ride at a local fair, where everything falls out of his pockets, but it doesn't mean anything special to us. Here's how Lowry described the same scene:

> Everything was falling out of his pockets, was being wrested from him, torn away, a fresh article at each whirligig, sickening, plunging, retreatable circuit, his notecase, pipe, keys, his dark glasses he had taken off . . . . There was a kind of fierce delight in this final acceptance. Let everything go! Everything particularly that provided the means of ingress or egress, went bond for, gave meaning or character, or purpose or identity to that frightful bloody nightmare he was forced to carry around with him everywhere on his back, that went by the name of Geoffrey Firmin . . . .

In the movie, this episode comes across as little more than a funny-sad lark. Huston has, however, done one shrewd thing; he's hewed the movie to Finney's performance, hoping, perhaps, that his acting would provide the passion that the rest of the film lacks. And Finney comes through, or at least as much as any actor could under the circumstances. We *do* get a sense of something larger—something more fearful and ominous and ruined—in his Consul; Finney's performance gives the movie a heavy, ambiguous weight. Strapped into his tux, with his dark sunglasses blanking out his eyes, his arms bent at his side like broken wings, Finney's Consul seems perpetually aghast, and yet he's a tough old lush. He may fall down stuporous in the street, but, when a British motorist drives by and inquires if he's all right, Geoffrey snaps to groggy attention—he even uses the occasion to satirize the motorist's upper-crust accent. Geoffrey's drinking is presented (as it also was in the novel) as a form of heroism. He never slobbers disgustingly over anyone, never throws up, never gets the DTs. He even frequents a whorehouse—he's surprisingly potent. But Geoffrey's spiritual impotence—his unwillingness to break out of his fantasies into the world of action—is what gnaws at him. And yet he prizes the way he is; he regards the world as too blighted to be worth his sobriety. He's proud to be among the damned.

It's amazing how much of this comes through in Finney's performance, considering how little he had to work with. Bisset and Andrews offer such slim support that he's practically doing a solo. Finney knows how to portray the various moods and levels of drunkenness; he knows how to use his voice so that it's a cracked quaver one moment and a booming instrument the next. He can slide imperceptibly into the sloughs. In Finney's most remarkable scene, he jabbers good-naturedly with Hugh and Yvonne and then, in a flash, almost apologetically, confronts them about their affair and then flees to his doom. We can see in this confrontation how Geoffrey's anger has fermented into self-hatred; in an earlier sequence, he and Yvonne talked of a paradisiacal future together, and now, with these belated accusations, he's junking that future—the future he cannot face.

Huston has made a career out of challenges, and he's often won. *Under the Volcano* was probably the biggest challenge of them all—even bigger than *Moby Dick*. He's made extraordinary movies out of books as disparate as the Bible and *The Red Badge of Courage* and *Reflections in a Golden Eye*, and, a few years ago, he entered into Flannery O'Connor's Southern Gothic nightmare world in *Wise Blood*. But *Under the Volcano* might have meant more to Huston thirty years ago, when he first wanted to make it. The movie needs the touch of a cracked, crazed visionary—a

Werner Herzog or an Orson Welles or a Luis Bunuel (who once wanted to adapt the book and then rejected the idea). At seventy-eight, age has transformed Huston's style into something which, at its late best, as in the 1975 *The Man Who Would Be King*, is contemplative and serene. (That's what Bunuel's last films were like, too.) In *Under the Volcano*, that serenity sometimes gives the film a fated, deliberate pull but, for the most part, it comes across as perfunctory. Huston can no longer connect with Geoffrey's cry: "Hell is my natural habitat." The best he can manage in *Under the Volcano* is purgatory.

(Los Angeles Herald Examiner, 1984)

Lolita

Vladimir Nabokov's *Lolita* still has the power to scare people off. Proof is the book's new movie adaptation, directed by Adrian Lyne, scripted by Stephen Schiff, and starring Jeremy Irons as the passionate pedophile Humbert Humbert—a man entranced by nymphets.

Completed more than two years ago, the movie went without a distributor in this country until the small, independent Samuel Goldwyn Films agreed to a limited theatrical release following the film's early-August airing on the TV cable network Showtime. (By then it had already played to a mixed reception in England and France and had a one-week Oscar-qualifying run in a small Los Angeles art house.) It's easy to understand why all the major Hollywood studios passed on this $58-million migraine—why risk hurting their corporate image promoting such a film when it was far from certain they would even retrieve their investment? Now that the movie has been released nationally, their worries, in cultural if not financial terms, appear unfounded.

As far as its subject matter goes, this *Lolita* is shocking, all right, but it's not exploitative. Neither, of course, was Nabokov's 1955 novel, or Stanley Kubrick's antic, brilliant 1962 movie version. *Lolita*, in whatever form it takes, *should* be shocking. But this new movie incarnation makes its appearance during a particularly muddled moment in our culture. Despite all of the media attention given over to the sexual exploitation of children, there has never been another time when the image of the nymphet has been so fawned over and commercialized. Nymphets peer out at us posselike from fashion pages and movie screens. What in the end may prove shocking to audiences of this new *Lolita* is not so much its cast of characters as the apparent seriousness of its intent.

But that very seriousness functions in the film as a kind of merit badge. In order to show off his deep-dish credentials, Lyne (1983's *Flashdance*, 1987's *Fatal Attraction*) has given us a lyrically lethargic *Lolita*. He has done to Nabokov's book what generations of Hollywood directors have always done to the "classics"—he's slicked it up with high purpose. What he has wrought is, in some ways, commendable—he connects with Humbert's racked longing and sorrow—but conceptually and stylistically, he's seized upon incendiary material, then taken the safe way out. What makes the novel such an extraordinary document is how it horrifies when it is at its most wheedlingly funny. Humbert isn't just a great tragic figure; he's a great comic figure, too. His lecherous folly for the twelve-year-old Lolita is a parody of passion that turns out to be the real thing. Nabokov's *Lolita*, as Lionel Trilling famously wrote, "is not about sex but about love." And yet there has never been another love story that had such a rotting, risible soul.

And so the chief complaint one can lodge against Lyne's film is central—it's not that *funny*. Which is another way of saying that, for all its controversy, it's not that daring. Much has been made of the fact that Lyne's film sticks much closer to Nabokov's novel than did Kubrick's version. In the most literal-minded sense this is true. But Kubrick's film—which in numerous published interviews has been the target of heavy-duty disparagement from Lyne and his collaborators—was a lot closer to Nabokov in spirit. (Nabokov himself has screenwriter credit on the earlier film, though most of his work wasn't used.) Kubrick captured—particularly in Peter Sellers's monologues as Humbert's bête noir Clare Quilty—the book's rhapsodic, nutbrain ghastliness.

There's another overarching problem in Lyne's film—it's all told from Humbert's unwavering point of view, *as if we were watching what really happened*. But although Humbert was also the narrator of Nabokov's book, he was no more reliable than any other species of madman. By framing the film as a transcription of reality—not simply Humbert's reality—the material becomes insuperably flattened out. It turns into a movie about a suffering, martyred romantic.

It's a highly conventional approach for a most unconventional "hero." Humbert's character is "explained" for us. For example, at age thirteen, while living at his father's hotel on the French Riviera, he falls for a twelve-year-old girl named Annabel, who dies of typhus a year later. These early flashback scenes are in the movie to demonstrate how this loss supposedly locked Humbert into a lifelong yearning for nymphets. But what comes across is just a fancy form of special pleading—a way to absolve Humbert of his sins. Surely there is more to Humbert's mania than this cut-and-paste Freudianism?

Years later in 1947, Humbert, now a professor of French literature, ventures to a small New England town to take a teaching post. There he encounters the overbearingly amorous widow Charlotte Haze (Melanie Griffith) and her daughter Lolita (Dominique Swain), the surrogate Annabel. She becomes his ruling passion, but the passion is dolorous from the start. Lolita is Humbert's temptress, his ruin, and we're never allowed to forget it. On the soundtrack are the composer Ennio Morricone's mournful phrasings. Humbert, stricken instantly when he first sees Lolita, is stricken ever after.

And let's face it, Jeremy Irons has been stricken in far too many movies lately. *Waterland, M. Butterfly, Damage, Stealing Beauty, The Chinese Box*—he's becoming a regular Garbo. As beautiful as his line readings often are, Irons isn't terribly interesting when he drizzles himself out in this way; his anguish is too decorous. In *Reversal of Fortune*, he was able to snap out of his fine-tuned funk because the character he was playing, Claus von Bülow, was a real rotter—a prize cad. But in *Lolita* he's much closer to the comatose Sunny von Bülow.

This elegant nothingness passing for grand passion saps the material of its power to disturb; Humbert is such a writhing wraith that he never comes close to being a predator. It is Lolita who is shown to be the initiator of their sexual folly. Because the film—as opposed to the book—is so intent on turning Humbert into an all-out tragic figure, it never even gives his lechery its due. Lyne is too high-minded for that. Or is it high-low-minded? We first see Lolita stretched out on the lawn as a sprinkler dapples her; we might as well be watching a commercial for a new perfume—"Nymphet," perhaps?

Dominique Swain at least has the right flip coyness for the role, and the movie's tartest scenes are those in which her Lolita exasperates the humbug Humbert with her lowdown tastes. Lolita is a child of pop culture, and in the movie's terms, her fetish for pulpy movie magazines and songs with lyrics like "Bongo, bongo, bongo/I don't want to leave the Congo" is distinctly all-American. But the contrast between Humbert's aggrieved European finesse—his extraction is primarily Swiss-English—and Lolita's slangy Americanism should be jauntier than it is. Lyne makes it bear too much metaphorical baggage.

It certainly is possible, though not entirely profitable, to regard *Lolita* as an allegory about how desiccated old postwar Europe was seduced and overwhelmed by the bright pop crud of the U.S. of A. But there should be more glee in this perception. Perhaps the reason there isn't is because Lyne is still on the side of the musty old Europeans. Nabokov, in his essay "On a Book Entitled *Lolita*," wrote: "Nothing is more exhilarating than philistine vulgarity." Lyne wants to expunge any vulgarity from *Lolita*. He wants to make an art film on the Continental model—sleek and somnambulistic. That's his idea of art.

It isn't just pop vulgarity that gets short shrift in this *Lolita*. Missing also is a strong sense of the absurd. Humbert and Lolita, crisscrossing the country by car and stopping at cheesy motels and remote gas stations, are a mock father-daughter duo. On the surface their spats sound like what any exasperated dad goes through with his kid—except, of course, the incestuous context is infernal. What the movie mostly misses is the awful comic irony in all this.

What it *does* capture, in the end, is the irony that Humbert would massacre another man for doing to Lolita what he himself has done. Quilty is the man who hounds Humbert and spirits Lolita away to his own casbah. As played by Frank Langella, he's a voluminously fetid creep whose depravities, in his few scenes, appear bottomless. He is Humbert's walking nightmare, his nemesis, his alter ego—which, of course, is why he must be destroyed. The final image of the bloodied Humbert—bereft beyond all care, mourning Lolita's lost innocence—is eloquent.

What all this means, I fear, is that Lyne's *Lolita* works best as a classy horror film. This approach is not inappropriate to the material, but it's a vast diminution of what might have been. I realize this movie is not intended as a substitute for the book, and I have attempted to discuss it with that in mind. But the book keeps calling me back. Nabokov's masterpiece touched on so many senses and caught the reader up in such a frightful whirligig of ardor and mischief and woe that it remains one of the most supremely unclassifiable great books. Lyne's version, by contrast, is essentially a long and lugubrious lamentation. It may be his *Lolita*, but it's not mine.

(*New Times*, 1998)

Fool for Love

I've seen more than a half-dozen Sam Shepard plays, read several more, and flipped through his auto-hypnotic jag, *Motel Chronicles,* and I'm still not sure what he's all about. He's the archetypal hip doctoral thesis. I suppose he's also the most "cinematic" of the major American playwrights to have emerged in the last twenty years. His language is full of imagery, and his productions often turn on the sort of fancies that seem more movie than stage-inspired. Shepard's high currency in the theater world may, in fact, be partly a backhanded tribute to movies; he writes free-form dramas for people whose heads are jampacked with movie-movie tidbits. But the movies Shepard draws on are a particular sort—the lonesome-cowboy-and-vintage-Chevy variety, movies about wayward wanderlust, anomie. *The Treasure of Sierra Madre* and *They Live By Night* and *Hud* hover wraithlike over many of Shepard's plays. So does the aroma of the hallucinogenic sixties. (Maybe *that's* why Shepard's plays seem moviel-ike—film states and dream-druggie states overlap.) The nostalgia for pop artifacts is so intense in Shepard's work that he practically turns kitsch into Zen worship. He's a hayseed conjurer.

    Fool for Love is the first Shepard play to be made into a movie, although he scripted a fragment of Antonioni's 1971 anomie bash, *Zabriskie Point,* and most of Wim Wenders's *Paris, Texas.* Of his major plays, *Fool for Love* is probably the best movie material, but it's booby-trapped. Robert Altman's movie version, starring Shepard himself, trips most of the traps. It's a beautifully made film around the edges, but the center is as weightless as dandelion puff. It lacks erotic charge.

    The couple in the center of the ring are Eddie (Shepard), a stunt man and rodeo rider, and May (Kim Basinger), his long-term, on-again-off-again lover. May is living in a motel on the edge of Southwest nowhere (that archetypal Shepard locale), and Eddie, hauling horses in a trailer hooked behind his pickup, tracks her down at the beginning of the film and kicks in the motel door. He's been out of May's life for a while, but now he's back and he wants her to come live with him on a patch of land in Wyoming.

Most of the film is taken up with their tussling. Eddie swears he won't leave May again, and May, in her slinky silk slip, rasps and accuses (Eddie once had a fling with a rich dame—the Countess) and knees his groin in the middle of an embrace. There's also a dust-caked old-timer (Harry Dean Stanton) who scoots around the motel grounds and pops into the Eddie-May confrontations like a prairie Tinker Bell. A couple check into the cabin next to May's and their little blond girl—a diminutive May—peeks through the windows.

This stuff may not hang together, but it sure is Mythic. Everything—from the people to the prairie to the flickering motel neon sign—is mystic and doomy. As the story glides along, the sky's twilight adobe browns and reds deepen into jet-black. Against this backdrop, the characters seem cut-out, their clothes and flesh tones are slightly lurid, hallucinatory.

It's a good thing that Altman and his cinematographer, Pierre Mignot, are so adept at filigree. *Fool for Love* needs all of its high style, because Shepard and Basinger don't connect. They might as well be fumbling around the motel floor looking for the movie's ignition key. Shepard isn't a bad actor when he's playing mum, cooled-out Gary Cooper types. But he's more effective an actor in stills than he is in motion; action dilutes his force. There's a skimpiness about Shepard's work in *Fool for Love*—he's so naturalistic he wafts away. We don't see the sexual avidity that propelled Eddie's search for May. (When he kicks in that door, he might as well be breaking in the toe of his boot.) Eddie should be a carnal hellion, which is how Ed Harris played him off-Broadway. So should May, although Basinger, despite her Brigitte-Bardot-on-the-range looks, is zonked and Shmoolike. (The only time I cared about her was when, terrified, she ducks Eddie's whirling, whistling lasso.) What's the point of making a movie about the ties that bind if your actors are tricked up in slipknots?

Onstage, *Fool for Love* took place entirely in May's motel room (where, according to Shepard's stage directions, the walls were miked to amplify the body blows). By "opening up" the play into the motel courtyard and beyond, Altman, working from Shepard's movie adaptation, loses the play's penned-in, romper-room intensity. Except that, with Shepard and Basinger, there's not much intensity to lose. Altman's visual pirouettes might have seemed intrusive if, say, Ed Harris and Debra Winger were cast. As it is, his little *divertissements* give the material its mite of soul.

Altman just may be the closest thing to a wizard the movies have yet produced. He can turn dross into gold. His 1982 *Come Back to the Five and Dime, Jimmy Dean, Jimmy Dean* was such a prize piece of sorcery that you left the theater believing Altman could turn *anything* into a great film. Even more, if he could get at the core of artistic truth in a third-rate play like Ed Graczyk's *Jimmy Dean,* imagine what he could do with a *great* play. Shepard's *Fool for Love* isn't particularly memorable but it's a much better play than *Jimmy Dean.* The writing and the situations have a spooky avidity. Why, then, is it not as good a movie as *Jimmy Dean?*

Perhaps it's because *Jimmy Dean,* that compost heap of Inge, Williams, O'Neill, Miller, and Shepard, provided the humus for Altman's art. *Fool for Love* is also impacted with pop-cult references, but Shepard doesn't leave any stickum on them. Everything is etherealized by Shepard's blend of cooled out melodrama. His vision is unmistakable, but it's not a *layered* vision. You can't pull richness out of it by the handful; you have to scout it, like hunting for fireflies. Altman can't do much with Shepard and Basinger in their one-on-one motel scenes, but he captures some of Shepard's fireflies when his camera moves outside, into the cool night air.

Shepard's plays often appear to take off from images, sometimes a single image (like the famous one at the end of *True West,* with the two brothers squaring off in a frozen, feral pose). Altman scores with those images in *Fool for Love* again and again. He and Mignot employ a gliding voyeuristic camera style, with the action often seen through windows, car windshields, mirrors. Altman is trying to *build in* the layers that Shepard's writing doesn't offer up, and most of the time, he steers it clear of preciousness. (I could have done without the contrapuntal woman-and-child May stuff; it reminded me of the Altman of *Images*—Altman the snookered dream-weaver.) I'm not sure how Altman manages his best effects in this movie. Maybe it's because he has as deep a feeling for the sad spaces of America as Shepard does. He can show us Eddie, his lasso twirling, galloping after a limo as gravel is kicked up into the night sky, and he makes the image emblematic. It's a montage of cracked Americana—a limo and a lasso—and, in some mysterious way, it seems to sum up what we've been watching. (It's the last image in the movie.)

It's typical of the film that this summation comes through in its imagery and not its words, despite a lot of monologue-jabbers near the end. *Fool for Love,* like most of Shepard's work, is unresolved (or weakly resolved). He doesn't have the storyteller's gift; halfway through the film, you get the mildly queasy feeling that all the prairie-dust mumbo-jumbo you've been witnessing isn't going to lead anywhere—that it's going to collapse into obscurity. I never thought I'd call Randy Quaid a breath of fresh air, but when he enters the movie halfway through, as May's bumpkin suitor, you immediately side with him against the wrasslin' loonies. He's our representative, the bewildered embodiment of our qualms. And his speech isn't drenched in mystic sauce. (Sometimes, in a few flashback scenes, people don't speak at all even though the voice-over narrator tells us they're wailing. You've heard of Silent Screams? In one flashback in a pasture, the cows, who are described as real noisy, give us Silent Moos.)

Actors love appearing in Sam Shepard plays because his characters are really actors' conceits (this is also true for John Cassavetes's movies). They're motivated less by dramatic logic than by their need to play emotional bumper-cars. That's one reason why Shepard's characters often seem brutish yet centerless, vague. Shepard isn't interested in psychology and, until *Fool for Love,* he wasn't much interested in women, either. The man-woman conflict in *Fool for Love* is supposed to be primal; Shepard even gives Eddie and May a blood link. And yet the movie isn't really about them. If it's about anything at all, it's about the creepy, pop-irradiated melancholia of the wide open spaces. Altman does a prodigious job of finger-painting in those open spaces. Like much of Shepard's work, the movie sometimes moved me without my knowing exactly why. But's it's a tall tale without a tale. It's a tall mood.

(*Los Angeles Herald Examiner,* 1985)

Kiss of the Spider Woman

We hear William Hurt in *Kiss of the Spider Woman* before we see him, lipsticked, his head wrapped turban-style in a large red towel. As Molina, the mother-fixated homosexual window dresser beginning a seven-year sentence in a South American prison for "relations with a minor," Hurt affects a fey voice that is both melancholy and impassioned. He's spinning a story for his cell-mate, Valentin (Raul Julia), a bearded political prisoner who's nursing bruises from a recent interrogation.

The story, Molina's version of a forties Nazi propaganda film about a French chanteuse who falls in love with a German captain and dies for the Fatherland, brings out the gaga in Molina. (It doesn't take much.) He doesn't register the story as propaganda; in the retelling, it's clear that he doesn't even realize the men with funny hats he's describing are actually Jews with yarmulkes. Molina responds to the story strictly as movie-movie glamour; its ardor functions as both an escape from his sordid surroundings and an intensification of his romantic longings. And, because Molina looks so rapt in the retelling, we can't really hate him for his political naiveté. He operates in an ozone layer of pure emotion.

For Molina, fantasy will forever supersede "reality." For Valentin the Marxist, who at first regards Molina with bemused suspicion, "the struggle" is all. "Fantasies are no escape," he tells Molina, but pretty soon he finds himself hooked on his cell-mate's imaginings.

For this movie to work, we have to be hooked as well. Except for a couple of sequences, I never was, although the film is definitely in the Intriguing Failure category. It's a pastiche—part mood-memory play, part camp charade, part political-prison drama. When Molina tells his movie stories—they're lullabies, really—the director, Hector Babenco, shows us what Molina is describing. That's one reason, I think, why the movie doesn't hook us. Instead of letting Hurt's acting rhythms set the scene for us, instead of allowing us to imagine the movie through his eyes, his words, Babenco gives us, in effect, a literal translation, in silvery sepia.

Sonia Braga is the French chanteuse and, later on, in another story, she's the mythological Spider Woman as well. These fantasy movie sequences, which constitute a fair amount of the movie, almost wreck it; they're ultrasleek pieces of camp archness, and the actors' deliberate overacting in them gets intended laughs from the audience where no laughs should be.

These sequences undercut Molina's ardor. It's one thing for *us* to think these movies silly, but Molina would never imagine them as camp. They mean too much to him. The movie is adapted by Leonard Schrader from Manuel Puig's 1976 novel, but there's more visual energy in Puig's movie descriptions (of, among several films, Val Lewton's *The Cat People*) than there is in all of Babenco's movie.

Babenco and Puig are both Argentinian exiles, but on the evidence of *Spider Woman,* movies don't hold the same fantastical allure for Babenco that they do for Puig—and that may account for the film's flatness. Babenco, whose last film was the extraordinary *Pixote,* comes out of a neorealist tradition that regards movie-making as a response to social injustice. Puig, who was an assistant director before becoming a writer, comes out of a modern South American novelists' tradition that draws heavily on the movies, particularly the Hollywood weepies and shoot-'em-ups and musical extravaganzas of the forties and fifties. (Puig has also written a novel called *Betrayed by Rita Hayworth* and, in his *The Buenos Aires Affair,* each chapter had a bit of Hollywood-movie dialogue as its epitaph; its heroine evoked Veronica Lake. Carlos Fuentes, a contemporary of Puig's, once dedicated one of his books to the actors of *The Maltese Falcon* "in order of their disappearance.") In *Spider Woman,* Molina is Puig's fantasy image of himself. Enraptured by make-believe passions, he dreams of being a splendiferous temptress who has the power to make strong men swoon. His ultimate compliment comes when Valentin imagines him as the Spider Woman.

The book is a coy, hallucinatory homosexual fantasy; the movie never works its way into Molina's psyche with comparable force. Babenco is a social realist toying with avant-garde exotica. Since most of the movie is taken up with Molina and Valentin disputing each other in their jail cell, the film seems unavoidably stagy as well. (The novel has, in fact, been successfully dramatized abroad.) Were it not for the strong performances, the movie might be pretty heavy going indeed.

Raul Julia is stuck with a somewhat inert role, actually—he has to grouse and throw up a lot. It's a *reactive* role, and even though we may appreciate this new low-key Julia, he doesn't draw us into his growing fascination and, ultimately, his love for Molina. Julia gives an honest, dignified performance, though; he roots William Hurt's flights of fancy. Hurt does some amazing work here (his acting won the Grand Prize at Cannes). He's not doing a camp cabaret act, he's creating a character; instead of swishing up the performance with acting exercises, he inhabits Molina's sweet, sad soul and lets the character uncoil slowly before us. (This will probably disappoint those in the audience expecting *La Cage aux Folles.*) Hurt shows us the star-struck lady of quality inside Molina, and he shows us jagged flashes of Molina's self-hatred, too. It's part of the movie's conception that, at the end, when the freed, blissfully apolitical window dresser has the opportunity to act out Valentin's political ideals, we also see in him a possibility for grandeur. We watch him in the process of discovering his own fortitude.

This last section is the most moving in the film; it actually improves on the novel, where Molina's political action is far more ambiguous than it is in the movie. In Babenco's film, Molina's political action is consistent with the film as love story; by aiding Valentin's friends while Valentin is still imprisoned, Molina is sounding his love. His act, which may be suicidally foolhardy, is his way of remaining intimate with Valentin.

Kiss of the Spider Woman would have been more satisfying if Babenco had used what he was best at—his lacerating realism—instead of reaching for Puig's fanzine-and-filigree mysticism. There's a propagandistic undercurrent to Puig's impassioned cool; a couple of nights in bed together, and Valentin and Molina are soul mates. It's a sentimental wish-fulfillment fantasy, and I wish Babenco had knocked some of the stardust from its eyes. Might not Molina, a "silly old queen" (his words) with a streak of self-loathing, also feel some loathing for Valentin once he turned out to be (if only momentarily) a homosexual just like himself? Molina's fantasy man is, after all, resolutely heterosexual. I realize that there are a lot of psychological convolutions involved here, and the South American macho mythos is an added complication. But the movie glosses over most of the material's psychosexual complexities. Molina's movie fantasies aren't only about grand-scale romantic longing. They're also about sexual terror; they're about men and women as betrayers, insects. That's what the movie misses out on—the terror inside Puig's conception. It's a web without a spider.

(*Los Angeles Herald Examiner*, 1985)

Prick Up Your Ears

The opening image in Stephen Frears's fine, damnably intelligent *Prick Up Your Ears* is the burnished, big Buddha's head of Kenneth Halliwell, who has just murdered Joe Orton, his lover and roommate of sixteen years. Lurid and bald-pated, he looks a bit like James Earl Jones's Jack Jefferson, but the murder has knocked out all his ferocity. He's imploring, gentle, bereft; violence has tenderized him. When he goes on to end his own life with an overdose of Nembutal, it's a mercy killing.

Halliwell's face in that scene is an emblem of abject, almost beatific misery, and Frears wants the image to stay with us—as the emblem of the movie. Everything flashes back from this scene; our awareness of the horror to come tinctures even the most larky passages. As in Orton's plays, the shards of smashed taboos litter the fierce frivolity. Even the title *Prick Up Your Ears* carries a shiv of double meaning.

Frears and his screenwriter, Alan Bennett, adapting John Lahr's 1978 Orton biography, have chosen not to make much use of Orton's plays. You don't get a sense of what Orton accomplished as a playwright, what a struggle he had even after he was "discovered," what he meant to the near-moribund British stage in the early sixties. (With plays like *Entertaining Mr. Sloane, Loot,* and his last, the posthumously produced *What the Butler Saw,* Orton was dubbed the Oscar Wilde of Welfare State gentility.) The filmmakers have made a movie about the playwright Joe Orton, but they don't give us the playwright. There's a brazenness to their method. By dealing mostly with Orton's life apart from the stage, they reinforce the notion that Orton's life was the raw, unaltered version of his art; a skeleton's key to his plays and novels and diaries and screenplays. (They also affix a dumb, disposable framing device with Wallace Shawn as John Lahr researching the Orton bio; Lahr's neglected wife/collaborator is supposed to remind us of Halliwell.)

Orton was seventeen when he met Halliwell—seven years older and solidly middle-class—in 1951 as an acting scholarship student at the Royal Academy of Dramatic Art. Orton was raised in drab, monotonous Leicester, in a family leaning toward the lower end of the middle-class; his mother wanted him to be a civil servant. Halliwell's mother was killed by a wasp sting when he was eleven; his father killed himself six years later. Halliwell was orphaned, and Orton considered himself an orphan, too. In the first ten years that they lived together in their cramped Islington bed-sitter, they collaborated on four novels (all unpublished); Halliwell taught Orton the classics and Shakespeare and mythology. They also defaced books in the local library with obscene dustjacket blurbs and scurrilous, re-worked covers, decorating their flat with a picture collage of pilfered snippets. For this they were arrested and incarcerated, in separate cells, for six months. (The sentence was absurdly harsh, but the defacements carry a disturbing, porno-Dadaist charge. They may well have been the most creative of the Orton/Halliwell collaborations.)

Away from Halliwell, Orton began to do his own writing. As his plays attracted notoriety, Halliwell was reduced to being Orton's "personal secretary." Orton in public would not acknowledge Halliwell's contributions to his career; Halliwell, in turn, demanded inordinate credit for Orton's successes. (All the plays' titles are his.) No longer Orton's mentor, Halliwell retreated ever further into gloomy bitchiness.

As Orton, Gary Oldman seems exactly right when he says: "Cheap clothes suit me. That's because I'm from the gutter." He wasn't, really, but he fancied himself a guttersnipe. Oldman gives Orton the bearing of a lower-middle-class homosexual cavalier who's trying very hard to be working-class. There's a taunt to his promiscuity; he's always poised for a spree.

As the hulking, prematurely bald Halliwell, Alfred Molina shows us how Orton's promiscuity might have provoked him. There's a racked, shamed quality to Halliwell's sexual jaunts with other men (all at Orton's instigation). He closes himself off from sympathy. Halliwell is the tortured, pre-liberated (and pre-AIDS) homosexual archetype. Orton is the priapic, unashamed cruiser—a modern libertine.

Orton's psychological ties to Halliwell lacked a sexual charge— Molina's drear, seething face tells us that. Orton probably stayed with Halliwell precisely *because* he felt no charge. The pairing seems all wrong on the surface, but their neuroses conjoined so perfectly that probably only murder could (and did) release them. (Halliwell showed the dramatic instinct in life that he lacked on the page, or on the stage.)

It's a *folie*, all right, but Frears and Bennett don't quite make it *à deux*. We don't see enough of Orton as Halliwell's callow, unformed acolyte, and so the flip-flop in their relationship when Orton becomes successful doesn't have resonance. Orton the bumbling acting student trying to lose his working-class accent is just an in-joke to us. (And, apparently, to Orton, too. He smirks with foreknowledge.) The characterization of Halliwell as a young man doesn't quite work, either. He's not that far from the twisted, half-mad brooder he became; it's not clear why Orton was drawn to him. (When Halliwell is handed an imaginary cat in acting class, he strangles it, and we in the audience laugh. Even then *he knew*.) We don't see how cowed and daunted Orton must have felt with Halliwell in the beginning, so the unacknowledgement of his debt to him later on doesn't seem like such a big deal. When Orton brings his agent, Peggy Ramsay (Vanessa Redgrave, in a great small performance), as his guest to an awards dinner, leaving Halliwell at home, there should be more cruelty in the mood.

Even so, Oldman and Molina work some minor miracles. For example, it's not clear from the early, flustered sequences with Orton's mother (Julie Walters) why he should be so unmoved at her death, but Oldman, as he also demonstrated in *Sid and Nancy,* has a genius for snarly, free-floating licentiousness. His implacable effrontery seems just right, even if we're not always sure where it comes from. When Orton hands his dead mother's false teeth to a horrified *Loot* cast member as a prop, the moment has a triumphant heartlessness. I think that's because Frears and Bennett don't really condemn Orton. His heartlessness is equated with his art. The film is saying that to be a writer you have to loot life, and that makes you something of a cur.

It's also saying that it's not enough to have the proper checklist of homosexual/orphan/outcast credentials in order to qualify as an artist. This is Halliwell's great lament at the end of the film, just before he murders. Molina does it full justice; his eyes sear inward at the brutality of the sick joke life has played on him. The achievement of *Prick Up Your Ears* is that you really feel for Halliwell by the end.

Our responses to Orton are more complicated, and that's as it should be. His homosexuality provided him with his outsider's subversive view—the view of a terrorist farceur. Without missing a beat, he could segue from a swank awards dinner to a public urinal for a pickup. What's disturbing about Orton in *Prick Up Your Ears* is that his actions don't seem to issue from rage or rebellion; as a playwright, Orton wrote in a state of hyper-awareness, but in life there was something pre-conscious about his demolitions. His union with Halliwell was bound to self-de-struct, because Halliwell was morbidly over-conscious of every slight, imagined or real. Why did they stick it out so long? Maybe it just proves the dictum—nothing is as compelling as a bad marriage.

(*Los Angeles Herald Examiner*, 1987)

Quills

Quills, about the Marquis de Sade, is a voluptuous impasto. Everything in it—the colors, the locations, the people—seems swirled with a mixture of decadence and grace. American movies don't often delineate with such rich ambiguity the demarcation between angels and demons, and the lack of clear-cut borders here can seem heady yet profoundly unsettling. Philip Kaufman, directing from a script by Doug Wright expanded from his Obie-winning play, makes a vivid, if finally somewhat compromised, show out of these ambiguities; he revels in them because he understands that his film is ultimately an attempt to describe what it means to be human.

Humanity's depraved, annihilating force is represented by the Marquis (Geoffrey Rush), the aristocratic libertine who barely survived the terrors of the French Revolution only to find himself incarcerated in its aftermath at the Charenton asylum for the insane, where he lives in a book-lined, velvet-draped bedchamber. A bewigged fop whose finery becomes ever more ragged, he uses Madeleine (Kate Winslet), a young laundress, to smuggle his scurrilous writings to a waiting public—much to the embarrassment of Napoleon. The emperor dispatches to Charenton Dr. Royer-Collard (Michael Caine), whose "treatments" for the insane are widely viewed as barbaric. Royer-Collard and Sade are linked by a deep, almost incestuous understanding of each other. Sade intuitively grasps the depravities strengthening Royer-Collard's iron will. The doctor, in turn, recognizes the subversion that Sade represents; he recognizes his Antichrist posturings, his masochistic obsession to draw out the torturer in his enemies. The black comedy of *Quills* is that the more Sade is crushed and humiliated, the more thrillingly righteous he gets; his abasement is a horror that doubles as erotic pleasure.

The intermediary in this face-off is Charenton's overseer, the abbé Coulmier (Joaquin Phoenix in yet another first-rate performance this year), whose benevolence toward his inmates has allowed Sade to stage theatricals in which they lewdly prance and chortle. In a series of quick philosophical exchanges with Sade, Coulmier tries to coax his illustrious tenant into exhibiting in his writing the good parts of life; he considers the Marquis his friend, incorrigible but not abhorrent. Sade, of course, interprets Coulmier's kindness as a veiled request to be brought into the illicit, and Coulmier's unadmitted love for Madeleine, which racks him, gives credence to Sade's suspicions.

Kaufman, who also directed *The Unbearable Lightness of Being* and *Henry and June* (the first studio film to receive an NC-17 rating), knows how to bring together intellectualism and carnality without losing the carnal bite. Sade is, for him, perhaps the archetypal protagonist, since the Marquis, despite all his ravenous carryings on, is a species of philosophe. Sade needs to play to an audience, which is why, when the doctor's intercessions deprive him of his writing implements, he can justifiably howl, "I've been raped!" Sade, even in rags, expects aristocratic privilege, and without a readership for his works, he sees himself brought down to commonness—a mere diddler. This is why he rages for his right to continue spewing his salacious screeds and why he ultimately obliterates himself rather than relent. In Kaufman and Wright's scheme, it doesn't really matter if Sade is a great artist or just a depraved scribbler; the point is that he has within himself the inextinguishable impulse to create, which summons all of the filmmakers' anguish and awe. (Wright, drawing an implicit parallel between then and now, wrote his play in 1996 in response to attacks on the NEA. Marquis de Sade, meet Andres Serrano.)

Quills isn't very seductive, nor does it try to be. Seductiveness implies a level of human interplay that is far more shared and intimate than anything on view here. Sade may be a libertine, but he is sealed off from everybody else by his own voraciousness. He has the spirited dullness of a pornographer in the grips of compulsion. For him, every interaction contains a sexual secret, and where none exists, he creates one. Geoffrey Rush brings an extraordinary density to Sade; between his tantrums and harangues, one can glimpse a man crazed by self-deceit and the wastefulness of his life (and perhaps, although it's not discussed, venereal disease). When Sade's wife, Reneé (Jane Menelaus, Rush's real-life wife), is brought into his cell, we are at first startled at her poise and concern; this is not the kind of woman we would have expected him to marry. Reneé mourns the wastefulness, too, and her reasoned sorrow gives us a new window on her husband. It exposes him—humanizes him.

Michael Caine so often plays characters who are sympathetic and good-natured that it's easy to forget how truly terrifying he can also be (as in *Mona Lisa*). What's horrifying about Royer-Collard is the placidity of his belief in his own barbarism—which, of course, he sees as benevolence. Caine understands the self-justifying nature of villainy. The doctor fears and loathes Sade because the Marquis is the one man who sees through that self-justification. Chaos for Royer-Collard, as for Coulmier, is an abyss to be avoided at all cost; but, unlike the abbé, he isn't tempted by degradation. Or by beauty either. His pretty, virginal young bride (Amelia Warner) is for him a "rare bird" he intends to keep caged in his clutches. Royer-Collard's understanding of baseness is perhaps as profound as Sade's. The difference between them is that Sade aches for liberation while Royer-Collard is all about repression. He suspects everyone of degeneracy, and those suspicions keep him in command. When his bride makes a fool of him, we get a momentary flash of the beast within; it's as if a statesman had suddenly gnarled himself into a gargoyle.

Kaufman goes deep in *Quills*, but in the end he may stand back from the abyss, too. He's a bit too much of the civil libertarian to do full justice to Sade, who, for all his preening decadence here, is never depicted in the full measure of his atrociousness. Sade cataloged and exulted in practically every perversion imaginable, but the words we hear spoken from his works are for the most part weak derivatives of the real thing; likewise Sade's monstrous crimes, while alluded to, are not emphasized. These crimes, which included the torture and mutilation of young women, with possible intent to murder, were at least as responsible for getting Sade repeatedly locked up as anything he wrote.

Quills is one of the few really good American movies of the year, and it's bursting with intellectual energy and standout performances and good old-fashioned Grand Guignol theatrics. But for all its attention to ambiguity, it's also pushing a rather neat formulation: in order to know virtue, we must know vice. The film is offered up to us as a kind of curative. But since Sade's vice has been adulterated by the filmmakers, our ensuing knowledge of virtue is a bit too easily won.

Kaufman doesn't completely avoid the deranging implications of Sade's words on others; in a riotous scene near the end, his words help bring about the death of someone close to him. Neither does Kaufman avoid those implications for the Marquis himself. The film practically says that Sade died for our sins. But his writing also occasions a lot of bawdy guffawing and groping among the groundlings and the hired help, and there's something a bit self-congratulatory about such scenes. They seem to be saying, "Look at how unshocked we are," when in fact there's nothing much that's spoken here to be shocked about. Madeleine, representing, it would appear, all free spirits, calls Sade's works her salvation. They allow her to fantasize; if she wasn't such a bad woman on the page, she says, she couldn't be such a good woman in real life. This is a dear conceit, and Kate Winslet's radiance as Madeleine—she has the soft glow of idealized youth—saves it from ickiness. But still. Kaufman may believe no man is beyond redemption; he may believe it necessary, as a formidable artist in his own right, to promote art as salvation, much as Coulmier did to salve his mad inmates. But in doing so he links art to the bromides of therapy and denies blackness its truest sheen.

(New York, 2000)

Affliction

In writer-director Paul Schrader's *Affliction*, small-town New Hampshire looks like hell frozen over. It's a vast meat locker of a locale, except the dead meat is walking around instead of hung up on hooks. The affliction here is metaphoric, but it's literal too. That's the Schrader specialty, and it's also the stock-in-trade of Russell Banks, upon whose 1989 novel the film is scrupulously based. The confluence of Schrader and Banks is almost too perfect—their dual oppressiveness wipes you out before the movie is ten minutes old.

Wade Whitehouse (Nick Nolte) is the chief afflictee of the piece. Divorced twice from the same woman (Mary Beth Hurt), he attempts to be a part-time father to his nine-year-old daughter, Jill (Brigid Tierney), who regards him in the same way her mother does—as a brawling, dangerous nuisance. His response, typically self-humiliating, is to sue for custody. As the town's sole police officer, Wade mostly acts as a crossing guard. To make ends meet, he does menial work for a local developer (Holmes Osborne), whose response to him isn't much more admiring than Jill's. Wade's father, Glen (James Coburn), is a roaring, vicious drunk, and just in case we thought this a recent incarnation, Schrader periodically intercuts flashbacks showing the brute pummeling his young son.

Barreling his way through his frostbitten inferno, Wade is the prototypical walking wounded, Schrader-Banks-style. He may try to wriggle out of his fate, but it's bigger than he is. In the film's take-no-prisoners view, this is the fate of all men, who must either self-destruct or visit their ills upon a new generation. What makes Wade such a heroic presence is that he's self-aware enough to know he's in torment. He's a good man gnarled by primal circumstance. He reaches out to his daughter because she represents for him the bliss of the normal; his sessions with her are botched and rancorous because he wants much more from her than she could ever give. Jill resents being used as an angel for her father's salvation. In his dotingness she spots the note of inauthenticity—Wade responds not to her but, rather, to his idealization of her.

Wade's waitress girlfriend, Margie (Sissy Spacek), is another of his angels-in-waiting. Her mercifulness toward him is the tenderest thing in the movie. If Wade is the archetypical male screw-up, Margie is the archetypal silent sufferer. In their scenes together, he has a ravaged calm and she looks ethereal from longing. She wants her bliss, too. Everybody in this movie—not just Wade and Margie—has a long-ago look in their eyes. They're pulled in by the past, by its damages. Wade's brother, Rolfe (Willem Dafoe), who also narrates the film, has a death's-head countenance. He's a Boston University history professor with no sense of his own history. Speaking to Wade about their father, he says, "At least I was never afflicted by that man's violence," and Wade responds, "That's what you think."

The last film to have this kind of marrow-deep glumness was Atom Egoyan's *The Sweet Hereafter,* also based on a Banks novel, in which a school-bus accident wipes out virtually all of a village's children. I wasn't such a big fan of that movie. Its horrors were displayed as an emanation of small-town anomie—as if its villagers deserved their tragedies because of the littleness of their lives. Schrader's film also suffers from a heavygoing approach to rural malaise; he's offering up a sophisticated intellectual's take on the material, and there's something distanced and diminishing about his methods. (At one point Wade holds up traffic by posturing as if crucified.) His people are all so fixed in their fates that there's no possibility for joy. There never is in his movies. He turns winter-bound New Hampshire into a Hieronymous Bosch canvas—blasted souls topped by Wade's father's leering-gargoyle grin.

And yet this film is far more roiling and powerful than *The Sweet Hereafter*. It has the indrawn obsessiveness of male mythology, and even if you reject most of what it's saying, it's tough to shake off. It transcends your better judgment. Movies like *Straw Dogs* and *Deliverance* also operated in this realm of hallucinatory machismo; the survivalist tactics on display were framed as crucibles of masculinity. *Affliction* shares with them a sense of the world as a battlefield of male privilege, but it has a much drearier and more tragic overview. *Affliction* is the long hangover to those films. Schrader and Banks are saying that it's impossible to break the long chain of brutality at the core of maleness. Rolfe's narration near the end of the novel, in which he speaks on behalf of himself and Wade, and which Schrader largely incorporates, talks of boys and men who, for thousands of years, "were beaten by their fathers, whose capacity for love and trust was crippled almost at birth and whose best hope for a connection to other human beings lay in elaborating for themselves an elegiac mode of relatedness, as if everyone's life was already over. It is how we keep from destroying in our turn our own children and terrorizing the women who have the misfortune to love us."

This is highfalutin pop-psych palaver, and it carries a cock-of-the-walk gloat—especially that business about the "women who have the misfortune to love us." But this sort of weepy-brawly riff has its deep-down appeal to men, and perhaps to women, too. It explains, and it explains away. Schrader lays the blame for Wade's sorry state on his father, but then he also casts the father as stand-in for a patriarchal line going back to the beginnings. Wade is both a special case and an unwitting player in a primordial procession. It's Freudian and it's biblical—quite a heavy load to lug.

But the film is blessed with a performance by Nolte that has real grace and sinew. Wade is the kind of character who is usually presented as a "type" in the movies—he's the Joe Six Pack we take for granted. It's Nolte's genius as an actor to bring out the delicacy and hurt in hunky parts. He's perfectly cast as Wade because he shows us how the man is miscast in his own life. Wade may be his father's Frankenstein monster, but his innards are his alone. He's too sensitive for the role he's been assigned. Wade wants to do the right thing in his world, but he's trapped not only by his own demons but by the unchangeable perception he has created in the town. When he sees a divorce lawyer about retaining custody of Jill, Wade halfheartedly tells him, "I'm not as dumb as I look." Wade knows it, but does anybody else? When, in torment, he looks in the mirror, a stranger stares back at him. The whipped boy is ever present in the adult, and Wade seems to be playing out some elaborate, furious penance for having been that boy. He's almost blithely unaware of his own need for protection; in a snowfall he's often hatless, and he has a raging toothache that he finally takes a pair of pliers to. The grimace on his face when he pulls the tooth is scarily identical to his broadest smiles. His smiles are like scars. He's afflicted, all right—beyond reckoning. The movie is his rightful dirge.

(*New York*, 1999)

The Tailor of Panama

If you think the spy-thriller genre has been streamlined and spoofed and subverted until nothing new can be done to it, think again. John Boorman's adaptation of John Le Carré's 1996 novel *The Tailor of Panama*, starring Pierce Brosnan as a swankily cynical British operative and Geoffrey Rush as the man he blackmails, is a tragicomic spree with hot and cold running water in its veins. Le Carré's novel was inspired by Graham Greene, especially his book *Our Man in Havana*, and Boorman, who co-scripted with Le Carré and Andrew Davies, has made a movie that often seems close in spirit to Greene's puckish woe. Boorman slips into the salsa rhythm of the Panamanian state; he gives corruption its sexy due. The glittering high-rise banks and luxe clubs and prostitute flop-houses all have an equivalency—they reek of foul money. Rarely do we see any travelogue-ish vistas of Panama's natural beauty, because Boorman has a keener eye for the beauty inside all this high-low squalor. He's spent enough time in rain forests in his career. In *The Tailor of Panama*, he's going after a different species of flora altogether.

Andy Osnard (Brosnan) has been exiled to Panama by his M16 superiors after too many indiscretions with the wives and mistresses of British ambassadors and too many gambling debts. Ordered to monitor money laundering and drug smuggling, he quickly gets the goods on Harry Pendel (Rush), a British subject who tailors the Panamanian elite. Harry pretends to have a Saville Row background when in fact his skills were picked up in prison while serving time for arson. In exchange for keeping mum about Harry's past, Osnard uses the tailor as an informant and as a guide to Panama's wicked ways. As odd couples go, the two men are a perfect match. Both are very good at creating illusions because, deep down, they have no illusions of their own. For Osnard, the absence of any humbuggery in his constitution is a source of pride; for Harry, it's a sorrowful lack.

The film is set in 1999, after the fall of Noriega and after the Panama Canal has been given back to Panama by the U.S. Harry feeds Osnard false information that the canal is on the block, perhaps to the Chinese or the Japanese (for that Yellow Peril effect). Unbelieving but maneuvering for a big payday, Osnard feeds the information to the British and Americans, who are only too willing to act on any excuse to take back the canal. The film starts out as a freewheeling farce and turns into a pitch-black burlesque with surprising depths of feeling. The concoctions of these two fabulists have mortal consequences. Real lives are lost when their spymaster fantasies are made flesh.

Pierce Brosnan's role here has been characterized in the press as that of the anti-James Bond, but that's not quite right. Osnard has the waxy, libidinous sheen of the early Sean Connery as 007—James Bond in his walking-phallus stage. (As the current Bond, Brosnan is more like a walking product endorsement for the good life.) For Osnard, getting the lowdown on anyone means tapping into that person's sexual secrets. His entire existence is toned by sex, which is why Panama City, which reeks of it, is practically Edenic for him. When he asks Harry's American wife, Louisa (Jamie Lee Curtis), how Harry won her heart, he's looking for a way to worm his way inside her. Just for the dirty sport of it. Osnard's life is lived without metaphor. He describes espionage as "dark, lonely work, like oral sex," and the joke is that, for him, the two are literally the same. (He's in on the joke.)

Geoffrey Rush's performance has a freakish passion unlike anything else I've ever seen in the movies. (His most famous acting job, in *Shine*, was for me more stunt than marvel.) He has a genius for showing us the still center in a whirligig. When Rush is at his best, in *Quills* and in this film, you really have to focus instant by instant on what he's doing because he's giving you much more than most actors ever do, and he's giving it to you all at once. What for most performers can end up looking like freneticism is, for Rush, something closer to an infatuation with the jumbled contrariness of character. What he does has the velocity of a drive-by performance—all bluster and high impact—but he gives each outburst its own emotional coloration. He may be a dervish, but he's a highly articulated one.

The Judas overtones in Harry's Jewishness made some critics uneasy with Le Carré's novel, but I don't think the movie will provoke the same discomfort. Rush's performance is far too rousing and complex to fit into any Semitic stereotype. Inventing ever more outrageous lies, Harry is both aghast at his treachery and mesmerized—tickled—by it. He lies not only because he is being blackmailed but because, until things spin out of control, he likes the way that fabricating makes him feel. He builds up the people he loves—especially the former anti-Noriega freedom fighter and current drunk Mickie Abraxas, played by the marvelous Brendan Gleeson—into what they by all rights *should* be. They are fantasized into being the best of who they are. Harry tries to do the same for his own depleted spirit; he hungers to be brought into his most ardent self. His fervent, deluded attempts at self-transformation give the film its richness. Like Osnard, Harry lives a life in which metaphor has become literal—he is quite aware that he is a tailor of souls.

In Le Carré's novel, Harry's end is less than sunny, but here, as if in tribute to Rush's performance and the life force he embodies, he has a better time of it. It's almost a romantic gesture on the part of the filmmakers; they want to pay homage to the man's capacity for folly. Harry isn't merely a lovable, blinkered rogue. He's the exemplar of the dreamer, and so he deserves our balm.

(*New York*, 2001)

Troy

It was around the time that the massed tribes of Greece launched their first major assault in *Troy* that the thought flashed through my mind: *Where are the orcs?* Because of the sheer oomph of its fantastical effects, *Lord of the Rings* may have poisoned the well for any subsequent battle epics involving plain old humans. Directed by Wolfgang Petersen and with a script by David Benioff "inspired by" Homer's *Iliad* (with snippets from *The Aeneid, The Odyssey*, Aeschylus, and, if memory serves, *Classics Illustrated* comics), *Troy* has to content itself with the comparatively mundane excitements of armored men clanging bronze swords. The results are grimly lifelike. Even the legendary warriors, like Brad Pitt's Achilles and Eric Bana's Hector, are mortal. Their dialogue certainly is. Hector, for example, helpfully informs us that this whole Trojan-war mess "is about power, not love." He's the Prince of Understatement.

Except for a few brilliant flashes, mostly from Peter O'Toole as Hector's father, the Trojans' magisterially woebegone King Priam, *Troy* is a fairly routine action picture with an advanced case of grandeuritis. (Its $175 million budget is, however, not routine—not yet, anyway.) The actors model their profiles as if they were going to be stamped on coins. Some are more successful at this than others. Hector, for instance, strikes noble poses even when he's nestling with wife and child. On the other hand, his brother, Paris (Orlando Bloom), whose seduction-abduction of Helen (Diane Kruger) from her husband, King Menelaus (Brendan Gleeson), kicks off the festivities, is supposed to be the image of romantic ardor—though most of the time he just looks flummoxed by what he has wrought. He's a nincompoop for the ages. Helen isn't much better. The face that launched a thousand ships would be more comfortable launching a new line of cosmetics. Helen's beauty is the center of the action, yet there is no ominous force in her features, just a bright prettiness. After Paris wimps out in his big public face-off with Menelaus, Helen reassures him that she doesn't want a hero, just a man she can "grow old with." Doesn't she know that dying young is an occupational hazard in his line of work?

Achilles, the world's greatest warrior, is initially reluctant to lead the attack against Troy under the banner of the perpetually snarling Agamemnon (Brian Cox), king of the Mycenaeans and brother of Menelaus.

Achilles detests Agamemnon for using the abduction of Helen as a transparent excuse to extend his empire. But Achilles's mother, Thetis (Julie Christie in a way-too-brief cameo), prophesizes that if he fights the Trojans, the world will forever remember his name. So that's that. Achilles is not only the first great hero in Western lit, he's also the first media whore.

Looking gold-dipped and leonine, Brad Pitt has an inchoate surliness. At times, he appears to be doing a Brando, especially when Achilles stands before the gates of Troy and yells, "Hector!" at the top of his lungs. (Presumably, Stella was unavailable.) Still, Pitt isn't bad in the role, and he (or someone) invented a marvelous leaping motion for Achilles when he moves in for the kill; for a split second, he seems to corkscrew through the air. His character has been cleaned up for the movies, though. For one thing, Patroclus (Garrett Hedlund), his dearest friend in *The Iliad*, whose death at the hands of Hector incites Achilles's vengeance, is now his cousin—just in case all that Greek male bonding seemed suspect. Achilles's elaborate funeral for Patroclus has been cleaned up, too. No human sacrifices here. And Briseis (Rose Byrne), a sexy Trojan priestess, is on hand to bring out Achilles's softer side—i.e., he doesn't kill her.

The filmmakers decided to leave out the many gods who populate *The Iliad*, and it's probably just as well. It would have been the height of camp to have, say, Sean Connery pop up as Zeus. But without them, the movie needs more than ever an infusion of mythic feeling, and we don't get it. Homer's unpitying recitation of war's awful allure is rendered as a series of confused skirmishes, and the Trojan horse looks like a gigantic wicker *objet d'art*. Maybe this is why the actors are forever striking classical poses; they're trying to memorialize the drama. But you can't force this kind of thing—either you're mythic or you're not. This is why the only characters in *Troy* who appear larger than life are those played by actors who *are* larger than life. Julie Christie makes you believe, in her scant screen time, that this mother is both fiercely proud of and afraid for her son. And the clouded eyes and fine-drawn El Greco features of Peter O'Toole, along with his peerlessly dolorous line readings, give Priam a great gravity. The horror on his face as he watches his son become carrion is equal to Homer's finest poetry.

But such imperishable moments are rare. One should not expect Homeric grandeur from Hollywood's *Troy*. What about a bit more relish, though? *Troy* is clearly a bid to capitalize on the success of *Gladiator*, and, like that film, it often misses the point of why we go to these armor-plated films in the first place. It's not just the pomp and circumstance of battle that draws us in—it's also the eye-candy production design and all those wiggy moments involving cuckoo kings. The hissy effrontery of Joaquin Phoenix's mad-for-eyeliner Commodus in *Gladiator* was every bit as necessary as Russell Crowe's he-man waddle. The people who made *Troy,* however, won't admit to the kitsch pleasures of the genre. On second thought, it *could* have used Sean Connery as Zeus.

(New York, 2004)

The Crucible

Why a movie of *The Crucible now*? Arthur Miller's play about the Salem witchcraft trials was first staged on Broadway in 1953, when McCarthyism was still in flower, and it was not a resounding success. Now, of course, it's a staple of rep theaters and high school and college drama societies—it's the warhorse in Miller's stable of righteously neighing nags.

I've never really believed Miller's assertion that the play was written as a response not only to McCarthyism but to *all* forms of hysterical political intimidation. I mean, not many arch-conservatives in 1953 went around championing *The Crucible* as a commentary on, say, the Stalin show trials in Czechoslovakia. If you hold a copy of the play up to the light, the words "House Un-American Activities Committee" clearly shine through.

And yet the dubious "universality" of *The Crucible*—which the great critic Robert Warshow dismantled in a 1953 essay reprinted in *The Immediate Experience*—turns out to have some credence after all. Except that the "universality" has less to do with the play's all-purpose political application than with its stagecraft. *The Crucible* is one hell of a contraption; all you have to do is give it a nudge, and it zooms off on its own power. Miller's gift for high-toned melodrama allows the play to work for audiences who don't know HUAC from a Humvee. The real "universality" in *The Crucible* is its mix of high dudgeon and low cunning.

If you are still thinking of *The Crucible* in terms of the McCarthy era, the movie will likely seem irrelevant. But why limit yourself to history? Miller, who adapted his play, and his director, Nicholas Hytner, realize there are always new fish to fry. Don't relate to the blacklist any more? Try repressed memory syndrome, fatal attraction syndrome, you name it.

Filmed in the clear wide open spaces of Salem (actually Hog Island, Massachusetts), the play reduces itself to a kind of domestic revenge fantasy. Despite all the political finger-pointing in the play, maybe it is this aspect—the adulterous hubby brought low by a jezebel and redeemed by a Good Wife—that explains its enduring appeal. It's *The Young and the Restless* with broomsticks.

The film opens with antic girls cavorting like a pack of pagans under a full moon. Abigail (Winona Ryder) smears chicken blood on her face; the Barbadian slave Tituba (Charlayne Woodard) bubbles her caldron; nearby and unseen, Abigail's uncle, Reverend Parris (Bruce Davison), watches aghast. Found out, the girls evade punishment by claiming the Devil made them do it—and since they finger many devils among Salem's Puritan elders, the community, which holds fast to a belief in witchcraft, comes apart in a scourge of trials and hysteria. Accused "witches" can save themselves from the gallows only by "confessing"—and accusing others.

Almost alone among the elders whom we see, John Proctor (Daniel Day-Lewis) sees through the sham. Miller makes Proctor a progenitor of the modern liberal free-thinker; it may be 1692, but he stands apart from the crowd of the panicked, the vengeful, the mad. It's easy for him to stand apart—Hytner hasn't exactly re-created Salem as a real-world place. It's a theatrical construct with everybody in it assigned their appointed roles in the moral shakedown. And, of course, Miller doesn't complicate matters by depicting Salem in the full flush of its Puritan sympathies. (As Warshow pointed out, the religious community of Salem was "quite as ready to hang a Quaker as a witch.") The film makes it easy to feel superior to these Satan-racked folk because we are made to understand that, like John Proctor, we too would have the liberality to break through superstition.

But Proctor has his own frightened core, and this also is presented to us in "modern" terms. It is not the Devil that racks Proctor, but adultery—with Abigail. Because he will have no more of her—she still pants for him—Abigail accuses his wife, Elizabeth (Joan Allen). Proctor's wailing and moaning over his wife's fate and, soon, his own, come across as the elaborate prostrations of a penitent philanderer. Elizabeth, frosty at the outset, becomes his saintly soulmate. Nothing like being accused of witchcraft to patch a bad marriage.

The British have been getting a lot of mileage in the past few years from their carefully appointed "literate" adaptations of Austen, Forster, Hardy, Shakespeare. Hytner, an English stage director who made his feature film debut with the more free-wheeling *The Madness of King George*, combines with Miller for some stateside classicism. *The Crucible* is America's rough-and-ready answer to all those carefully mounted British museum pieces. It has the heft of an American "classic." With its air of moral rectitude, its blazing-eyed performances by A-list actors, and its political pedigree, *The Crucible* is Oscar-ready.

Given the creeping retroism in movies right now, the resurfacing of *The Crucible* isn't so strange after all. It presents us with a four-square hero who finally refuses to knuckle under to the State. Miller's view of Proctor posits a world in which a single individual *can* make a difference. And all that jazz. Proctor martyrs himself for a greater good. His redemption redeems society. It's an exalted view of the common man that also comes across as an exalted view of Arthur Miller.

Of course, Proctor is presented as just about the only hale fellow in all of Salem. In fact, just to be on the safe side, Salem seems bereft of boys, too. It's a wonder that Proctor, striding about open-shirted and fashionably unshaven, has only Abigail on his tail. Day-Lewis acts as if he hasn't quite shaken off *The Last of the Mohicans*, but at least he's not musty. He knows how to play a character in period and still keep him vibrant. (His teeth are browned and rottenish, though—a concession to period accuracy I could have lived without.)

Winona Ryder fits less successfully into period, and her role never transcends vengeful vixenhood. Nevertheless, she brings something extra to Abigail's hurt—a frenzied bewilderment—that isn't on the page. You believe the damages this girl is capable of.

Joan Allen is magnificent as Elizabeth. It's tough playing a saint, but Allen gives this one so many layers of hurt and pride that you kind of wish the movie had been all about her. Allen inhabits her characters so thoroughly she seems to have lived her whole life in each of them. In *Nixon*, she transformed Pat Nixon into an almost tragic figure. In *The Crucible*, the tragedy on view in Salem is best reflected in her resigned, beseeching eyes.

The other actors—including Paul Scofield as the hanging judge, Danforth; George Gaynes as Danforth's less austere cohort, Sewall; Rob Campbell as Reverend Hale, the cleric who slowly awakes to reason; Peter Vaughan as the magnificently pig-headed farmer Gilles Corey; and Bruce Davison—also do extremely well trying to inhabit their roles fully, even though Miller doesn't give them much room to shimmy.

Miller wrote several years after the play's premiere that he thought he erred in not making the judges even *more* villainous. Get thee behind me, Satan! What *The Crucible* needs more of—and what these actors try to provide—is a *greater* sense of human ambiguity. But if *The Crucible* were richer, it wouldn't be *The Crucible*, would it?

(New Times, 1996)

Hamlet

It's not every day that you encounter a *Hamlet* in which you hear the voice of Mr. Moviefone. Or hear "To be or not to be" recited as the Prince of Denmark (Ethan Hawke) wanders the Action section at Blockbuster Video. It's also not often that you catch the ghost of Hamlet's father (Sam Shepard) disappearing into a Pepsi machine. Yet these dissonances, seemingly facetious, are also weirdly apt. Michael Almereyda, who directed the film in Super 16 mm and did the stripped-down, contemporary adaptation, sets the play in a ghastly, gleaming, fortresslike New York that is all video monitors and mirrored surfaces and product logos. *Hamlet* is a play about paranoia (along with a million other things), and this latest movie incarnation—coming after the Zeffirelli-Mel Gibson drearfest and Kenneth Branagh's bigger, longer, and uncut version—readily lends itself to a high-tech consumerist culture where everyone is watching and being watched. No matter how covert their designs, everybody will be found out.

Denmark here is not a country but a megaconglomerate whose CEO, Claudius (Kyle MacLachlan), has the square-jawed forthrightness of a captain of industry. In other words, he's already a villain even without the added bonus of being the murderer of Hamlet's father. Hamlet is a tatty romantic who slumps his way about the city in a furiously alienated funk. He's the most grad-studentish of all movie Hamlets, and also, I believe, the youngest—a *Reality Bites* Hamlet and a hippie Hamlet, too, with some James Dean thrown in. (Dean's image is invoked in the movie.) The more one sees of this loquacious moper, the more he resembles a refugee from the counterculture wars. Corporatism in this movie is the big bad wolf. At large in a global media culture, Hamlet is as dewy a rebel as any flower-powered precursor. A would-be digital filmmaker, he fights the enemy with its own weapons; his version of *The Mousetrap,* the play-within-the-play that captures Claudius's conscience and leaves him aghast, is rendered here as a movie-within-a-movie.

If the success of any *Hamlet* ultimately rests on the quality of its lead performance, then Almereyda's version is middling. Hawke isn't terrible. His lines are delivered unaffectedly, in a way that allows the poetry to come through without seeming either too familiar or arch. Plus, as he also demonstrated in Richard Linklater's great, neglected *Before Sunrise,* he has a scruffy, moonstruck quality that works well all by itself. But it's difficult to find a way into Hamlet's torrential musings in a production as overstocked as this one. Hawke doesn't have the formidableness to break through the jabber of experimental-film imagery and shock cuts and surfaces reflecting back on surfaces. Maybe no actor could have broken through. But what is missing from this performance, and this production, is the sense that Hamlet is, as Mark Van Doren wrote, "trying to be more than a man can possibly be."

At times it seems as if Hawke's Hamlet were a bit player in his own extravaganza, a counterpart to Rosencrantz and Guildenstern. This effect may be intentional, of course, but that doesn't make it laudable. There is a tendency to overpraise Shakespeare productions (whether for stage or film) proffering some imposing, overarching concept, as if the only way to prove his universality is to bend his drama into a Möbius strip of newfangled meanings. There are times in this new *Hamlet,* as with so many other hepped-up Shakespearean productions, when I just wanted to clear the decks of all the conceptualizing and folderol and get back to the beauty of the lines, of the emotions. Sometimes the most radical way to interpret a text is simply to serve it up unadorned.

Nevertheless, this *Hamlet* is not a movie to place beside, say, Baz

Luhrmann's *Romeo + Juliet* or similar travesties. Almereyda isn't pandering to youth the way that film did. You can be less than ecstatic about what he's trying for here and still respect the attempt. By equating the garish feudalism of the play's original setting with the megalopolis of today's New York, he's at least on the right track. The problem is, it's just about his *only* track. And for New Yorkers, the equation between the two may be less than shocking anyway. So what else is new?

There are still plenty of reasons to check out this new *Hamlet*. There's a marvelous mad scene in which Ophelia (a Fiona Appleish-looking Julia Stiles) screams like a banshee within the coiled tiers of the Guggenheim. If Ethan Hawkes's performance doesn't carry the day, there are others that do, chiefly Liev Schreiber's elegantly seething Laertes, Sam Shepard's rude, startlingly present Ghost, Diane Venora's Gertrude, and (yes) Bill Murray's Polonius. Murray gives his lines a slightly skewed twist that makes them seem both eccentric and naturalistic. His Polonius is a voluble old fud who is also immensely touching; his murder is the only time in the film when one feels a life has been extinguished. Diane Venora is the cast's most experienced Shakespearean performer—she once played the Melancholy Dane for Joe Papp and recently returned to Papp's New York Shakespeare Festival as Gertrude opposite Liev Schreiber's Hamlet—and she demonstrates yet again that she is one of the most gifted (and underused) actresses around. Her Gertrude is both solicitous and passionate, a queen gravely troubled by what is going on all around her and inside herself. She is a worthy counterpart to Hamlet, and her depth-charged brooding makes it clearer than ever how closely blood-linked this woman is to her son. For all of Almereyda's nouveau overconceptualizing, his *Hamlet* ultimately comes down to a story about a boy and his mother.

(*New York*, 2000)

Seize the Day

The movies have not been kind to first-rank American novelists. De-boned, trashed, gussied up, their books are too often reduced to commemorative stamps in a mogul's photo album, with the spittle still sticky on the page. Even the labor-of-love adaptations are sticky; the filmmakers are so reverent toward the material that what might have some depth and tone and snap ends up with all the allure of Currier and Ives.

This doesn't mean that writers like E. L. Doctorow, Philip Roth, Norman Mailer, and John Updike have stopped selling their books to the movies. Movie sales give many of these writers the financial independence to do nothing but write novels—which then get wrecked in the movies. Besides, it's the odd novelist who doesn't harbor the secret wish to see his creations come to new life, replenished and monumental, on the big screen.

But Saul Bellow, the most honored living American writer, has been conspicuously—embarrassingly—absent from the movie adaptation daisy-chain. Absent except for the *Great Performances* TV production of his novella *Seize the Day,* starring Robin Williams, televised two years ago, and then almost immediately forgotten. Now it's available for rental in the video stores, at the same time that Bellow's new novella, *A Theft,* is in the bookstores. It's worth an in-depth second look, both as an achievement in its own right and for what it says about his art.

If Bellow's books have been excluded from filmic adaptation, it's not, as is commonly supposed, because he's refused to allow his books to be optioned, in the manner of J. D. Salinger. Actually, according to Bellow's literary agent, Harriet Wasserman, all of his novels except *Herzog* and *Mr. Sammler's Planet* have been sold at least once to the movies, as has the 1977 short story *A Silver Dish.*

No, the problem lies elsewhere; Bellow is one tough literary nut to crack, and most filmmakers have a difficult enough time with the pistachios and filberts and sunflower seeds that litter the best-seller lists and drugstore paperback carousels.

In the past, Bellow's distinctive tang could be felt in movies with no literal connection to his work. There was a Bellow moment in Paul Mazursky's *Harry and Tonto,* with the enraged, evicted Harry spouting *King Lear* as he's hauled from his apartment. The movies of Irvin Kershner, particularly *Loving,* have some of Bellow's quality of feeling. So do such early Fred Wiseman documentaries as *Hospital* and *Welfare,* with their bracing, plangent sympathy for the human predicament.

It's not surprising that *Seize the Day,* which is flooded with such sympathy, would become the first and, so far, only Bellow novel to be adapted for the screen. Of all his works, *Seize the Day* has perhaps the most marvelous movie possibilities. The antic, rapt picaresque *The Adventures of Augie March* would make a good TV miniseries, but it would probably end up looking like Howard Fast.

Henderson the Rain King, which Jack Nicholson once optioned, is easily the most "cinematic" of Bellow's fictions; and the least "Jewish." What a movie pair this novel offers up: the roaring, stomping Henderson, his chest full of wants, and the leonine, metaphysical King Dahfu!

(In an earlier era, Burt Lancaster and Ossie Davis could have played them.)

The big books that followed *Seize the Day* and *Henderson,* the ones that weighted Bellow's reputation, like *Herzog* and *Humboldt's Gift,* are less marvelous movie material. Sometimes it's possible for a filmmaker to scour the intellectualizing from "idea" novels, until you're left with the bare, exposed plumbing of plot. But this scouring only works if there's a strong plot to begin with (as John Huston discovered to his dismay when he filmed *Under the Volcano*). It's certainly not Bellow's *plots* that pull you through his books; neither does he have the movie-inspired prose of many of his contemporaries.

Bellow doesn't impose a visual style on you; he imposes his raucous, ruminative approach to character. And Bellow characters like Moses Herzog and Arthur Sammler don't really mesh with the surrounding cast; their antennae are tuned to an inner pulsar, so they all seem a bit mad, stenciled against the wash of their own suffering. Obsessive characters can propel a movie, give the flux of images a magnetic core. But Bellow's characters are at the core of their stories in ways that don't always translate into action—at least not movie action.

Still, for an actor, there's strong seltzer in Bellow's lusty spritz of wants and ideas; and *Seize the Day,* with its murderers' row of great roles, is a far more manageable and elegant piece of movie material than, say, *Herzog.* It also makes sense that it finally came to life in the public-television arena, which has become a gathering place for small-scale, frankly ethnic and racial, actor-dominated dramas. The Jewish material that makes it to the big screen nowadays is often show-biz Jewish; it carries an imprimatur—Woody Allen, Neil Simon, Barbra Streisand. Bellow stands a better chance of being Bellow on the small screen.

The TV *Seize the Day,* directed by Fielder Cook and scripted by

Ronald Ribman, has the faint bloom of "quality" television. But the actors are really on to something. Robin Williams, as the despairing, throttled Tommy Wilhelm, and Jerry Stiller, as Dr. Tamkin, are at each other's
nerve-endings, like a great vaudeville team, and Joseph Wiseman, as Dr.
Adler, is on hand to deliver the coup de grace over and over again. These
performers understand the book better than the filmmakers (or most literary critics). For *Seize the Day* is certainly a species of comedy, of the ancient grievances between parent and child. Wilhelm, big, blond, bearish,
in his early forties, can no longer withstand his life. The novel, which the
movie follows closely, recounts his day of reckoning.

Born Wilky Adler, Tommy dropped out of college and changed his
name when a flim-flamming agent suggested he might have an acting career in Hollywood. (Aside from a couple of walk-ons, he spent most of
his seven years in Los Angeles as a hospital orderly.) Now, many years
later, he has stormed off his job as a traveling children's furniture salesman after a row with his boss. Separated from his unconsoling wife, from
whom he desperately wants a divorce, and his two boys, whom he adores,
he lives in the same Upper West Side hotel as his father, the retired, widowed Dr. Adler, who looks down on his failure of a son with a withering
rage. Tommy's only solace is his adoring *shiksa* mistress in Roxbury; she's
willing to leave the Catholic Church for him.

Tommy can't even make rent, but he invests his last seven hundred
dollars in the commodities market, in partnership with another hotel
resident, Dr. Tamkin, a psychologist without apparent portfolio, who
patents crackpot inventions and claims to have once treated Egyptian
royalty. Tommy gives to others the kindness he craves for himself. His father treats him like a patient whose illness is of no consequence. Tommy
reaches out to the old man and Tamkin steps in—Tamkin the bamboozler, the healer.

Robin Williams at first seems an odd choice to play Wilhelm; one
envisions an aging, husky handsomeness. But, if Williams doesn't have
the look for Tommy, he's just right for Wilky; he's brought the inner man,
the pained, failed dissimulator, right to the surface. His vulnerabilities
are shockingly, comically evident. When Tommy is eating breakfast with
his father (a ritual they both abhor), sitting across from the impeccably
dressed autocrat, he demeans himself by playing the kid; he lets his voice
dip and squeak, as if he were a ventriloquist jamming with his puppet.

Throughout the movie, Dr. Adler is, in effect, imploring his son to comfort him for having such a son, and Williams shows us how Tommy is choked by the indignity. (Their scenes together suggest an assimilation comedy as well, with Dr. Adler playing the Jewish usurer to Tommy's gentile borrower.)

Courted by Tamkin, Williams slows down Tommy's words and gives them an extra beat—as if he were thirsting to be mesmerized and brought out of this world. When Tommy speaks to one of his sons on the phone, he can't find the right tone. He's fatherly but he's also beseeching; he's looking for succor. Near the end, when Tommy is about to be wiped out in the commodities market, he turns to a cranky, wealthy, old trader and entreats, quickly and under his breath, "How do you make money, Mr. Rappaport?" and we can see in Williams's stung, slack face that Tommy is looking for redemption on the sly—redemption in the form of a hot tip. He's looking for the one clue that will change things around. Rebuffed, he assumes the warped features, the slat-mouth and inward-burning eyes of a man about to convulse.

Onstage, the montage of Williams's comic rhythms—like fast-cutting in the movies—often has a delirious, ecstatic quality. Here, he fills those rhythms out, gives them an emotional towline. His acting sometimes lapses into a fussbudget's fervor; a better director might have encouraged him to trust the quietness of his moods more. But you can respond to what Williams is reaching for. He's startled, bewildered by his own poignancy.

In the movie's other major performance, Jerry Stiller, too, seems entranced by the possibilities he's discovered in himself. Tamkin is a great character on the page; you don't necessarily think of Stiller as a casting possibility when you read the book, but, in retrospect, his interpretation is indispensable. His performance is like an argument, a communion with Bellow's inspiration. With his greasy, marcelled hair and blobby, big-ribbed frame, he's like some dandified sea mammal. He's reprehensibly, voluptuously hypnotic—a liar who sometimes tells the truth. (That "truth" part is what makes the character great.) You can understand his gravitational pull on Tommy.

Tamkin lives in the money culture and yet speaks of the primacy of feelings—that's a strategy that would certainly appeal to Tommy. The story's Upper West Side location is like an urban *shtetl*, but, for Tommy, the city is full of cynical strangers speaking a code he can't decipher. Tamkin offers himself as the decipherer. "My real calling is to be a healer," he says, and Stiller gives the words a ritualistic, matter-of-fact gravity—a con man's gravity. Tommy recognizes the con; he just can't accept it. The dark jest in this material is that Tommy has a greater comprehension of loneliness than Tamkin, and yet he can't *do* anything with that comprehension, except suffer. He's grist for Tamkin, who *can* do something with it.

Williams and Stiller give you all of this, and that's a large achievement. And yet the production that pinions them is not transcendent. For one thing, it has no ending. In Bellow's novel, Tommy, broke and broken, pursues a man he believes to be Tamkin into a Jewish funeral home; stepping outside the line moving past the open coffin, Tommy looks at the powdered skin and formal shirt of the dead man, a stranger to him, and begins to cry uncontrollably. He hears the organ music and sinks "deeper than sorrow, through torn sobs and cries toward the consummation of his heart's ultimate need." In the movie, Tommy races into the parlor, does a pratfall, plunks himself down in the gallery while the service is going on, and begins to wail. Freeze frame. The End.

It's not just that this ending seems rushed and skimpy. It's that, the way the filmmakers have conceived Tommy, he just isn't grand enough for a consummation. Williams's characterization has its deep resonances, but it's thumbtacked to the posterboard of a quick-fix psychology. There's a scene near the end where Tommy and Tamkin, taking a break from the commodities market, eat in a nearby cafeteria; and Tamkin, sucking pot roast juice from his fingers, tells Tommy that the reason he punishes himself is for "failing to make your parents love you." The scene is played excruciatingly well, but you can tell by the camera's dead-set gaze that this is one of Tamkin's honest-to-God truths we're hearing.

But not, certainly, the final defining truth for Tommy? (This bit of dialogue is not in the book.) Fielder Cook and Ronald Ribman, alas, have been taken in by Tamkin. Their Tommy is ultimately an arrested adolescent. And a junior-league Willy Loman, too; we see Tommy turned down by a succession of smiley-callous employers. But it's wrong for the filmmakers to lay in the meanings for us here, Arthur Miller-style. The meanings in the material are far too harsh and ambiguous and restorative for that.

We can't "understand" Tommy the way we might understand a case history, or a theorem. The highest ambition of this production is to make us feel sorry for Tommy, to make us feel protective. That's not enough. What's missing is Tommy the holy fool. What's missing is the manifestation of Bellow's love for the sanctity of his foolishness—*our* foolishness.

Still, the impulse to bring Bellow's work to the screen is not disreputable. It comes from a desire to bring a new tone, a new range of feeling to American film. The impulse, of course, is booby-trapped. On film, Bellow's characters, deprived of the novelist's thick webbing of commentary and insight, risk becoming all-too-easily comprehensible—the reduction of their obsessions.

But what riches some of these characters are! For an actor, their emotional layering is like life-blood. You see Jerry Stiller in *Seize the Day,* and you are reminded that major actors can give us the same quality of insight, embodied, as major writers; they're dramatists of the flesh. (Olivier doesn't merely act Othello, he *fulfills* Othello.) Think of actors, most of them now languishing, who would be great in Bellow: Bill Macy, Bob Dishy, Alan Arkin, Tyne Daly, George Segal, Debra Winger, Jerry Orbach, Eli Wallach. Think of directors: Kershner, Mazursky, Ivan Passer, Barry Levinson, the Alan Parker who made *Shoot the Moon*. Think how wonderful it would be if, say, *A Silver Dish* were filmed, and even half of the story's fierce anguish made it to the screen. For those of us who love literature and movies, why should we be so deprived?

(*Los Angeles Herald Examiner*, 1989)

CHAPTER 11

MISCELLANY:
BOOK REVIEWS
AND
CRUISE SHIPS

The Complete Essays by Michel de Montaigne

We are awash in the era of the essay—in the cult of the essay. In our newspapers and our magazines, on our airwaves, between covers hard and soft, the current proliferation of the essay certifies the notion that every thought, no matter how stray, is eminently airable. The cult of the essay is really the cult of personality; the particular popularity of the "personal" essay, rife with the superannuated Me Generation fulminations of the Robert Fulghums and the Alice Kahns, represents a narcissist's swoon-a-thon in which any ego can play.

The appearance of a new edition of the complete essays of Michel de Montaigne, translated and edited by Oxford scholar M. A. Screech (a name to tickle a Monty Pythonite!), should go a long way in redeeming the "personal" essay for a generation untutored in the richness of the form. Montaigne was not only its inventor but also its greatest practitioner; he justified the essay not because he deigned to voice his own piping philosophies and innermost musings, but because he contained within himself the protean dimensions of all mankind.

Montaigne first published his *Essays* in 1580, when he was forty-seven, adding new editions in 1582 and 1588, four years before his death. He came late to writing—later, perhaps, than any other comparable literary giant. He sometimes regrets in his *Essays* that he didn't begin his project earlier, but maybe the riches needed to be stored up before they could spill over.

By the time Montaigne retreated with his wife to his family estate to read and meditate and write his essays—he had previously studied law at the University of Toulouse and served on the parliament of Bordeaux—he had already absorbed the humors and horrors of the Late

Renaissance. His worldview was bracketed by the explorations of the New World, which deepened his far-flung sympathies and fascination for the human condition, and the wars of religion, with their protracted cruelties.

Although the popular image of Montaigne is that of a solitary, almost ascetic scrivener esconced in his tower line with thousands of books and decorated with an ever-changing array of Greek and Latin inscriptions, he was far from a hermit. He ran his estate, he traveled to Germany, Italy, Austria. (His notebooks were published in 1774 as *Journal de Voyage,* the only non-essay writings, except for some letters, in the Montaigne canon.) Like his father before him, he was elected mayor of Bordeaux. He became the confidant of both Henry III and Henry IV.

"I myself am the subject of my book," writes Montaigne in his opening note to the reader, quickly adding, "It is not reasonable that you should employ your leisure on a topic so frivolous and vain."

This is a classic double-whammy from Montaigne—the stout proclamation followed by a self-deprecating blush. It's a coy tactic, but throughout the essays, Montaigne's immodest modesty has an endearing genuineness. He can't hold back from the thrill of what he is doing, the sheer novelty of it, and as the essays accumulate and resound and become increasingly personal, his philosophical forays and digressions—on everything from cannibals to friendship to children's education to thumbs—begin to cohere and circulate about each other. As mammoth as the collected essays are—more than 1,200 tightly packed pages in the Screech edition—they form a unified force field of experience. They take on the shape of a human life. We grow old with Montaigne, and his deepening presence is like a balm.

No matter how loftily his essays are billed, Montaigne recognizes in the mundane particulars of our lives the sweetmeats of existence. He was a celebrant—a sensualist—of our routine humors, of our habits, our vanity, our melancholy. Montaigne is perhaps the one great exemplar of sanity in literature, the most voluminous demonstration of how art can reside in the quotidian. Yet—and this is a quality even his admirers sometimes miss—he a had a profound tragic sense. (That's why we trust his sanity.) His credo may have been that "The greatness of the soul is dignified in the Mean," but he was painfully aware of the treacheries on either side of that mean. There is no more sorrowful passage in literature than the brief paragraph that closes the essay "On Coaches," with its description of the Spanish army's capture of the King of Peru as he was "borne seated on a golden chair suspended from shafts of gold." Each sentence follows the next like a deadfall, as the slaughter takes hold and then abruptly passes from our eyes.

"I am better at friendship than anything else," Montaigne writes in one of the earliest essays ("On Liars"), and it was a loss, through death, of a great friendship with fellow parliamentarian Etienne de la Boetie that encouraged Montaigne to retreat inside himself. Dutiful Renaissance man that he was, Montaigne peppers his essays liberally with borrowings from antiquity, but his spiritual muses were not really Plutarch and Plato. Etienne, and Montaigne's beloved father, are his true touchstones. They recur like revenants throughout the work.

The friendship Montaigne creates with us is based on an extraordinary directness and honesty; his study of the weakness of others is almost always a prelude to a study of his own. He pinned much of man's voyagings on the vagaries of Fortune, but his comprehension of the totality of the human condition makes his *Essays,* in addition to everything else, the first great breakthrough in modern psychology. "We are fashioned out of oddments put together," he wrote, and he exulted in the alloy of elements, the maddening polarities, that went into making up a man. Despite his Catholic faith, he had an almost pantheistic openness to experience. Like any good ex-lawyer, he disdained the law: "Nature always gives us happier laws than those we give ourselves."

The enormousness of Montaigne's achievement creeps up on us because he's not a pontificator or even a philosopher, really; you could fill half of *Bartlett's* with his quotations but, ripped out of the amble and ramble of the essays, Montaigne's pensées don't begin to suggest the book's value. Montaigne was no La Rochefoucauld, nor, as he once feared, does his volume survive as an ornament in a ladies' salon.

Montaigne's great creation was, in effect, himself—the universe of possibilities he contained. And he conveyed those possibilities in a limpid, unvarnished prose that was all of a piece with the mettle of his mind. For us, the unassuming directness of Montaigne's prose is a gesture of amity; he wants to be understood, to be recognized for telling the truth, because, for Montaigne, truth-telling is the highest moral good. He is forever on the lookout for anything in his writing that smacks of cant or pretense, because he wants nothing phony to intercede between us. He doesn't want to rattle the communion.

To some extent, Montaigne's "honesty" was, of course, a literary effect. He tells us very little, for example, about his wife, his political participants, his religion. But the effect has its own integrity beyond the particular evasions of Montaigne's work. And perhaps we would trust him less if he pretended to "tell all."

One explanation for Montaigne's amazing candor is his unmasked delight in himself; he insisted that in any just consideration of man, the body is at least equal to the soul, and so we are treated to all manner of descriptions about the kidney stones which plagued him; about the raptures of sexual intercourse; about how he eats ravenously with his hands ("In my haste I often bite my tongue and occasionally my fingers"). He informs us matter-of-factly that "My bowels and I never fail to keep our rendezvous." (*Essays,* incidentally, is probably the greatest bathroom book ever written, except it's too heavy.)

Montaigne's preoccupation with bodily experiences was tagged to his central preoccupation with death and dying. Early in the *Essays,* he adopts a stoical posture when he writes that life's continual task is to build for death—for the separation of the soul from the body. But in one of his later essays, "On Repenting," we want to cheer when he writes: "It is my conviction that what makes for human happiness is not, as Antithenes said, dying happily but living happily." Death is the great subject of the *Essays* because it informs everything, cuts across everything.

Montaigne's attitude toward his own death (summed up in his final, sublime essay "On Experience") was by turns raggedy, beseeching, cranky, philosophic. The book is both a fortification against mortality and a coming to terms with it. It shouldn't matter to our response to the *Essays*—but it does—to know that Montaigne died peacefully, surrounded by his friends and family, while hearing Mass in his room.

(*Los Angeles Times,* 1992)

The Primary Colors:
Three Essays by Alexander Theroux

"It is strange how deeply colors seem to penetrate man, like scent."
This quote from "Middlemarch"—the frontispiece to Alexander Theroux's *The Primary Colors*—is the most apt of intros for this playfully profound, one-of-a-kind book. Theroux's lengthy essays on blue, yellow, and red—one essay per color—spring from an almost pagan worship of everything that color can inspire in us. Reading the book can be a heady, intoxicating experience—you have to put it down every ten pages or so and take a deep breath—because Theroux gives his words the same tactile, almost talismanic shimmer as the colors he invokes.

The invocation draws on personal memories and literary anecdotes, fragments of art history, military history, politics, movie references, archeological tidbits, gossip, poetry, prejudices, scientific arcana, sporting lore. It draws on just about everything, promiscuously.

Theroux's style is a puzzlement—discursive and singsong, yet ferociously driven. There's real propulsion to his free-associative japes and apercus. He probably could have continued adding association to association forever, but he knows when to draw the curtain on his three acts. This is no rambling, dolled-up database of a book, no mere cataloguing of caprice. It's something far stranger than that—despite its surface calm, it's almost a mad book. For Theroux, there's something anthropomorphic about color; color has its own life in a way that's powerfully unsettling and sensual. His feeling for the primary colors (for all color, really) is so piercingly intimate that it's creepy. He makes us feel pretty stupid for looking at, say, the color blue in our everyday lives and seeing . . . the color blue.

When Theroux looks at the primary colors, he sees an entire latticework of connections. (His book is a mansion of filaments.) Here is Theroux on yellow:

> It is the color of cowardice, third prize, the caution flag on auto speedways, adipose tissue, scones and honey, the nimbus of saints, school buses, urine, New Mexico license plates, illness, the cheeks of penguins, the sixth dog's livery in greyhound racing, highway signs, Pennzoil, and the oddly lit hair of all Ab-

origines. Easter is yellow, so is spring, and much of the beauty of autumn. It is redolent of old horn, dead coins, southernwood, and the generous sun . . . .

This is more than a checklist; it's practically an incantation. Theroux has written novels and poetry, and there's a novelist's ardor for the precise detail in these words, as well as a poet's unblinkered eye ("the cheeks of a penguin"). His perceptions call up overwhelming emotions for us because he recognizes how color and feeling are twinned. Colors are our madeleines. Theroux doesn't really create new emotions in us; he connects us to our own private emulsion of mood and memory. He makes us register images we never thought we knew ("the cheeks of a penguin"). We don't necessarily make the same connections he does, but we can recognize his passion for getting it all out. It's a passion that goes beyond will, as if he were a medium for a torrent of imagery that, finally, has its own wild, whorled life.

This may explain why *The Primary Colors,* while it may seem to be a species of personal memoir, is also an oddly disjointed book. We don't feel we really "know" Theroux after we've read it, and that may be a part of his magician's act. Now you see him, now you don't. The book is both intimate and imperial. It's something of a tease. He brings us very close to the root of his mood; he writes how the snowfall was blue the day he was engaged to be married, of a blue bistro he remembers in Montparnasse. But he also talks—in virtually the same breath—of how hallucinations on mescaline are supposed to be blue, how blue is not mentioned in the Bible, how a blue spot (which gradually disappears) can be found on the lower back of newborn Asian babies. There's something closed-off about Theroux's openness. Perhaps it's because he's employing his own life as a kind of poetic conceit. His fantasies are experienced on the same level as his privacies.

Theroux doesn't have a generalizing mind; he's not trying for a Unified Color Field Theory. Even though his book deals with primary colors—colors that can't be made by mixing other colors together and from which nearly all other colors are mixed—he understands that a color can be too pure. He prefers a mongrelization of tones in his primary hues; it suits his poetic-mongrel style. Impurity brings out the portraitist in him. He quotes an L. E. Sissman poem that begins, "My mother, with a skin of crepe de Chine/Predominantly yellow-colored, sheer/Enough to let the venous blue show through." He cites Melville on Queequeg's face in *Moby Dick*, "of a dark, purplish yellow color, here and there struck over with large, blackish squares." (Theroux has a great instinct for the unfamiliar quotation from the familiar writer.)

The sheer catholicity of colors—the way they can embrace a yin and yang of form and feeling—has an engulfing power for Theroux. Yellow, he writes, can accommodate size—a ten-wheeler truck or a kernel of corn. Red symbolizes east to the Chippewa, the direction west in Tibet. It is "a color with a strange gigantic life, an enigma encompassing everything from sunsets to the roseate tint of our insides." Blue is "primordial simplicity and infinite space which, being empty, can contain everything and nothing."

Theroux has his chichi, mushy-mystic side—everything and nothing don't always add up to something. But he's set himself a large and fundamental task here. He's trying to get across how colors affect us in ways we can't fully acknowledge. He's trying to find a language to express the inexplicable, and he's probably right in reaching for a fervid fanciness in the prose.

At least the fanciness is grounded. Theroux isn't afraid of examining colors in the light of hard scientific fact. For him, analyzing the chemical composition of a color only *increases* its strangeness. The further you delve into science, the more you get into philosophy—into the inexplicable. *The Primary Colors* doesn't close out our interest in the subject; it's an opening out into a numinous mystery.

(*Los Angeles Times*, 1994)

License to Thrill: A Movie-ish Cruise

"What club is that?" he asks. The logo on my cap reads *Austin Powers in Goldmember,* and the sixtyish tourist aboard our SeaDream II mega-yacht in Monaco wants to know more. "It's not a club," I say. "It's from that movie." His expression goes blank. I try another tack: "You know the James Bond movie *Goldfinger*? It's a joke—finger, member?" He gets it—sort of. He also seems relieved. For a moment there, it looked like there might be a club too exclusive even for him.

I, in turn, feel less flattered than mystified since, except for the fluted champagne glass nestled inside my pinkie, I could pass for a deckhand. Dressed in nondescript shorts and T-shirt, sneakers, and cap, I am barely clinging to the cusp of "yacht casual." In my regular capacity as a film writer and critic, I've been around Bel-Air often enough to know that the schlumpiest dressers often carry the thickest wad. Still, this is different—a weeklong Mediterranean five-star cruise, with nowhere to hide except one's stateroom (stocked with Bulgari emollients in pleasing shades of jade). The glossy SeaDream brochure, although nobody pictured in it seems to have surmounted age thirty-five, does not otherwise mischaracterize the experience—luxe people in luxe places.

It's been many years since I've clapped eyes on Nice, Cannes, Cap Ferrat, Aix-en-Provence, St. Paul de Vence. Some of our other destinations, like Portofino and Cassis and St. Tropez, are new to me. Monaco I remember from the late eighties when, having come over by train from the Cannes Film Festival, I found myself barred from the casino for wearing cut-offs. Since my last name is close enough to "Rainier" to create a moderate frisson in these climes, I considered pulling rank, then thought better of it. I did not wish to be incarcerated or caned or whatever it is they do. (Torture by repeated viewing of *Herbie Goes to Monte Carlo*?) Instead, I changed into long pants and spent a pleasant afternoon pretending to be James Bond in a roomful of Omar Sharif lookalikes.

On SeaDream, 007 was pretty much confined to the DVD library, which was stocked with too many Roger Moores, not enough Sean Connerys. (*GoldenEye*, which features a scene in a Monte Carlo casino, was missing in action.) And so, I once again contrived to be my own Bond—this time aboard my own yacht. I could recline topside and sip limoncellos as ports faded from view and dusk twinkled into darkness; the backgammon tables on the upper deck were often busy well past midnight. The movie-ness of it all was easy to imagine. The difficult part, especially whenever I ventured off the ship, was in seeing the ports and the people as they really are, without the pop-cult paraphernalia. Or the high-art paraphernalia, for that matter. Whether it's Bond or Bonnard, something's always getting in the way.

I tried to sample everything, high, low, and in-between. Mostly low. I indulged my shallowness. With Bardot on my mind, I wound my way around the alleys and quays of St. Tropez. (Never mind that Bardot has become a semi-reclusive animal-rights nut and National Front sympathizer.) I would peer into Provençal faces for telltale traces of quaintness. (They usually did not peer back.) On a rainy, overcast October day in Portofino, hiking up the steep slopes to the Castello di San Giorgio high above the harbor, I gasped at blank-faced Italians in dark jackets and shades. So Antonioni-esque! (Few things are sexier than alienation in bad weather.) Portofino was our first stop on the cruise, and it set the tone for all that followed; as I looked out at the moody grandeur of the landscape, the hills that the mighty Greeks once inhabited and the Romans fortified, a guide informed me that Pavarotti had a house there.

Well, why wouldn't he? Apparently so did Prada and Pirelli. The impossibly elegant Hotel Splendido overlooking the bay is so pricey that room fees are available only "upon request." It was all I could do, after much wheezing, to reach the hotel's Corniche-clogged driveway. (And I'm in pretty good shape—for a writer.) Portofino humbles you. It soon becomes bracingly clear that you are not jet-set material. Even more humiliating is the archetypal experience of panting for air on that three hundredth step toward the Church of Saint Giacomo di Corte while a bandy-legged local, a stogie protruding from his ancient face, whizzes past you on his way to the summit.

At times like these, the SeaDream became a kind of oasis for me—a floating retreat where I could sustain the fantasy of being intimate with glamour. On board were only ninety-two guests and an equal number of crew, so it was possible to feel personally tended to. There was an Asian spa and a golf simulator, and a watersports marina for those few souls hardy (i.e. nuts) enough to buck the slaphappy waves in their Jet Skis. I stuck to simpler enjoyments, going pleasantly ga-ga as I watched a typical late afternoon's entertainment, a Norah Jones concert video in the main lounge, while tippling from my endlessly re-filled glass of fine Cabernet. "Norah," I muse to myself, "would you like to have dinner with me and the captain tonight? He's Norwegian. Would you like to walk with me across the smooth pebbles of the Baie des Anges and slip inside the cobalt waves at twilight? How are your sea legs? The reason I ask is because, last night, the yacht swayed and thumped for so long that a third of the passengers, including your ardent admirer, discovered a whole new galaxy of gods to pray to."

The movie showing in the lounge that fateful night was *The Alamo,* an especially inappropriate choice. Forget *Remember the Alamo.* Did anyone remember the Dramamine? Movies and ships, like movies on airplanes, generally don't go well together even under the best of circumstances. I once had been hired as the Italian film expert for an Italian cruise line in the Caribbean, and I still remember how pole-axed everybody looked on the first day as I attempted to lecture them on neo-realism. When I opened it up for questions, there was only one: "Is Sophia Loren still married to Carlo Ponti?" Then there was the time a loud-speaker announcement for shuffleboard on Deck Three instantly emptied the theater midway through *The Bicycle Thief.* Stuff like this stays with you a long time.

Leo Kasun, a curator at Washington's National Gallery, encountered (as far as I could tell) no such humiliations aboard the SeaDream. He and thirty art lovers—a bustling subculture of youngish couples and retirees, definitely not the silk pajama set—had come along to inspect the Mediterranean *musées.* Attempting to douse my swank fantasias, I attended lectures like "Southern Light: The Impressionist Invasion in Provence." (Of course, the going rate for Impressionist canvases brings us back to *Lifestyles of the Rich and Famous,* but that's an irony for another day.) In St. Tropez, shortly before I inadvertently wandered into an alfresco microbrew beer blast celebrating the day's regatta victors, I toured the converted chapel L'Annonciade and found myself encircled by world-class art: Fauvist masterpieces by Braque and Dufy, Pointillist miniatures by Seurat. Oils and watercolors by Paul Signac, a yachtsman who so loved the light in St. Tropez that he ended up living there, are positioned right next to windows overlooking almost identical waterfront vistas. The glitterati may have descended like locusts since Signac's time, but the light outside is still the same, so honeyed and delicate that the wide world itself resembles a lustrous open air gallery. I had the same experience in St. Paul de Vence, with its panorama of high peaks and olive groves. Matisse seemed everywhere around me.

But all this was becoming a bit too aestheticized for my mood, so I signed up with SeaDream's activities director for lessons in how to maneuver the Segway Human Transporter, which was touted as something

Q might have concocted for 007. A two-wheeled device with no acceler-
ator and no brakes and speeds of up to twenty mph, it responds to changes in body position—lean forward and you move forward; straighten up
and you stop. At least that's the theory. When I descended the gangway
and gave it a run, the thing pirouetted to my every whim and then, battery beeping, promptly plopped headfirst like a *Looney Tunes* character
with its eyes X-ed out. Clearly, this would not feed my need for speed, so
I opted next for the "Biking and Adventure Along the Loup River."

The biking part was fine—a mile and a half of lovely rustic paths
about an hour's drive from Nice, ending in what is ominously referred
to in the SeaDream literature as "adventure camp." Now, I've never spent
quality time on rope bridges and I've never crossed a river while hooked to
a harness. I've never rapelled, and I'm still not even sure what that means.
The instructor spoke very little English. "You place your hands *où*?" I
asked him as I epoxied myself to the steel cable. It's amazing how quickly your high-school French comes back to you in moments like these.
"*Aidez-moi!*" While my attempt at high-wire performance art was going
on, much to the amusement of some jeering and no doubt anti-Ameri-
can *enfants* below me, my yacht companions were having a high old time
rapelling—even the chunky, chain-smoking bakery magnate who two
months earlier had spinal fusion surgery. (He showed me the scar.)

I'll say this much for my little eco-challenge—it sure scared up an
appetite. In general, I ate my lunches ashore and dinnered on the yacht;
and although I was often ravenous by nightfall, I was rarely sated when I
finally pushed off from the dining room. Truman Capote once said that
what truly separates the rich from the rest of us is the size of their dinner portions: baby peas, baby lamb, baby everything. SeaDream is not
one of those floating emporiums that goes in for midnight buffets; it's a
quality-not-quantity establishment, which is probably just as well since it
simply wouldn't do to heap a plate with *marinade acidulée au parfum de
manque-passion.*

Besides, there were other compensations. If you chose your company
right, or if you were lucky, every dinner gathering was like a novella. In
the space of an hour or two, people would roll out their lives for you
(whether they meant to or not). The baker boasted that he restored a
famous gray-green Rolls, the Lady Olivier, that once belonged to Vivien
Leigh. A Bahamanian airline pilot, seated next to his formidable bride,

passed around posed photos of her in bodybuilding competitions. A burly Florida tycoon nicknamed The Commodore, who had known Burt Reynolds in high school, ordered only non-alcoholic drinks. He had long ago given up smoking, too. Near the end of the meal, he looked over at his wife and then leaned in to me and said softly, "If she ever died, I would go out onto my front porch that night with a carton of cigarettes and a bottle of gin." He paused to let it sink in. "But I have children," he went on, "so I hope I wouldn't."

I began the cruise believing that if I ever had the opportunity to live a long time in these ports, I might be able to dismiss the glitz and see things pure and whole. But nothing is pure and whole anymore, not for anybody, and least of all in the Côte d'Azur—where Fragonard is more reknowned as the name of a *parfum* than as an artist and autographed headshots of Yanni are staples in the photo shops. By the time we disembarked in Monaco, I came to the conclusion that maybe purity isn't all it's cracked up to be. It's more fun pretending to be a secret agent than a saint.

Waiting at Heathrow for my plane back to JFK, I opened the Sunday *Times* and couldn't believe my eyes. Here was an article about something called Spyland, "the world's first espionage theme park," located fifty miles south of Lyon, which is scheduled to kick off in the spring of 2007: "A tourist attraction to open in France will invite visitors to race a motorised gondola [à la *Thunderball*], crack a safe, and save the world from destruction by defusing a nuclear bomb." Presumably not a real one. It goes on to say that tourists will participate in spy games involving coded messages and secret liaisons with other "agents" played by professional actors. Cars will be souped up to look like Astin Martins, complete with "special gadgets."

Can GoldMembers get a discount?

(*Virtuoso Travel + Life*, 2005)

INDEX

ACKNOWLEDGMENTS

I have been fortunate over the years in having worked with a variety of editors who, perhaps without realizing it, brought out whatever is best in me. The late, great Mary Cantwell at *Mademoiselle* gave me my first regular gig (my first professional review was of *Chinatown*, no less). Editor Mary Anne Dolan at the *Los Angeles Herald Examiner* ushered me into the glorious world of ink-stained wretches and frantic deadlines. Robert Sam Anson and Mike Caruso provided a happy home for me at *Los Angeles* magazine when I was much in need of it. Profuse thanks to publisher Mike Lacey and editor Rick Barrs for the extraordinary space and freedom they provided me at *New Times*. I wrote my heart out for them. Brett Israel and Tim Swanson at the *Los Angeles Times* were always tremendously encouraging. I loved writing essays for their pages. Caroline Miller at *New York* magazine was a model editor in every way; ditto Jeremy Gerard, with whom I am re-teamed at Bloomberg. At the *Christian Science Monitor*, editor Richard Bergenheim and managing editor Marshall Ingwerson, with Stephen Humphries, were responsible for bringing me into that venerable institution. Along with Marshall, *Monitor* editor John Yemma and weekly edition editor Clay Collins believe in the arts and arts criticism, a double rarity in the world of journalism these days. They, along with former editor Su Leach, have my great gratitude.

I would also like to give a shout-out to various friends, editors, and colleagues who have supported me along the way: Jay Carr, Brian Rose, Richard Schickel, David Denby, Manuela Hoelterhoff, Anne Taylor Fleming, Robert Wilonsky, Scott Timberg, Trish Reynales, Mary Tawiah, Dave Kehr, the late Roger Ebert, Ann Louise Bardach, Caroline

Graham, Paul Coates, Jeanine Basinger, Ann Herold, Hamilton Fish, Tim Mangan, Naomi Foner, Peter Jones, Donna Perlmutter, David Kuhn, Lewis Lapham, Howie Kuperberg, Art Tobinick, Larry Mantle, and Annette Insdorf.

I am extremely grateful to Amy Inouye of Future Studio for her marvelous cover design for this book, and to Kate Murray, editorial director of Santa Monica Press, for her expert editing of the manuscript. My deepest thanks goes to my publisher, Jeffrey Goldman, who believed in me and made this book happen.

My beloved family is my touchstone: my parents forever and always, to whom this book is dedicated, my brother Jeff, my niece Marta, my nephews Jeremy and Alex, my sister-in-law Iwona, my uncle Lester, and, through the veils of time, my grandma Eva.

PERMISSIONS

Grateful acknowledgment is made to the following publications, in whose pages these articles originally appeared: the *Los Angeles Herald Examiner*, the *Los Angeles Times*, Village Voice Media (*New Times*), the *Christian Science Monitor*, *Virtuoso Travel + Life*, *Esquire Gentleman*, *Los Angeles* magazine, *New York* magazine, and LACE.

For those interested, a complete archive of my reviews from the *Monitor*, *New York* magazine, Village Voice Media, and the *Los Angeles Times* can be accessed via their respective websites.

ABOUT THE AUTHOR

Peter Rainer is the film critic for the *Christian Science Monitor*, a columnist for Bloomberg News, the president of the National Society of Film Critics, and a regular reviewer for *FilmWeek* on National Public Radio. Previously, he was the film critic at the *Los Angeles Herald Examiner*, the *Los Angeles Times*, *Los Angeles* magazine, *New York* magazine, and *New Times Los Angeles,* where he was a finalist in 1998 for the Pulitzer Prize in Criticism. He edited the critics' anthology *Love and Hisses*, co-wrote the unjustly neglected 1977 AIP picture *Joyride*, and wrote and co-produced documentaries for A&E on Sidney Poitier and the Hustons. His writing has also appeared in numerous critical anthologies and in the *New York Times Magazine, Vogue,* and *GQ,* and he has appeared as a film commentator on *Nightline, ABC World News,* and *CNN.* He has lectured at film societies and colleges around the world, and has taught film criticism in the graduate division of the University of Southern California School of Cinematic Arts. He also served on the main juries of the Venice and Montreal film festivals. In 2010, he won the National Entertainment Journalism Award for Best Online Entertainment Critic.